READ IT IN THE ROCKET
ASTRO LAFFS by Scott Kurtz
BRIING... BRIING...
HUFF!
PUFF!
HUP!
HELLO?
YES, IS THIS THE SECRET UNDERGROUND HEADQUARTERS OF THE HONOR GUARD?
YES IT IS...
I KNEW IT! BWAH HA! HA HAAA!
CLICK
RATS!
WE'RE MOVING AGAIN, AREN'T WE?
www.pvponline.com

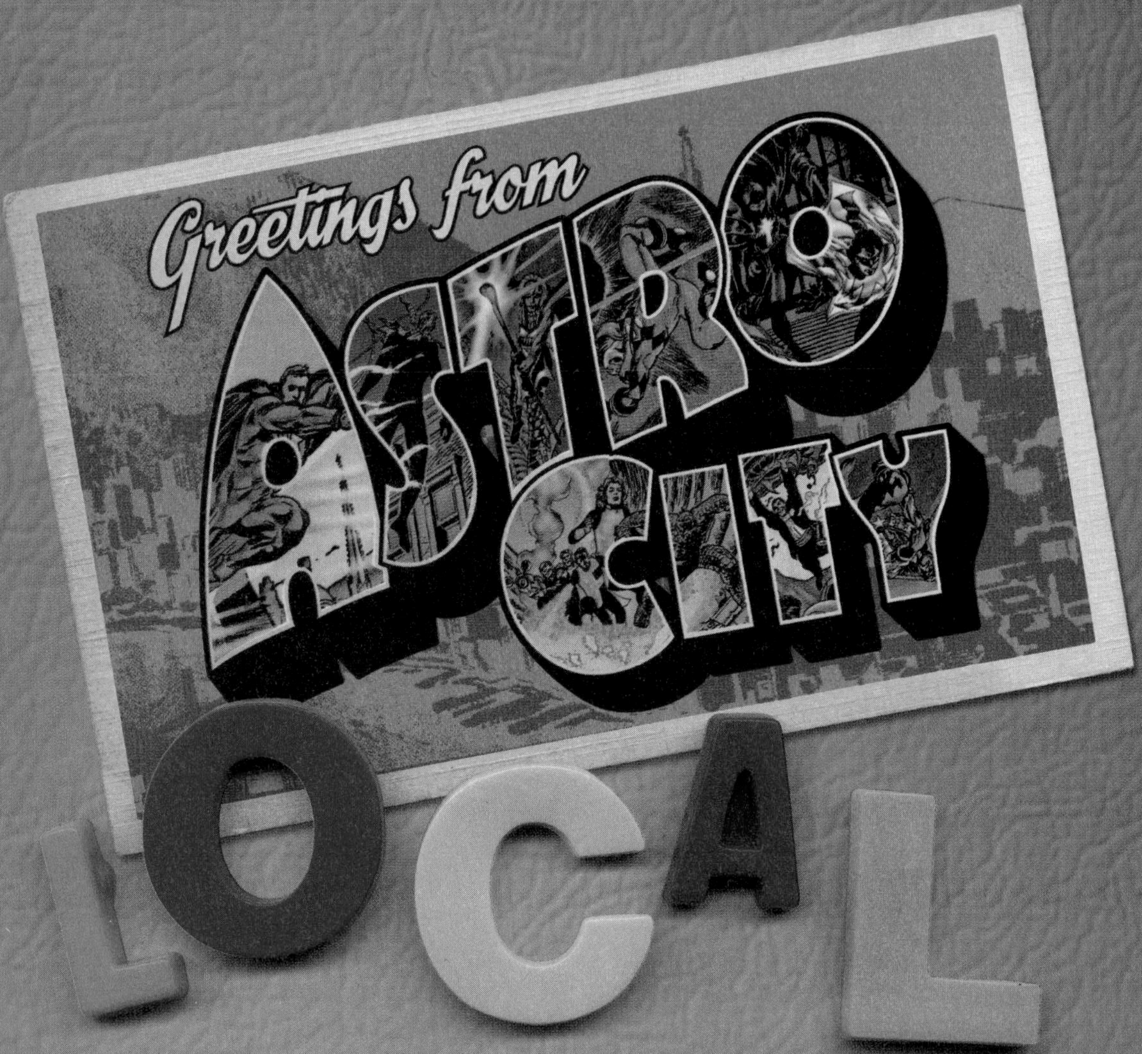
Greetings from
ASTRO CITY
LOCAL

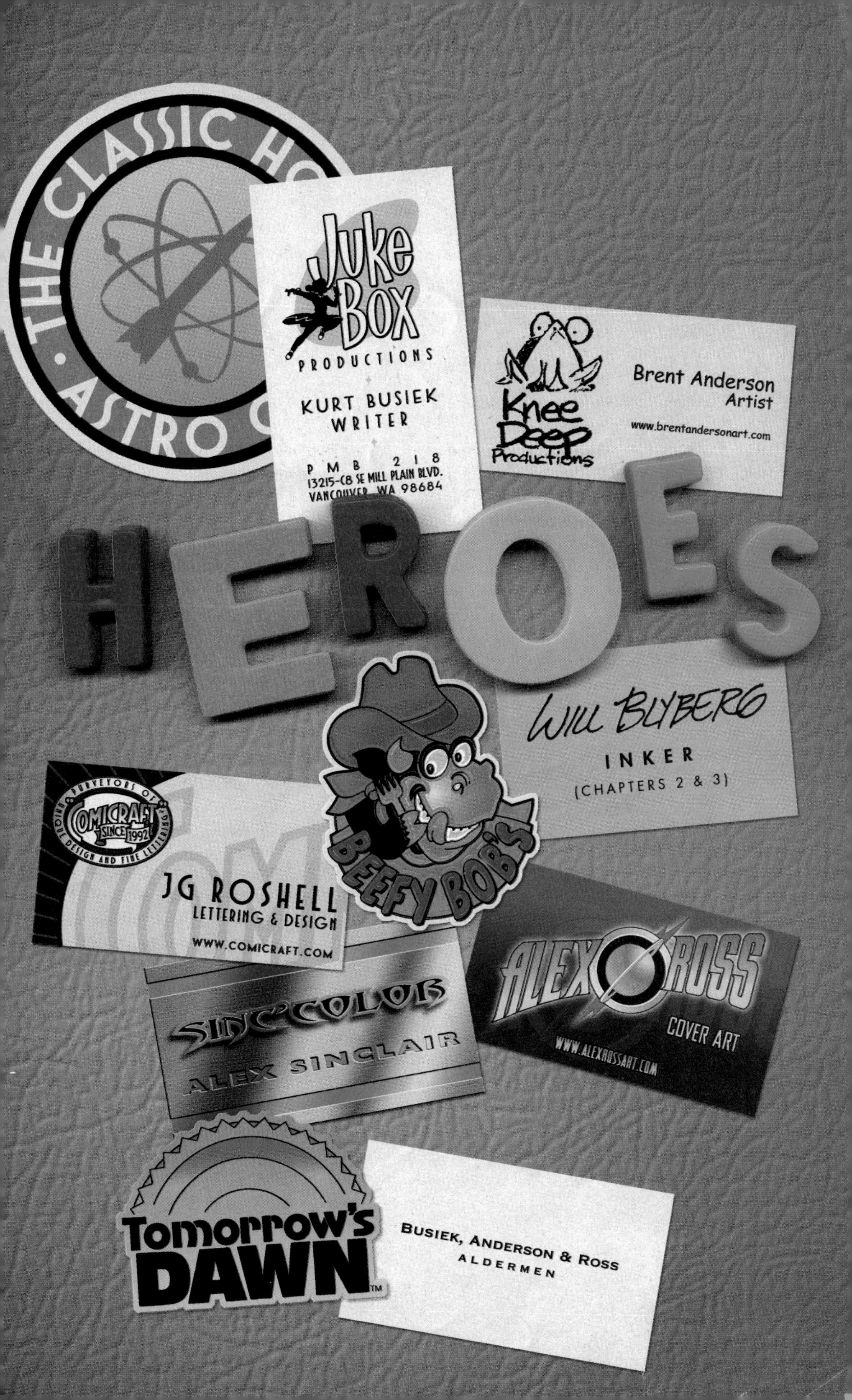

THE CLASSIC
ASTRO
Juke Box
PRODUCTIONS
KURT BUSIEK
WRITER
P M B 2 1 8
13215-C8 SE MILL PLAIN BLVD.
VANCOUVER WA 98684
Knee Deep Productions
Brent Anderson
Artist
www.brentandersonart.com
HEROES
WILL BLYBERG
INKER
(CHAPTERS 2 & 3)
PURVEYORS OF COMICRAFT SINCE 1992 UNIQUE DESIGN AND FINE LETTERING
JG ROSHELL
LETTERING & DESIGN
WWW.COMICRAFT.COM
BEEFY BOB'S
ALEX ROSS
COVER ART
WWW.ALEXROSSART.COM
SINC'COLOR
ALEX SINCLAIR
Tomorrow's DAWN™
BUSIEK, ANDERSON & ROSS
ALDERMEN

CITYWIDE THEATRES

See our website for tickets & information - www.astrocity.us

FEATURES & SHOWTIMES LISTED PLAY THRU SATURDAY ONLY

JUKE BOX
Productions

Ann Huntington Busiek
MANAGING EDITOR (PG)
(1:00) 3:50) 6:40 9:30

COMICRAFT
Purveyors of Unique Design

Richard Starkings
ART DIRECTOR (R)
(1:30 4:10) 6:40 9:10

DC COMICS MEGAPLEX 18   Features Stadium Seating
A Warner Bros. Entertainment Company

Jim Lee
EDITORIAL DIRECTOR
(PG-13) (1:10 3:30) 6:10

John Nee
VP-BUSINESS DEVELOPMENT (R)
(1:40 4:15) 6:50 9:20

Scott Dunbier
EXECUTIVE EDITOR
(G) (1:00 3:40) 6:20 9:00

John Layman & Ben Abernathy
EDITORS - ORIGINAL SERIES (PG)
(1:15 3:45) 6:30 9:15

Kristy Quinn
ASSISTANT EDITOR - ORIGINAL SERIES (R)
Fri- 7:00   Sat- (2:30) 7:00

Ben Abernathy
EDITOR - COLLECTED EDITION (G)
(1:20 4:30) 7:45 9:30

Robbin Brosterman
SENIOR ART DIRECTOR (PG-13)
(1:00 3:40) 6:10 8:40

Ed Roeder
ART DIRECTOR (PG)
(1:00 3:15) 6:00 8:30

Paul Levitz
PRESIDENT & PUBLISHER
(G) (1:30 4:00) 6:30 8:50

Georg Brewer
VP-DESIGN & RETAIL PRODUCT DEVELOPMENT (PG)
Fri- 7:00   Sat- (1:45) 7:00

Richard Bruning
SENIOR VP- CREATIVE DIRECTOR (R) (2:00) 7:15

Patrick Caldon
SENIOR VP-FINANCE & OPERATIONS (PG)
(1:00 3:40) 6:10 8:40

Chris Caramalis
VP-FINANCE (PG-13)
(1:30 4:10) 6:40 9:10

Terri Cunningham
VP-MANAGING EDITOR
(R) (1:40) 6:45 9:00

Dan DiDio
VP-EDITORIAL (PG)
(1:20 4:00) 6:20 9:00

Alison Gill
VP-MANUFACTURING
(PG) 5:00 7:30

Rich Johnson
VP-BOOK TRADE SALES (R) (1:15) 6:30

Hank Kanalz
VP-GENERAL MANAGER, WILDSTORM (PG-13)
Fri- 7:30   Sat- (2:15) 7:30

Lillian Laserson
SENIOR VP & GENERAL COUNSEL (R) (4:30) 7:45

David McKillips
VP-ADVERTISING & CUSTOM PUBLISHING
(PG-13) (1:45 4:20) 7:00

Gregory Noveck
SENIOR VP-CREATIVE AFFAIRS (PG) (4:40) 7:30

Cheryl Rubin
SENIOR VP-BRAND MANAGEMENT (R)
(1:20 4:00) 6:40 9:10

Bob Wayne
VP-SALES & MARKETING
(PG) (1:00 3:30) 6:00 8:20

Features are Available at All Citywide Theatres Locations

Assisted Listening Systems are Available at All Citywide Theatres Locations

Dark Streets...Dark Times...Dar[k]

STARTS TO

MOVIE REVIEW

'Indicia' a mix of laughs, thrills

ASTRO CITY: LOCAL HEROES, published by WildStorm Productions. 888 Prospect St. #240, La Jolla, CA 92037. Cover, introduction and compilation copyright © 2005 Juke Box Productions. All Rights Reserved. Astro City, its logos, symbols, prominent characters featured in this issue and the distinctive likenesses thereof, are trademarks of Juke Box Productions. WildStorm and logo are TM DC Comics. Any similiarity to institutions or persons living or dead is unintentional and purely coincidental. Printed on recyclable paper. WildStorm does not read or accept unsolicited submissions of ideas, stories or artwork. Printed in Canada. Second Printing.

Originally Published in Kurt Busiek's Astro City volume 2 #21-22, Astro City: Local Heroes #1-5, Astro City Special #1, 9-11 - The World's Finest Comic Book Writers & Artists Tell Stories To Remember (vol. 2) and various Feb 2002 WildStorm releases.

DC Comics, a Warner Bros. Entertainment Company.
ISBN: 1-4012-0284-5
ISBN-13: 978-1-4012-0284-2

NOW PLAYING

A GUIDE TO WHAT'S AVAILABLE IN YOUR LOCAL COMIC SHOP

DC BOOKS BY THE SAME CREATORS:
Astro City: Life in the Big City
Astro City: Confession
Astro City: Family Album
Astro City: The Tarnished Angel

BY KURT BUSIEK
Arrowsmith: So Smart in Their Fine Uniforms (with Carlos Pacheco)
JLA/Avengers (with George Pérez)
Superman: Secret Identity (with Stuart Immonen)
The Wizard's Tale (with David Wenzel)

BY BRENT ANDERSON
Legacy: The Last Will and Testament of Hal Jordan (with Joe Kelly)

BY ALEX ROSS
Batman: War on Crime (with Paul Dini)
JLA: Liberty and Justice (with Paul Dini)
Kingdom Come

(with Mark Waid)
Mythology: The DC Comics Art of Alex Ross
Shazam: Powe[r] of Hope (with Paul Dini)
Superman: Peace on Earth (with Paul Dini)
Uncle Sam (with Steve Darnall)
Wonder Woma[n]: Spirit of Truth (with Paul Din[i])

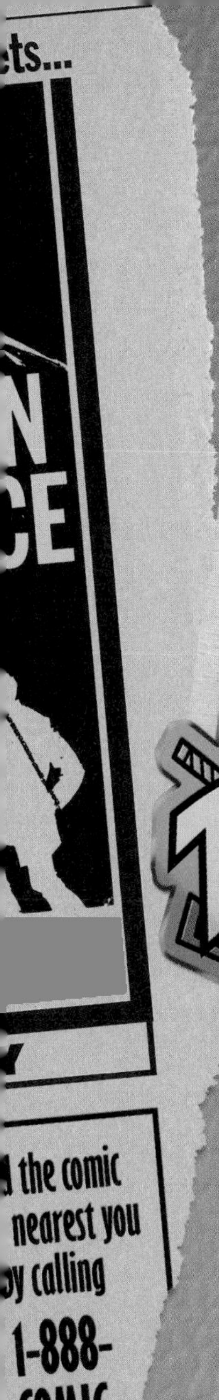
...ets...
N
CE
the comic
nearest you
by calling
1-888-
COMIC
BOOK
toll fre

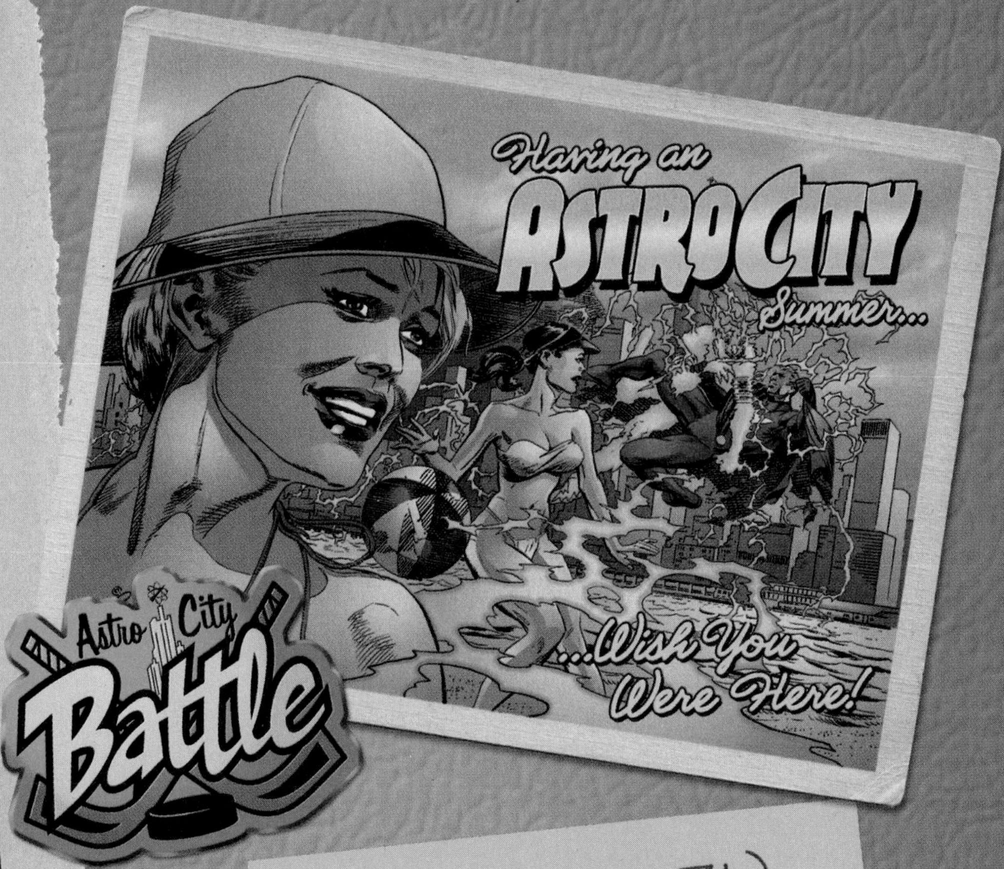
Having an
ASTRO CITY
Summer...
...Wish You
Were Here!
Astro City
Battle

FOR STEVE HUNTINGTON
& CAROLYN SLINEY—
Miracle workers with food
and local heroes par excellence.
—KURT

For all the local heroes at Cali Calmecac Charter School, the administrators, staff, parent volunteers, teachers and students who work tirelessly to teach and promote peace, tolerance, social justice, universal community and personal achievement. You are all heroes to me.

—Brent

FOR BEN,
MY LOCAL HERO.
Alex Ross

ASTRO Mart

SHOPPING LIST

INTRO

TABLE of CONTENTS:

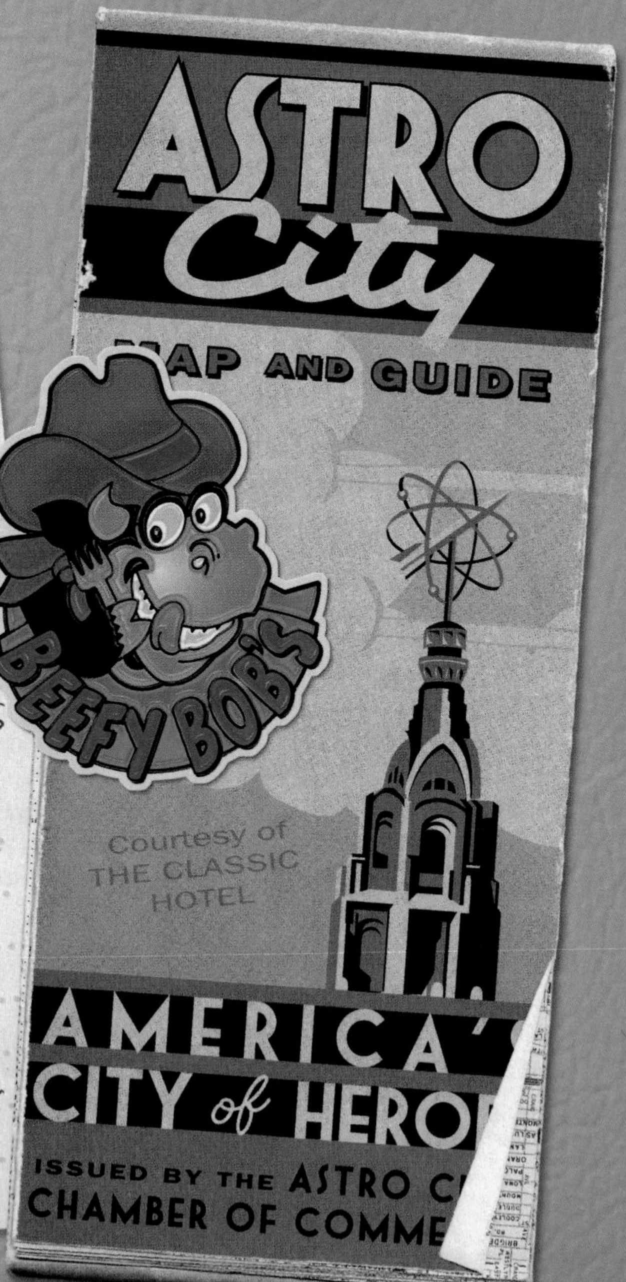

ASTRO City
AP AND GUIDE
BEEFY BOB'S
Courtesy of THE CLASSIC HOTEL
AMERICA'S
CITY of HERO
ISSUED BY THE ASTRO C
CHAMBER OF COMME

DUCTION

Current

Bulldog Comics

Around Town
with James Robinson

HOW LONG WOULD IT take to read every issue of *The Avengers?* How many hours, days, weeks? Knowing that for every great story there was one or two of questionable merit. Plowing through tales where the writer and/or artist were clearly more concerned with paying their rent than they were adding to the superteam's halcyon lore. Slogging through issue after issue, all those deaths and resurrections, characters of note and those best forgotten. How long would such a task take? And at the cost of what?—in terms of free time, in terms of one's life? I have no idea. Nor is the desire to learn firsthand so very important I ever intend to try. I'm happy somebody else undertook the task.

Kurt Busiek.

Perhaps in order to better formulate his ideas for his run writing *The Avengers* and the fantastic maxi-series *Avengers Forever.* Perhaps. Perhaps he merely did it for fun. Or for a better understanding of the medium he has chosen for his life. Or maybe just for the sheer obsessive Hell of it. The fact is, Kurt did it. And I'm sure he's equally as versed in the sagas that comprise the Fantastic Four, Thor and his Asgardian brethren, Tony Stark's battle with "Mister Booze" and the many theaters of combat seen by Sgt. Fury and his Howling Commandos. It appears that Kurt has read it all. (Which made him the perfect writer for *Marvels*—all those oblique visual references, subtly layered through the larger narrative.)

Then we have DC Comics, where Kurt appears as versed in the history of the JLA, the life and death of Barry Allen and the seventeen million revamps of the Legion of Superheroes.

I haven't dared question him about Charlton Comics' repertoire of heroes nor the work of Charles Biro nor Larry Lieber's short-lived line of Atlas Comics nor Gold Key's stab at super heroics. But I'm sure Kurt knows. I'm sure he knows the nuances of Judomaster and Airboy and Son of Vulcan and Brain Boy. It seems like Kurt has read every germane comic imaginable (I add germane because I have no idea as to his overview of *Millie the Model, Binky and his Buddies* or an opinion on where "Jason's Quest" would have taken him had he appeared in more than one issue of *Showcase*.)

AND YET, UNLIKE SOME walking comic book encyclopedias, Kurt isn't what one might uncharitably refer as a drooling fanboy. (Incidentally, has anyone actually seen a fanboy drool? I've seen a few of them eat pizza. I glanced at one or two drink too many cans of Coke. And God help me, I've shared an elevator and had to smell one or two of the more extreme avatars of the breed. Never, though, have I seen even a drop of drool on a fanboy's greasy lips. Ahh, one can dare to dream, I suppose.)

Anyway, where was I—oh yes, Kurt—I recall one time, talking to Kurt, I forget where, probably a comic convention, it certainly wasn't during a sex tour holiday of Southeast Asia (I remember distinctly that Kurt sprained his ankle and couldn't make it, so me, Tony Isabella and Maggie Thompson went to Thailand without him). Anyway, in the course of our chat, Kurt dropped some arcane piece of comic book trivia, in the absent, off-hand manner mere mortals might comment on the weather or their favorite ice cream flavor. I forget exactly what Kurt said—how 3-D Man's cologne fragrance in 1954 caused a ripple effect throughout Marvel continuity that led to the Kree-Skrull War—or maybe not. Whatever it was it was both profound and Byzantine enough for me to proclaim—"Kurt, you're the Martin Scorsese of comics. And I mean that in a good way."

By that I meant how, in interviews, in DVD commentaries, Scorsese is an abundance of references, contrasting film makers' techniques with his own where no nuance of cinematic technique, no shot framing or storytelling device, no thematic subtext or recurring auteurist themes is dismissed—even from the most obscure of B-movie directors—names that you or I have never thought to catalogue. And yet Scorsese isn't the cinematic equivalent of a drooling fanboy. No, he's maybe the world's coolest living director in terms of his body of work. And in the aforementioned commentary he may talk about how this camera framing or that dolly move were influenced by William Wellman or Sam Fuller or whoever, but his work is never anyone's but his own. There are no slavish tributes, nothing that screams the influence of prior filmmakers in the way that for instance Brian DePalma for a long time wore his love of Hitchcock on his sleeve in every film he made.

Kurt is, to me, the same—aware of the comic book medium to a microscopic degree, the characters, the creators, the stories. But never is his work an ode to any prior creator's canon. I've watched Kurt find a voice very much his own, over the years from his lowly days finishing up series such as *Power Man and Iron Fist,* already earmarked for cancellation, through to the glory of *Marvels* and beyond.

And of course the highpoint of that ascent is *Astro City.*

A*STRO CITY* WORKS PERFECTLY for many reasons. One of them is consistency. Kurt's scripts, the art of Brent and Will. Alex's covers. Every issue. Consistent. Quality.

At the same time this is a comic that

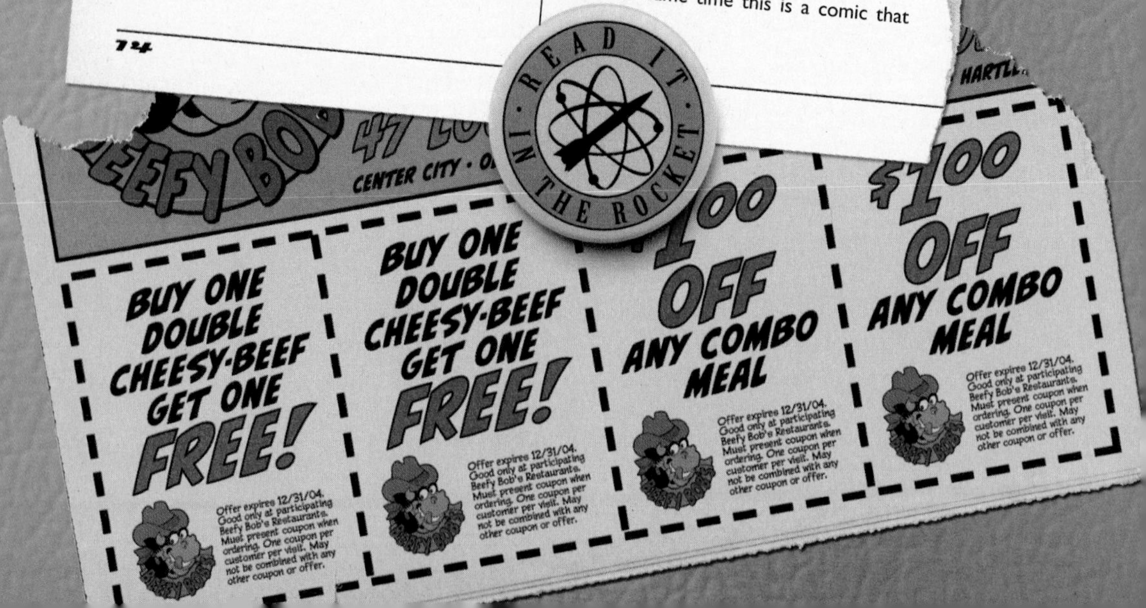
READ IT IN THE ROCKET
BEEFY BOB'S
BUY ONE DOUBLE CHEESY-BEEF GET ONE FREE!
Offer expires 12/31/04. Good only at participating Beefy Bob's Restaurants. Must present coupon when ordering. One coupon per customer per visit. May not be combined with any other coupon or offer.
BUY ONE DOUBLE CHEESY-BEEF GET ONE FREE!
Offer expires 12/31/04. Good only at participating Beefy Bob's Restaurants. Must present coupon when ordering. One coupon per customer per visit. May not be combined with any other coupon or offer.
OFF ANY COMBO MEAL
Offer expires 12/31/04. Good only at participating Beefy Bob's Restaurants. Must present coupon when ordering. One coupon per customer per visit. May not be combined with any other coupon or offer.
$1.00 OFF ANY COMBO MEAL
Offer expires 12/31/04. Good only at participating Beefy Bob's Restaurants. Must present coupon when ordering. One coupon per customer per visit. May not be combined with any other coupon or offer.

Tomorrow's DAWN™

couldn't exist forty years ago. Why? Because of the comic book readers' shared consciousness (and no, I don't mean like Starro). Rather, we understand the formulas. Back in the 1960s, those rules, the formulas and character archetypes that worked, were still being developed. We, as comic book readers, weren't as familiar. Now, we know.

• We know the dynamic of the "family" as superteam—different versions of it have existed since the 1950s—*Boys' Ranch, The Challengers of the Unknown, Sea Devils,* Rip Hunter's crew (did they ever have a name?), and of course the epitome of this, *The Fantastic Four.* And somehow their adventures in our imagination add texture and fill out what little we actually know about the First Family.

• Equally the superteam as an alliance of individuals, a la Justice Society, Justice League, Avengers, etc. We know how this works, the mixture of complementary and confrontational personalities, the internal drama even as the world's most powerful villains get in line to fight them. And thereby we already know the adventures of Honor Guard, no matter how obliquely we see them in Kurt's stories.

• We understand the figure of the "uberman," the pinnacle of any superhero universe. We've read *Superman* for decades, so little need be said of Samaritan, we understand him. We know what his adventures are, without ever being told them.

• We understand the convention of the "patriotic hero," be it Captain America, DC's Uncle Sam or *Astro City's* Old Soldier.

• The capering "fun" hero—Spider-Man, Jack-In-The Box.

• The dark hero and his/her bright sidekick—Batman and Robin, *Astro City's* Nightingale and Sunbird.

And on and on. We know the conventions. We've seen the adventures told over and over by greater and lesser talents, published by greater and lesser companies. And therein is the genius of *Astro City* the comic book. Kurt "Scorsese" Busiek applies these formulas, not as the derivative forefront, but rather as the color and dressing. And that's all it needs. The underlying palette.

How many uninspired copies of the X-Men have been published over the years, how many carbon copy heroes and teams, more of the same, more, more, more of the same? Rather, under Kurt's expert hand, this comic is about the city itself and to a larger degree the human condition—what it's like as an ordinary person to live among giants, or what it's like (as a person) to don the mantle of giants with its responsibilities and woes. A lesser writer would have made this book about the fights and the powers and everything we've already read. Kurt allows us to tell those stories ourselves in our imaginations from every comic book we've ever read, while he concentrates rather on the stories we haven't seen before.

I LOVE THIS BOOK. I love the characters. I love Kurt's ability to shift viewpoint from issue to issue, new lives, new personalities, but always accessible—lives you want to know.

The ASTRO CITY CLASSIC
By any measure... a classic.
BETWEEN CENTER CITY AND OLD TOWN

Current

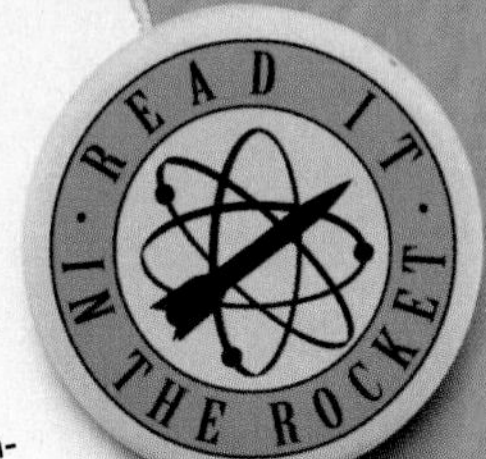
READ IT IN THE ROCKET

In the collection you now hold Kurt takes us into more diverse points of view.

• The comic book writer of "real" superhero adventures, spotlighting the irony of the comic book in a world of the fantastic while at the same time focusing on the personality of old time comic book publishing.

• The actor playing a superhero thrust into the reality of adventure.

• The doorman of a hotel in Astro City, always looking, noting the world changing day by day, people and superheroes coming, going. And at the same time we see why a man can love this place and how the vagaries of it can make anyone a hero at least for a moment.

• Astro City and the courts of law—when the logic of eyewitnesses and physical evidence breaks down in the face of the fantastic.

• An old hero brought back from retirement, illustrating the contrast between the fun of the past and the harsh reality of the time ticking down.

• And my favorite story, "Pastoral." A girl away from the city, hating life, until she allows herself to see the beauty of a simpler place and simpler heroes.

All of these stories are perfect examples of Kurt Busiek's talents, the adventures obliquely referred to, using comic book conventions as dressing for deeper tales of reflection and self-realization. Great stories, great people. With another delight being that Kurt clearly has a great many more tales to tell in the amazing world of *Astro City.*

And God willing, maybe one day Kurt will get around to telling us what happened to the Silver Agent.

—*James Robinson*
September 2004

JAMES ROBINSON BROKE INTO COMICS WITH THE SUPERBLY MOODY GRAPHIC NOVEL *LONDON'S DARK*, IMMEDIATELY DRAWING THE ATTENTION OF MAJOR EDITORS AND PUBLISHERS. BEST KNOWN IN COMICS AS THE CREATOR AND WRITER OF THE AWARD-WINNING *STARMAN* AND *THE GOLDEN AGE*, HE HAS IN RECENT YEARS TURNED HIS ATTENTION TO THE FILM INDUSTRY, WRITING THE SCREENPLAYS FOR *THE LEAGUE OF EXTRAORDINARY GENTLEMEN* AND *COMIC BOOK VILLAINS*, WHICH HE DIRECTED HIMSELF. KURT FEELS CONSTRAINED TO NOTE THAT "JASON'S QUEST" APPEARED IN THREE ISSUES OF *SHOWCASE*.

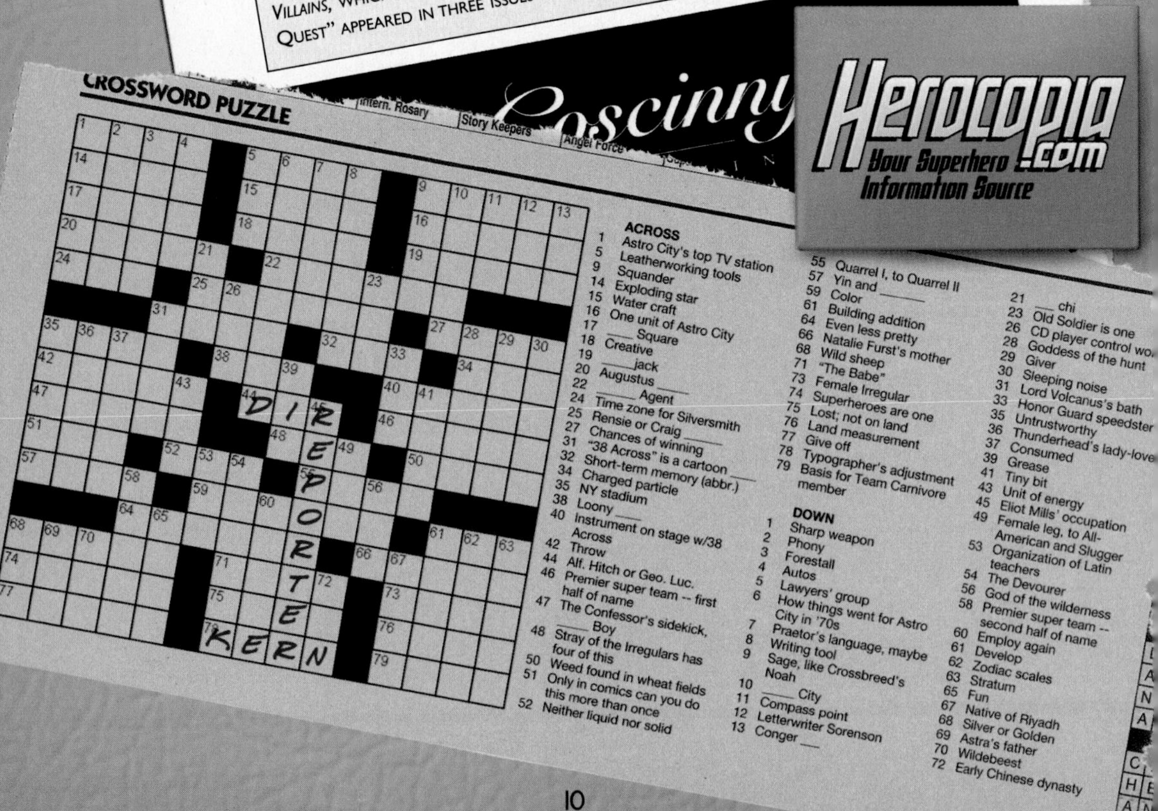
Herocopia.com
Your Superhero Information Source
CROSSWORD PUZZLE
Intern. Rosary
Story Keepers
Angel Force
DIREPORTER
KERN
ACROSS
1 Astro City's top TV station
5 Leatherworking tools
9 Squander
14 Exploding star
15 Water craft
16 One unit of Astro City
17 ____ Square
18 Creative
19 ____jack
20 Augustus ____
22 ____ Agent
24 Time zone for Silversmith
25 Rensie or Craig ____
27 Chances of winning
31 "38 Across" is a cartoon ____
32 Short-term memory (abbr.)
34 Charged particle
35 NY stadium
38 Loony ____
40 Instrument on stage w/38 Across
42 Throw
44 Alf. Hitch or Geo. Luc.
46 Premier super team -- first half of name
47 The Confessor's sidekick, ____ Boy
48 Stray of the Irregulars has four of this
50 Weed found in wheat fields
51 Only in comics can you do this more than once
52 Neither liquid nor solid
55 Quarrel I, to Quarrel II
57 Yin and ____
59 Color
61 Building addition
64 Even less pretty
66 Natalie Furst's mother
68 Wild sheep
71 "The Babe"
73 Female Irregular
74 Superheroes are one
75 Lost; not on land
76 Land measurement
77 Give off
78 Typographer's adjustment
79 Basis for Team Carnivore member
DOWN
1 Sharp weapon
2 Phony
3 Forestall
4 Autos
5 Lawyers' group
6 How things went for Astro City in '70s
7 Praetor's language, maybe
8 Writing tool
9 Sage, like Crossbreed's Noah
10 ____ City
11 Compass point
12 Letterwriter Sorenson
13 Conger ____
21 ___ chi
23 Old Soldier is one
26 CD player control wo
28 Goddess of the hunt
29 Giver
30 Sleeping noise
31 Lord Volcanus's bath
33 Honor Guard speedster
35 Untrustworthy
36 Thunderhead's lady-love
37 Consumed
39 Grease
41 Tiny bit
43 Unit of energy
45 Eliot Mills' occupation
49 Female leg. to All-American and Slugger
53 Organization of Latin teachers
54 The Devourer
56 God of the wilderness
58 Premier super team -- second half of name
60 Employ again
61 Develop
62 Zodiac scales
63 Stratum
65 Fun
67 Native of Riyadh
68 Silver or Golden
69 Astra's father
70 Wildebeest
72 Early Chinese dynasty

ONE
NEWCOMERS

CKET ✻ D R 20

ALIEN CONQUEROR CAPTURED IN SUBURBS

ASTRO CITY—The alien invader Kroseth IV of Antares was captured Tuesday by Honor Guard, after spending almost a year disguised as a ranch-style home in the Goldwater neighborhood. Though the creature put up a stiff battle, it was subdued and taken into custody with no loss of life.

The extraterrestrial had been home to retiree Rosemary Lucey, at 414 DeCarlo Avenue, for ten months. Late last year, Mrs. Lucey's longtime home was inadvertently destroyed during a battle between Samaritan and the Glowworm. After the battle, Honor Guard reconstructed Mrs. Lucey's home, using the Repli-Matrix crystal captured from Tritonian slavers early in their career, which they have so often used for reconstruction purposes.

"Unfortunately," said Honor Guard spokesman MPH, "Kroseth hadn't been destroyed after our last clash with him, as it had appeared. He'd infused his essence with the Repli-Matrix, and the next time we used it—pow!, there he was. A two-bedroom house." Honor Guard realized the deception when Kroseth began mentally controlling area civil servants, forming them into a strikeforce.

The house's unusual nature hadn't gone completely unnoticed, however.

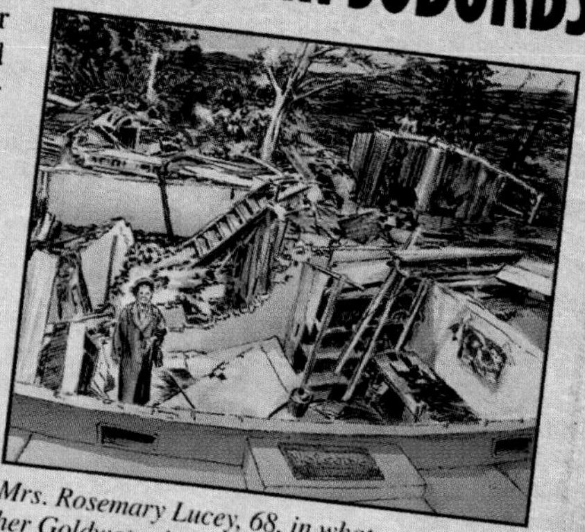

Mrs. Rosemary Lucey, 68, in what remains of her Goldwater home. Photo by Brent Anderson

"We used to have such a squirrel problem all through the block," said Mrs. Lucey. "They hogged the birdseed we put out for the birds, no matter what we did. But after Honor Guard built my new house, they weren't a problem any more. I think it was eating them.

"Still," she added, "I had no idea it had enslaved Frank, our mailman. It was quite good company, most of the time. It would sing me to sleep in its own language... lovely, lovely songs. And it was a great help with the crossword puzzle."

Honor Guard begins construction on Mrs. Lucey's new home—by more conventional building methods—on Monday.

SPRANG
MUSEUM OF POPULAR ADVERTISING
To my Sidekick Buddy
Crackerjack
Non-Transferable
Order No:
14811327302 7

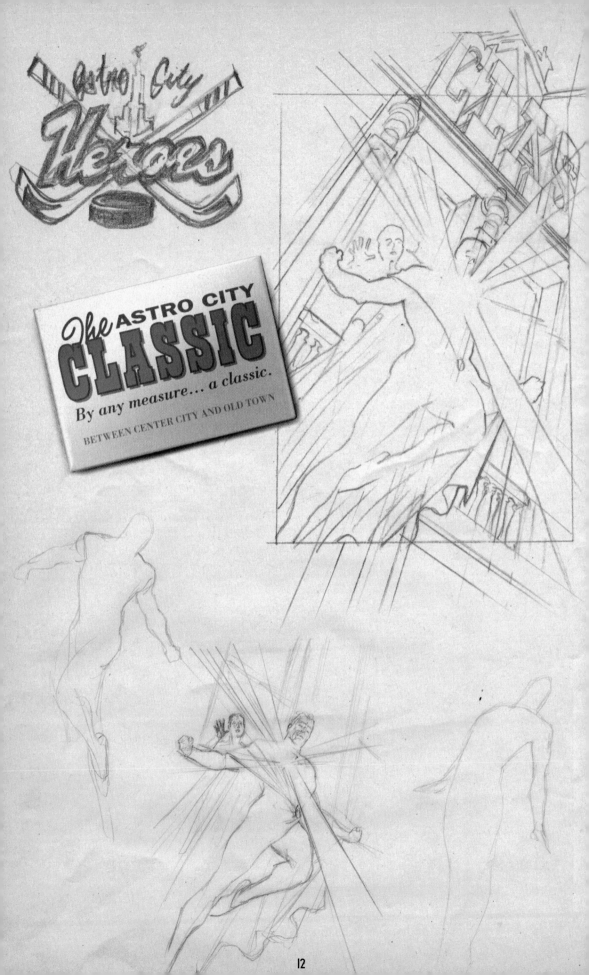

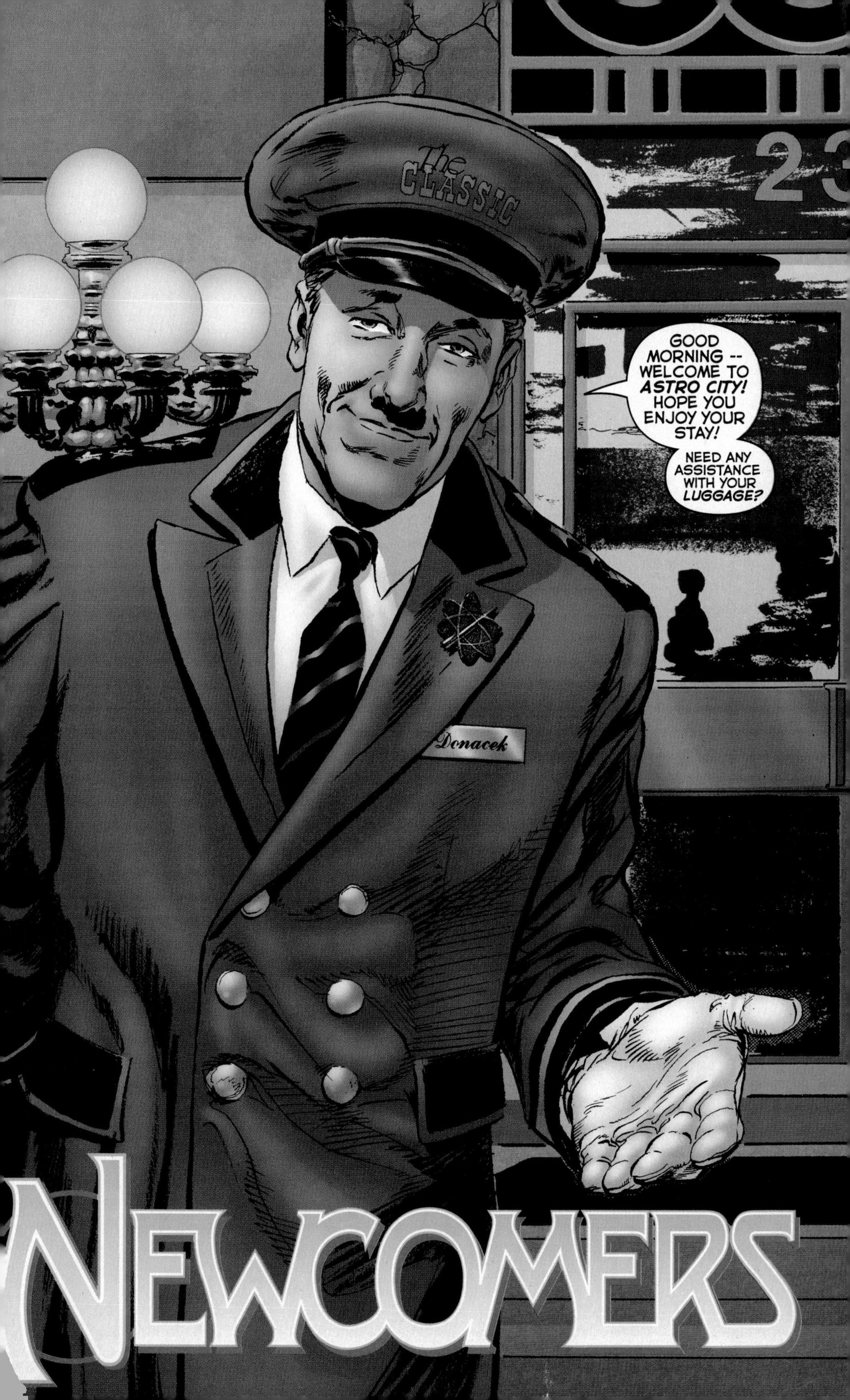

The CLASSIC
23
GOOD MORNING -- WELCOME TO ASTRO CITY! HOPE YOU ENJOY YOUR STAY!
NEED ANY ASSISTANCE WITH YOUR LUGGAGE?
Donacek
NEWCOMERS

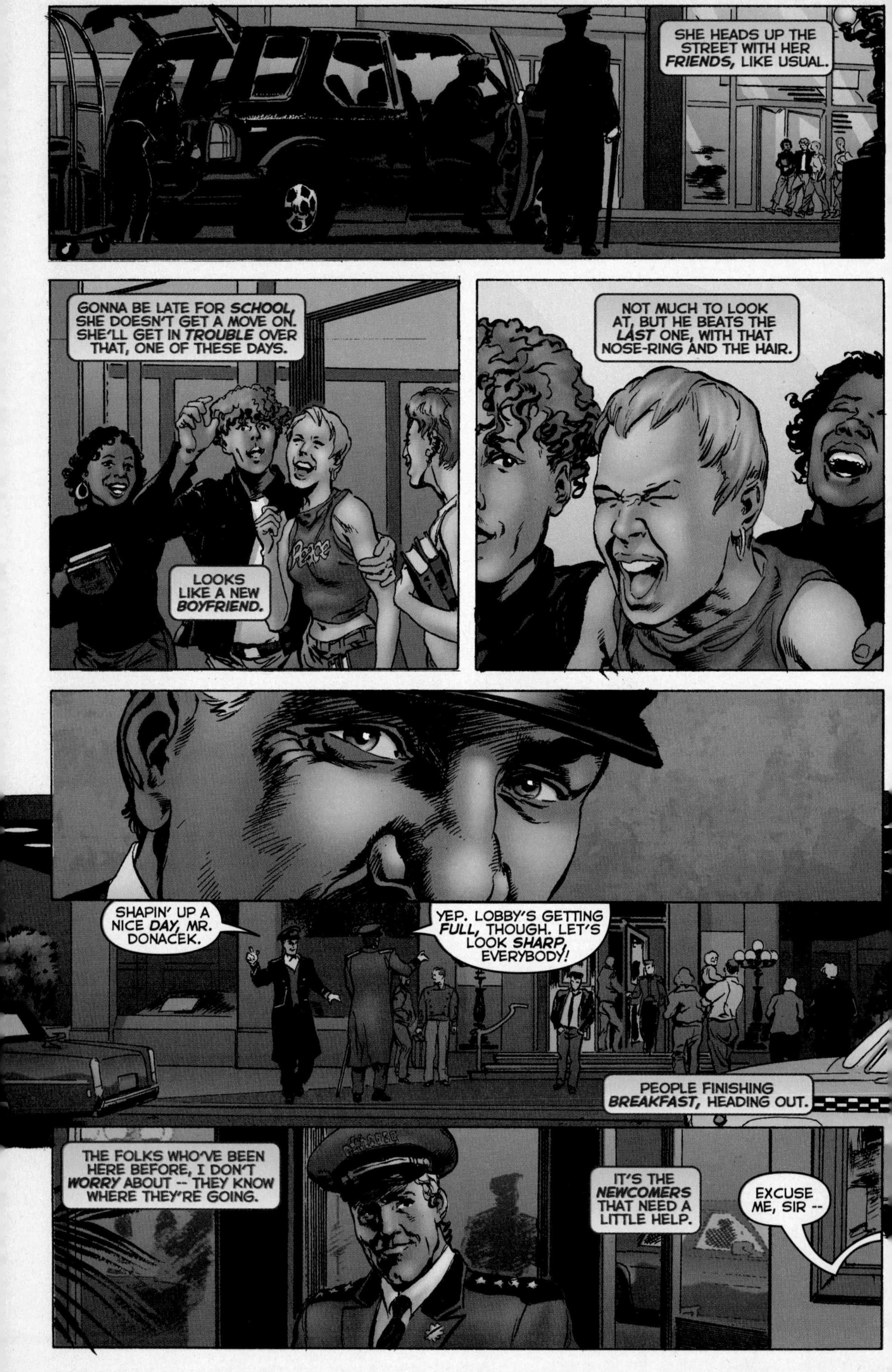
SHE HEADS UP THE STREET WITH HER FRIENDS, LIKE USUAL.
GONNA BE LATE FOR SCHOOL, SHE DOESN'T GET A MOVE ON. SHE'LL GET IN TROUBLE OVER THAT, ONE OF THESE DAYS.
LOOKS LIKE A NEW BOYFRIEND.
PEACE
NOT MUCH TO LOOK AT, BUT HE BEATS THE LAST ONE, WITH THAT NOSE-RING AND THE HAIR.
SHAPIN' UP A NICE DAY, MR. DONACEK.
YEP. LOBBY'S GETTING FULL, THOUGH. LET'S LOOK SHARP, EVERYBODY!
PEOPLE FINISHING BREAKFAST, HEADING OUT.
THE FOLKS WHO'VE BEEN HERE BEFORE, I DON'T WORRY ABOUT -- THEY KNOW WHERE THEY'RE GOING.
IT'S THE NEWCOMERS THAT NEED A LITTLE HELP.
EXCUSE ME, SIR --

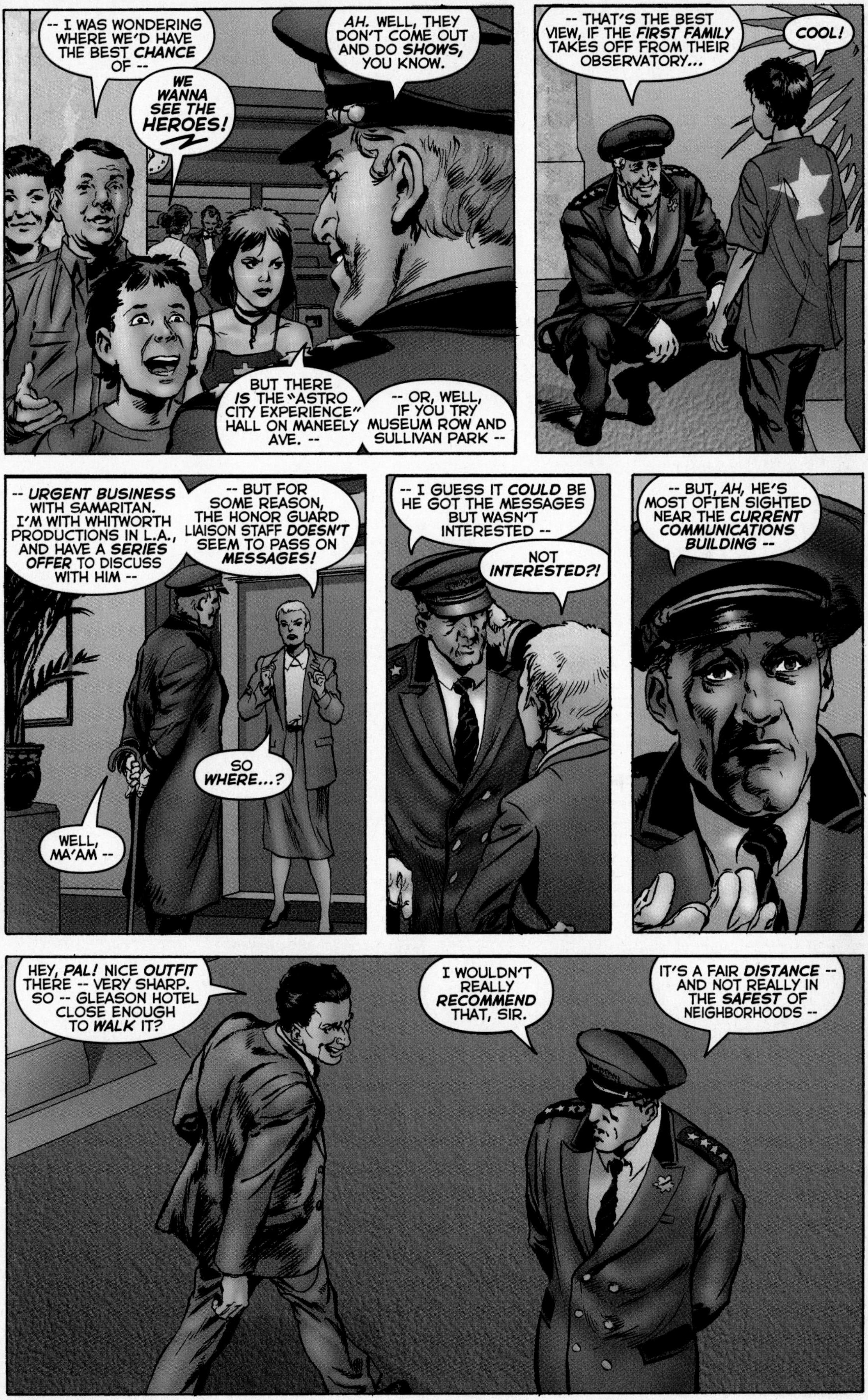
-- I WAS WONDERING WHERE WE'D HAVE THE BEST CHANCE OF --
WE WANNA SEE THE HEROES!
AH. WELL, THEY DON'T COME OUT AND DO SHOWS, YOU KNOW.
BUT THERE IS THE "ASTRO CITY EXPERIENCE" HALL ON MANEELY AVE. --
-- OR, WELL, IF YOU TRY MUSEUM ROW AND SULLIVAN PARK --
-- THAT'S THE BEST VIEW, IF THE FIRST FAMILY TAKES OFF FROM THEIR OBSERVATORY...
COOL!
-- URGENT BUSINESS WITH SAMARITAN. I'M WITH WHITWORTH PRODUCTIONS IN L.A., AND HAVE A SERIES OFFER TO DISCUSS WITH HIM --
-- BUT FOR SOME REASON, THE HONOR GUARD LIAISON STAFF DOESN'T SEEM TO PASS ON MESSAGES!
SO WHERE...?
WELL, MA'AM --
-- I GUESS IT COULD BE HE GOT THE MESSAGES BUT WASN'T INTERESTED --
NOT INTERESTED?!
-- BUT, AH, HE'S MOST OFTEN SIGHTED NEAR THE CURRENT COMMUNICATIONS BUILDING --
HEY, PAL! NICE OUTFIT THERE -- VERY SHARP. SO -- GLEASON HOTEL CLOSE ENOUGH TO WALK IT?
I WOULDN'T REALLY RECOMMEND THAT, SIR.
IT'S A FAIR DISTANCE -- AND NOT REALLY IN THE SAFEST OF NEIGHBORHOODS --

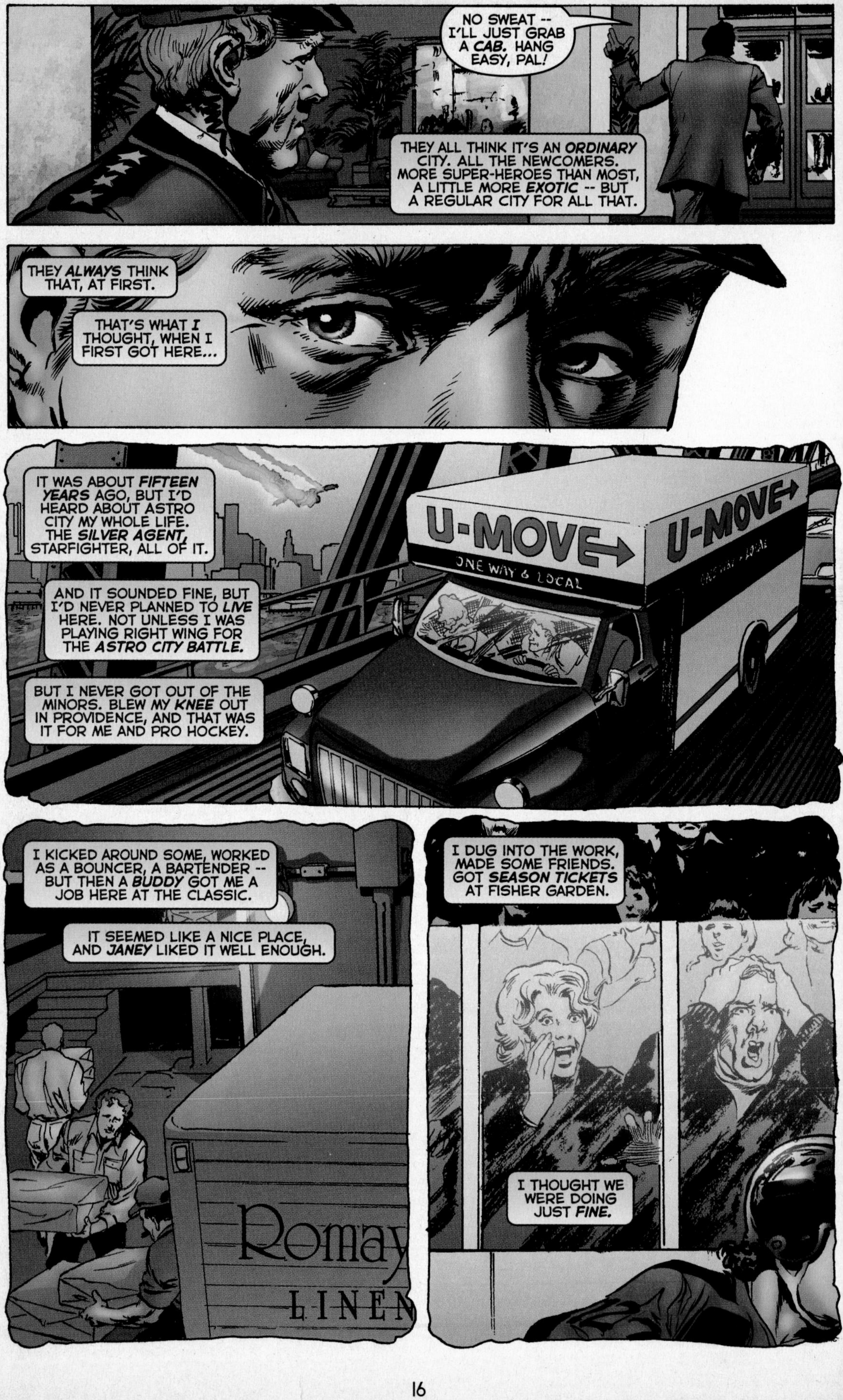
NO SWEAT -- I'LL JUST GRAB A CAB. HANG EASY, PAL!
THEY ALL THINK IT'S AN ORDINARY CITY. ALL THE NEWCOMERS. MORE SUPER-HEROES THAN MOST, A LITTLE MORE EXOTIC -- BUT A REGULAR CITY FOR ALL THAT.
THEY ALWAYS THINK THAT, AT FIRST.
THAT'S WHAT I THOUGHT, WHEN I FIRST GOT HERE...
IT WAS ABOUT FIFTEEN YEARS AGO, BUT I'D HEARD ABOUT ASTRO CITY MY WHOLE LIFE. THE SILVER AGENT, STARFIGHTER, ALL OF IT.
U-MOVE
ONE WAY & LOCAL
AND IT SOUNDED FINE, BUT I'D NEVER PLANNED TO LIVE HERE. NOT UNLESS I WAS PLAYING RIGHT WING FOR THE ASTRO CITY BATTLE.
BUT I NEVER GOT OUT OF THE MINORS. BLEW MY KNEE OUT IN PROVIDENCE, AND THAT WAS IT FOR ME AND PRO HOCKEY.
I KICKED AROUND SOME, WORKED AS A BOUNCER, A BARTENDER -- BUT THEN A BUDDY GOT ME A JOB HERE AT THE CLASSIC.
IT SEEMED LIKE A NICE PLACE, AND JANEY LIKED IT WELL ENOUGH.
Romay
LINEN
I DUG INTO THE WORK, MADE SOME FRIENDS. GOT SEASON TICKETS AT FISHER GARDEN.
I THOUGHT WE WERE DOING JUST FINE.

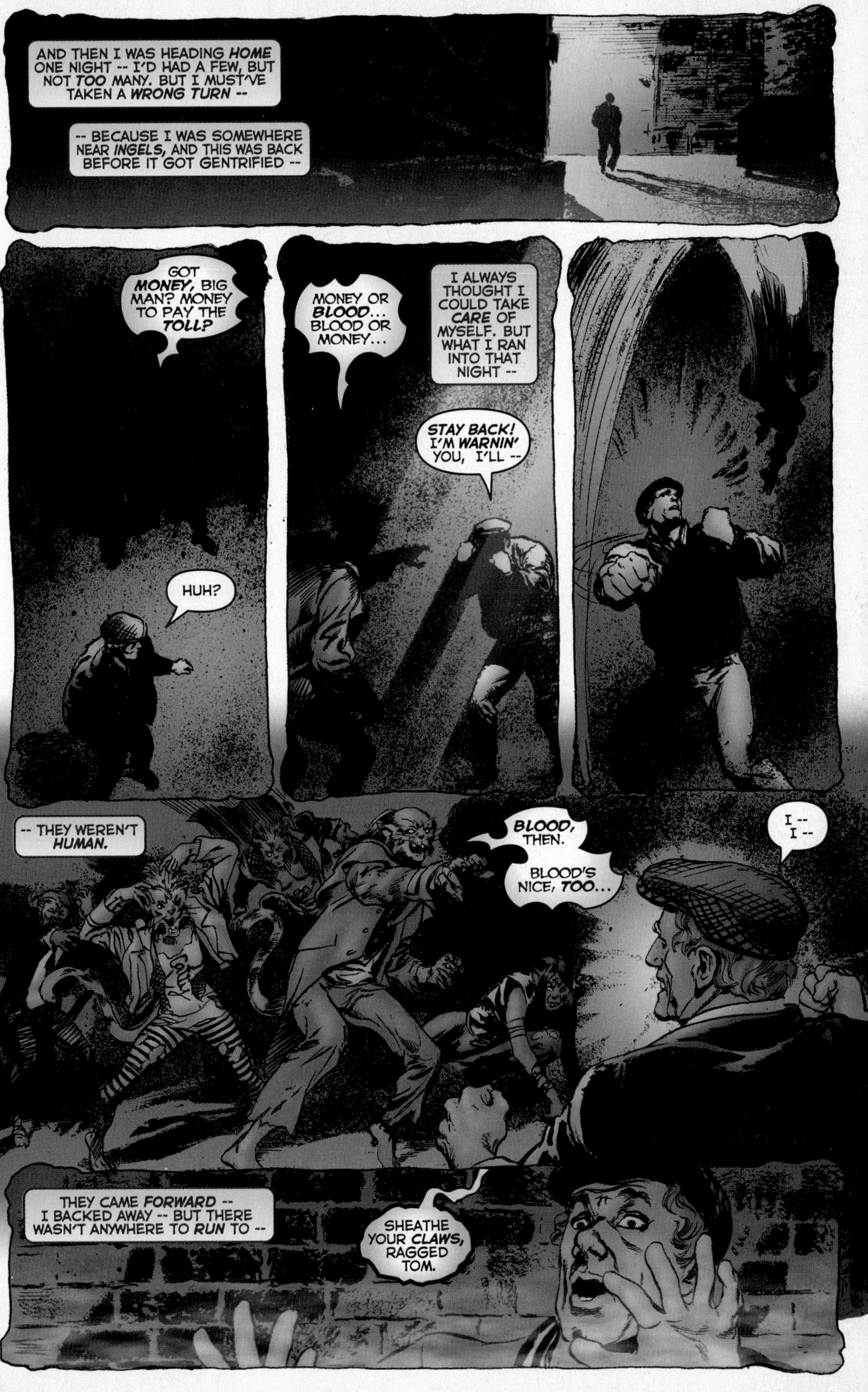
AND THEN I WAS HEADING HOME ONE NIGHT -- I'D HAD A FEW, BUT NOT TOO MANY. BUT I MUST'VE TAKEN A WRONG TURN --
-- BECAUSE I WAS SOMEWHERE NEAR INGELS, AND THIS WAS BACK BEFORE IT GOT GENTRIFIED --
GOT MONEY, BIG MAN? MONEY TO PAY THE TOLL?
HUH?
MONEY OR BLOOD... BLOOD OR MONEY...
I ALWAYS THOUGHT I COULD TAKE CARE OF MYSELF. BUT WHAT I RAN INTO THAT NIGHT --
STAY BACK! I'M WARNIN' YOU, I'LL --
-- THEY WEREN'T HUMAN.
BLOOD, THEN.
BLOOD'S NICE, TOO...
I -- I --
THEY CAME FORWARD -- I BACKED AWAY -- BUT THERE WASN'T ANYWHERE TO RUN TO --
SHEATHE YOUR CLAWS, RAGGED TOM.

SHEATHE THEM, ALL OF YOU. YOUR HUNTING DAYS ARE DONE.
IT WAS THE CONFESSOR.
I'D HEARD OF HIM, OF COURSE, BUT THERE'D NEVER BEEN A PICTURE OF HIM. LOTS OF PEOPLE SAID HE DIDN'T EXIST.
HE'S BACK, THESE DAYS -- OR MAYBE IT'S A NEW ONE. EITHER WAY, THERE'S PICTURES, NOW --
-- BUT BACK THEN, NOTHING. STILL, I'D HEARD THE STORIES. AND HE WAS REAL.

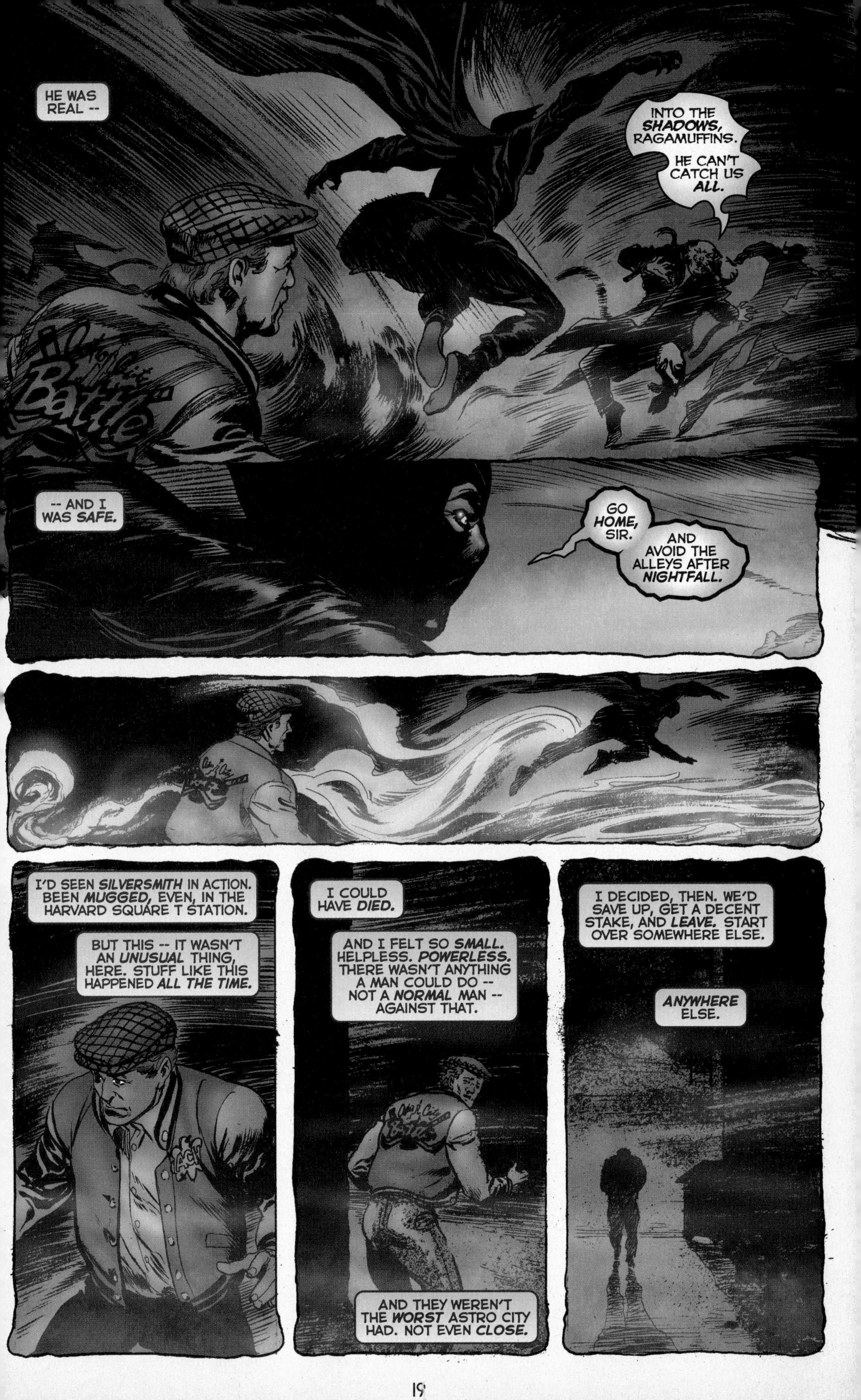
HE WAS REAL --
INTO THE SHADOWS, RAGAMUFFINS.
HE CAN'T CATCH US ALL.
-- AND I WAS SAFE.
GO HOME, SIR.
AND AVOID THE ALLEYS AFTER NIGHTFALL.
I'D SEEN SILVERSMITH IN ACTION. BEEN MUGGED, EVEN, IN THE HARVARD SQUARE T STATION.
BUT THIS -- IT WASN'T AN UNUSUAL THING, HERE. STUFF LIKE THIS HAPPENED ALL THE TIME.
I COULD HAVE DIED.
AND I FELT SO SMALL. HELPLESS. POWERLESS. THERE WASN'T ANYTHING A MAN COULD DO -- NOT A NORMAL MAN -- AGAINST THAT.
AND THEY WEREN'T THE WORST ASTRO CITY HAD. NOT EVEN CLOSE.
I DECIDED, THEN. WE'D SAVE UP, GET A DECENT STAKE, AND LEAVE. START OVER SOMEWHERE ELSE.
ANYWHERE ELSE.

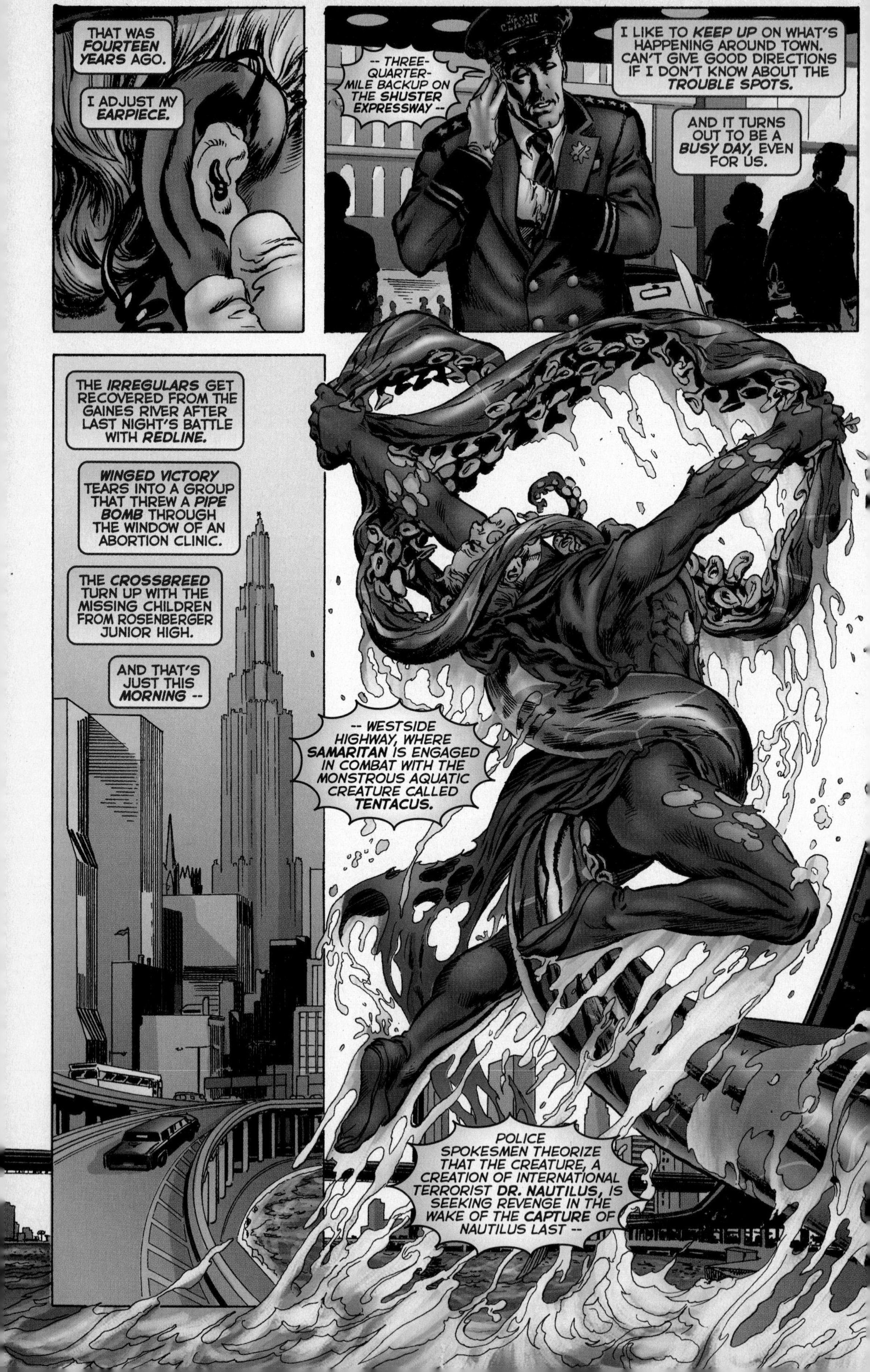
THAT WAS FOURTEEN YEARS AGO.
I ADJUST MY EARPIECE.
-- THREE-QUARTER-MILE BACKUP ON THE SHUSTER EXPRESSWAY --
I LIKE TO KEEP UP ON WHAT'S HAPPENING AROUND TOWN. CAN'T GIVE GOOD DIRECTIONS IF I DON'T KNOW ABOUT THE TROUBLE SPOTS.
AND IT TURNS OUT TO BE A BUSY DAY, EVEN FOR US.
THE IRREGULARS GET RECOVERED FROM THE GAINES RIVER AFTER LAST NIGHT'S BATTLE WITH REDLINE.
WINGED VICTORY TEARS INTO A GROUP THAT THREW A PIPE BOMB THROUGH THE WINDOW OF AN ABORTION CLINIC.
THE CROSSBREED TURN UP WITH THE MISSING CHILDREN FROM ROSENBERGER JUNIOR HIGH.
AND THAT'S JUST THIS MORNING --
-- WESTSIDE HIGHWAY, WHERE SAMARITAN IS ENGAGED IN COMBAT WITH THE MONSTROUS AQUATIC CREATURE CALLED TENTACUS.
POLICE SPOKESMEN THEORIZE THAT THE CREATURE, A CREATION OF INTERNATIONAL TERRORIST DR. NAUTILUS, IS SEEKING REVENGE IN THE WAKE OF THE CAPTURE OF NAUTILUS LAST --

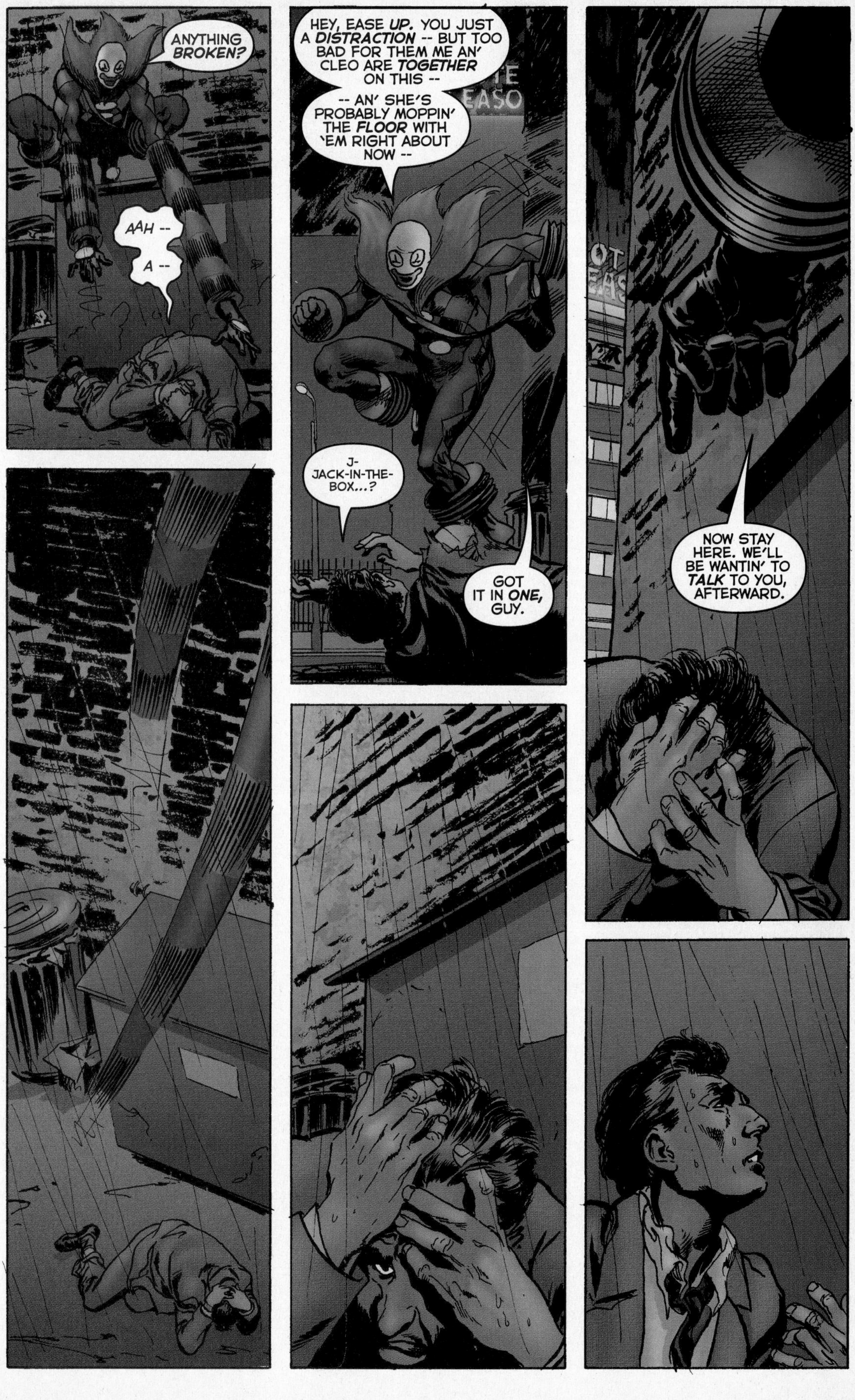
ANYTHING BROKEN?
AAH -- A --
HEY, EASE UP. YOU JUST A DISTRACTION -- BUT TOO BAD FOR THEM ME AN' CLEO ARE TOGETHER ON THIS --
-- AN' SHE'S PROBABLY MOPPIN' THE FLOOR WITH 'EM RIGHT ABOUT NOW --
J-JACK-IN-THE-BOX...?
GOT IT IN ONE, GUY.
NOW STAY HERE. WE'LL BE WANTIN' TO TALK TO YOU, AFTERWARD.

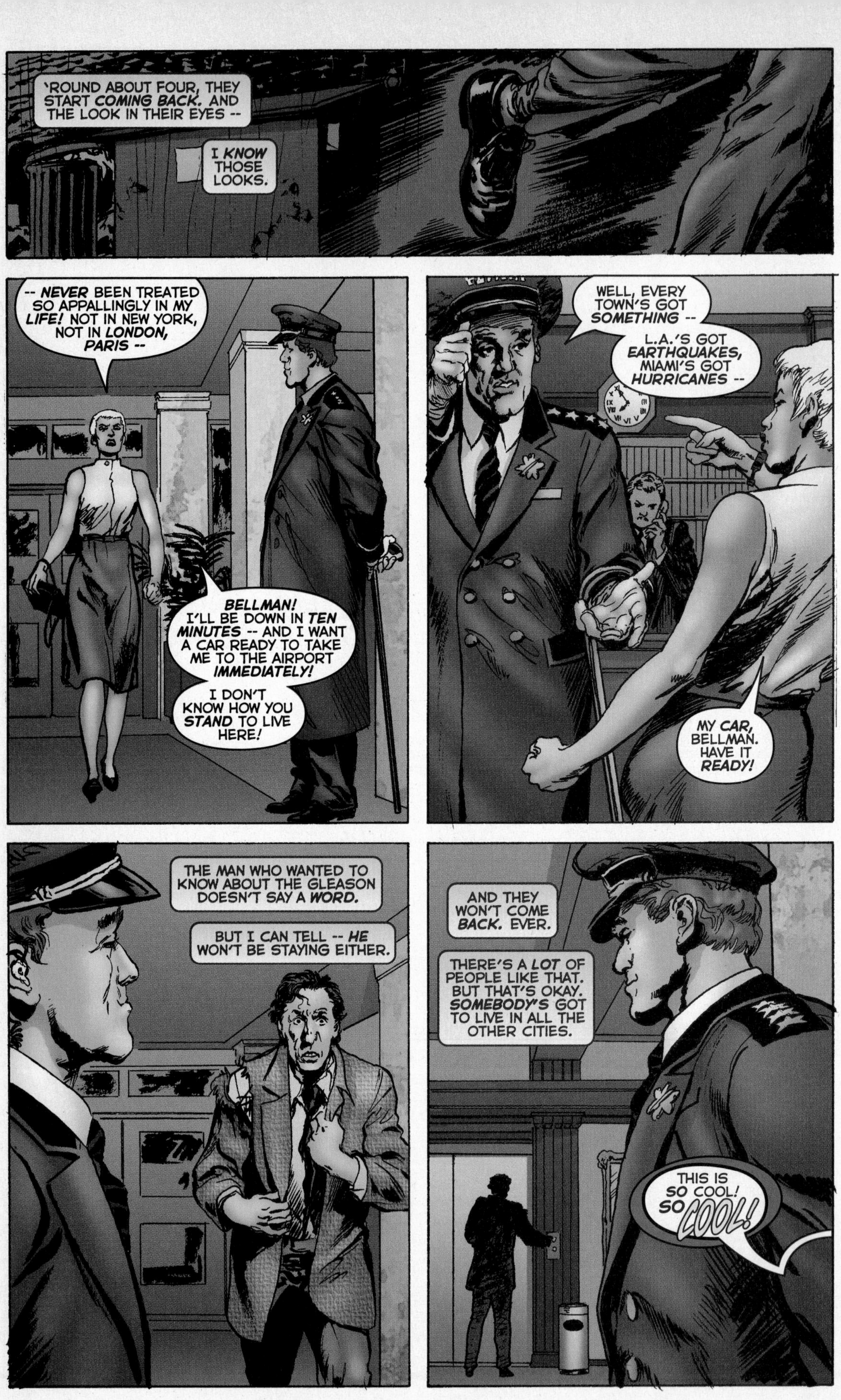

'ROUND ABOUT FOUR, THEY START COMING BACK. AND THE LOOK IN THEIR EYES --
I KNOW THOSE LOOKS.
-- NEVER BEEN TREATED SO APPALLINGLY IN MY LIFE! NOT IN NEW YORK, NOT IN LONDON, PARIS --
BELLMAN! I'LL BE DOWN IN TEN MINUTES -- AND I WANT A CAR READY TO TAKE ME TO THE AIRPORT IMMEDIATELY!
I DON'T KNOW HOW YOU STAND TO LIVE HERE!
WELL, EVERY TOWN'S GOT SOMETHING --
L.A.'S GOT EARTHQUAKES, MIAMI'S GOT HURRICANES --
MY CAR, BELLMAN. HAVE IT READY!
THE MAN WHO WANTED TO KNOW ABOUT THE GLEASON DOESN'T SAY A WORD.
BUT I CAN TELL -- HE WON'T BE STAYING EITHER.
AND THEY WON'T COME BACK. EVER.
THERE'S A LOT OF PEOPLE LIKE THAT. BUT THAT'S OKAY. SOMEBODY'S GOT TO LIVE IN ALL THE OTHER CITIES.
THIS IS SO COOL! SO COOL!

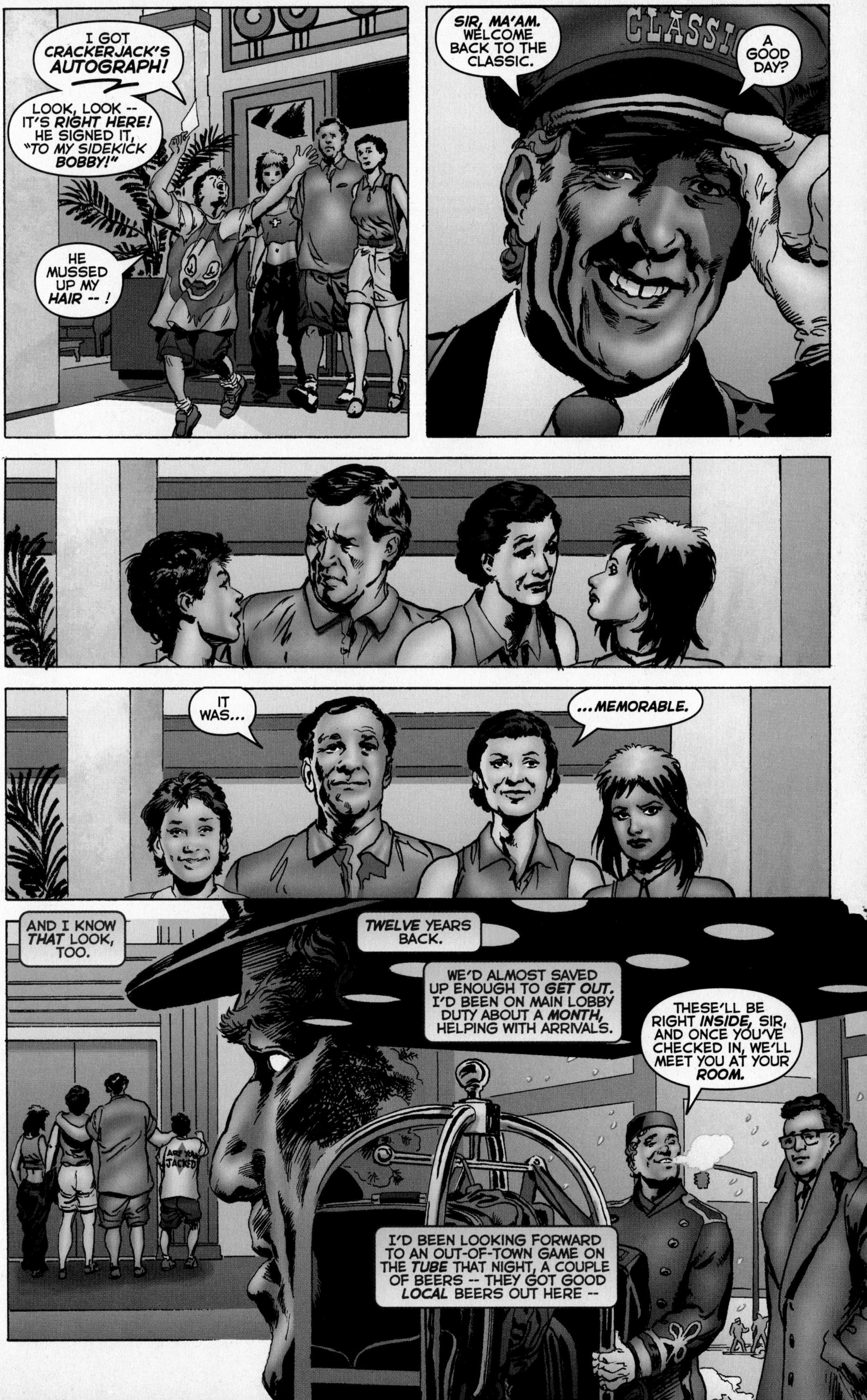
I GOT CRACKERJACK'S AUTOGRAPH!
LOOK, LOOK -- IT'S RIGHT HERE! HE SIGNED IT, "TO MY SIDEKICK BOBBY!"
HE MUSSED UP MY HAIR -- !
SIR, MA'AM. WELCOME BACK TO THE CLASSIC.
A GOOD DAY?
IT WAS...
...MEMORABLE.
AND I KNOW THAT LOOK, TOO.
TWELVE YEARS BACK.
WE'D ALMOST SAVED UP ENOUGH TO GET OUT. I'D BEEN ON MAIN LOBBY DUTY ABOUT A MONTH, HELPING WITH ARRIVALS.
THESE'LL BE RIGHT INSIDE, SIR, AND ONCE YOU'VE CHECKED IN, WE'LL MEET YOU AT YOUR ROOM.
I'D BEEN LOOKING FORWARD TO AN OUT-OF-TOWN GAME ON THE TUBE THAT NIGHT, A COUPLE OF BEERS -- THEY GOT GOOD LOCAL BEERS OUT HERE --

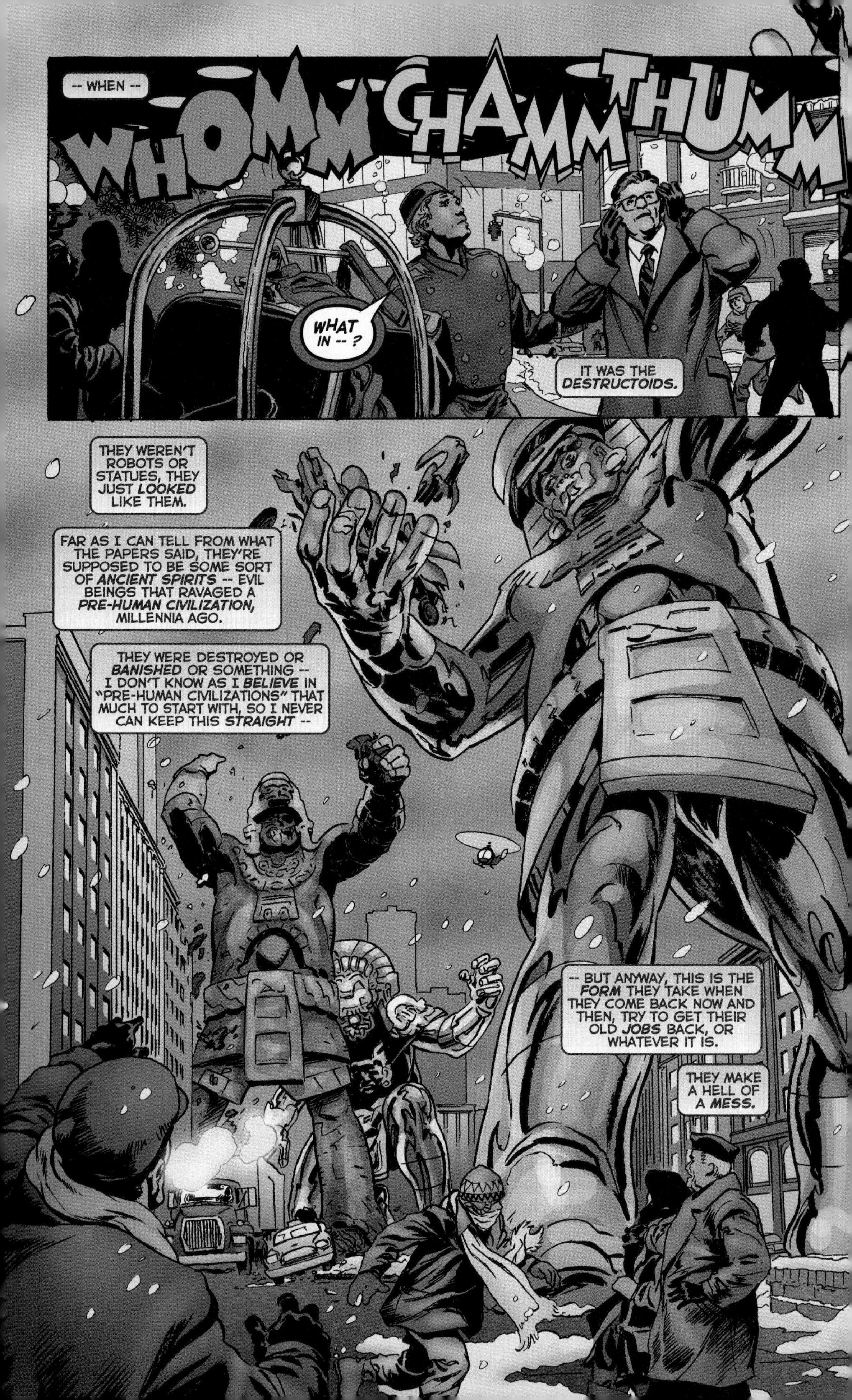
-- WHEN --
WHOMM
CHAMM
THUMM
WHAT IN -- ?
IT WAS THE *DESTRUCTOIDS.*
THEY WEREN'T ROBOTS OR STATUES, THEY JUST *LOOKED* LIKE THEM.
FAR AS I CAN TELL FROM WHAT THE PAPERS SAID, THEY'RE SUPPOSED TO BE SOME SORT OF *ANCIENT SPIRITS* -- EVIL BEINGS THAT RAVAGED A *PRE-HUMAN CIVILIZATION,* MILLENNIA AGO.
THEY WERE DESTROYED OR *BANISHED* OR SOMETHING -- I DON'T KNOW AS I *BELIEVE* IN "PRE-HUMAN CIVILIZATIONS" THAT MUCH TO START WITH, SO I NEVER CAN KEEP THIS *STRAIGHT* --
-- BUT ANYWAY, THIS IS THE *FORM* THEY TAKE WHEN THEY COME BACK NOW AND THEN, TRY TO GET THEIR OLD *JOBS* BACK, OR WHATEVER IT IS.
THEY MAKE A HELL OF A *MESS.*

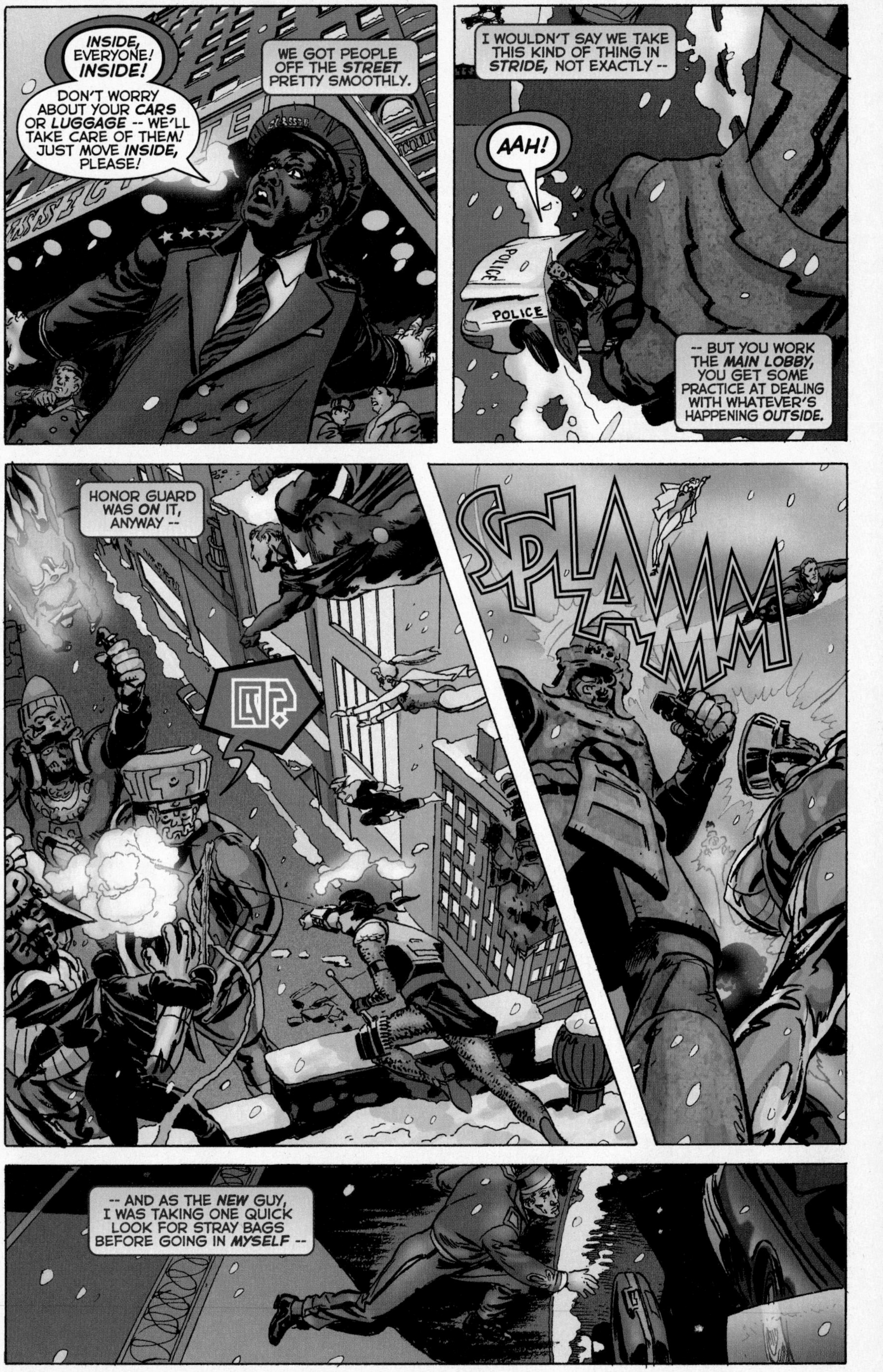
INSIDE, EVERYONE! INSIDE!
DON'T WORRY ABOUT YOUR CARS OR LUGGAGE -- WE'LL TAKE CARE OF THEM! JUST MOVE INSIDE, PLEASE!
WE GOT PEOPLE OFF THE STREET PRETTY SMOOTHLY.
I WOULDN'T SAY WE TAKE THIS KIND OF THING IN STRIDE, NOT EXACTLY --
AAH!
POLICE
-- BUT YOU WORK THE MAIN LOBBY, YOU GET SOME PRACTICE AT DEALING WITH WHATEVER'S HAPPENING OUTSIDE.
HONOR GUARD WAS ON IT, ANYWAY --
SPLAMMM
-- AND AS THE NEW GUY, I WAS TAKING ONE QUICK LOOK FOR STRAY BAGS BEFORE GOING IN MYSELF --

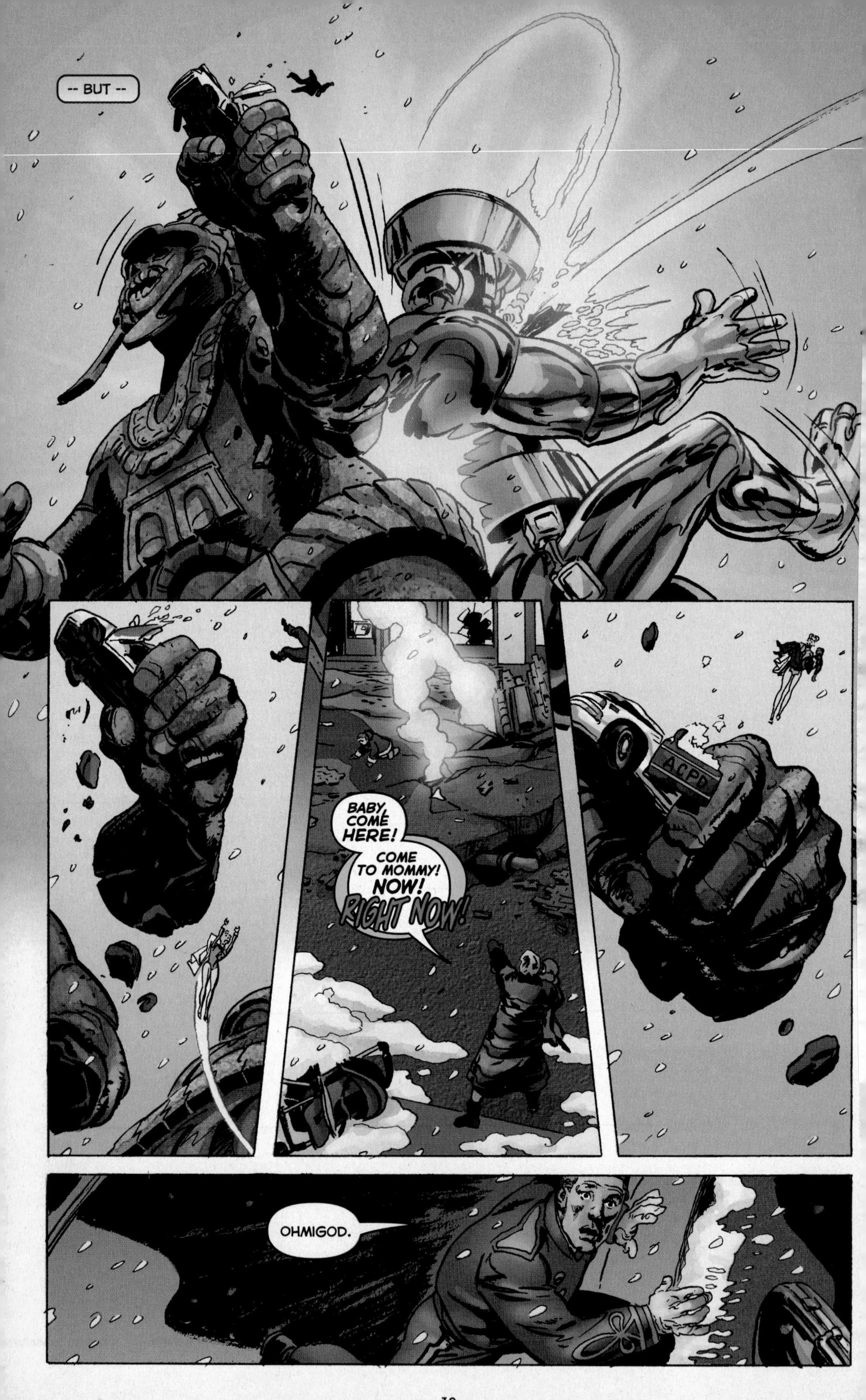
-- BUT --
ACPD
BABY, COME HERE!
COME TO MOMMY! NOW! RIGHT NOW!
OHMIGOD.

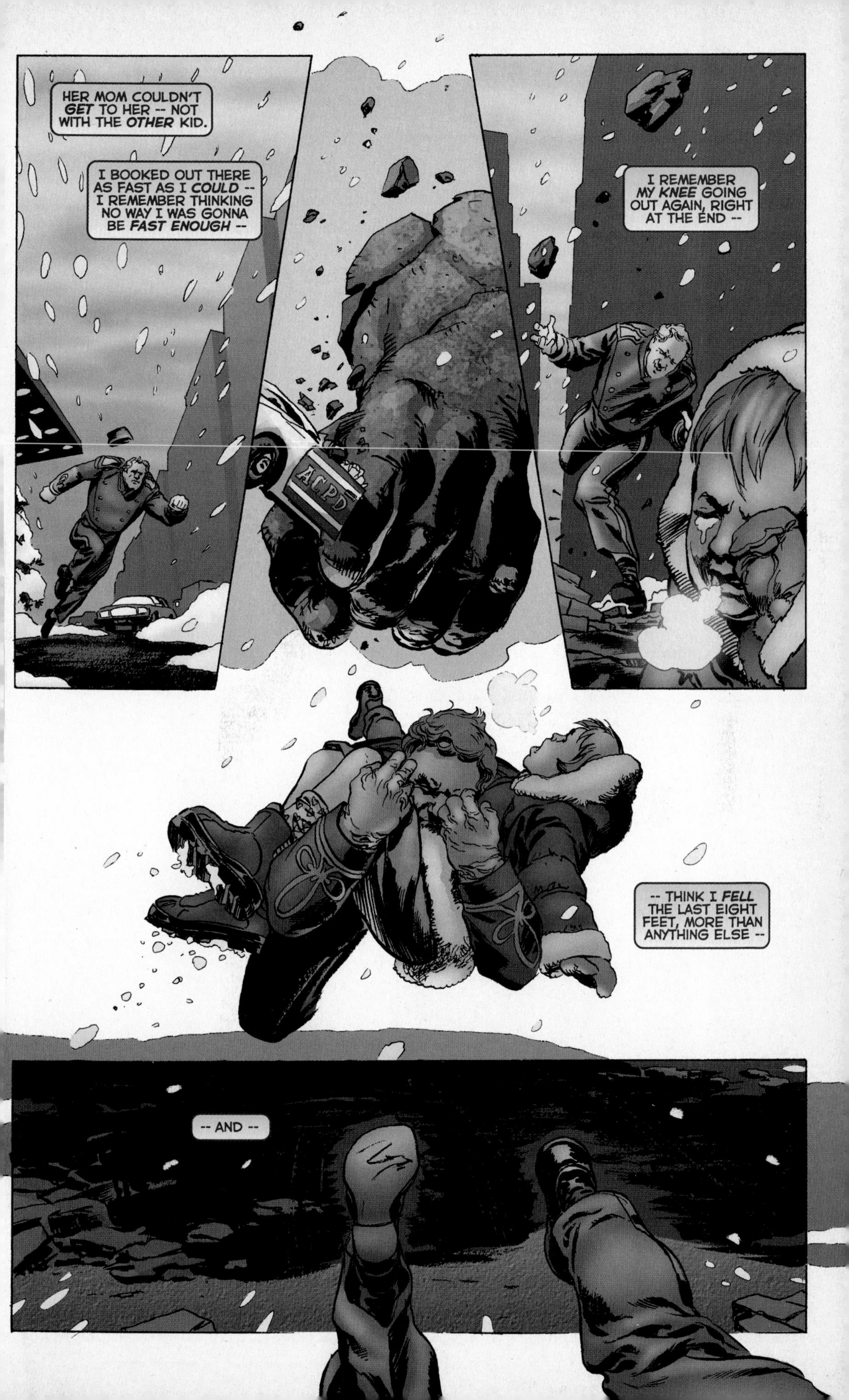
HER MOM COULDN'T GET TO HER -- NOT WITH THE OTHER KID.
I BOOKED OUT THERE AS FAST AS I COULD -- I REMEMBER THINKING NO WAY I WAS GONNA BE FAST ENOUGH --
ACPD
I REMEMBER MY KNEE GOING OUT AGAIN, RIGHT AT THE END --
-- THINK I FELL THE LAST EIGHT FEET, MORE THAN ANYTHING ELSE --
-- AND --

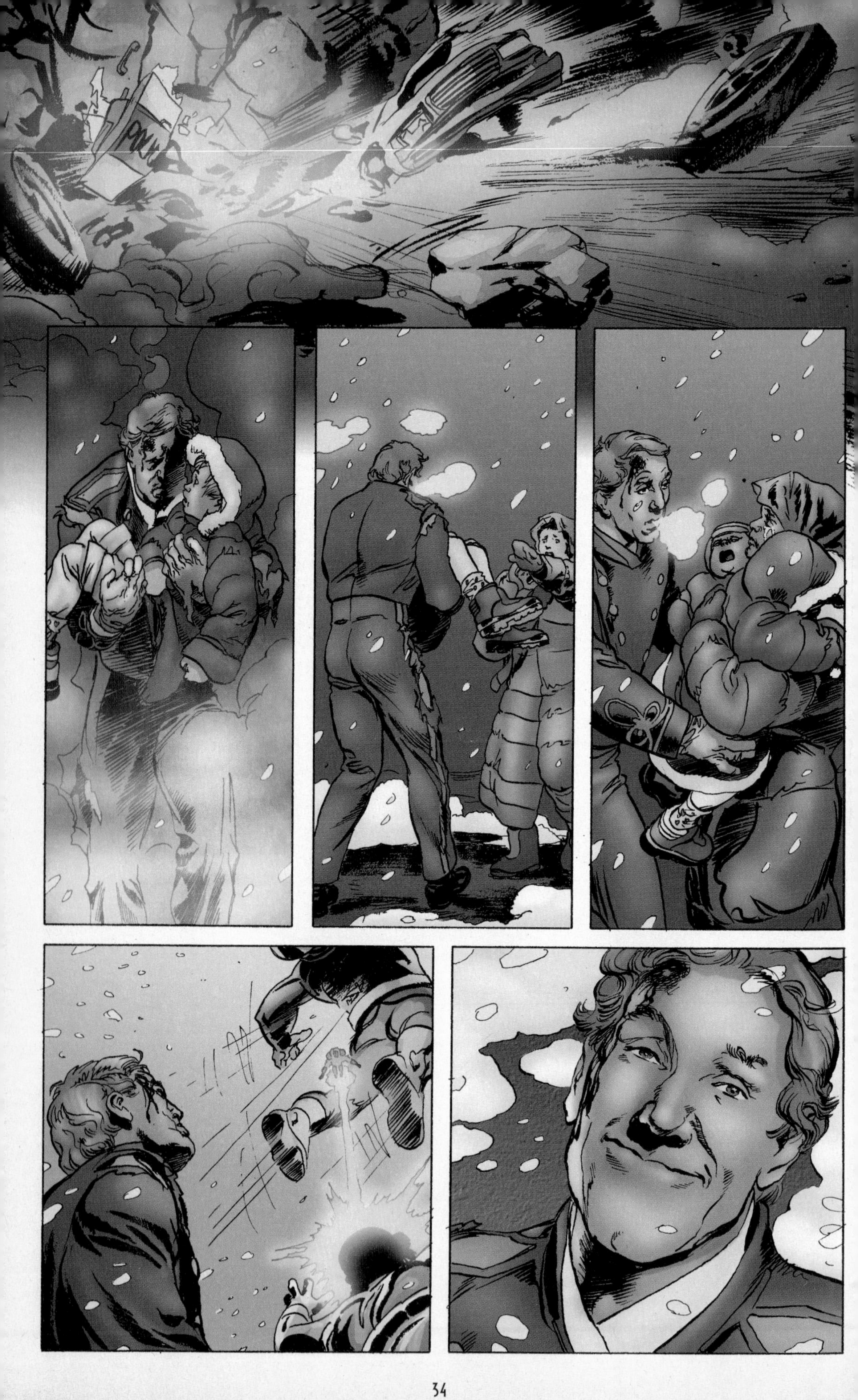

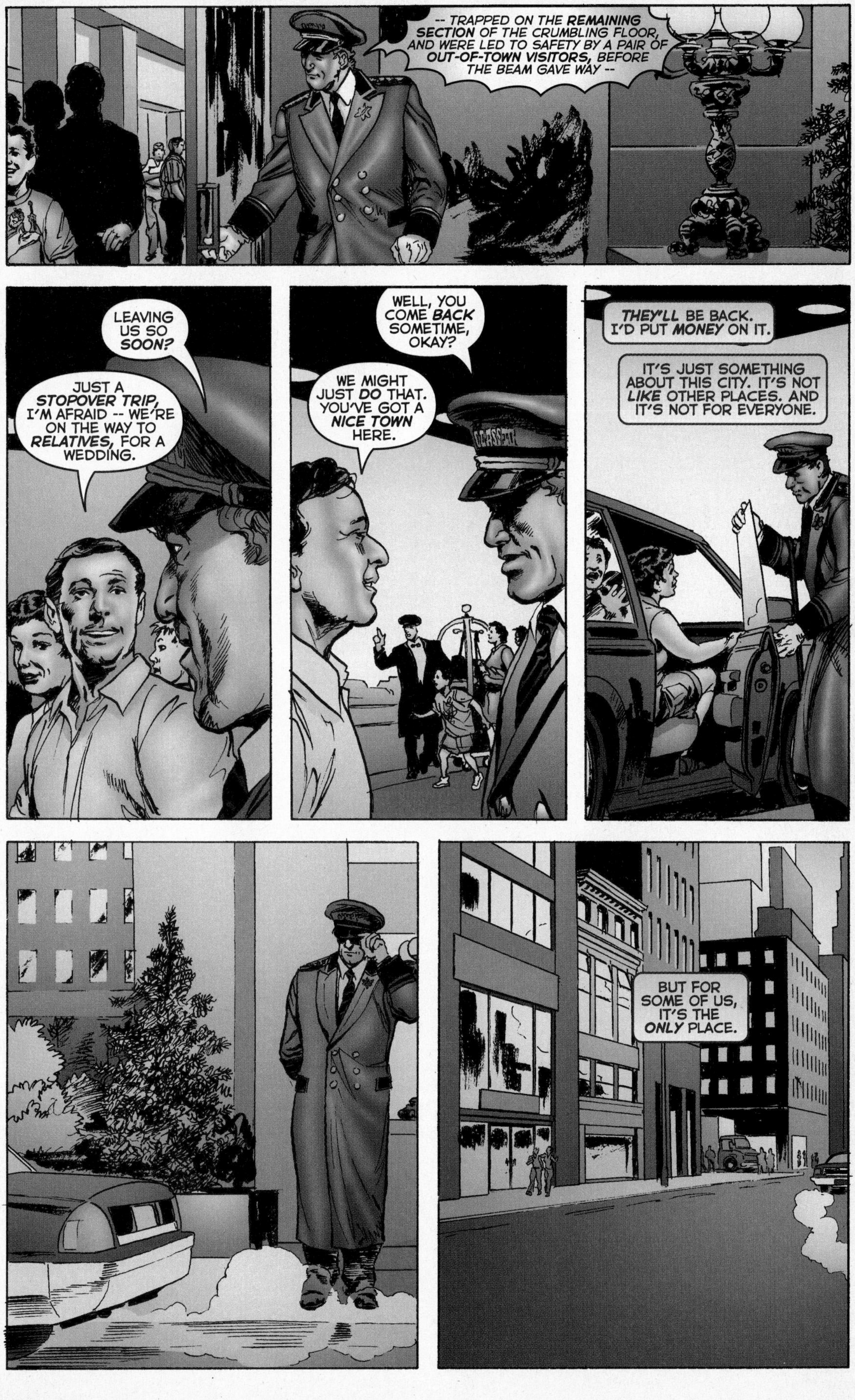
-- TRAPPED ON THE REMAINING SECTION OF THE CRUMBLING FLOOR, AND WERE LED TO SAFETY BY A PAIR OF OUT-OF-TOWN VISITORS, BEFORE THE BEAM GAVE WAY --
LEAVING US SO SOON?
JUST A STOPOVER TRIP, I'M AFRAID -- WE'RE ON THE WAY TO RELATIVES, FOR A WEDDING.
WELL, YOU COME BACK SOMETIME, OKAY?
WE MIGHT JUST DO THAT. YOU'VE GOT A NICE TOWN HERE.
THEY'LL BE BACK. I'D PUT MONEY ON IT.
IT'S JUST SOMETHING ABOUT THIS CITY. IT'S NOT LIKE OTHER PLACES. AND IT'S NOT FOR EVERYONE.
BUT FOR SOME OF US, IT'S THE ONLY PLACE.

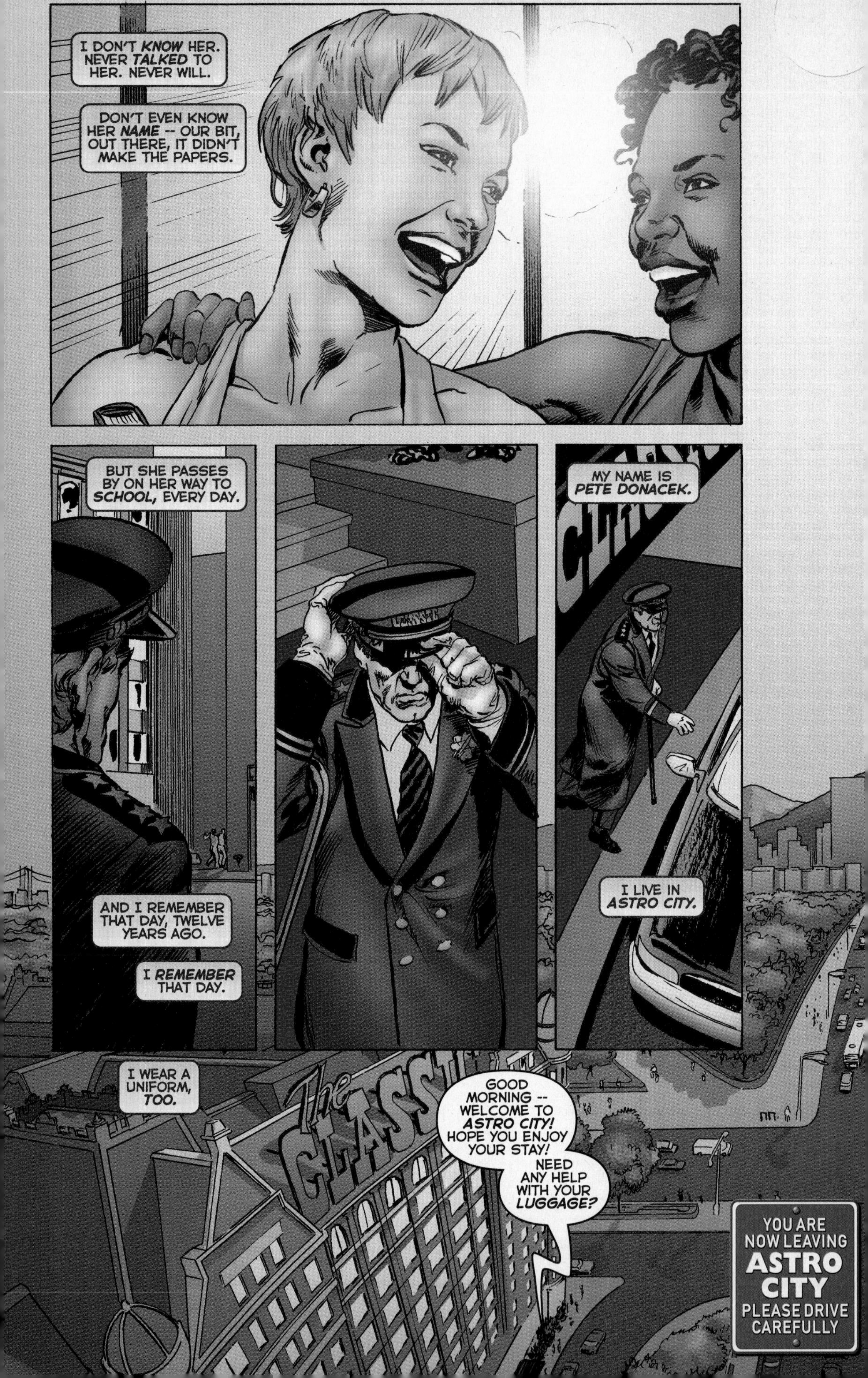
I DON'T KNOW HER. NEVER TALKED TO HER. NEVER WILL.
DON'T EVEN KNOW HER NAME -- OUR BIT, OUT THERE, IT DIDN'T MAKE THE PAPERS.
BUT SHE PASSES BY ON HER WAY TO SCHOOL, EVERY DAY.
AND I REMEMBER THAT DAY, TWELVE YEARS AGO.
I REMEMBER THAT DAY.
MY NAME IS PETE DONACEK.
I LIVE IN ASTRO CITY.
I WEAR A UNIFORM, TOO.
GOOD MORNING -- WELCOME TO ASTRO CITY! HOPE YOU ENJOY YOUR STAY!
NEED ANY HELP WITH YOUR LUGGAGE?
YOU ARE NOW LEAVING ASTRO CITY PLEASE DRIVE CAREFULLY

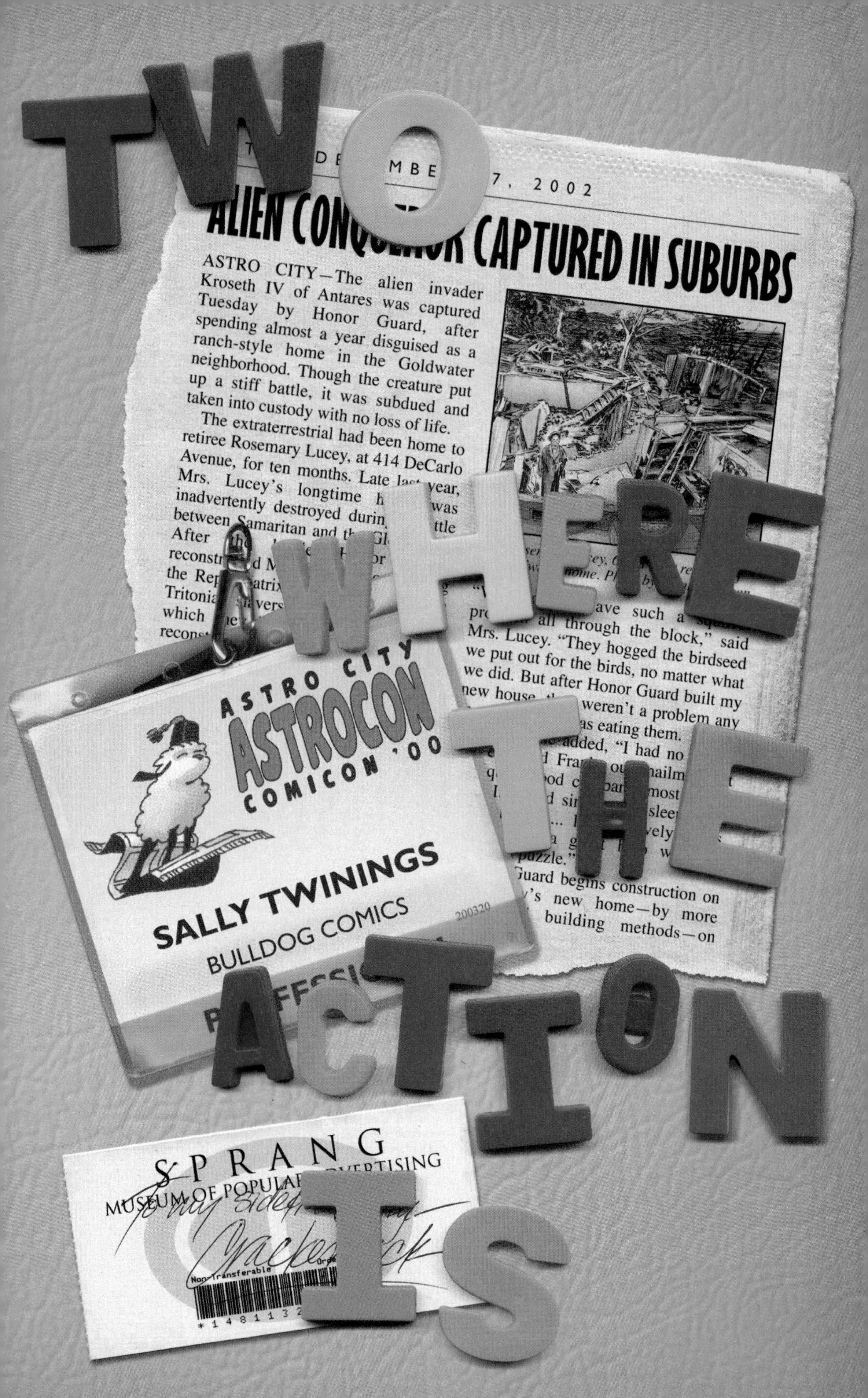
TWO
ALIEN CON CAPTURED IN SUBURBS
7, 2002
ASTRO CITY—The alien invader Kroseth IV of Antares was captured Tuesday by Honor Guard, after spending almost a year disguised as a ranch-style home in the Goldwater neighborhood. Though the creature put up a stiff battle, it was subdued and taken into custody with no loss of life.
The extraterrestrial had been home to retiree Rosemary Lucey, at 414 DeCarlo Avenue, for ten months.
all through the block," said Mrs. Lucey. "They hogged the birdseed we put out for the birds, no matter what we did. But after Honor Guard built my new house,
weren't a problem any
as eating them.
added, "I had no
puzzle."
Guard begins construction on
's new home—by more
building methods—on
WHERE
THE
ASTRO CITY
ASTROCON
COMICON '00
SALLY TWININGS
BULLDOG COMICS
200320
ACTION
SPRANG
MUSEUM OF POPULAR ADVERTISING
Non-Transferable
IS

Bulldog Comics

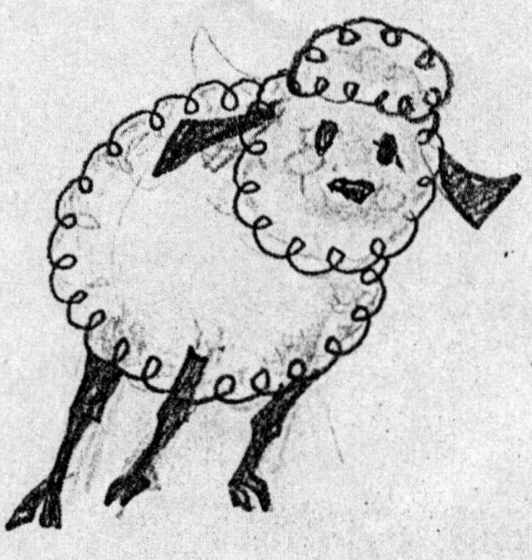

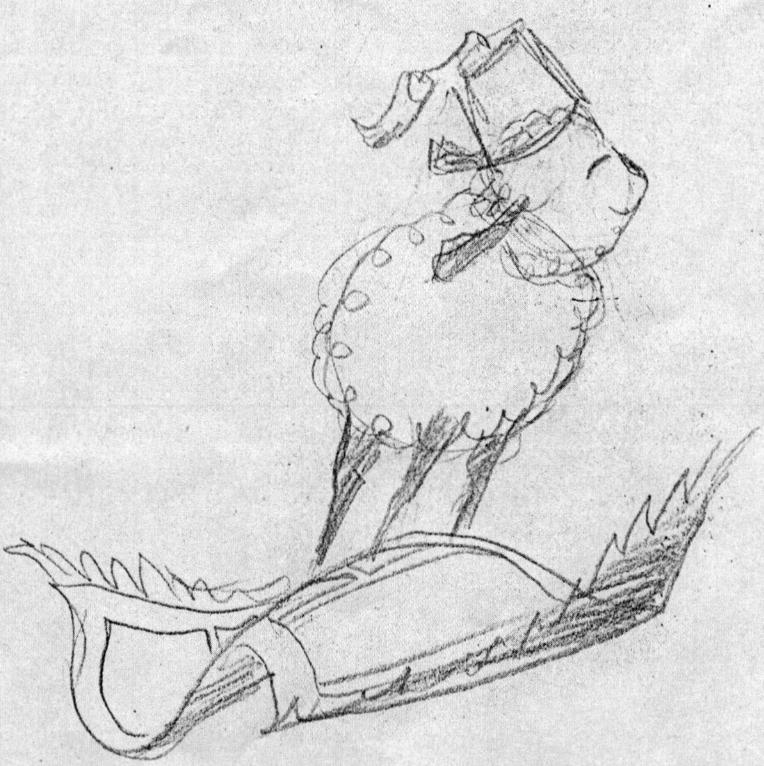

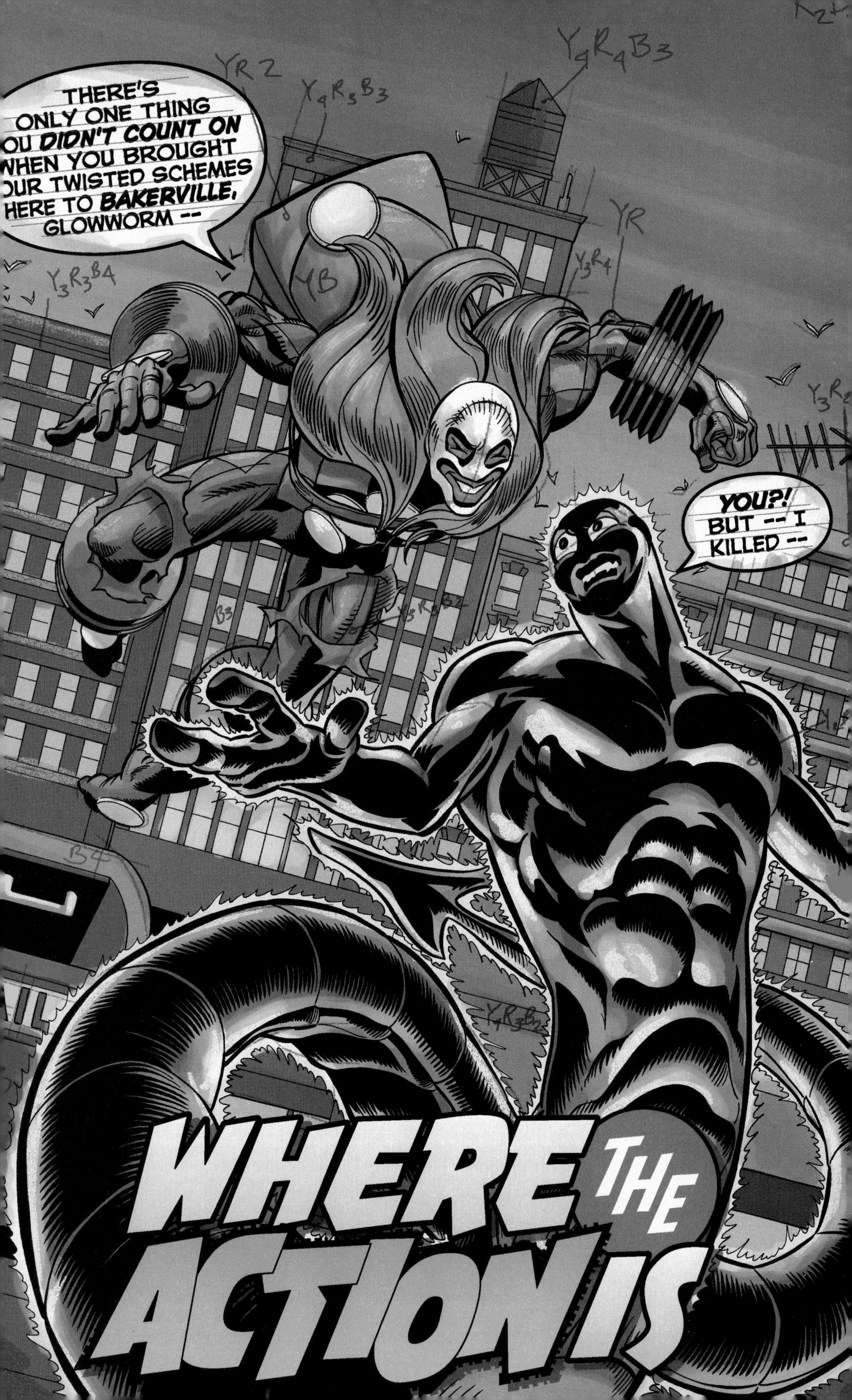
THERE'S ONLY ONE THING OU DIDN'T COUNT ON WHEN YOU BROUGHT OUR TWISTED SCHEMES HERE TO BAKERVILLE, GLOWWORM --
YOU?! BUT -- I KILLED --
WHERE THE ACTION IS

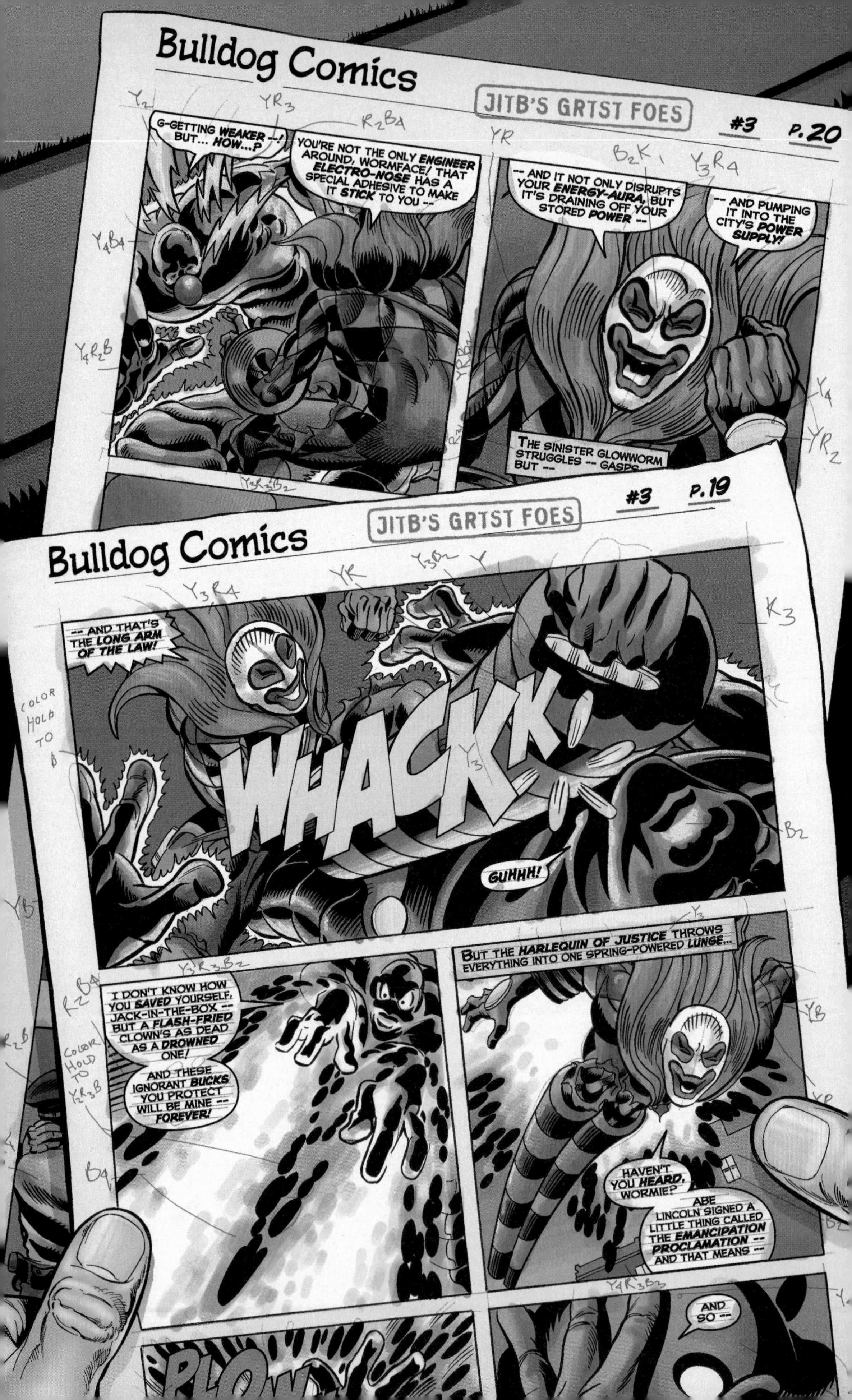

Bulldog Comics
JITB'S GRTST FOES
#3 P.20
G-GETTING WEAKER --! BUT... HOW...?
YOU'RE NOT THE ONLY ENGINEER AROUND, WORMFACE! THAT ELECTRO-NOSE HAS A SPECIAL ADHESIVE TO MAKE IT STICK TO YOU --
-- AND IT NOT ONLY DISRUPTS YOUR ENERGY-AURA, BUT IT'S DRAINING OFF YOUR STORED POWER --
-- AND PUMPING IT INTO THE CITY'S POWER SUPPLY!
THE SINISTER GLOWWORM STRUGGLES -- GASPS BUT --
#3 P.19
JITB'S GRTST FOES
Bulldog Comics
-- AND THAT'S THE LONG ARM OF THE LAW!
COLOR HOLD TO B
WHACKK
GUHHH!
I DON'T KNOW HOW YOU SAVED YOURSELF, JACK-IN-THE-BOX -- BUT A FLASH-FRIED CLOWN'S AS DEAD AS A DROWNED ONE!
AND THESE IGNORANT BUCKS YOU PROTECT WILL BE MINE -- FOREVER!
COLOR HOLD TO Y2R3B
BUT THE HARLEQUIN OF JUSTICE THROWS EVERYTHING INTO ONE SPRING-POWERED LUNGE...
HAVEN'T YOU HEARD, WORMIE?
ABE LINCOLN SIGNED A LITTLE THING CALLED THE EMANCIPATION PROCLAMATION -- AND THAT MEANS --
AND SO --

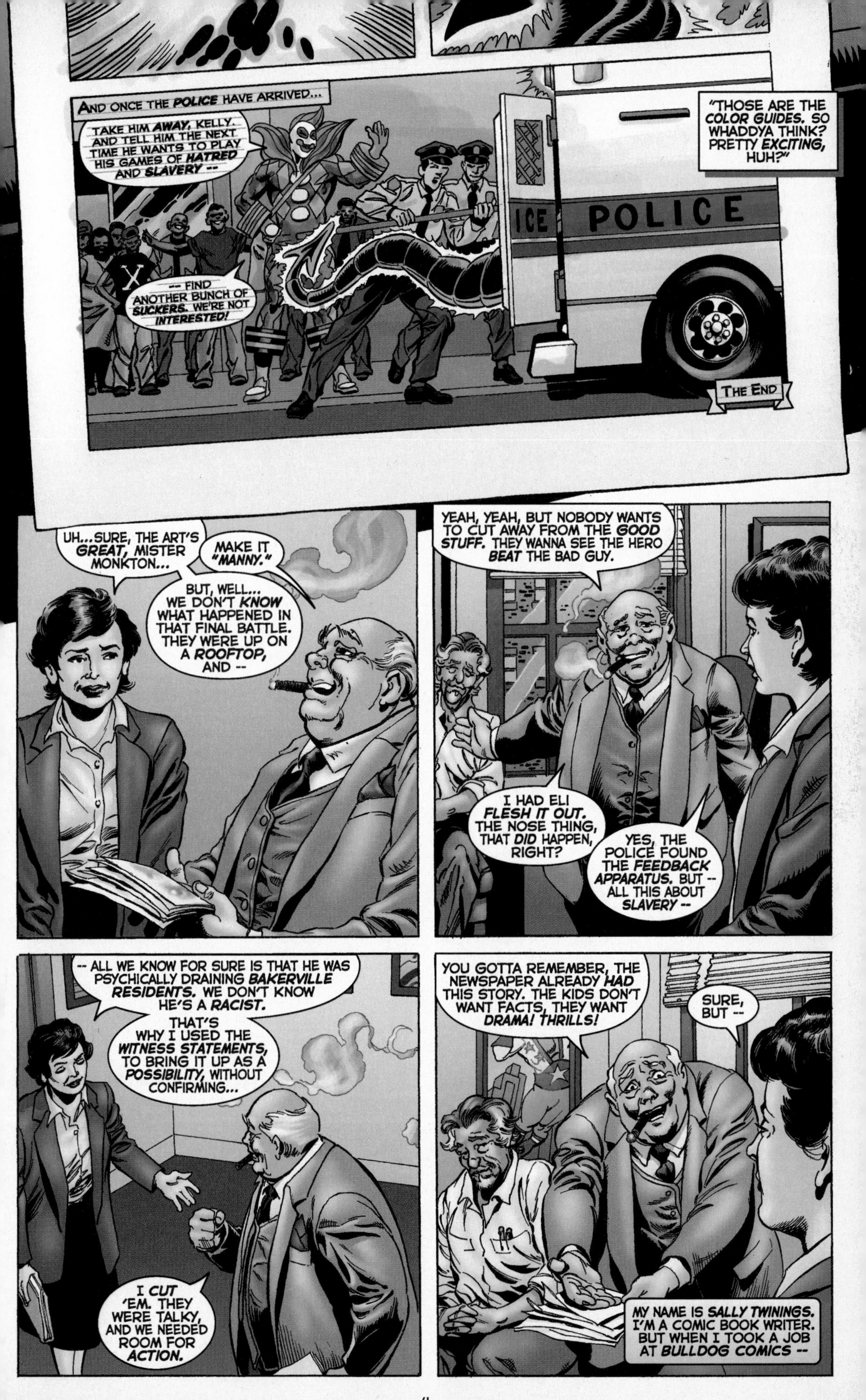
AND ONCE THE POLICE HAVE ARRIVED...
TAKE HIM AWAY, KELLY. AND TELL HIM THE NEXT TIME HE WANTS TO PLAY HIS GAMES OF HATRED AND SLAVERY --
-- FIND ANOTHER BUNCH OF SUCKERS. WE'RE NOT INTERESTED!
ICE POLICE
"THOSE ARE THE COLOR GUIDES. SO WHADDYA THINK? PRETTY EXCITING, HUH?"
THE END
UH...SURE, THE ART'S GREAT, MISTER MONKTON...
MAKE IT "MANNY."
BUT, WELL... WE DON'T KNOW WHAT HAPPENED IN THAT FINAL BATTLE. THEY WERE UP ON A ROOFTOP, AND --
YEAH, YEAH, BUT NOBODY WANTS TO CUT AWAY FROM THE GOOD STUFF. THEY WANNA SEE THE HERO BEAT THE BAD GUY.
I HAD ELI FLESH IT OUT. THE NOSE THING, THAT DID HAPPEN, RIGHT?
YES, THE POLICE FOUND THE FEEDBACK APPARATUS. BUT -- ALL THIS ABOUT SLAVERY --
-- ALL WE KNOW FOR SURE IS THAT HE WAS PSYCHICALLY DRAINING BAKERVILLE RESIDENTS. WE DON'T KNOW HE'S A RACIST.
THAT'S WHY I USED THE WITNESS STATEMENTS, TO BRING IT UP AS A POSSIBILITY, WITHOUT CONFIRMING...
I CUT 'EM. THEY WERE TALKY, AND WE NEEDED ROOM FOR ACTION.
YOU GOTTA REMEMBER, THE NEWSPAPER ALREADY HAD THIS STORY. THE KIDS DON'T WANT FACTS, THEY WANT DRAMA! THRILLS!
SURE, BUT --
MY NAME IS SALLY TWININGS. I'M A COMIC BOOK WRITER. BUT WHEN I TOOK A JOB AT BULLDOG COMICS --

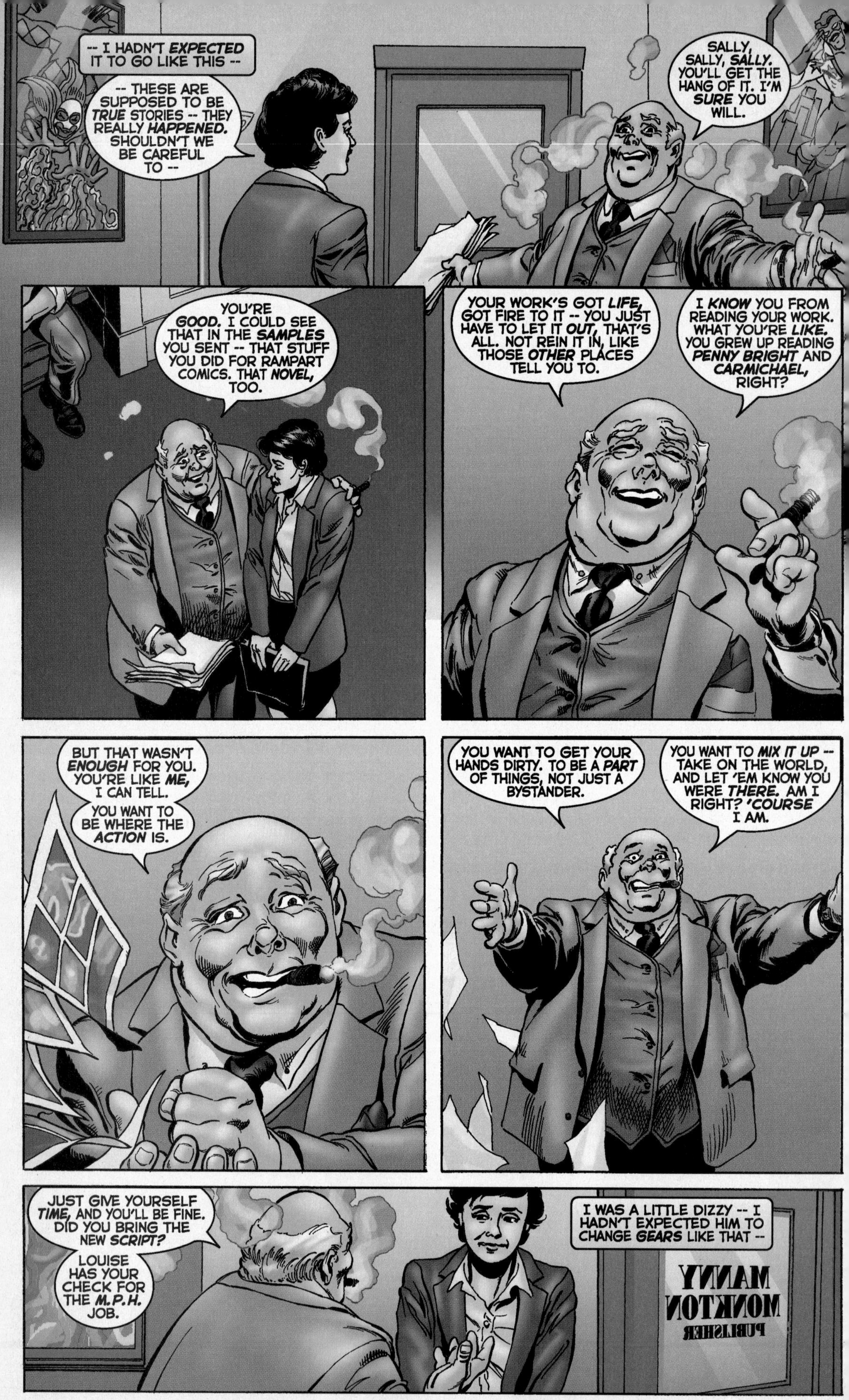
-- I HADN'T EXPECTED IT TO GO LIKE THIS --
-- THESE ARE SUPPOSED TO BE TRUE STORIES -- THEY REALLY HAPPENED. SHOULDN'T WE BE CAREFUL TO --
SALLY, SALLY, SALLY. YOU'LL GET THE HANG OF IT. I'M SURE YOU WILL.
YOU'RE GOOD. I COULD SEE THAT IN THE SAMPLES YOU SENT -- THAT STUFF YOU DID FOR RAMPART COMICS. THAT NOVEL, TOO.
YOUR WORK'S GOT LIFE, GOT FIRE TO IT -- YOU JUST HAVE TO LET IT OUT, THAT'S ALL. NOT REIN IT IN, LIKE THOSE OTHER PLACES TELL YOU TO.
I KNOW YOU FROM READING YOUR WORK. WHAT YOU'RE LIKE. YOU GREW UP READING PENNY BRIGHT AND CARMICHAEL, RIGHT?
BUT THAT WASN'T ENOUGH FOR YOU. YOU'RE LIKE ME, I CAN TELL.
YOU WANT TO BE WHERE THE ACTION IS.
YOU WANT TO GET YOUR HANDS DIRTY. TO BE A PART OF THINGS, NOT JUST A BYSTANDER.
YOU WANT TO MIX IT UP -- TAKE ON THE WORLD, AND LET 'EM KNOW YOU WERE THERE. AM I RIGHT? 'COURSE I AM.
JUST GIVE YOURSELF TIME, AND YOU'LL BE FINE. DID YOU BRING THE NEW SCRIPT?
LOUISE HAS YOUR CHECK FOR THE M.P.H. JOB.
I WAS A LITTLE DIZZY -- I HADN'T EXPECTED HIM TO CHANGE GEARS LIKE THAT --
MANNY MONKTON PUBLISHER

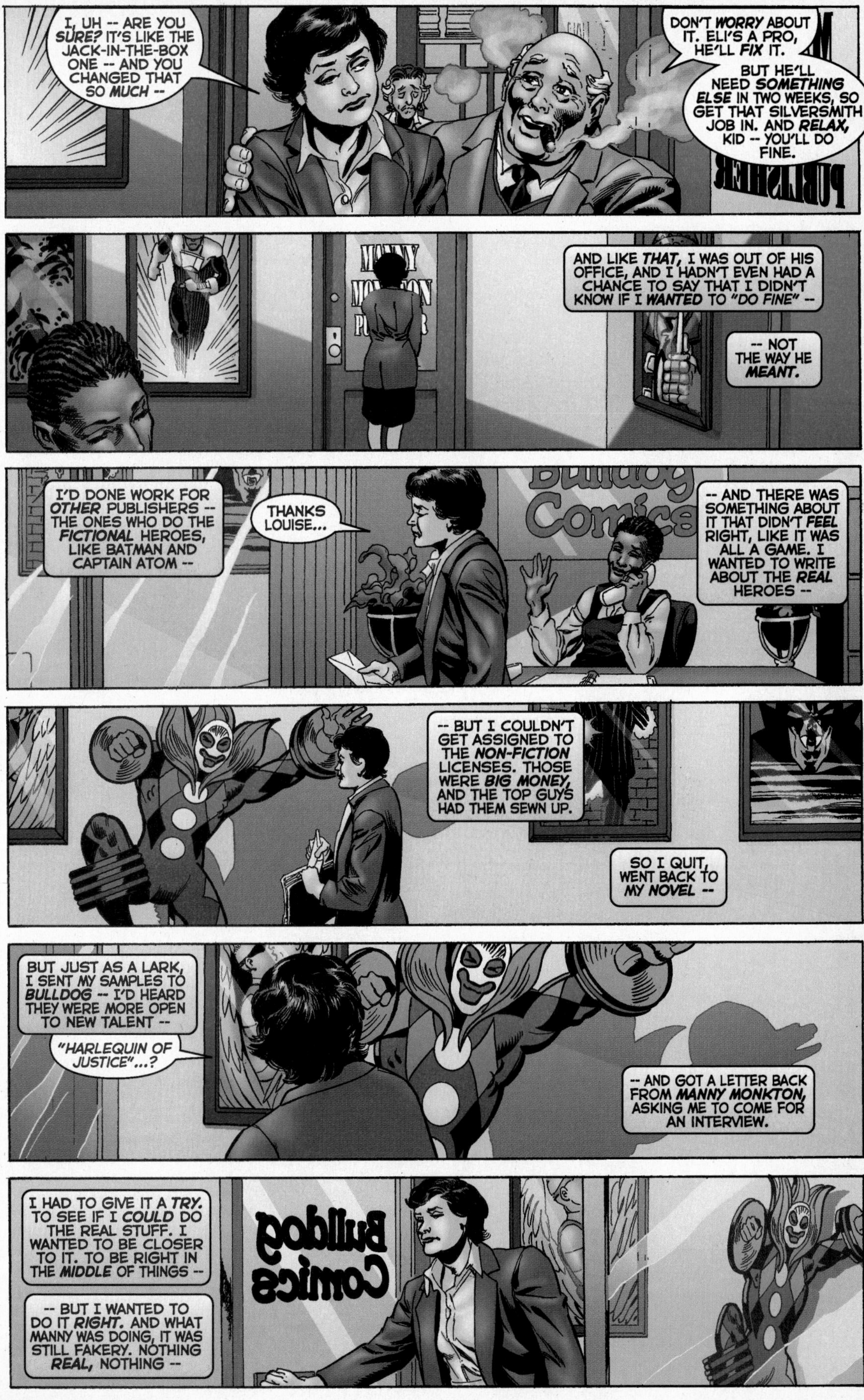

I, UH -- ARE YOU SURE? IT'S LIKE THE JACK-IN-THE-BOX ONE -- AND YOU CHANGED THAT SO MUCH --
DON'T WORRY ABOUT IT. ELI'S A PRO, HE'LL FIX IT.
BUT HE'LL NEED SOMETHING ELSE IN TWO WEEKS, SO GET THAT SILVERSMITH JOB IN. AND RELAX, KID -- YOU'LL DO FINE.
PUBLISHER
MANNY MONKTON PUBLISHER
AND LIKE THAT, I WAS OUT OF HIS OFFICE, AND I HADN'T EVEN HAD A CHANCE TO SAY THAT I DIDN'T KNOW IF I WANTED TO "DO FINE" --
-- NOT THE WAY HE MEANT.
I'D DONE WORK FOR OTHER PUBLISHERS -- THE ONES WHO DO THE FICTIONAL HEROES, LIKE BATMAN AND CAPTAIN ATOM --
THANKS LOUISE...
Bulldog Comics
-- AND THERE WAS SOMETHING ABOUT IT THAT DIDN'T FEEL RIGHT, LIKE IT WAS ALL A GAME. I WANTED TO WRITE ABOUT THE REAL HEROES --
-- BUT I COULDN'T GET ASSIGNED TO THE NON-FICTION LICENSES. THOSE WERE BIG MONEY, AND THE TOP GUYS HAD THEM SEWN UP.
SO I QUIT, WENT BACK TO MY NOVEL --
BUT JUST AS A LARK, I SENT MY SAMPLES TO BULLDOG -- I'D HEARD THEY WERE MORE OPEN TO NEW TALENT --
"HARLEQUIN OF JUSTICE"...?
-- AND GOT A LETTER BACK FROM MANNY MONKTON, ASKING ME TO COME FOR AN INTERVIEW.
I HAD TO GIVE IT A TRY. TO SEE IF I COULD DO THE REAL STUFF. I WANTED TO BE CLOSER TO IT. TO BE RIGHT IN THE MIDDLE OF THINGS --
Bulldog Comics
-- BUT I WANTED TO DO IT RIGHT. AND WHAT MANNY WAS DOING, IT WAS STILL FAKERY. NOTHING REAL, NOTHING --

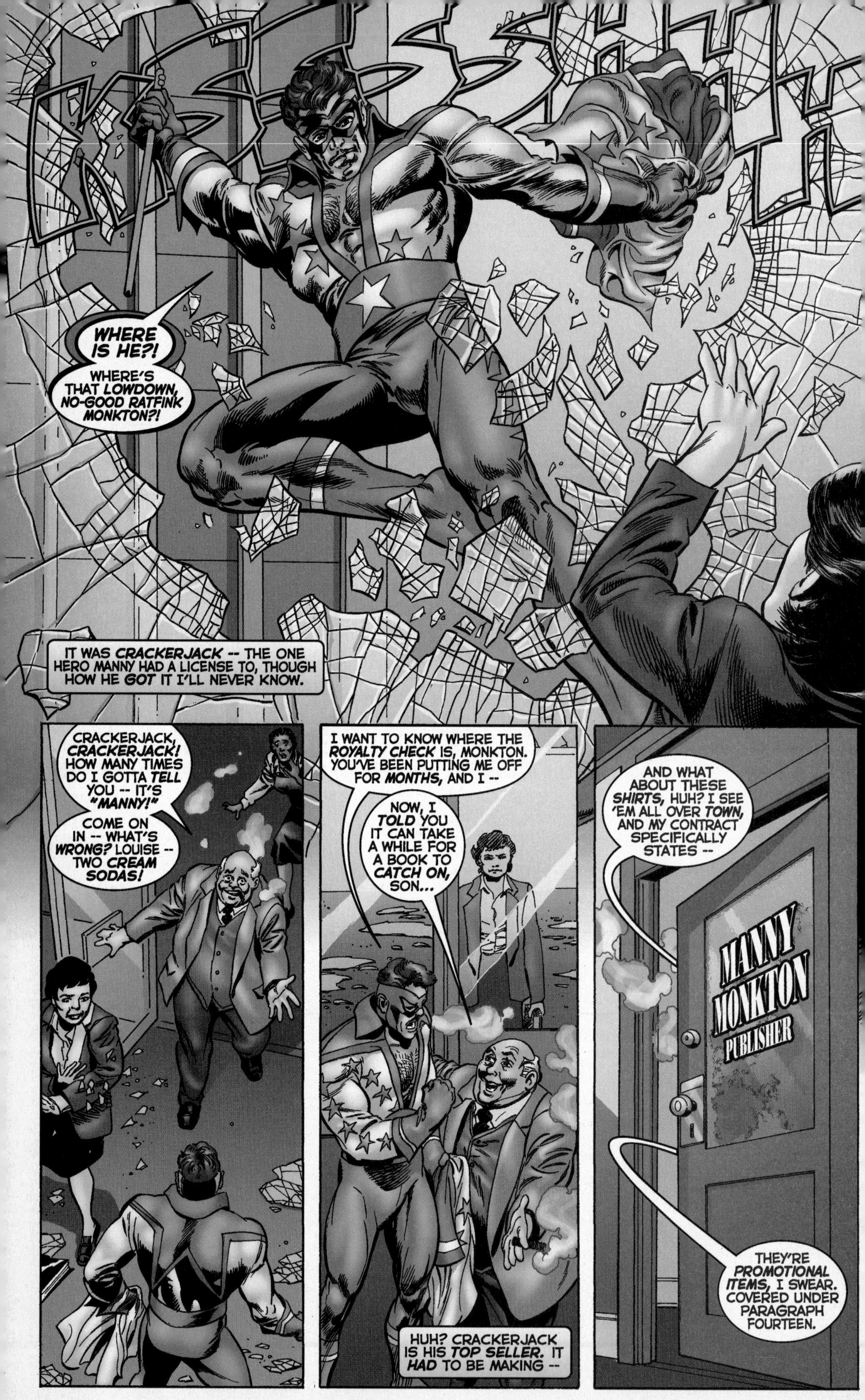

WHERE IS HE?!
WHERE'S THAT LOWDOWN, NO-GOOD RATFINK MONKTON?!
IT WAS CRACKERJACK -- THE ONE HERO MANNY HAD A LICENSE TO, THOUGH HOW HE GOT IT I'LL NEVER KNOW.
CRACKERJACK, CRACKERJACK! HOW MANY TIMES DO I GOTTA TELL YOU -- IT'S "MANNY!"
COME ON IN -- WHAT'S WRONG? LOUISE -- TWO CREAM SODAS!
I WANT TO KNOW WHERE THE ROYALTY CHECK IS, MONKTON. YOU'VE BEEN PUTTING ME OFF FOR MONTHS, AND I --
NOW, I TOLD YOU IT CAN TAKE A WHILE FOR A BOOK TO CATCH ON, SON...
HUH? CRACKERJACK IS HIS TOP SELLER. IT HAD TO BE MAKING --
AND WHAT ABOUT THESE SHIRTS, HUH? I SEE 'EM ALL OVER TOWN, AND MY CONTRACT SPECIFICALLY STATES --
MANNY MONKTON PUBLISHER
THEY'RE PROMOTIONAL ITEMS, I SWEAR. COVERED UNDER PARAGRAPH FOURTEEN.

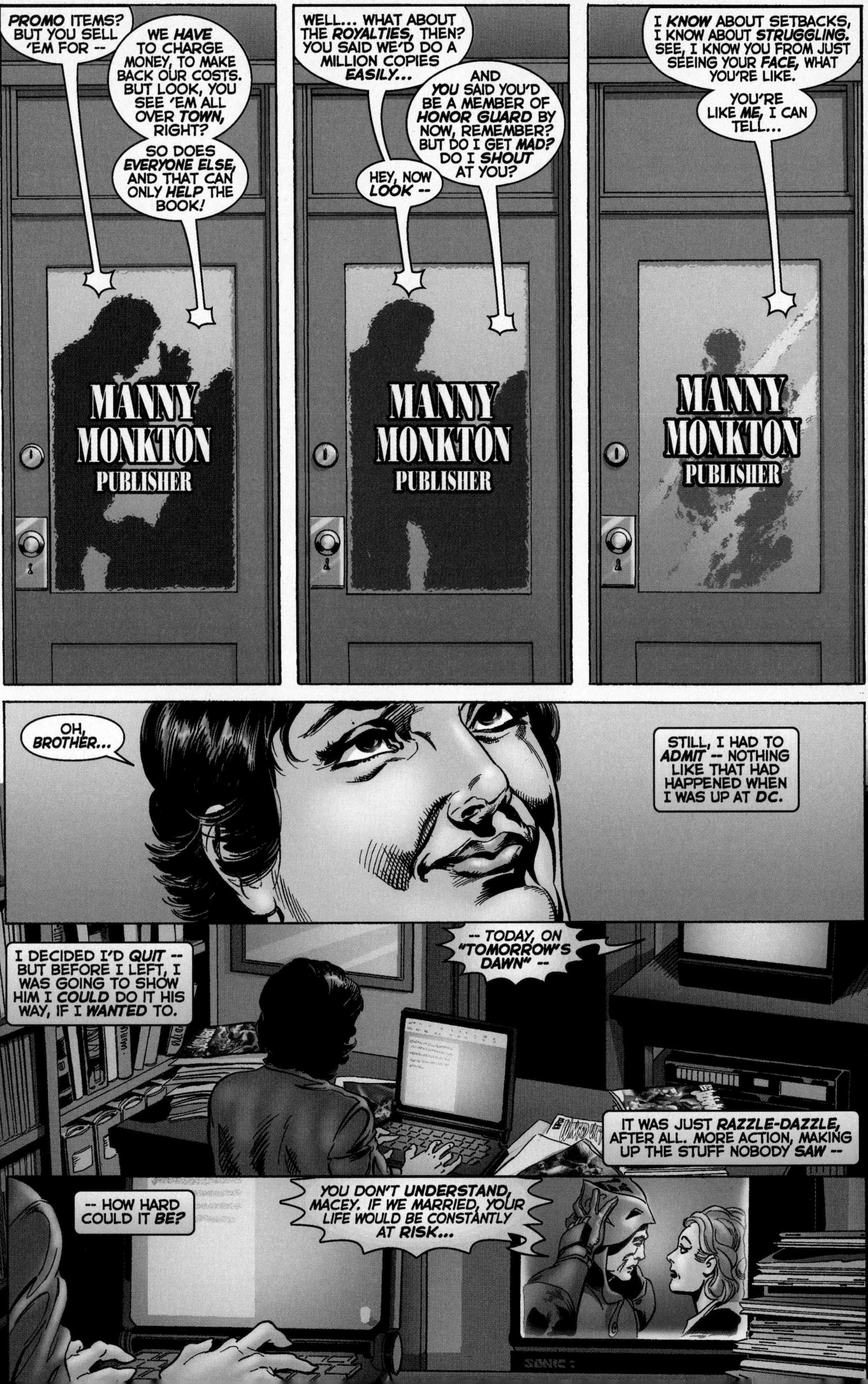

PROMO ITEMS? BUT YOU SELL 'EM FOR --
WE HAVE TO CHARGE MONEY, TO MAKE BACK OUR COSTS. BUT LOOK, YOU SEE 'EM ALL OVER TOWN, RIGHT?
SO DOES EVERYONE ELSE, AND THAT CAN ONLY HELP THE BOOK!
MANNY MONKTON PUBLISHER
WELL... WHAT ABOUT THE ROYALTIES, THEN? YOU SAID WE'D DO A MILLION COPIES EASILY...
AND YOU SAID YOU'D BE A MEMBER OF HONOR GUARD BY NOW, REMEMBER? BUT DO I GET MAD? DO I SHOUT AT YOU?
HEY, NOW LOOK --
MANNY MONKTON PUBLISHER
I KNOW ABOUT SETBACKS, I KNOW ABOUT STRUGGLING. SEE, I KNOW YOU FROM JUST SEEING YOUR FACE, WHAT YOU'RE LIKE.
YOU'RE LIKE ME, I CAN TELL...
MANNY MONKTON PUBLISHER
OH, BROTHER...
STILL, I HAD TO ADMIT -- NOTHING LIKE THAT HAD HAPPENED WHEN I WAS UP AT DC.
I DECIDED I'D QUIT -- BUT BEFORE I LEFT, I WAS GOING TO SHOW HIM I COULD DO IT HIS WAY, IF I WANTED TO.
-- TODAY, ON "TOMORROW'S DAWN" --
IT WAS JUST RAZZLE-DAZZLE, AFTER ALL. MORE ACTION, MAKING UP THE STUFF NOBODY SAW --
-- HOW HARD COULD IT BE?
YOU DON'T UNDERSTAND, MACEY. IF WE MARRIED, YOUR LIFE WOULD BE CONSTANTLY AT RISK...

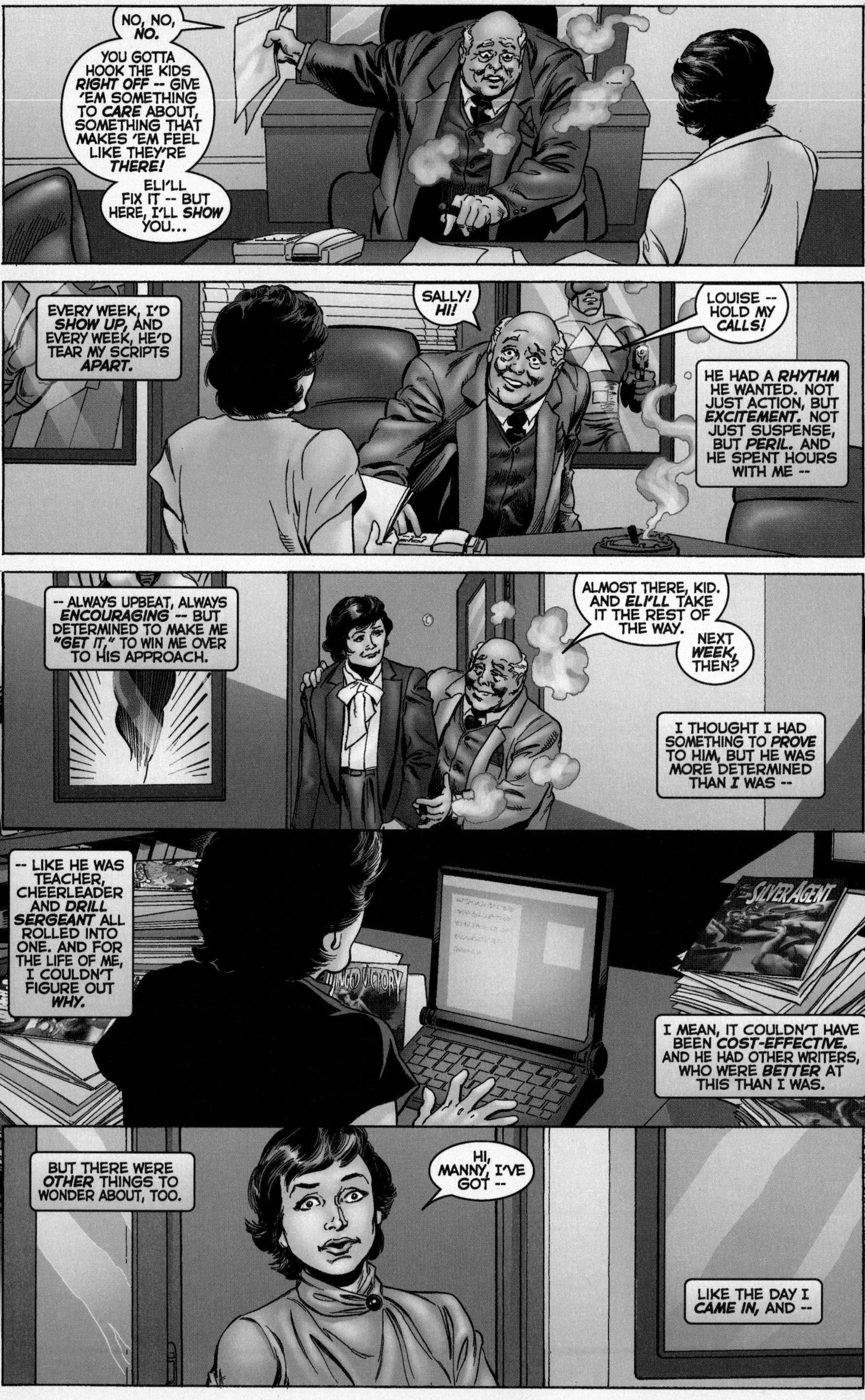
NO, NO, NO.
YOU GOTTA HOOK THE KIDS RIGHT OFF -- GIVE 'EM SOMETHING TO CARE ABOUT, SOMETHING THAT MAKES 'EM FEEL LIKE THEY'RE THERE!
ELI'LL FIX IT -- BUT HERE, I'LL SHOW YOU...
EVERY WEEK, I'D SHOW UP, AND EVERY WEEK, HE'D TEAR MY SCRIPTS APART.
SALLY! HI!
LOUISE -- HOLD MY CALLS!
HE HAD A RHYTHM HE WANTED. NOT JUST ACTION, BUT EXCITEMENT. NOT JUST SUSPENSE, BUT PERIL. AND HE SPENT HOURS WITH ME --
-- ALWAYS UPBEAT, ALWAYS ENCOURAGING -- BUT DETERMINED TO MAKE ME "GET IT," TO WIN ME OVER TO HIS APPROACH.
ALMOST THERE, KID. AND ELI'LL TAKE IT THE REST OF THE WAY.
NEXT WEEK, THEN?
I THOUGHT I HAD SOMETHING TO PROVE TO HIM, BUT HE WAS MORE DETERMINED THAN I WAS --
-- LIKE HE WAS TEACHER, CHEERLEADER AND DRILL SERGEANT ALL ROLLED INTO ONE. AND FOR THE LIFE OF ME, I COULDN'T FIGURE OUT WHY.
SILVER AGENT
WINGED VICTORY
I MEAN, IT COULDN'T HAVE BEEN COST-EFFECTIVE. AND HE HAD OTHER WRITERS, WHO WERE BETTER AT THIS THAN I WAS.
BUT THERE WERE OTHER THINGS TO WONDER ABOUT, TOO.
HI, MANNY, I'VE GOT --
LIKE THE DAY I CAME IN, AND --

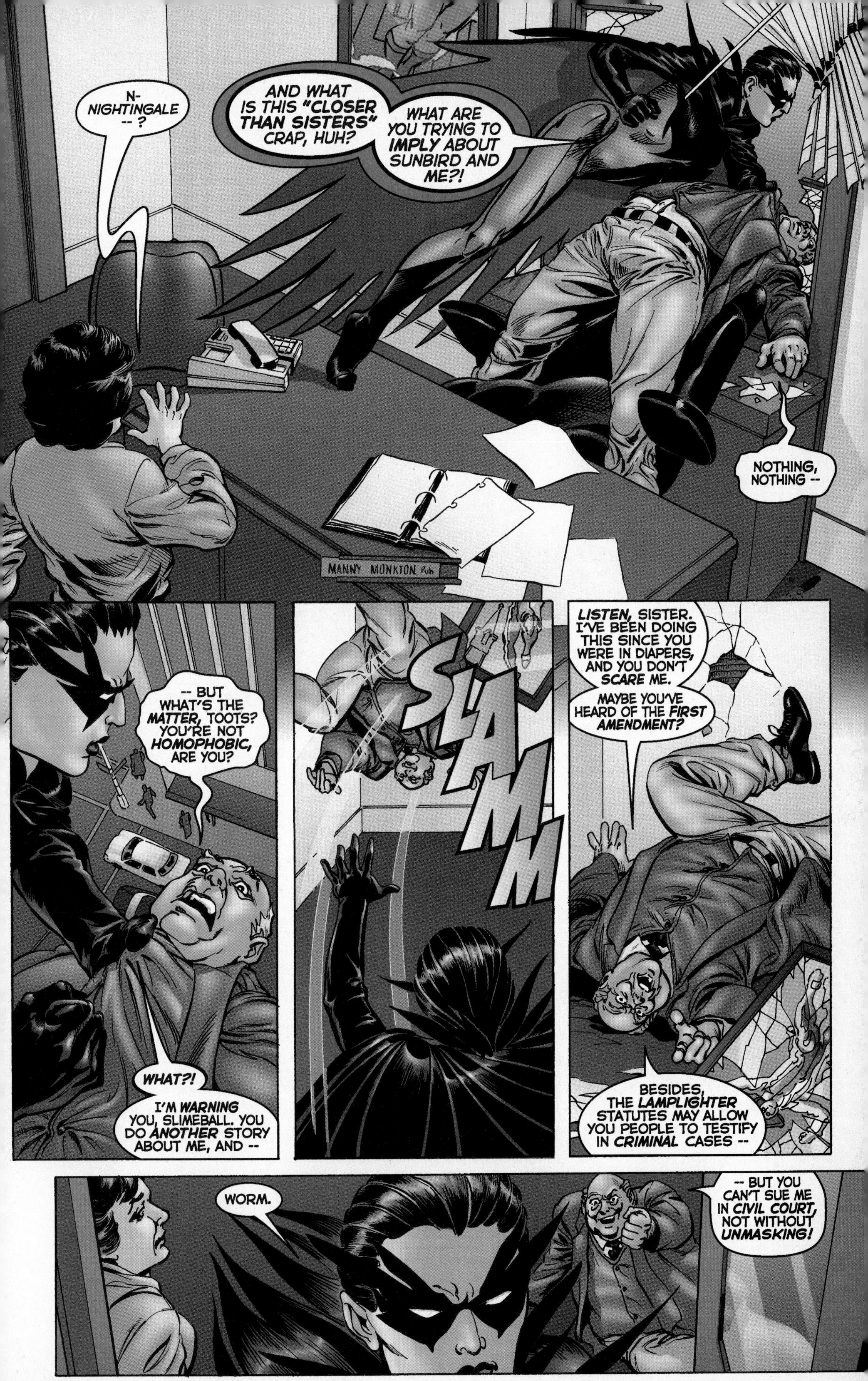
N-NIGHTINGALE --?
AND WHAT IS THIS "CLOSER THAN SISTERS" CRAP, HUH?
WHAT ARE YOU TRYING TO IMPLY ABOUT SUNBIRD AND ME?!
NOTHING, NOTHING --
MANNY MONKTON Pub
-- BUT WHAT'S THE MATTER, TOOTS? YOU'RE NOT HOMOPHOBIC, ARE YOU?
WHAT?!
I'M WARNING YOU, SLIMEBALL. YOU DO ANOTHER STORY ABOUT ME, AND --
SLAMM
LISTEN, SISTER. I'VE BEEN DOING THIS SINCE YOU WERE IN DIAPERS, AND YOU DON'T SCARE ME.
MAYBE YOU'VE HEARD OF THE FIRST AMENDMENT?
BESIDES, THE LAMPLIGHTER STATUTES MAY ALLOW YOU PEOPLE TO TESTIFY IN CRIMINAL CASES --
WORM.
-- BUT YOU CAN'T SUE ME IN CIVIL COURT, NOT WITHOUT UNMASKING!

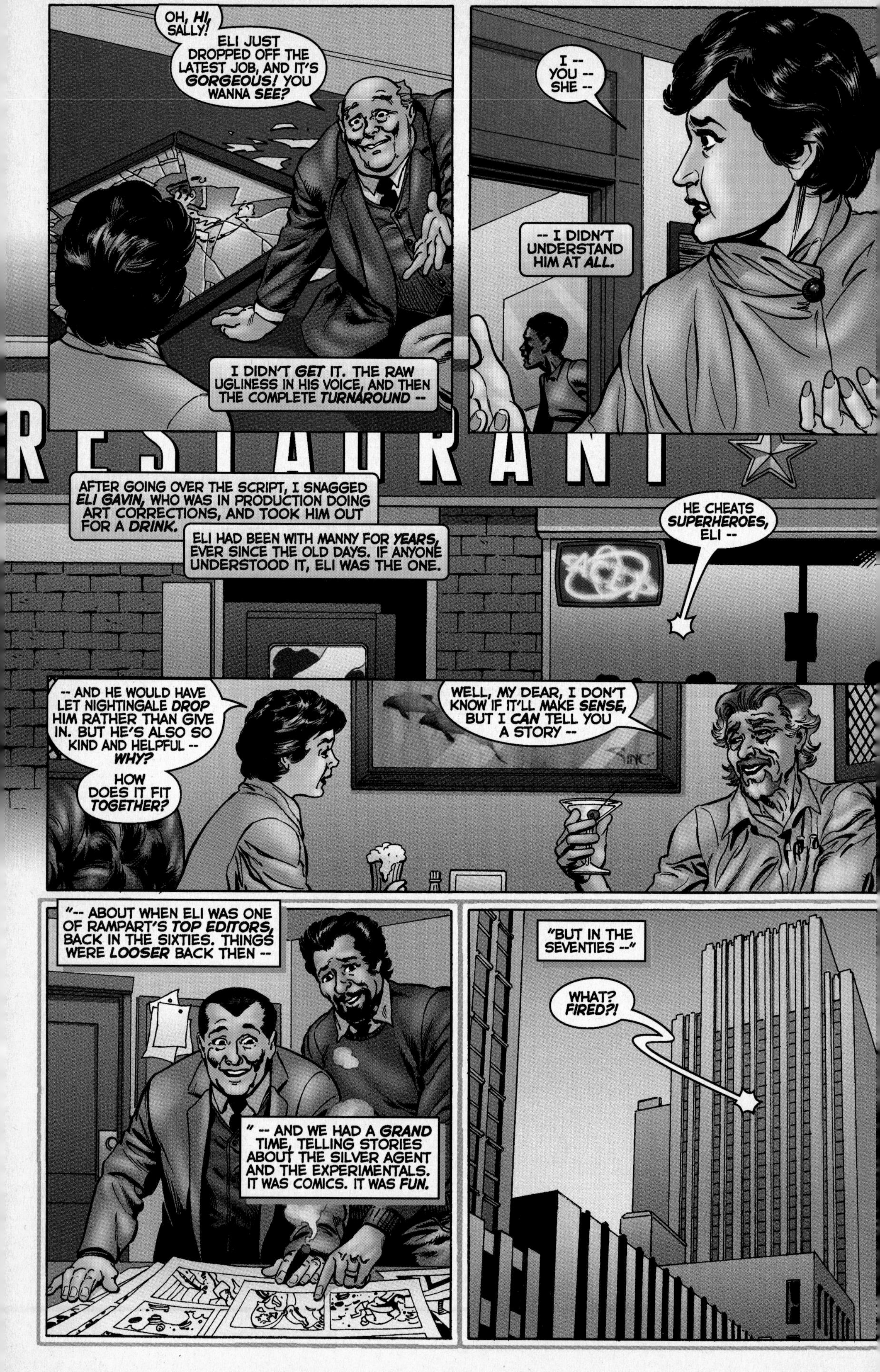

OH, HI, SALLY! ELI JUST DROPPED OFF THE LATEST JOB, AND IT'S GORGEOUS! YOU WANNA SEE?
I DIDN'T GET IT. THE RAW UGLINESS IN HIS VOICE, AND THEN THE COMPLETE TURNAROUND --
I -- YOU -- SHE --
-- I DIDN'T UNDERSTAND HIM AT ALL.
RESTAURANT
AFTER GOING OVER THE SCRIPT, I SNAGGED ELI GAVIN, WHO WAS IN PRODUCTION DOING ART CORRECTIONS, AND TOOK HIM OUT FOR A DRINK.
ELI HAD BEEN WITH MANNY FOR YEARS, EVER SINCE THE OLD DAYS. IF ANYONE UNDERSTOOD IT, ELI WAS THE ONE.
HE CHEATS SUPERHEROES, ELI --
-- AND HE WOULD HAVE LET NIGHTINGALE DROP HIM RATHER THAN GIVE IN. BUT HE'S ALSO SO KIND AND HELPFUL -- WHY?
HOW DOES IT FIT TOGETHER?
WELL, MY DEAR, I DON'T KNOW IF IT'LL MAKE SENSE, BUT I CAN TELL YOU A STORY --
"-- ABOUT WHEN ELI WAS ONE OF RAMPART'S TOP EDITORS, BACK IN THE SIXTIES. THINGS WERE LOOSER BACK THEN --
" -- AND WE HAD A GRAND TIME, TELLING STORIES ABOUT THE SILVER AGENT AND THE EXPERIMENTALS. IT WAS COMICS. IT WAS FUN.
"BUT IN THE SEVENTIES --"
WHAT? FIRED?!

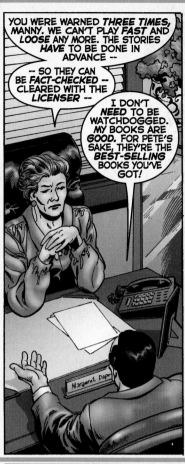

YOU WERE WARNED *THREE TIMES,* MANNY. WE CAN'T PLAY *FAST* AND *LOOSE* ANY MORE. THE STORIES *HAVE* TO BE DONE IN ADVANCE --

-- SO THEY CAN BE *FACT-CHECKED* -- CLEARED WITH THE *LICENSER* --

I DON'T *NEED* TO BE WATCHDOGGED. MY BOOKS ARE *GOOD.* FOR PETE'S SAKE, THEY'RE THE *BEST-SELLING* BOOKS YOU'VE GOT!

:SIGH: THE HEROES AREN'T AS POPULAR AS THEY *USED* TO BE, MANNY. THE PUBLIC IS *WARY,* SUSPICIOUS -- OF *US,* TOO.

WE'VE HAD *LAWSUITS.* WE'RE AN EASIER TARGET THAN THE HEROES. THE ONLY WAY WE CAN *PROTECT* OURSELVES --

-- IS TO *BLAND* EVERYTHING DOWN, AND DRAIN THE *LIFE* OUT OF IT. GET THE FACTS RIGHT -- FORGET THE *DRAMA.* THE *FUN!*

NOTHING I CAN *DO* ABOUT IT, MANNY.

YEAH? WELL, I *CAN!* YOU JUST KEEP ON *HIDING,* MARGARET --

-- AND I'LL *SHOW* YOU *HOW IT'S DONE!*

"HE STARTED UP BULLDOG A FEW MONTHS LATER. HE ALWAYS WAS A GOOD TALKER, AND HIS RESUMÉ LOOKED GOOD TO INVESTORS.

AND SINCE THEN, HE'S BEEN SURROUNDED BY *TURMOIL,* BUT HE SEEMS TO *THRIVE* ON IT. THERE'S *ALWAYS* A LAWSUIT OR TWO --

-- BUT, WELL, HE'S STILL *HERE.*

THERE'S A *REASON* HE CALLED IT *"BULLDOG COMICS,"* AFTER ALL.

AND... *WHY YOU?* YOU COULD HAVE STAYED AT *RAMPART...*

HE'S A GOOD *TALKER.* BESIDES, I'M *USED* TO HIM. AND LIFE, WELL --

-- LIFE WOULD BE A LOT *DULLER* WITHOUT HIM AROUND --

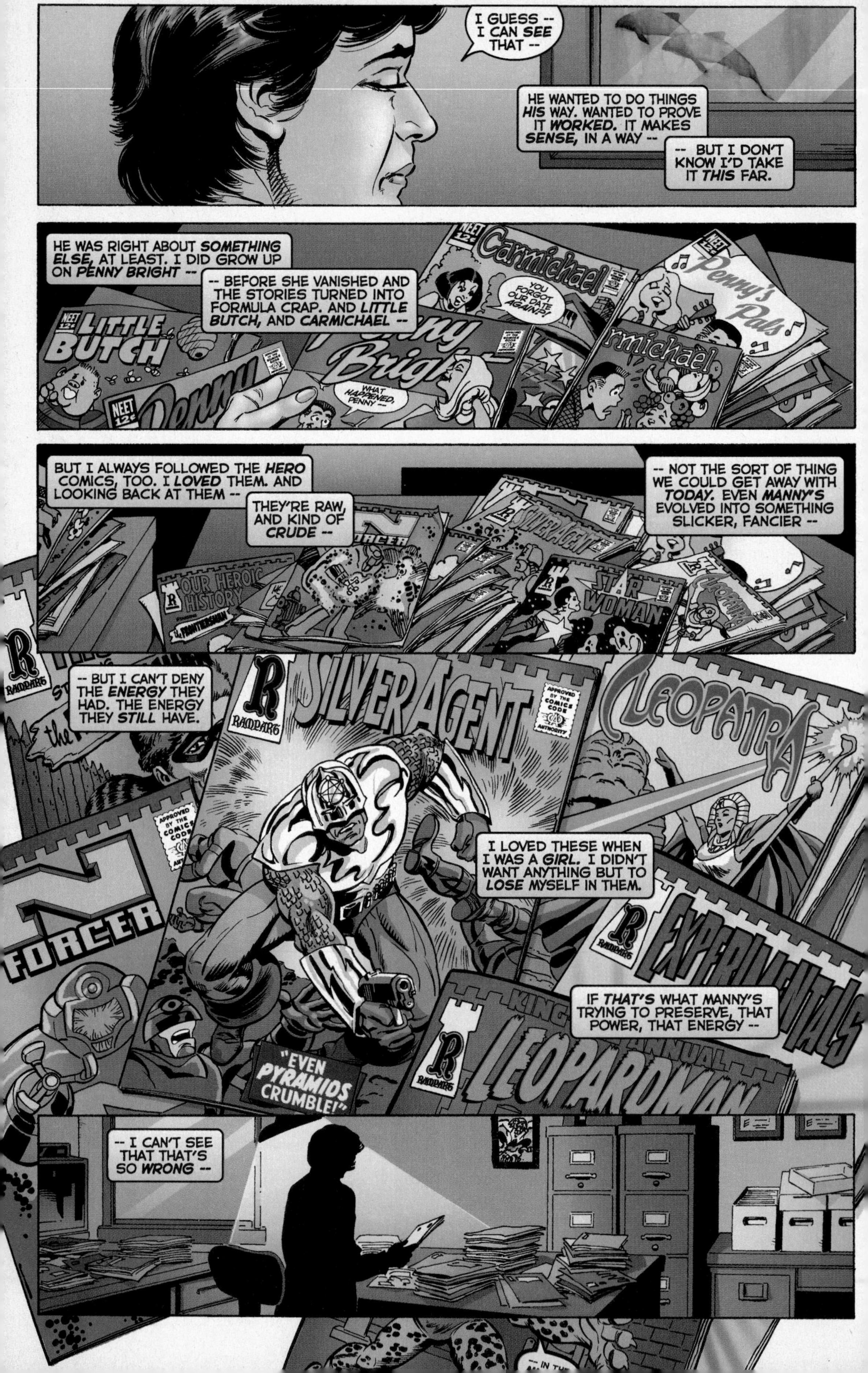

I GUESS -- I CAN SEE THAT --
HE WANTED TO DO THINGS HIS WAY. WANTED TO PROVE IT WORKED. IT MAKES SENSE, IN A WAY --
-- BUT I DON'T KNOW I'D TAKE IT THIS FAR.
HE WAS RIGHT ABOUT SOMETHING ELSE, AT LEAST. I DID GROW UP ON PENNY BRIGHT --
-- BEFORE SHE VANISHED AND THE STORIES TURNED INTO FORMULA CRAP. AND LITTLE BUTCH, AND CARMICHAEL --
Carmichael
YOU FORGOT OUR DATE AGAIN?!
Penny's Pals
NEET 12¢
LITTLE BUTCH
WHAT HAPPENED, PENNY ---
BUT I ALWAYS FOLLOWED THE HERO COMICS, TOO. I LOVED THEM. AND LOOKING BACK AT THEM --
THEY'RE RAW, AND KIND OF CRUDE --
-- NOT THE SORT OF THING WE COULD GET AWAY WITH TODAY. EVEN MANNY'S EVOLVED INTO SOMETHING SLICKER, FANCIER --
OUR HEROIC HISTORY
STAR WOMAN
-- BUT I CAN'T DENY THE ENERGY THEY HAD. THE ENERGY THEY STILL HAVE.
SILVER AGENT
RAMPART
APPROVED BY THE COMICS CODE AUTHORITY
CLEOPATRA
I LOVED THESE WHEN I WAS A GIRL. I DIDN'T WANT ANYTHING BUT TO LOSE MYSELF IN THEM.
FORCER
EXPERIMENTALS
IF THAT'S WHAT MANNY'S TRYING TO PRESERVE, THAT POWER, THAT ENERGY --
KING-SIZE ANNUAL
LEOPARDMAN
"EVEN PYRAMIDS CRUMBLE!"
-- I CAN'T SEE THAT THAT'S SO WRONG --

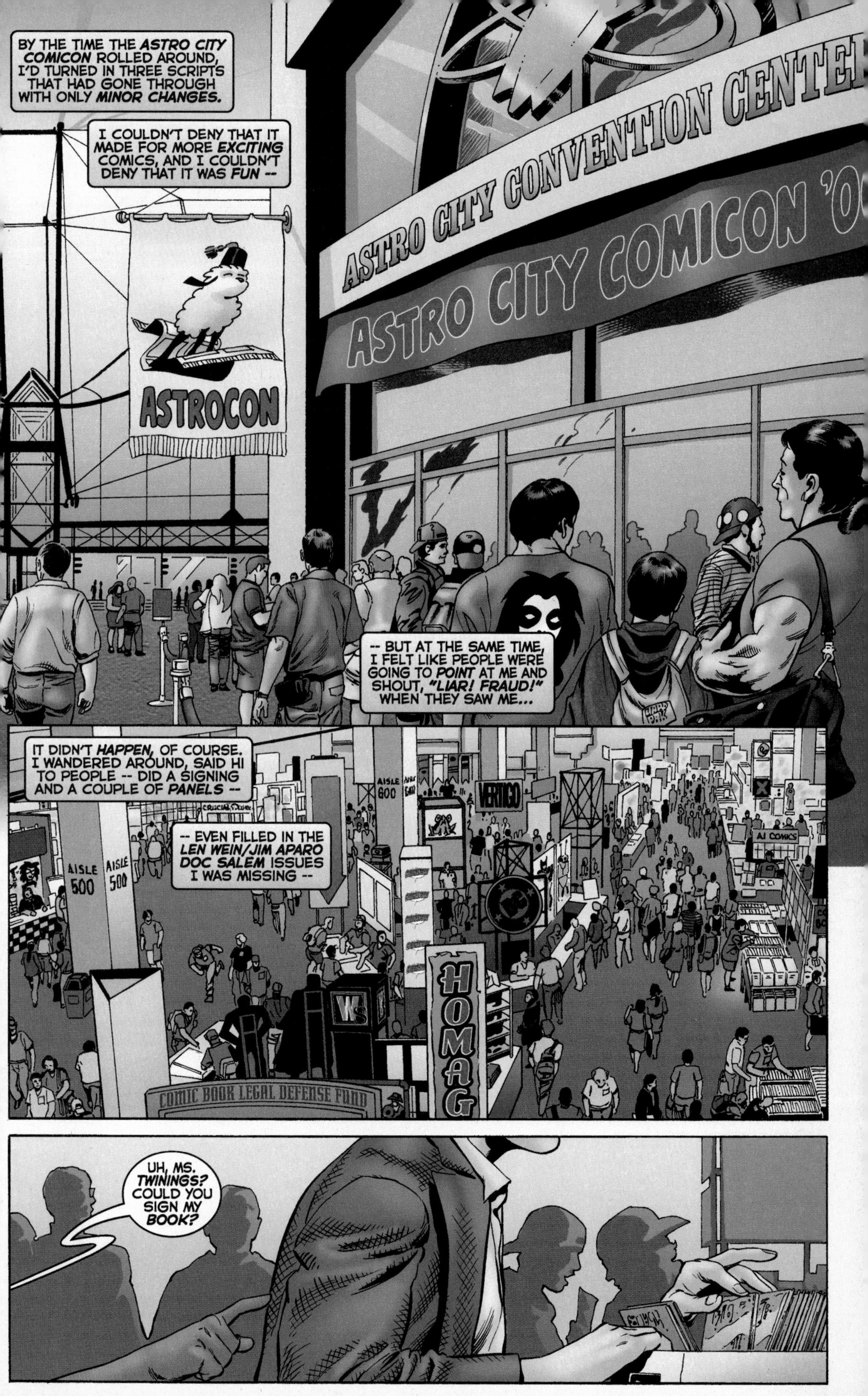
BY THE TIME THE ASTRO CITY COMICON ROLLED AROUND, I'D TURNED IN THREE SCRIPTS THAT HAD GONE THROUGH WITH ONLY MINOR CHANGES.
I COULDN'T DENY THAT IT MADE FOR MORE EXCITING COMICS, AND I COULDN'T DENY THAT IT WAS FUN --
ASTRO CITY CONVENTION CENTE
ASTRO CITY COMICON '0
ASTRO CITY COMICON
ASTROCON
-- BUT AT THE SAME TIME, I FELT LIKE PEOPLE WERE GOING TO POINT AT ME AND SHOUT, "LIAR! FRAUD!" WHEN THEY SAW ME...
IT DIDN'T HAPPEN, OF COURSE. I WANDERED AROUND, SAID HI TO PEOPLE -- DID A SIGNING AND A COUPLE OF PANELS --
-- EVEN FILLED IN THE LEN WEIN/JIM APARO DOC SALEM ISSUES I WAS MISSING --
AISLE 500
AISLE 500
AISLE 800
VERTIGO
AJ COMICS
HOMAG
COMIC BOOK LEGAL DEFENSE FUND
UH, MS. TWININGS? COULD YOU SIGN MY BOOK?

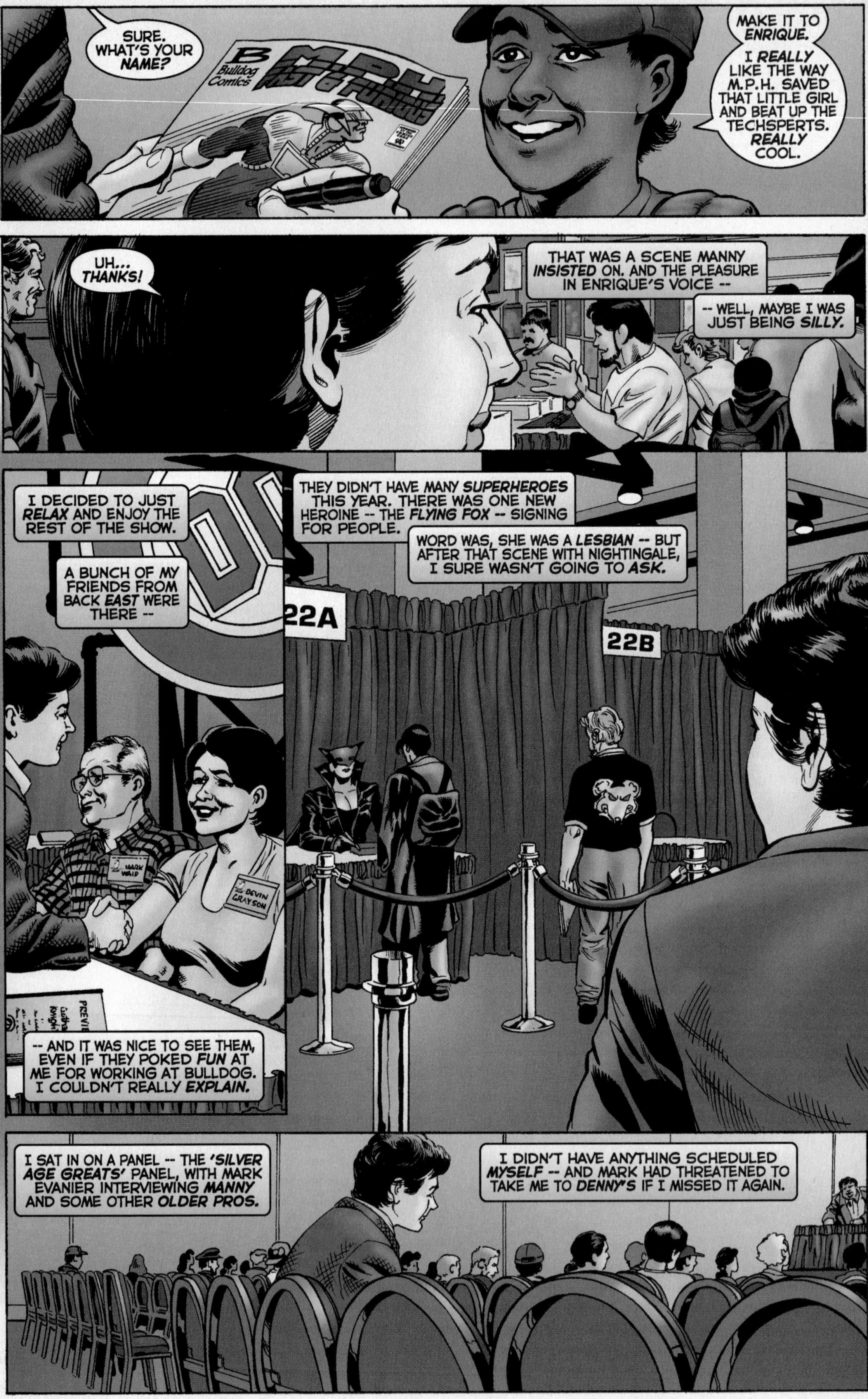
SURE. WHAT'S YOUR NAME?
Bulldog Comics
MAKE IT TO ENRIQUE.
I REALLY LIKE THE WAY M.P.H. SAVED THAT LITTLE GIRL AND BEAT UP THE TECHSPERTS. REALLY COOL.
UH... THANKS!
THAT WAS A SCENE MANNY INSISTED ON. AND THE PLEASURE IN ENRIQUE'S VOICE --
-- WELL, MAYBE I WAS JUST BEING SILLY.
I DECIDED TO JUST RELAX AND ENJOY THE REST OF THE SHOW.
A BUNCH OF MY FRIENDS FROM BACK EAST WERE THERE --
MARK WAID
DEVIN GRAYSON
-- AND IT WAS NICE TO SEE THEM, EVEN IF THEY POKED FUN AT ME FOR WORKING AT BULLDOG. I COULDN'T REALLY EXPLAIN.
THEY DIDN'T HAVE MANY SUPERHEROES THIS YEAR. THERE WAS ONE NEW HEROINE -- THE FLYING FOX -- SIGNING FOR PEOPLE.
WORD WAS, SHE WAS A LESBIAN -- BUT AFTER THAT SCENE WITH NIGHTINGALE, I SURE WASN'T GOING TO ASK.
22A
22B
I SAT IN ON A PANEL -- THE 'SILVER AGE GREATS' PANEL, WITH MARK EVANIER INTERVIEWING MANNY AND SOME OTHER OLDER PROS.
I DIDN'T HAVE ANYTHING SCHEDULED MYSELF -- AND MARK HAD THREATENED TO TAKE ME TO DENNY'S IF I MISSED IT AGAIN.

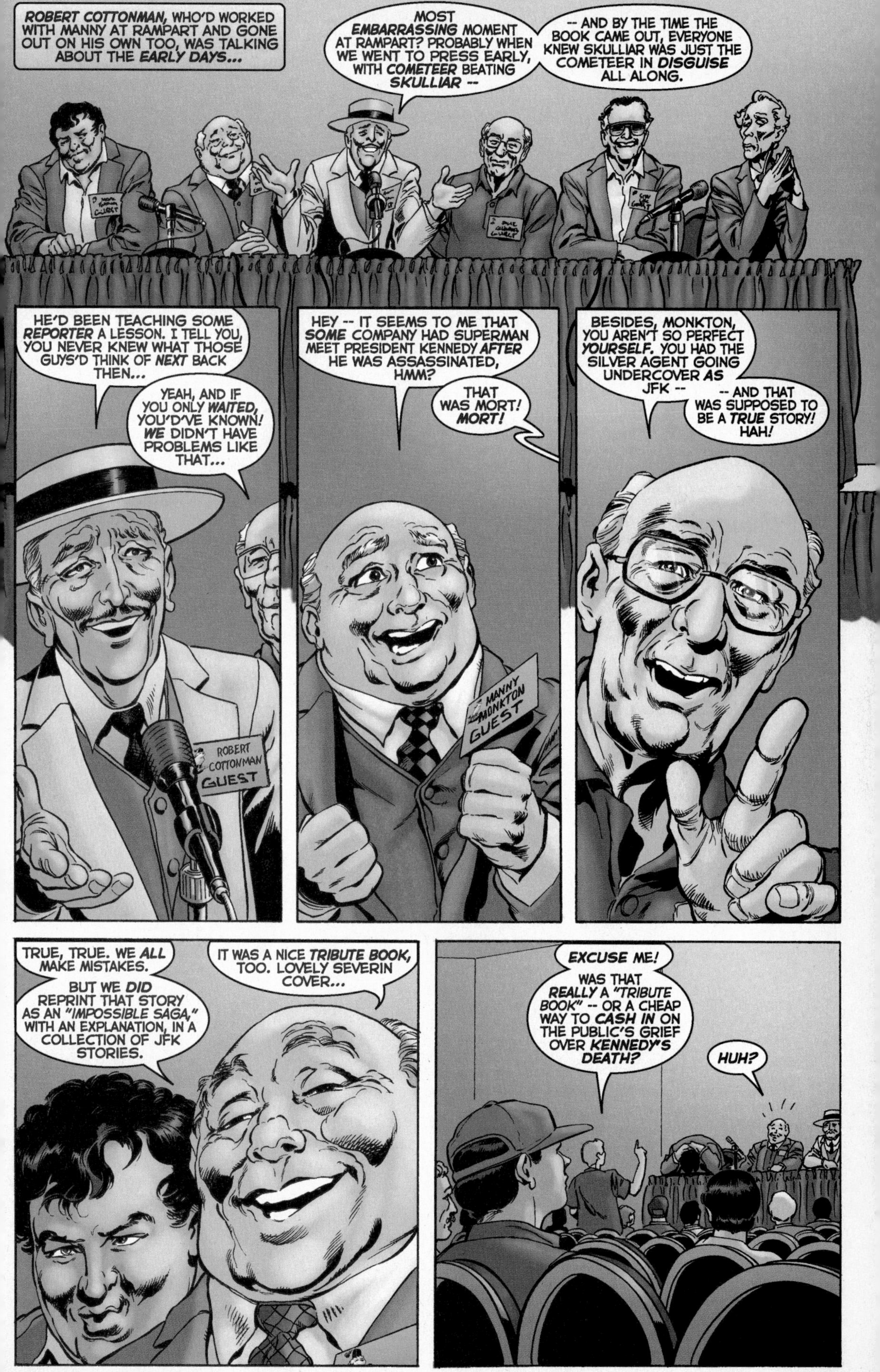

ROBERT COTTONMAN, WHO'D WORKED WITH MANNY AT RAMPART AND GONE OUT ON HIS OWN TOO, WAS TALKING ABOUT THE EARLY DAYS...
MOST EMBARRASSING MOMENT AT RAMPART? PROBABLY WHEN WE WENT TO PRESS EARLY, WITH COMETEER BEATING SKULLIAR --
-- AND BY THE TIME THE BOOK CAME OUT, EVERYONE KNEW SKULLIAR WAS JUST THE COMETEER IN DISGUISE ALL ALONG.
HE'D BEEN TEACHING SOME REPORTER A LESSON. I TELL YOU, YOU NEVER KNEW WHAT THOSE GUYS'D THINK OF NEXT BACK THEN...
YEAH, AND IF YOU ONLY WAITED, YOU'D'VE KNOWN! WE DIDN'T HAVE PROBLEMS LIKE THAT...
ROBERT COTTONMAN GUEST
HEY -- IT SEEMS TO ME THAT SOME COMPANY HAD SUPERMAN MEET PRESIDENT KENNEDY AFTER HE WAS ASSASSINATED, HMM?
THAT WAS MORT! MORT!
MANNY MONKTON GUEST
BESIDES, MONKTON, YOU AREN'T SO PERFECT YOURSELF. YOU HAD THE SILVER AGENT GOING UNDERCOVER AS JFK --
-- AND THAT WAS SUPPOSED TO BE A TRUE STORY! HAH!
TRUE, TRUE. WE ALL MAKE MISTAKES.
BUT WE DID REPRINT THAT STORY AS AN "IMPOSSIBLE SAGA," WITH AN EXPLANATION, IN A COLLECTION OF JFK STORIES.
IT WAS A NICE TRIBUTE BOOK, TOO. LOVELY SEVERIN COVER...
EXCUSE ME!
WAS THAT REALLY A "TRIBUTE BOOK" -- OR A CHEAP WAY TO CASH IN ON THE PUBLIC'S GRIEF OVER KENNEDY'S DEATH?
HUH?

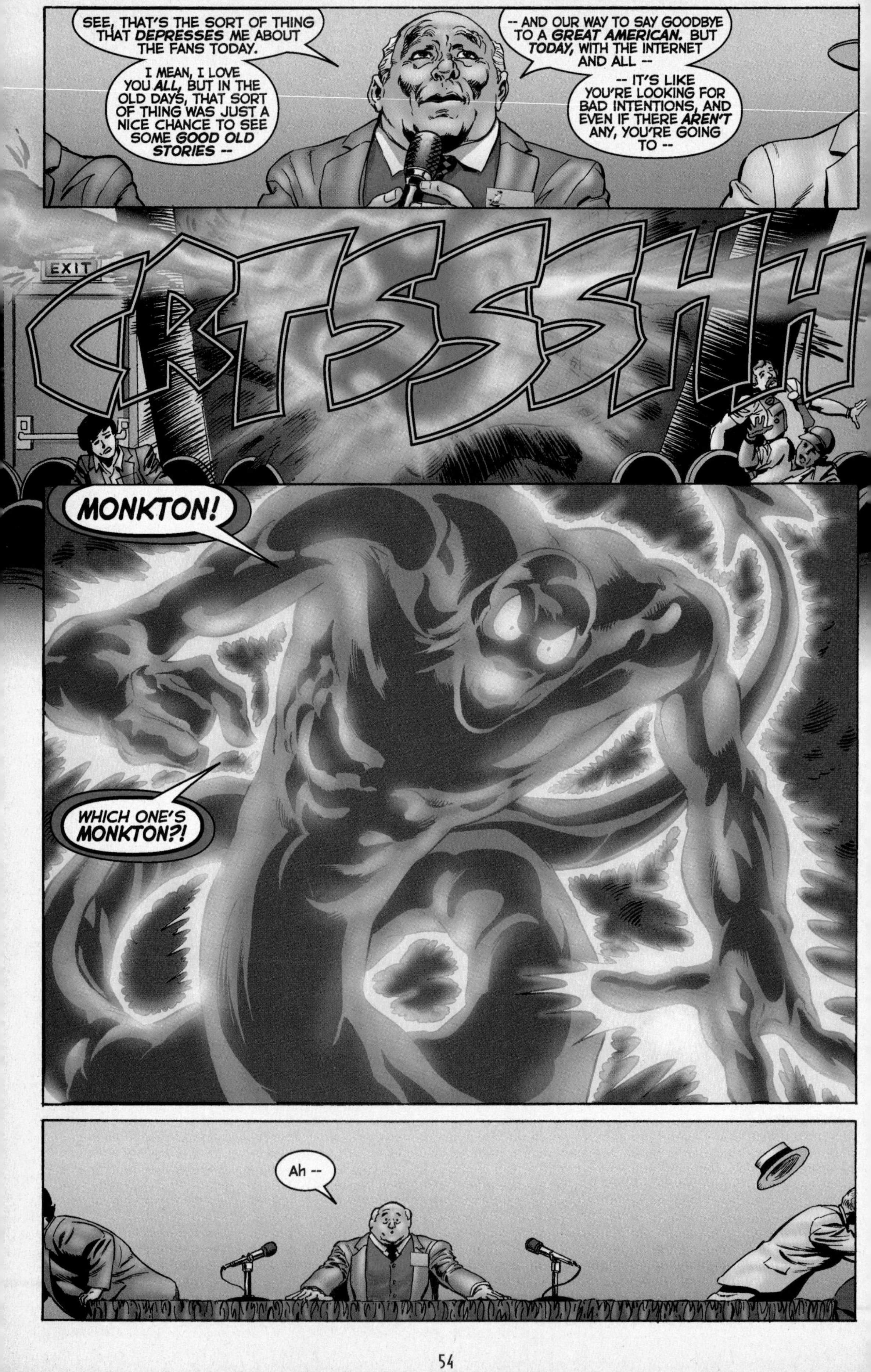

SEE, THAT'S THE SORT OF THING THAT DEPRESSES ME ABOUT THE FANS TODAY.
I MEAN, I LOVE YOU ALL, BUT IN THE OLD DAYS, THAT SORT OF THING WAS JUST A NICE CHANCE TO SEE SOME GOOD OLD STORIES --
-- AND OUR WAY TO SAY GOODBYE TO A GREAT AMERICAN. BUT TODAY, WITH THE INTERNET AND ALL --
-- IT'S LIKE YOU'RE LOOKING FOR BAD INTENTIONS, AND EVEN IF THERE AREN'T ANY, YOU'RE GOING TO --
EXIT
CRTSSHH
MONKTON!
WHICH ONE'S MONKTON?!
Ah --

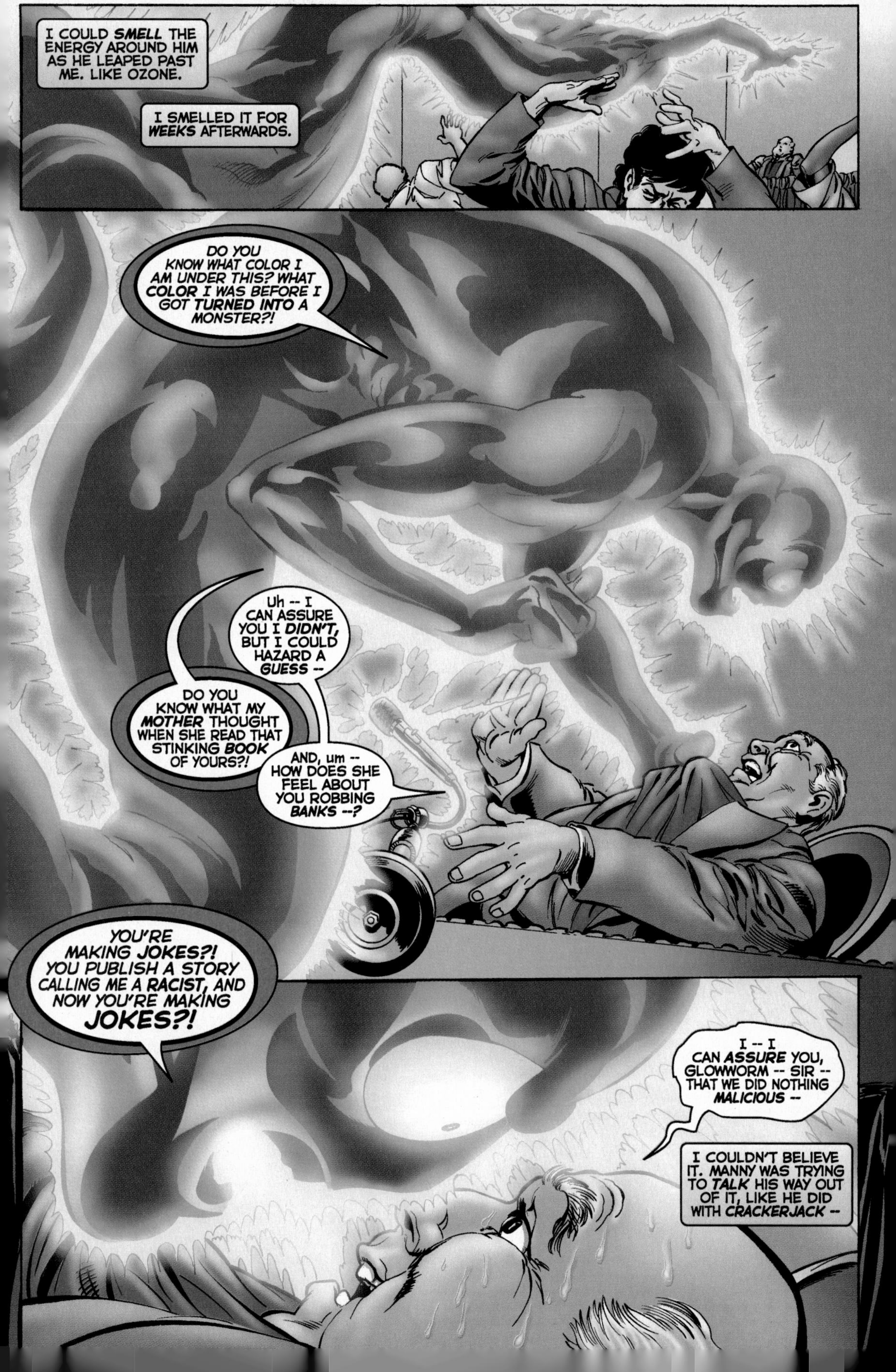

I COULD SMELL THE ENERGY AROUND HIM AS HE LEAPED PAST ME. LIKE OZONE.
I SMELLED IT FOR WEEKS AFTERWARDS.
DO YOU KNOW WHAT COLOR I AM UNDER THIS? WHAT COLOR I WAS BEFORE I GOT TURNED INTO A MONSTER?!
Uh -- I CAN ASSURE YOU I DIDN'T, BUT I COULD HAZARD A GUESS --
DO YOU KNOW WHAT MY MOTHER THOUGHT WHEN SHE READ THAT STINKING BOOK OF YOURS?!
AND, um -- HOW DOES SHE FEEL ABOUT YOU ROBBING BANKS --?
YOU'RE MAKING JOKES?! YOU PUBLISH A STORY CALLING ME A RACIST, AND NOW YOU'RE MAKING JOKES?!
I -- I CAN ASSURE YOU, GLOWWORM -- SIR -- THAT WE DID NOTHING MALICIOUS --
I COULDN'T BELIEVE IT. MANNY WAS TRYING TO TALK HIS WAY OUT OF IT, LIKE HE DID WITH CRACKERJACK --

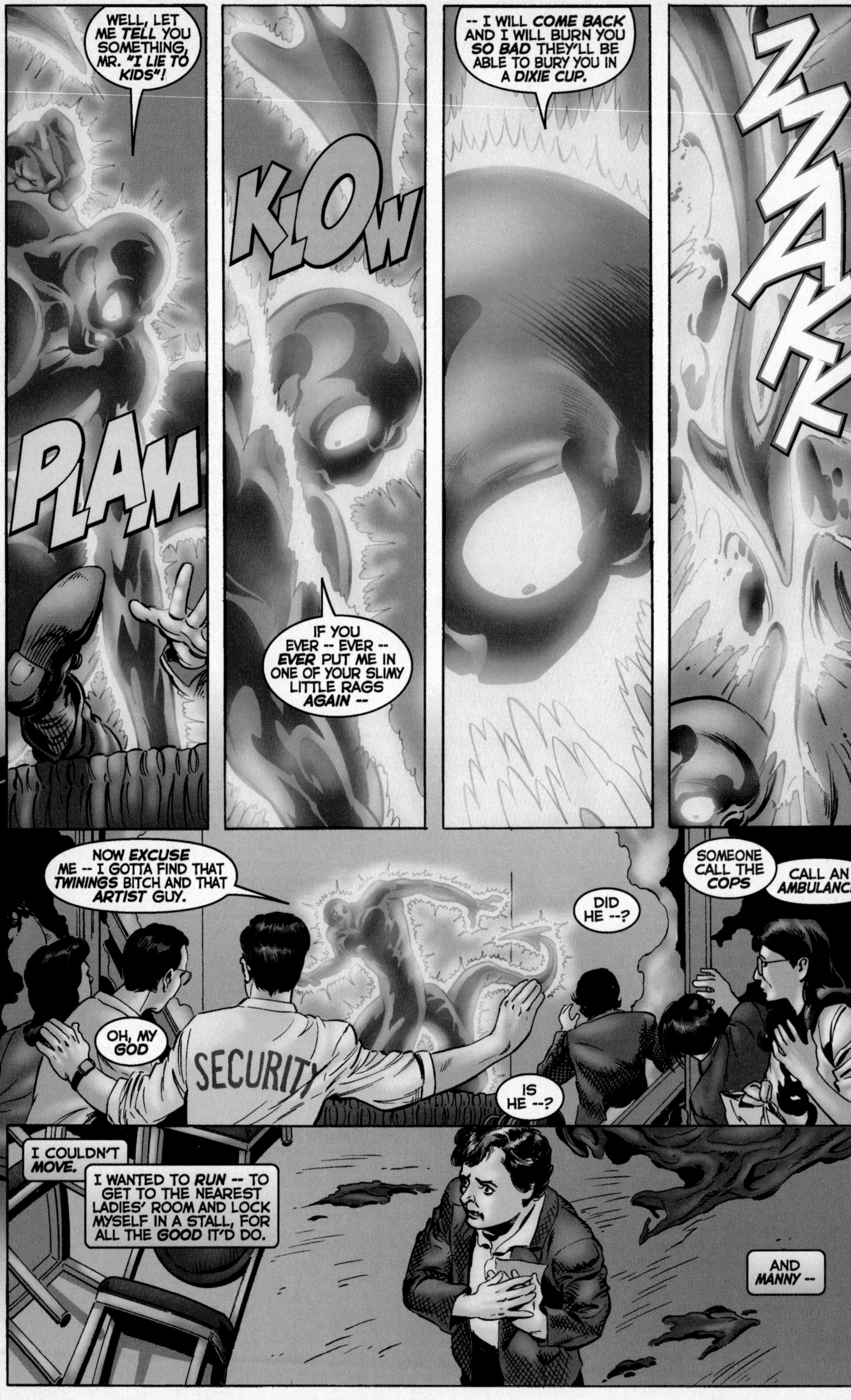
WELL, LET ME TELL YOU SOMETHING, MR. "I LIE TO KIDS"!
PLAM
KLOW
IF YOU EVER -- EVER -- EVER PUT ME IN ONE OF YOUR SLIMY LITTLE RAGS AGAIN --
-- I WILL COME BACK AND I WILL BURN YOU SO BAD THEY'LL BE ABLE TO BURY YOU IN A DIXIE CUP.
ZZAKK
NOW EXCUSE ME -- I GOTTA FIND THAT TWININGS BITCH AND THAT ARTIST GUY.
OH, MY GOD
SECURITY
DID HE --?
IS HE --?
SOMEONE CALL THE COPS
CALL AN AMBULANCE
I COULDN'T MOVE.
I WANTED TO RUN -- TO GET TO THE NEAREST LADIES' ROOM AND LOCK MYSELF IN A STALL, FOR ALL THE GOOD IT'D DO.
AND MANNY --

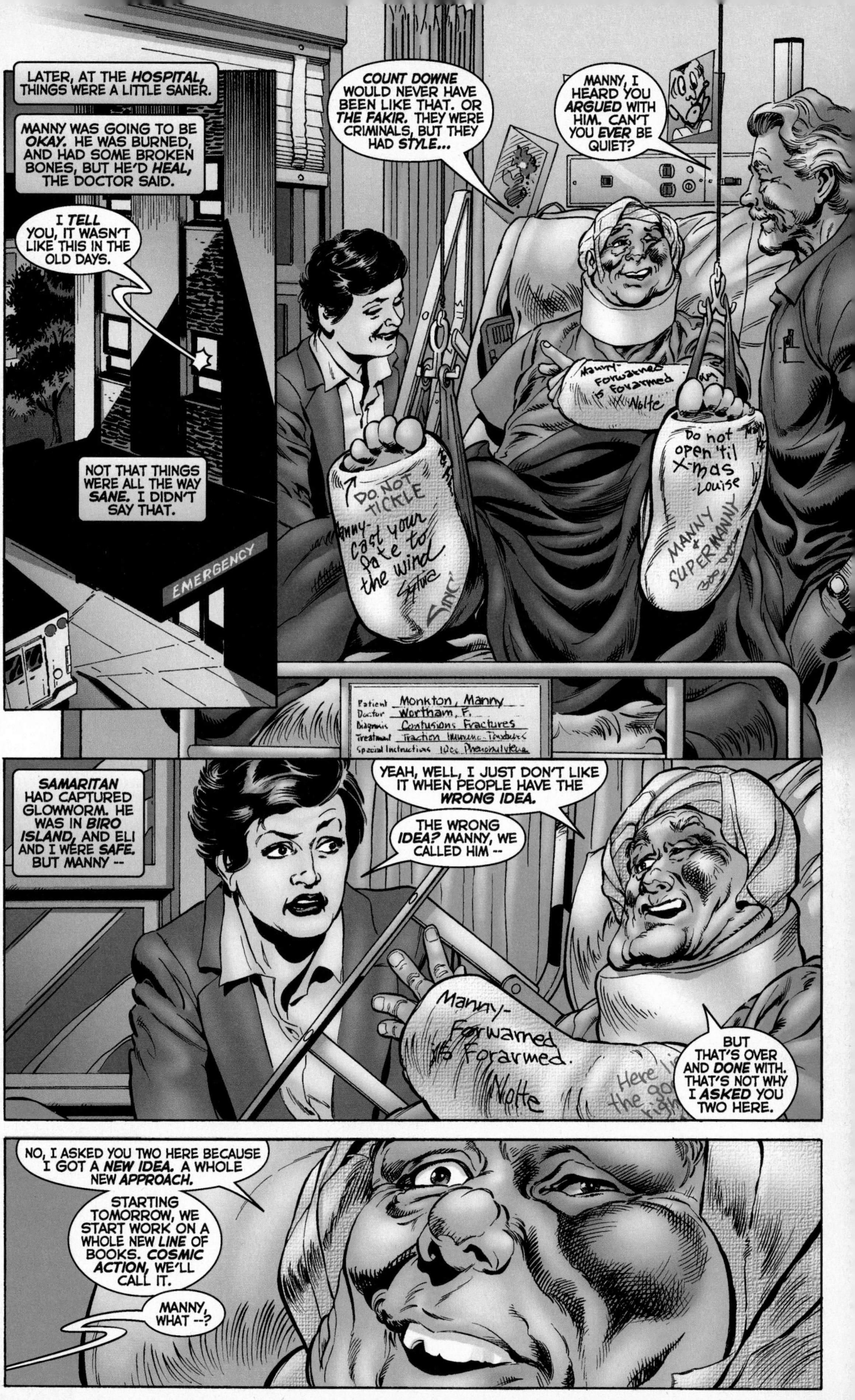
LATER, AT THE HOSPITAL, THINGS WERE A LITTLE SANER.
MANNY WAS GOING TO BE OKAY. HE WAS BURNED, AND HAD SOME BROKEN BONES, BUT HE'D HEAL, THE DOCTOR SAID.
I TELL YOU, IT WASN'T LIKE THIS IN THE OLD DAYS.
NOT THAT THINGS WERE ALL THE WAY SANE. I DIDN'T SAY THAT.
EMERGENCY
COUNT DOWNE WOULD NEVER HAVE BEEN LIKE THAT. OR THE FAKIR. THEY WERE CRIMINALS, BUT THEY HAD STYLE...
MANNY, I HEARD YOU ARGUED WITH HIM. CAN'T YOU EVER BE QUIET?
Manny- Forwarned is Forarmed Nolte
DO NOT TICKLE
Manny- cast your fate to the wind
Do not open 'til X-mas -Louise
MANNY & SUPERMANNY
Patient Monkton, Manny
Doctor Wortham, F.
Diagnosis Contusions Fractures
SAMARITAN HAD CAPTURED GLOWWORM. HE WAS IN BIRO ISLAND, AND ELI AND I WERE SAFE. BUT MANNY --
YEAH, WELL, I JUST DON'T LIKE IT WHEN PEOPLE HAVE THE WRONG IDEA.
THE WRONG IDEA? MANNY, WE CALLED HIM --
Manny- Forwarned is Forarmed. Nolte
BUT THAT'S OVER AND DONE WITH. THAT'S NOT WHY I ASKED YOU TWO HERE.
NO, I ASKED YOU TWO HERE BECAUSE I GOT A NEW IDEA. A WHOLE NEW APPROACH.
STARTING TOMORROW, WE START WORK ON A WHOLE NEW LINE OF BOOKS. COSMIC ACTION, WE'LL CALL IT.
MANNY, WHAT --?

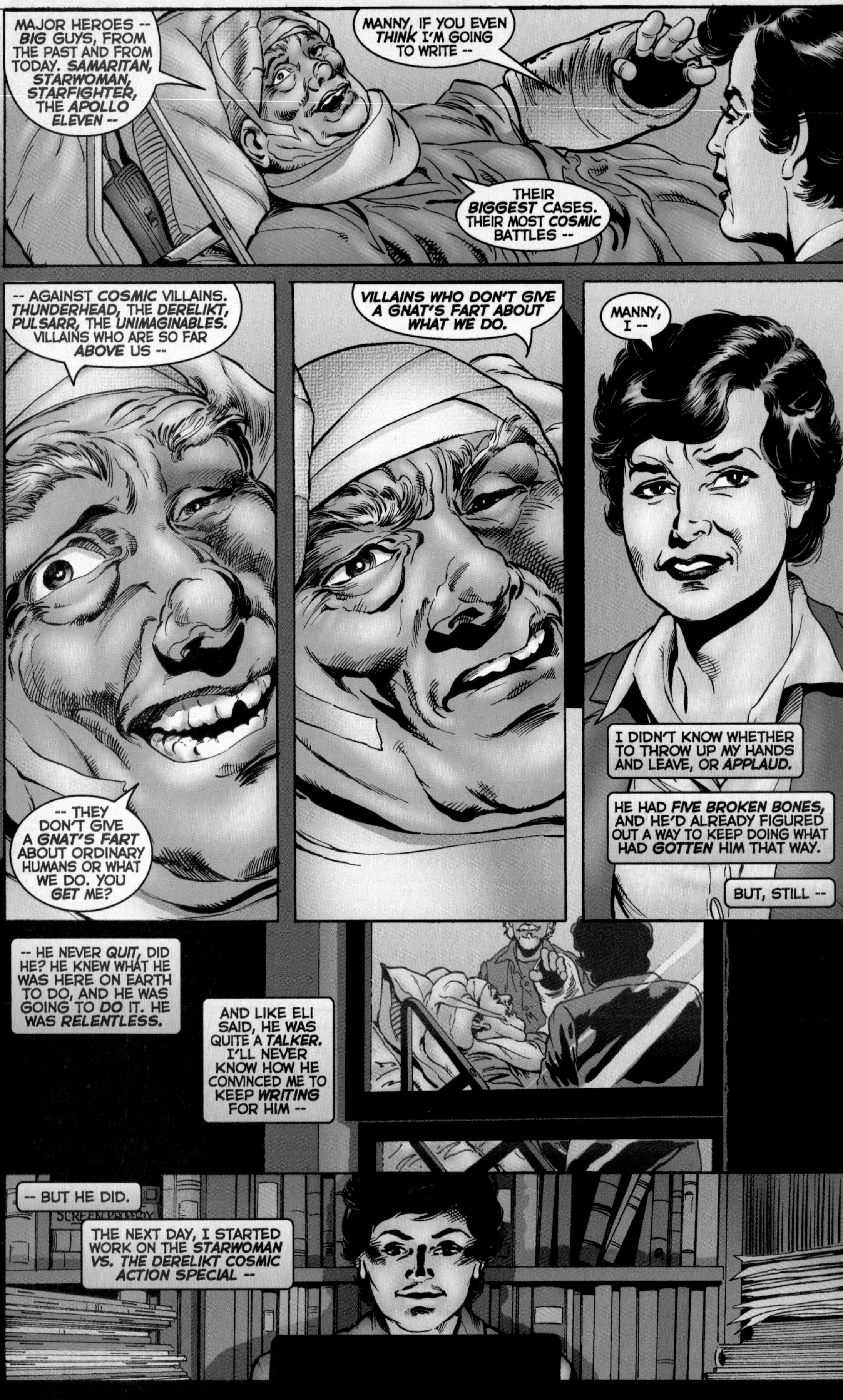
MAJOR HEROES -- BIG GUYS, FROM THE PAST AND FROM TODAY. SAMARITAN, STARWOMAN, STARFIGHTER, THE APOLLO ELEVEN --
MANNY, IF YOU EVEN THINK I'M GOING TO WRITE --
THEIR BIGGEST CASES. THEIR MOST COSMIC BATTLES --
-- AGAINST COSMIC VILLAINS. THUNDERHEAD, THE DERELIKT, PULSARR, THE UNIMAGINABLES. VILLAINS WHO ARE SO FAR ABOVE US --
-- THEY DON'T GIVE A GNAT'S FART ABOUT ORDINARY HUMANS OR WHAT WE DO. YOU GET ME?
VILLAINS WHO DON'T GIVE A GNAT'S FART ABOUT WHAT WE DO.
MANNY, I --
I DIDN'T KNOW WHETHER TO THROW UP MY HANDS AND LEAVE, OR APPLAUD.
HE HAD FIVE BROKEN BONES, AND HE'D ALREADY FIGURED OUT A WAY TO KEEP DOING WHAT HAD GOTTEN HIM THAT WAY.
BUT, STILL --
-- HE NEVER QUIT, DID HE? HE KNEW WHAT HE WAS HERE ON EARTH TO DO, AND HE WAS GOING TO DO IT. HE WAS RELENTLESS.
AND LIKE ELI SAID, HE WAS QUITE A TALKER. I'LL NEVER KNOW HOW HE CONVINCED ME TO KEEP WRITING FOR HIM --
-- BUT HE DID.
THE NEXT DAY, I STARTED WORK ON THE STARWOMAN VS. THE DERELIKT COSMIC ACTION SPECIAL --

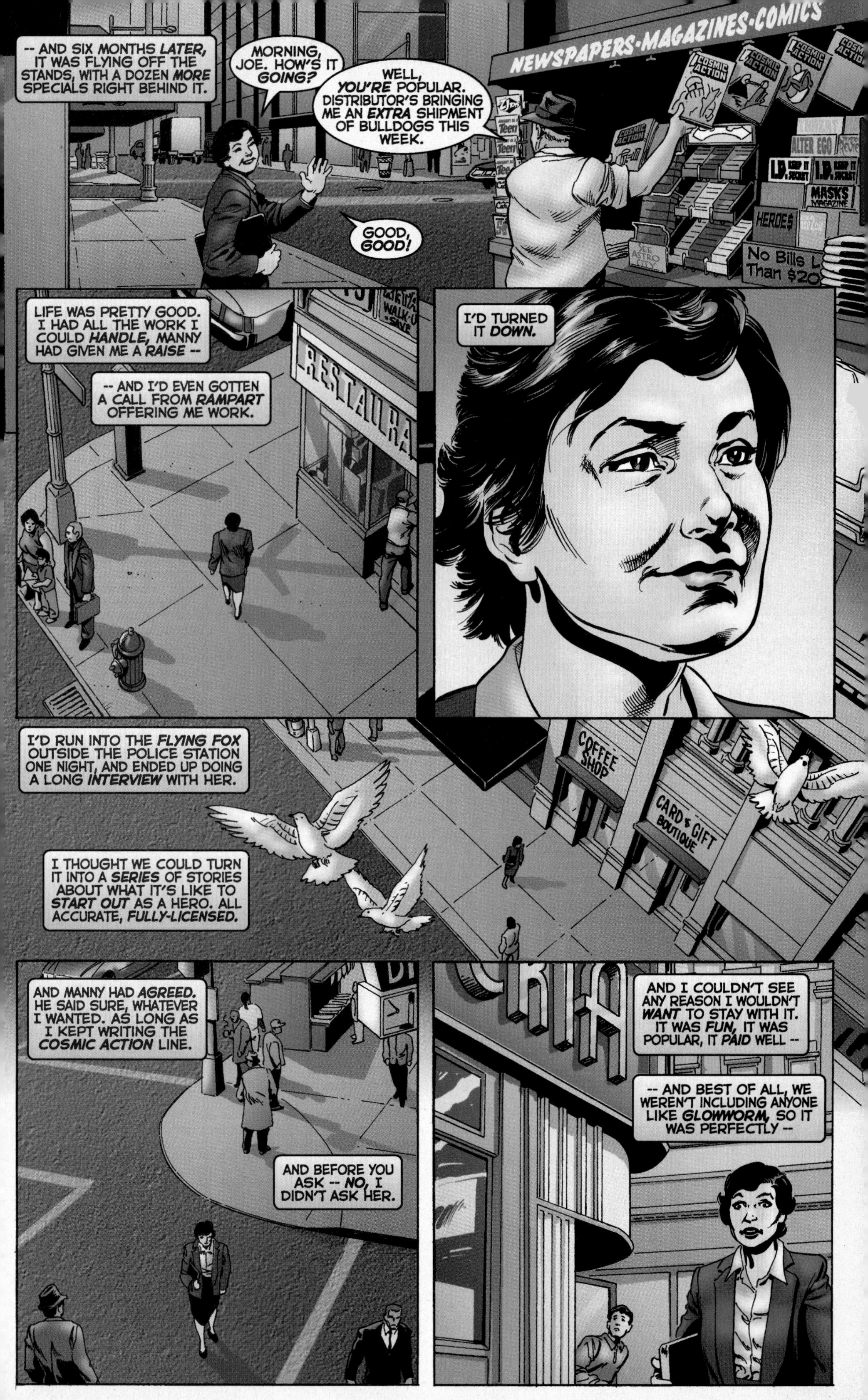
NEWSPAPERS·MAGAZINES·COMICS
-- AND SIX MONTHS LATER, IT WAS FLYING OFF THE STANDS, WITH A DOZEN MORE SPECIALS RIGHT BEHIND IT.
MORNING, JOE. HOW'S IT GOING?
WELL, YOU'RE POPULAR. DISTRIBUTOR'S BRINGING ME AN EXTRA SHIPMENT OF BULLDOGS THIS WEEK.
GOOD, GOOD!
COSMIC ACTION
ALTER EGO
I.D. KEEP IT SECRET
MASKS MAGAZINE
HEROE$
SEE ASTRO CITY
No Bills L Than $20
LIFE WAS PRETTY GOOD. I HAD ALL THE WORK I COULD HANDLE, MANNY HAD GIVEN ME A RAISE --
-- AND I'D EVEN GOTTEN A CALL FROM RAMPART OFFERING ME WORK.
RESTAURA
I'D TURNED IT DOWN.
I'D RUN INTO THE FLYING FOX OUTSIDE THE POLICE STATION ONE NIGHT, AND ENDED UP DOING A LONG INTERVIEW WITH HER.
I THOUGHT WE COULD TURN IT INTO A SERIES OF STORIES ABOUT WHAT IT'S LIKE TO START OUT AS A HERO. ALL ACCURATE, FULLY-LICENSED.
COFFEE SHOP
CARD & GIFT BOUTIQUE
AND MANNY HAD AGREED. HE SAID SURE, WHATEVER I WANTED. AS LONG AS I KEPT WRITING THE COSMIC ACTION LINE.
AND BEFORE YOU ASK -- NO, I DIDN'T ASK HER.
AND I COULDN'T SEE ANY REASON I WOULDN'T WANT TO STAY WITH IT. IT WAS FUN, IT WAS POPULAR, IT PAID WELL --
-- AND BEST OF ALL, WE WEREN'T INCLUDING ANYONE LIKE GLOWWORM, SO IT WAS PERFECTLY --

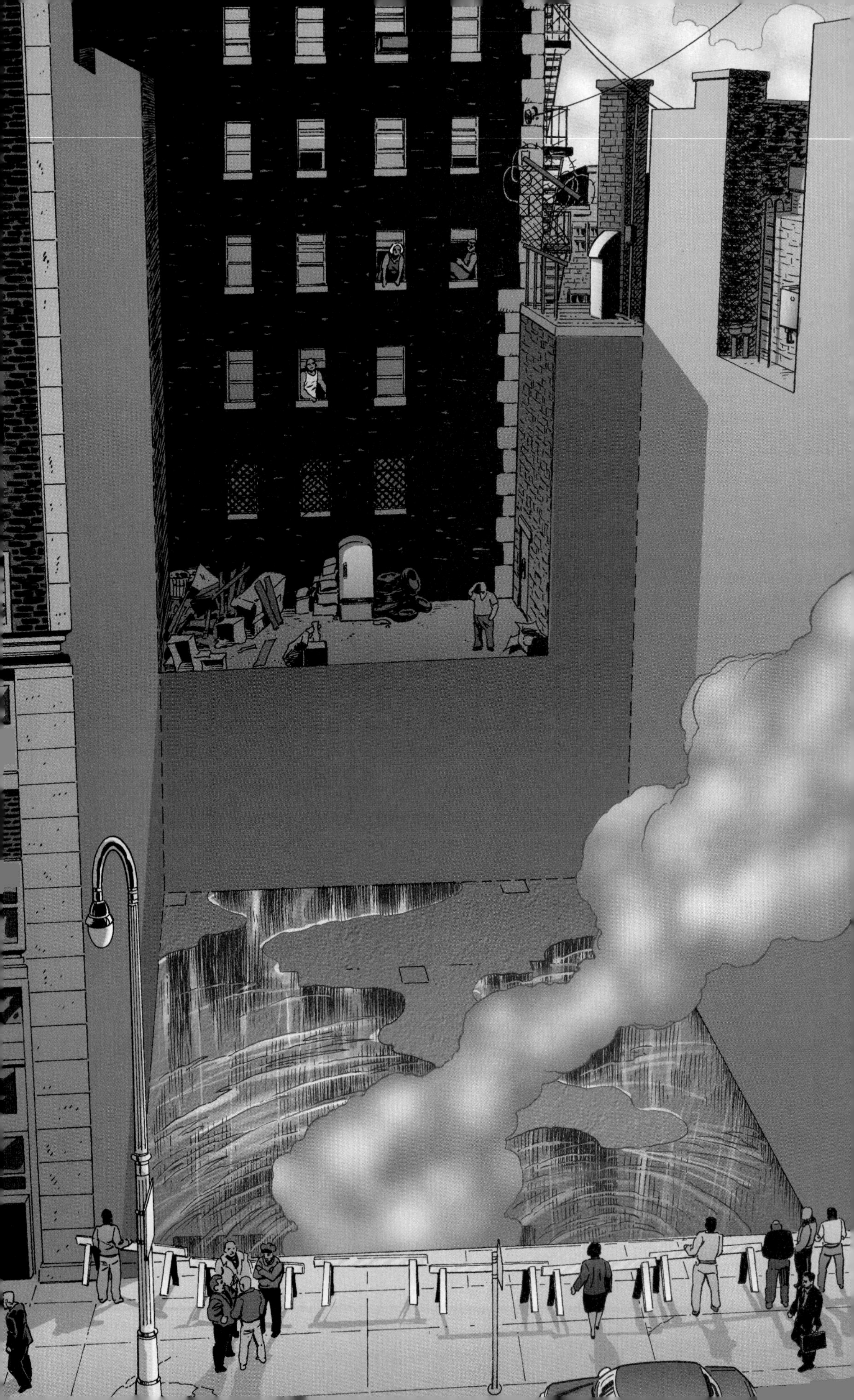

IT HAD JUST *VANISHED*. THE *WHOLE* BUILDING.

THEY SAID MANNY GOT THERE A LITTLE BEFORE *SEVEN*, LIKE USUAL, AND THERE WAS NO ONE ELSE IN THE BUILDING.

AND THEN LIKE THAT -- IT WAS *GONE*.

WE NEVER SAW HIM *AGAIN*. NEVER FOUND OUT WHAT *HAPPENED*.

THERE WAS A *SMELL* LEFT BEHIND, A SMELL I'LL NEVER FORGET. NOT OZONE, *NOTHING* LIKE OZONE.

MAYBE IT WAS A *GNAT'S FART*.

A TRAGEDY, A *TERRIBLE* TRAGEDY. I JUST *HEARD*.

Huh?

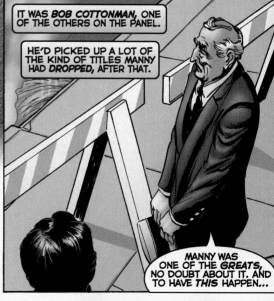

IT WAS *BOB COTTONMAN*, ONE OF THE OTHERS ON THE PANEL.

HE'D PICKED UP A LOT OF THE KIND OF TITLES MANNY HAD *DROPPED*, AFTER THAT.

MANNY WAS ONE OF THE *GREATS*, NO DOUBT ABOUT IT. AND TO HAVE *THIS* HAPPEN...

YOU KNOW, YOU MUST HAVE HAD BOOKS IN THE PIPELINE -- AT THE PRINTER, OR THE *SEPARATOR'S* AT LEAST. WHAT, FOUR, *FIVE* OF THEM?

MY COMPANY COULD BRING THEM OUT. WE'RE MOVING *OFFICES* SOON, AND WE COULD USE THE CURRENT ADDRESS --

-- AND BY THE TIME THE BOOKS HIT THE *STANDS*, WE'D BE IN THE *NEW* PLACE. MAYBE EVEN ANOTHER *NAME*.

WE COULD EVEN DO A *TRIBUTE BOOK* TO MANNY -- ALL HIS BACK *FILM'S* IN STORAGE IN CANADA.

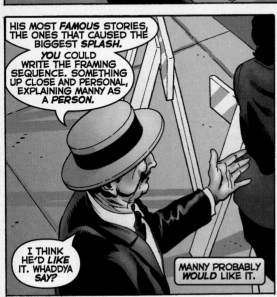

HIS MOST *FAMOUS* STORIES, THE ONES THAT CAUSED THE BIGGEST *SPLASH*.

YOU COULD WRITE THE FRAMING SEQUENCE. SOMETHING UP CLOSE AND PERSONAL, EXPLAINING MANNY AS A *PERSON*.

I THINK HE'D *LIKE* IT. WHADDYA *SAY*?

MANNY PROBABLY *WOULD* LIKE IT.

YOU *KNOW*, MISTER COTTONMAN --

BOB. MAKE IT *BOB*.

HE'D CERTAINLY HAVE *DONE* IT. HE WOULDN'T HAVE THOUGHT *TWICE*.

IT WAS WHAT HE LIVED FOR. IT WAS EVERYTHING HE WAS, EVERYTHING HE WANTED TO BE. HE'D DO IT FOR THE *JOY* OF IT --

-- OR JUST TO SHOW IT COULD BE *DONE*. BUT I HAD MY NOVEL -- HAD THAT OFFER FROM *RAMPART* --

YOU KNOW, BOB --

-- I DON'T *THINK* SO.

YOU ARE NOW LEAVING **ASTRO CITY** PLEASE DRIVE CAREFULLY

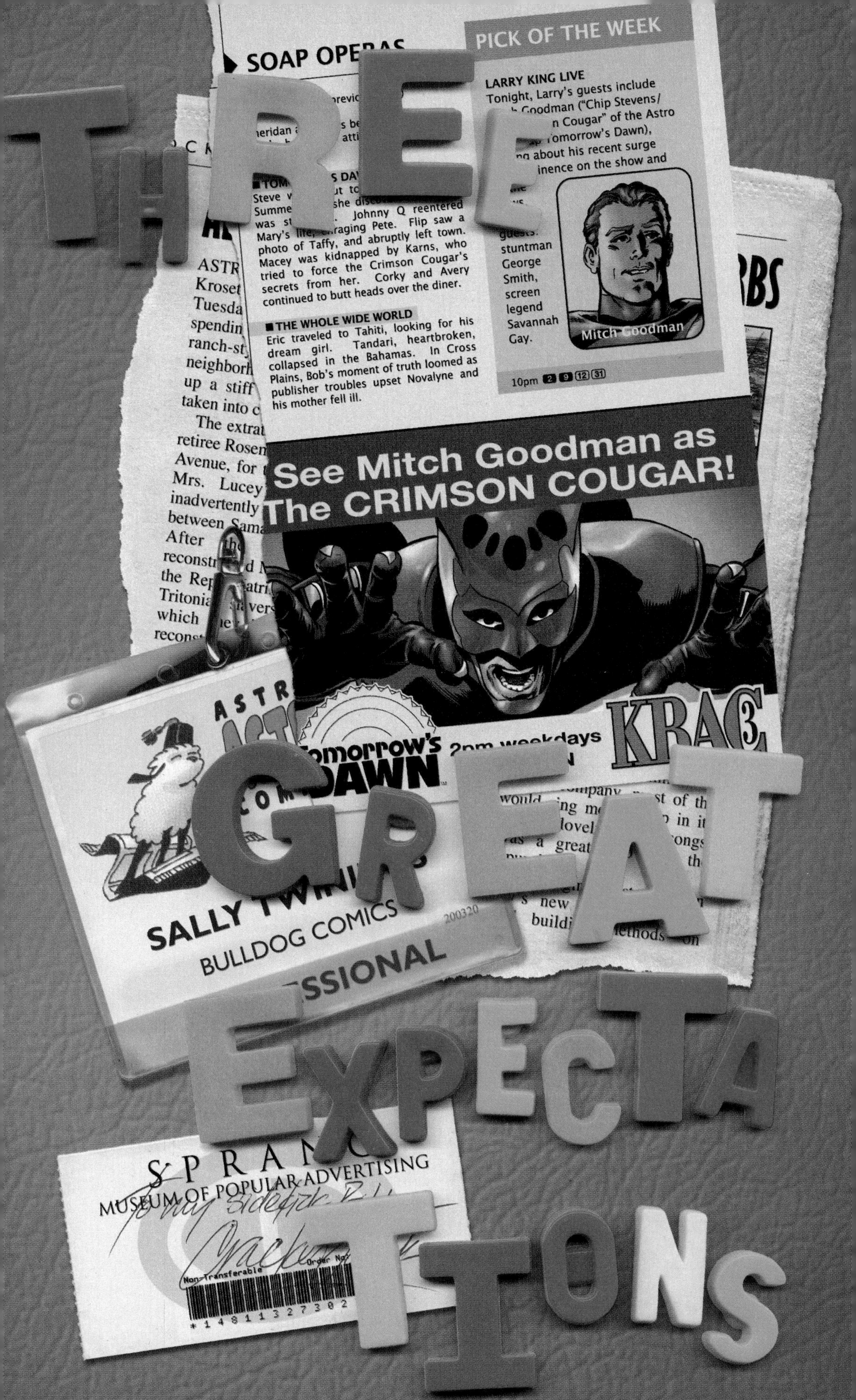
THREE
GREAT
EXPECTATIONS
SOAP OPERAS
PICK OF THE WEEK
LARRY KING LIVE
Tonight, Larry's guests include
Smith,
screen
legend
Savannah
Gay.
Mitch Goodman
10pm 2 9 12 31
Eric traveled to Tahiti, looking for his dream girl. Tandari, heartbroken, collapsed in the Bahamas. In Cross Plains, Bob's moment of truth loomed as publisher troubles upset Novalyne and his mother fell ill.
See Mitch Goodman as The CRIMSON COUGAR!
Tomorrow's DAWN
2pm weekdays
KRAC
SALLY
BULLDOG COMICS
MUSEUM OF POPULAR ADVERTISING
Non-Transferable

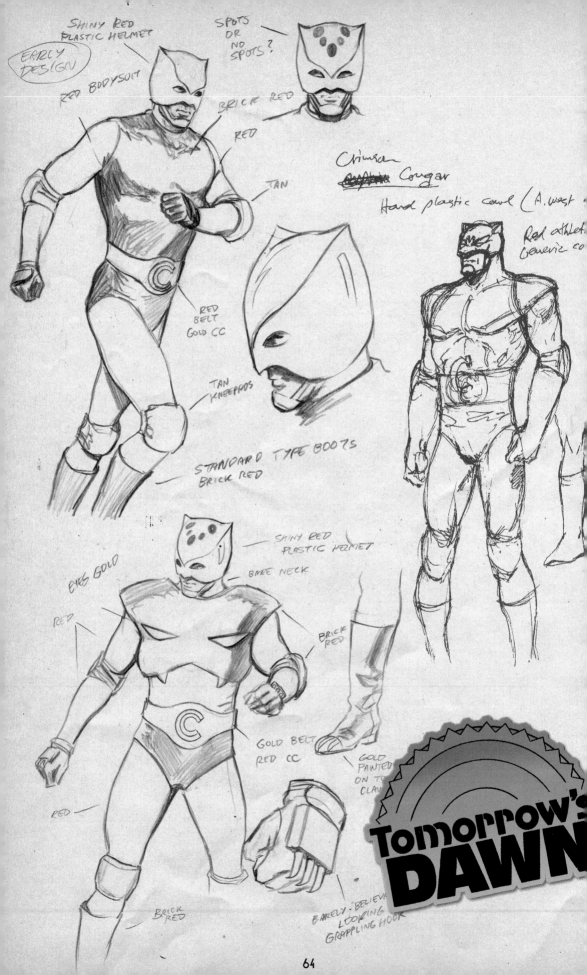

SHINY RED
PLASTIC HELMET

EARLY
DESIGN

RED BODYSUIT

SPOTS
OR
NO
SPOTS?

BRICK RED

RED

TAN

Crimson
~~CAT~~ Cougar

Hard plastic cowl (A. West

Red athlet.
Generic co

RED
BELT
GOLD CC

TAN
KNEEPADS

STANDARD TYPE BOOTS
BRICK RED

EYES GOLD

RED

SHINY RED
PLASTIC HELMET

BARE NECK

BRICK
RED

GOLD BELT
RED CC

RED

GOLD
PAINTED
ON TO
CLAW

BRICK
RED

BARELY BELIEVA
LOOKING
GRAPPLING HOOK

Tomorrow's DAWN

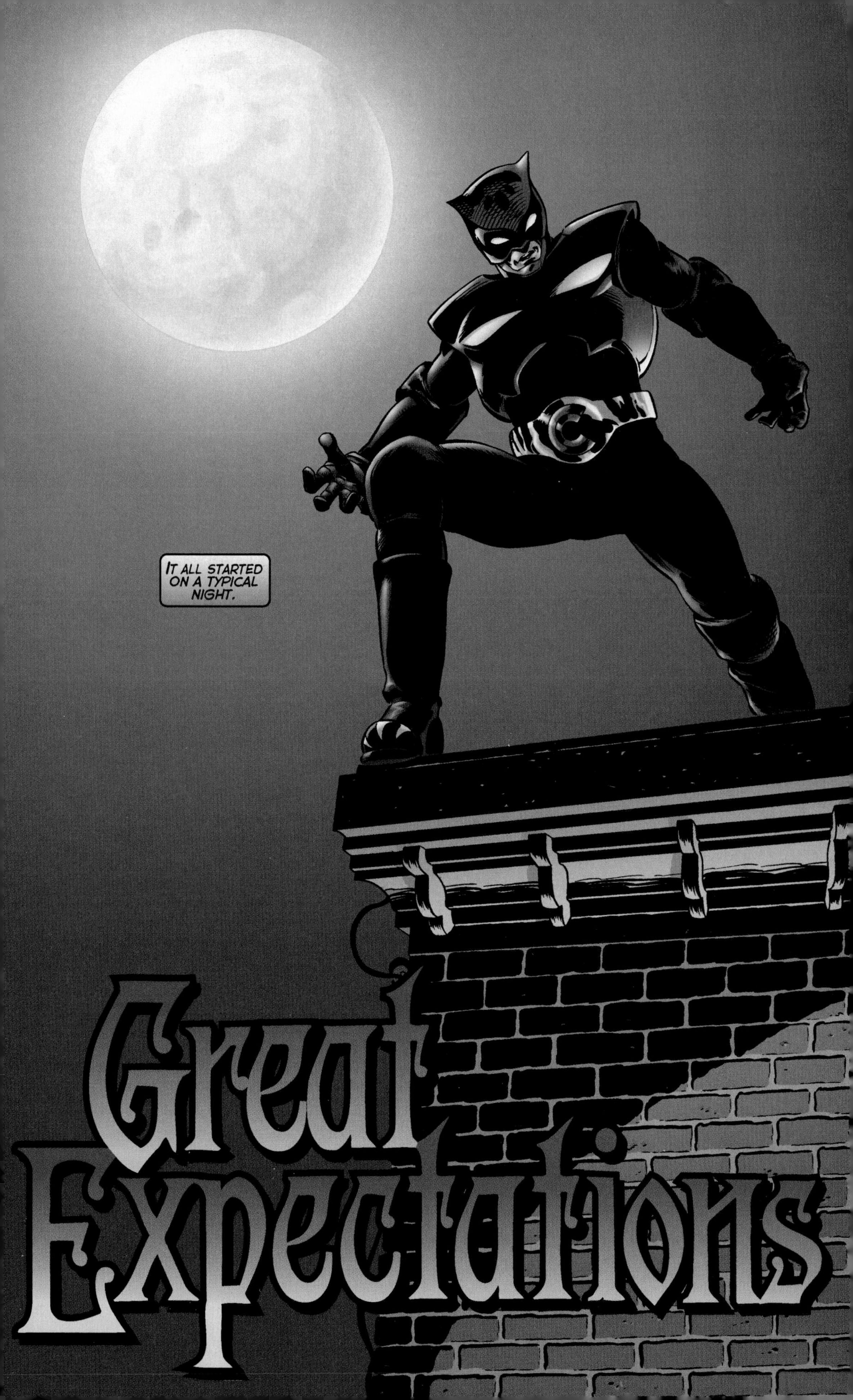
It all started on a typical night.
Great Expectations

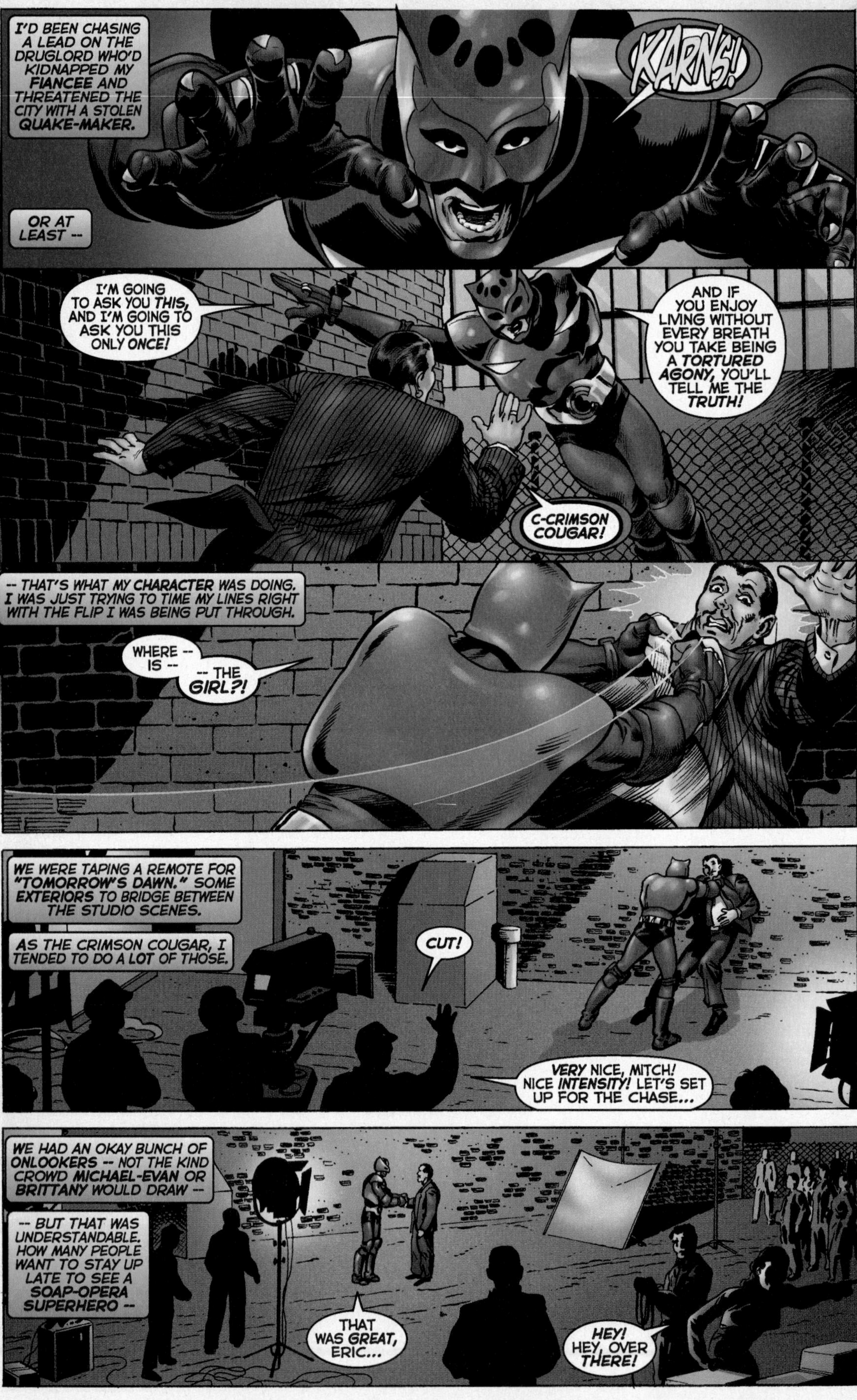
I'D BEEN CHASING A LEAD ON THE DRUGLORD WHO'D KIDNAPPED MY FIANCEE AND THREATENED THE CITY WITH A STOLEN QUAKE-MAKER.
KARNS!
OR AT LEAST --
I'M GOING TO ASK YOU THIS, AND I'M GOING TO ASK YOU THIS ONLY ONCE!
AND IF YOU ENJOY LIVING WITHOUT EVERY BREATH YOU TAKE BEING A TORTURED AGONY, YOU'LL TELL ME THE TRUTH!
C-CRIMSON COUGAR!
-- THAT'S WHAT MY CHARACTER WAS DOING. I WAS JUST TRYING TO TIME MY LINES RIGHT WITH THE FLIP I WAS BEING PUT THROUGH.
WHERE --
IS --
-- THE GIRL?!
WE WERE TAPING A REMOTE FOR "TOMORROW'S DAWN." SOME EXTERIORS TO BRIDGE BETWEEN THE STUDIO SCENES.
AS THE CRIMSON COUGAR, I TENDED TO DO A LOT OF THOSE.
CUT!
VERY NICE, MITCH! NICE INTENSITY! LET'S SET UP FOR THE CHASE...
WE HAD AN OKAY BUNCH OF ONLOOKERS -- NOT THE KIND CROWD MICHAEL-EVAN OR BRITTANY WOULD DRAW --
-- BUT THAT WAS UNDERSTANDABLE. HOW MANY PEOPLE WANT TO STAY UP LATE TO SEE A SOAP-OPERA SUPERHERO --
THAT WAS GREAT, ERIC...
HEY! HEY, OVER THERE!

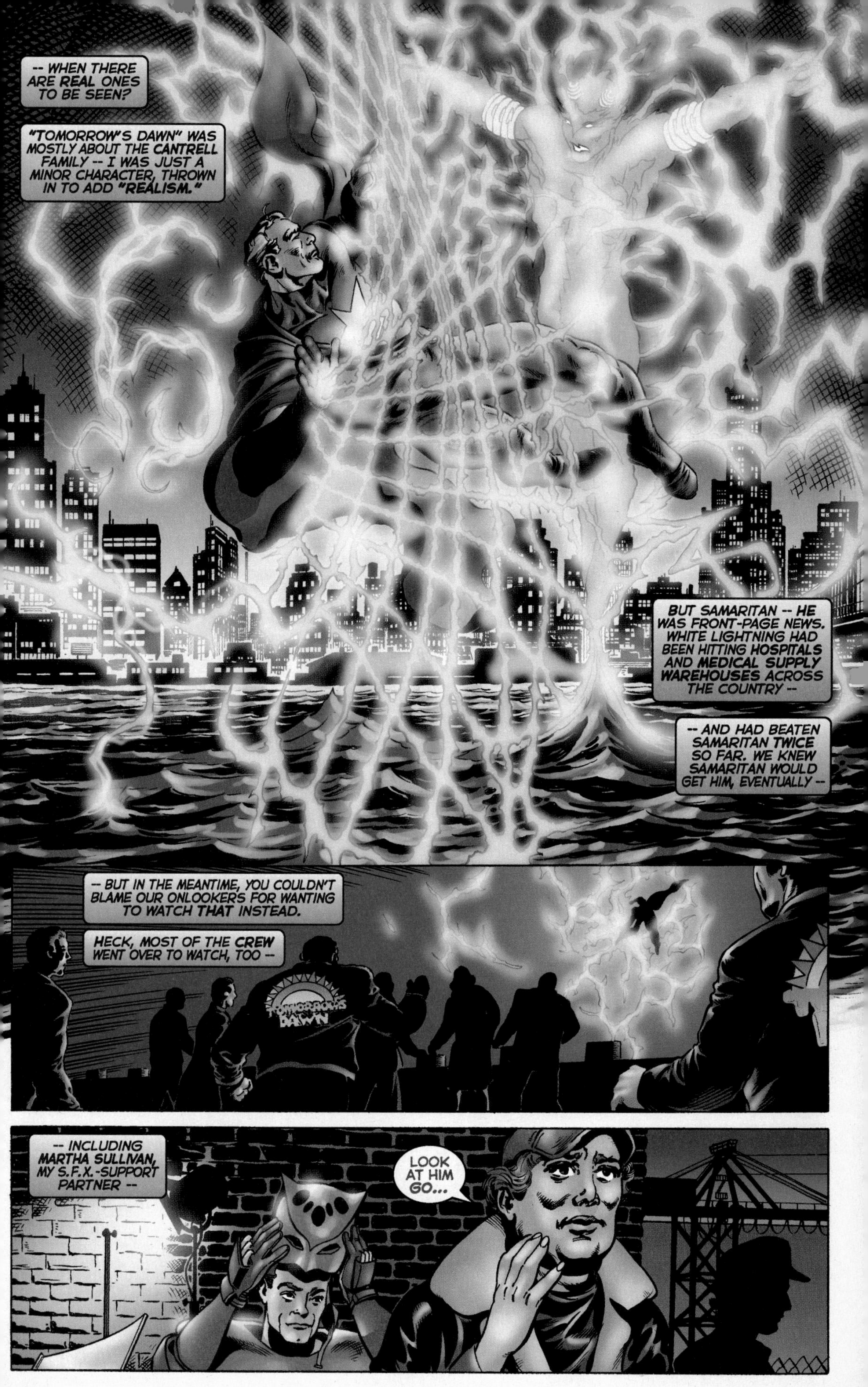
-- WHEN THERE ARE REAL ONES TO BE SEEN?
"TOMORROW'S DAWN" WAS MOSTLY ABOUT THE CANTRELL FAMILY -- I WAS JUST A MINOR CHARACTER, THROWN IN TO ADD "REALISM."
BUT SAMARITAN -- HE WAS FRONT-PAGE NEWS. WHITE LIGHTNING HAD BEEN HITTING HOSPITALS AND MEDICAL SUPPLY WAREHOUSES ACROSS THE COUNTRY --
-- AND HAD BEATEN SAMARITAN TWICE SO FAR. WE KNEW SAMARITAN WOULD GET HIM, EVENTUALLY --
-- BUT IN THE MEANTIME, YOU COULDN'T BLAME OUR ONLOOKERS FOR WANTING TO WATCH THAT INSTEAD.
HECK, MOST OF THE CREW WENT OVER TO WATCH, TOO --
TOMORROW'S DAWN
-- INCLUDING MARTHA SULLIVAN, MY S.F.X.-SUPPORT PARTNER --
LOOK AT HIM GO...

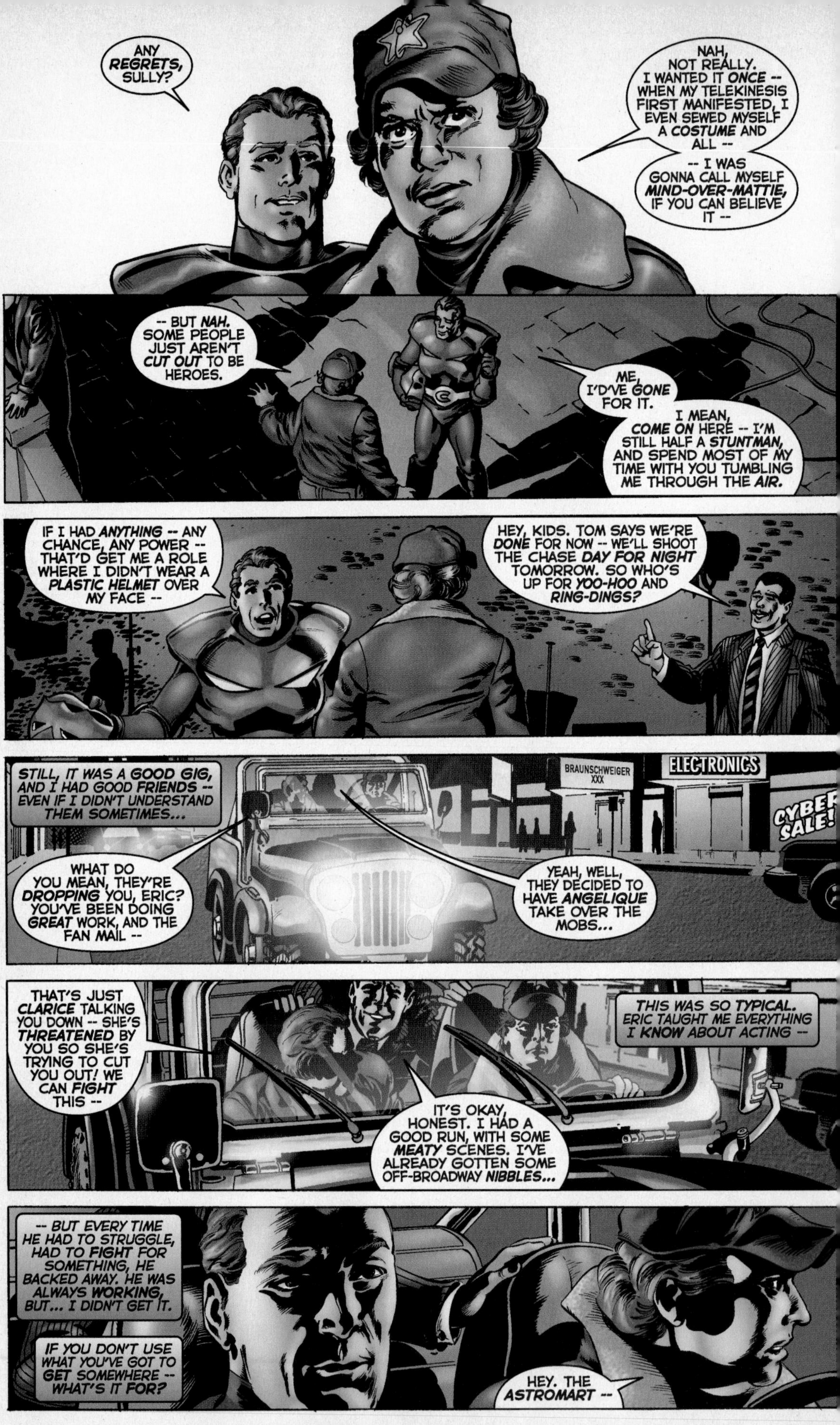
ANY REGRETS, SULLY?
NAH, NOT REALLY. I WANTED IT ONCE -- WHEN MY TELEKINESIS FIRST MANIFESTED, I EVEN SEWED MYSELF A COSTUME AND ALL --
-- I WAS GONNA CALL MYSELF MIND-OVER-MATTIE, IF YOU CAN BELIEVE IT --
-- BUT NAH. SOME PEOPLE JUST AREN'T CUT OUT TO BE HEROES.
ME, I'D'VE GONE FOR IT.
I MEAN, COME ON HERE -- I'M STILL HALF A STUNTMAN, AND SPEND MOST OF MY TIME WITH YOU TUMBLING ME THROUGH THE AIR.
IF I HAD ANYTHING -- ANY CHANCE, ANY POWER -- THAT'D GET ME A ROLE WHERE I DIDN'T WEAR A PLASTIC HELMET OVER MY FACE --
HEY, KIDS. TOM SAYS WE'RE DONE FOR NOW -- WE'LL SHOOT THE CHASE DAY FOR NIGHT TOMORROW. SO WHO'S UP FOR YOO-HOO AND RING-DINGS?
STILL, IT WAS A GOOD GIG, AND I HAD GOOD FRIENDS -- EVEN IF I DIDN'T UNDERSTAND THEM SOMETIMES...
BRAUNSCHWEIGER XXX
ELECTRONICS
CYBER SALE!
WHAT DO YOU MEAN, THEY'RE DROPPING YOU, ERIC? YOU'VE BEEN DOING GREAT WORK, AND THE FAN MAIL --
YEAH, WELL, THEY DECIDED TO HAVE ANGELIQUE TAKE OVER THE MOBS...
THAT'S JUST CLARICE TALKING YOU DOWN -- SHE'S THREATENED BY YOU SO SHE'S TRYING TO CUT YOU OUT! WE CAN FIGHT THIS --
THIS WAS SO TYPICAL. ERIC TAUGHT ME EVERYTHING I KNOW ABOUT ACTING --
IT'S OKAY, HONEST. I HAD A GOOD RUN, WITH SOME MEATY SCENES. I'VE ALREADY GOTTEN SOME OFF-BROADWAY NIBBLES...
-- BUT EVERY TIME HE HAD TO STRUGGLE, HAD TO FIGHT FOR SOMETHING, HE BACKED AWAY. HE WAS ALWAYS WORKING, BUT... I DIDN'T GET IT.
IF YOU DON'T USE WHAT YOU'VE GOT TO GET SOMEWHERE -- WHAT'S IT FOR?
HEY. THE ASTROMART --

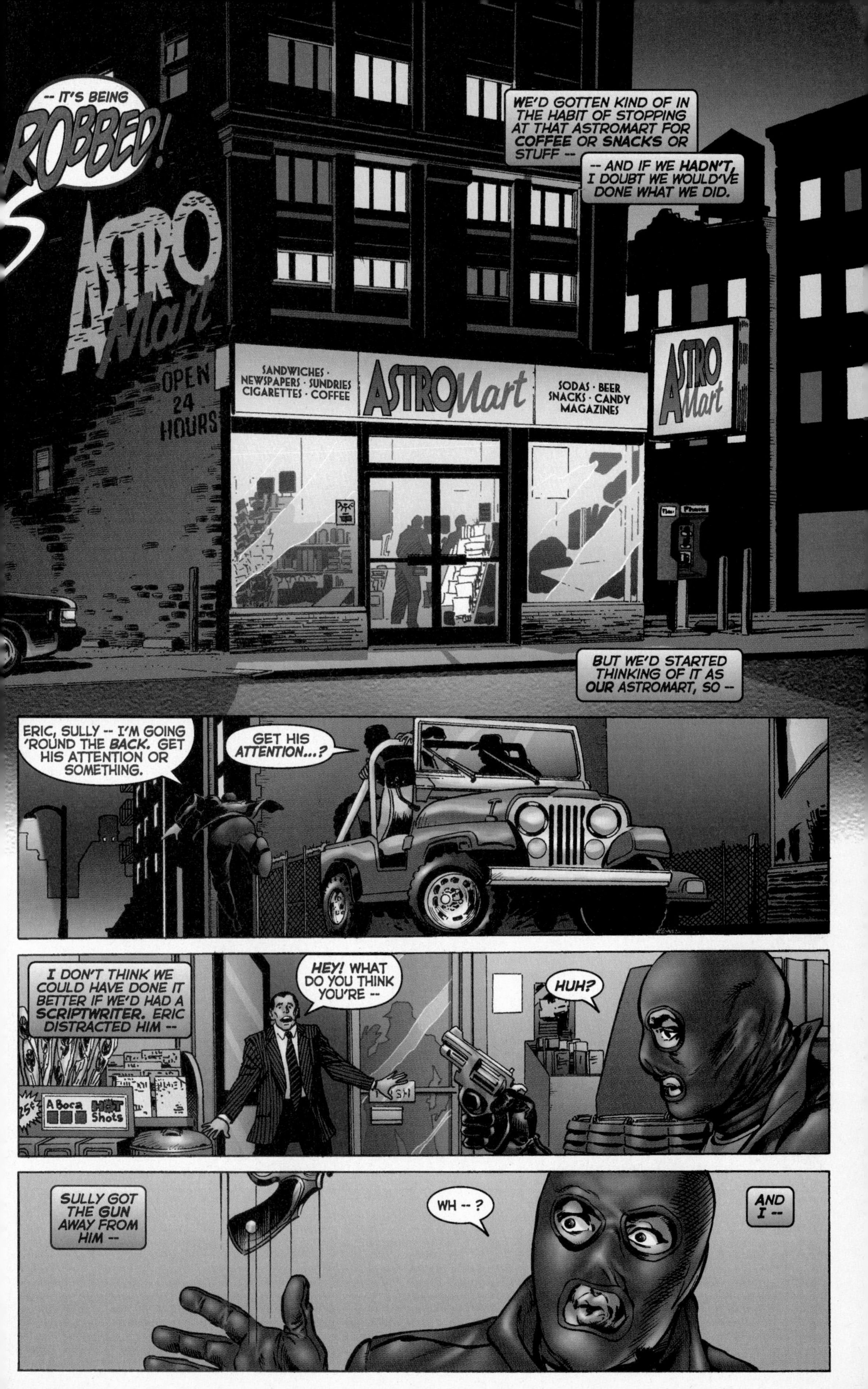

-- IT'S BEING ROBBED!
WE'D GOTTEN KIND OF IN THE HABIT OF STOPPING AT THAT ASTROMART FOR COFFEE OR SNACKS OR STUFF --
-- AND IF WE HADN'T, I DOUBT WE WOULD'VE DONE WHAT WE DID.
ASTRO Mart
OPEN 24 HOURS
SANDWICHES · NEWSPAPERS · SUNDRIES CIGARETTES · COFFEE
ASTRO Mart
SODAS · BEER SNACKS · CANDY MAGAZINES
ASTRO Mart
BUT WE'D STARTED THINKING OF IT AS OUR ASTROMART, SO --
ERIC, SULLY -- I'M GOING 'ROUND THE BACK. GET HIS ATTENTION OR SOMETHING.
GET HIS ATTENTION...?
I DON'T THINK WE COULD HAVE DONE IT BETTER IF WE'D HAD A SCRIPTWRITER. ERIC DISTRACTED HIM --
HEY! WHAT DO YOU THINK YOU'RE --
HUH?
25¢ A Boca HOT Shots
SULLY GOT THE GUN AWAY FROM HIM --
WH -- ?
AND I --

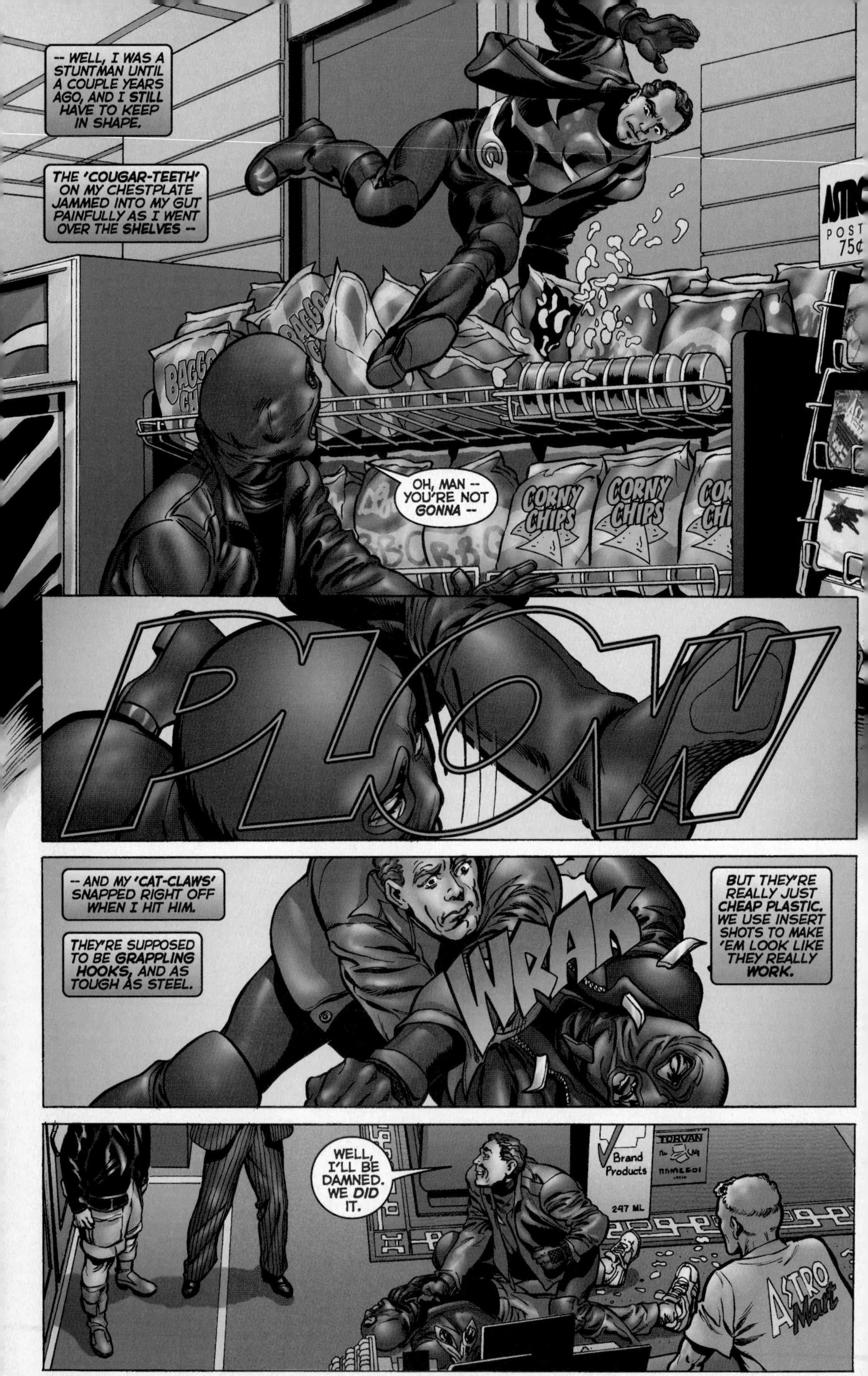
-- WELL, I WAS A STUNTMAN UNTIL A COUPLE YEARS AGO, AND I STILL HAVE TO KEEP IN SHAPE.
THE 'COUGAR-TEETH' ON MY CHESTPLATE JAMMED INTO MY GUT PAINFULLY AS I WENT OVER THE SHELVES --
POST 75¢
CORNY CHIPS
OH, MAN -- YOU'RE NOT GONNA --
PLOW
-- AND MY 'CAT-CLAWS' SNAPPED RIGHT OFF WHEN I HIT HIM.
THEY'RE SUPPOSED TO BE GRAPPLING HOOKS, AND AS TOUGH AS STEEL.
WRAK
BUT THEY'RE REALLY JUST CHEAP PLASTIC. WE USE INSERT SHOTS TO MAKE 'EM LOOK LIKE THEY REALLY WORK.
WELL, I'LL BE DAMNED. WE DID IT.
Brand Products
TORVAN
247 ML
ASTRO Mart

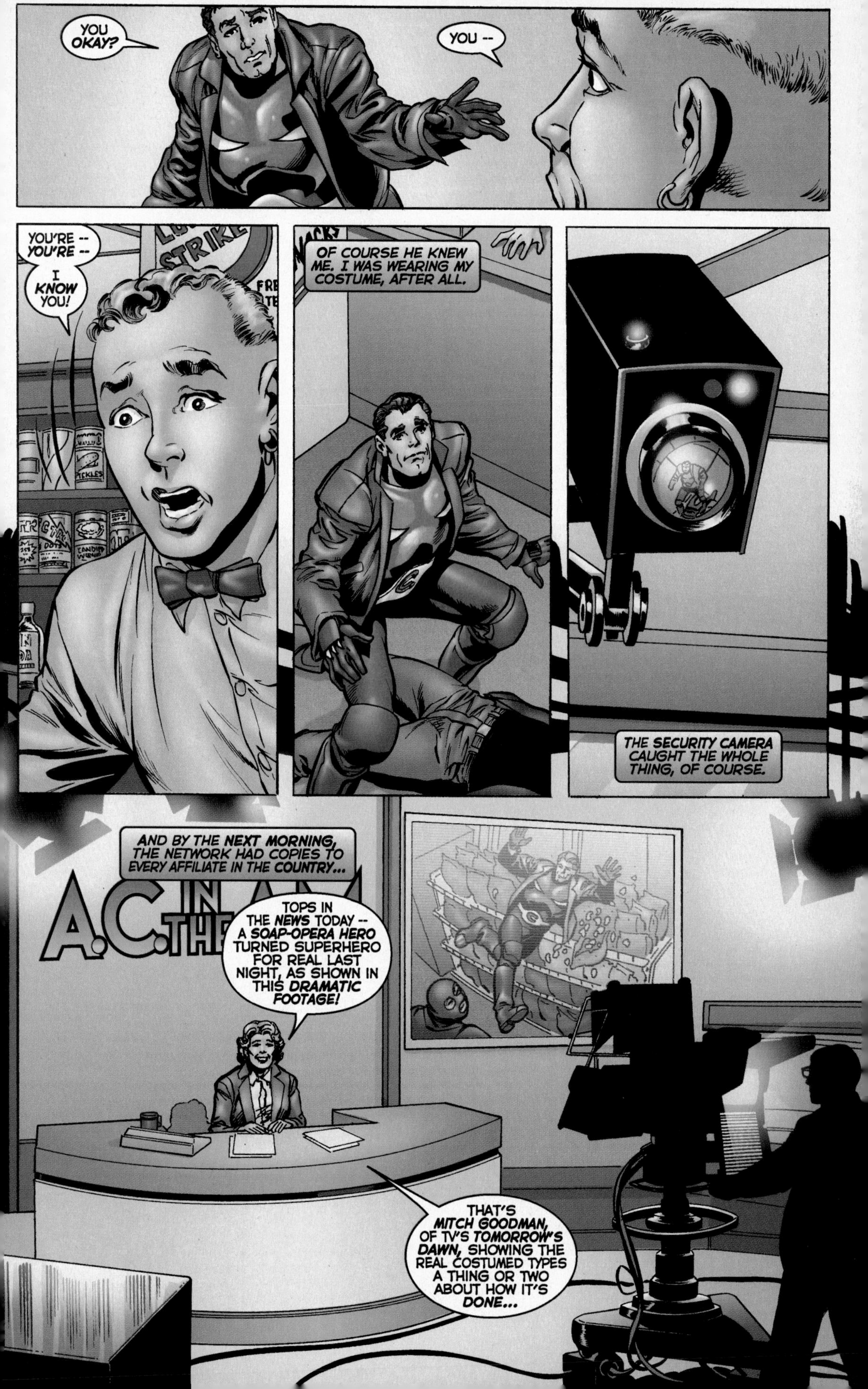
YOU OKAY?
YOU --
YOU'RE -- YOU'RE --
I KNOW YOU!
OF COURSE HE KNEW ME. I WAS WEARING MY COSTUME, AFTER ALL.
THE SECURITY CAMERA CAUGHT THE WHOLE THING, OF COURSE.
AND BY THE NEXT MORNING, THE NETWORK HAD COPIES TO EVERY AFFILIATE IN THE COUNTRY...
TOPS IN THE NEWS TODAY -- A SOAP-OPERA HERO TURNED SUPERHERO FOR REAL LAST NIGHT, AS SHOWN IN THIS DRAMATIC FOOTAGE!
THAT'S MITCH GOODMAN, OF TV'S TOMORROW'S DAWN, SHOWING THE REAL COSTUMED TYPES A THING OR TWO ABOUT HOW IT'S DONE...

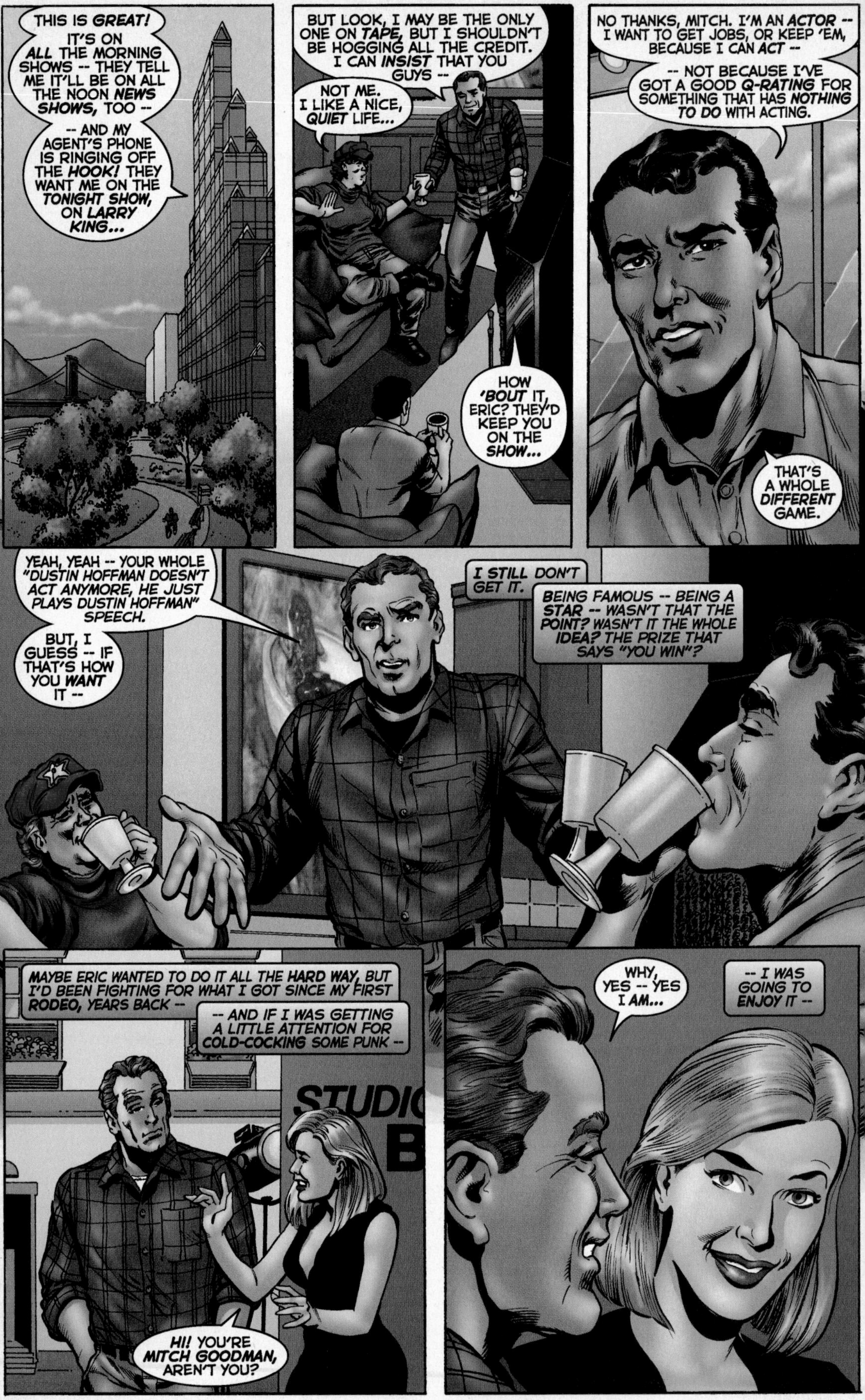
THIS IS GREAT! IT'S ON ALL THE MORNING SHOWS -- THEY TELL ME IT'LL BE ON ALL THE NOON NEWS SHOWS, TOO --
-- AND MY AGENT'S PHONE IS RINGING OFF THE HOOK! THEY WANT ME ON THE TONIGHT SHOW, ON LARRY KING...
BUT LOOK, I MAY BE THE ONLY ONE ON TAPE, BUT I SHOULDN'T BE HOGGING ALL THE CREDIT. I CAN INSIST THAT YOU GUYS --
NOT ME. I LIKE A NICE, QUIET LIFE...
HOW 'BOUT IT, ERIC? THEY'D KEEP YOU ON THE SHOW...
NO THANKS, MITCH. I'M AN ACTOR -- I WANT TO GET JOBS, OR KEEP 'EM, BECAUSE I CAN ACT --
-- NOT BECAUSE I'VE GOT A GOOD Q-RATING FOR SOMETHING THAT HAS NOTHING TO DO WITH ACTING.
THAT'S A WHOLE DIFFERENT GAME.
YEAH, YEAH -- YOUR WHOLE "DUSTIN HOFFMAN DOESN'T ACT ANYMORE, HE JUST PLAYS DUSTIN HOFFMAN" SPEECH.
BUT, I GUESS -- IF THAT'S HOW YOU WANT IT --
I STILL DON'T GET IT.
BEING FAMOUS -- BEING A STAR -- WASN'T THAT THE POINT? WASN'T IT THE WHOLE IDEA? THE PRIZE THAT SAYS "YOU WIN"?
MAYBE ERIC WANTED TO DO IT ALL THE HARD WAY, BUT I'D BEEN FIGHTING FOR WHAT I GOT SINCE MY FIRST RODEO, YEARS BACK --
-- AND IF I WAS GETTING A LITTLE ATTENTION FOR COLD-COCKING SOME PUNK --
STUDIO B
HI! YOU'RE MITCH GOODMAN, AREN'T YOU?
WHY, YES -- YES I AM...
-- I WAS GOING TO ENJOY IT --

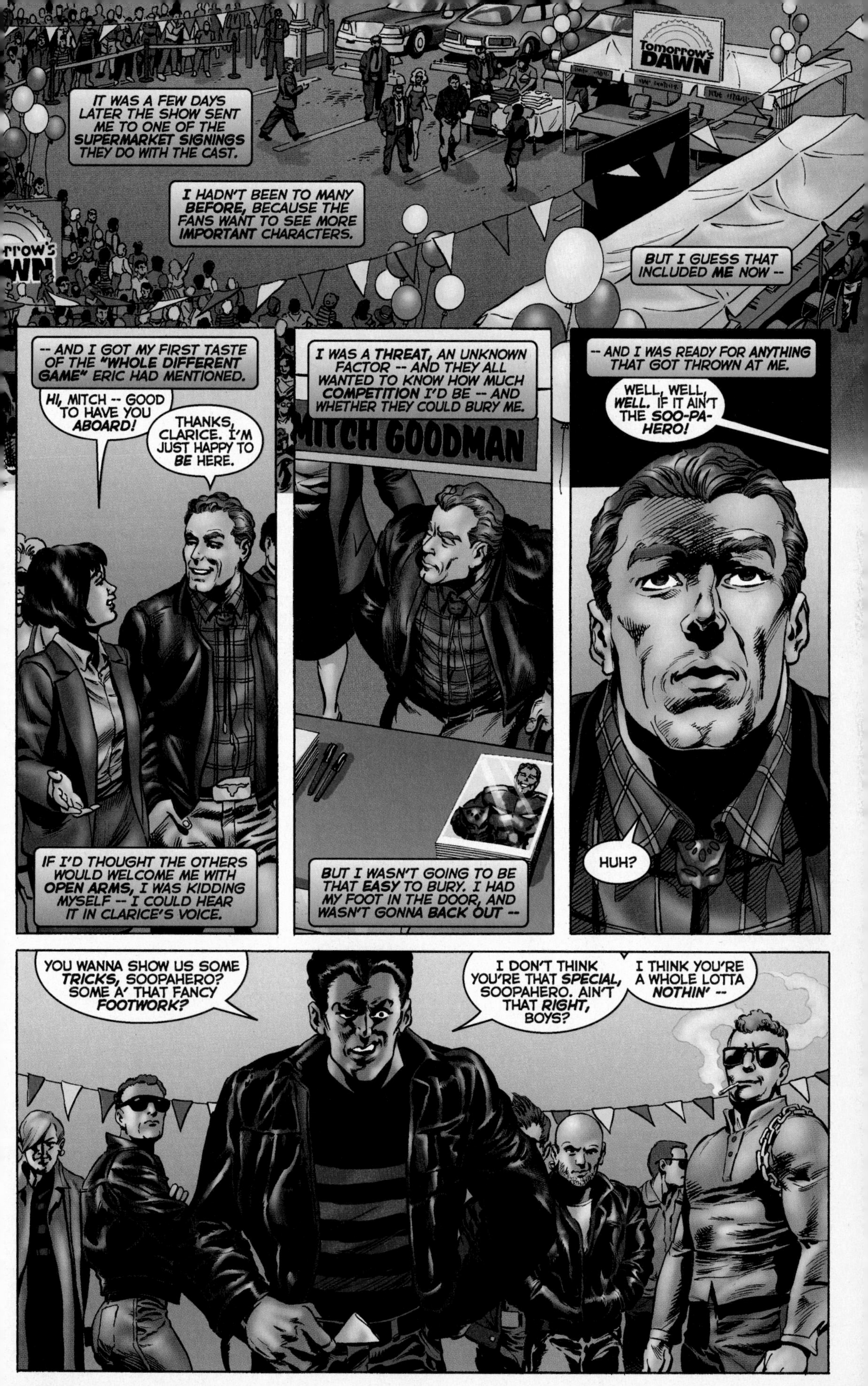
IT WAS A FEW DAYS LATER THE SHOW SENT ME TO ONE OF THE SUPERMARKET SIGNINGS THEY DO WITH THE CAST.
Tomorrow's DAWN
I HADN'T BEEN TO MANY BEFORE, BECAUSE THE FANS WANT TO SEE MORE IMPORTANT CHARACTERS.
BUT I GUESS THAT INCLUDED ME NOW --
-- AND I GOT MY FIRST TASTE OF THE "WHOLE DIFFERENT GAME" ERIC HAD MENTIONED.
HI, MITCH -- GOOD TO HAVE YOU ABOARD!
THANKS, CLARICE. I'M JUST HAPPY TO BE HERE.
IF I'D THOUGHT THE OTHERS WOULD WELCOME ME WITH OPEN ARMS, I WAS KIDDING MYSELF -- I COULD HEAR IT IN CLARICE'S VOICE.
I WAS A THREAT, AN UNKNOWN FACTOR -- AND THEY ALL WANTED TO KNOW HOW MUCH COMPETITION I'D BE -- AND WHETHER THEY COULD BURY ME.
MITCH GOODMAN
BUT I WASN'T GOING TO BE THAT EASY TO BURY. I HAD MY FOOT IN THE DOOR, AND WASN'T GONNA BACK OUT --
-- AND I WAS READY FOR ANYTHING THAT GOT THROWN AT ME.
WELL, WELL, WELL. IF IT AIN'T THE SOO-PA-HERO!
HUH?
YOU WANNA SHOW US SOME TRICKS, SOOPAHERO? SOME A' THAT FANCY FOOTWORK?
I DON'T THINK YOU'RE THAT SPECIAL, SOOPAHERO. AIN'T THAT RIGHT, BOYS?
I THINK YOU'RE A WHOLE LOTTA NOTHIN' --

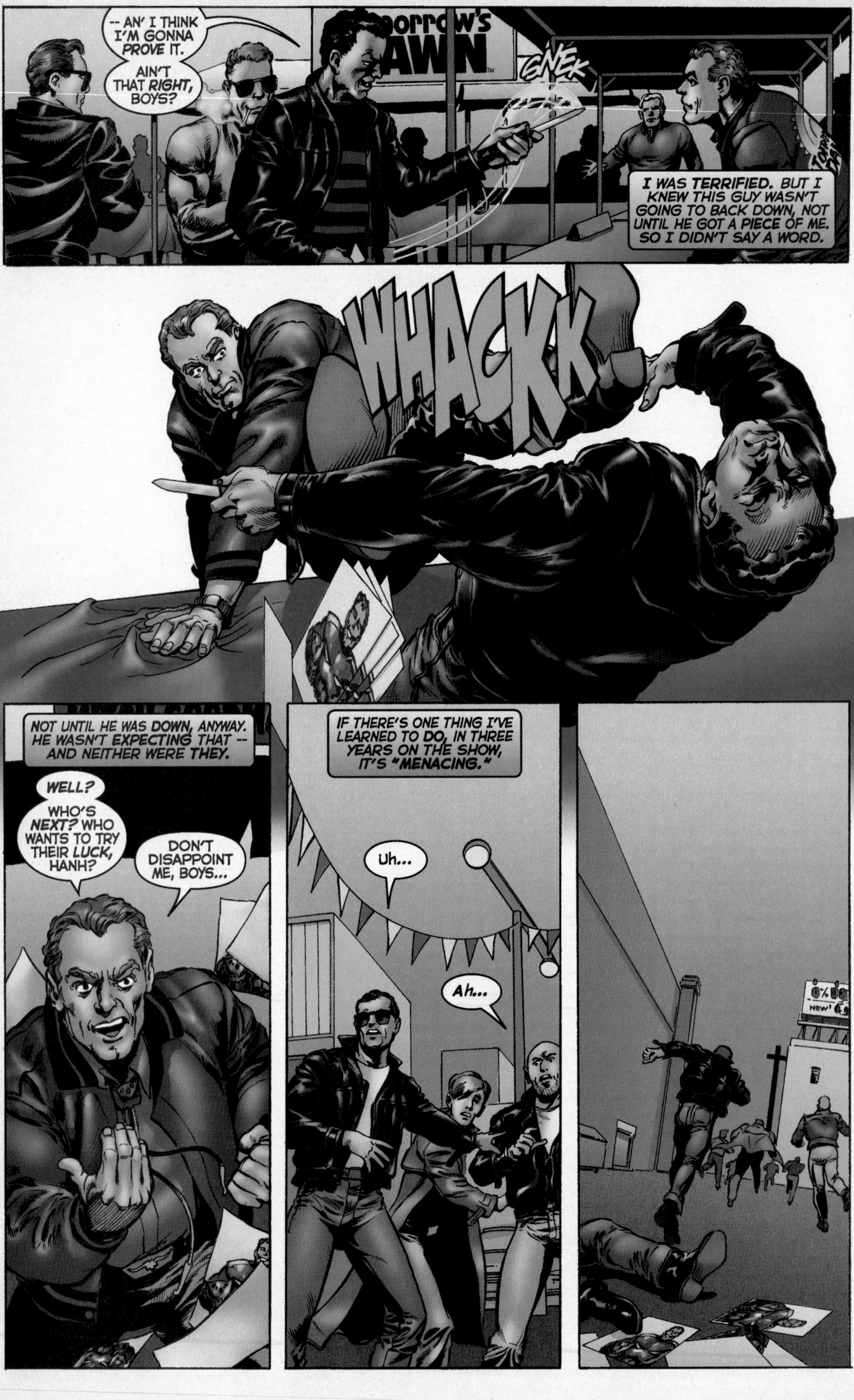
-- AN' I THINK I'M GONNA PROVE IT.
AIN'T THAT RIGHT, BOYS?
SNEK
I WAS TERRIFIED. BUT I KNEW THIS GUY WASN'T GOING TO BACK DOWN, NOT UNTIL HE GOT A PIECE OF ME. SO I DIDN'T SAY A WORD.
WHACKK
NOT UNTIL HE WAS DOWN, ANYWAY. HE WASN'T EXPECTING THAT -- AND NEITHER WERE THEY.
WELL?
WHO'S NEXT? WHO WANTS TO TRY THEIR LUCK, HANH?
DON'T DISAPPOINT ME, BOYS...
IF THERE'S ONE THING I'VE LEARNED TO DO, IN THREE YEARS ON THE SHOW, IT'S "MENACING."
Uh...
Ah...

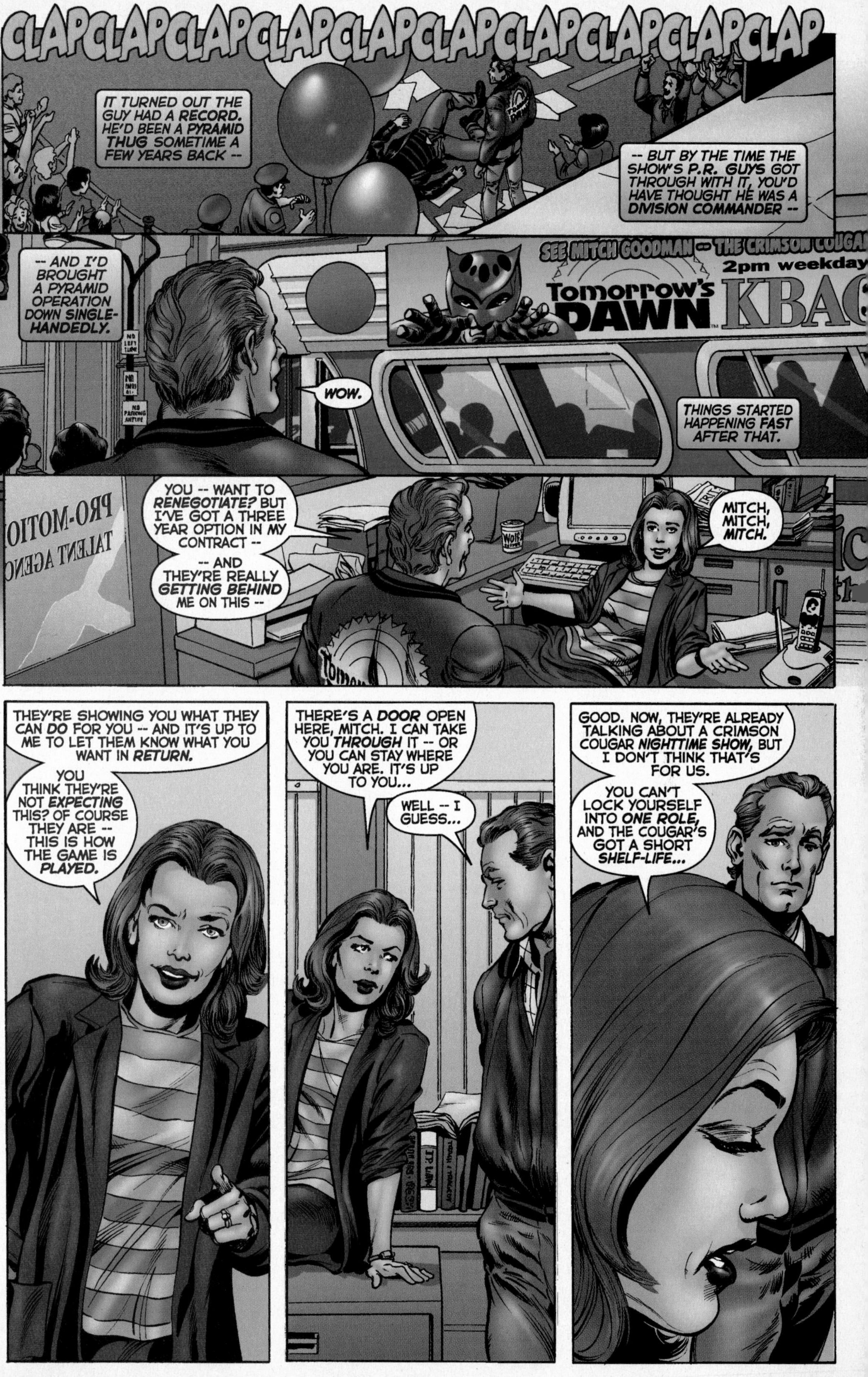
CLAPCLAPCLAPCLAPCLAPCLAPCLAPCLAPCLAPCLAP
IT TURNED OUT THE GUY HAD A RECORD. HE'D BEEN A PYRAMID THUG SOMETIME A FEW YEARS BACK --
-- BUT BY THE TIME THE SHOW'S P.R. GUYS GOT THROUGH WITH IT, YOU'D HAVE THOUGHT HE WAS A DIVISION COMMANDER --
-- AND I'D BROUGHT A PYRAMID OPERATION DOWN SINGLE-HANDEDLY.
SEE MITCH GOODMAN — THE CRIMSON COUGAR
2pm weekday
Tomorrow's DAWN
KBAC
WOW.
THINGS STARTED HAPPENING FAST AFTER THAT.
YOU -- WANT TO RENEGOTIATE? BUT I'VE GOT A THREE YEAR OPTION IN MY CONTRACT --
-- AND THEY'RE REALLY GETTING BEHIND ME ON THIS --
MITCH, MITCH, MITCH.
THEY'RE SHOWING YOU WHAT THEY CAN DO FOR YOU -- AND IT'S UP TO ME TO LET THEM KNOW WHAT YOU WANT IN RETURN.
YOU THINK THEY'RE NOT EXPECTING THIS? OF COURSE THEY ARE -- THIS IS HOW THE GAME IS PLAYED.
THERE'S A DOOR OPEN HERE, MITCH. I CAN TAKE YOU THROUGH IT -- OR YOU CAN STAY WHERE YOU ARE. IT'S UP TO YOU...
WELL -- I GUESS...
GOOD. NOW, THEY'RE ALREADY TALKING ABOUT A CRIMSON COUGAR NIGHTTIME SHOW, BUT I DON'T THINK THAT'S FOR US.
YOU CAN'T LOCK YOURSELF INTO ONE ROLE, AND THE COUGAR'S GOT A SHORT SHELF-LIFE...

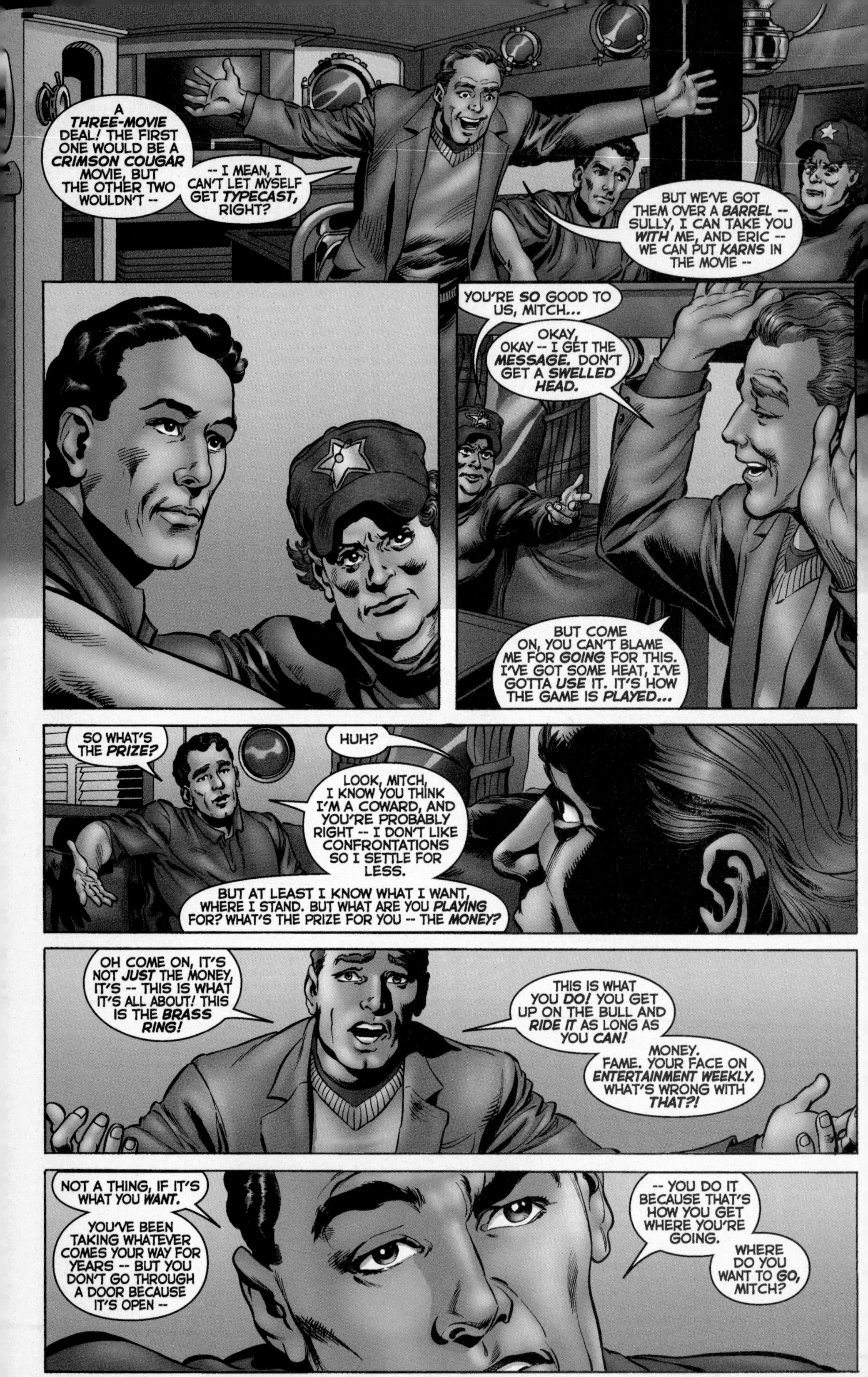
A THREE-MOVIE DEAL! THE FIRST ONE WOULD BE A CRIMSON COUGAR MOVIE, BUT THE OTHER TWO WOULDN'T --
-- I MEAN, I CAN'T LET MYSELF GET TYPECAST, RIGHT?
BUT WE'VE GOT THEM OVER A BARREL -- SULLY, I CAN TAKE YOU WITH ME, AND ERIC -- WE CAN PUT KARNS IN THE MOVIE --
YOU'RE SO GOOD TO US, MITCH...
OKAY, OKAY -- I GET THE MESSAGE. DON'T GET A SWELLED HEAD.
BUT COME ON, YOU CAN'T BLAME ME FOR GOING FOR THIS. I'VE GOT SOME HEAT, I'VE GOTTA USE IT. IT'S HOW THE GAME IS PLAYED...
SO WHAT'S THE PRIZE?
HUH?
LOOK, MITCH, I KNOW YOU THINK I'M A COWARD, AND YOU'RE PROBABLY RIGHT -- I DON'T LIKE CONFRONTATIONS SO I SETTLE FOR LESS.
BUT AT LEAST I KNOW WHAT I WANT, WHERE I STAND. BUT WHAT ARE YOU PLAYING FOR? WHAT'S THE PRIZE FOR YOU -- THE MONEY?
OH COME ON, IT'S NOT JUST THE MONEY, IT'S -- THIS IS WHAT IT'S ALL ABOUT! THIS IS THE BRASS RING!
THIS IS WHAT YOU DO! YOU GET UP ON THE BULL AND RIDE IT AS LONG AS YOU CAN!
MONEY. FAME. YOUR FACE ON ENTERTAINMENT WEEKLY. WHAT'S WRONG WITH THAT?!
NOT A THING, IF IT'S WHAT YOU WANT.
YOU'VE BEEN TAKING WHATEVER COMES YOUR WAY FOR YEARS -- BUT YOU DON'T GO THROUGH A DOOR BECAUSE IT'S OPEN --
-- YOU DO IT BECAUSE THAT'S HOW YOU GET WHERE YOU'RE GOING.
WHERE DO YOU WANT TO GO, MITCH?

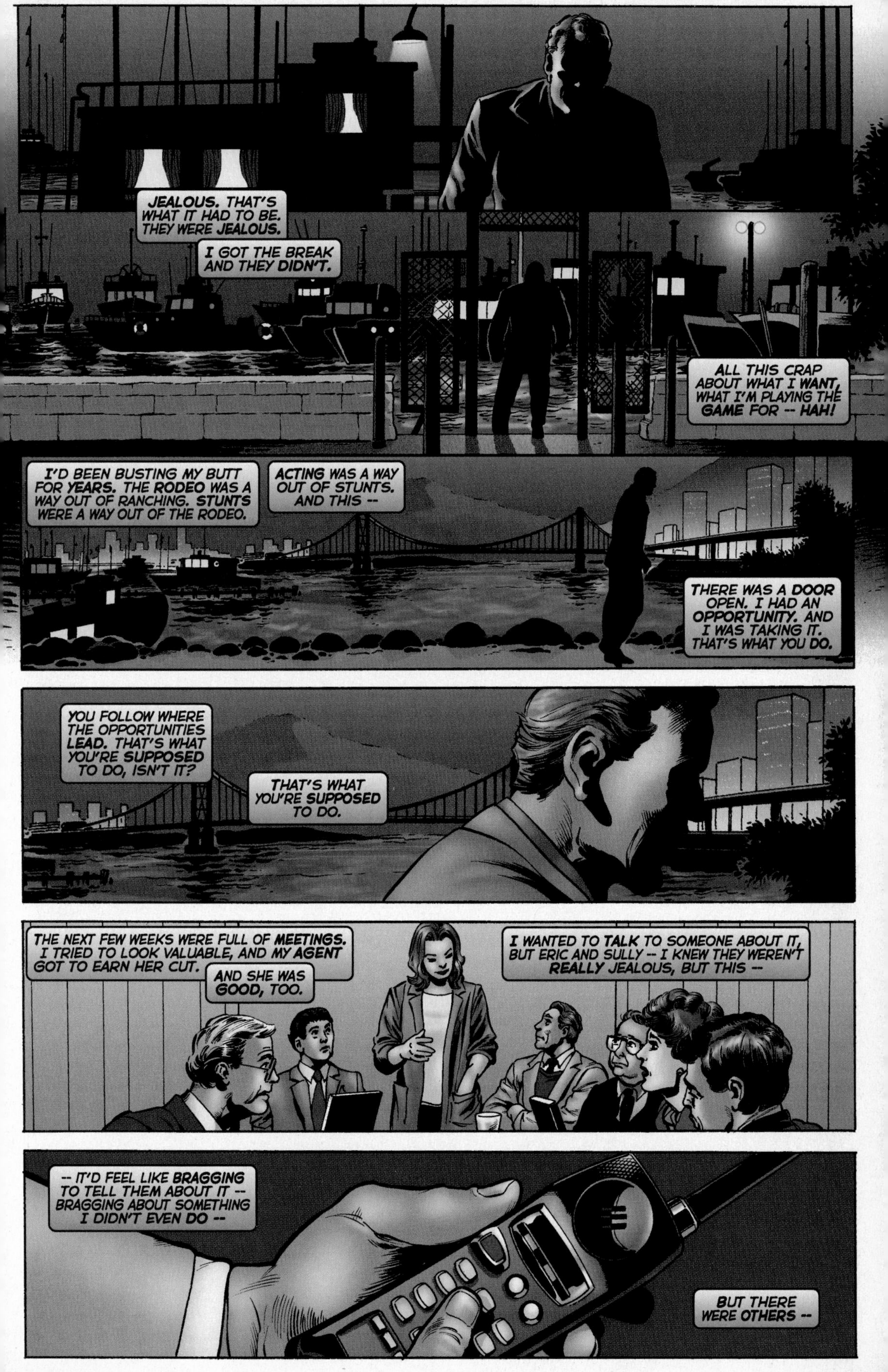
JEALOUS. THAT'S WHAT IT HAD TO BE. THEY WERE JEALOUS.
I GOT THE BREAK AND THEY DIDN'T.
ALL THIS CRAP ABOUT WHAT I WANT, WHAT I'M PLAYING THE GAME FOR -- HAH!
I'D BEEN BUSTING MY BUTT FOR YEARS. THE RODEO WAS A WAY OUT OF RANCHING. STUNTS WERE A WAY OUT OF THE RODEO.
ACTING WAS A WAY OUT OF STUNTS. AND THIS --
THERE WAS A DOOR OPEN. I HAD AN OPPORTUNITY. AND I WAS TAKING IT. THAT'S WHAT YOU DO.
YOU FOLLOW WHERE THE OPPORTUNITIES LEAD. THAT'S WHAT YOU'RE SUPPOSED TO DO, ISN'T IT?
THAT'S WHAT YOU'RE SUPPOSED TO DO.
THE NEXT FEW WEEKS WERE FULL OF MEETINGS. I TRIED TO LOOK VALUABLE, AND MY AGENT GOT TO EARN HER CUT.
AND SHE WAS GOOD, TOO.
I WANTED TO TALK TO SOMEONE ABOUT IT, BUT ERIC AND SULLY -- I KNEW THEY WEREN'T REALLY JEALOUS, BUT THIS --
-- IT'D FEEL LIKE BRAGGING TO TELL THEM ABOUT IT -- BRAGGING ABOUT SOMETHING I DIDN'T EVEN DO --
BUT THERE WERE OTHERS --

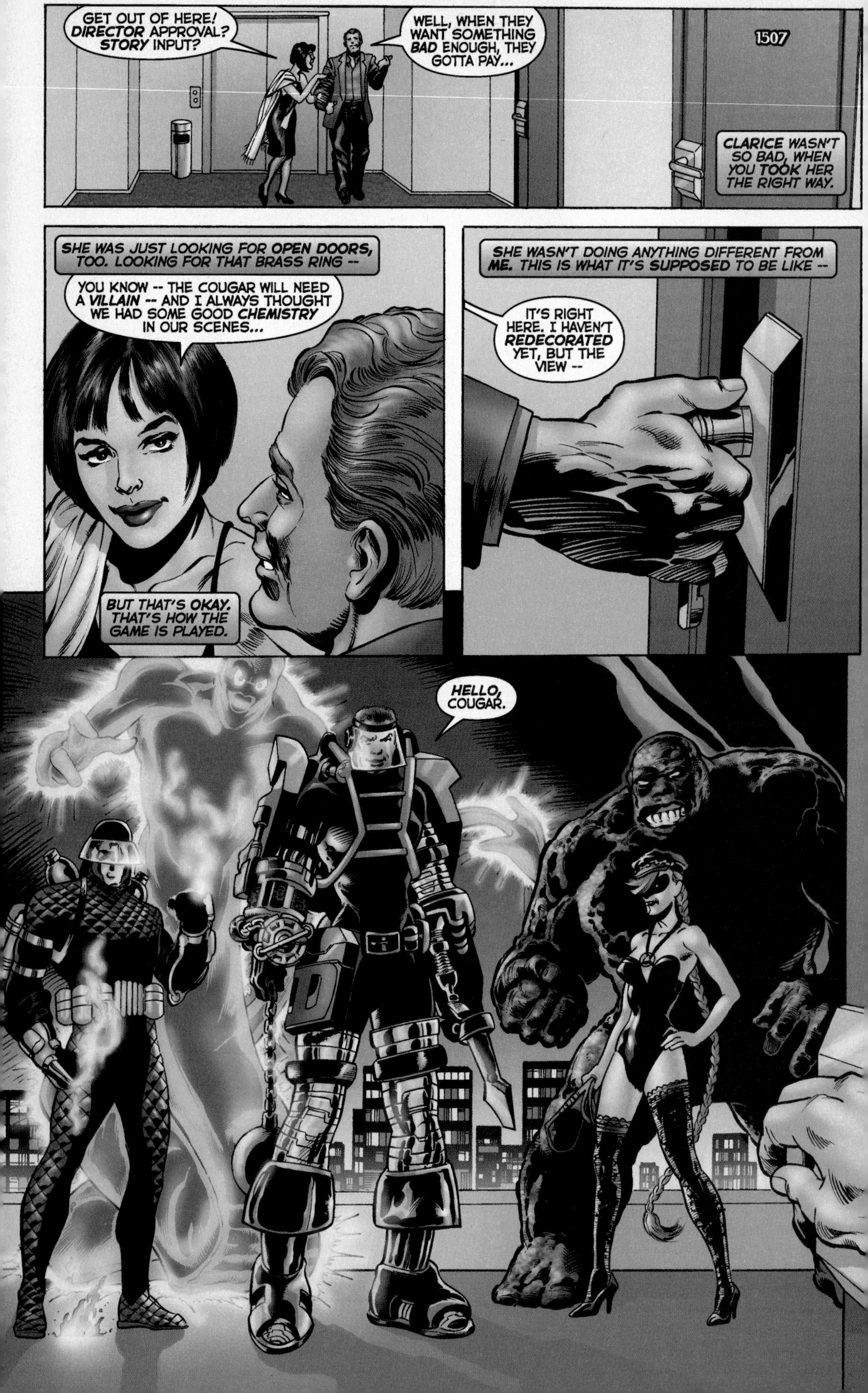
GET OUT OF HERE! DIRECTOR APPROVAL? STORY INPUT?
WELL, WHEN THEY WANT SOMETHING BAD ENOUGH, THEY GOTTA PAY...
1507
CLARICE WASN'T SO BAD, WHEN YOU TOOK HER THE RIGHT WAY.
SHE WAS JUST LOOKING FOR OPEN DOORS, TOO. LOOKING FOR THAT BRASS RING --
YOU KNOW -- THE COUGAR WILL NEED A VILLAIN -- AND I ALWAYS THOUGHT WE HAD SOME GOOD CHEMISTRY IN OUR SCENES...
BUT THAT'S OKAY. THAT'S HOW THE GAME IS PLAYED.
SHE WASN'T DOING ANYTHING DIFFERENT FROM ME. THIS IS WHAT IT'S SUPPOSED TO BE LIKE --
IT'S RIGHT HERE. I HAVEN'T REDECORATED YET, BUT THE VIEW --
HELLO, COUGAR.

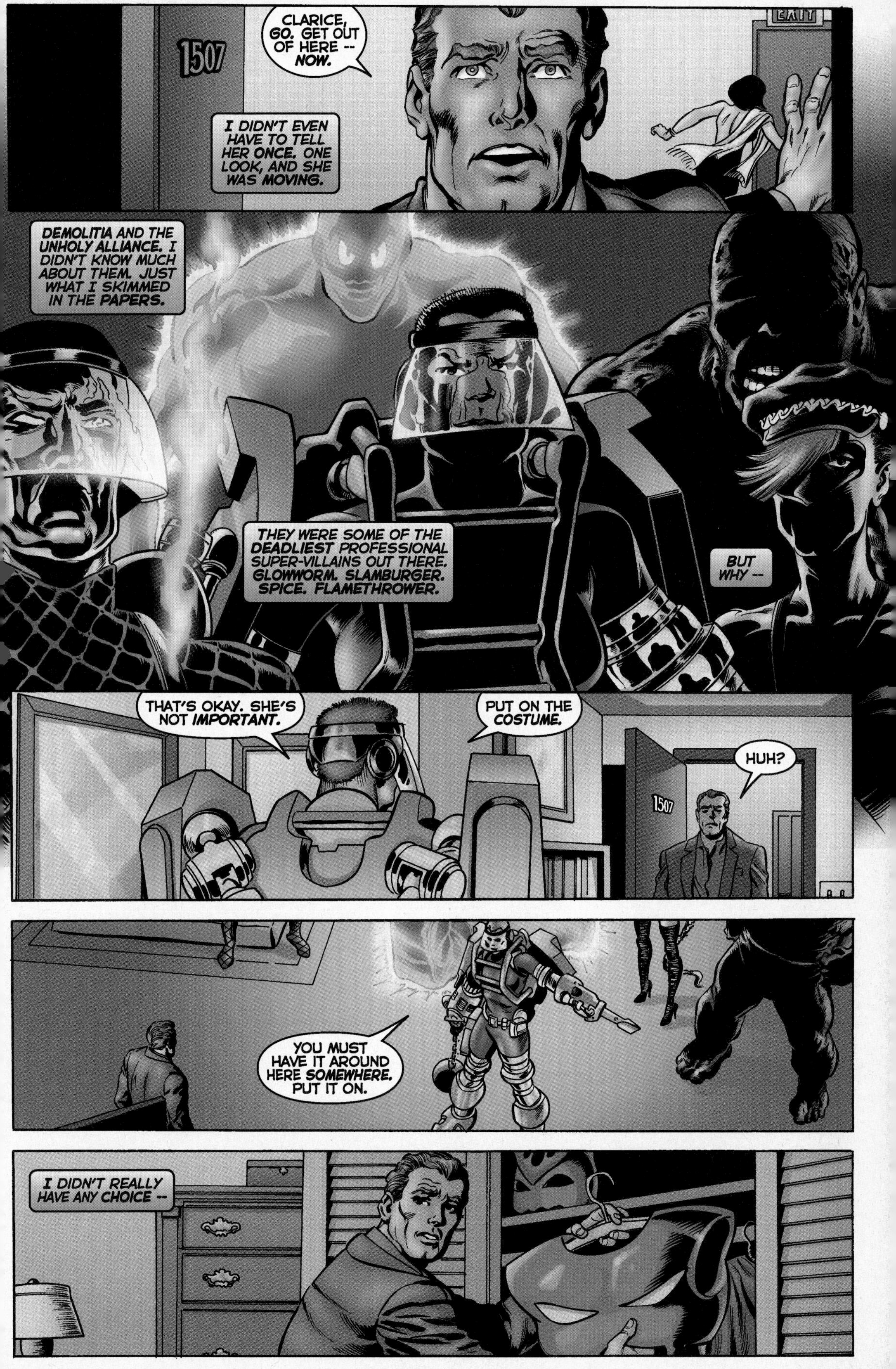
1507
CLARICE, GO. GET OUT OF HERE -- NOW.
EXIT
I DIDN'T EVEN HAVE TO TELL HER ONCE. ONE LOOK, AND SHE WAS MOVING.
DEMOLITIA AND THE UNHOLY ALLIANCE. I DIDN'T KNOW MUCH ABOUT THEM. JUST WHAT I SKIMMED IN THE PAPERS.
THEY WERE SOME OF THE DEADLIEST PROFESSIONAL SUPER-VILLAINS OUT THERE. GLOWWORM. SLAMBURGER. SPICE. FLAMETHROWER.
BUT WHY --
THAT'S OKAY. SHE'S NOT IMPORTANT.
PUT ON THE COSTUME.
1507
HUH?
YOU MUST HAVE IT AROUND HERE SOMEWHERE. PUT IT ON.
I DIDN'T REALLY HAVE ANY CHOICE --

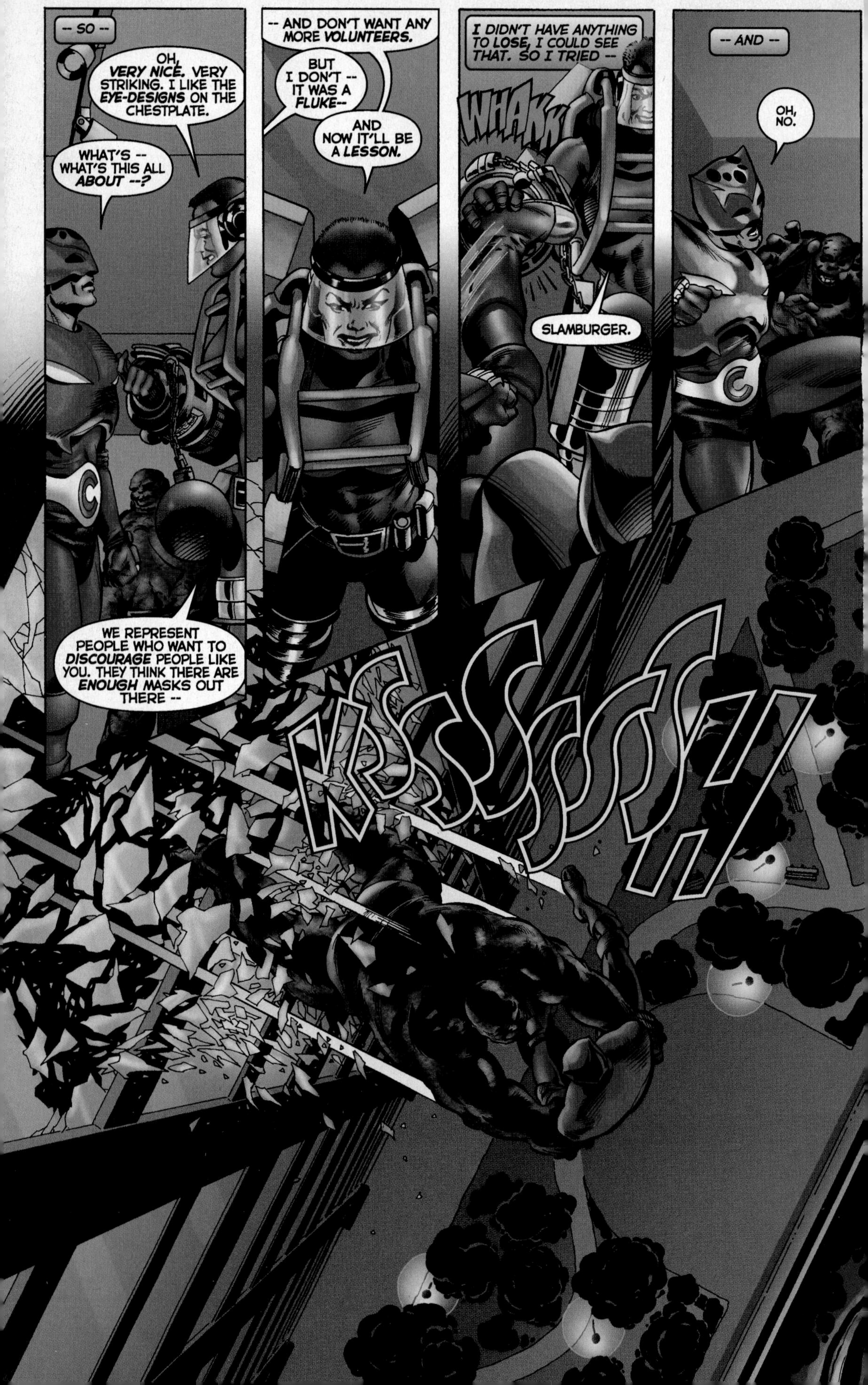
-- SO --
OH, VERY NICE. VERY STRIKING. I LIKE THE EYE-DESIGNS ON THE CHESTPLATE.
WHAT'S -- WHAT'S THIS ALL ABOUT --?
WE REPRESENT PEOPLE WHO WANT TO DISCOURAGE PEOPLE LIKE YOU. THEY THINK THERE ARE ENOUGH MASKS OUT THERE --
-- AND DON'T WANT ANY MORE VOLUNTEERS.
BUT I DON'T -- IT WAS A FLUKE--
AND NOW IT'LL BE A LESSON.
I DIDN'T HAVE ANYTHING TO LOSE, I COULD SEE THAT. SO I TRIED --
WHAKK
SLAMBURGER.
-- AND --
OH, NO.
KRSSSSSSH!

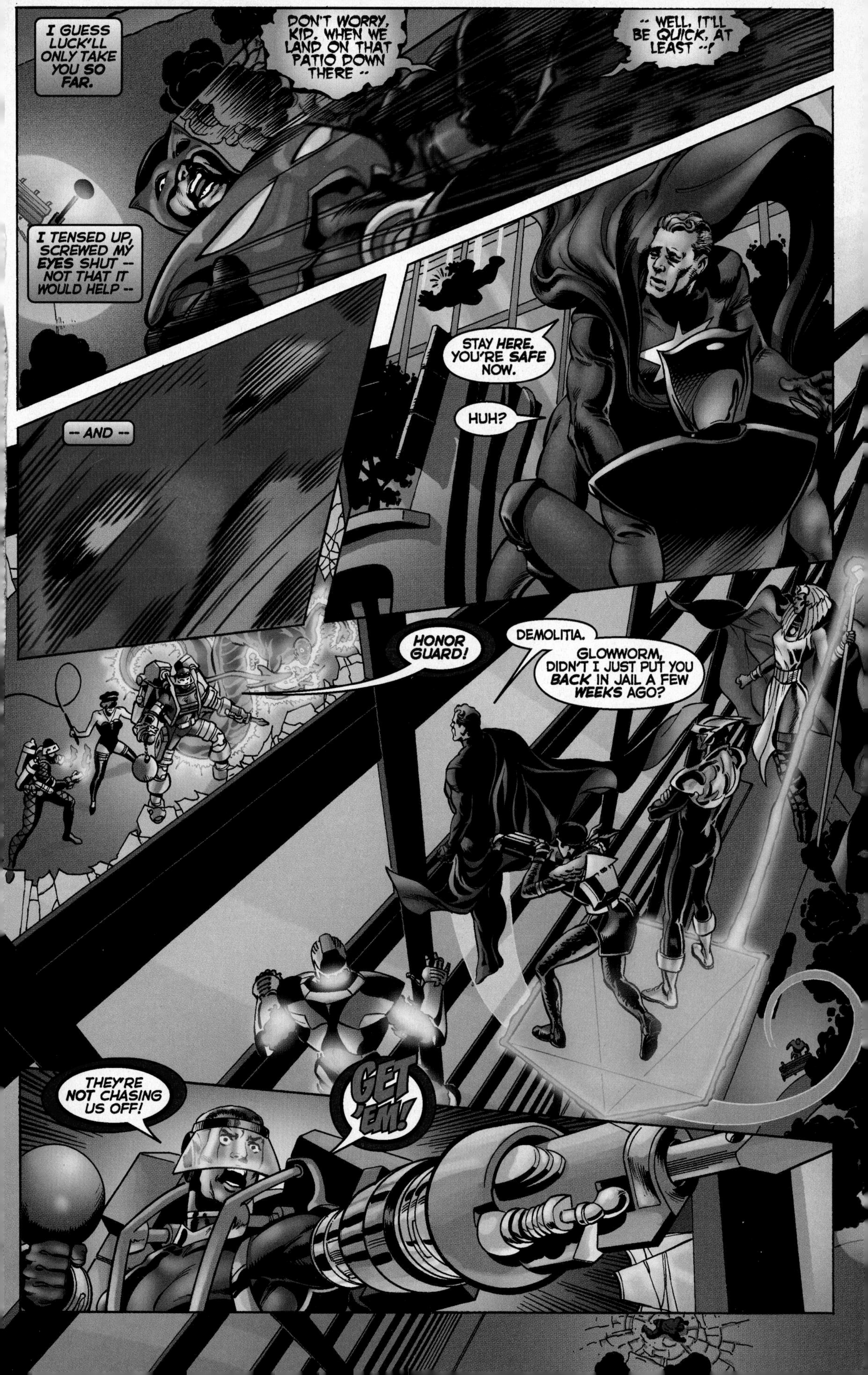

I GUESS LUCK'LL ONLY TAKE YOU SO FAR.
DON'T WORRY, KID. WHEN WE LAND ON THAT PATIO DOWN THERE --
-- WELL, IT'LL BE QUICK, AT LEAST --!
I TENSED UP, SCREWED MY EYES SHUT -- NOT THAT IT WOULD HELP --
-- AND --
STAY HERE. YOU'RE SAFE NOW.
HUH?
HONOR GUARD!
DEMOLITIA.
GLOWWORM, DIDN'T I JUST PUT YOU BACK IN JAIL A FEW WEEKS AGO?
THEY'RE NOT CHASING US OFF!
GET 'EM!

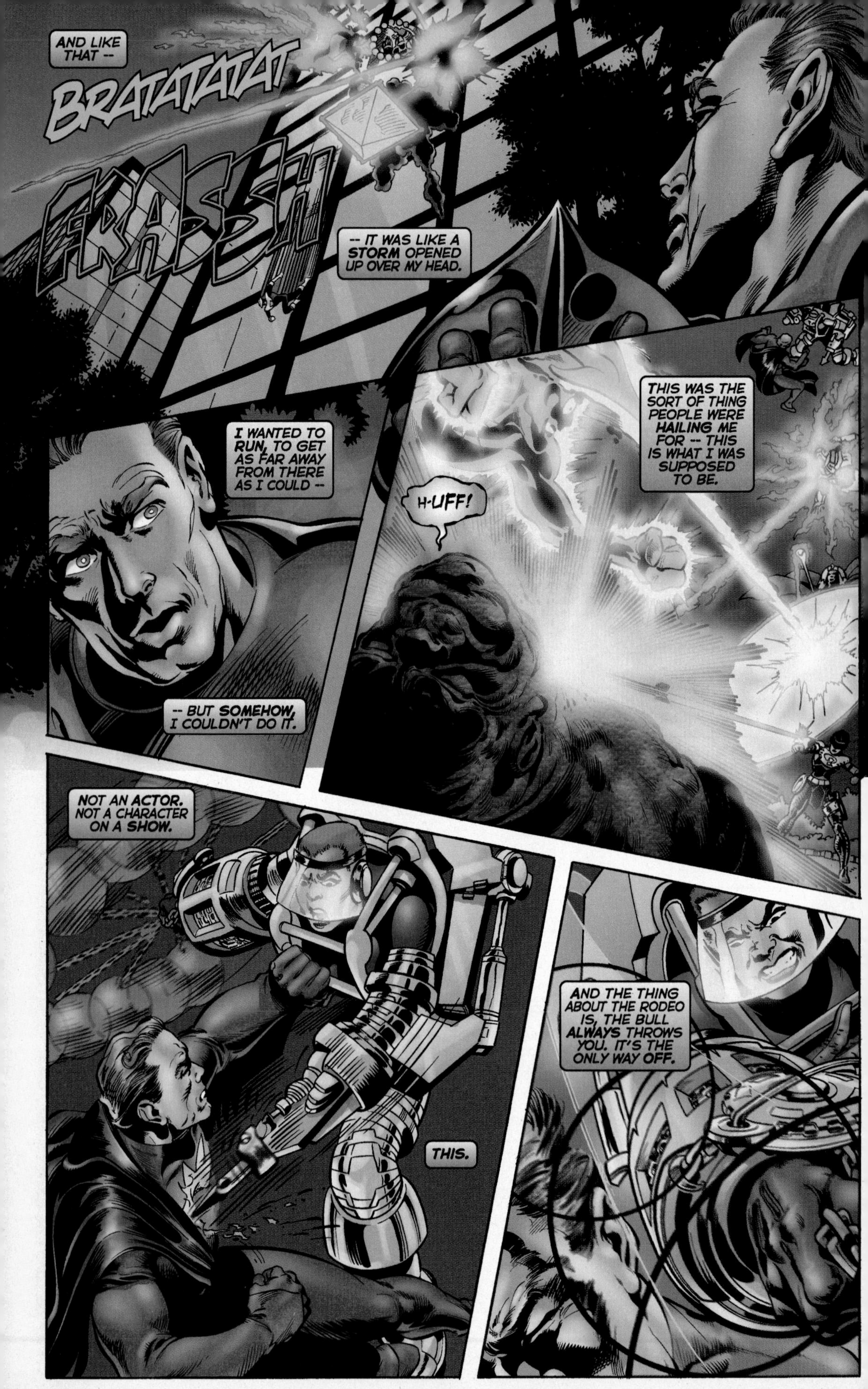

AND LIKE THAT --
BRATATATAT
CRASSH
-- IT WAS LIKE A STORM OPENED UP OVER MY HEAD.
I WANTED TO RUN, TO GET AS FAR AWAY FROM THERE AS I COULD --
-- BUT SOMEHOW, I COULDN'T DO IT.
H-UFF!
THIS WAS THE SORT OF THING PEOPLE WERE HAILING ME FOR -- THIS IS WHAT I WAS SUPPOSED TO BE.
NOT AN ACTOR. NOT A CHARACTER ON A SHOW.
THIS.
AND THE THING ABOUT THE RODEO IS, THE BULL ALWAYS THROWS YOU. IT'S THE ONLY WAY OFF.

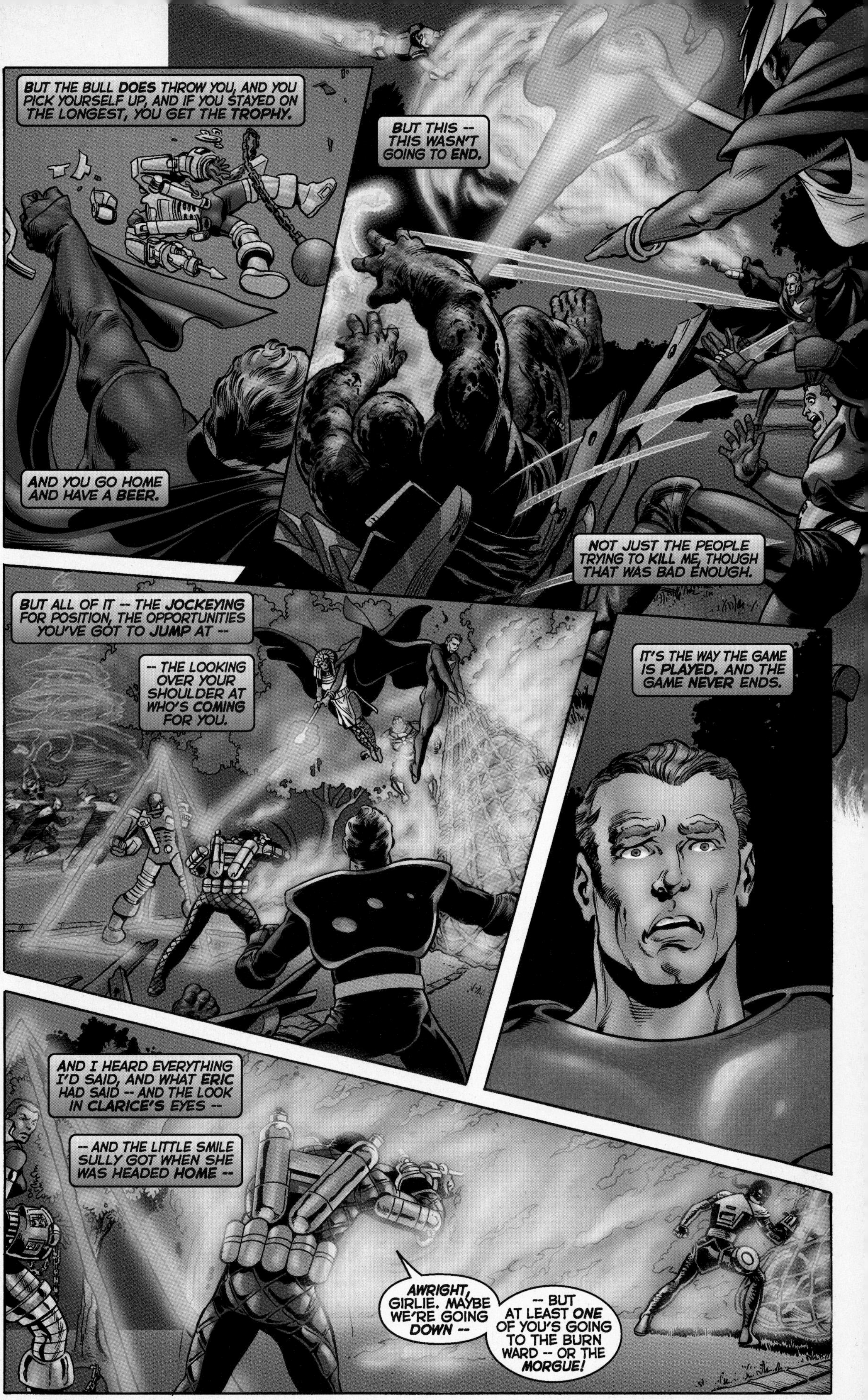
BUT THE BULL DOES THROW YOU, AND YOU PICK YOURSELF UP, AND IF YOU STAYED ON THE LONGEST, YOU GET THE TROPHY.
AND YOU GO HOME AND HAVE A BEER.
BUT THIS -- THIS WASN'T GOING TO END.
NOT JUST THE PEOPLE TRYING TO KILL ME, THOUGH THAT WAS BAD ENOUGH.
BUT ALL OF IT -- THE JOCKEYING FOR POSITION, THE OPPORTUNITIES YOU'VE GOT TO JUMP AT --
-- THE LOOKING OVER YOUR SHOULDER AT WHO'S COMING FOR YOU.
IT'S THE WAY THE GAME IS PLAYED. AND THE GAME NEVER ENDS.
AND I HEARD EVERYTHING I'D SAID, AND WHAT ERIC HAD SAID -- AND THE LOOK IN CLARICE'S EYES --
-- AND THE LITTLE SMILE SULLY GOT WHEN SHE WAS HEADED HOME --
AWRIGHT, GIRLIE. MAYBE WE'RE GOING DOWN --
-- BUT AT LEAST ONE OF YOU'S GOING TO THE BURN WARD -- OR THE MORGUE!

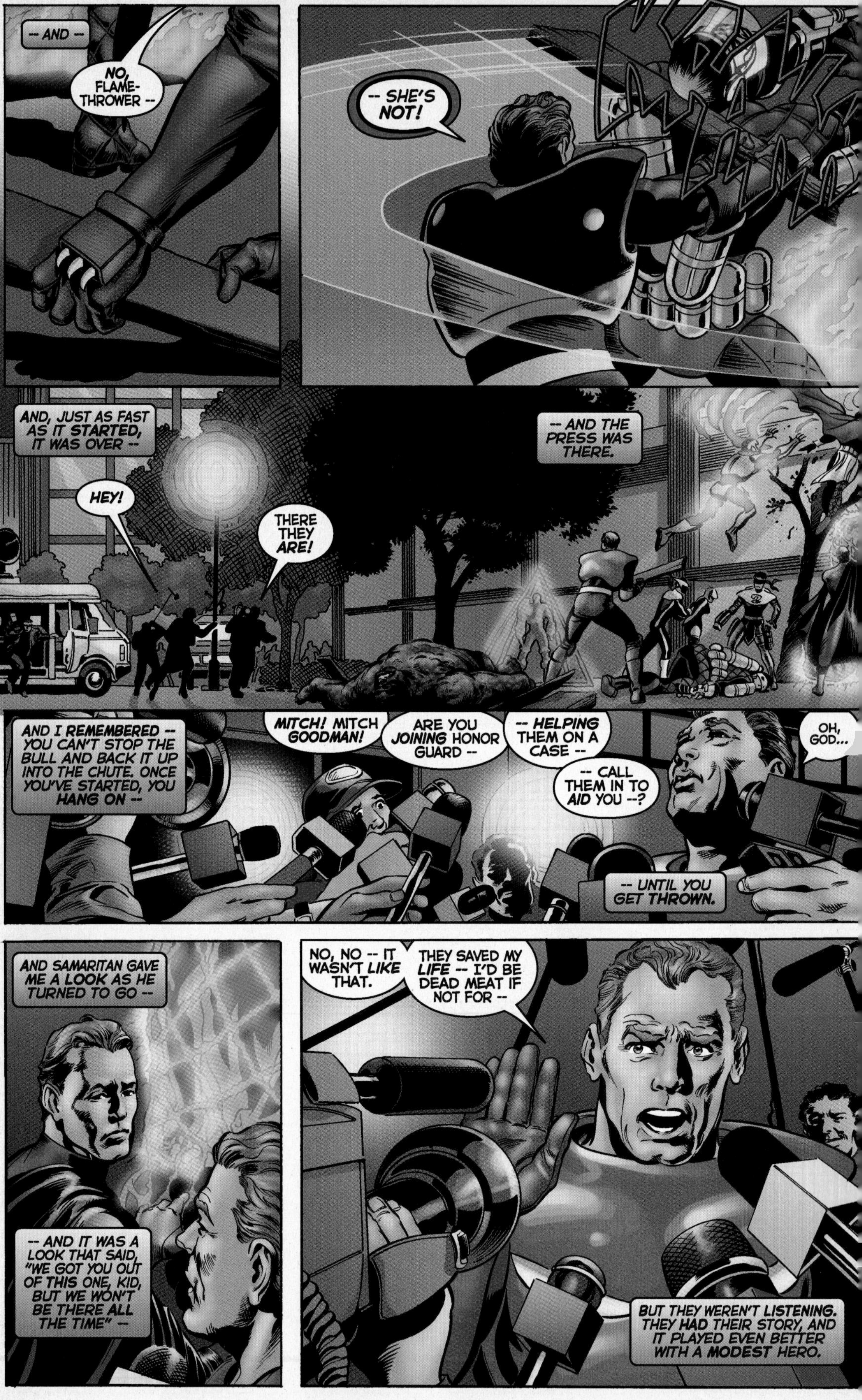
-- AND --
NO, FLAME-THROWER --
-- SHE'S NOT!
AND, JUST AS FAST AS IT STARTED, IT WAS OVER --
HEY!
THERE THEY ARE!
-- AND THE PRESS WAS THERE.
AND I REMEMBERED -- YOU CAN'T STOP THE BULL AND BACK IT UP INTO THE CHUTE. ONCE YOU'VE STARTED, YOU HANG ON --
MITCH! MITCH GOODMAN!
ARE YOU JOINING HONOR GUARD --
-- HELPING THEM ON A CASE --
-- CALL THEM IN TO AID YOU --?
OH, GOD...
-- UNTIL YOU GET THROWN.
AND SAMARITAN GAVE ME A LOOK AS HE TURNED TO GO --
-- AND IT WAS A LOOK THAT SAID, "WE GOT YOU OUT OF THIS ONE, KID, BUT WE WON'T BE THERE ALL THE TIME" --
NO, NO -- IT WASN'T LIKE THAT.
THEY SAVED MY LIFE -- I'D BE DEAD MEAT IF NOT FOR --
BUT THEY WEREN'T LISTENING. THEY HAD THEIR STORY, AND IT PLAYED EVEN BETTER WITH A MODEST HERO.

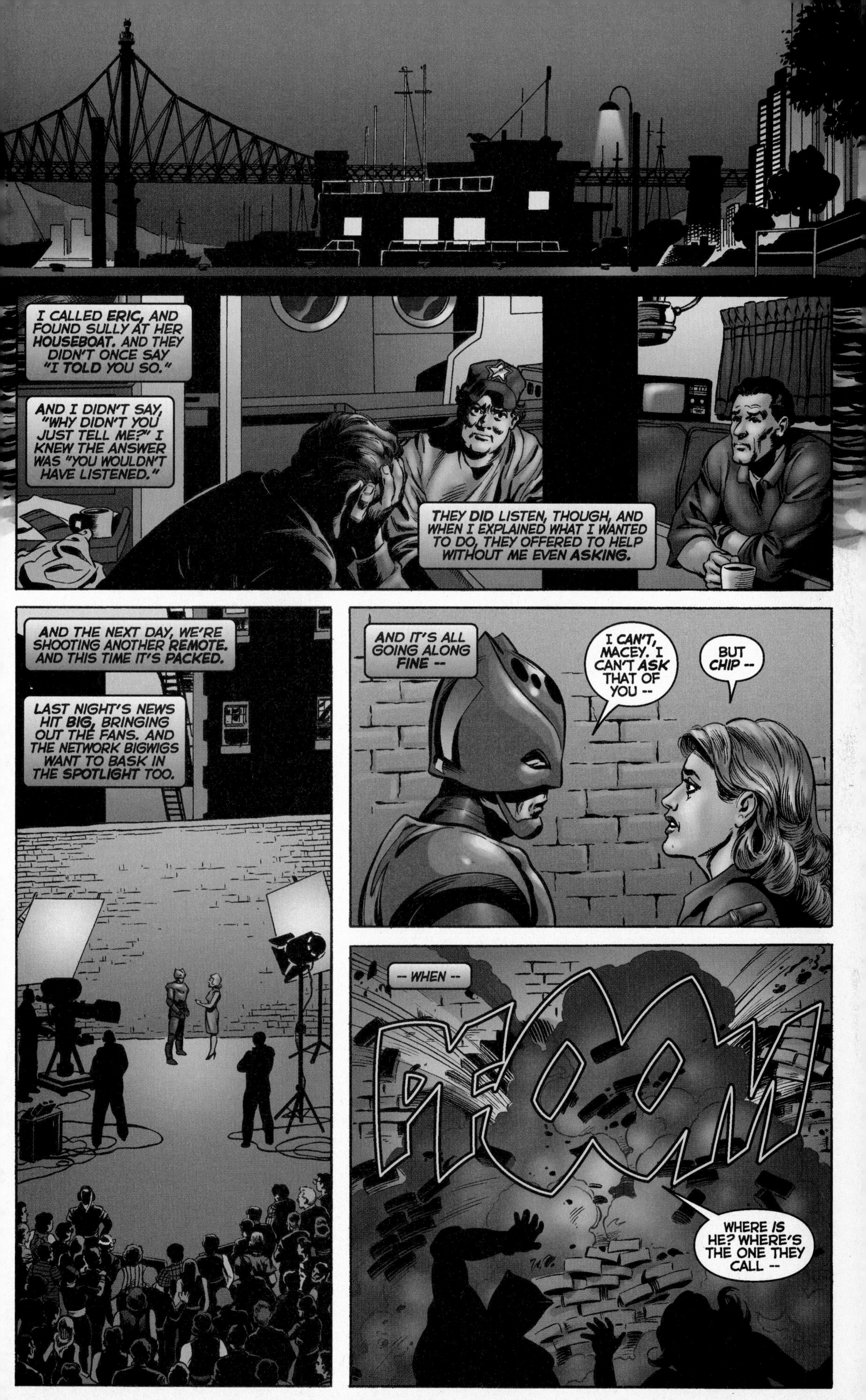
I CALLED ERIC, AND FOUND SULLY AT HER HOUSEBOAT. AND THEY DIDN'T ONCE SAY "I TOLD YOU SO."
AND I DIDN'T SAY, "WHY DIDN'T YOU JUST TELL ME?" I KNEW THE ANSWER WAS "YOU WOULDN'T HAVE LISTENED."
THEY DID LISTEN, THOUGH, AND WHEN I EXPLAINED WHAT I WANTED TO DO, THEY OFFERED TO HELP WITHOUT ME EVEN ASKING.
AND THE NEXT DAY, WE'RE SHOOTING ANOTHER REMOTE. AND THIS TIME IT'S PACKED.
LAST NIGHT'S NEWS HIT BIG, BRINGING OUT THE FANS. AND THE NETWORK BIGWIGS WANT TO BASK IN THE SPOTLIGHT TOO.
AND IT'S ALL GOING ALONG FINE --
I CAN'T, MACEY. I CAN'T ASK THAT OF YOU --
BUT CHIP --
-- WHEN --
WHERE IS HE? WHERE'S THE ONE THEY CALL --

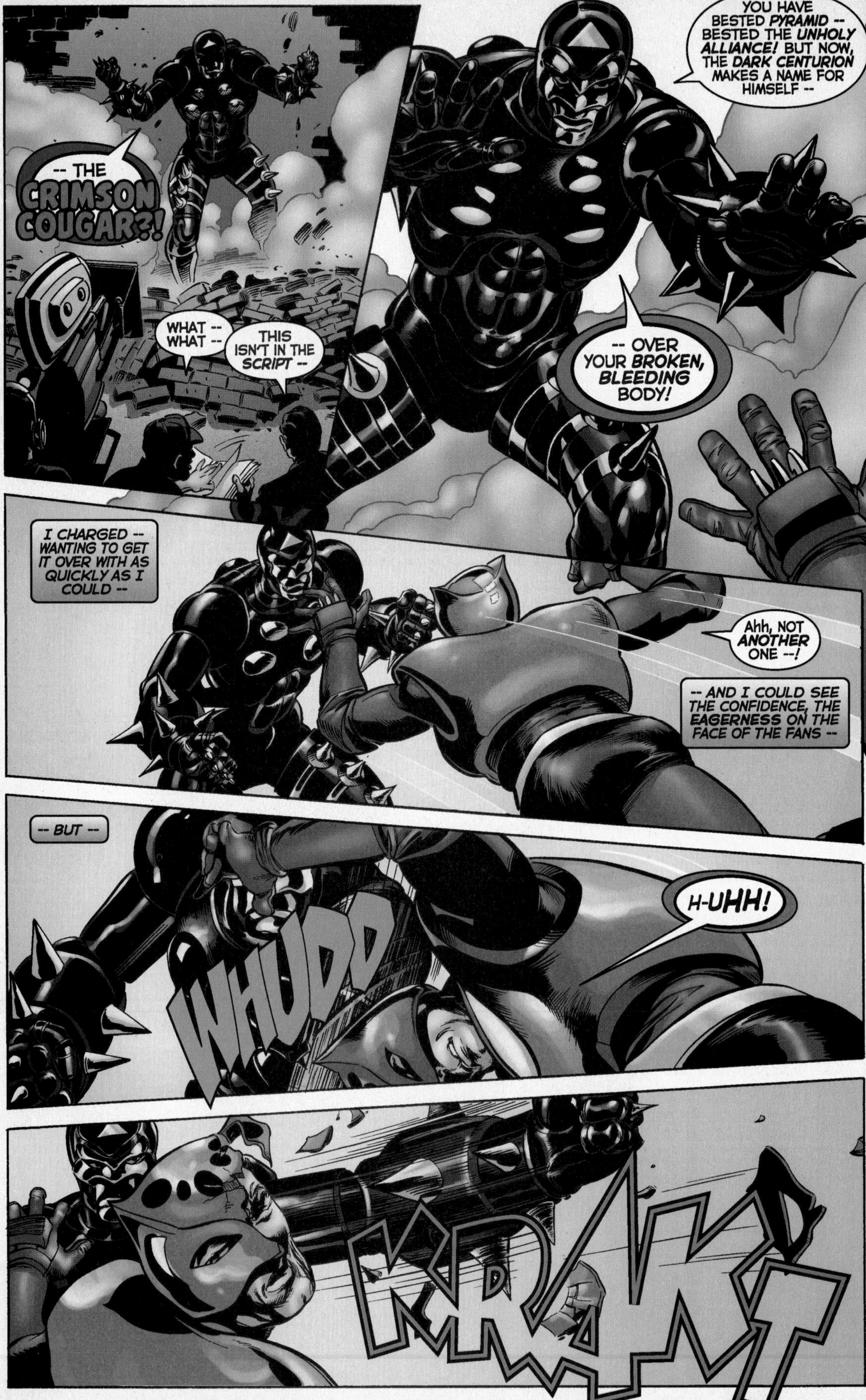
-- THE CRIMSON COUGAR?!
WHAT -- WHAT --
THIS ISN'T IN THE SCRIPT --
YOU HAVE BESTED PYRAMID -- BESTED THE UNHOLY ALLIANCE! BUT NOW, THE DARK CENTURION MAKES A NAME FOR HIMSELF --
-- OVER YOUR BROKEN, BLEEDING BODY!
I CHARGED -- WANTING TO GET IT OVER WITH AS QUICKLY AS I COULD --
Ahh, NOT ANOTHER ONE --!
-- AND I COULD SEE THE CONFIDENCE, THE EAGERNESS ON THE FACE OF THE FANS --
-- BUT --
H-UHH!
WHUDD
KRAKT

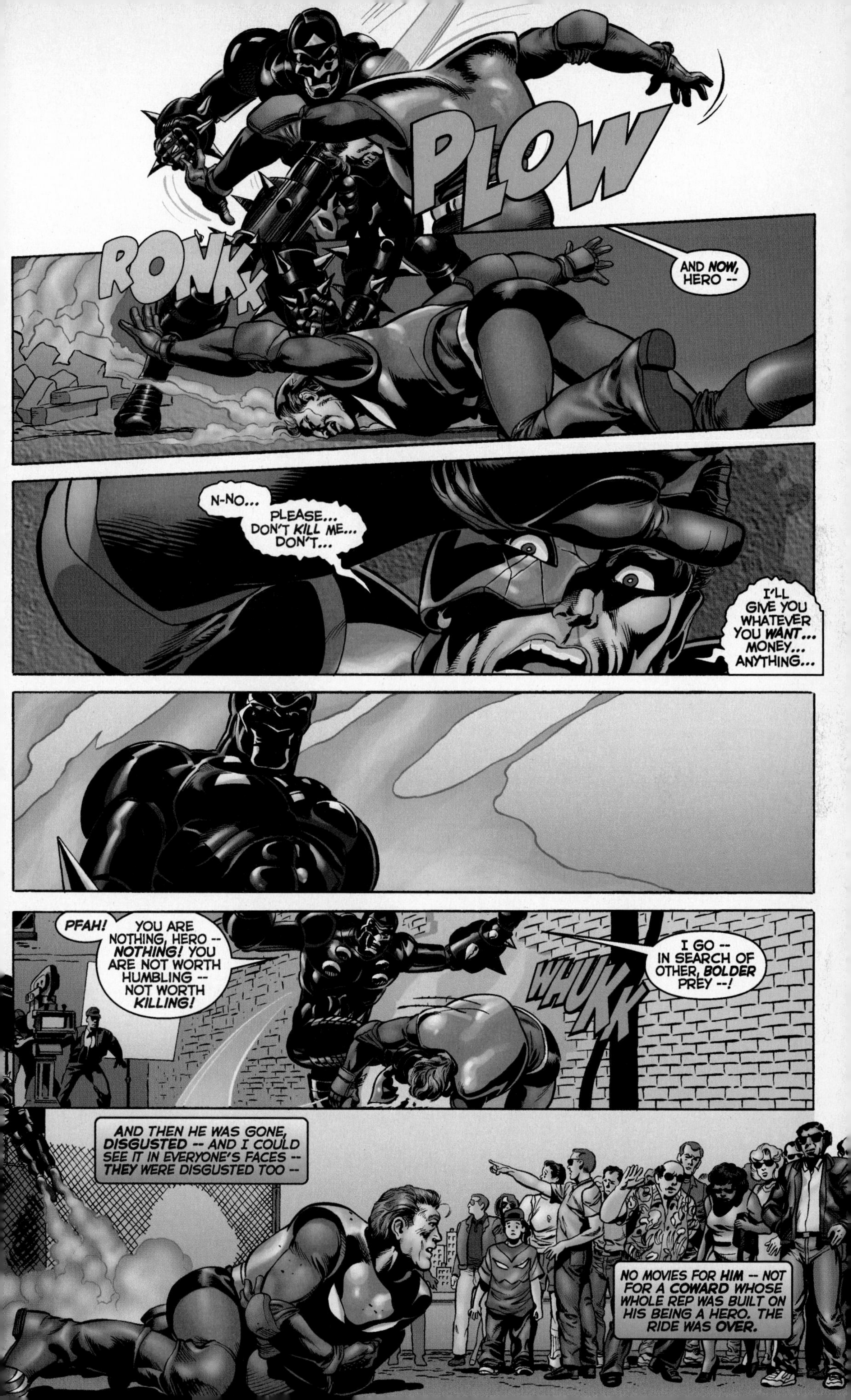
PLOW
RONKK
AND NOW, HERO --
N-NO... PLEASE... DON'T KILL ME... DON'T...
I'LL GIVE YOU WHATEVER YOU WANT... MONEY... ANYTHING...
PFAH!
YOU ARE NOTHING, HERO -- NOTHING! YOU ARE NOT WORTH HUMBLING -- NOT WORTH KILLING!
WHUKK
I GO -- IN SEARCH OF OTHER, BOLDER PREY --!
AND THEN HE WAS GONE, DISGUSTED -- AND I COULD SEE IT IN EVERYONE'S FACES -- THEY WERE DISGUSTED TOO --
NO MOVIES FOR HIM -- NOT FOR A COWARD WHOSE WHOLE REP WAS BUILT ON HIS BEING A HERO. THE RIDE WAS OVER.

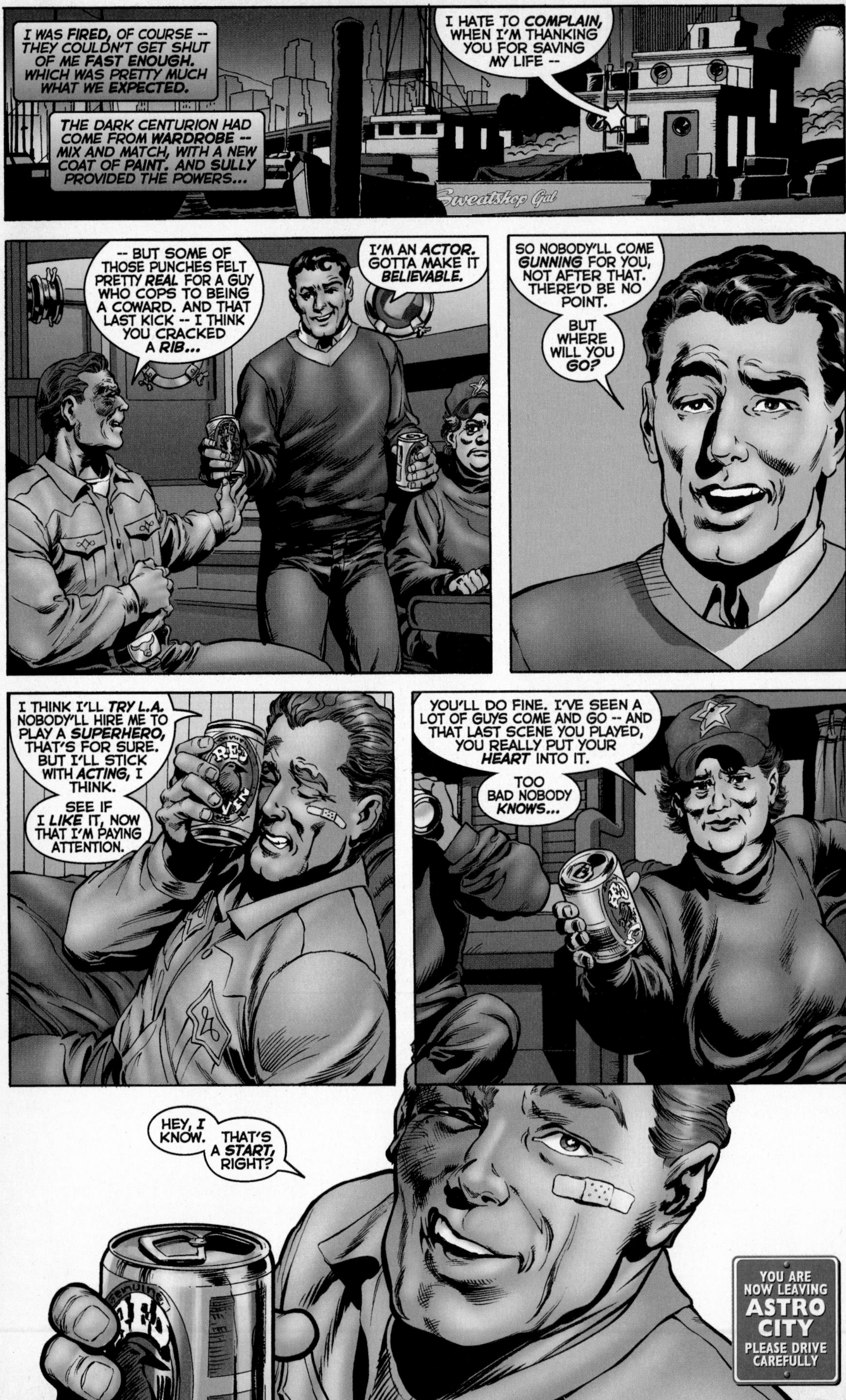
I WAS FIRED, OF COURSE -- THEY COULDN'T GET SHUT OF ME FAST ENOUGH. WHICH WAS PRETTY MUCH WHAT WE EXPECTED.
THE DARK CENTURION HAD COME FROM WARDROBE -- MIX AND MATCH, WITH A NEW COAT OF PAINT. AND SULLY PROVIDED THE POWERS...
I HATE TO COMPLAIN, WHEN I'M THANKING YOU FOR SAVING MY LIFE --
Sweatshop Gal
-- BUT SOME OF THOSE PUNCHES FELT PRETTY REAL FOR A GUY WHO COPS TO BEING A COWARD. AND THAT LAST KICK -- I THINK YOU CRACKED A RIB...
I'M AN ACTOR. GOTTA MAKE IT BELIEVABLE.
SO NOBODY'LL COME GUNNING FOR YOU, NOT AFTER THAT. THERE'D BE NO POINT.
BUT WHERE WILL YOU GO?
I THINK I'LL TRY L.A. NOBODY'LL HIRE ME TO PLAY A SUPERHERO, THAT'S FOR SURE. BUT I'LL STICK WITH ACTING, I THINK.
SEE IF I LIKE IT, NOW THAT I'M PAYING ATTENTION.
YOU'LL DO FINE. I'VE SEEN A LOT OF GUYS COME AND GO -- AND THAT LAST SCENE YOU PLAYED, YOU REALLY PUT YOUR HEART INTO IT.
TOO BAD NOBODY KNOWS...
HEY, I KNOW.
THAT'S A START, RIGHT?
YOU ARE NOW LEAVING ASTRO CITY PLEASE DRIVE CAREFULLY

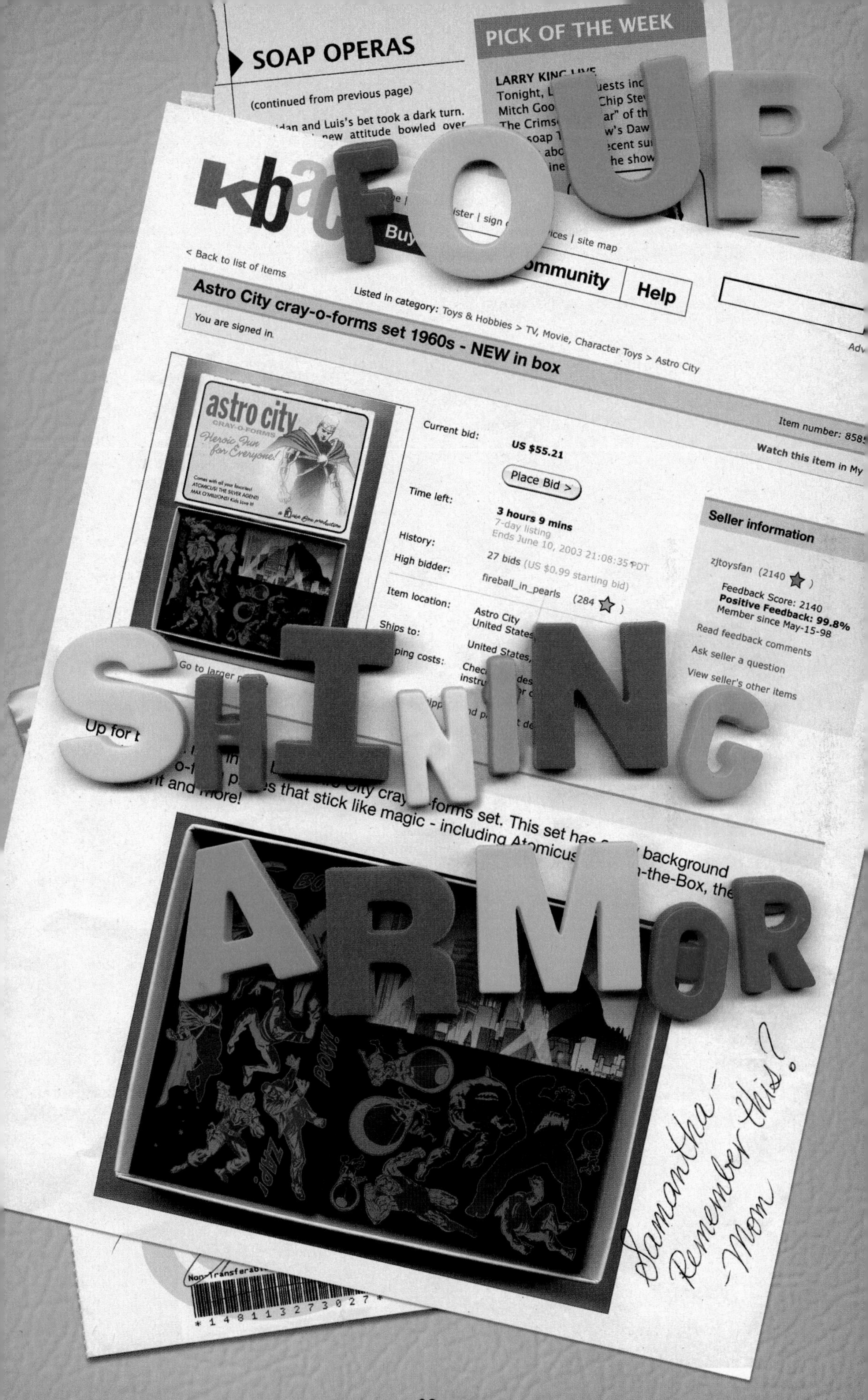
SOAP OPERAS
(continued from previous page)
PICK OF THE WEEK
LARRY KING LIVE
FOUR
< Back to list of items
Help
Astro City cray-o-forms set 1960s - NEW in box
Listed in category: Toys & Hobbies > TV, Movie, Character Toys > Astro City
You are signed in.
astro city
CRAY-O-FORMS
Heroic Fun for Everyone!
Current bid:
US $55.21
Place Bid >
Time left:
3 hours 9 mins
7-day listing
Ends June 10, 2003 21:08:35 PDT
History:
27 bids (US $0.99 starting bid)
High bidder:
fireball_in_pearls (284)
Item location:
Astro City
United States
Ships to:
United States
Item number:
Watch this item in My
Seller information
zjtoysfan (2140)
Feedback Score: 2140
Positive Feedback: 99.8%
Member since May-15-98
Read feedback comments
Ask seller a question
View seller's other items
SHINING
s that stick like magic - including Atomicus
background
-the-Box, the
ARMOR
BOOM!
POW!
ZAP!
Samantha-
Remember this?
-Mom
Non-Transferable
* 1 4 8 1 1 3 2 7 3 0 2 7 *

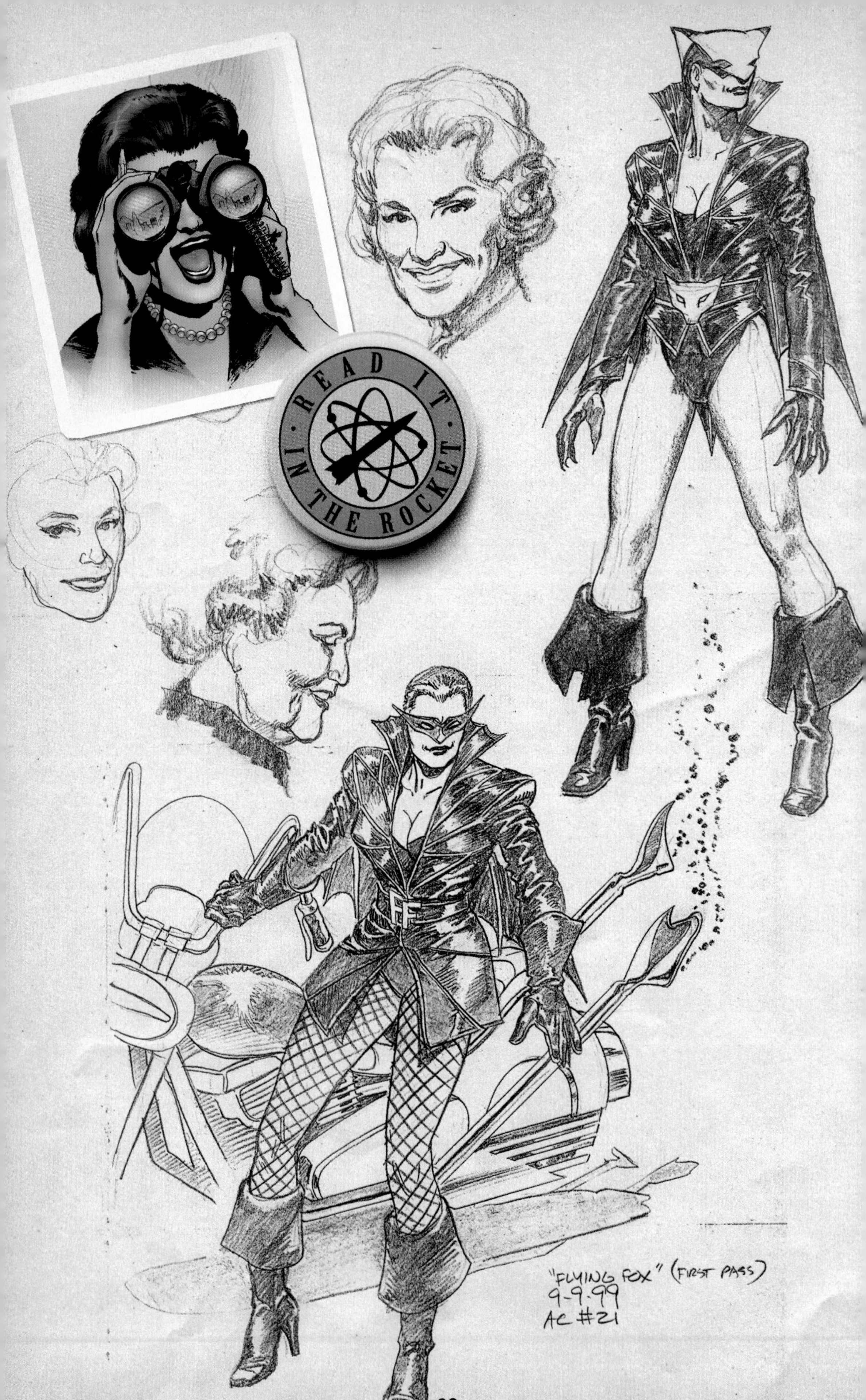
READ IT · IN THE ROCKET ·
"FLYING FOX" (FIRST PASS)
9-9-99
AC #21

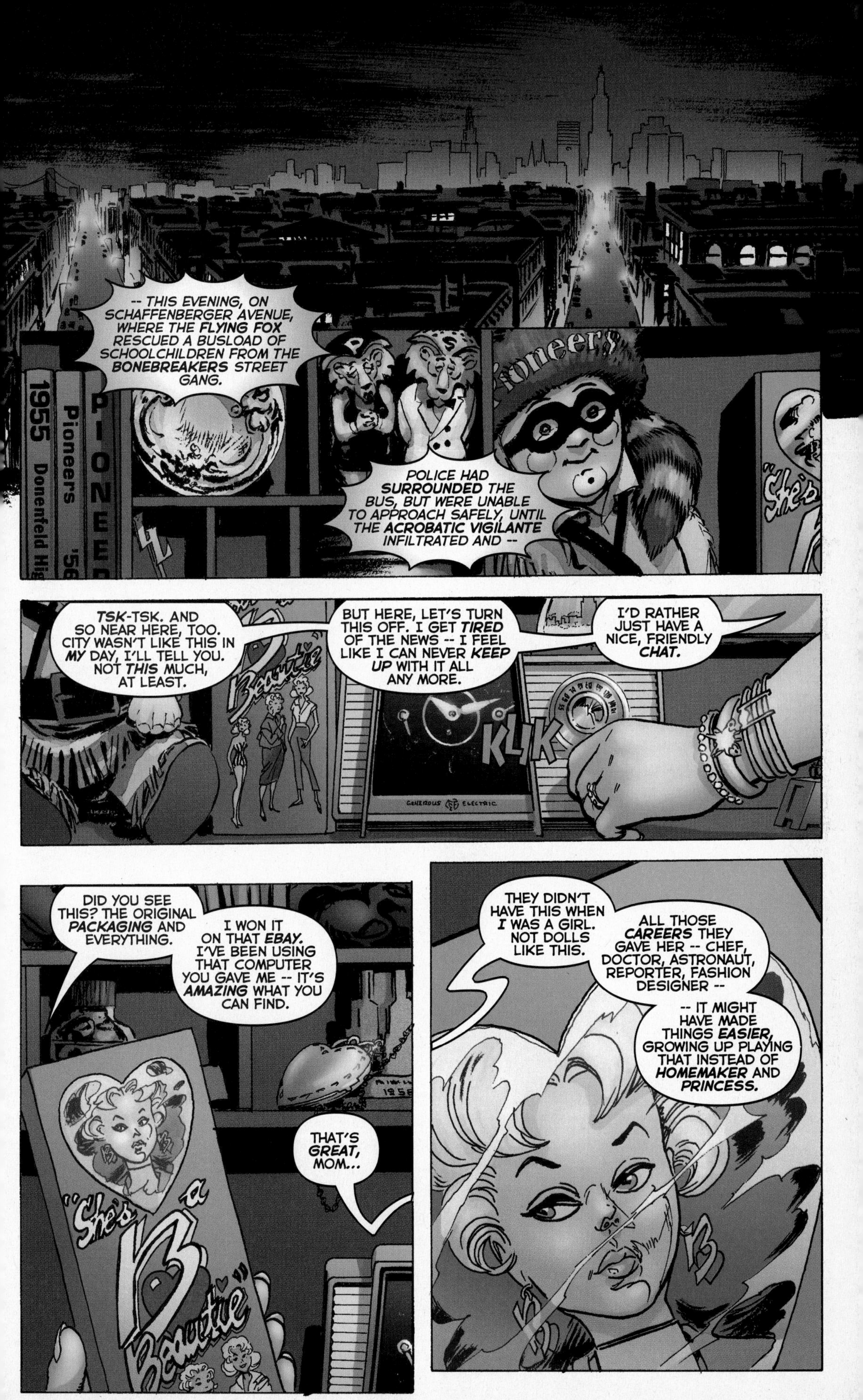
-- THIS EVENING, ON SCHAFFENBERGER AVENUE, WHERE THE FLYING FOX RESCUED A BUSLOAD OF SCHOOLCHILDREN FROM THE BONEBREAKERS STREET GANG.
POLICE HAD SURROUNDED THE BUS, BUT WERE UNABLE TO APPROACH SAFELY, UNTIL THE ACROBATIC VIGILANTE INFILTRATED AND --
1955 Pioneers Donenfeld Hig
Pioneers '56
PIONEER
Pioneers
TSK-TSK. AND SO NEAR HERE, TOO. CITY WASN'T LIKE THIS IN MY DAY, I'LL TELL YOU. NOT THIS MUCH, AT LEAST.
BUT HERE, LET'S TURN THIS OFF. I GET TIRED OF THE NEWS -- I FEEL LIKE I CAN NEVER KEEP UP WITH IT ALL ANY MORE.
I'D RATHER JUST HAVE A NICE, FRIENDLY CHAT.
KLIK
GENEROUS ELECTRIC
DID YOU SEE THIS? THE ORIGINAL PACKAGING AND EVERYTHING.
I WON IT ON THAT EBAY. I'VE BEEN USING THAT COMPUTER YOU GAVE ME -- IT'S AMAZING WHAT YOU CAN FIND.
THAT'S GREAT, MOM...
"She's a B Beautie"
THEY DIDN'T HAVE THIS WHEN I WAS A GIRL. NOT DOLLS LIKE THIS.
ALL THOSE CAREERS THEY GAVE HER -- CHEF, DOCTOR, ASTRONAUT, REPORTER, FASHION DESIGNER --
-- IT MIGHT HAVE MADE THINGS EASIER, GROWING UP PLAYING THAT INSTEAD OF HOMEMAKER AND PRINCESS.

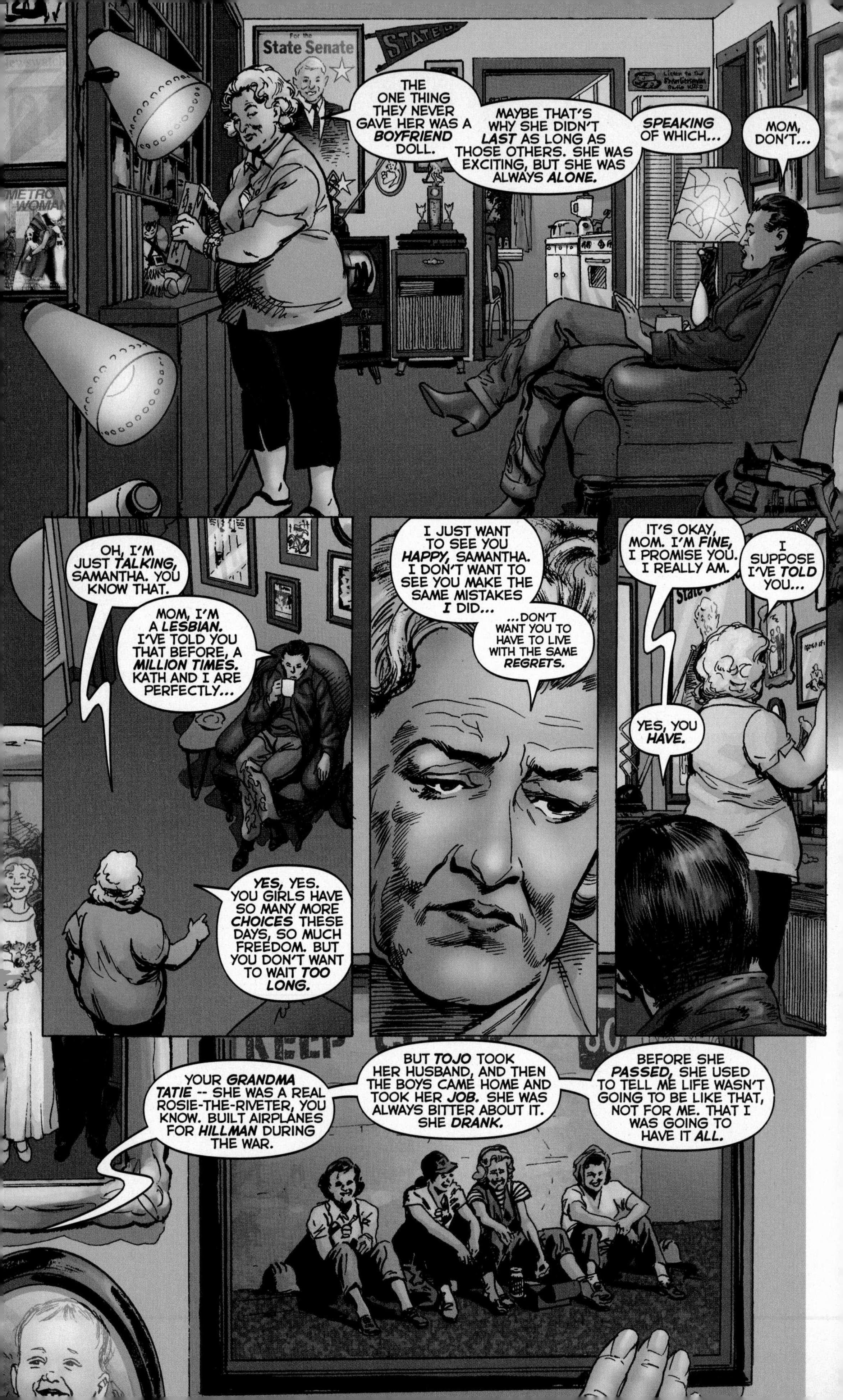
State Senate
STATE
METRO WOMAN
THE ONE THING THEY NEVER GAVE HER WAS A BOYFRIEND DOLL.
MAYBE THAT'S WHY SHE DIDN'T LAST AS LONG AS THOSE OTHERS. SHE WAS EXCITING, BUT SHE WAS ALWAYS ALONE.
SPEAKING OF WHICH...
MOM, DON'T...
OH, I'M JUST TALKING, SAMANTHA. YOU KNOW THAT.
MOM, I'M A LESBIAN. I'VE TOLD YOU THAT BEFORE, A MILLION TIMES. KATH AND I ARE PERFECTLY...
YES, YES. YOU GIRLS HAVE SO MANY MORE CHOICES THESE DAYS, SO MUCH FREEDOM. BUT YOU DON'T WANT TO WAIT TOO LONG.
I JUST WANT TO SEE YOU HAPPY, SAMANTHA. I DON'T WANT TO SEE YOU MAKE THE SAME MISTAKES I DID...
...DON'T WANT YOU TO HAVE TO LIVE WITH THE SAME REGRETS.
IT'S OKAY, MOM. I'M FINE, I PROMISE YOU. I REALLY AM.
I SUPPOSE I'VE TOLD YOU...
YES, YOU HAVE.
YOUR GRANDMA TATIE -- SHE WAS A REAL ROSIE-THE-RIVETER, YOU KNOW. BUILT AIRPLANES FOR HILLMAN DURING THE WAR.
BUT TOJO TOOK HER HUSBAND, AND THEN THE BOYS CAME HOME AND TOOK HER JOB. SHE WAS ALWAYS BITTER ABOUT IT. SHE DRANK.
BEFORE SHE PASSED, SHE USED TO TELL ME LIFE WASN'T GOING TO BE LIKE THAT, NOT FOR ME. THAT I WAS GOING TO HAVE IT ALL.

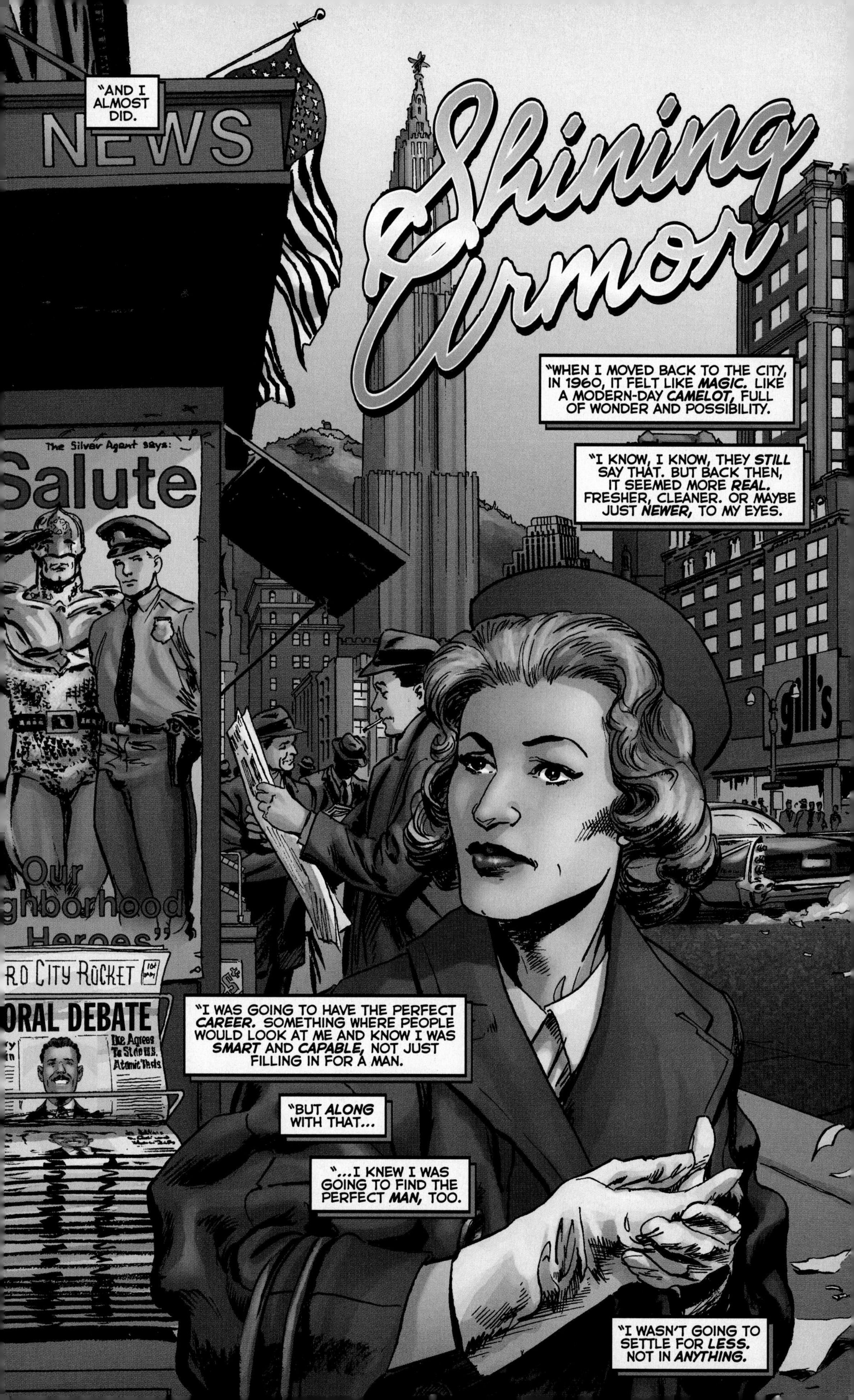
"AND I ALMOST DID.
NEWS
Shining Armor
"WHEN I MOVED BACK TO THE CITY, IN 1960, IT FELT LIKE MAGIC. LIKE A MODERN-DAY CAMELOT, FULL OF WONDER AND POSSIBILITY.
"I KNOW, I KNOW, THEY STILL SAY THAT. BUT BACK THEN, IT SEEMED MORE REAL. FRESHER, CLEANER. OR MAYBE JUST NEWER, TO MY EYES.
The Silver Agent says:
Salute
Our
ghborhood
Heroes"
RO CITY ROCKET
ORAL DEBATE
Ike Agrees To St do U.S. Atomic Tests
gill's
"I WAS GOING TO HAVE THE PERFECT CAREER. SOMETHING WHERE PEOPLE WOULD LOOK AT ME AND KNOW I WAS SMART AND CAPABLE, NOT JUST FILLING IN FOR A MAN.
"BUT ALONG WITH THAT...
"...I KNEW I WAS GOING TO FIND THE PERFECT MAN, TOO.
"I WASN'T GOING TO SETTLE FOR LESS. NOT IN ANYTHING.

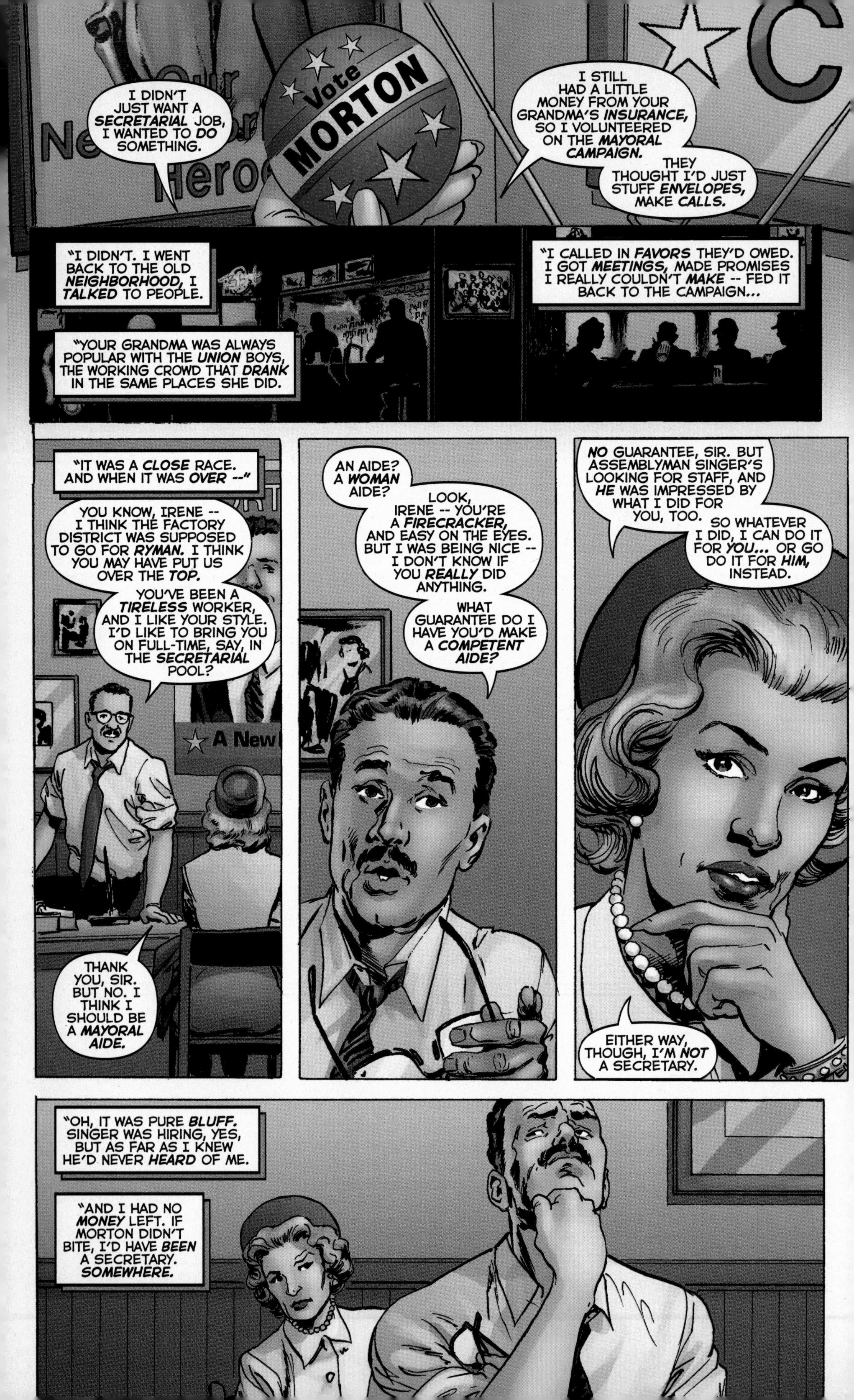
I DIDN'T JUST WANT A *SECRETARIAL* JOB, I WANTED TO *DO* SOMETHING.
Vote MORTON
I STILL HAD A LITTLE MONEY FROM YOUR GRANDMA'S *INSURANCE,* SO I VOLUNTEERED ON THE *MAYORAL CAMPAIGN.*
THEY THOUGHT I'D JUST STUFF *ENVELOPES,* MAKE *CALLS.*
"I DIDN'T. I WENT BACK TO THE OLD *NEIGHBORHOOD,* I *TALKED* TO PEOPLE.
"YOUR GRANDMA WAS ALWAYS POPULAR WITH THE *UNION* BOYS, THE WORKING CROWD THAT *DRANK* IN THE SAME PLACES SHE DID.
"I CALLED IN *FAVORS* THEY'D OWED. I GOT *MEETINGS,* MADE PROMISES I REALLY COULDN'T *MAKE* -- FED IT BACK TO THE CAMPAIGN...
"IT WAS A *CLOSE* RACE. AND WHEN IT WAS *OVER* --"
YOU KNOW, IRENE -- I THINK THE FACTORY DISTRICT WAS SUPPOSED TO GO FOR *RYMAN.* I THINK YOU MAY HAVE PUT US OVER THE *TOP.*
YOU'VE BEEN A *TIRELESS* WORKER, AND I LIKE YOUR STYLE. I'D LIKE TO BRING YOU ON FULL-TIME, SAY, IN THE *SECRETARIAL* POOL?
A New
THANK YOU, SIR. BUT NO. I THINK I SHOULD BE A *MAYORAL AIDE.*
AN AIDE? A *WOMAN* AIDE?
LOOK, IRENE -- YOU'RE A *FIRECRACKER,* AND EASY ON THE EYES. BUT I WAS BEING NICE -- I DON'T KNOW IF YOU *REALLY* DID ANYTHING.
WHAT GUARANTEE DO I HAVE YOU'D MAKE A *COMPETENT AIDE?*
NO GUARANTEE, SIR. BUT ASSEMBLYMAN SINGER'S LOOKING FOR STAFF, AND *HE* WAS IMPRESSED BY WHAT I DID FOR YOU, TOO.
SO WHATEVER I DID, I CAN DO IT FOR *YOU*... OR GO DO IT FOR *HIM,* INSTEAD.
EITHER WAY, THOUGH, I'M *NOT* A SECRETARY.
"OH, IT WAS PURE *BLUFF.* SINGER WAS HIRING, YES, BUT AS FAR AS I KNEW HE'D NEVER *HEARD* OF ME.
"AND I HAD NO *MONEY* LEFT. IF MORTON DIDN'T BITE, I'D HAVE *BEEN* A SECRETARY. *SOMEWHERE.*

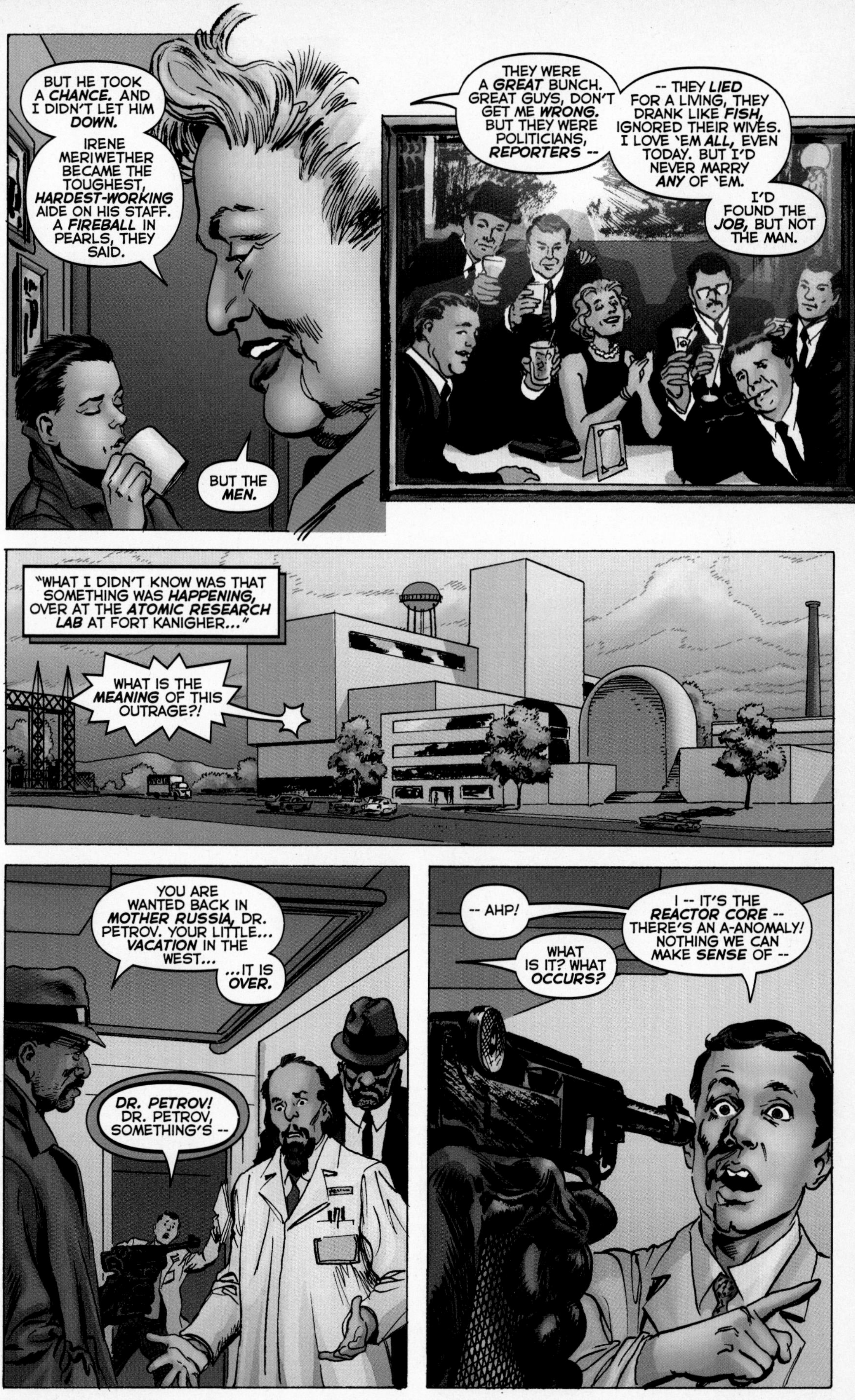
BUT HE TOOK A CHANCE. AND I DIDN'T LET HIM DOWN.
IRENE MERIWETHER BECAME THE TOUGHEST, HARDEST-WORKING AIDE ON HIS STAFF. A FIREBALL IN PEARLS, THEY SAID.
BUT THE MEN.
THEY WERE A GREAT BUNCH. GREAT GUYS, DON'T GET ME WRONG. BUT THEY WERE POLITICIANS, REPORTERS --
-- THEY LIED FOR A LIVING, THEY DRANK LIKE FISH, IGNORED THEIR WIVES. I LOVE 'EM ALL, EVEN TODAY. BUT I'D NEVER MARRY ANY OF 'EM.
I'D FOUND THE JOB, BUT NOT THE MAN.
"WHAT I DIDN'T KNOW WAS THAT SOMETHING WAS HAPPENING, OVER AT THE ATOMIC RESEARCH LAB AT FORT KANIGHER..."
WHAT IS THE MEANING OF THIS OUTRAGE?!
YOU ARE WANTED BACK IN MOTHER RUSSIA, DR. PETROV. YOUR LITTLE... VACATION IN THE WEST...
...IT IS OVER.
DR. PETROV! DR. PETROV, SOMETHING'S --
-- AHP!
I -- IT'S THE REACTOR CORE -- THERE'S AN A-ANOMALY! NOTHING WE CAN MAKE SENSE OF --
WHAT IS IT? WHAT OCCURS?

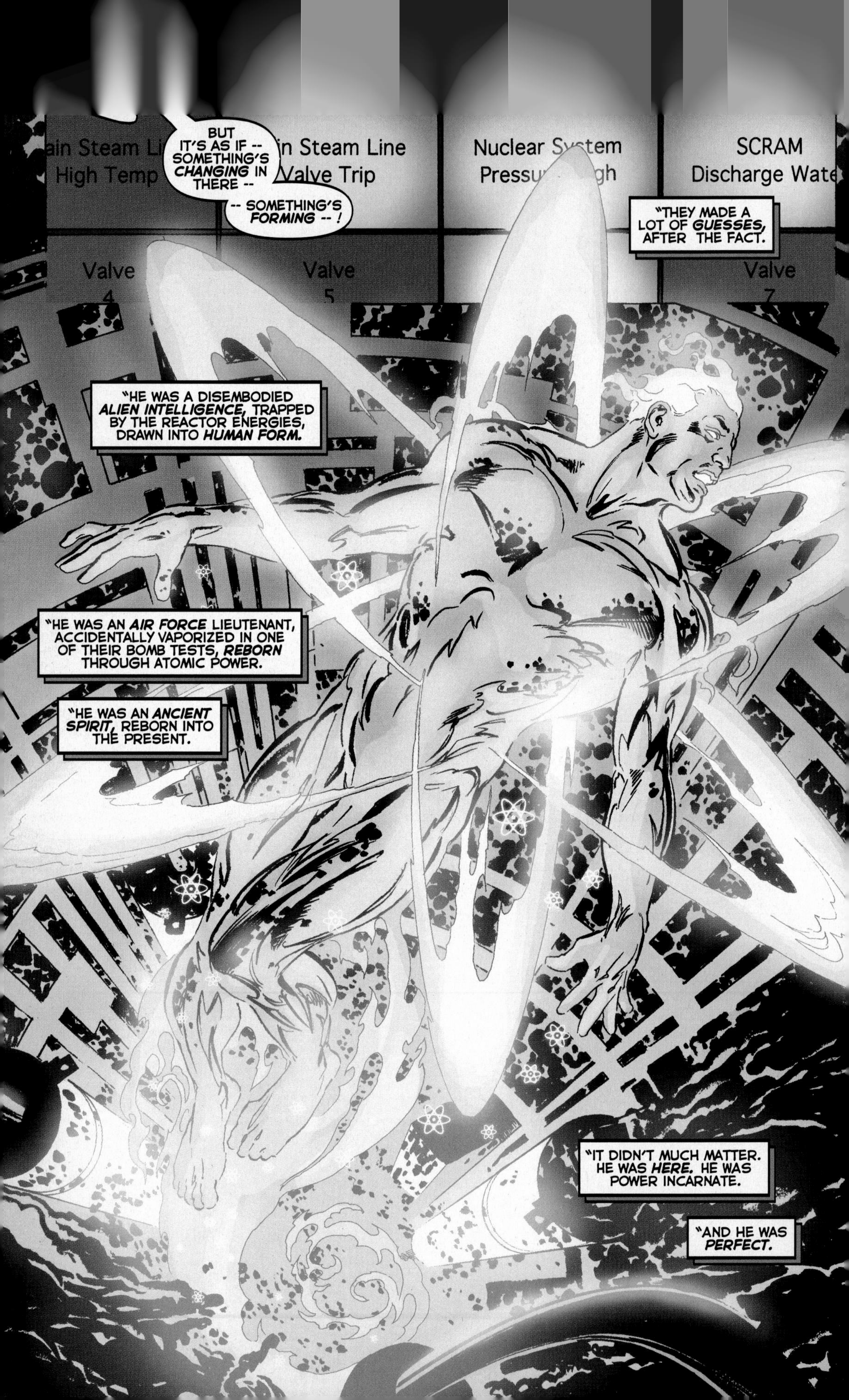

BUT IT'S AS IF -- SOMETHING'S *CHANGING* IN THERE --
-- SOMETHING'S *FORMING* -- !
High Temp
Valve Trip
Nuclear System
SCRAM
"THEY MADE A LOT OF *GUESSES,* AFTER THE FACT.
Valve 4
Valve 5
Valve
"HE WAS A DISEMBODIED *ALIEN INTELLIGENCE,* TRAPPED BY THE REACTOR ENERGIES, DRAWN INTO *HUMAN FORM.*
"HE WAS AN *AIR FORCE* LIEUTENANT, ACCIDENTALLY VAPORIZED IN ONE OF THEIR BOMB TESTS, *REBORN* THROUGH ATOMIC POWER.
"HE WAS AN *ANCIENT SPIRIT,* REBORN INTO THE PRESENT.
"IT DIDN'T MUCH MATTER. HE WAS *HERE.* HE WAS POWER INCARNATE.
"AND HE WAS *PERFECT.*

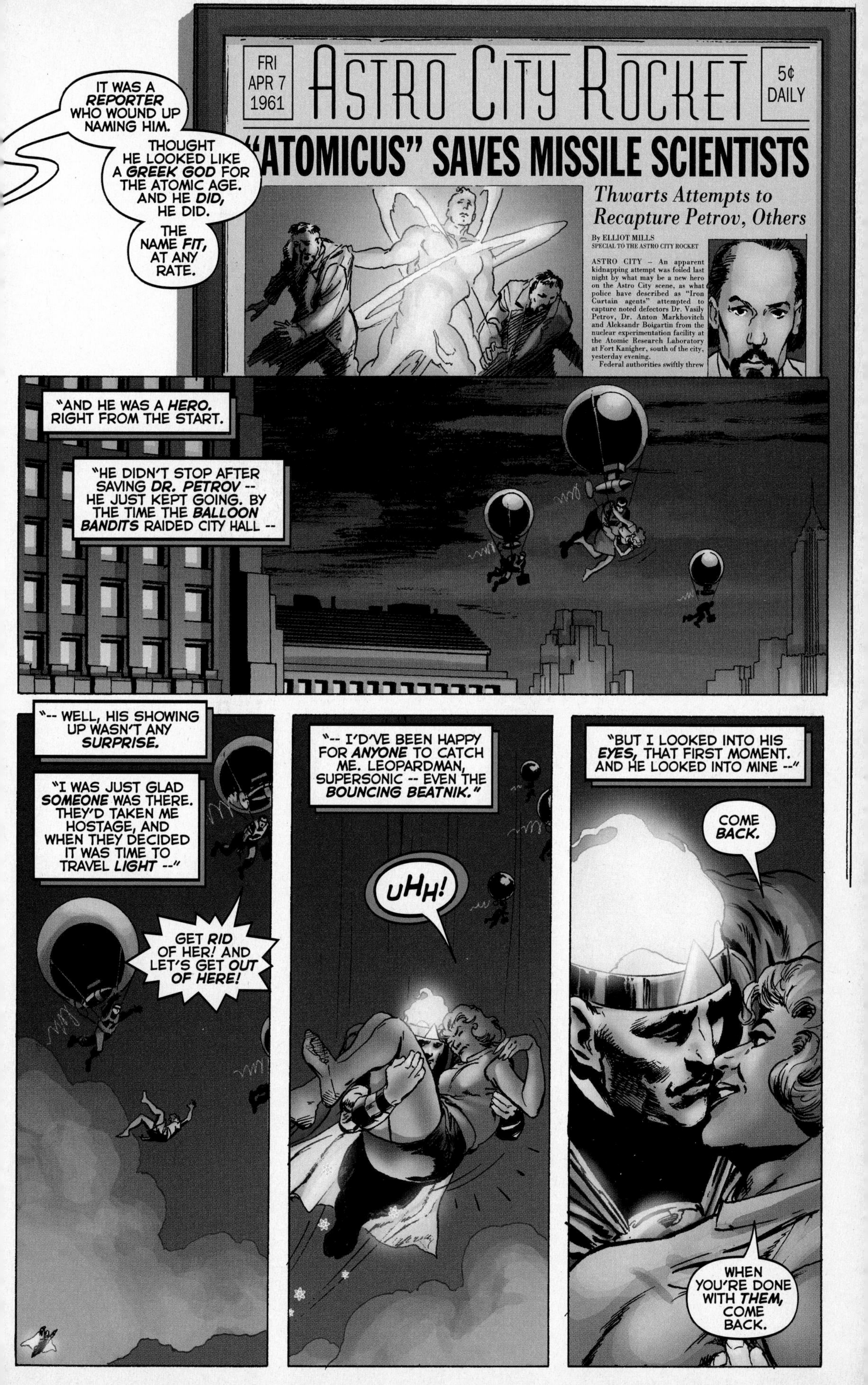
IT WAS A REPORTER WHO WOUND UP NAMING HIM.
THOUGHT HE LOOKED LIKE A GREEK GOD FOR THE ATOMIC AGE. AND HE DID, HE DID.
THE NAME FIT, AT ANY RATE.
FRI APR 7 1961
ASTRO CITY ROCKET
5¢ DAILY
"ATOMICUS" SAVES MISSILE SCIENTISTS
Thwarts Attempts to Recapture Petrov, Others
By ELLIOT MILLS
SPECIAL TO THE ASTRO CITY ROCKET
ASTRO CITY – An apparent kidnapping attempt was foiled last night by what may be a new hero on the Astro City scene, as what police have described as "Iron Curtain agents" attempted to capture noted defectors Dr. Vasily Petrov, Dr. Anton Markhovitch and Aleksandr Boigartin from the nuclear experimentation facility at the Atomic Research Laboratory at Fort Kanigher, south of the city, yesterday evening.
Federal authorities swiftly threw
"AND HE WAS A HERO. RIGHT FROM THE START.
"HE DIDN'T STOP AFTER SAVING DR. PETROV -- HE JUST KEPT GOING. BY THE TIME THE BALLOON BANDITS RAIDED CITY HALL --
"-- WELL, HIS SHOWING UP WASN'T ANY SURPRISE.
"I WAS JUST GLAD SOMEONE WAS THERE. THEY'D TAKEN ME HOSTAGE, AND WHEN THEY DECIDED IT WAS TIME TO TRAVEL LIGHT --"
GET RID OF HER! AND LET'S GET OUT OF HERE!
"-- I'D'VE BEEN HAPPY FOR ANYONE TO CATCH ME. LEOPARDMAN, SUPERSONIC -- EVEN THE BOUNCING BEATNIK."
UHH!
"BUT I LOOKED INTO HIS EYES, THAT FIRST MOMENT. AND HE LOOKED INTO MINE --"
COME BACK.
WHEN YOU'RE DONE WITH THEM, COME BACK.

"AND HE DID."

-- BUT WHY DO YOU *DO* IT?

NOT THAT I'M NOT *GRATEFUL*, BUT --

I... DON'T *KNOW*.

I WAS BORN ABLE TO *TALK*, TO THINK -- BUT I KNOW SO *LITTLE* OF THIS WORLD, OF HOW IT AND IT'S PEOPLE ARE --

I JUST FEEL --

THERE IS A *SIGN* NEAR WHERE I CAME AWARE. *"BETTER LIVING THROUGH ATOMIC POWER,"* IT SAYS. AND *THAT'S* WHAT I FEEL.

MY POWER WAS INTENDED TO *IMPROVE* LIFE. TO SERVE *HUMANITY,* SERVE AMERICA.

SO THAT IS WHAT I *DO.*

BUT SOMETIMES IT ALL SEEMS SO *BIG* -- SO CONFUSING --

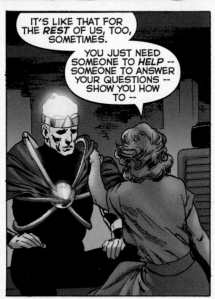

IT'S LIKE THAT FOR THE *REST* OF US, TOO, SOMETIMES.

YOU JUST NEED SOMEONE TO *HELP* -- SOMEONE TO ANSWER YOUR QUESTIONS -- SHOW YOU HOW TO --

"WE TALKED FOR *HOURS,* THAT NIGHT.

"WE TALKED --

"AND I KNEW. HE WAS *RIGHT* FOR ME. I WAS RIGHT FOR *HIM.*

"I *KNEW* IT.

"I HELPED him, AFTER that -- HELPED HIM HOWEVER I COULD.

"WHEN THE COMPUTERMEN CAME, OR WHEN DR. CYCLOTRON KIDNAPPED THE MAYOR, I WAS THERE --

"-- I DID THE DETECTIVE WORK, AND ALERTED HIM --

"-- AND HE TOOK IT FROM THERE."

THATAWAY, TOMMIE!

YOU TELL 'EM!

"WE MADE A GREAT TEAM."

DELIVERY FOR THE CHIEF, OFFICER. THE MAYOR'S FINE --

-- THANKS TO THE PLUCK AND DETERMINATION OF A VERY SPECIAL LADY.

"A GREAT TEAM --

METRO WOMAN

Atomicus Girl Friend?

-- AND SOMETHING MORE.

The Best & The Lightest
10 Slimming Recipes for the New Era!
QUEEN ELIZABETH'S FABULOUS CLOTHES
Five Wars Wives Fail • Home Shampooing Tricks

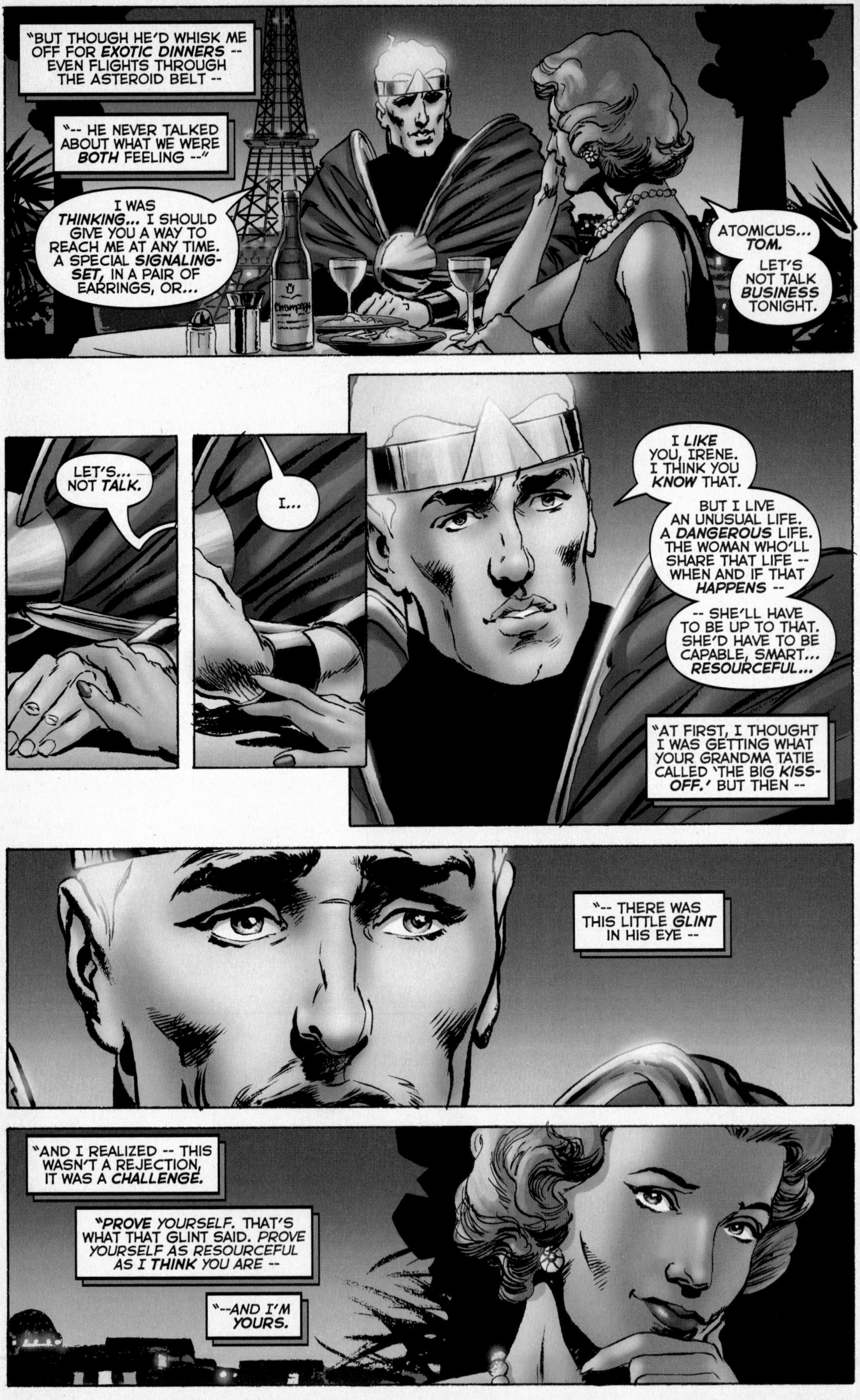

"BUT THOUGH HE'D WHISK ME OFF FOR EXOTIC DINNERS -- EVEN FLIGHTS THROUGH THE ASTEROID BELT --
"-- HE NEVER TALKED ABOUT WHAT WE WERE BOTH FEELING --"
I WAS THINKING... I SHOULD GIVE YOU A WAY TO REACH ME AT ANY TIME. A SPECIAL SIGNALING-SET, IN A PAIR OF EARRINGS, OR...
ATOMICUS... TOM.
LET'S NOT TALK BUSINESS TONIGHT.
LET'S... NOT TALK.
I...
I LIKE YOU, IRENE. I THINK YOU KNOW THAT.
BUT I LIVE AN UNUSUAL LIFE. A DANGEROUS LIFE. THE WOMAN WHO'LL SHARE THAT LIFE -- WHEN AND IF THAT HAPPENS --
-- SHE'LL HAVE TO BE UP TO THAT. SHE'D HAVE TO BE CAPABLE, SMART... RESOURCEFUL...
"AT FIRST, I THOUGHT I WAS GETTING WHAT YOUR GRANDMA TATIE CALLED 'THE BIG KISS-OFF.' BUT THEN --
"-- THERE WAS THIS LITTLE GLINT IN HIS EYE --
"AND I REALIZED -- THIS WASN'T A REJECTION, IT WAS A CHALLENGE.
"PROVE YOURSELF. THAT'S WHAT THAT GLINT SAID. PROVE YOURSELF AS RESOURCEFUL AS I THINK YOU ARE --
"--AND I'M YOURS.

"IT WASN'T LONG AFTER *THAT*..."

SAY HELLO TO *ADAM PETERSON*, ALL! HE'LL BE JOINING US.

HE'S A PROMISING YOUNG FELLA FROM BACK *EAST* -- AND I'M SURE WE'LL BE SEEING *GREAT THINGS* FROM HIM.

"BUT IF HE WAS THAT GOOD, IT DIDN'T SHOW --"

UHH, IRENE? THESE REPORTS -- WHERE DO I...?

I LOOK LIKE YOUR *SECRETARY*, PETERSON?

"CAN'T SAY I HAD MUCH *USE* FOR HIM.

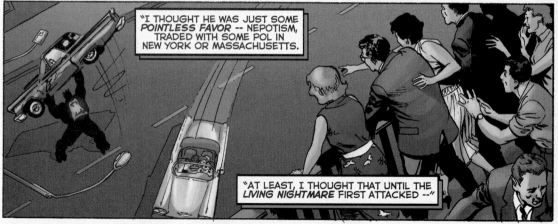

"I THOUGHT HE WAS JUST SOME *POINTLESS FAVOR* -- NEPOTISM, TRADED WITH SOME POL IN NEW YORK OR MASSACHUSETTS.

"AT LEAST, I THOUGHT THAT UNTIL THE *LIVING NIGHTMARE* FIRST ATTACKED --"

LORD, WHAT *IS* THAT THING?! PETERSON, LET'S *BLOW* THIS -- PETERSON?

ADAM?

"-- THEN THE *IMPERIAL* --"

ADAM?

"-- THEN THE *DIMENSION HOUNDS* --"

OH-*HO!*

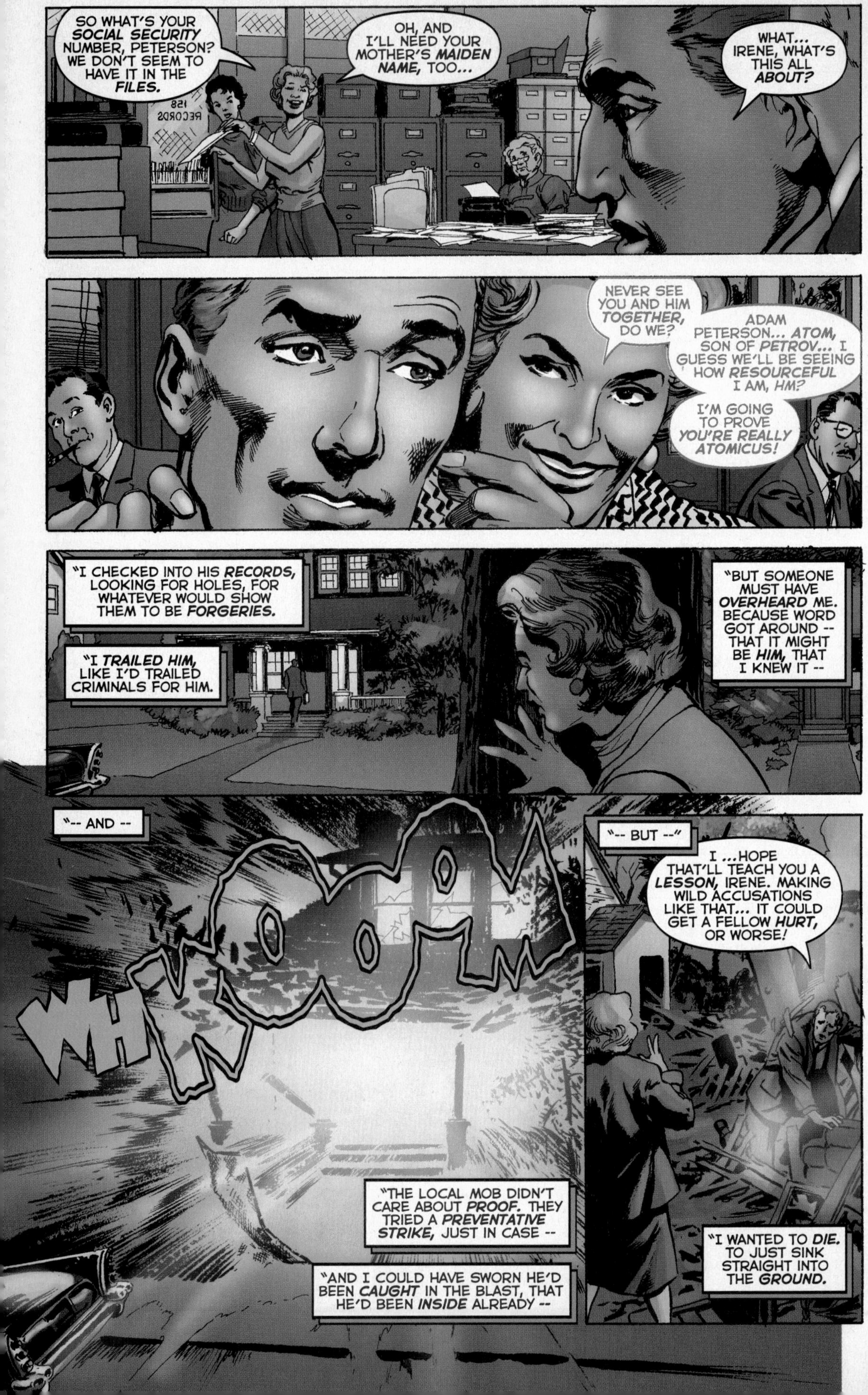
SO WHAT'S YOUR SOCIAL SECURITY NUMBER, PETERSON? WE DON'T SEEM TO HAVE IT IN THE FILES.
OH, AND I'LL NEED YOUR MOTHER'S MAIDEN NAME, TOO...
WHAT... IRENE, WHAT'S THIS ALL ABOUT?
158 RECORDS
NEVER SEE YOU AND HIM TOGETHER, DO WE?
ADAM PETERSON... ATOM, SON OF PETROV... I GUESS WE'LL BE SEEING HOW RESOURCEFUL I AM, HM?
I'M GOING TO PROVE YOU'RE REALLY ATOMICUS!
"I CHECKED INTO HIS RECORDS, LOOKING FOR HOLES, FOR WHATEVER WOULD SHOW THEM TO BE FORGERIES.
"I TRAILED HIM, LIKE I'D TRAILED CRIMINALS FOR HIM.
"BUT SOMEONE MUST HAVE OVERHEARD ME. BECAUSE WORD GOT AROUND -- THAT IT MIGHT BE HIM, THAT I KNEW IT --
"-- AND --
WHOOOM
"THE LOCAL MOB DIDN'T CARE ABOUT PROOF. THEY TRIED A PREVENTATIVE STRIKE, JUST IN CASE --
"AND I COULD HAVE SWORN HE'D BEEN CAUGHT IN THE BLAST, THAT HE'D BEEN INSIDE ALREADY --
"-- BUT --"
I ...HOPE THAT'LL TEACH YOU A LESSON, IRENE. MAKING WILD ACCUSATIONS LIKE THAT... IT COULD GET A FELLOW HURT, OR WORSE!
"I WANTED TO DIE. TO JUST SINK STRAIGHT INTO THE GROUND.

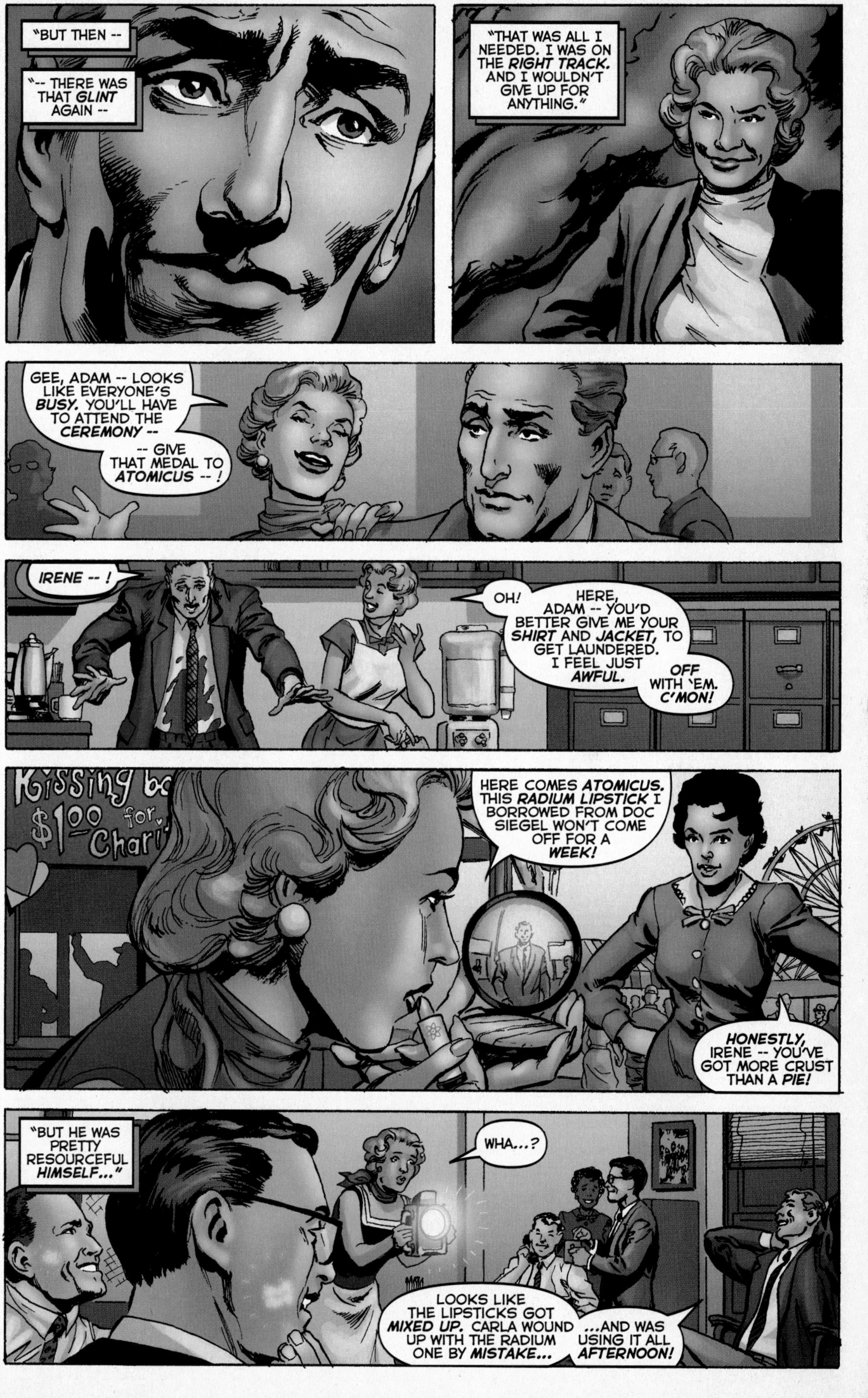
"BUT THEN --
"-- THERE WAS THAT GLINT AGAIN --
"THAT WAS ALL I NEEDED. I WAS ON THE RIGHT TRACK. AND I WOULDN'T GIVE UP FOR ANYTHING."
GEE, ADAM -- LOOKS LIKE EVERYONE'S BUSY. YOU'LL HAVE TO ATTEND THE CEREMONY --
-- GIVE THAT MEDAL TO ATOMICUS -- !
IRENE -- !
OH!
HERE, ADAM -- YOU'D BETTER GIVE ME YOUR SHIRT AND JACKET, TO GET LAUNDERED. I FEEL JUST AWFUL.
OFF WITH 'EM. C'MON!
HERE COMES ATOMICUS. THIS RADIUM LIPSTICK I BORROWED FROM DOC SIEGEL WON'T COME OFF FOR A WEEK!
HONESTLY, IRENE -- YOU'VE GOT MORE CRUST THAN A PIE!
"BUT HE WAS PRETTY RESOURCEFUL HIMSELF..."
WHA...?
LOOKS LIKE THE LIPSTICKS GOT MIXED UP. CARLA WOUND UP WITH THE RADIUM ONE BY MISTAKE...
...AND WAS USING IT ALL AFTERNOON!

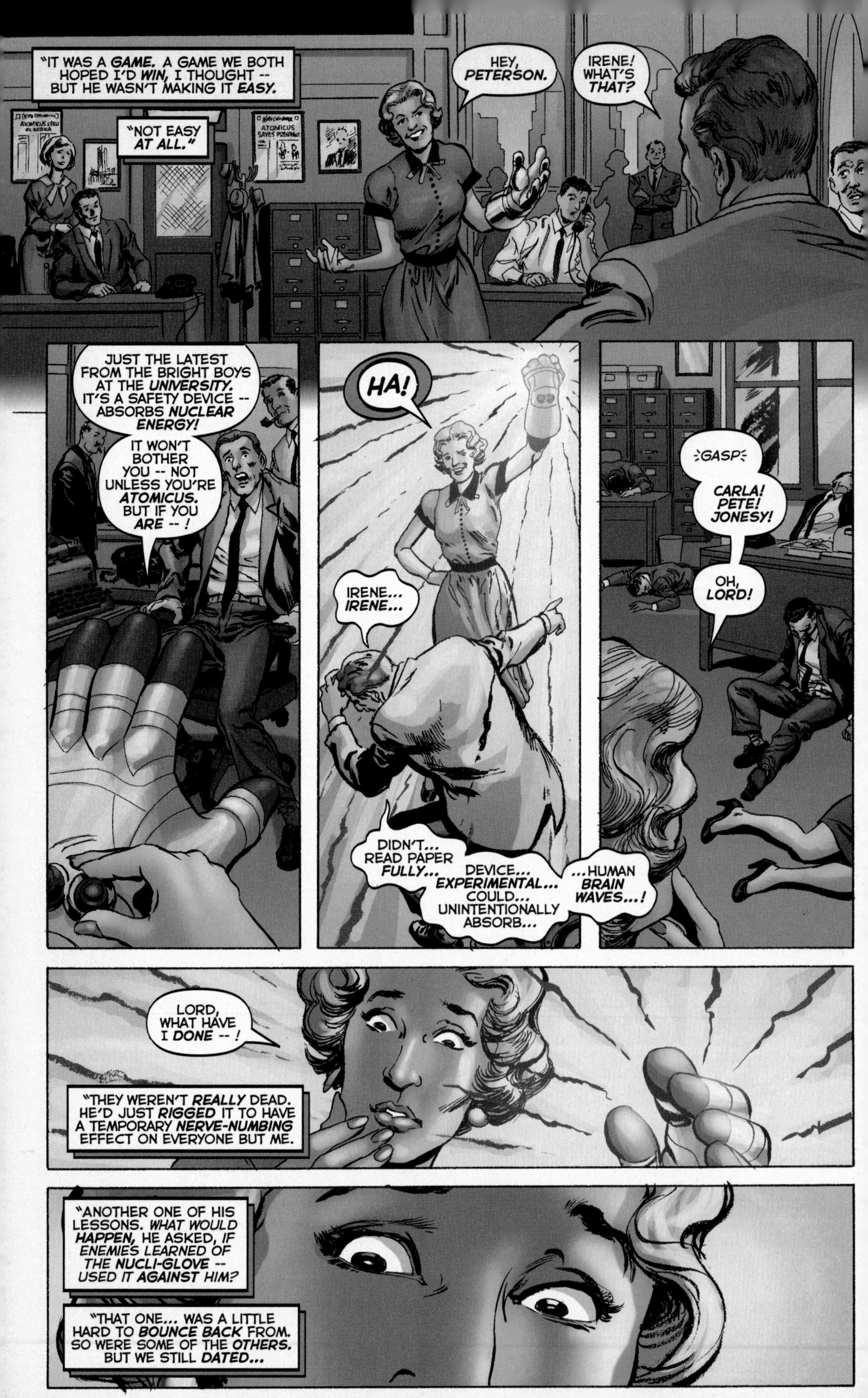
"IT WAS A GAME. A GAME WE BOTH HOPED I'D WIN, I THOUGHT -- BUT HE WASN'T MAKING IT EASY.
"NOT EASY AT ALL."
HEY, PETERSON.
IRENE! WHAT'S THAT?
ATOMICUS SAYES PIZZA
JUST THE LATEST FROM THE BRIGHT BOYS AT THE UNIVERSITY. IT'S A SAFETY DEVICE -- ABSORBS NUCLEAR ENERGY!
IT WON'T BOTHER YOU -- NOT UNLESS YOU'RE ATOMICUS. BUT IF YOU ARE -- !
HA!
IRENE... IRENE...
DIDN'T... READ PAPER FULLY...
DEVICE... EXPERIMENTAL... COULD... UNINTENTIONALLY ABSORB...
...HUMAN BRAIN WAVES...!
GASP
CARLA! PETE! JONESY!
OH, LORD!
LORD, WHAT HAVE I DONE -- !
"THEY WEREN'T REALLY DEAD. HE'D JUST RIGGED IT TO HAVE A TEMPORARY NERVE-NUMBING EFFECT ON EVERYONE BUT ME.
"ANOTHER ONE OF HIS LESSONS. WHAT WOULD HAPPEN, HE ASKED, IF ENEMIES LEARNED OF THE NUCLI-GLOVE -- USED IT AGAINST HIM?
"THAT ONE... WAS A LITTLE HARD TO BOUNCE BACK FROM. SO WERE SOME OF THE OTHERS. BUT WE STILL DATED...

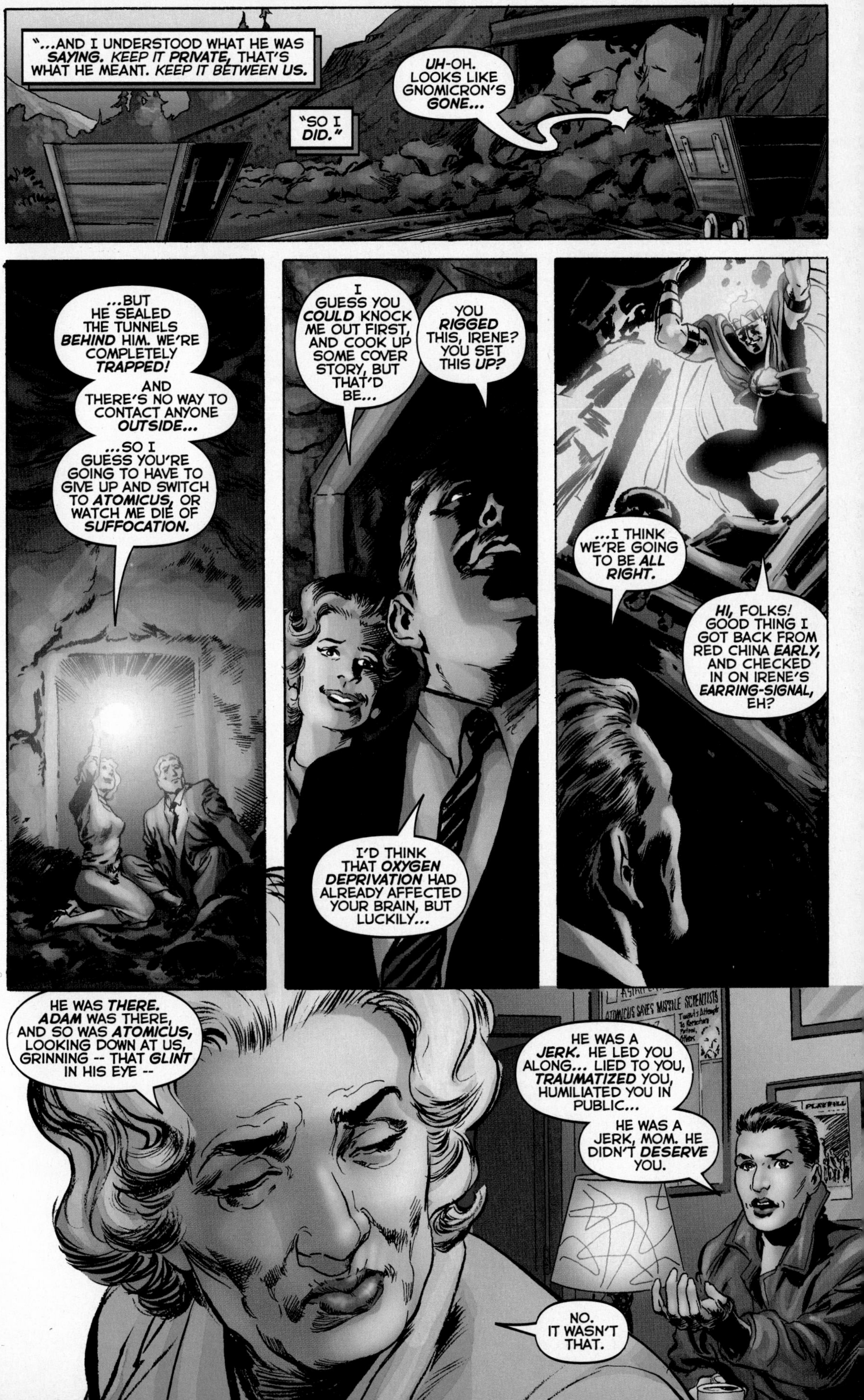
"...AND I UNDERSTOOD WHAT HE WAS SAYING. KEEP IT PRIVATE, THAT'S WHAT HE MEANT. KEEP IT BETWEEN US.
"SO I DID."
UH-OH. LOOKS LIKE GNOMICRON'S GONE...
...BUT HE SEALED THE TUNNELS BEHIND HIM. WE'RE COMPLETELY TRAPPED!
AND THERE'S NO WAY TO CONTACT ANYONE OUTSIDE...
...SO I GUESS YOU'RE GOING TO HAVE TO GIVE UP AND SWITCH TO ATOMICUS, OR WATCH ME DIE OF SUFFOCATION.
YOU RIGGED THIS, IRENE? YOU SET THIS UP?
I GUESS YOU COULD KNOCK ME OUT FIRST, AND COOK UP SOME COVER STORY, BUT THAT'D BE...
I'D THINK THAT OXYGEN DEPRIVATION HAD ALREADY AFFECTED YOUR BRAIN, BUT LUCKILY...
...I THINK WE'RE GOING TO BE ALL RIGHT.
HI, FOLKS! GOOD THING I GOT BACK FROM RED CHINA EARLY, AND CHECKED IN ON IRENE'S EARRING-SIGNAL, EH?
HE WAS THERE. ADAM WAS THERE, AND SO WAS ATOMICUS, LOOKING DOWN AT US, GRINNING -- THAT GLINT IN HIS EYE --
ATOMICUS SAVES MISSILE SCIENTISTS
PLAYBILL
HE WAS A JERK. HE LED YOU ALONG... LIED TO YOU, TRAUMATIZED YOU, HUMILIATED YOU IN PUBLIC...
HE WAS A JERK, MOM. HE DIDN'T DESERVE YOU.
NO. IT WASN'T THAT.

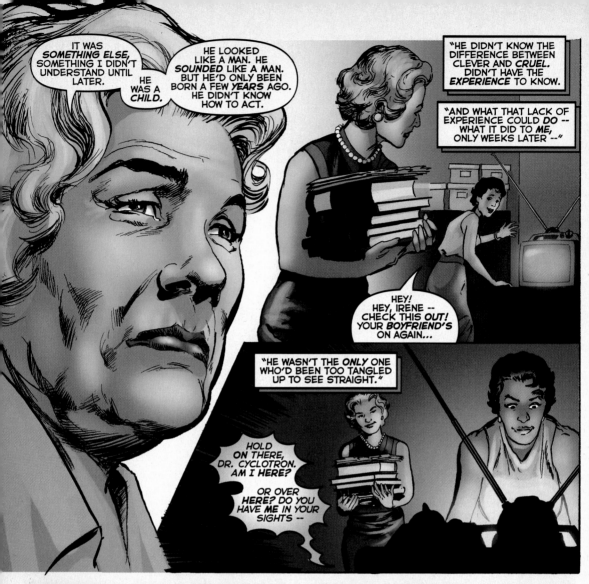

IT WAS *SOMETHING ELSE,* SOMETHING I DIDN'T UNDERSTAND UNTIL LATER.

HE WAS A *CHILD.*

HE LOOKED LIKE A MAN. HE *SOUNDED* LIKE A MAN. BUT HE'D ONLY BEEN BORN A FEW *YEARS* AGO. HE DIDN'T KNOW HOW TO ACT.

"HE DIDN'T KNOW THE DIFFERENCE BETWEEN CLEVER AND *CRUEL.* DIDN'T HAVE THE *EXPERIENCE* TO KNOW.

"AND WHAT THAT LACK OF EXPERIENCE COULD *DO* -- WHAT IT DID TO *ME,* ONLY WEEKS LATER --"

HEY! HEY, IRENE -- CHECK THIS *OUT!* YOUR *BOYFRIEND'S* ON AGAIN...

"HE WASN'T THE *ONLY* ONE WHO'D BEEN TOO TANGLED UP TO SEE STRAIGHT."

HOLD ON THERE, DR. CYCLOTRON. AM I HERE? OR OVER *HERE?* DO YOU HAVE ME IN YOUR SIGHTS --

-- OR ONE OF MY *ATOMIC DUPLICATES?*

ATOMIC DUPLICATES?

ATOMIC DUPLICATES?

"I'D BEEN TAKEN IN *COMPLETELY.* AND I'D BEEN SO SURE HE'D WANTED ME TO FIGURE IT OUT -- SO *SURE* --

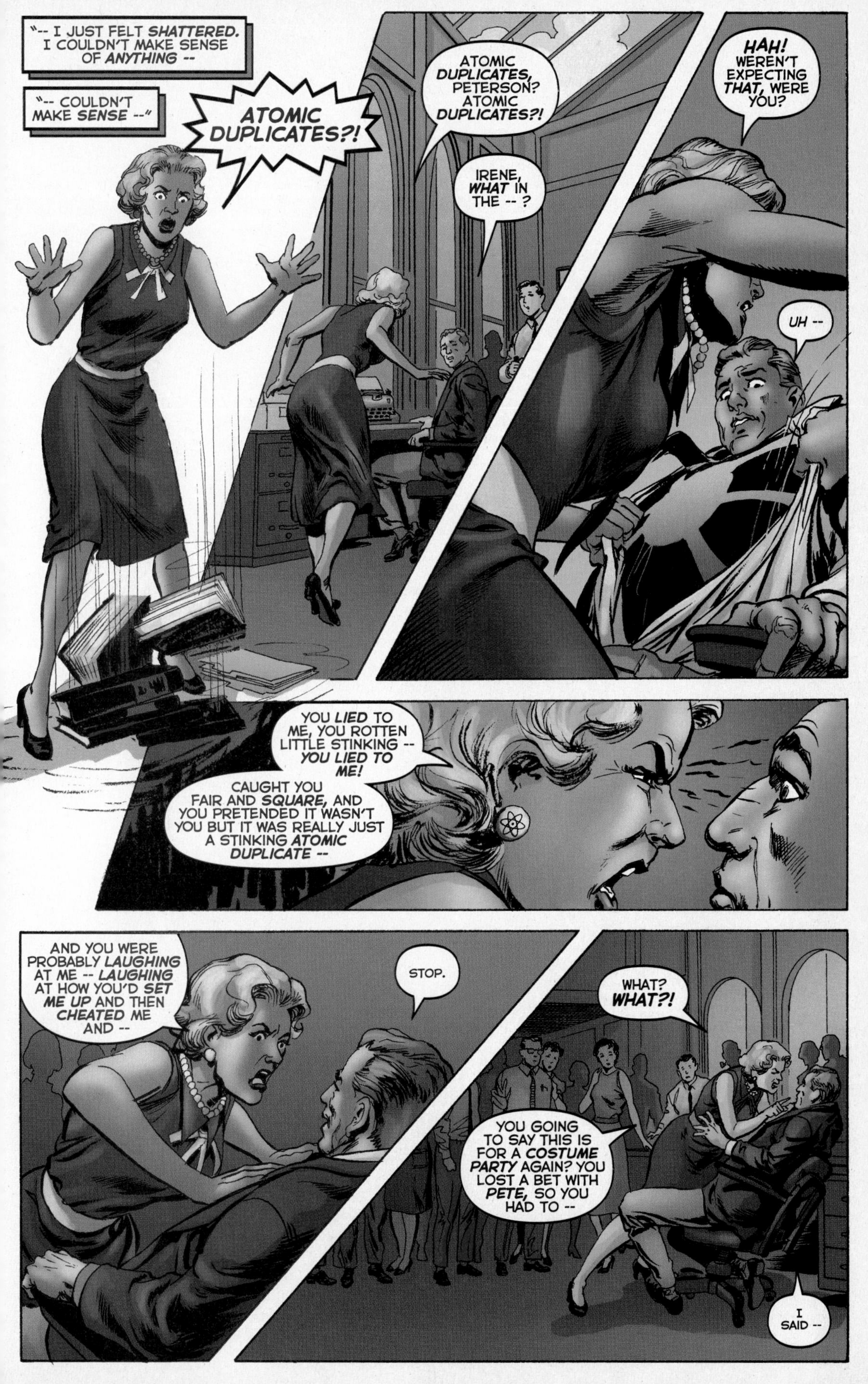
"-- I JUST FELT SHATTERED. I COULDN'T MAKE SENSE OF ANYTHING --
"-- COULDN'T MAKE SENSE --"
ATOMIC DUPLICATES?!
ATOMIC DUPLICATES, PETERSON? ATOMIC DUPLICATES?!
IRENE, WHAT IN THE -- ?
HAH! WEREN'T EXPECTING THAT, WERE YOU?
UH --
YOU LIED TO ME, YOU ROTTEN LITTLE STINKING -- YOU LIED TO ME!
CAUGHT YOU FAIR AND SQUARE, AND YOU PRETENDED IT WASN'T YOU BUT IT WAS REALLY JUST A STINKING ATOMIC DUPLICATE --
AND YOU WERE PROBABLY LAUGHING AT ME -- LAUGHING AT HOW YOU'D SET ME UP AND THEN CHEATED ME AND --
STOP.
WHAT? WHAT?!
YOU GOING TO SAY THIS IS FOR A COSTUME PARTY AGAIN? YOU LOST A BET WITH PETE, SO YOU HAD TO --
I SAID --

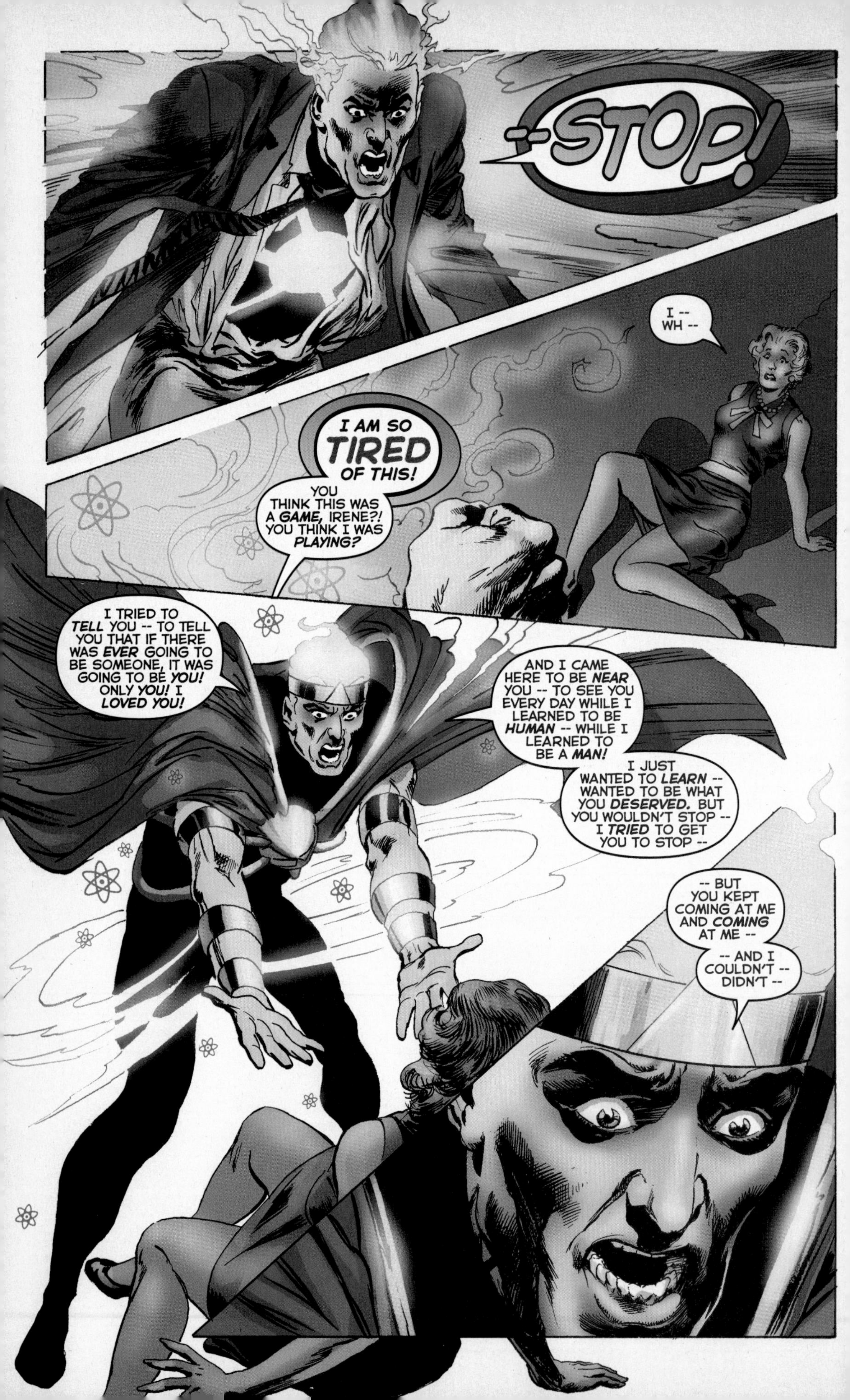

--STOP!
I -- WH --
I AM SO TIRED OF THIS!
YOU THINK THIS WAS A GAME, IRENE?! YOU THINK I WAS PLAYING?
I TRIED TO TELL YOU -- TO TELL YOU THAT IF THERE WAS EVER GOING TO BE SOMEONE, IT WAS GOING TO BE YOU! ONLY YOU! I LOVED YOU!
AND I CAME HERE TO BE NEAR YOU -- TO SEE YOU EVERY DAY WHILE I LEARNED TO BE HUMAN -- WHILE I LEARNED TO BE A MAN!
I JUST WANTED TO LEARN -- WANTED TO BE WHAT YOU DESERVED. BUT YOU WOULDN'T STOP -- I TRIED TO GET YOU TO STOP --
-- BUT YOU KEPT COMING AT ME AND COMING AT ME --
-- AND I COULDN'T -- DIDN'T --

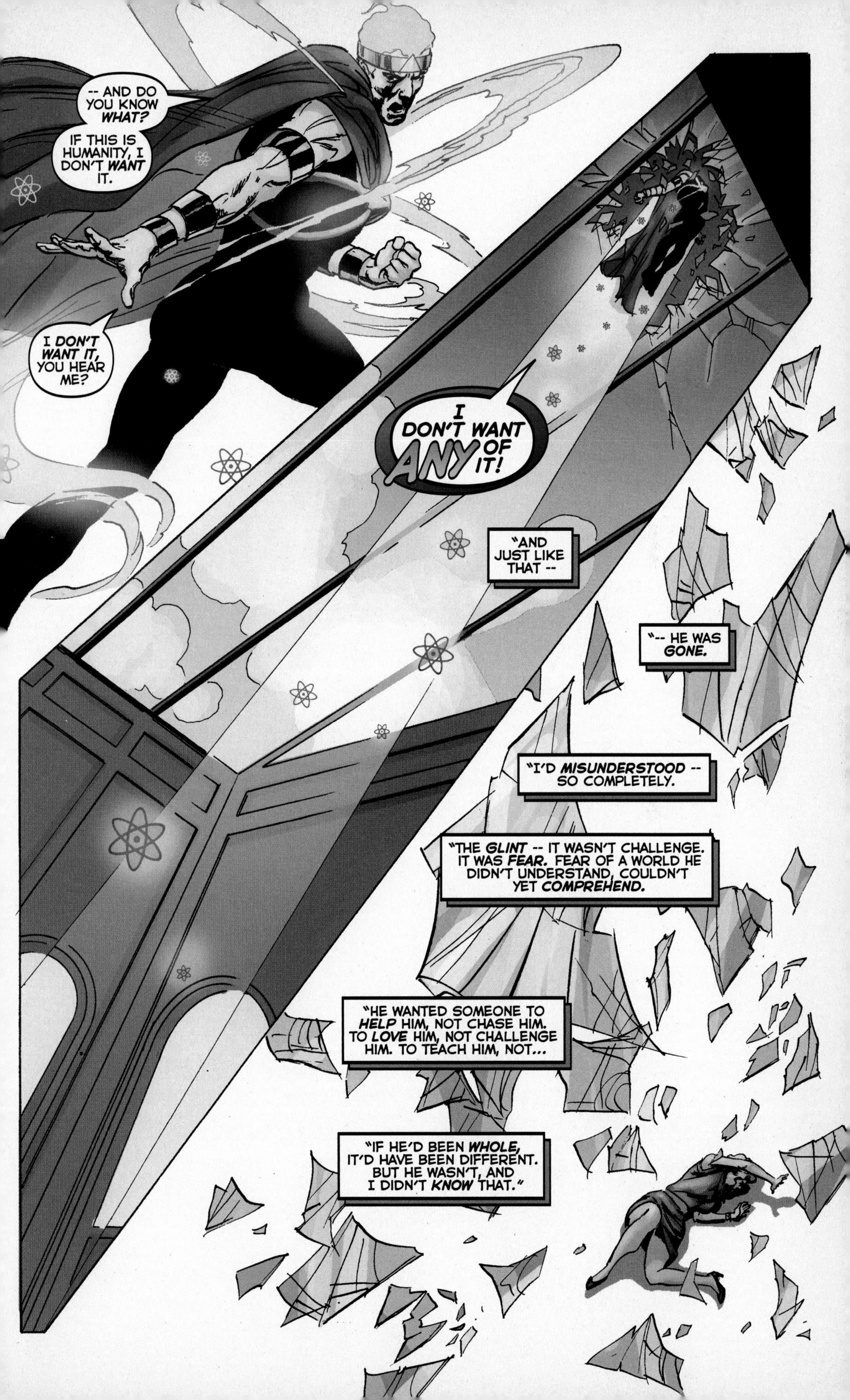
-- AND DO YOU KNOW WHAT?
IF THIS IS HUMANITY, I DON'T WANT IT.
I DON'T WANT IT, YOU HEAR ME?
I DON'T WANT ANY OF IT!
"AND JUST LIKE THAT --
"-- HE WAS GONE.
"I'D MISUNDERSTOOD -- SO COMPLETELY.
"THE GLINT -- IT WASN'T CHALLENGE. IT WAS FEAR. FEAR OF A WORLD HE DIDN'T UNDERSTAND, COULDN'T YET COMPREHEND.
"HE WANTED SOMEONE TO HELP HIM, NOT CHASE HIM. TO LOVE HIM, NOT CHALLENGE HIM. TO TEACH HIM, NOT...
"IF HE'D BEEN WHOLE, IT'D HAVE BEEN DIFFERENT. BUT HE WASN'T, AND I DIDN'T KNOW THAT."

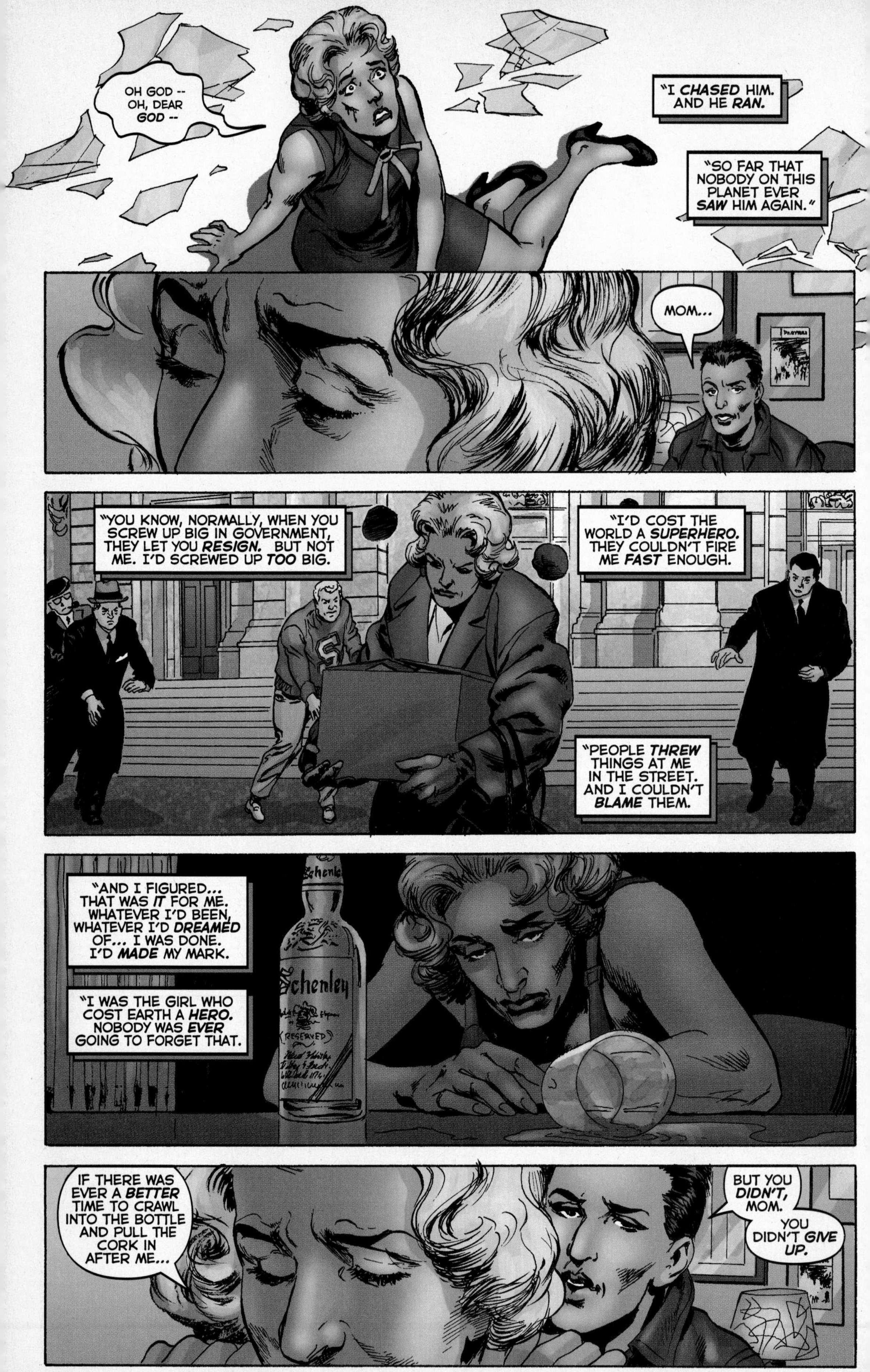
OH GOD -- OH, DEAR GOD --
"I CHASED HIM. AND HE RAN.
"SO FAR THAT NOBODY ON THIS PLANET EVER SAW HIM AGAIN."
MOM...
"YOU KNOW, NORMALLY, WHEN YOU SCREW UP BIG IN GOVERNMENT, THEY LET YOU RESIGN. BUT NOT ME. I'D SCREWED UP TOO BIG.
"I'D COST THE WORLD A SUPERHERO. THEY COULDN'T FIRE ME FAST ENOUGH.
"PEOPLE THREW THINGS AT ME IN THE STREET. AND I COULDN'T BLAME THEM.
"AND I FIGURED... THAT WAS IT FOR ME. WHATEVER I'D BEEN, WHATEVER I'D DREAMED OF... I WAS DONE. I'D MADE MY MARK.
"I WAS THE GIRL WHO COST EARTH A HERO. NOBODY WAS EVER GOING TO FORGET THAT.
Schenley
RESERVED
IF THERE WAS EVER A BETTER TIME TO CRAWL INTO THE BOTTLE AND PULL THE CORK IN AFTER ME...
BUT YOU DIDN'T, MOM.
YOU DIDN'T GIVE UP.

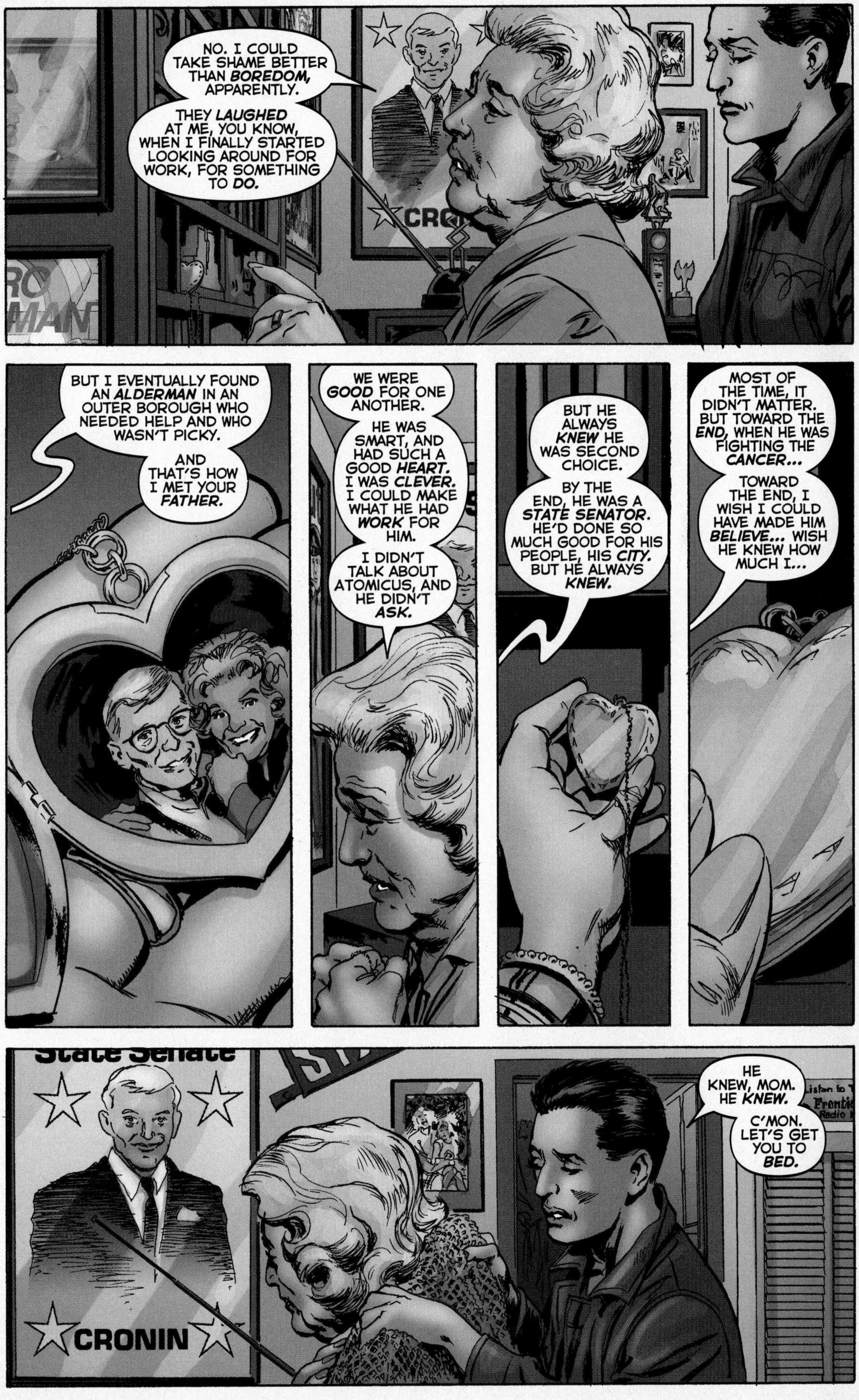
NO. I COULD TAKE SHAME BETTER THAN BOREDOM, APPARENTLY.
THEY LAUGHED AT ME, YOU KNOW, WHEN I FINALLY STARTED LOOKING AROUND FOR WORK, FOR SOMETHING TO DO.
BUT I EVENTUALLY FOUND AN ALDERMAN IN AN OUTER BOROUGH WHO NEEDED HELP AND WHO WASN'T PICKY.
AND THAT'S HOW I MET YOUR FATHER.
WE WERE GOOD FOR ONE ANOTHER.
HE WAS SMART, AND HAD SUCH A GOOD HEART. I WAS CLEVER. I COULD MAKE WHAT HE HAD WORK FOR HIM.
I DIDN'T TALK ABOUT ATOMICUS, AND HE DIDN'T ASK.
BUT HE ALWAYS KNEW HE WAS SECOND CHOICE.
BY THE END, HE WAS A STATE SENATOR. HE'D DONE SO MUCH GOOD FOR HIS PEOPLE, HIS CITY. BUT HE ALWAYS KNEW.
MOST OF THE TIME, IT DIDN'T MATTER. BUT TOWARD THE END, WHEN HE WAS FIGHTING THE CANCER...
TOWARD THE END, I WISH I COULD HAVE MADE HIM BELIEVE... WISH HE KNEW HOW MUCH I...
State Senate
CRONIN
HE KNEW, MOM. HE KNEW.
C'MON. LET'S GET YOU TO BED.

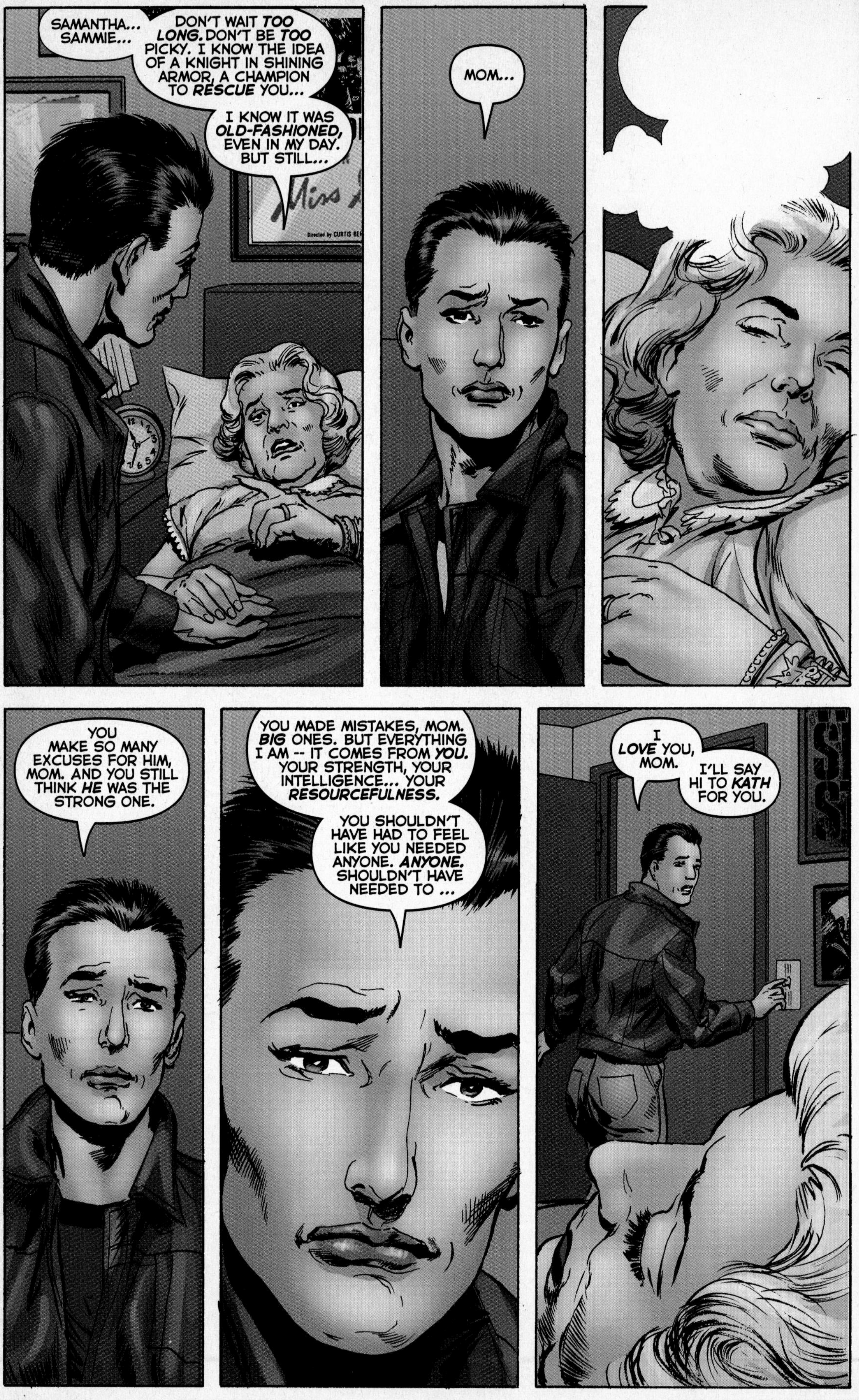
SAMANTHA... SAMMIE...
DON'T WAIT TOO LONG. DON'T BE TOO PICKY. I KNOW THE IDEA OF A KNIGHT IN SHINING ARMOR, A CHAMPION TO RESCUE YOU...
I KNOW IT WAS OLD-FASHIONED, EVEN IN MY DAY. BUT STILL...
Directed by CURTIS BE
MOM...
YOU MAKE SO MANY EXCUSES FOR HIM, MOM. AND YOU STILL THINK HE WAS THE STRONG ONE.
YOU MADE MISTAKES, MOM. BIG ONES. BUT EVERYTHING I AM -- IT COMES FROM YOU. YOUR STRENGTH, YOUR INTELLIGENCE... YOUR RESOURCEFULNESS.
YOU SHOULDN'T HAVE HAD TO FEEL LIKE YOU NEEDED ANYONE. ANYONE. SHOULDN'T HAVE NEEDED TO ...
I LOVE YOU, MOM.
I'LL SAY HI TO KATH FOR YOU.

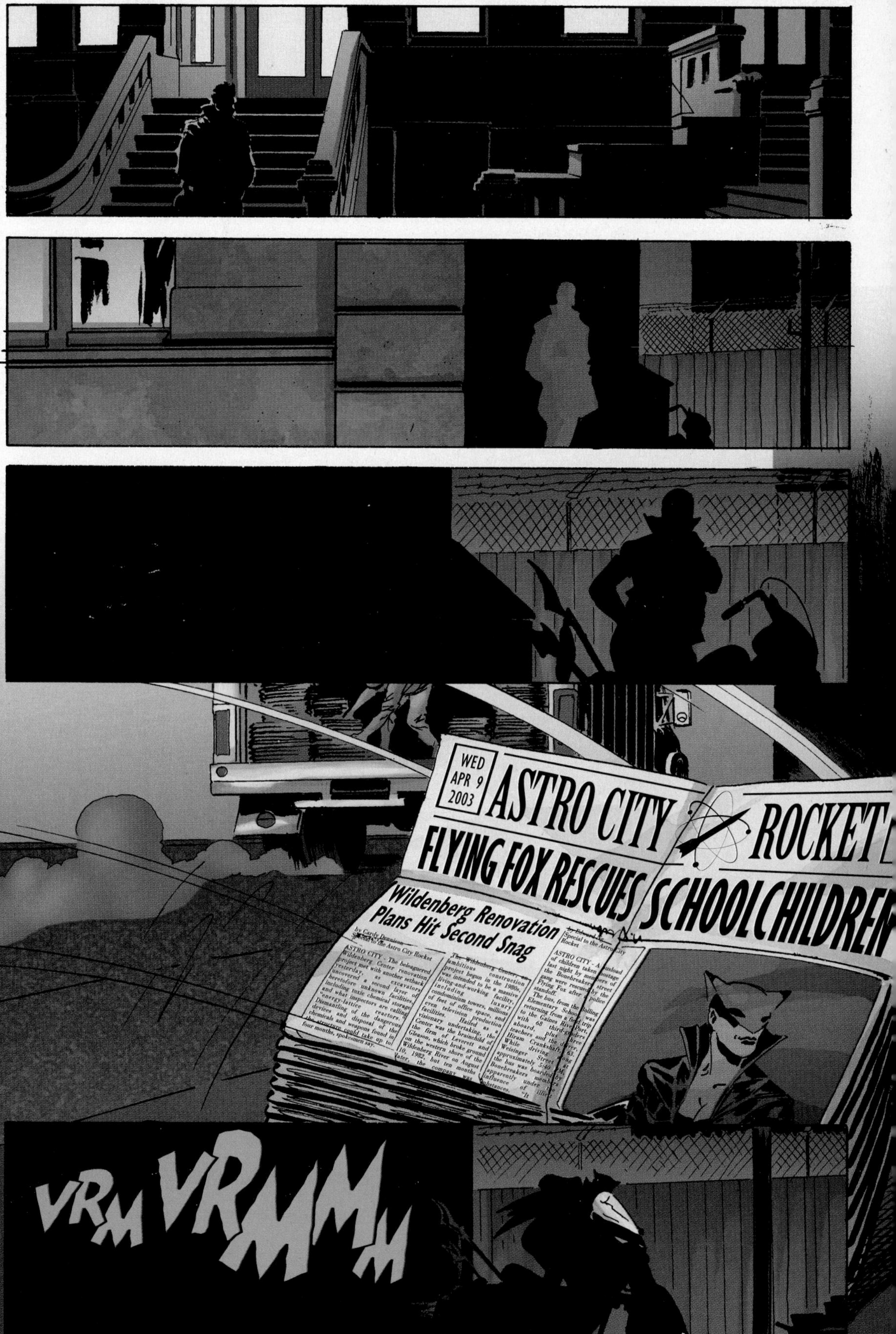
WED APR 9 2003
ASTRO CITY ROCKET
FLYING FOX RESCUES SCHOOLCHILDREN
Wildenberg Renovation Plans Hit Second Snag
VRM VRAMMM

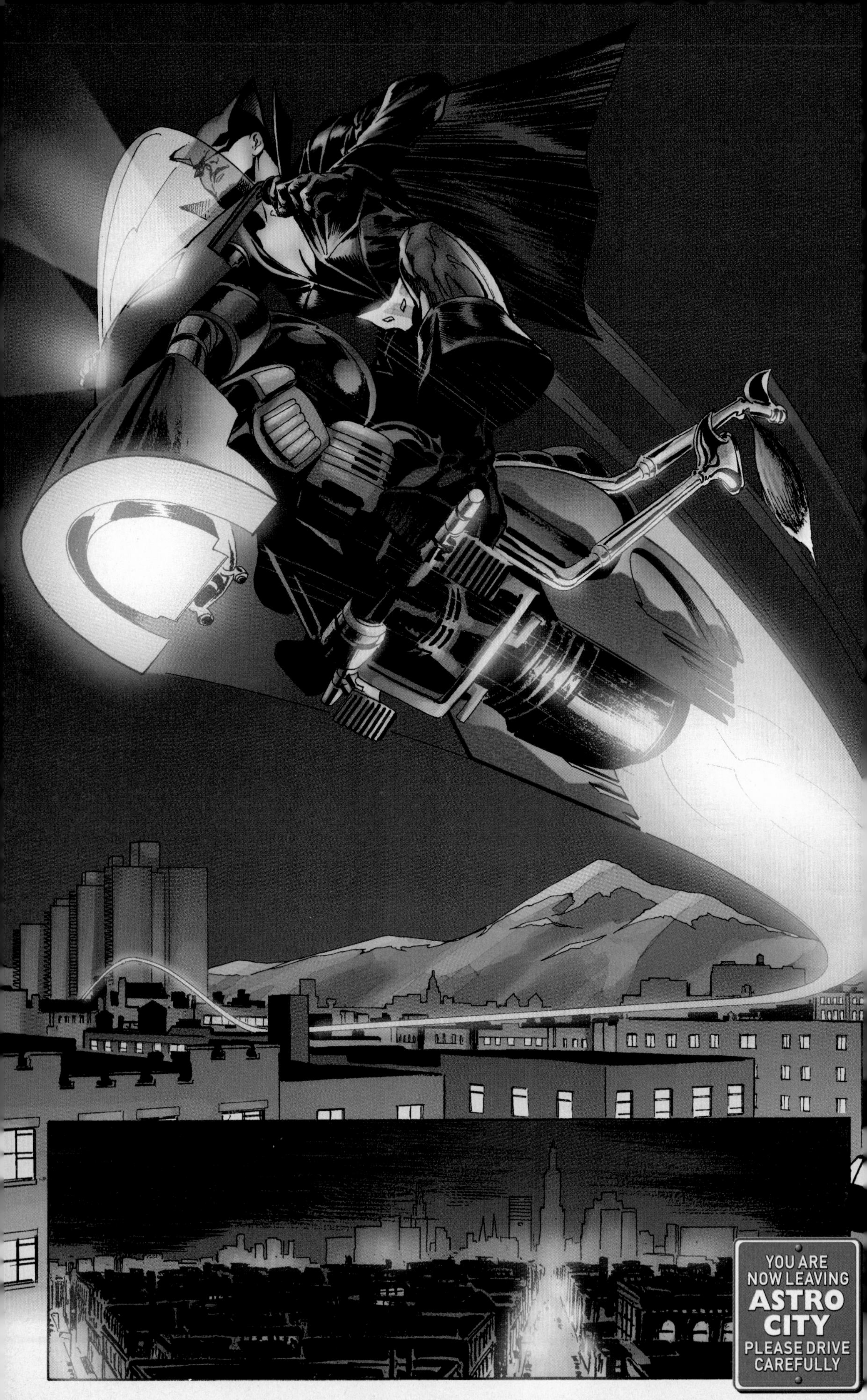
YOU ARE
NOW LEAVING
ASTRO
CITY
PLEASE DRIVE
CAREFULLY

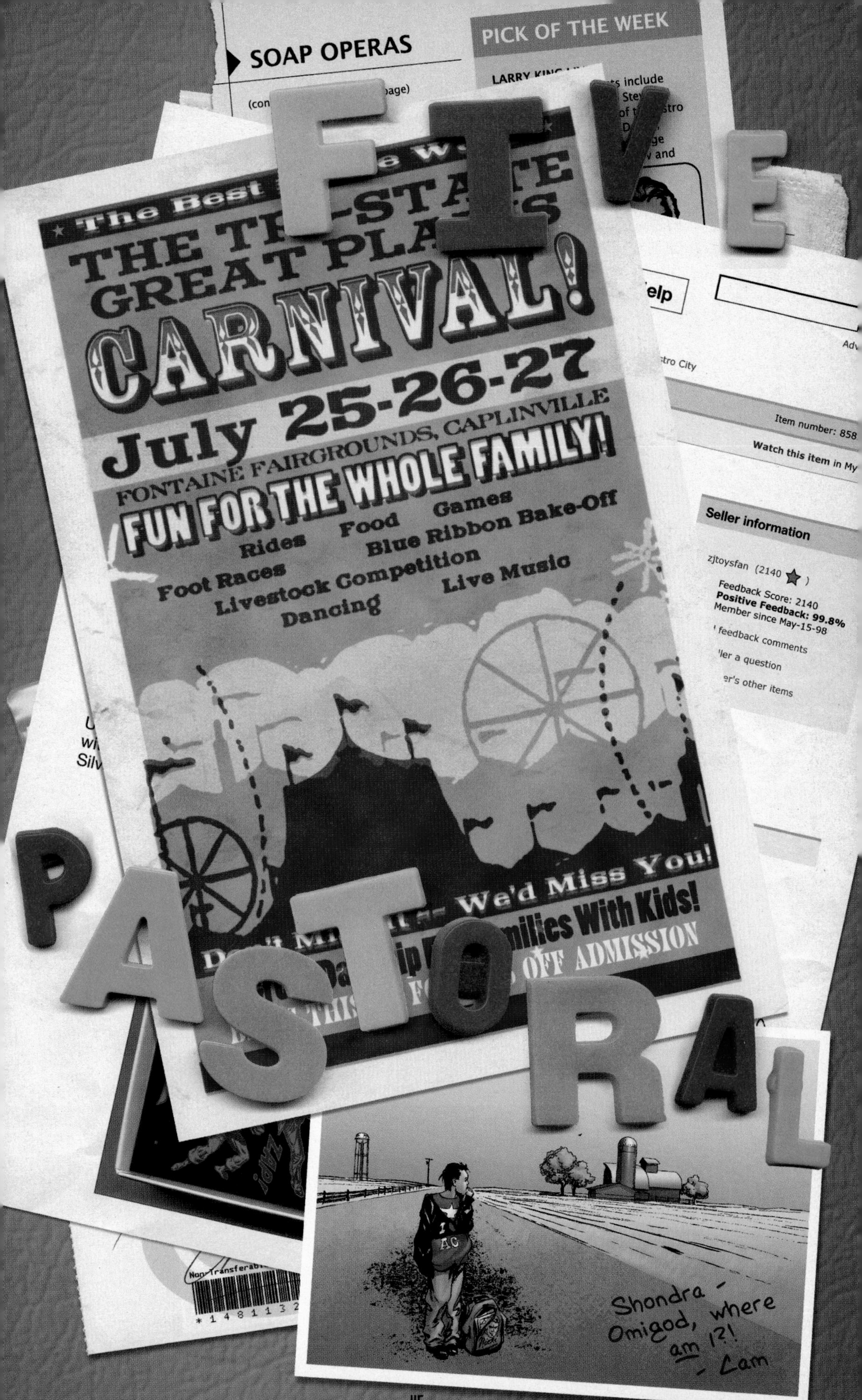
SOAP OPERAS
PICK OF THE WEEK
FIVE
CARNIVAL!
July 25-26-27
FONTAINE FAIRGROUNDS, CAPLINVILLE
FUN FOR THE WHOLE FAMILY!
Rides Food Games
Blue Ribbon Bake-Off
Foot Races
Livestock Competition
Live Music
Dancing
We'd Miss You!
OFF ADMISSION
Seller information
zjtoysfan (2140)
Feedback Score: 2140
Positive Feedback: 99.8%
Member since May-15-98
PASTORAL
Shondra -
Omigod, where am I?!
- Cam

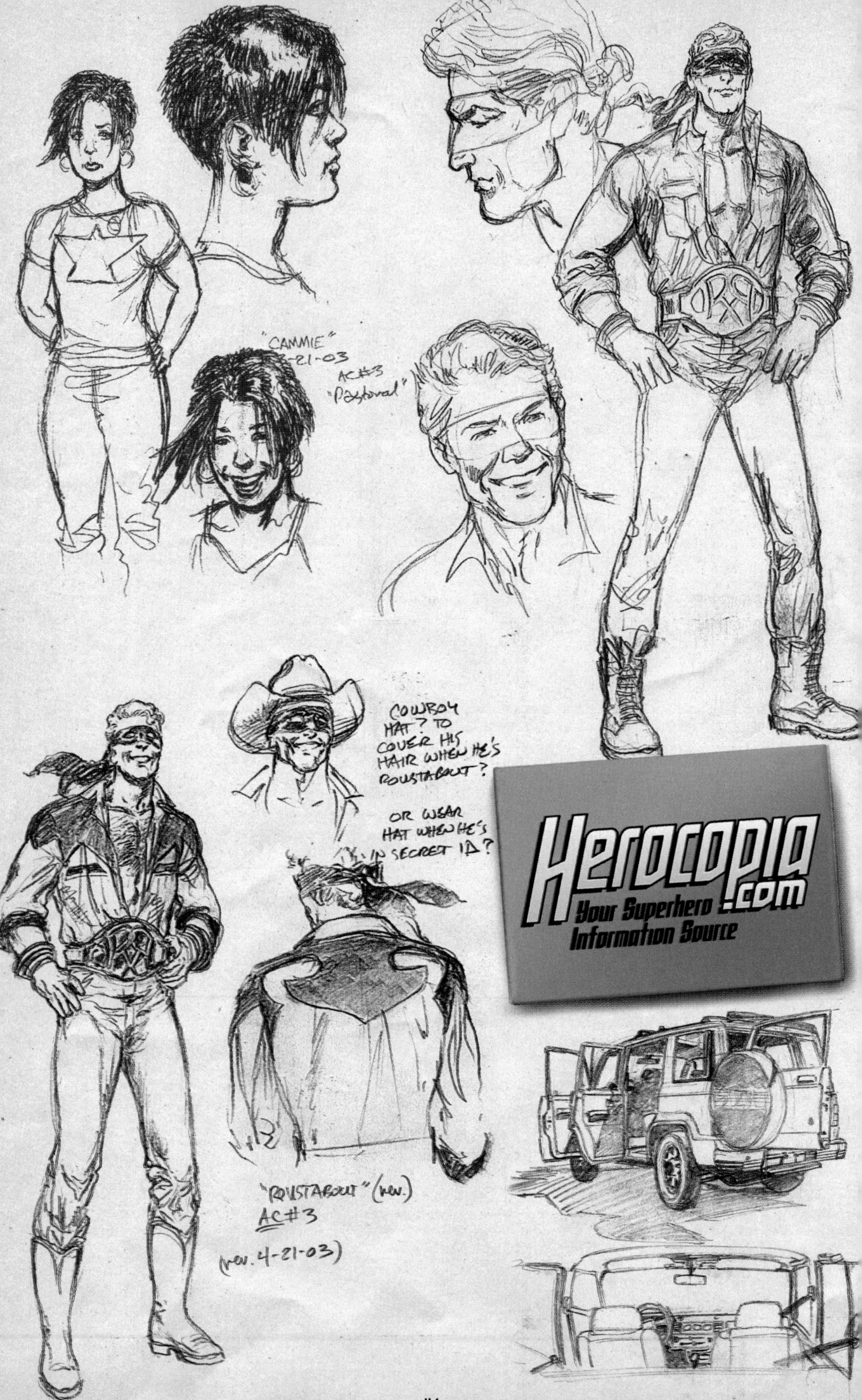
"CAMMIE"
-21-03
AC#3
"Pastoral"
COWBOY HAT? TO COVER HIS HAIR WHEN HE'S ROUSTABOUT?
OR WEAR HAT WHEN HE'S IN SECRET ID?
"ROUSTABOUT" (rev.)
AC#3
(rev. 4-21-03)

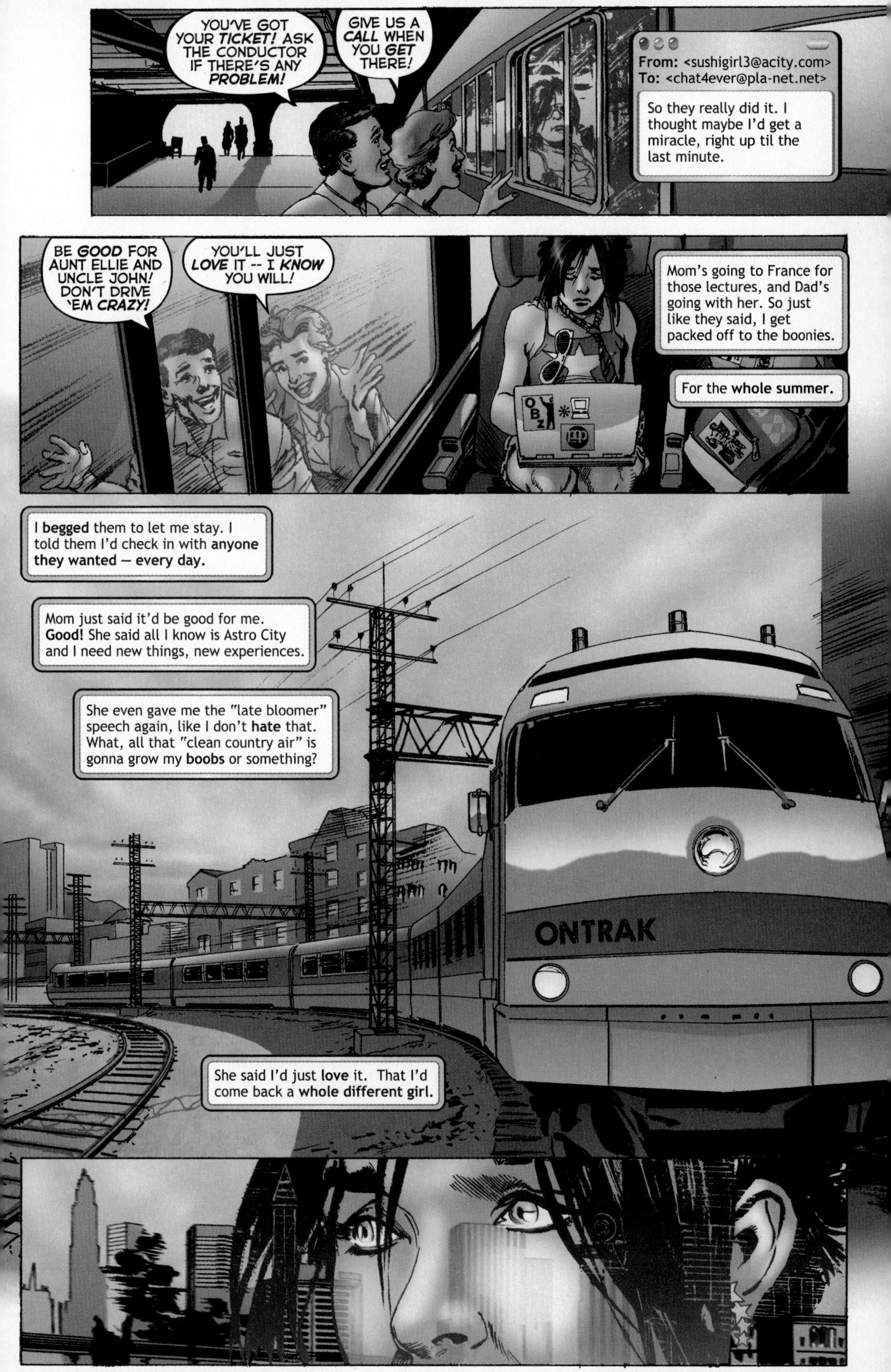
YOU'VE GOT YOUR TICKET! ASK THE CONDUCTOR IF THERE'S ANY PROBLEM!
GIVE US A CALL WHEN YOU GET THERE!
From: <sushigirl3@acity.com>
To: <chat4ever@pla-net.net>
So they really did it. I thought maybe I'd get a miracle, right up til the last minute.
BE GOOD FOR AUNT ELLIE AND UNCLE JOHN! DON'T DRIVE 'EM CRAZY!
YOU'LL JUST LOVE IT -- I KNOW YOU WILL!
Mom's going to France for those lectures, and Dad's going with her. So just like they said, I get packed off to the boonies.
For the whole summer.
I begged them to let me stay. I told them I'd check in with anyone they wanted — every day.
Mom just said it'd be good for me. Good! She said all I know is Astro City and I need new things, new experiences.
She even gave me the "late bloomer" speech again, like I don't hate that. What, all that "clean country air" is gonna grow my boobs or something?
ONTRAK
She said I'd just love it. That I'd come back a whole different girl.

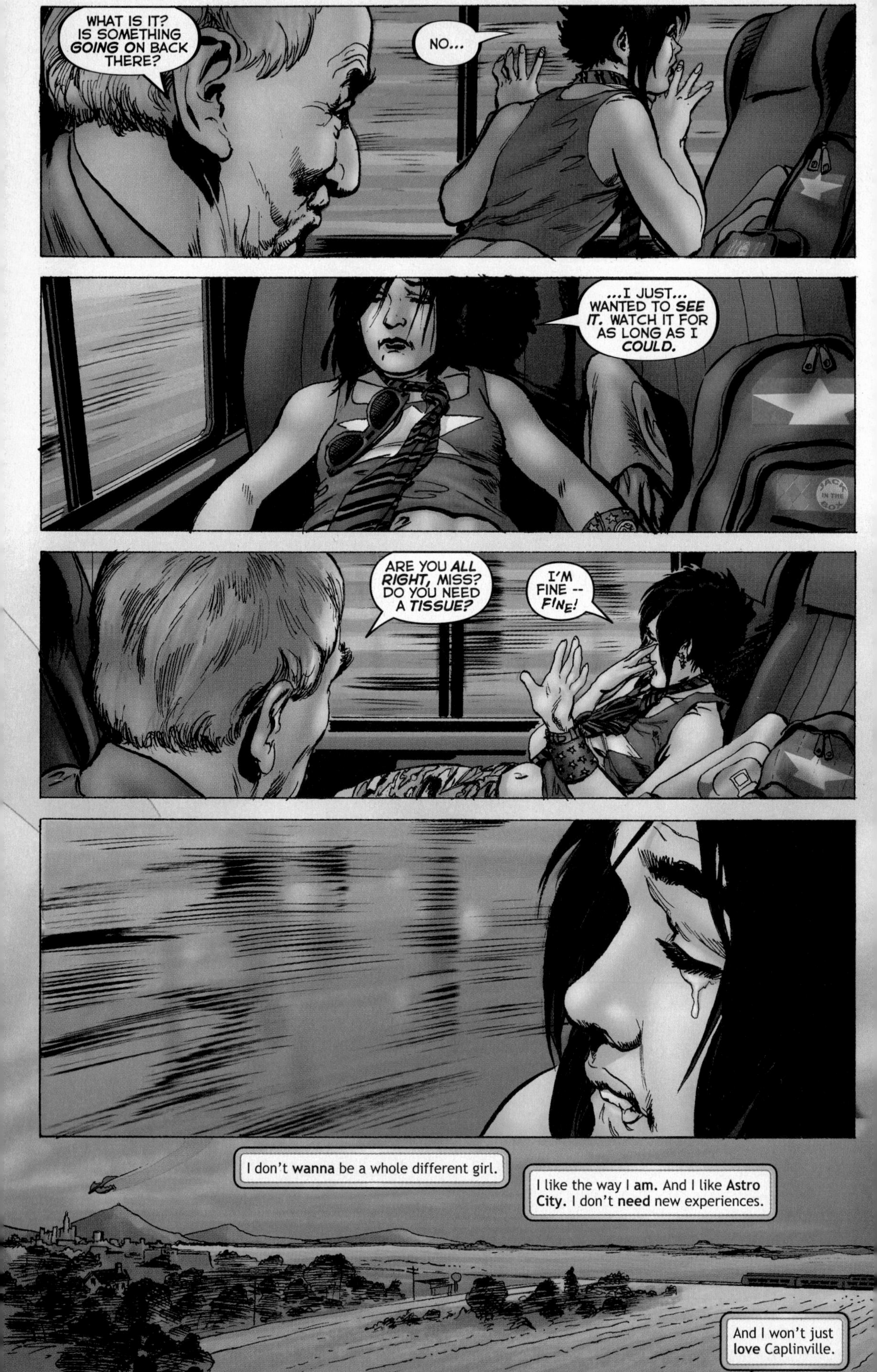

WHAT IS IT? IS SOMETHING *GOING ON* BACK THERE?
NO...
...I JUST... WANTED TO *SEE IT.* WATCH IT FOR AS LONG AS I *COULD.*
ARE YOU *ALL RIGHT,* MISS? DO YOU NEED A *TISSUE?*
I'M FINE -- *FINE!*
I don't **wanna** be a whole different girl.
I like the way I **am.** And I like **Astro City.** I don't **need** new experiences.
And I won't just **love** Caplinville.
JACK IN THE BOX

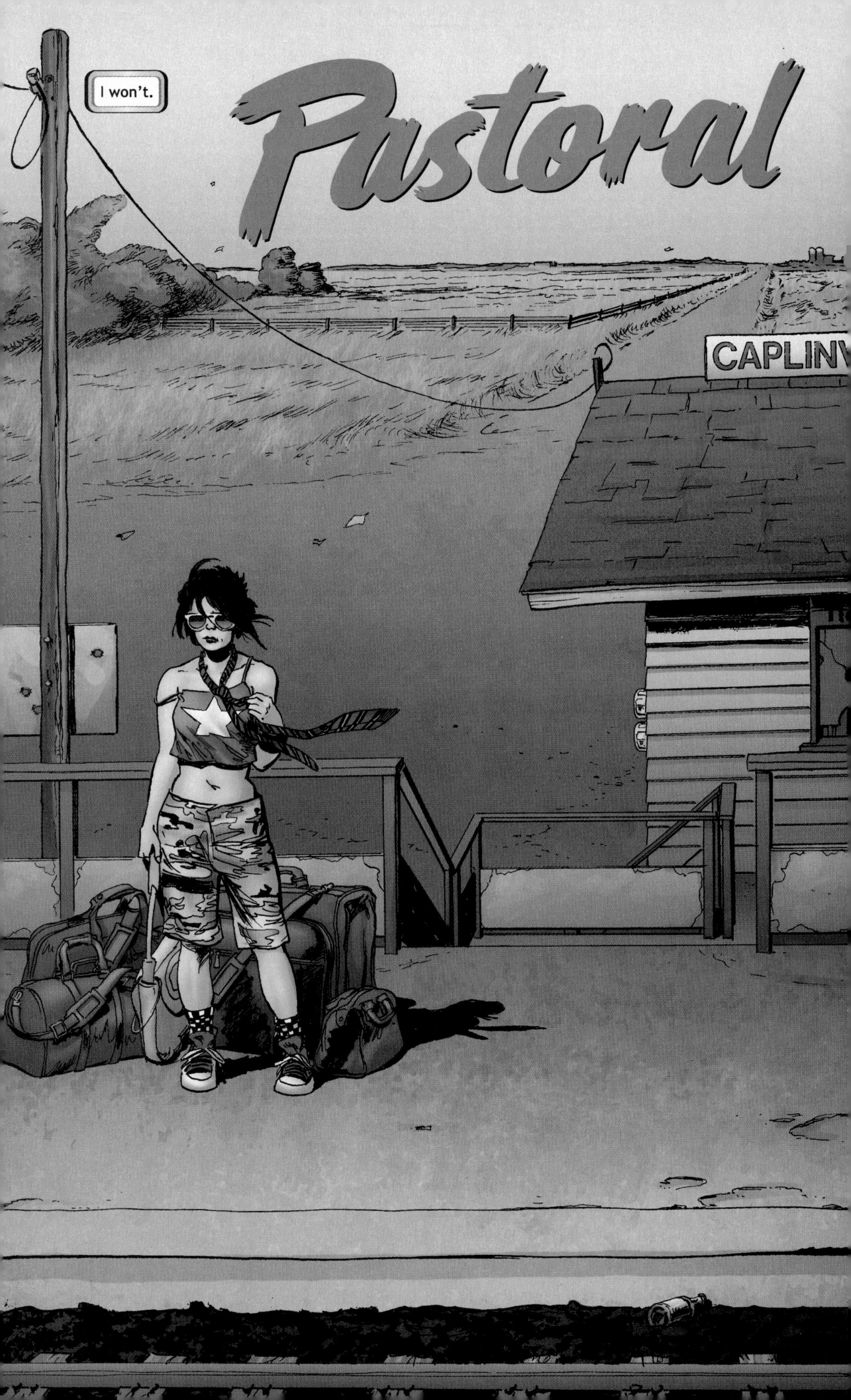

I won't.
Pastoral
CAPLINV

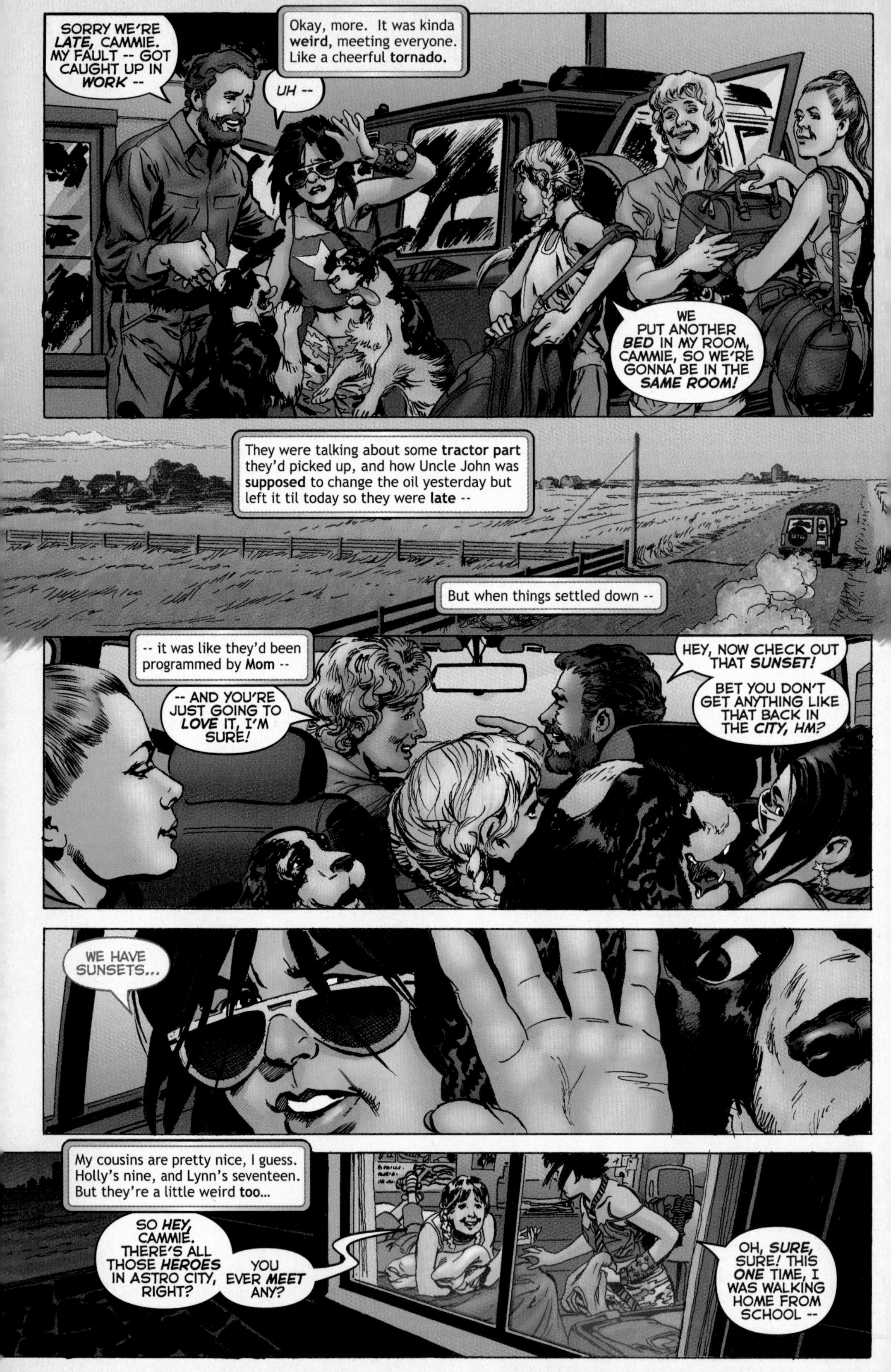
SORRY WE'RE LATE, CAMMIE. MY FAULT -- GOT CAUGHT UP IN WORK --
Okay, more. It was kinda weird, meeting everyone. Like a cheerful tornado.
UH --
WE PUT ANOTHER BED IN MY ROOM, CAMMIE, SO WE'RE GONNA BE IN THE SAME ROOM!
They were talking about some tractor part they'd picked up, and how Uncle John was supposed to change the oil yesterday but left it til today so they were late --
But when things settled down --
-- it was like they'd been programmed by Mom --
-- AND YOU'RE JUST GOING TO LOVE IT, I'M SURE!
HEY, NOW CHECK OUT THAT SUNSET!
BET YOU DON'T GET ANYTHING LIKE THAT BACK IN THE CITY, HM?
WE HAVE SUNSETS...
My cousins are pretty nice, I guess. Holly's nine, and Lynn's seventeen. But they're a little weird too...
SO HEY, CAMMIE. THERE'S ALL THOSE HEROES IN ASTRO CITY, RIGHT?
YOU EVER MEET ANY?
OH, SURE, SURE! THIS ONE TIME, I WAS WALKING HOME FROM SCHOOL --

"-- AND THERE'S THE *N-FORCER*, FIGHTING IT OUT WITH *SCARGOYLE*, RIGHT UP OVER MY HEAD!"

"HIS *FORCE-BLASTS* SHOOK THE *WHOLE BLOCK!*"

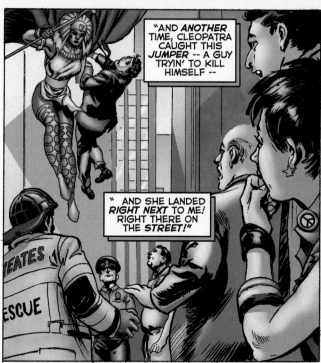

"AND *ANOTHER* TIME, CLEOPATRA CAUGHT THIS *JUMPER* -- A GUY TRYIN' TO KILL HIMSELF --"

"AND SHE LANDED *RIGHT NEXT* TO ME! RIGHT THERE ON THE *STREET!*"

YEAH? SO THEN WHAT HAPPENED? WHAT'D SHE *SAY* TO YOU? WHAT'S SHE *LIKE?*

HUH? NO, THAT WAS IT. WHY WOULD SHE *TALK* TO ME?

BUT --

HOLLY. I'M SURE CLEOPATRA'S *VERY NICE.* BUT IT'S BEDTIME.

Yeah, they're weird. What did Holly expect -- we **hang out** with the heroes? **Chat** with them? And ... "very **nice**"?

I guess they just don't know. But at least they didn't say I'd **love** it here. I'll send this in the morning. Write me, okay? I need linkage. -- cam

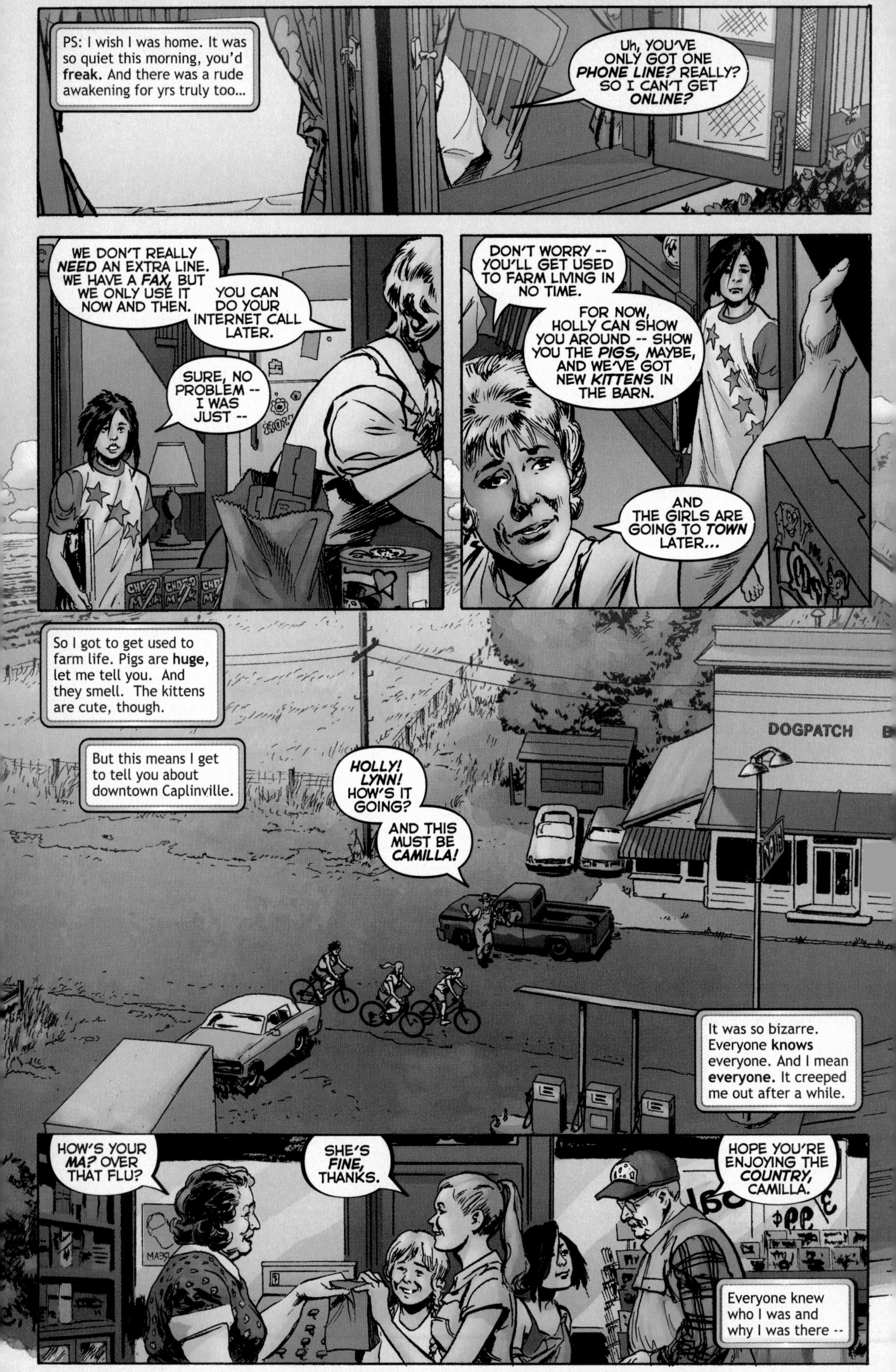
PS: I wish I was home. It was so quiet this morning, you'd **freak.** And there was a rude awakening for yrs truly too...
Uh, YOU'VE ONLY GOT ONE *PHONE LINE?* REALLY? SO I CAN'T GET *ONLINE?*
WE DON'T REALLY *NEED* AN EXTRA LINE. WE HAVE A *FAX,* BUT WE ONLY USE IT NOW AND THEN.
YOU CAN DO YOUR INTERNET CALL LATER.
SURE, NO PROBLEM -- I WAS JUST --
DON'T WORRY -- YOU'LL GET USED TO FARM LIVING IN NO TIME.
FOR NOW, HOLLY CAN SHOW YOU AROUND -- SHOW YOU THE *PIGS,* MAYBE, AND WE'VE GOT NEW *KITTENS* IN THE BARN.
AND THE GIRLS ARE GOING TO *TOWN* LATER...
So I got to get used to farm life. Pigs are **huge,** let me tell you. And they smell. The kittens are cute, though.
But this means I get to tell you about downtown Caplinville.
DOGPATCH
HOLLY! LYNN! HOW'S IT GOING?
AND THIS MUST BE *CAMILLA!*
It was so bizarre. Everyone **knows** everyone. And I mean **everyone.** It creeped me out after a while.
HOW'S YOUR *MA?* OVER THAT FLU?
SHE'S *FINE,* THANKS.
HOPE YOU'RE ENJOYING THE *COUNTRY,* CAMILLA.
Everyone knew who I was and why I was there --

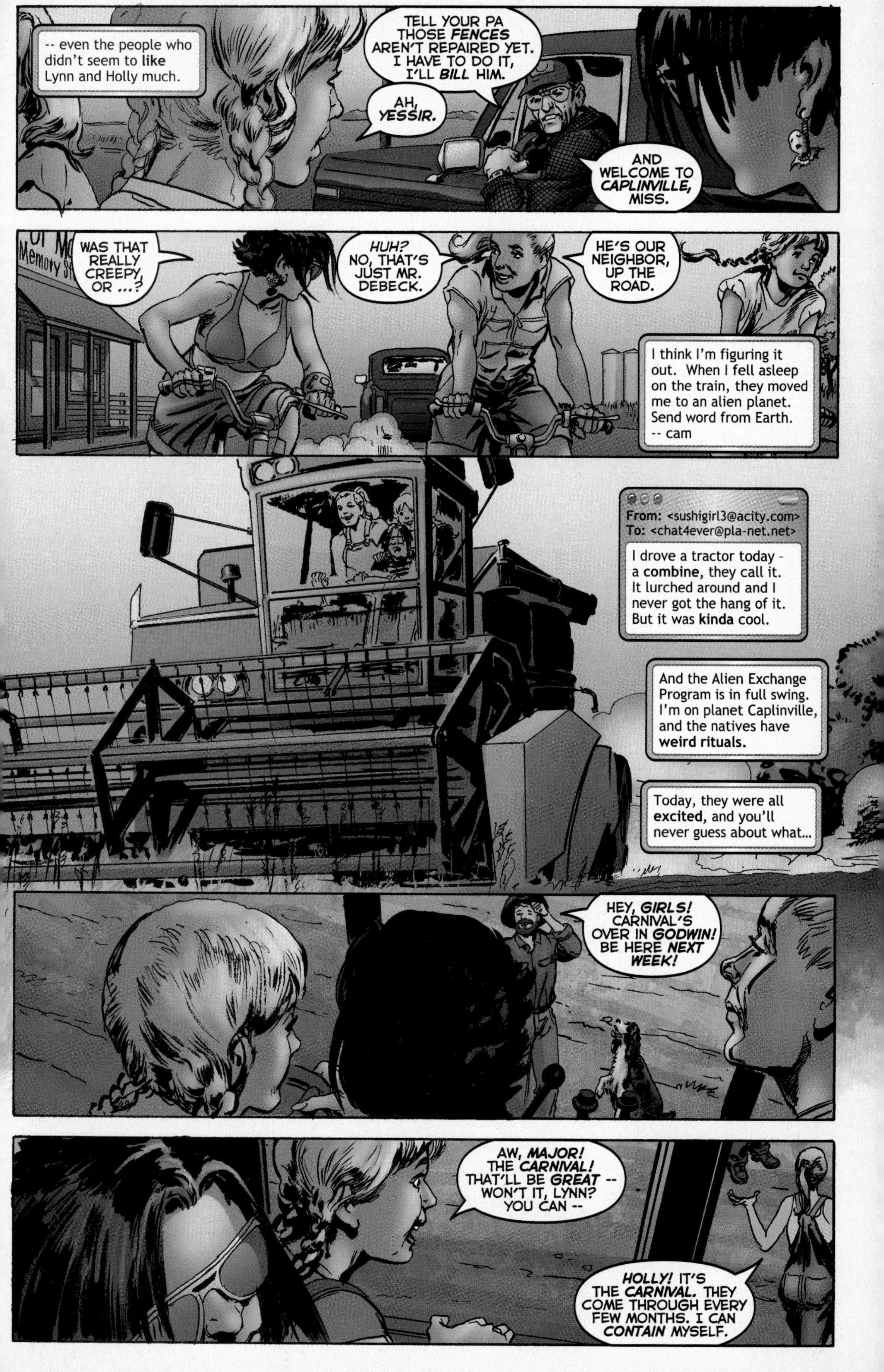
-- even the people who didn't seem to **like** Lynn and Holly much.
TELL YOUR PA THOSE *FENCES* AREN'T REPAIRED YET. I HAVE TO DO IT, I'LL *BILL* HIM.
AH, *YESSIR.*
AND WELCOME TO *CAPLINVILLE,* MISS.
WAS THAT REALLY CREEPY, OR ...?
HUH? NO, THAT'S JUST MR. DEBECK.
HE'S OUR NEIGHBOR, UP THE ROAD.
I think I'm figuring it out. When I fell asleep on the train, they moved me to an alien planet. Send word from Earth. -- cam
From: <sushigirl3@acity.com>
To: <chat4ever@pla-net.net>
I drove a tractor today - a **combine,** they call it. It lurched around and I never got the hang of it. But it was **kinda** cool.
And the Alien Exchange Program is in full swing. I'm on planet Caplinville, and the natives have **weird rituals.**
Today, they were all **excited,** and you'll never guess about what...
HEY, *GIRLS!* CARNIVAL'S OVER IN *GODWIN!* BE HERE *NEXT WEEK!*
AW, *MAJOR!* THE *CARNIVAL!* THAT'LL BE *GREAT* -- WON'T IT, LYNN? YOU CAN --
HOLLY! IT'S THE *CARNIVAL.* THEY COME THROUGH EVERY FEW MONTHS. I CAN *CONTAIN* MYSELF.

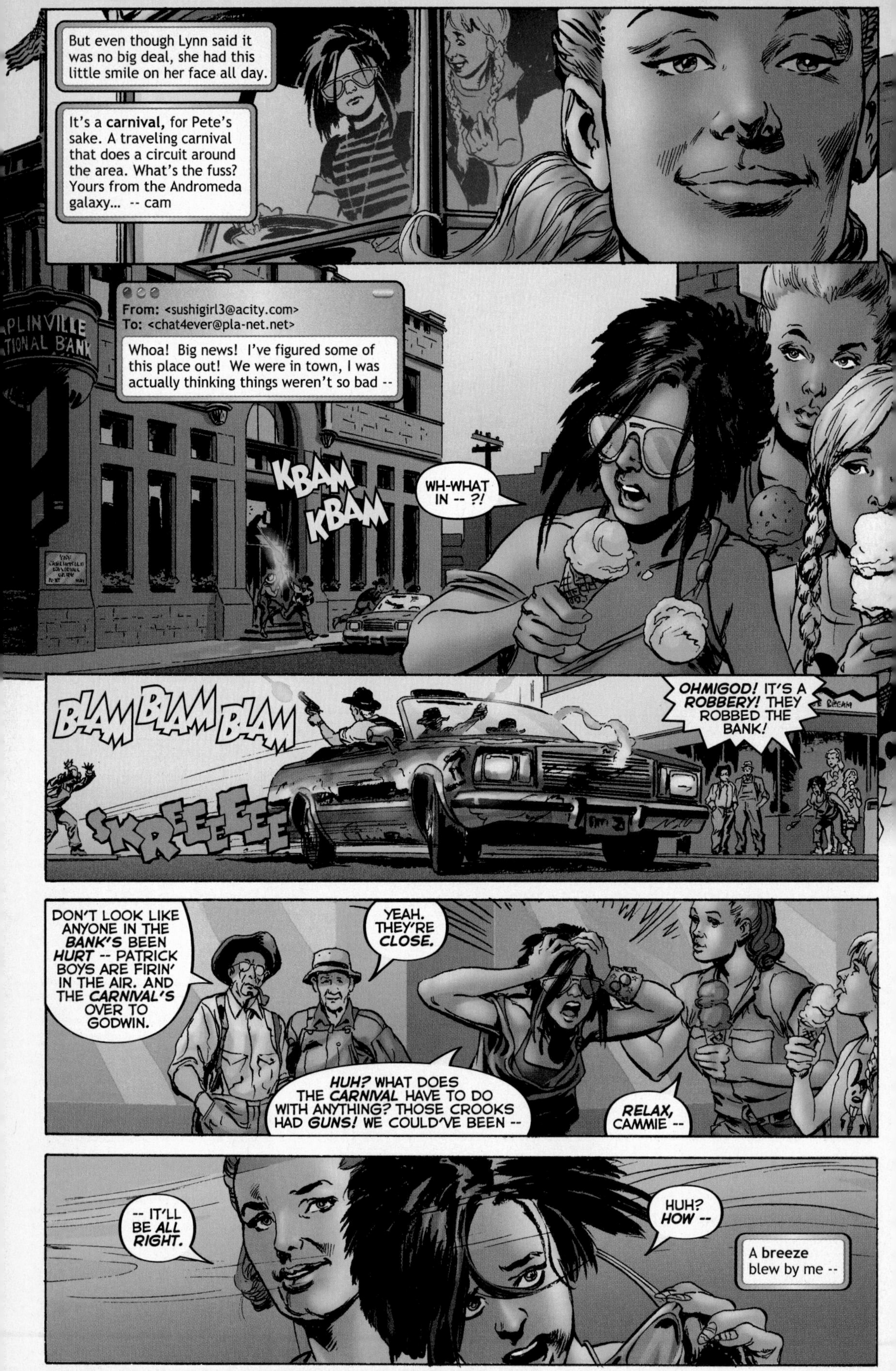

But even though Lynn said it was no big deal, she had this little smile on her face all day.
It's a **carnival,** for Pete's sake. A traveling carnival that does a circuit around the area. What's the fuss? Yours from the Andromeda galaxy... -- cam
From: <sushigirl3@acity.com>
To: <chat4ever@pla-net.net>
Whoa! Big news! I've figured some of this place out! We were in town, I was actually thinking things weren't so bad --
PLINVILLE
TIONAL BANK
KBAM KBAM
WH-WHAT IN -- ?!
BLAM BLAM BLAM
SKREEEEEE
OHMIGOD! IT'S A ROBBERY! THEY ROBBED THE BANK!
DON'T LOOK LIKE ANYONE IN THE BANK'S BEEN HURT -- PATRICK BOYS ARE FIRIN' IN THE AIR. AND THE CARNIVAL'S OVER TO GODWIN.
YEAH. THEY'RE CLOSE.
HUH? WHAT DOES THE CARNIVAL HAVE TO DO WITH ANYTHING? THOSE CROOKS HAD GUNS! WE COULD'VE BEEN --
RELAX, CAMMIE --
-- IT'LL BE ALL RIGHT.
HUH? HOW --
A **breeze** blew by me --

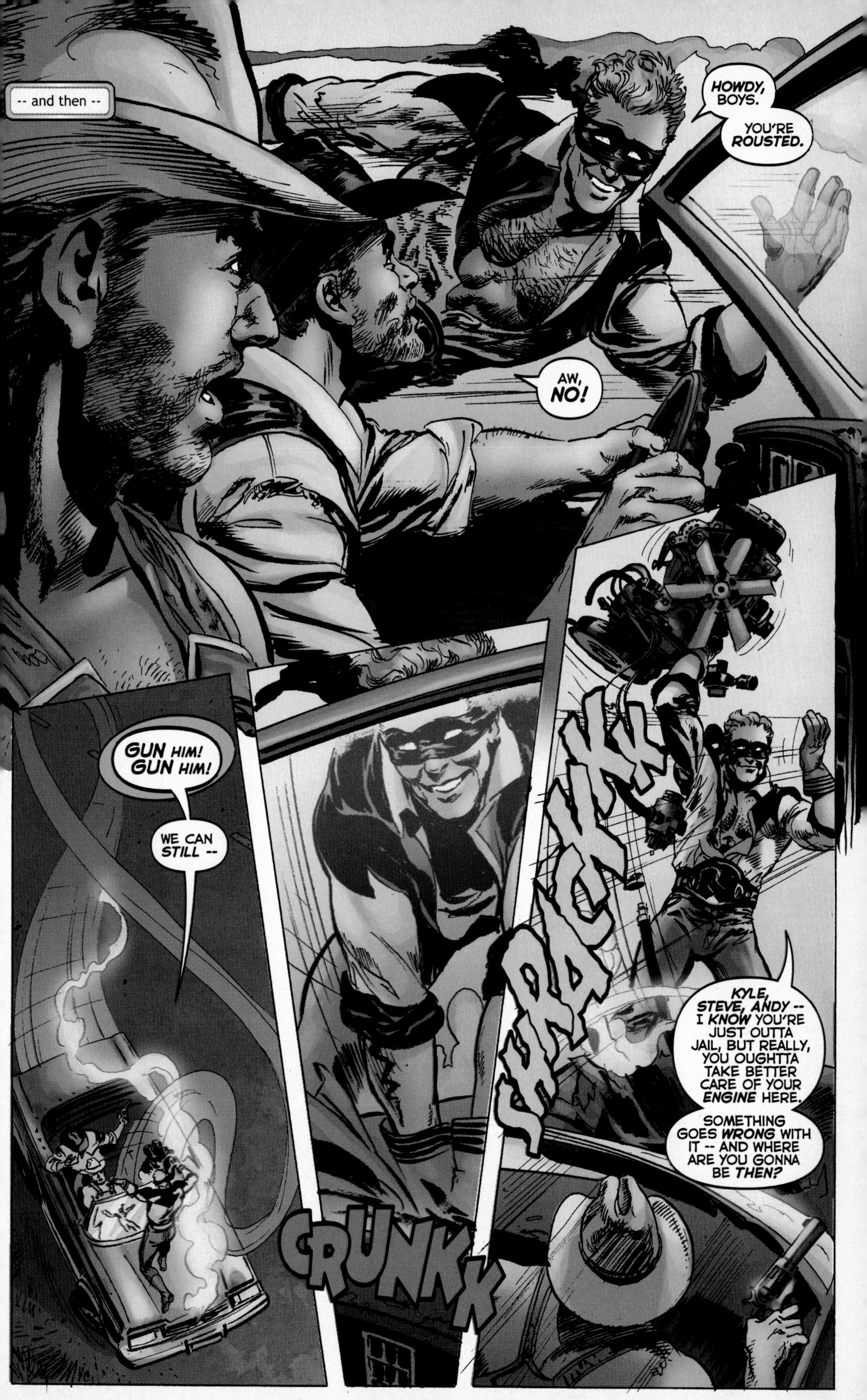
-- and then --
HOWDY, BOYS.
YOU'RE ROUSTED.
AW, NO!
GUN HIM! GUN HIM!
WE CAN STILL --
SHRACK
KYLE, STEVE, ANDY -- I KNOW YOU'RE JUST OUTTA JAIL, BUT REALLY, YOU OUGHTTA TAKE BETTER CARE OF YOUR ENGINE HERE.
SOMETHING GOES WRONG WITH IT -- AND WHERE ARE YOU GONNA BE THEN?
CRUNKK

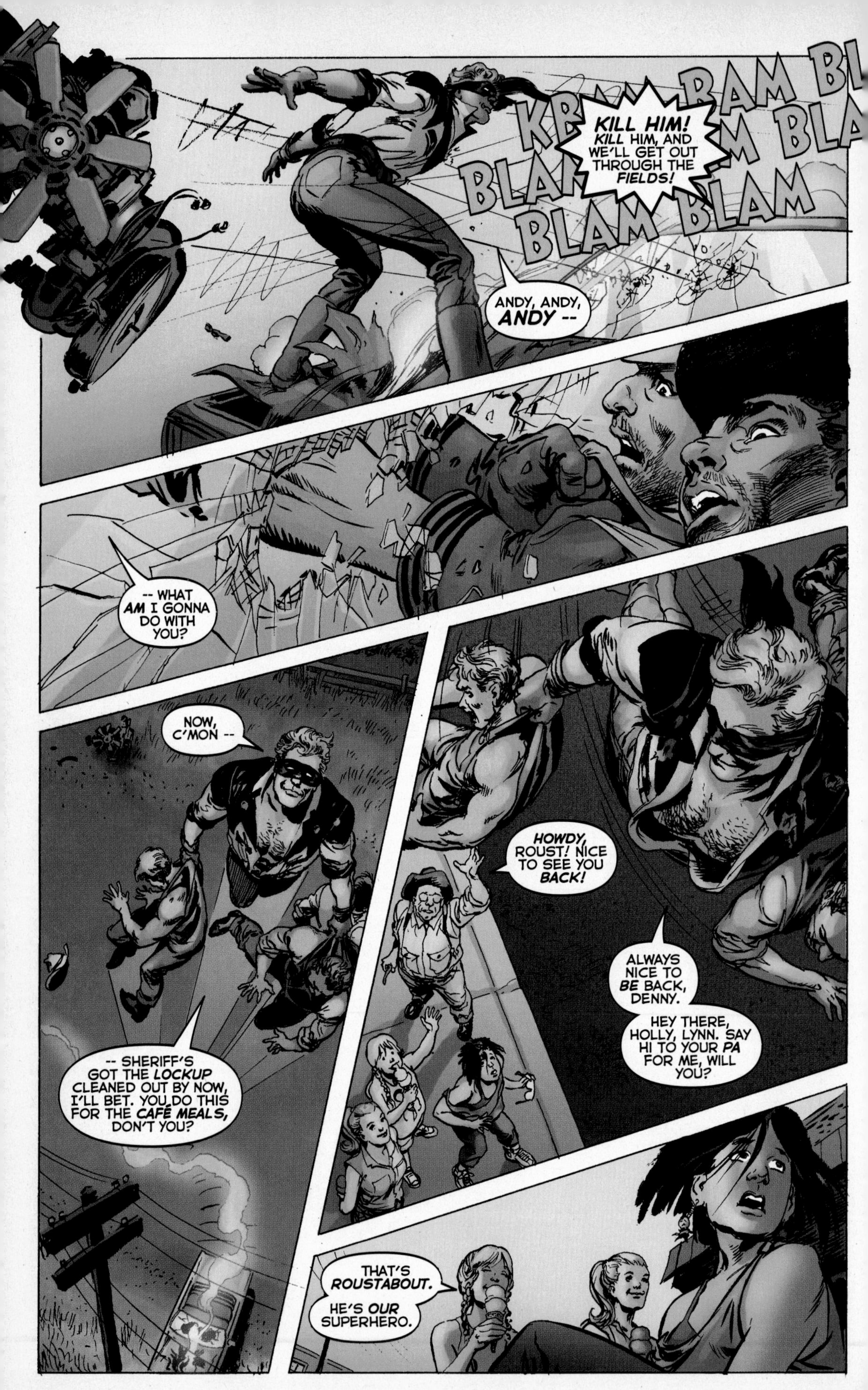
KRAM RAM BLAM BLAM BLAM BLAM BLAM
KILL HIM! KILL HIM, AND WE'LL GET OUT THROUGH THE FIELDS!
ANDY, ANDY, ANDY --
-- WHAT AM I GONNA DO WITH YOU?
NOW, C'MON --
-- SHERIFF'S GOT THE LOCKUP CLEANED OUT BY NOW, I'LL BET. YOU DO THIS FOR THE CAFÉ MEALS, DON'T YOU?
HOWDY, ROUST! NICE TO SEE YOU BACK!
ALWAYS NICE TO BE BACK, DENNY.
HEY THERE, HOLLY, LYNN. SAY HI TO YOUR PA FOR ME, WILL YOU?
THAT'S ROUSTABOUT.
HE'S OUR SUPERHERO.

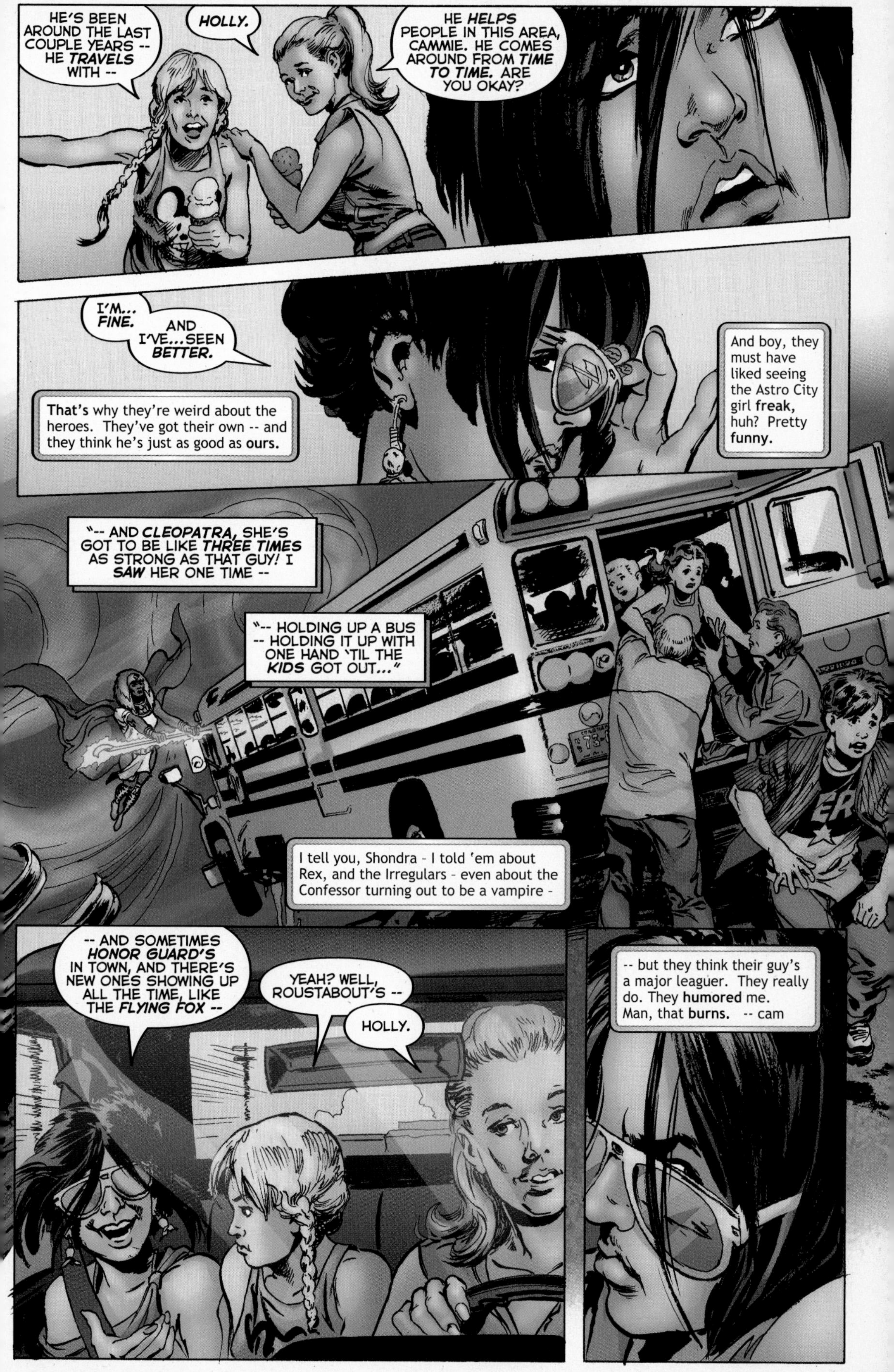
HE'S BEEN AROUND THE LAST COUPLE YEARS -- HE TRAVELS WITH --
HOLLY.
HE HELPS PEOPLE IN THIS AREA, CAMMIE. HE COMES AROUND FROM TIME TO TIME. ARE YOU OKAY?
I'M... FINE.
AND I'VE...SEEN BETTER.
That's why they're weird about the heroes. They've got their own -- and they think he's just as good as ours.
And boy, they must have liked seeing the Astro City girl freak, huh? Pretty funny.
"-- AND CLEOPATRA, SHE'S GOT TO BE LIKE THREE TIMES AS STRONG AS THAT GUY! I SAW HER ONE TIME --
"-- HOLDING UP A BUS -- HOLDING IT UP WITH ONE HAND 'TIL THE KIDS GOT OUT..."
I tell you, Shondra - I told 'em about Rex, and the Irregulars - even about the Confessor turning out to be a vampire -
-- AND SOMETIMES HONOR GUARD'S IN TOWN, AND THERE'S NEW ONES SHOWING UP ALL THE TIME, LIKE THE FLYING FOX --
YEAH? WELL, ROUSTABOUT'S --
HOLLY.
-- but they think their guy's a major leaguer. They really do. They humored me. Man, that burns. -- cam

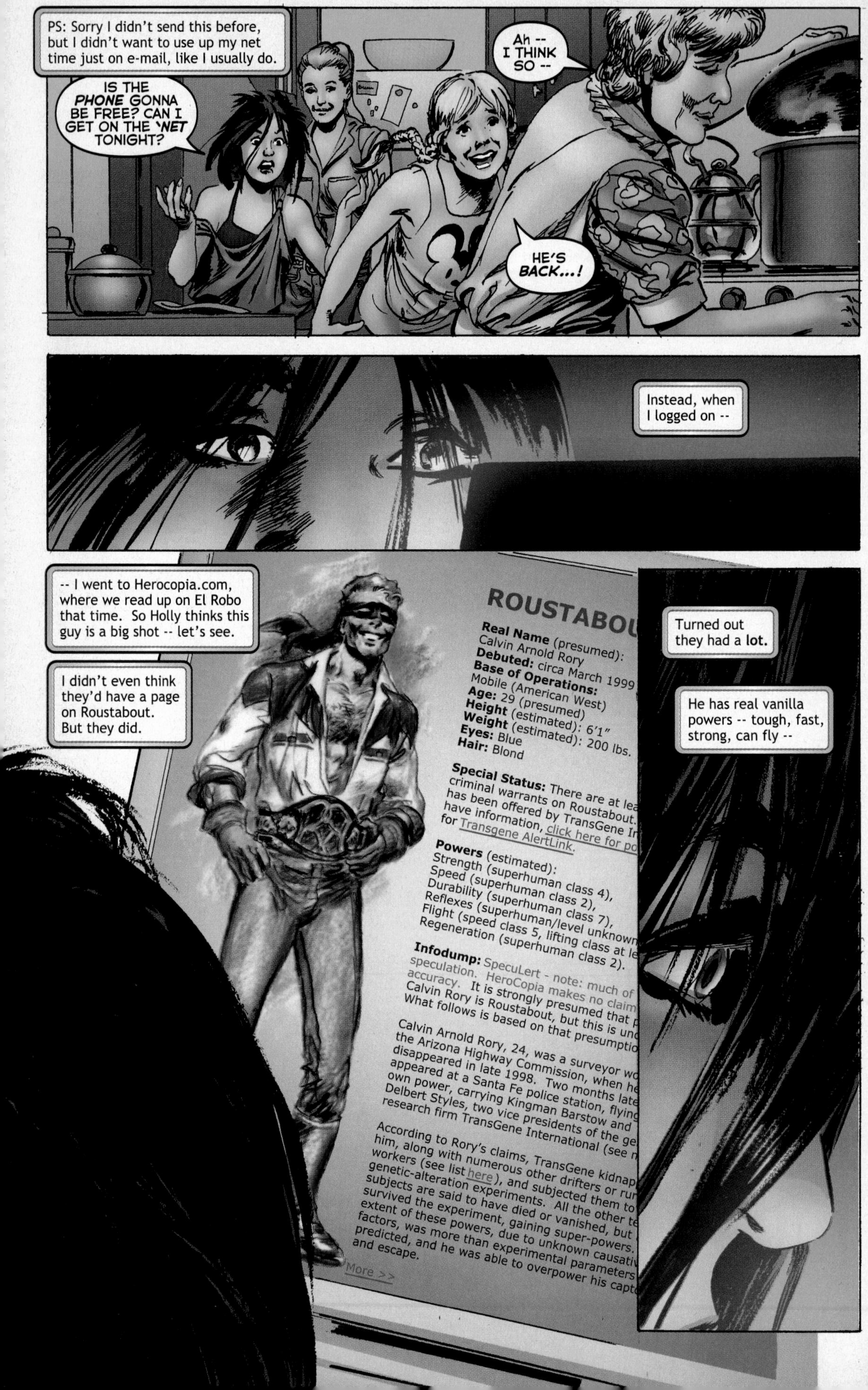

PS: Sorry I didn't send this before, but I didn't want to use up my net time just on e-mail, like I usually do.
IS THE PHONE GONNA BE FREE? CAN I GET ON THE 'NET TONIGHT?
Ah -- I THINK SO --
HE'S BACK...!
Instead, when I logged on --
-- I went to Herocopia.com, where we read up on El Robo that time. So Holly thinks this guy is a big shot -- let's see.
I didn't even think they'd have a page on Roustabout. But they did.
ROUSTABOU
Real Name (presumed): Calvin Arnold Rory
Debuted: circa March 1999
Base of Operations: Mobile (American West)
Age: 29 (presumed)
Height (estimated): 6'1"
Weight (estimated): 200 lbs.
Eyes: Blue
Hair: Blond
Powers (estimated):
Strength (superhuman class 4),
Speed (superhuman class 2),
Durability (superhuman class 7),
Reflexes (superhuman/level unknown
Regeneration (superhuman class 2).
More >>
Turned out they had a lot.
He has real vanilla powers -- tough, fast, strong, can fly --

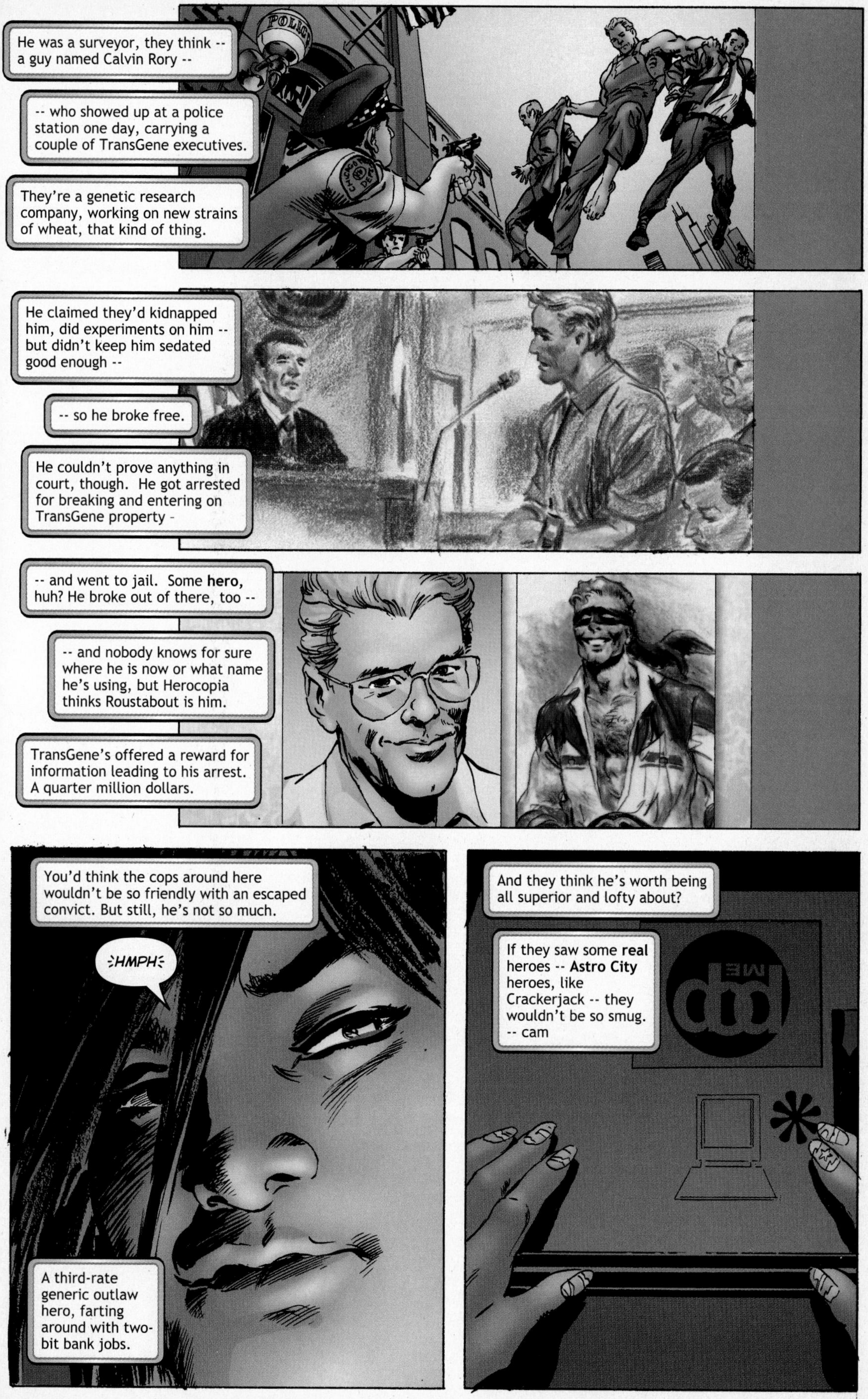
He was a surveyor, they think -- a guy named Calvin Rory --
-- who showed up at a police station one day, carrying a couple of TransGene executives.
They're a genetic research company, working on new strains of wheat, that kind of thing.
He claimed they'd kidnapped him, did experiments on him -- but didn't keep him sedated good enough --
-- so he broke free.
He couldn't prove anything in court, though. He got arrested for breaking and entering on TransGene property –
-- and went to jail. Some **hero,** huh? He broke out of there, too --
-- and nobody knows for sure where he is now or what name he's using, but Herocopia thinks Roustabout is him.
TransGene's offered a reward for information leading to his arrest. A quarter million dollars.
You'd think the cops around here wouldn't be so friendly with an escaped convict. But still, he's not so much.
HMPH
A third-rate generic outlaw hero, farting around with two-bit bank jobs.
And they think he's worth being all superior and lofty about?
If they saw some **real** heroes -- **Astro City** heroes, like Crackerjack -- they wouldn't be so smug. -- cam

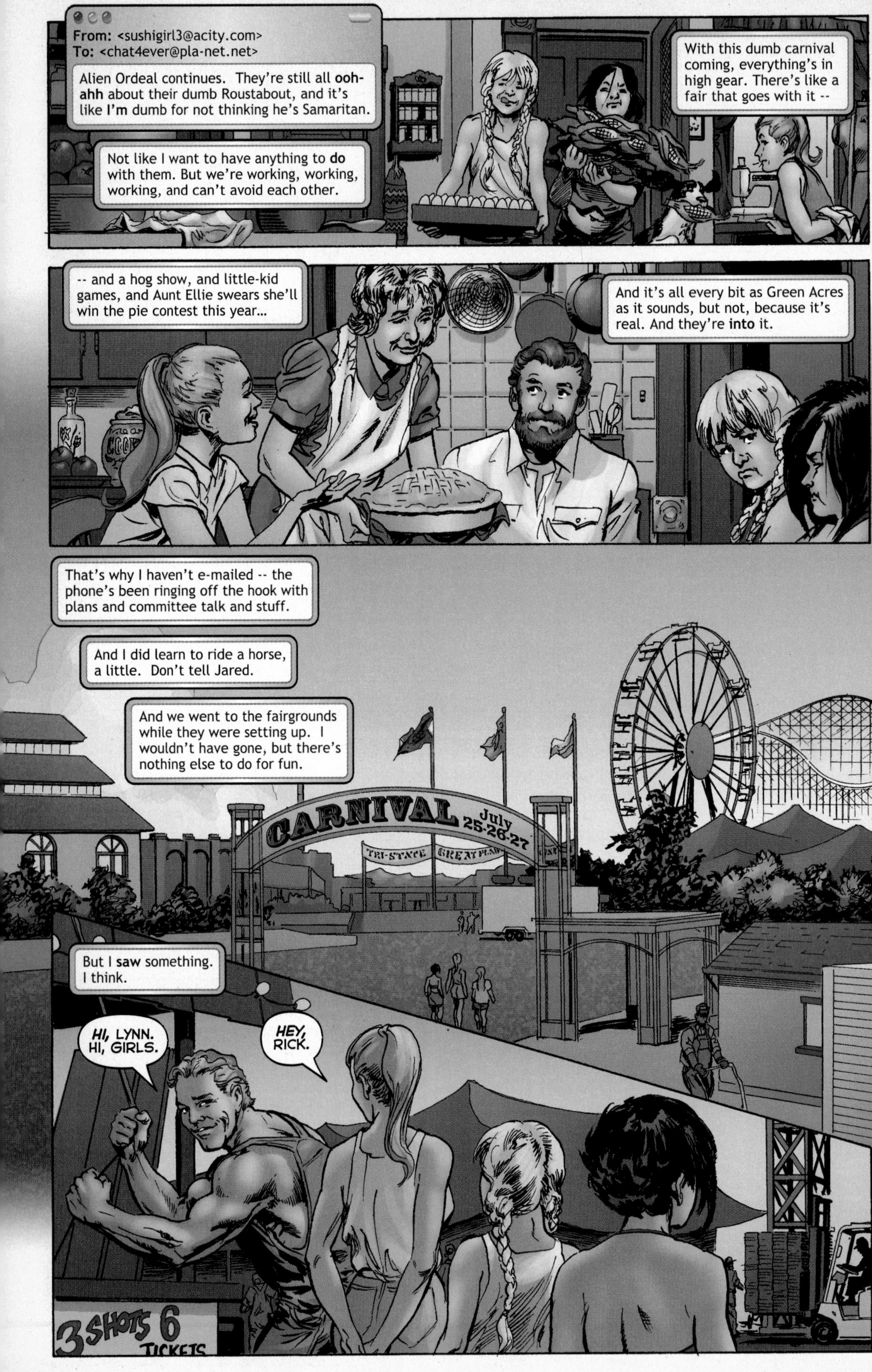
From: <sushigirl3@acity.com>
To: <chat4ever@pla-net.net>
Alien Ordeal continues. They're still all ooh-ahh about their dumb Roustabout, and it's like I'm dumb for not thinking he's Samaritan.
Not like I want to have anything to do with them. But we're working, working, working, and can't avoid each other.
With this dumb carnival coming, everything's in high gear. There's like a fair that goes with it --
-- and a hog show, and little-kid games, and Aunt Ellie swears she'll win the pie contest this year...
And it's all every bit as Green Acres as it sounds, but not, because it's real. And they're into it.
That's why I haven't e-mailed -- the phone's been ringing off the hook with plans and committee talk and stuff.
And I did learn to ride a horse, a little. Don't tell Jared.
And we went to the fairgrounds while they were setting up. I wouldn't have gone, but there's nothing else to do for fun.
CARNIVAL July 25-26-27
TRI-STATE GREAT PLA
But I saw something. I think.
HI, LYNN. HI, GIRLS.
HEY, RICK.
3 SHOTS 6 TICKETS

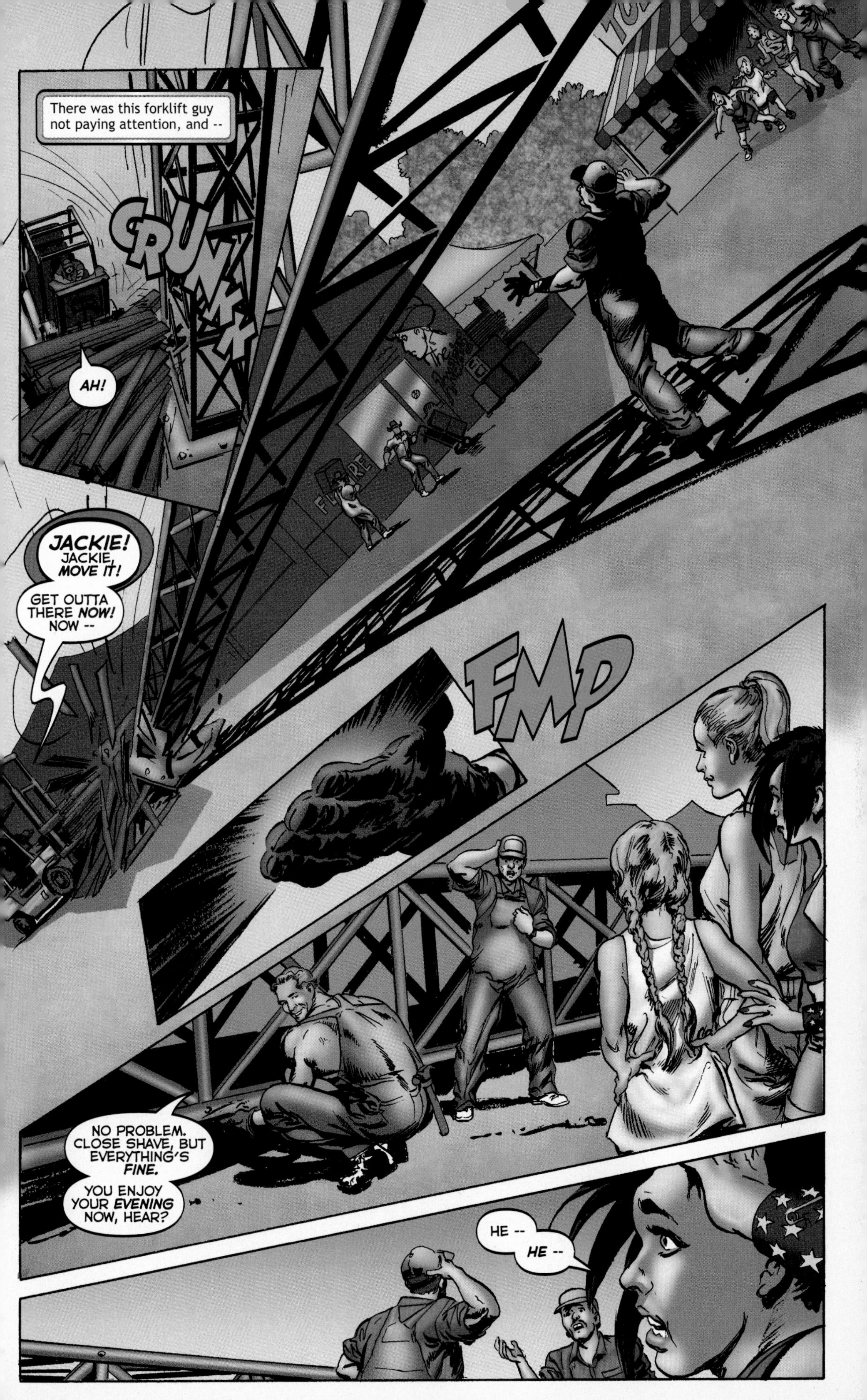
There was this forklift guy not paying attention, and --
CRUNKK
AH!
JACKIE! JACKIE, MOVE IT!
GET OUTTA THERE NOW! NOW --
FMP
NO PROBLEM. CLOSE SHAVE, BUT EVERYTHING'S FINE.
YOU ENJOY YOUR EVENING NOW, HEAR?
HE --
HE --

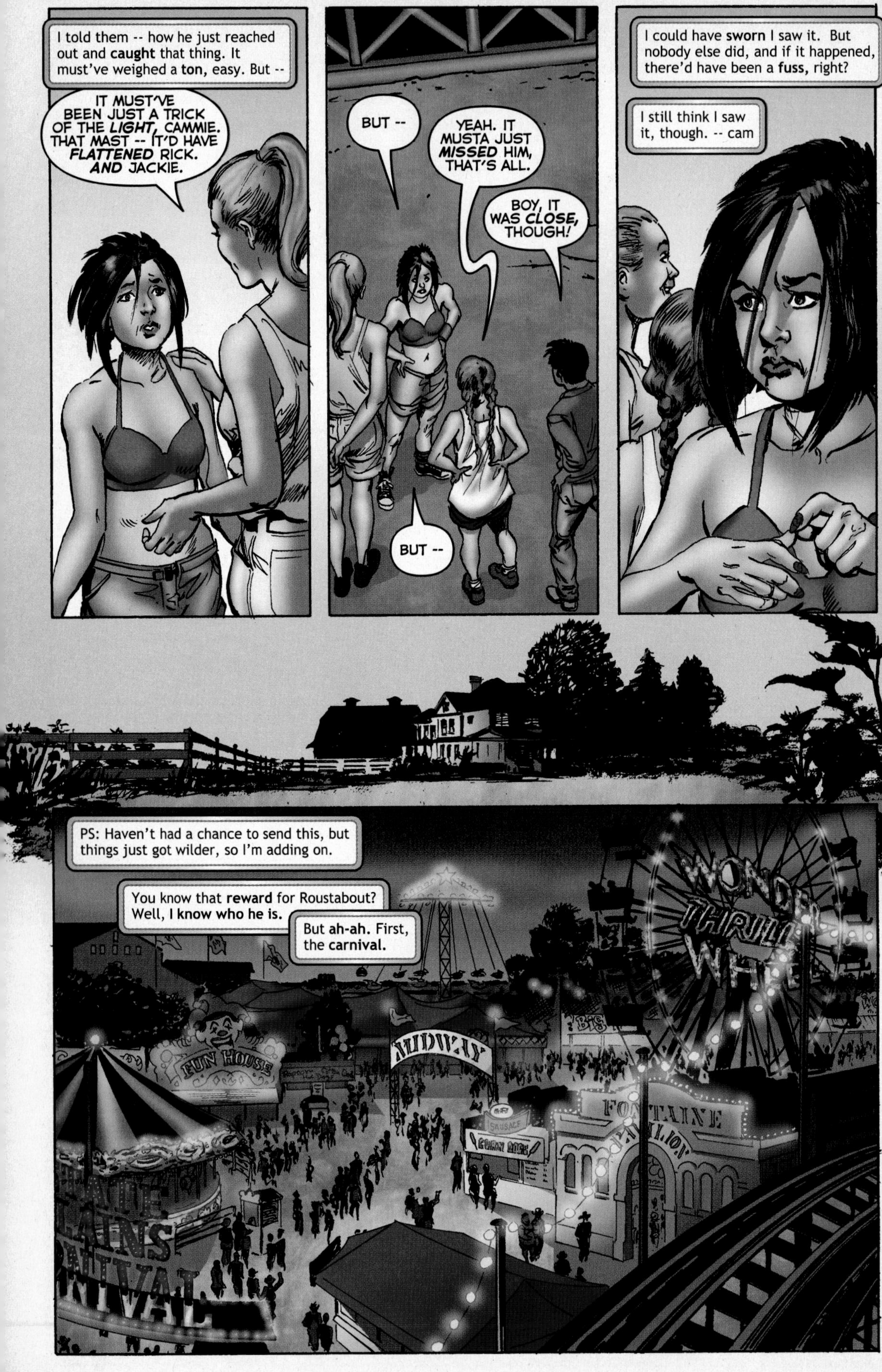

I told them -- how he just reached out and caught that thing. It must've weighed a ton, easy. But --
IT MUST'VE BEEN JUST A TRICK OF THE LIGHT, CAMMIE. THAT MAST -- IT'D HAVE FLATTENED RICK. AND JACKIE.
BUT --
YEAH. IT MUSTA JUST MISSED HIM, THAT'S ALL.
BOY, IT WAS CLOSE, THOUGH!
BUT --
I could have sworn I saw it. But nobody else did, and if it happened, there'd have been a fuss, right?
I still think I saw it, though. -- cam
PS: Haven't had a chance to send this, but things just got wilder, so I'm adding on.
You know that reward for Roustabout? Well, I know who he is.
But ah-ah. First, the carnival.
FUN HOUSE
MIDWAY
SAUSAGE
CORN DOGS
FONTAINE

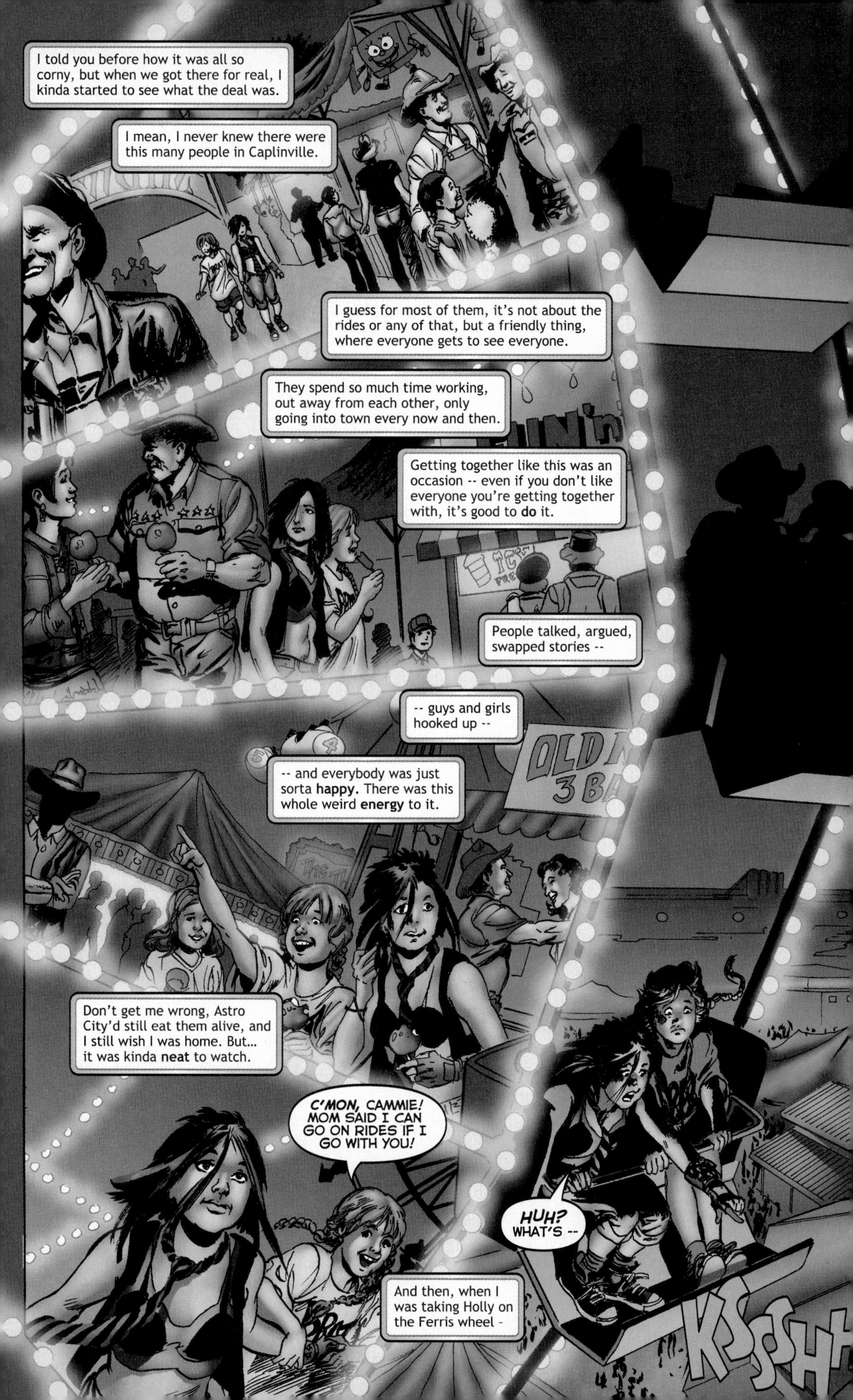
I told you before how it was all so corny, but when we got there for real, I kinda started to see what the deal was.
I mean, I never knew there were this many people in Caplinville.
I guess for most of them, it's not about the rides or any of that, but a friendly thing, where everyone gets to see everyone.
They spend so much time working, out away from each other, only going into town every now and then.
Getting together like this was an occasion -- even if you don't like everyone you're getting together with, it's good to **do** it.
People talked, argued, swapped stories --
-- guys and girls hooked up --
-- and everybody was just sorta **happy.** There was this whole weird **energy** to it.
Don't get me wrong, Astro City'd still eat them alive, and I still wish I was home. But... it was kinda **neat** to watch.
C'MON, CAMMIE! MOM SAID I CAN GO ON RIDES IF I GO WITH YOU!
And then, when I was taking Holly on the Ferris wheel -
HUH? WHAT'S --
KSSSH

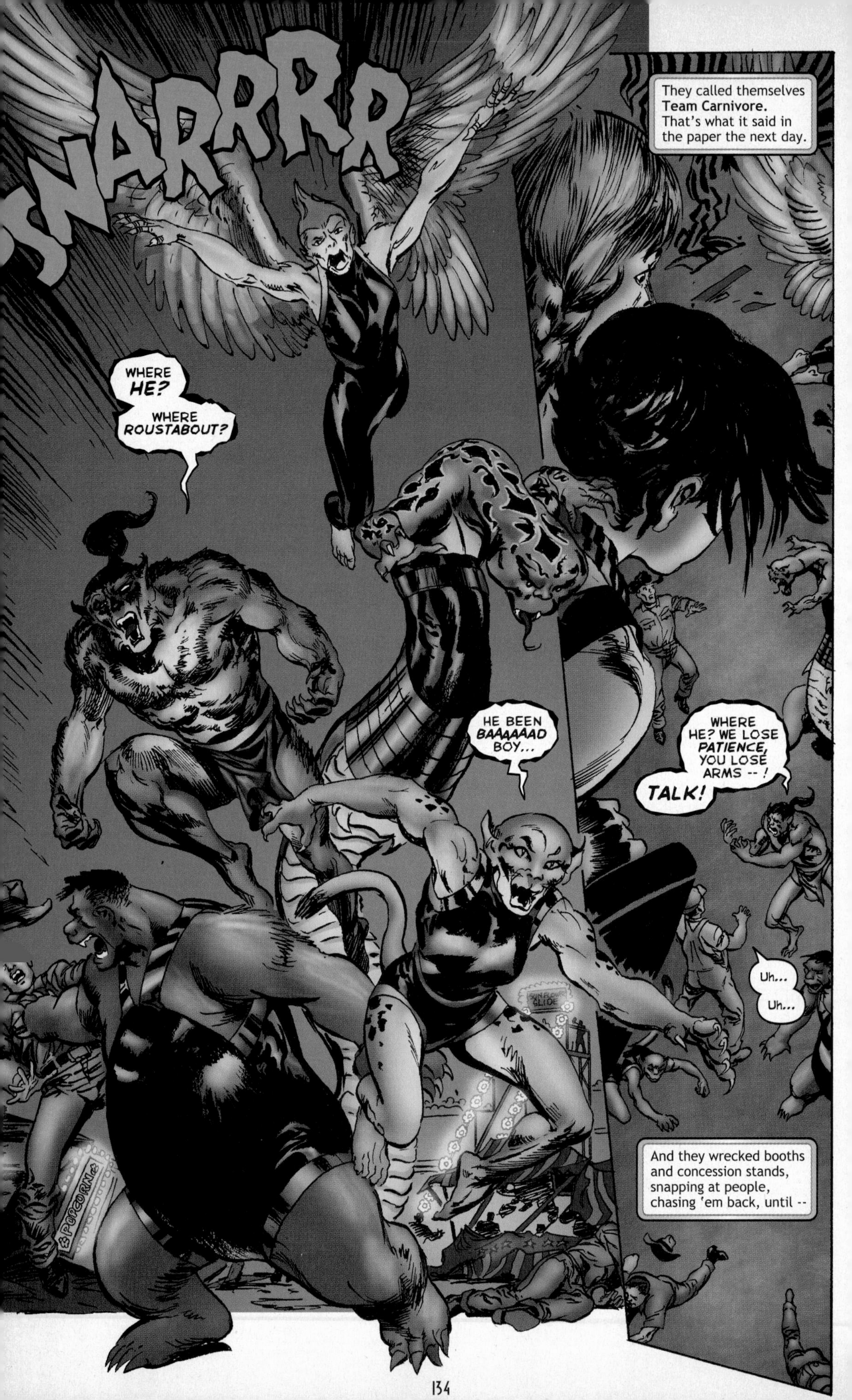
SNARRRR
They called themselves Team Carnivore. That's what it said in the paper the next day.
WHERE HE? WHERE ROUSTABOUT?
HE BEEN BAAAAAAD BOY...
WHERE HE? WE LOSE PATIENCE, YOU LOSE ARMS -- ! TALK!
Uh...
Uh...
And they wrecked booths and concession stands, snapping at people, chasing 'em back, until --

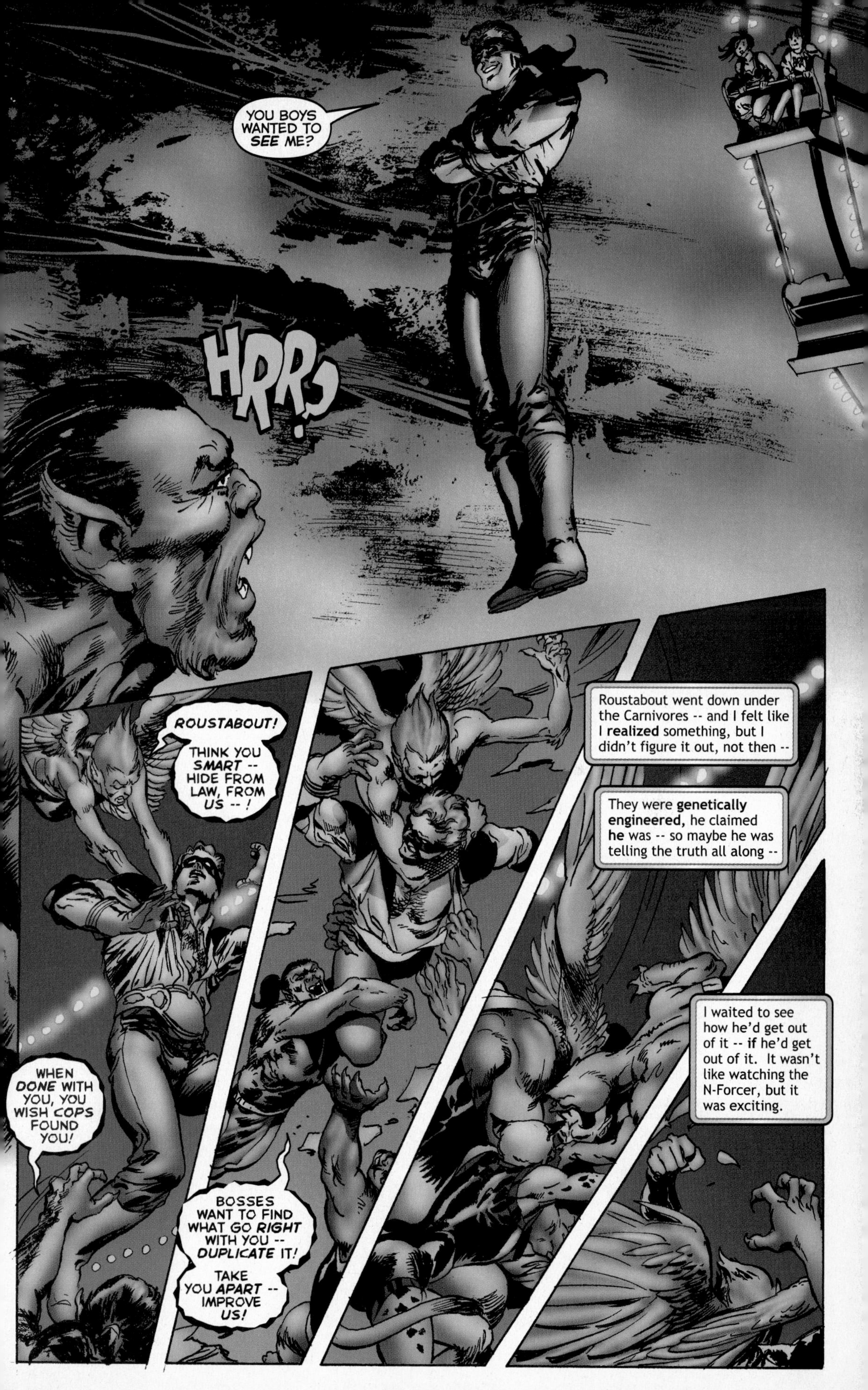
YOU BOYS WANTED TO SEE ME?
HRR?!
ROUSTABOUT!
THINK YOU SMART -- HIDE FROM LAW, FROM US -- !
WHEN DONE WITH YOU, YOU WISH COPS FOUND YOU!
BOSSES WANT TO FIND WHAT GO RIGHT WITH YOU -- DUPLICATE IT!
TAKE YOU APART -- IMPROVE US!
Roustabout went down under the Carnivores -- and I felt like I realized something, but I didn't figure it out, not then --
They were genetically engineered, he claimed he was -- so maybe he was telling the truth all along --
I waited to see how he'd get out of it -- if he'd get out of it. It wasn't like watching the N-Forcer, but it was exciting.

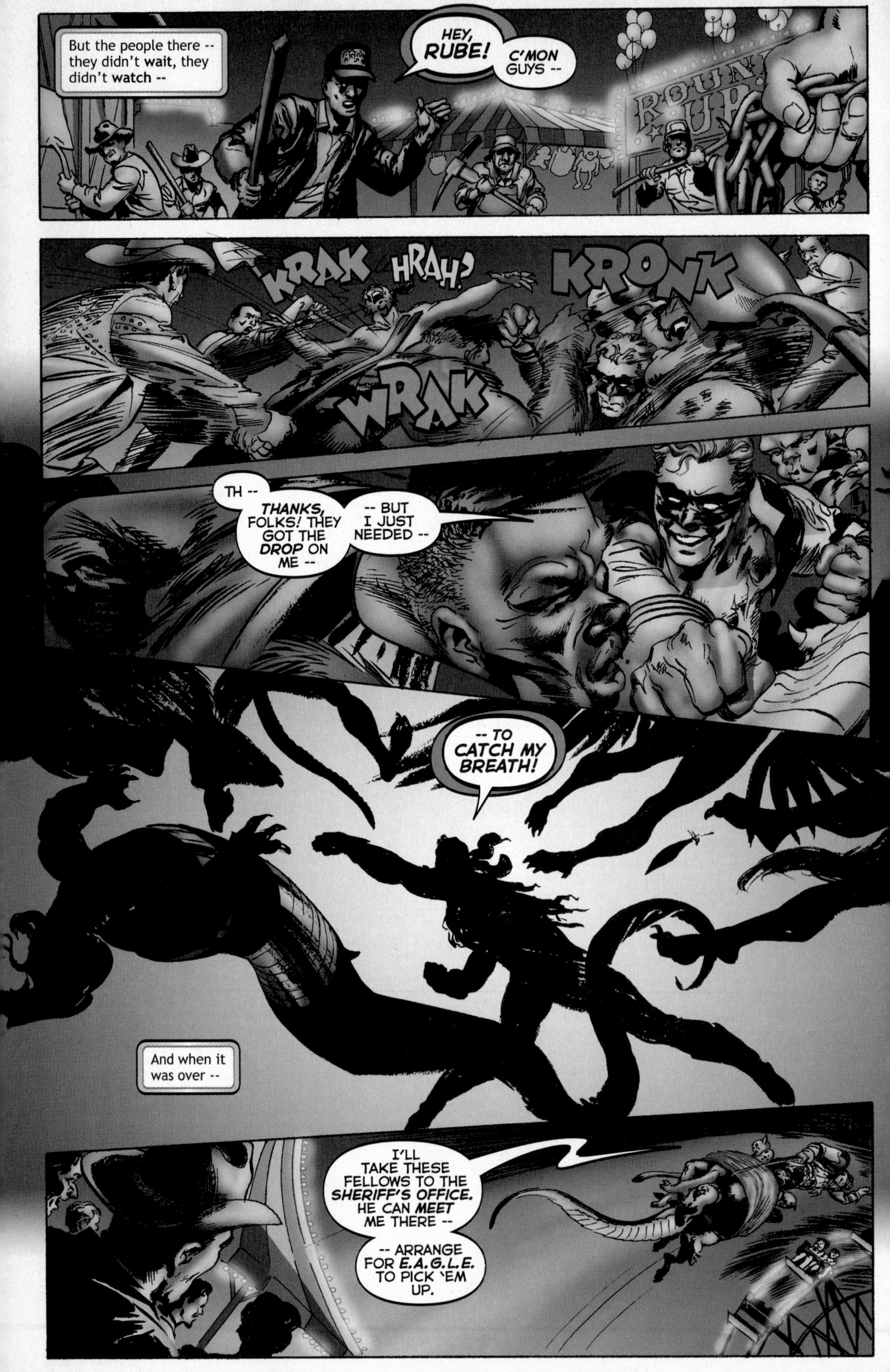
But the people there -- they didn't **wait,** they didn't **watch** --
HEY, RUBE!
C'MON GUYS --
KRAK
HRAH?
KRONK
WRAK
TH --
THANKS, FOLKS! THEY GOT THE DROP ON ME --
-- BUT I JUST NEEDED --
-- TO CATCH MY BREATH!
And when it was over --
I'LL TAKE THESE FELLOWS TO THE SHERIFF'S OFFICE. HE CAN MEET ME THERE --
-- ARRANGE FOR E.A.G.L.E. TO PICK 'EM UP.

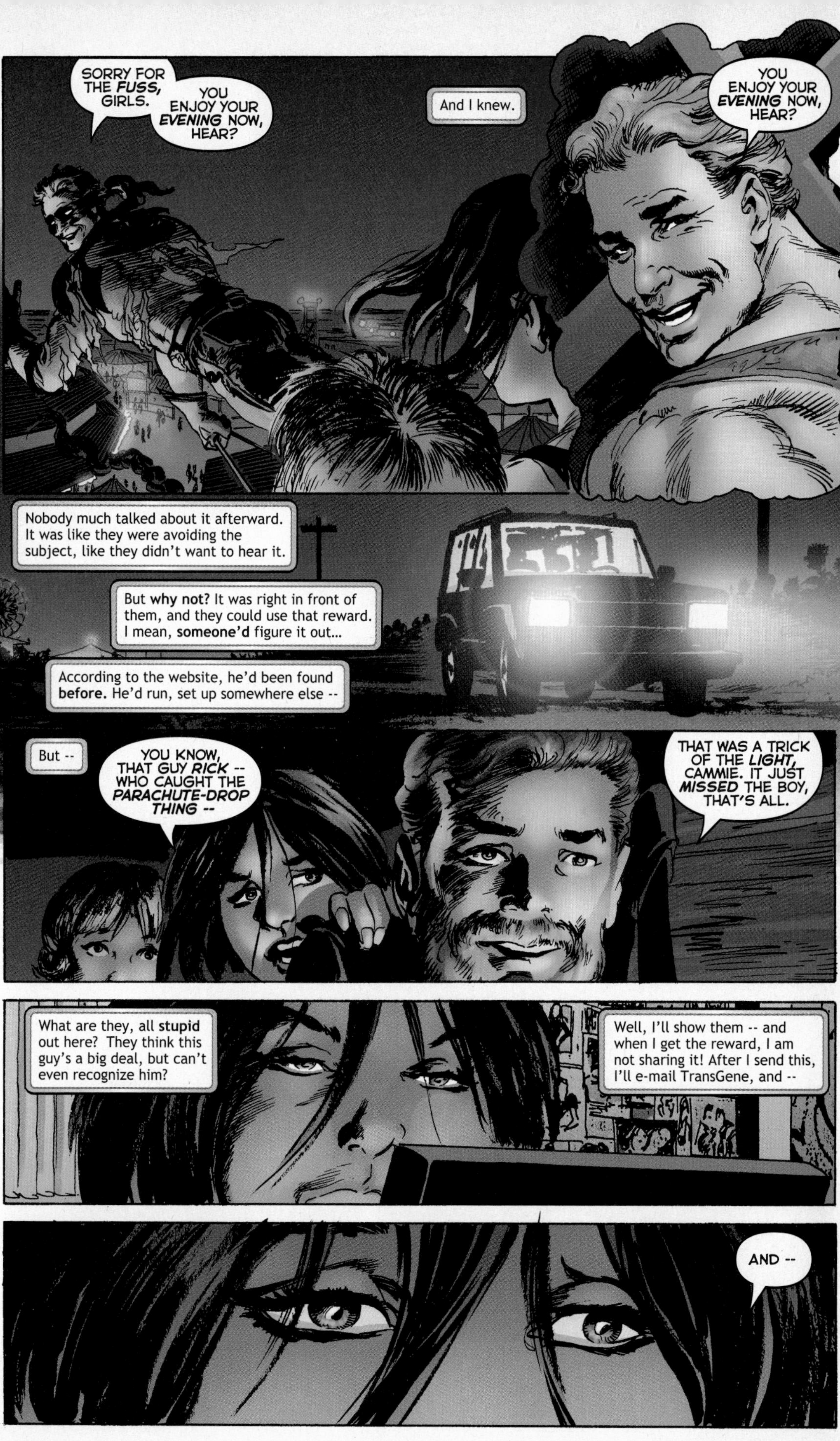
SORRY FOR THE FUSS, GIRLS.
YOU ENJOY YOUR EVENING NOW, HEAR?
And I knew.
YOU ENJOY YOUR EVENING NOW, HEAR?
Nobody much talked about it afterward. It was like they were avoiding the subject, like they didn't want to hear it.
But why not? It was right in front of them, and they could use that reward. I mean, someone'd figure it out...
According to the website, he'd been found before. He'd run, set up somewhere else --
But --
YOU KNOW, THAT GUY RICK -- WHO CAUGHT THE PARACHUTE-DROP THING --
THAT WAS A TRICK OF THE LIGHT, CAMMIE. IT JUST MISSED THE BOY, THAT'S ALL.
What are they, all stupid out here? They think this guy's a big deal, but can't even recognize him?
Well, I'll show them -- and when I get the reward, I am not sharing it! After I send this, I'll e-mail TransGene, and --
AND --

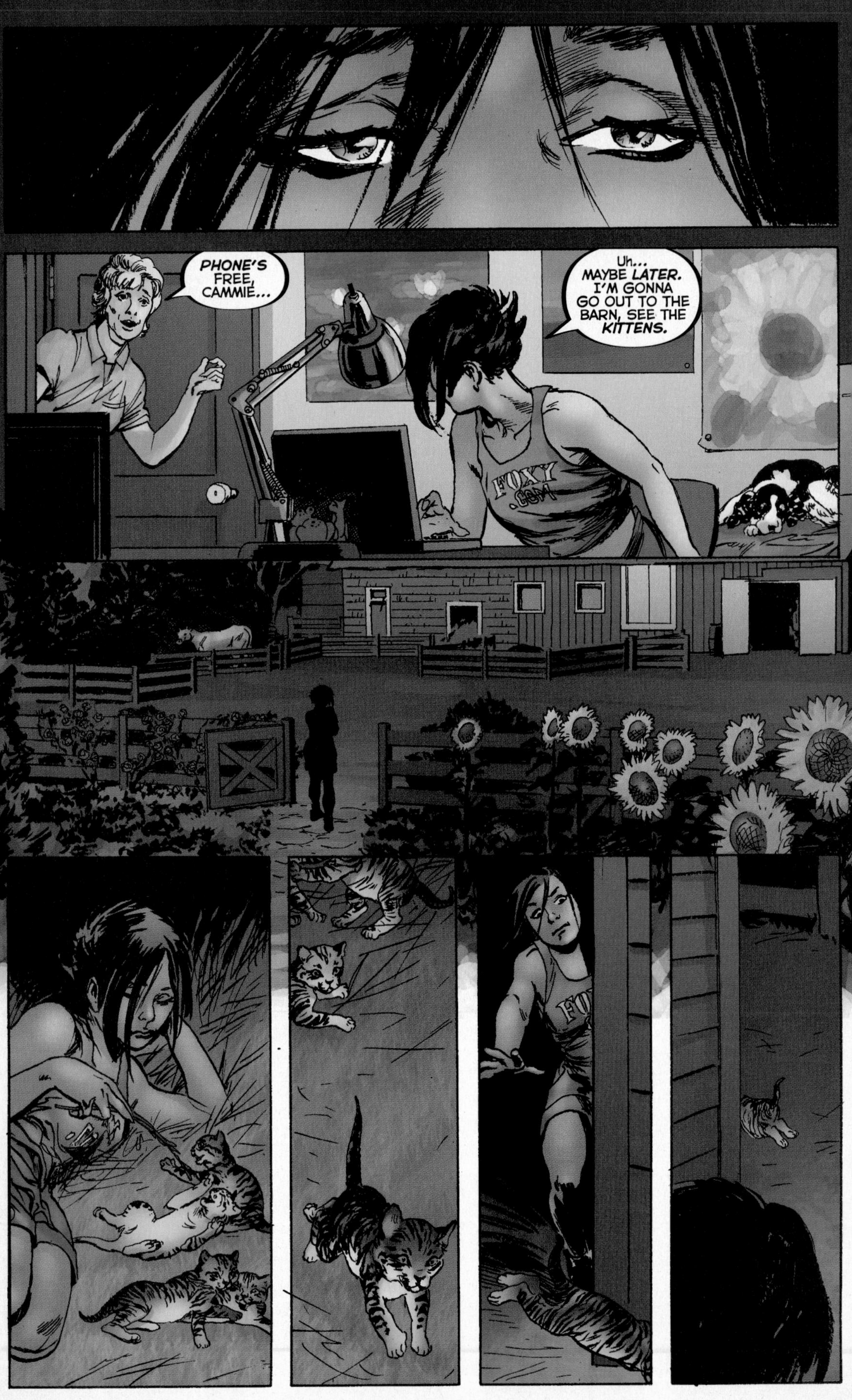
PHONE'S FREE, CAMMIE...
Uh... MAYBE LATER. I'M GONNA GO OUT TO THE BARN, SEE THE KITTENS.
FOXY .COM

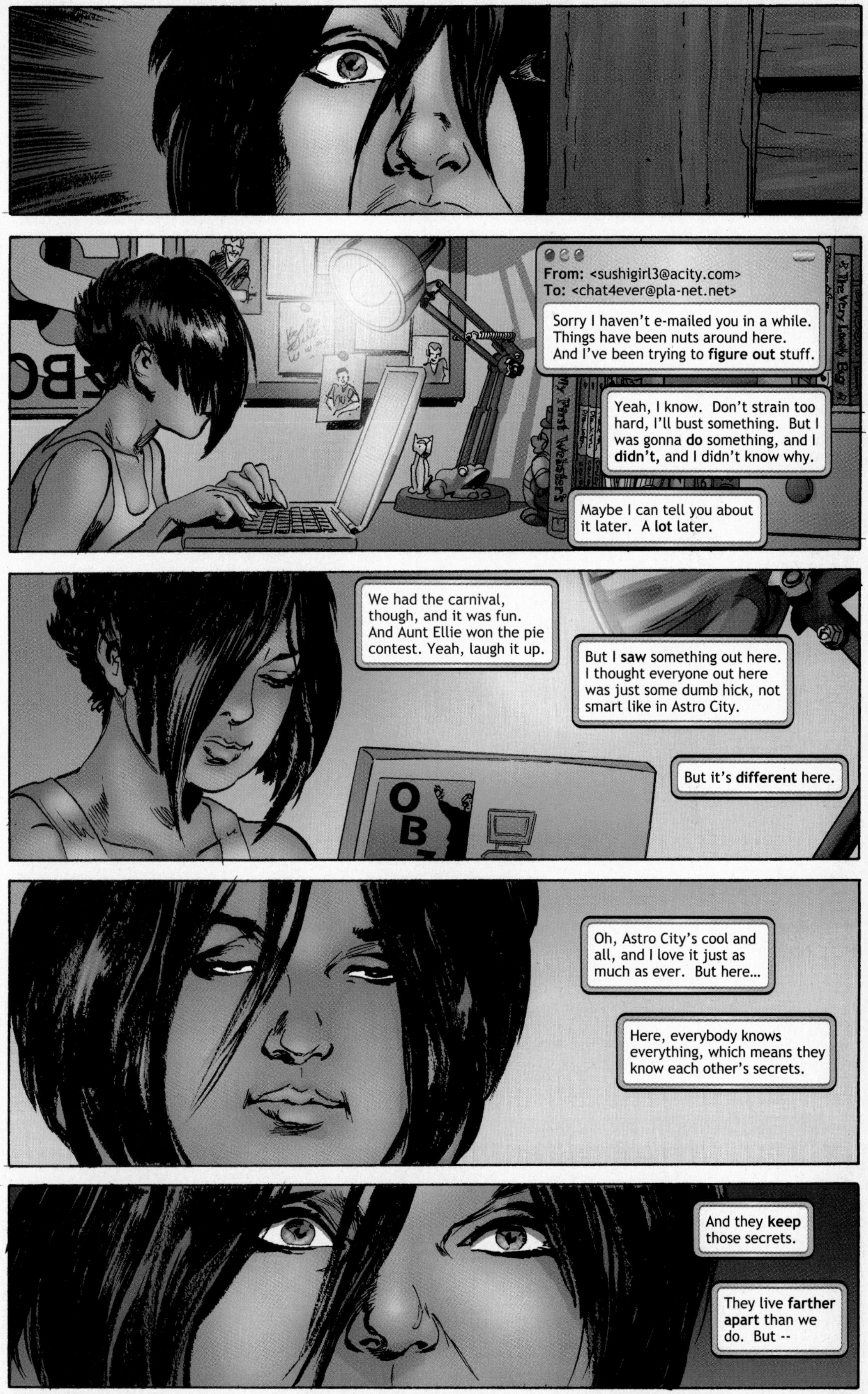
From: <sushigirl3@acity.com>
To: <chat4ever@pla-net.net>
Sorry I haven't e-mailed you in a while. Things have been nuts around here. And I've been trying to **figure out** stuff.
Yeah, I know. Don't strain too hard, I'll bust something. But I was gonna **do** something, and I **didn't**, and I didn't know why.
Maybe I can tell you about it later. A **lot** later.
We had the carnival, though, and it was fun. And Aunt Ellie won the pie contest. Yeah, laugh it up.
But I **saw** something out here. I thought everyone out here was just some dumb hick, not smart like in Astro City.
But it's **different** here.
Oh, Astro City's cool and all, and I love it just as much as ever. But here...
Here, everybody knows everything, which means they know each other's secrets.
And they **keep** those secrets.
They live **farther apart** than we do. But --

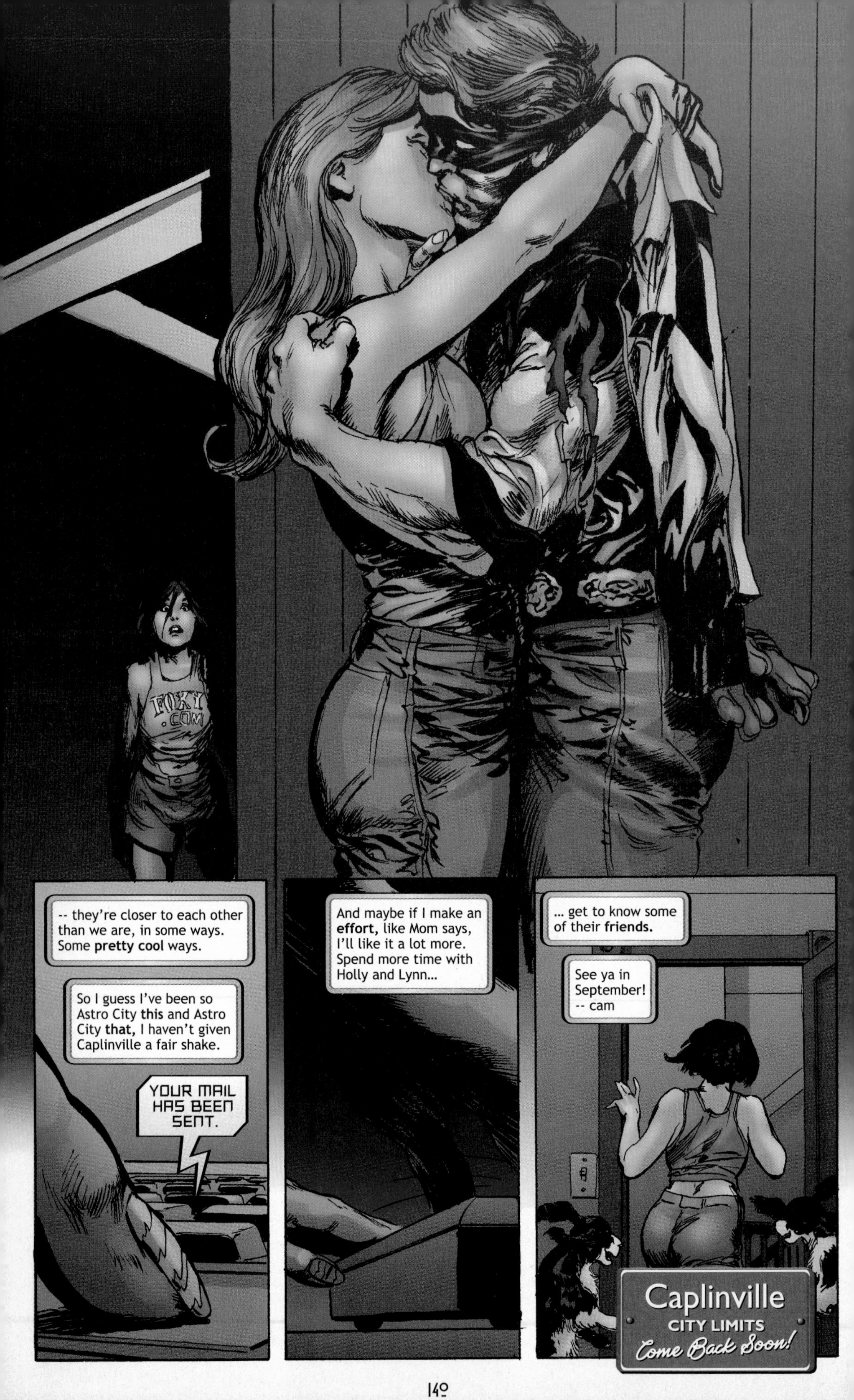
FOXY
.COM
-- they're closer to each other than we are, in some ways. Some pretty cool ways.
So I guess I've been so Astro City this and Astro City that, I haven't given Caplinville a fair shake.
YOUR MAIL HAS BEEN SENT.
And maybe if I make an effort, like Mom says, I'll like it a lot more. Spend more time with Holly and Lynn...
... get to know some of their friends.
See ya in September! -- cam
Caplinville
CITY LIMITS
Come Back Soon!

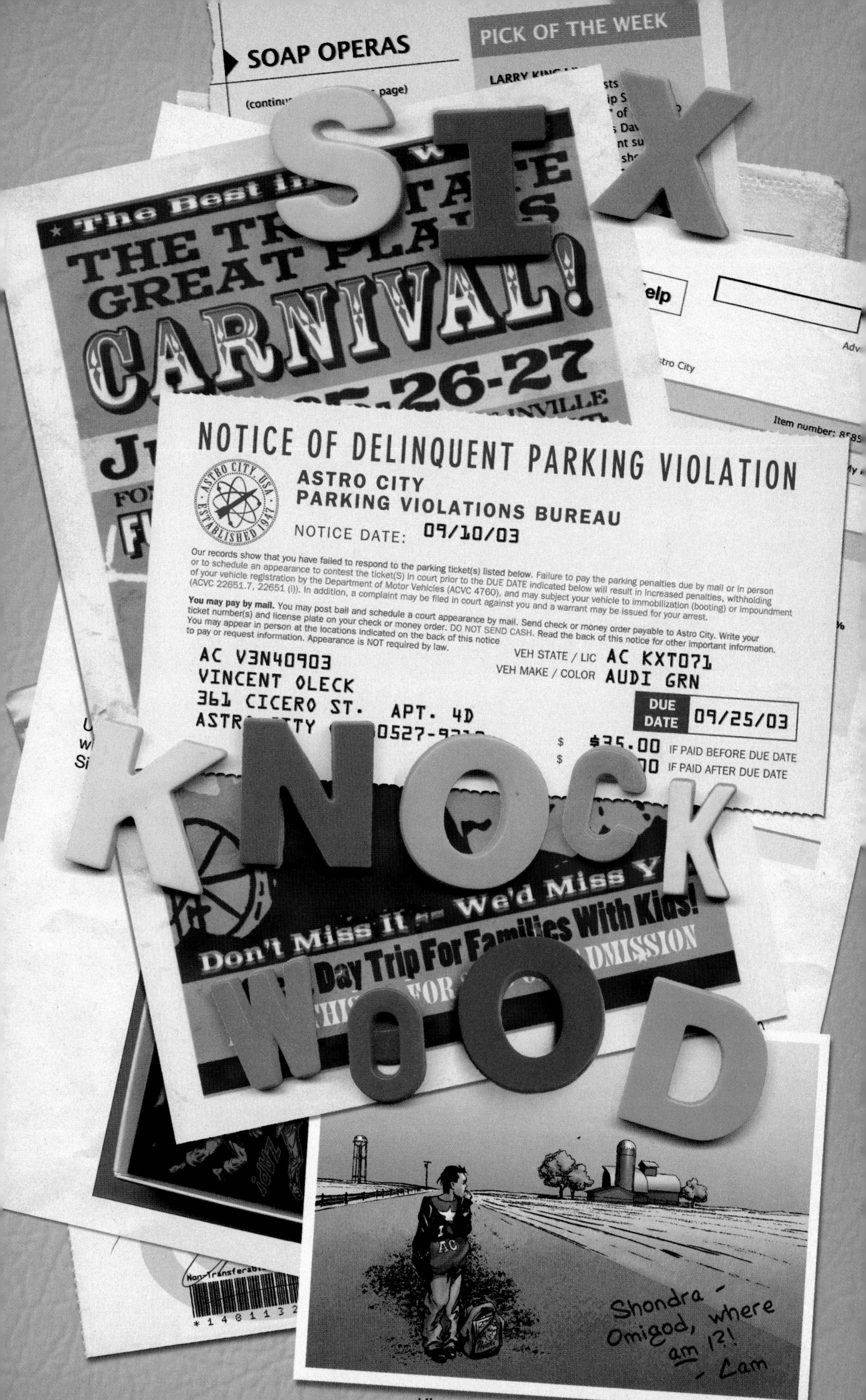
SIX
KNOCK
WOOD
SOAP OPERAS
PICK OF THE WEEK
THE GREAT CARNIVAL!
26-27
NOTICE OF DELINQUENT PARKING VIOLATION
ASTRO CITY, USA · ESTABLISHED 1947
ASTRO CITY
PARKING VIOLATIONS BUREAU
NOTICE DATE: 09/10/03
Our records show that you have failed to respond to the parking ticket(s) listed below. Failure to pay the parking penalties due by mail or in person or to schedule an appearance to contest the ticket(S) in court prior to the DUE DATE indicated below will result in increased penalties, withholding of your vehicle registration by the Department of Motor Vehicles (ACVC 4760), and may subject your vehicle to immobilization (booting) or impoundment (ACVC 22651.7, 22651 (i)). In addition, a complaint may be filed in court against you and a warrant may be issued for your arrest.
You may pay by mail. You may post bail and schedule a court appearance by mail. Send check or money order payable to Astro City. Write your ticket number(s) and license plate on your check or money order. DO NOT SEND CASH. Read the back of this notice for other important information. You may appear in person at the locations indicated on the back of this notice to pay or request information. Appearance is NOT required by law.
AC V3N40903
VINCENT OLECK
361 CICERO ST. APT. 4D
VEH STATE / LIC AC KXT071
VEH MAKE / COLOR AUDI GRN
DUE DATE 09/25/03
IF PAID BEFORE DUE DATE
IF PAID AFTER DUE DATE
Don't Miss It -- We'd Miss
Day Trip For Families With Kids!
Non-Transferable
Shondra - Omigod, where am I?! - Cam

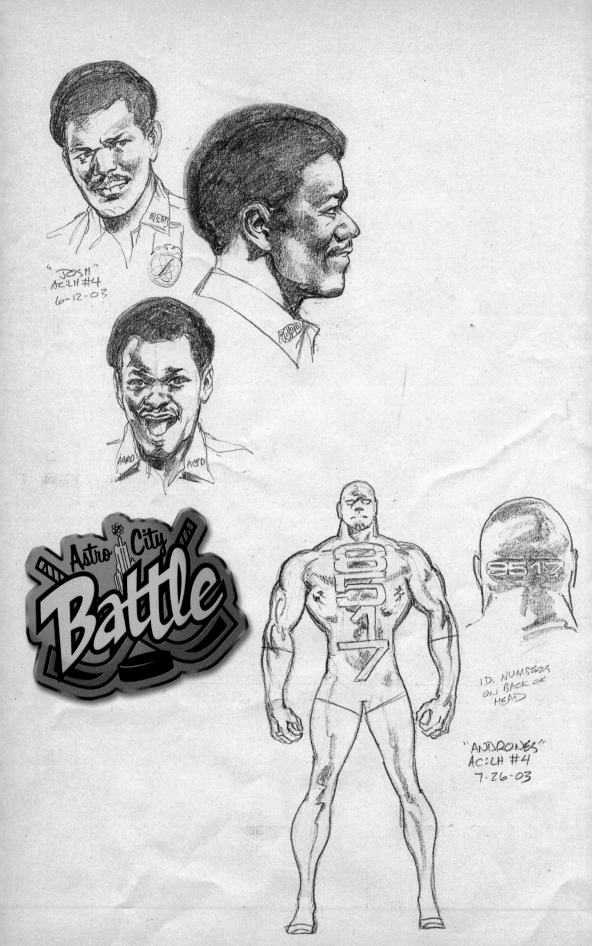

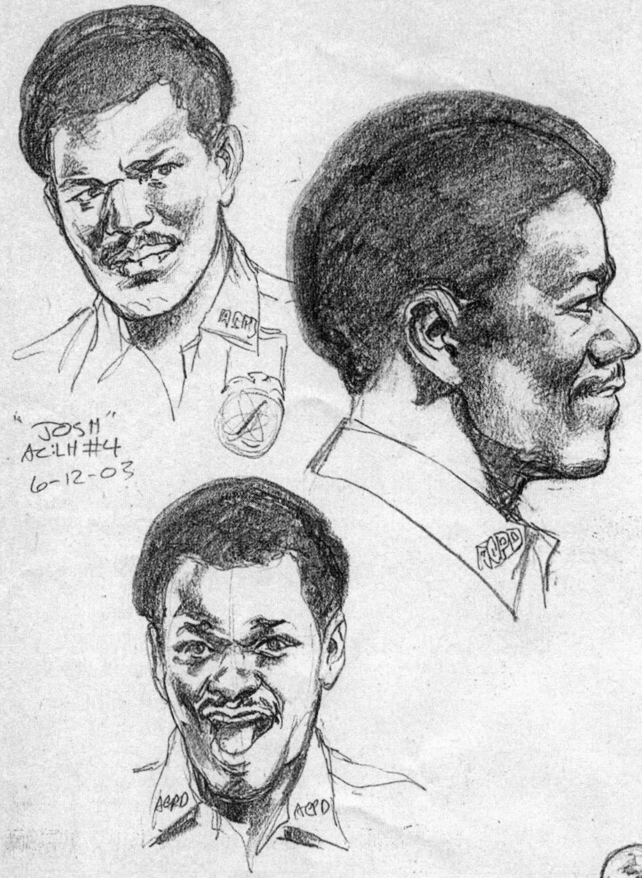
"JOSH"
AC:LH #4
6-12-03
ACPD
ACPD
ACPD
ACPD

Astro City Battle

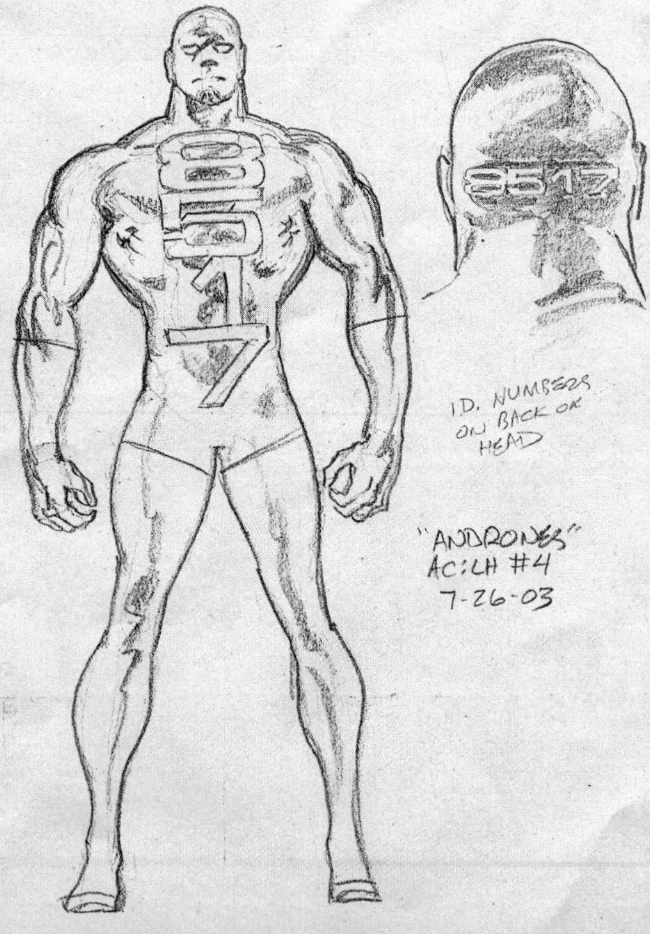
8517
8517
I.D. NUMBERS ON BACK OF HEAD
"ANDRONES"
AC:LH #4
7-26-03

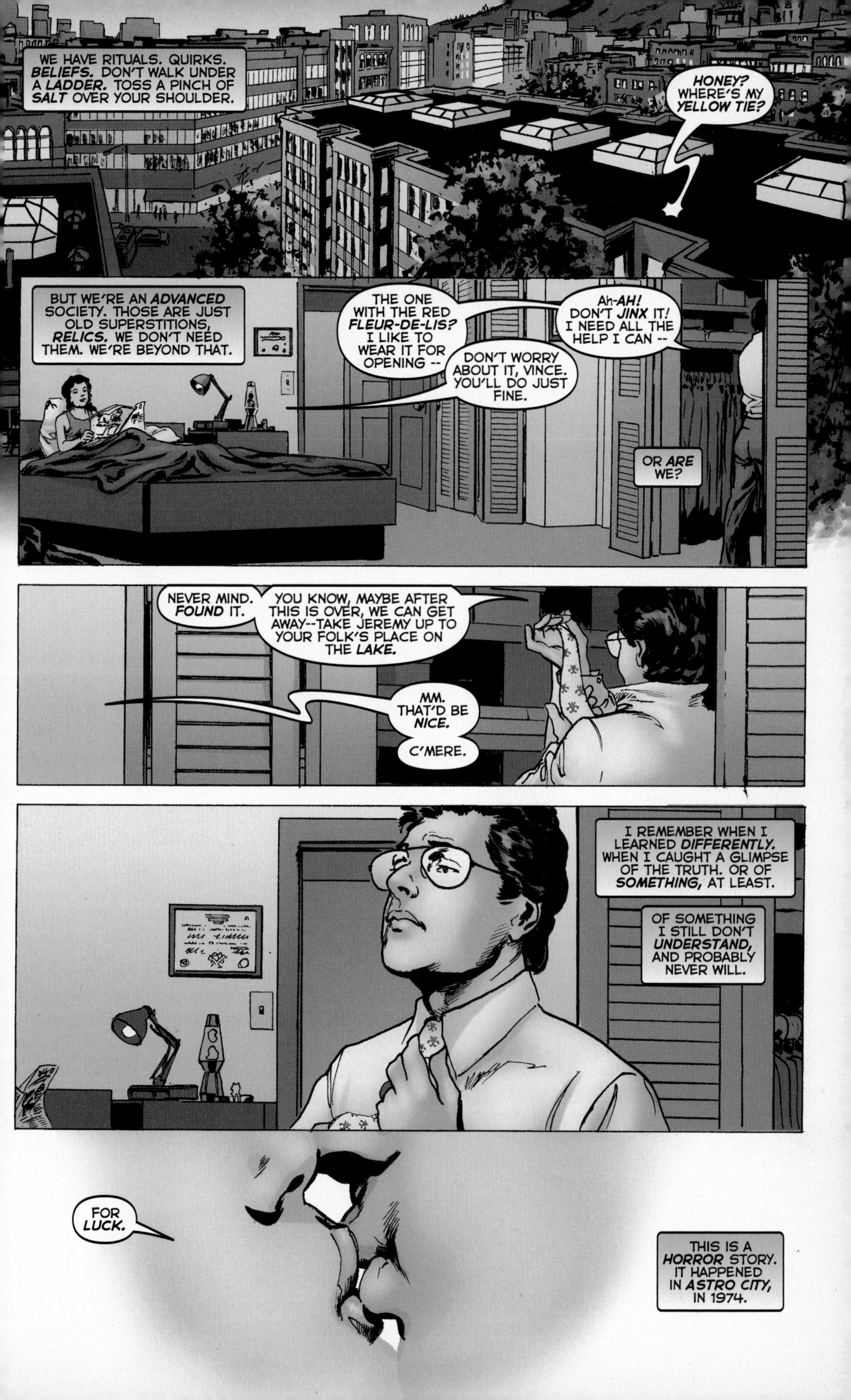
WE HAVE RITUALS. QUIRKS. BELIEFS. DON'T WALK UNDER A LADDER. TOSS A PINCH OF SALT OVER YOUR SHOULDER.
HONEY? WHERE'S MY YELLOW TIE?
BUT WE'RE AN ADVANCED SOCIETY. THOSE ARE JUST OLD SUPERSTITIONS, RELICS. WE DON'T NEED THEM. WE'RE BEYOND THAT.
THE ONE WITH THE RED FLEUR-DE-LIS? I LIKE TO WEAR IT FOR OPENING --
Ah-AH! DON'T JINX IT! I NEED ALL THE HELP I CAN --
DON'T WORRY ABOUT IT, VINCE. YOU'LL DO JUST FINE.
OR ARE WE?
NEVER MIND. FOUND IT.
YOU KNOW, MAYBE AFTER THIS IS OVER, WE CAN GET AWAY--TAKE JEREMY UP TO YOUR FOLK'S PLACE ON THE LAKE.
MM. THAT'D BE NICE.
C'MERE.
I REMEMBER WHEN I LEARNED DIFFERENTLY. WHEN I CAUGHT A GLIMPSE OF THE TRUTH. OR OF SOMETHING, AT LEAST.
OF SOMETHING I STILL DON'T UNDERSTAND, AND PROBABLY NEVER WILL.
FOR LUCK.
THIS IS A HORROR STORY. IT HAPPENED IN ASTRO CITY, IN 1974.

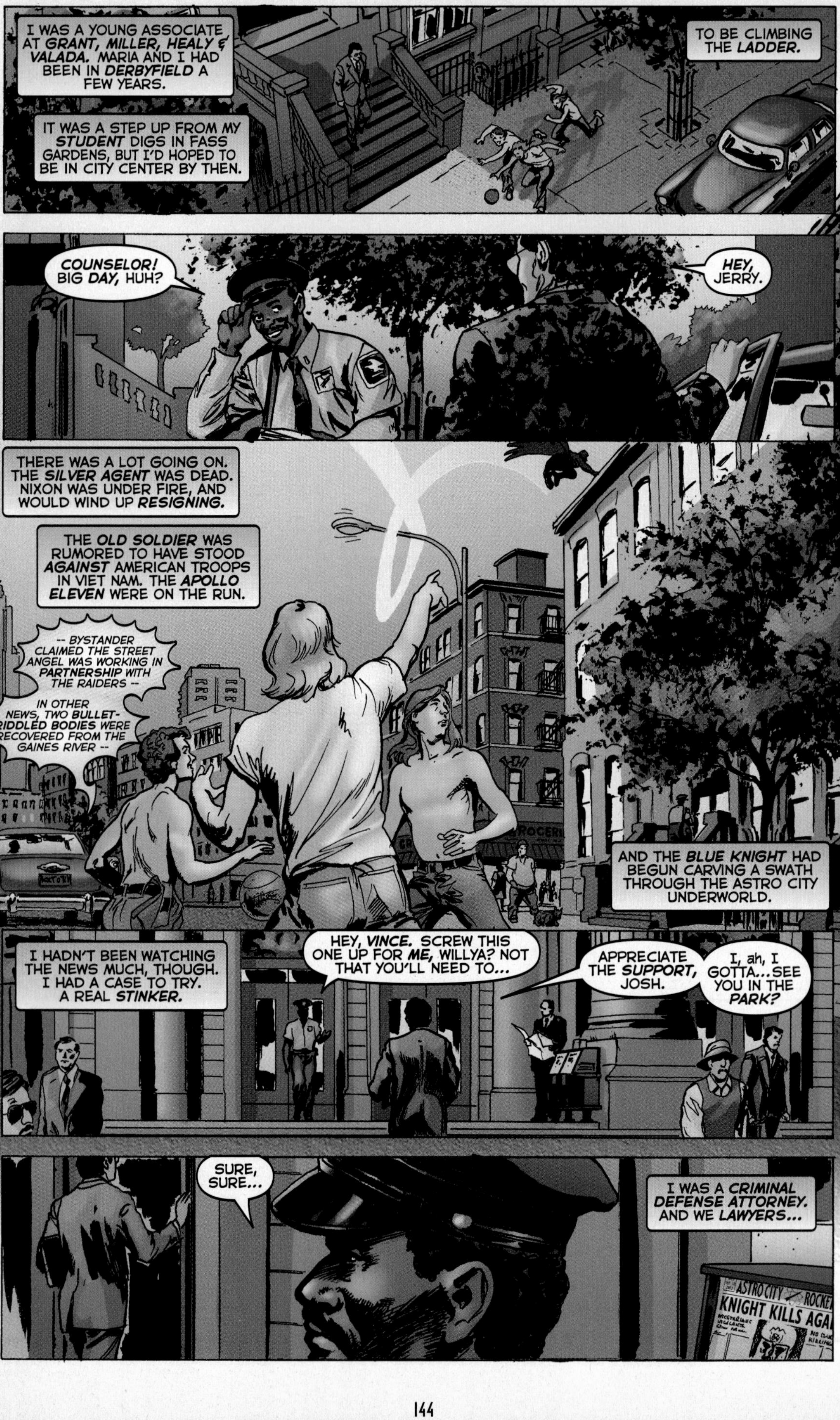
I WAS A YOUNG ASSOCIATE AT GRANT, MILLER, HEALY & VALADA. MARIA AND I HAD BEEN IN DERBYFIELD A FEW YEARS.
IT WAS A STEP UP FROM MY STUDENT DIGS IN FASS GARDENS, BUT I'D HOPED TO BE IN CITY CENTER BY THEN.
TO BE CLIMBING THE LADDER.
COUNSELOR! BIG DAY, HUH?
HEY, JERRY.
THERE WAS A LOT GOING ON. THE SILVER AGENT WAS DEAD. NIXON WAS UNDER FIRE, AND WOULD WIND UP RESIGNING.
THE OLD SOLDIER WAS RUMORED TO HAVE STOOD AGAINST AMERICAN TROOPS IN VIET NAM. THE APOLLO ELEVEN WERE ON THE RUN.
-- BYSTANDER CLAIMED THE STREET ANGEL WAS WORKING IN PARTNERSHIP WITH THE RAIDERS --
IN OTHER NEWS, TWO BULLET-RIDDLED BODIES WERE RECOVERED FROM THE GAINES RIVER --
AND THE BLUE KNIGHT HAD BEGUN CARVING A SWATH THROUGH THE ASTRO CITY UNDERWORLD.
I HADN'T BEEN WATCHING THE NEWS MUCH, THOUGH. I HAD A CASE TO TRY. A REAL STINKER.
HEY, VINCE. SCREW THIS ONE UP FOR ME, WILLYA? NOT THAT YOU'LL NEED TO...
APPRECIATE THE SUPPORT, JOSH.
I, ah, I GOTTA...SEE YOU IN THE PARK?
SURE, SURE...
I WAS A CRIMINAL DEFENSE ATTORNEY. AND WE LAWYERS...
ASTRO CITY
KNIGHT KILLS

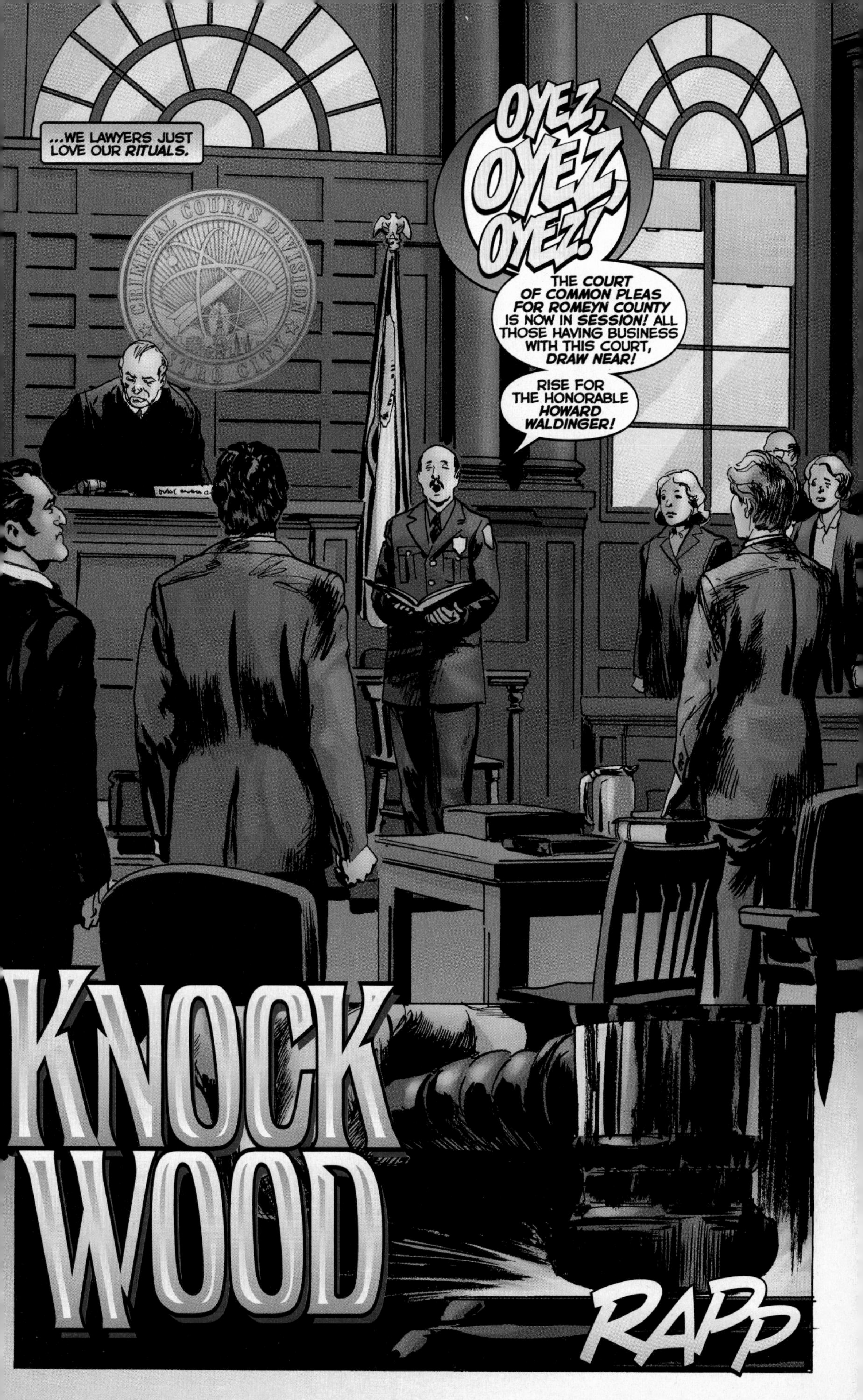
...WE LAWYERS JUST LOVE OUR RITUALS.
CRIMINAL COURTS DIVISION
OYEZ, OYEZ, OYEZ!
THE COURT OF COMMON PLEAS FOR ROMEYN COUNTY IS NOW IN SESSION! ALL THOSE HAVING BUSINESS WITH THIS COURT, DRAW NEAR!
RISE FOR THE HONORABLE HOWARD WALDINGER!
KNOCK WOOD
RAPP

YOUR HONOR, LADIES AND GENTLEMEN OF THE *JURY.*

WE WILL SHOW *BEYOND* A REASONABLE DOUBT THAT ON MARCH 15TH, THE DEFENDANT DID *KNOWINGLY* AND *BRUTALLY* --

THE FACTS OF THE CASE LOOKED DEPRESSINGLY *SIMPLE.*

ON *MARCH 15, 1974,* A YOUNG, ATTRACTIVE COUPLE STOPPED IN AT *TALLARICO'S,* A DINNER AND DANCE PLACE NEAR KAMEN STREET.

THEY *ARGUED.* OVER HER ALLEGED FRIENDSHIP WITH ANOTHER *MAN.*

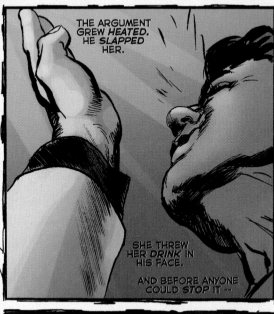

THE ARGUMENT GREW *HEATED.* HE *SLAPPED* HER.

SHE THREW HER *DRINK* IN HIS FACE.

AND BEFORE ANYONE COULD *STOP* IT --

-- HE CLUBBED HER TO DEATH WITH A BOTTLE OF *1924 BOLLE-HOLLINGSWORTH,* IN FRONT OF 59 WITNESSES.

SHE WAS IDENTIFIED AS *LISETTE PALAIS,* A SECRETARY.

HE WAS IDENTIFIED AS *RICHIE FORGIONE,* SECOND SON OF *"JUNIOR"* FORGIONE. THE REPUTED EASTSIDE *MOB BOSS.*

-- *TESTIMONY* AND *FORENSIC EVIDENCE* WILL SHOW --

RICHIE WAS MY *CLIENT,* AND MY READING ON IT WAS HE WAS *GUILTY* AS HELL.

BUT I WAS A *DEFENSE ATTORNEY.* MY JOB WASN'T TO *JUDGE* THE CASE, BUT TO PUT THE BURDEN OF PROOF ON THE *PROSECUTOR* --

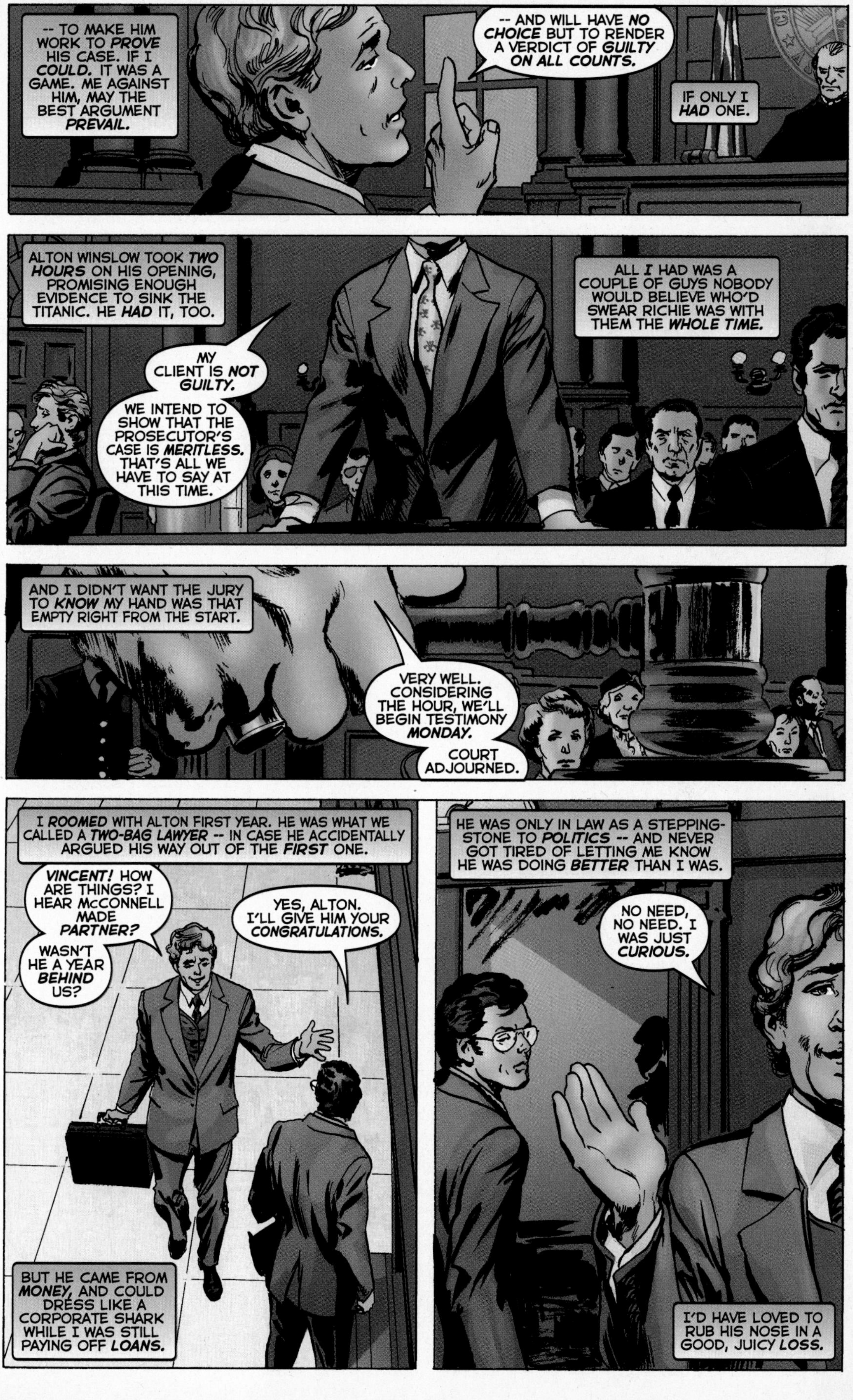
-- TO MAKE HIM WORK TO PROVE HIS CASE. IF I COULD. IT WAS A GAME. ME AGAINST HIM, MAY THE BEST ARGUMENT PREVAIL.
-- AND WILL HAVE NO CHOICE BUT TO RENDER A VERDICT OF GUILTY ON ALL COUNTS.
IF ONLY I HAD ONE.
ALTON WINSLOW TOOK TWO HOURS ON HIS OPENING, PROMISING ENOUGH EVIDENCE TO SINK THE TITANIC. HE HAD IT, TOO.
ALL I HAD WAS A COUPLE OF GUYS NOBODY WOULD BELIEVE WHO'D SWEAR RICHIE WAS WITH THEM THE WHOLE TIME.
MY CLIENT IS NOT GUILTY.
WE INTEND TO SHOW THAT THE PROSECUTOR'S CASE IS MERITLESS. THAT'S ALL WE HAVE TO SAY AT THIS TIME.
AND I DIDN'T WANT THE JURY TO KNOW MY HAND WAS THAT EMPTY RIGHT FROM THE START.
VERY WELL. CONSIDERING THE HOUR, WE'LL BEGIN TESTIMONY MONDAY.
COURT ADJOURNED.
I ROOMED WITH ALTON FIRST YEAR. HE WAS WHAT WE CALLED A TWO-BAG LAWYER -- IN CASE HE ACCIDENTALLY ARGUED HIS WAY OUT OF THE FIRST ONE.
VINCENT! HOW ARE THINGS? I HEAR McCONNELL MADE PARTNER?
WASN'T HE A YEAR BEHIND US?
YES, ALTON. I'LL GIVE HIM YOUR CONGRATULATIONS.
BUT HE CAME FROM MONEY, AND COULD DRESS LIKE A CORPORATE SHARK WHILE I WAS STILL PAYING OFF LOANS.
HE WAS ONLY IN LAW AS A STEPPING-STONE TO POLITICS -- AND NEVER GOT TIRED OF LETTING ME KNOW HE WAS DOING BETTER THAN I WAS.
NO NEED, NO NEED. I WAS JUST CURIOUS.
I'D HAVE LOVED TO RUB HIS NOSE IN A GOOD, JUICY LOSS.

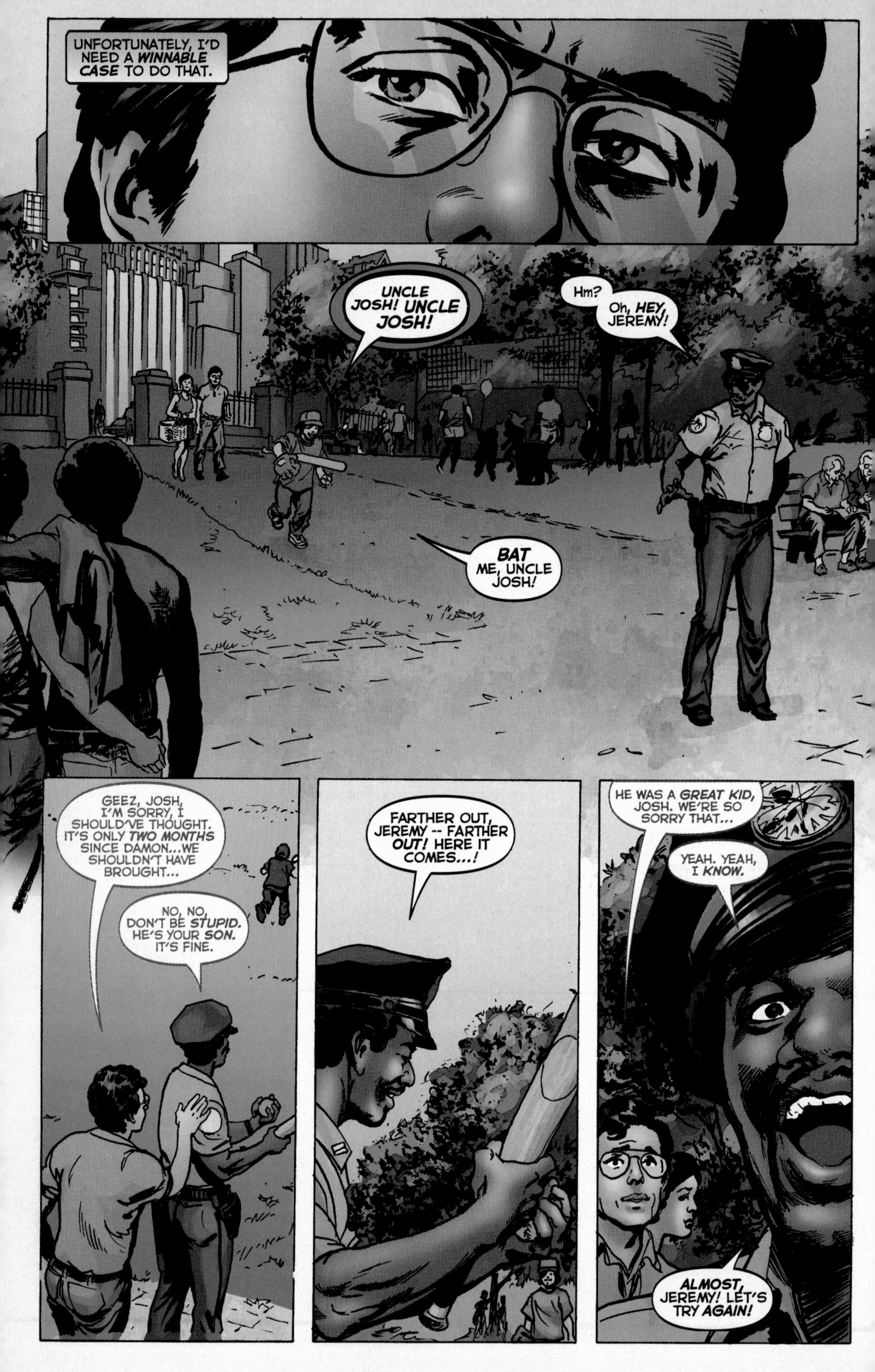
UNFORTUNATELY, I'D NEED A WINNABLE CASE TO DO THAT.
UNCLE JOSH! UNCLE JOSH!
Hm?
Oh, HEY, JEREMY!
BAT ME, UNCLE JOSH!
GEEZ, JOSH, I'M SORRY, I SHOULD'VE THOUGHT. IT'S ONLY TWO MONTHS SINCE DAMON...WE SHOULDN'T HAVE BROUGHT...
NO, NO, DON'T BE STUPID. HE'S YOUR SON. IT'S FINE.
FARTHER OUT, JEREMY -- FARTHER OUT! HERE IT COMES...!
HE WAS A GREAT KID, JOSH. WE'RE SO SORRY THAT...
YEAH. YEAH, I KNOW.
ALMOST, JEREMY! LET'S TRY AGAIN!

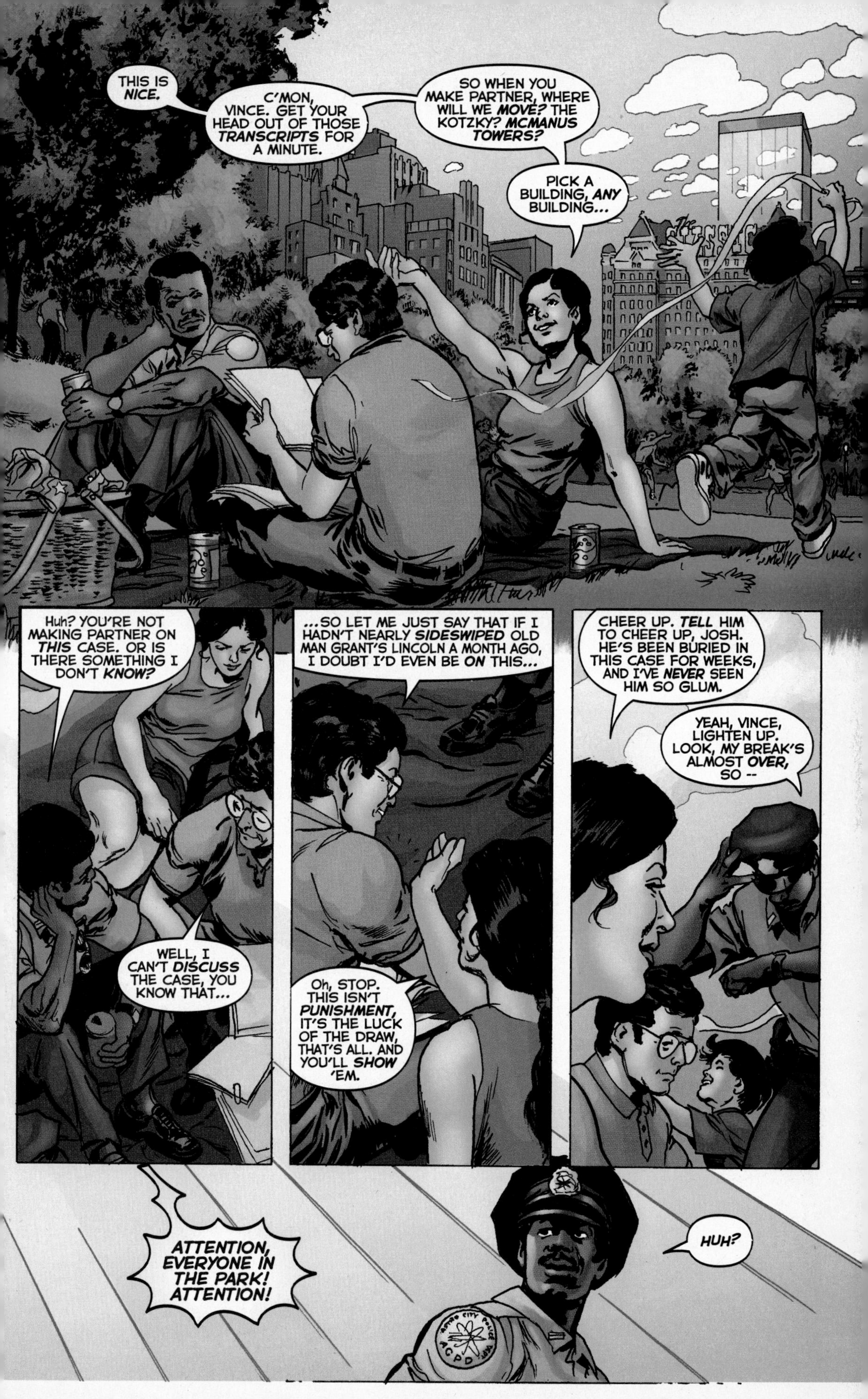
THIS IS NICE.
C'MON, VINCE. GET YOUR HEAD OUT OF THOSE TRANSCRIPTS FOR A MINUTE.
SO WHEN YOU MAKE PARTNER, WHERE WILL WE MOVE? THE KOTZKY? MCMANUS TOWERS?
PICK A BUILDING, ANY BUILDING...
Huh? YOU'RE NOT MAKING PARTNER ON THIS CASE. OR IS THERE SOMETHING I DON'T KNOW?
WELL, I CAN'T DISCUSS THE CASE, YOU KNOW THAT...
...SO LET ME JUST SAY THAT IF I HADN'T NEARLY SIDESWIPED OLD MAN GRANT'S LINCOLN A MONTH AGO, I DOUBT I'D EVEN BE ON THIS...
Oh, STOP. THIS ISN'T PUNISHMENT, IT'S THE LUCK OF THE DRAW, THAT'S ALL. AND YOU'LL SHOW 'EM.
CHEER UP. TELL HIM TO CHEER UP, JOSH. HE'S BEEN BURIED IN THIS CASE FOR WEEKS, AND I'VE NEVER SEEN HIM SO GLUM.
YEAH, VINCE, LIGHTEN UP. LOOK, MY BREAK'S ALMOST OVER, SO --
ATTENTION, EVERYONE IN THE PARK! ATTENTION!
HUH?
ACPD

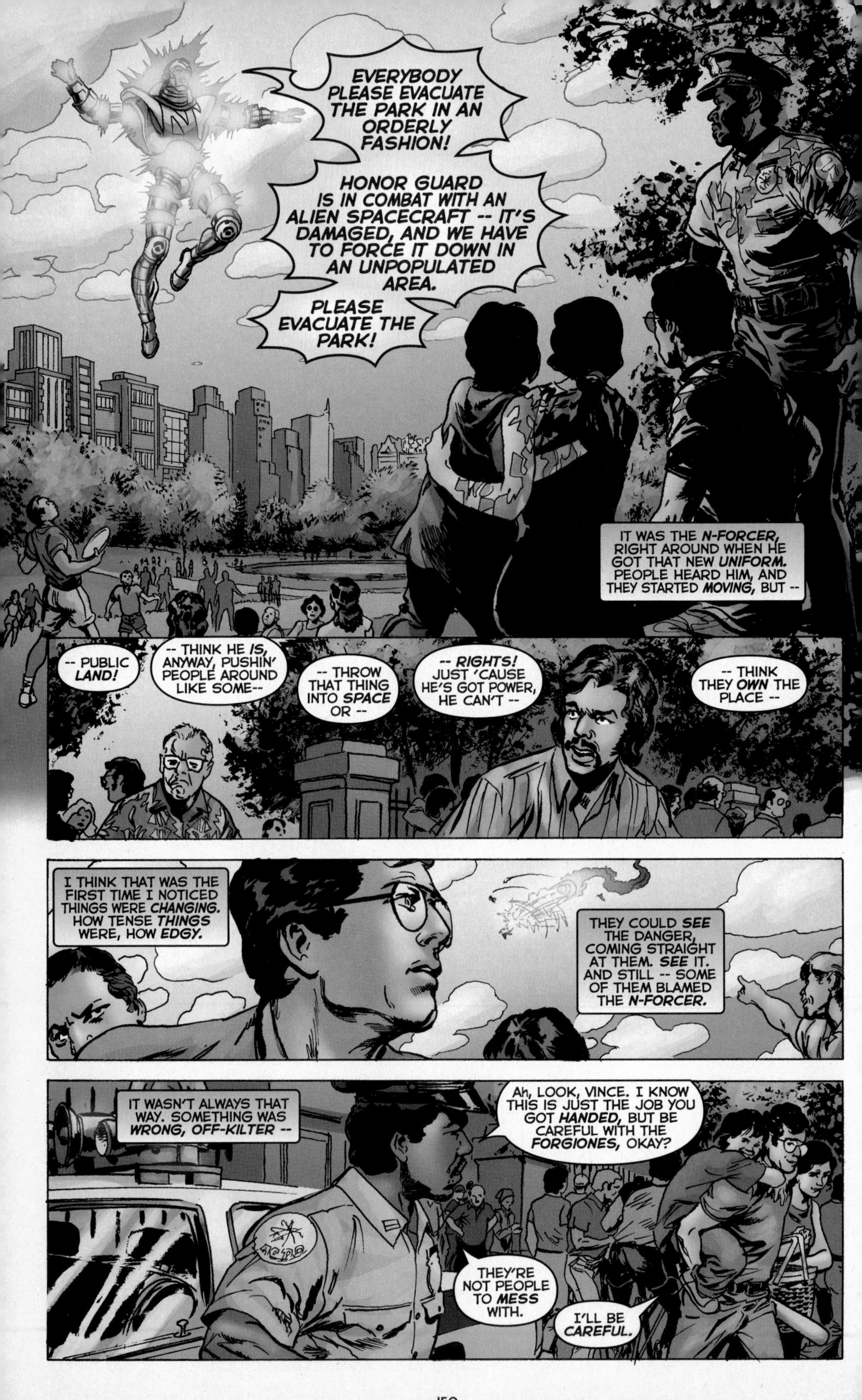
EVERYBODY PLEASE EVACUATE THE PARK IN AN ORDERLY FASHION!
HONOR GUARD IS IN COMBAT WITH AN ALIEN SPACECRAFT -- IT'S DAMAGED, AND WE HAVE TO FORCE IT DOWN IN AN UNPOPULATED AREA.
PLEASE EVACUATE THE PARK!
IT WAS THE N-FORCER, RIGHT AROUND WHEN HE GOT THAT NEW UNIFORM. PEOPLE HEARD HIM, AND THEY STARTED MOVING, BUT --
-- PUBLIC LAND!
-- THINK HE IS, ANYWAY, PUSHIN' PEOPLE AROUND LIKE SOME--
-- THROW THAT THING INTO SPACE OR --
-- RIGHTS! JUST 'CAUSE HE'S GOT POWER, HE CAN'T --
-- THINK THEY OWN THE PLACE --
I THINK THAT WAS THE FIRST TIME I NOTICED THINGS WERE CHANGING. HOW TENSE THINGS WERE, HOW EDGY.
THEY COULD SEE THE DANGER, COMING STRAIGHT AT THEM. SEE IT. AND STILL -- SOME OF THEM BLAMED THE N-FORCER.
IT WASN'T ALWAYS THAT WAY. SOMETHING WAS WRONG, OFF-KILTER --
Ah, LOOK, VINCE. I KNOW THIS IS JUST THE JOB YOU GOT HANDED, BUT BE CAREFUL WITH THE FORGIONES, OKAY?
THEY'RE NOT PEOPLE TO MESS WITH.
I'LL BE CAREFUL.

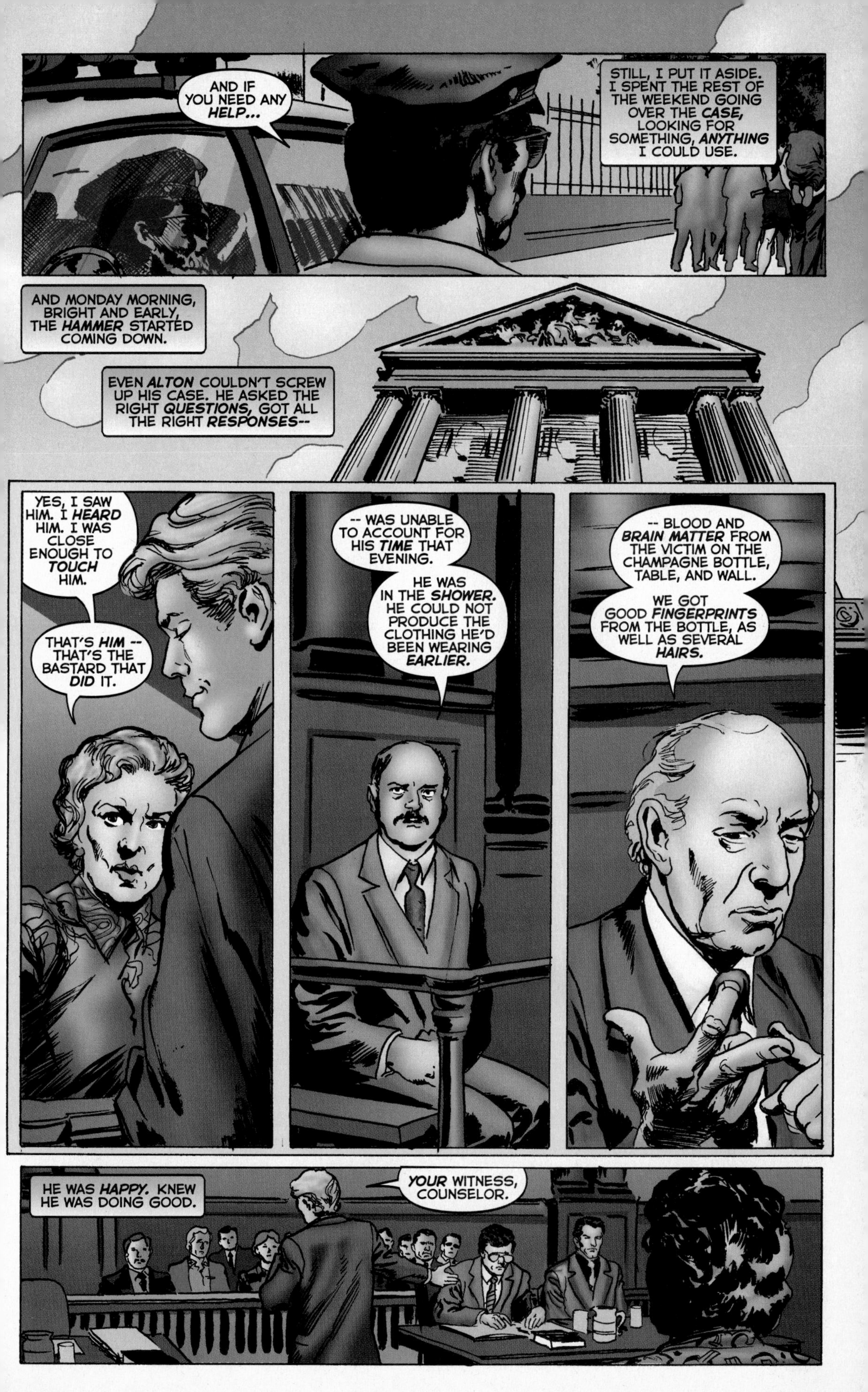
AND IF YOU NEED ANY HELP...
STILL, I PUT IT ASIDE. I SPENT THE REST OF THE WEEKEND GOING OVER THE CASE, LOOKING FOR SOMETHING, ANYTHING I COULD USE.
AND MONDAY MORNING, BRIGHT AND EARLY, THE HAMMER STARTED COMING DOWN.
EVEN ALTON COULDN'T SCREW UP HIS CASE. HE ASKED THE RIGHT QUESTIONS, GOT ALL THE RIGHT RESPONSES--
YES, I SAW HIM. I HEARD HIM. I WAS CLOSE ENOUGH TO TOUCH HIM.
THAT'S HIM -- THAT'S THE BASTARD THAT DID IT.
-- WAS UNABLE TO ACCOUNT FOR HIS TIME THAT EVENING.
HE WAS IN THE SHOWER. HE COULD NOT PRODUCE THE CLOTHING HE'D BEEN WEARING EARLIER.
-- BLOOD AND BRAIN MATTER FROM THE VICTIM ON THE CHAMPAGNE BOTTLE, TABLE, AND WALL.
WE GOT GOOD FINGERPRINTS FROM THE BOTTLE, AS WELL AS SEVERAL HAIRS.
HE WAS HAPPY. KNEW HE WAS DOING GOOD.
YOUR WITNESS, COUNSELOR.

THANK YOU.

ME? NOT SO MUCH.

YOU SAID THE RESTAURANT WAS *CROWDED*. THERE WAS PANIC, *CONFUSION...*?

IT WAS THE *NEXT TABLE*, MISTER.

I COULDA REACHED OUT AND *TOUCHED* HIM, I TELL YOU.

-- ARRESTED HIM WITHOUT *ANY* PHYSICAL EVIDENCE AT HIS *HOME*?

WE HAD *TWENTY-FOUR* CLEAR STATEMENTS, AND A GUY WITH NO *ALIBI* WHO'D JUST HOPPED IN THE *SHOWER* FRIDAY NIGHT AT TEN.

YOU *BET* WE ARRESTED HIM.

TWO OF THE FINGERPRINTS WERE IN HER *BLOOD*, MR. OLECK.

THERE WAS *NO* MISTAKING THAT.

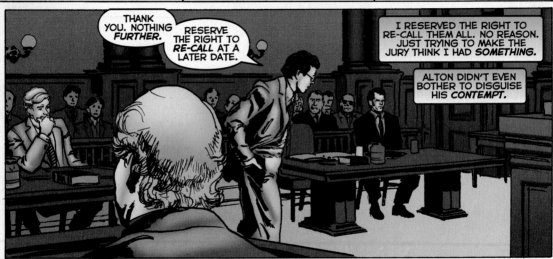

THANK YOU. NOTHING *FURTHER*.

RESERVE THE RIGHT TO *RE-CALL* AT A LATER DATE.

I RESERVED THE RIGHT TO RE-CALL THEM ALL. NO REASON. JUST TRYING TO MAKE THE JURY THINK I HAD *SOMETHING*.

ALTON DIDN'T EVEN BOTHER TO DISGUISE HIS *CONTEMPT*.

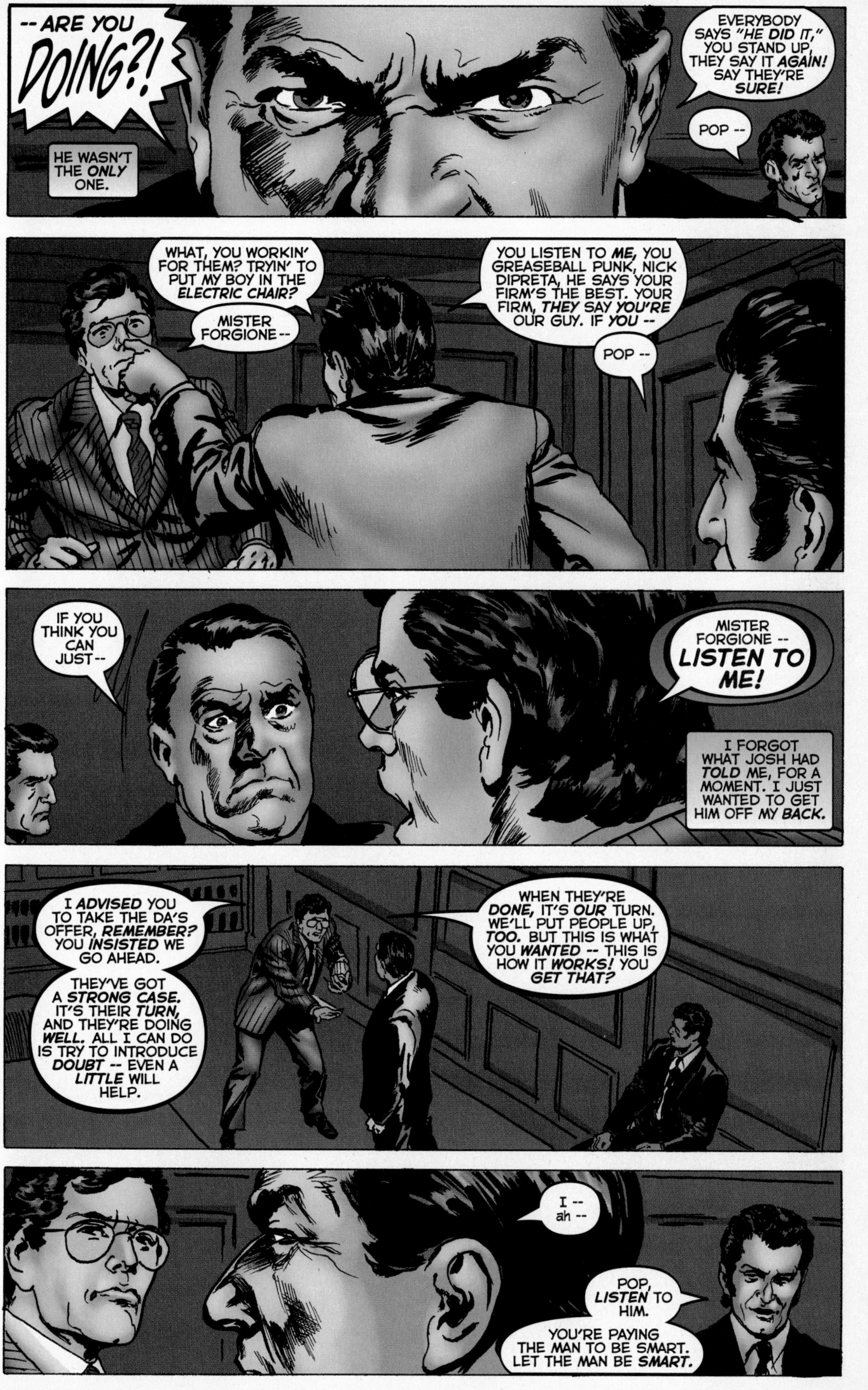
-- ARE YOU DOING?!
HE WASN'T THE ONLY ONE.
EVERYBODY SAYS "HE DID IT," YOU STAND UP, THEY SAY IT AGAIN! SAY THEY'RE SURE!
POP --
WHAT, YOU WORKIN' FOR THEM? TRYIN' TO PUT MY BOY IN THE ELECTRIC CHAIR?
MISTER FORGIONE --
YOU LISTEN TO ME, YOU GREASEBALL PUNK, NICK DIPRETA, HE SAYS YOUR FIRM'S THE BEST. YOUR FIRM, THEY SAY YOU'RE OUR GUY. IF YOU --
POP --
IF YOU THINK YOU CAN JUST --
MISTER FORGIONE -- LISTEN TO ME!
I FORGOT WHAT JOSH HAD TOLD ME, FOR A MOMENT. I JUST WANTED TO GET HIM OFF MY BACK.
I ADVISED YOU TO TAKE THE DA'S OFFER, REMEMBER? YOU INSISTED WE GO AHEAD.
THEY'VE GOT A STRONG CASE. IT'S THEIR TURN, AND THEY'RE DOING WELL. ALL I CAN DO IS TRY TO INTRODUCE DOUBT -- EVEN A LITTLE WILL HELP.
WHEN THEY'RE DONE, IT'S OUR TURN. WE'LL PUT PEOPLE UP, TOO. BUT THIS IS WHAT YOU WANTED -- THIS IS HOW IT WORKS! YOU GET THAT?
I -- ah --
POP, LISTEN TO HIM.
YOU'RE PAYING THE MAN TO BE SMART. LET THE MAN BE SMART.

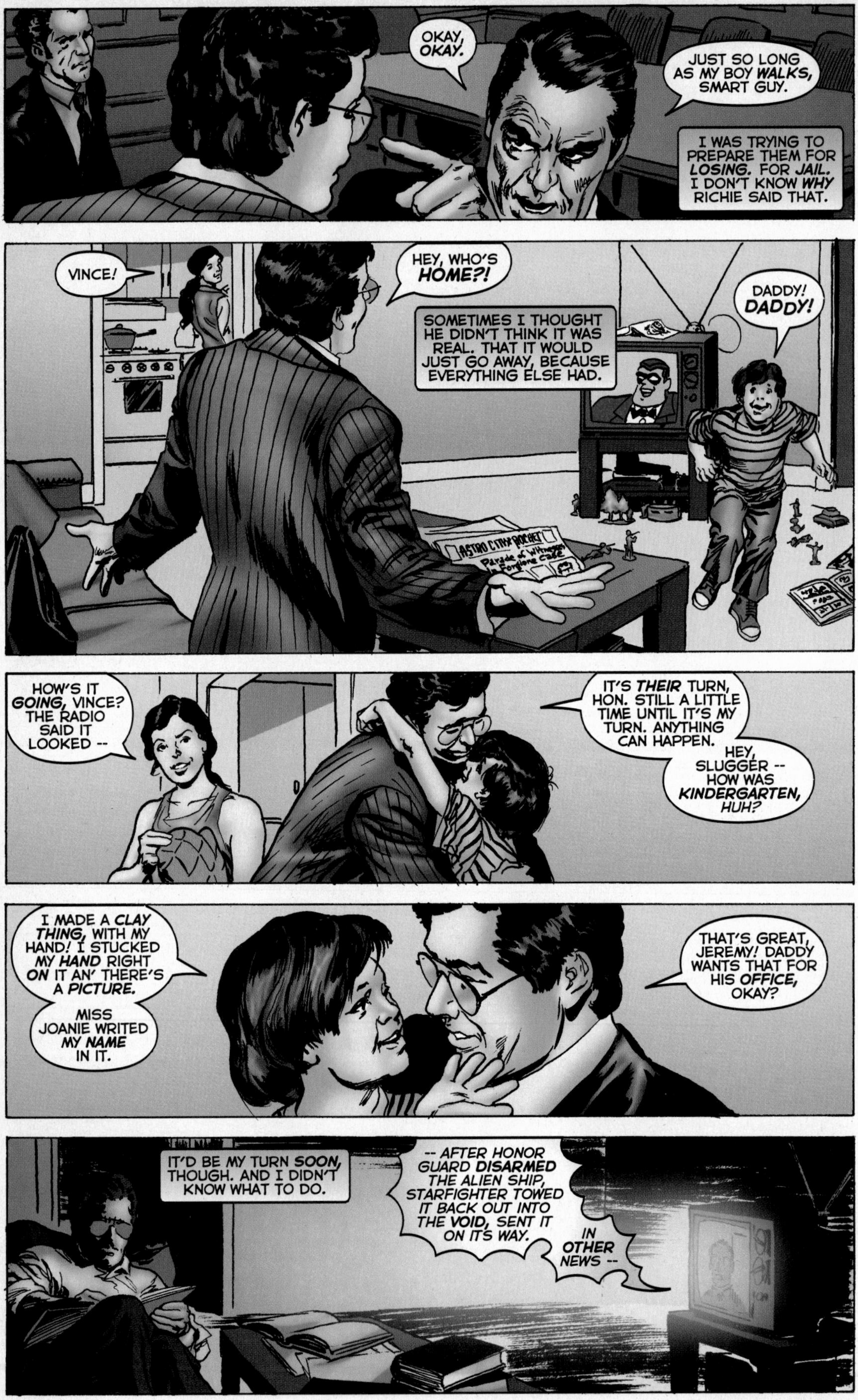
OKAY, OKAY.
JUST SO LONG AS MY BOY WALKS, SMART GUY.
I WAS TRYING TO PREPARE THEM FOR LOSING. FOR JAIL. I DON'T KNOW WHY RICHIE SAID THAT.
VINCE!
HEY, WHO'S HOME?!
SOMETIMES I THOUGHT HE DIDN'T THINK IT WAS REAL. THAT IT WOULD JUST GO AWAY, BECAUSE EVERYTHING ELSE HAD.
DADDY! DADDY!
HOW'S IT GOING, VINCE? THE RADIO SAID IT LOOKED --
IT'S THEIR TURN, HON. STILL A LITTLE TIME UNTIL IT'S MY TURN. ANYTHING CAN HAPPEN.
HEY, SLUGGER -- HOW WAS KINDERGARTEN, HUH?
I MADE A CLAY THING, WITH MY HAND! I STUCKED MY HAND RIGHT ON IT AN' THERE'S A PICTURE.
MISS JOANIE WRITED MY NAME IN IT.
THAT'S GREAT, JEREMY! DADDY WANTS THAT FOR HIS OFFICE, OKAY?
IT'D BE MY TURN SOON, THOUGH. AND I DIDN'T KNOW WHAT TO DO.
-- AFTER HONOR GUARD DISARMED THE ALIEN SHIP, STARFIGHTER TOWED IT BACK OUT INTO THE VOID, SENT IT ON IT'S WAY.
IN OTHER NEWS --

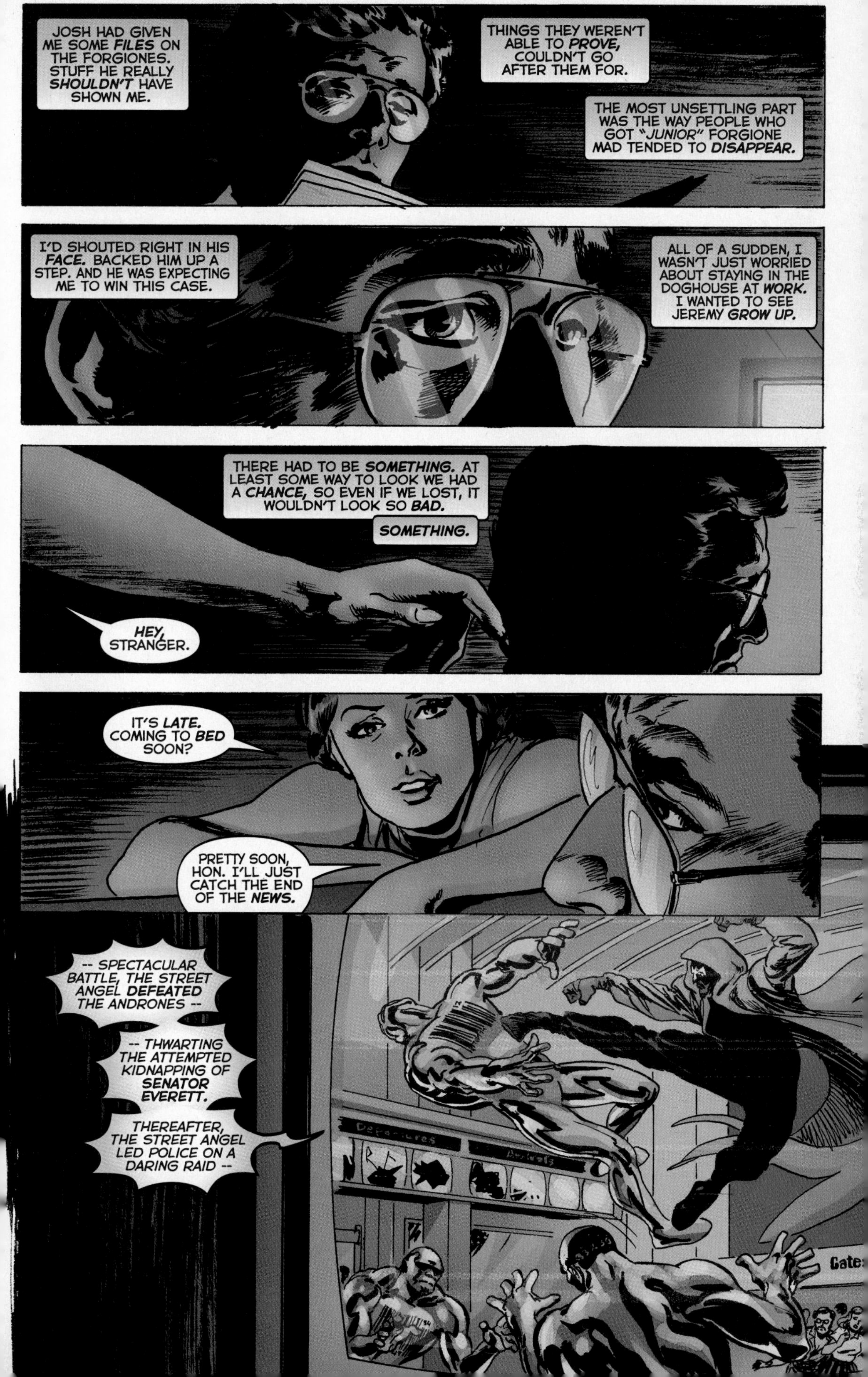
JOSH HAD GIVEN ME SOME FILES ON THE FORGIONES. STUFF HE REALLY SHOULDN'T HAVE SHOWN ME.
THINGS THEY WEREN'T ABLE TO PROVE, COULDN'T GO AFTER THEM FOR.
THE MOST UNSETTLING PART WAS THE WAY PEOPLE WHO GOT "JUNIOR" FORGIONE MAD TENDED TO DISAPPEAR.
I'D SHOUTED RIGHT IN HIS FACE. BACKED HIM UP A STEP. AND HE WAS EXPECTING ME TO WIN THIS CASE.
ALL OF A SUDDEN, I WASN'T JUST WORRIED ABOUT STAYING IN THE DOGHOUSE AT WORK. I WANTED TO SEE JEREMY GROW UP.
THERE HAD TO BE SOMETHING. AT LEAST SOME WAY TO LOOK WE HAD A CHANCE, SO EVEN IF WE LOST, IT WOULDN'T LOOK SO BAD.
SOMETHING.
HEY, STRANGER.
IT'S LATE. COMING TO BED SOON?
PRETTY SOON, HON. I'LL JUST CATCH THE END OF THE NEWS.
-- SPECTACULAR BATTLE, THE STREET ANGEL DEFEATED THE ANDRONES --
-- THWARTING THE ATTEMPTED KIDNAPPING OF SENATOR EVERETT.
THEREAFTER, THE STREET ANGEL LED POLICE ON A DARING RAID --
Departures
Arrivals
Gate

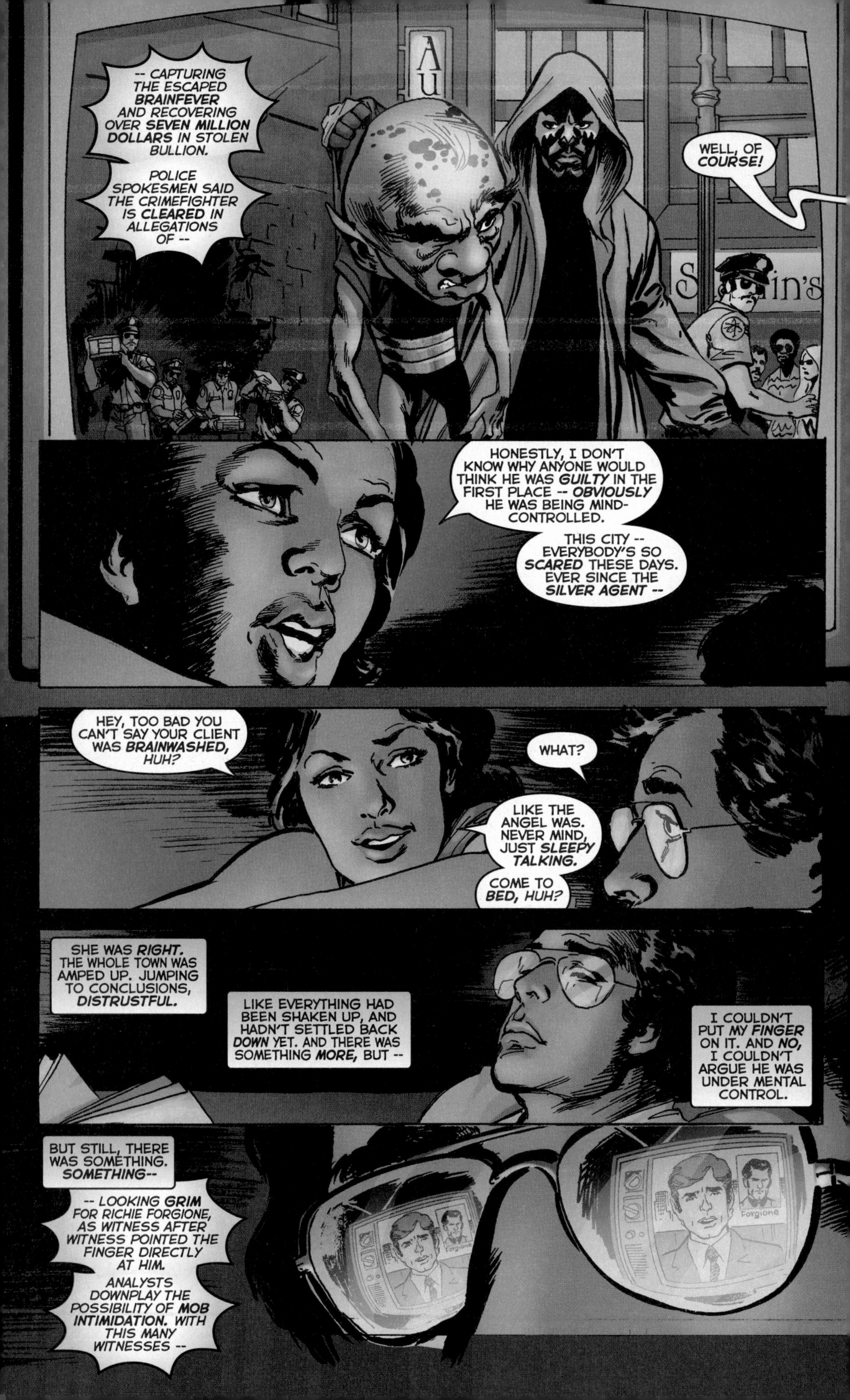
-- CAPTURING THE ESCAPED BRAINFEVER AND RECOVERING OVER SEVEN MILLION DOLLARS IN STOLEN BULLION.
POLICE SPOKESMEN SAID THE CRIMEFIGHTER IS CLEARED IN ALLEGATIONS OF --
WELL, OF COURSE!
HONESTLY, I DON'T KNOW WHY ANYONE WOULD THINK HE WAS GUILTY IN THE FIRST PLACE -- OBVIOUSLY HE WAS BEING MIND-CONTROLLED.
THIS CITY -- EVERYBODY'S SO SCARED THESE DAYS. EVER SINCE THE SILVER AGENT --
HEY, TOO BAD YOU CAN'T SAY YOUR CLIENT WAS BRAINWASHED, HUH?
WHAT?
LIKE THE ANGEL WAS. NEVER MIND, JUST SLEEPY TALKING.
COME TO BED, HUH?
SHE WAS RIGHT. THE WHOLE TOWN WAS AMPED UP. JUMPING TO CONCLUSIONS, DISTRUSTFUL.
LIKE EVERYTHING HAD BEEN SHAKEN UP, AND HADN'T SETTLED BACK DOWN YET. AND THERE WAS SOMETHING MORE, BUT --
I COULDN'T PUT MY FINGER ON IT. AND NO, I COULDN'T ARGUE HE WAS UNDER MENTAL CONTROL.
BUT STILL, THERE WAS SOMETHING. SOMETHING--
-- LOOKING GRIM FOR RICHIE FORGIONE, AS WITNESS AFTER WITNESS POINTED THE FINGER DIRECTLY AT HIM.
ANALYSTS DOWNPLAY THE POSSIBILITY OF MOB INTIMIDATION. WITH THIS MANY WITNESSES --

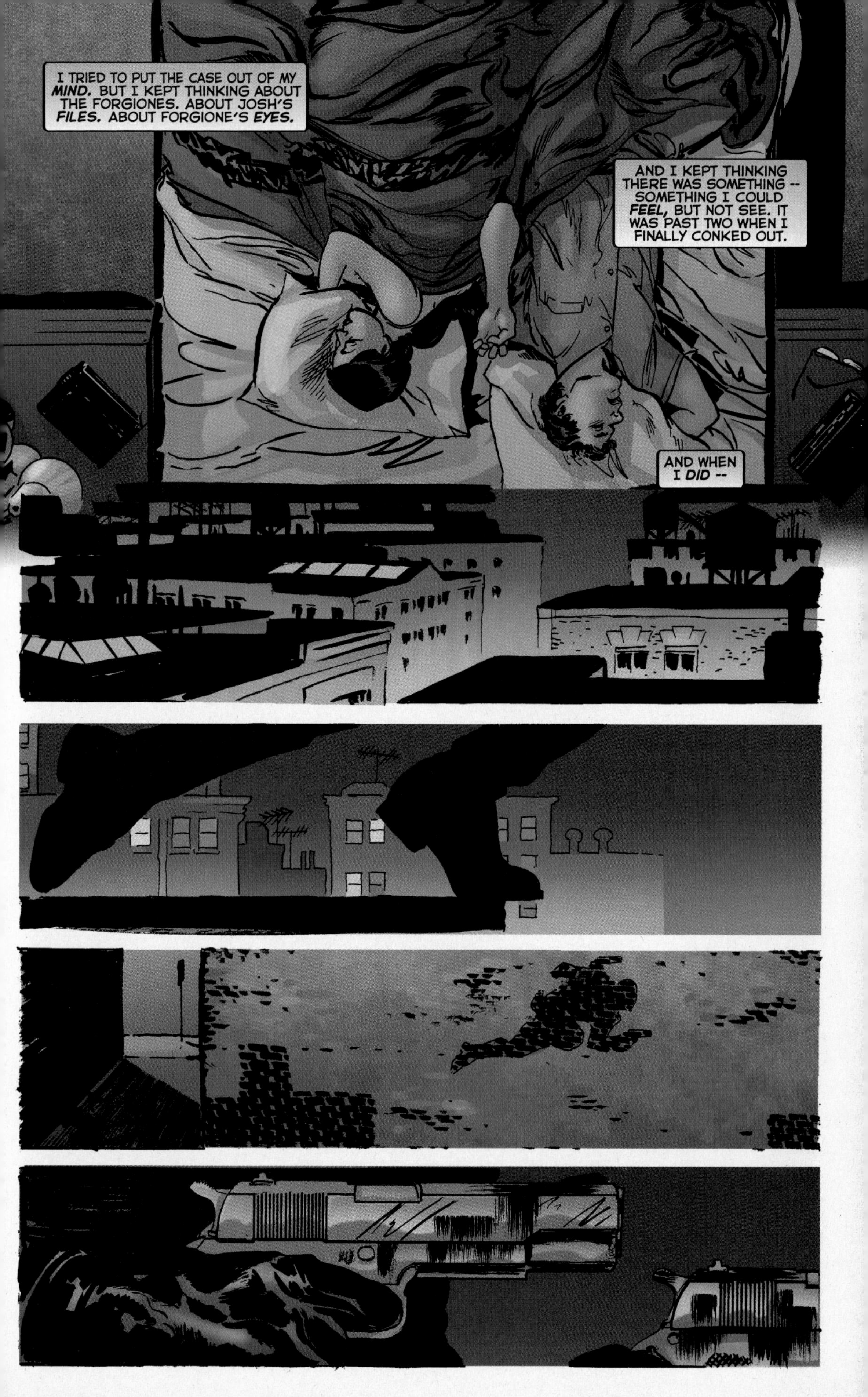
I TRIED TO PUT THE CASE OUT OF MY MIND. BUT I KEPT THINKING ABOUT THE FORGIONES. ABOUT JOSH'S FILES. ABOUT FORGIONE'S EYES.
AND I KEPT THINKING THERE WAS SOMETHING -- SOMETHING I COULD FEEL, BUT NOT SEE. IT WAS PAST TWO WHEN I FINALLY CONKED OUT.
AND WHEN I DID --

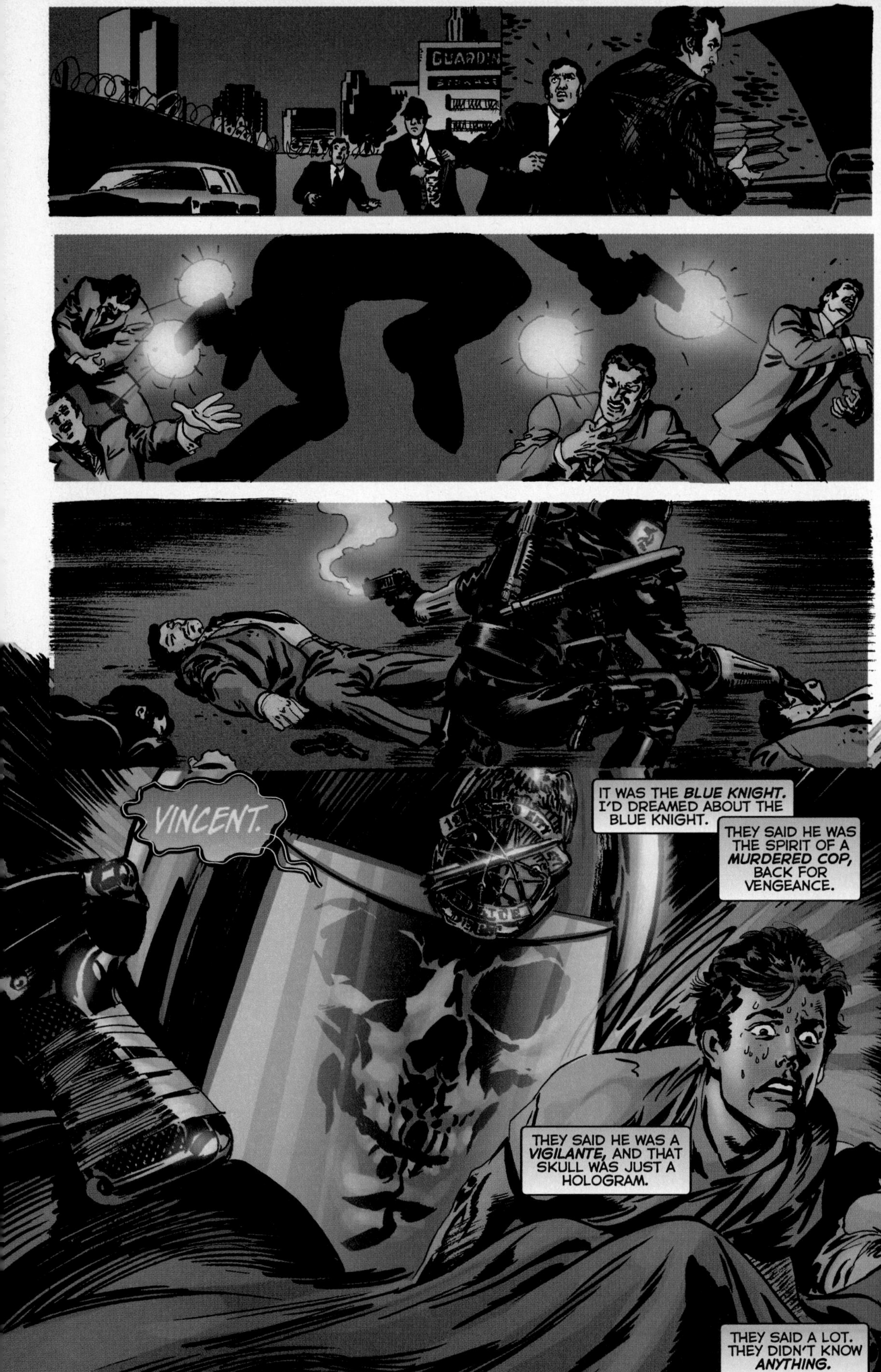
GUARDIN
VINCENT.
IT WAS THE BLUE KNIGHT. I'D DREAMED ABOUT THE BLUE KNIGHT.
THEY SAID HE WAS THE SPIRIT OF A MURDERED COP, BACK FOR VENGEANCE.
THEY SAID HE WAS A VIGILANTE, AND THAT SKULL WAS JUST A HOLOGRAM.
THEY SAID A LOT. THEY DIDN'T KNOW ANYTHING.

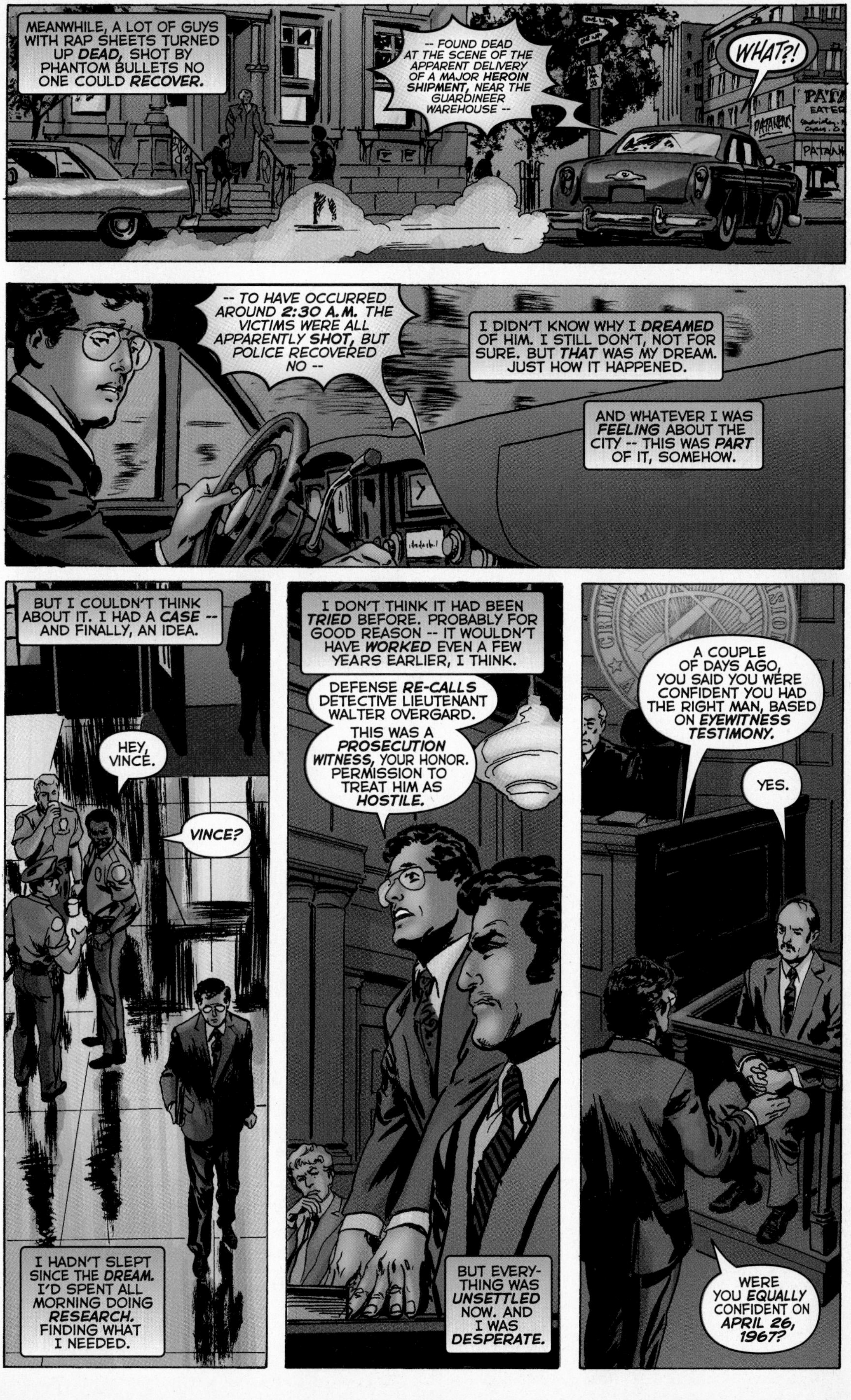
MEANWHILE, A LOT OF GUYS WITH RAP SHEETS TURNED UP DEAD, SHOT BY PHANTOM BULLETS NO ONE COULD RECOVER.
-- FOUND DEAD AT THE SCENE OF THE APPARENT DELIVERY OF A MAJOR HEROIN SHIPMENT, NEAR THE GUARDINEER WAREHOUSE --
WHAT?!
-- TO HAVE OCCURRED AROUND 2:30 A.M. THE VICTIMS WERE ALL APPARENTLY SHOT, BUT POLICE RECOVERED NO --
I DIDN'T KNOW WHY I DREAMED OF HIM. I STILL DON'T, NOT FOR SURE. BUT THAT WAS MY DREAM. JUST HOW IT HAPPENED.
AND WHATEVER I WAS FEELING ABOUT THE CITY -- THIS WAS PART OF IT, SOMEHOW.
BUT I COULDN'T THINK ABOUT IT. I HAD A CASE -- AND FINALLY, AN IDEA.
HEY, VINCE.
VINCE?
I HADN'T SLEPT SINCE THE DREAM. I'D SPENT ALL MORNING DOING RESEARCH. FINDING WHAT I NEEDED.
I DON'T THINK IT HAD BEEN TRIED BEFORE. PROBABLY FOR GOOD REASON -- IT WOULDN'T HAVE WORKED EVEN A FEW YEARS EARLIER, I THINK.
DEFENSE RE-CALLS DETECTIVE LIEUTENANT WALTER OVERGARD.
THIS WAS A PROSECUTION WITNESS, YOUR HONOR. PERMISSION TO TREAT HIM AS HOSTILE.
BUT EVERYTHING WAS UNSETTLED NOW. AND I WAS DESPERATE.
A COUPLE OF DAYS AGO, YOU SAID YOU WERE CONFIDENT YOU HAD THE RIGHT MAN, BASED ON EYEWITNESS TESTIMONY.
YES.
WERE YOU EQUALLY CONFIDENT ON APRIL 26, 1967?

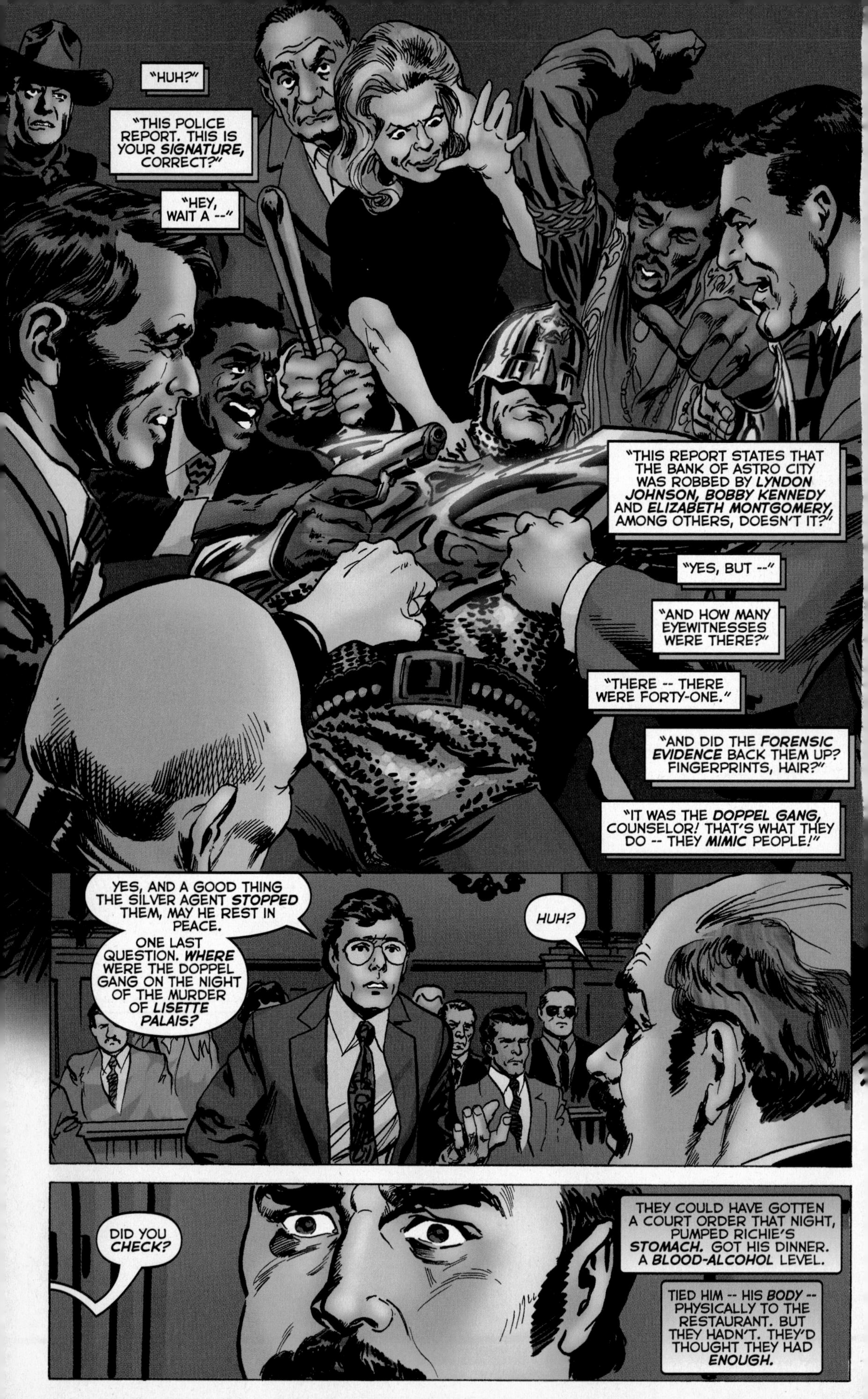
"HUH?"
"THIS POLICE REPORT. THIS IS YOUR SIGNATURE, CORRECT?"
"HEY, WAIT A --"
"THIS REPORT STATES THAT THE BANK OF ASTRO CITY WAS ROBBED BY LYNDON JOHNSON, BOBBY KENNEDY AND ELIZABETH MONTGOMERY, AMONG OTHERS, DOESN'T IT?"
"YES, BUT --"
"AND HOW MANY EYEWITNESSES WERE THERE?"
"THERE -- THERE WERE FORTY-ONE."
"AND DID THE FORENSIC EVIDENCE BACK THEM UP? FINGERPRINTS, HAIR?"
"IT WAS THE DOPPEL GANG, COUNSELOR! THAT'S WHAT THEY DO -- THEY MIMIC PEOPLE!"
YES, AND A GOOD THING THE SILVER AGENT STOPPED THEM, MAY HE REST IN PEACE.
ONE LAST QUESTION. WHERE WERE THE DOPPEL GANG ON THE NIGHT OF THE MURDER OF LISETTE PALAIS?
HUH?
DID YOU CHECK?
THEY COULD HAVE GOTTEN A COURT ORDER THAT NIGHT, PUMPED RICHIE'S STOMACH. GOT HIS DINNER. A BLOOD-ALCOHOL LEVEL.
TIED HIM -- HIS BODY -- PHYSICALLY TO THE RESTAURANT. BUT THEY HADN'T. THEY'D THOUGHT THEY HAD ENOUGH.

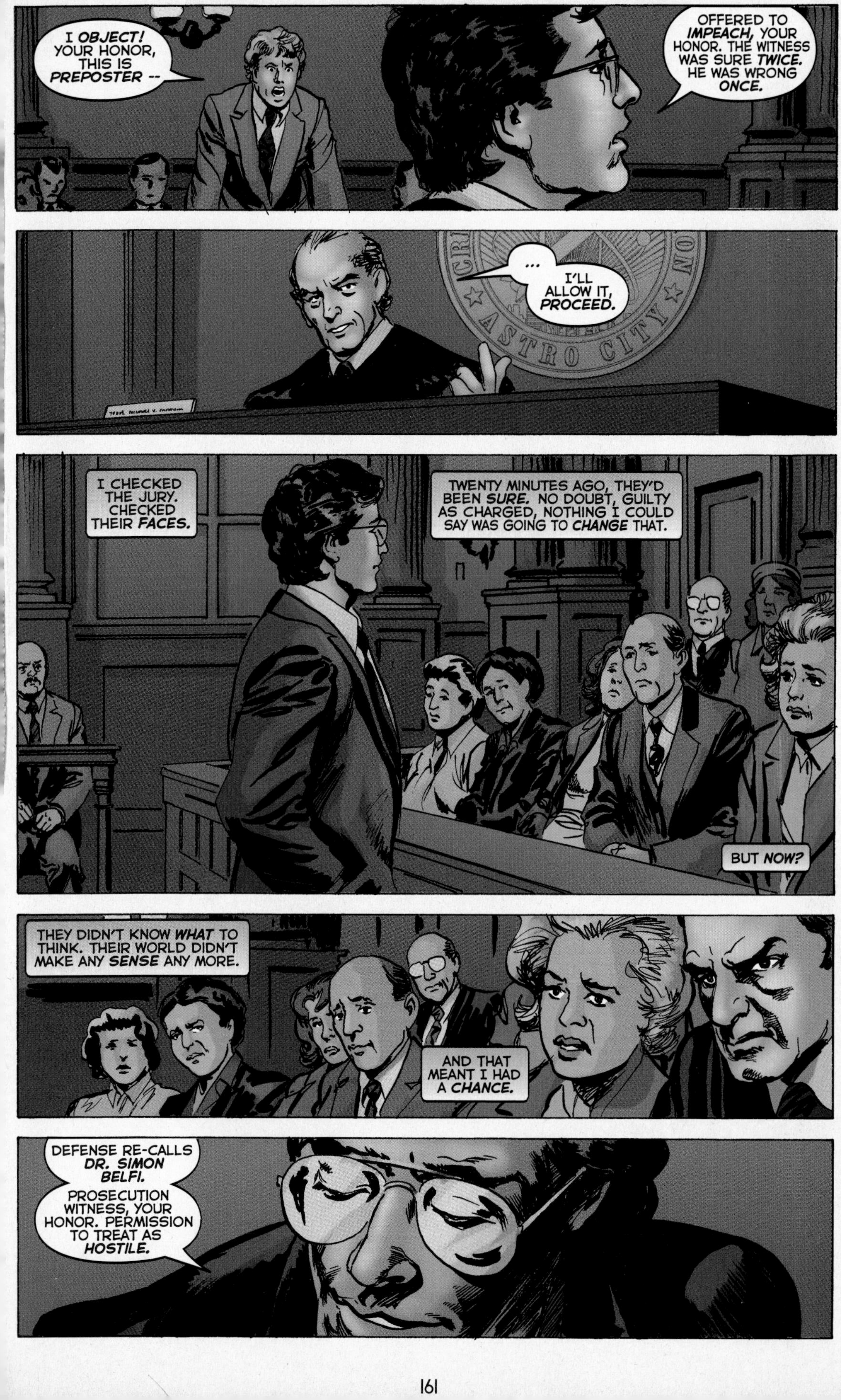
I OBJECT! YOUR HONOR, THIS IS PREPOSTER --
OFFERED TO IMPEACH, YOUR HONOR. THE WITNESS WAS SURE TWICE. HE WAS WRONG ONCE.
... I'LL ALLOW IT, PROCEED.
ASTRO CITY
I CHECKED THE JURY. CHECKED THEIR FACES.
TWENTY MINUTES AGO, THEY'D BEEN SURE. NO DOUBT, GUILTY AS CHARGED, NOTHING I COULD SAY WAS GOING TO CHANGE THAT.
BUT NOW?
THEY DIDN'T KNOW WHAT TO THINK. THEIR WORLD DIDN'T MAKE ANY SENSE ANY MORE.
AND THAT MEANT I HAD A CHANCE.
DEFENSE RE-CALLS DR. SIMON BELFI.
PROSECUTION WITNESS, YOUR HONOR. PERMISSION TO TREAT AS HOSTILE.

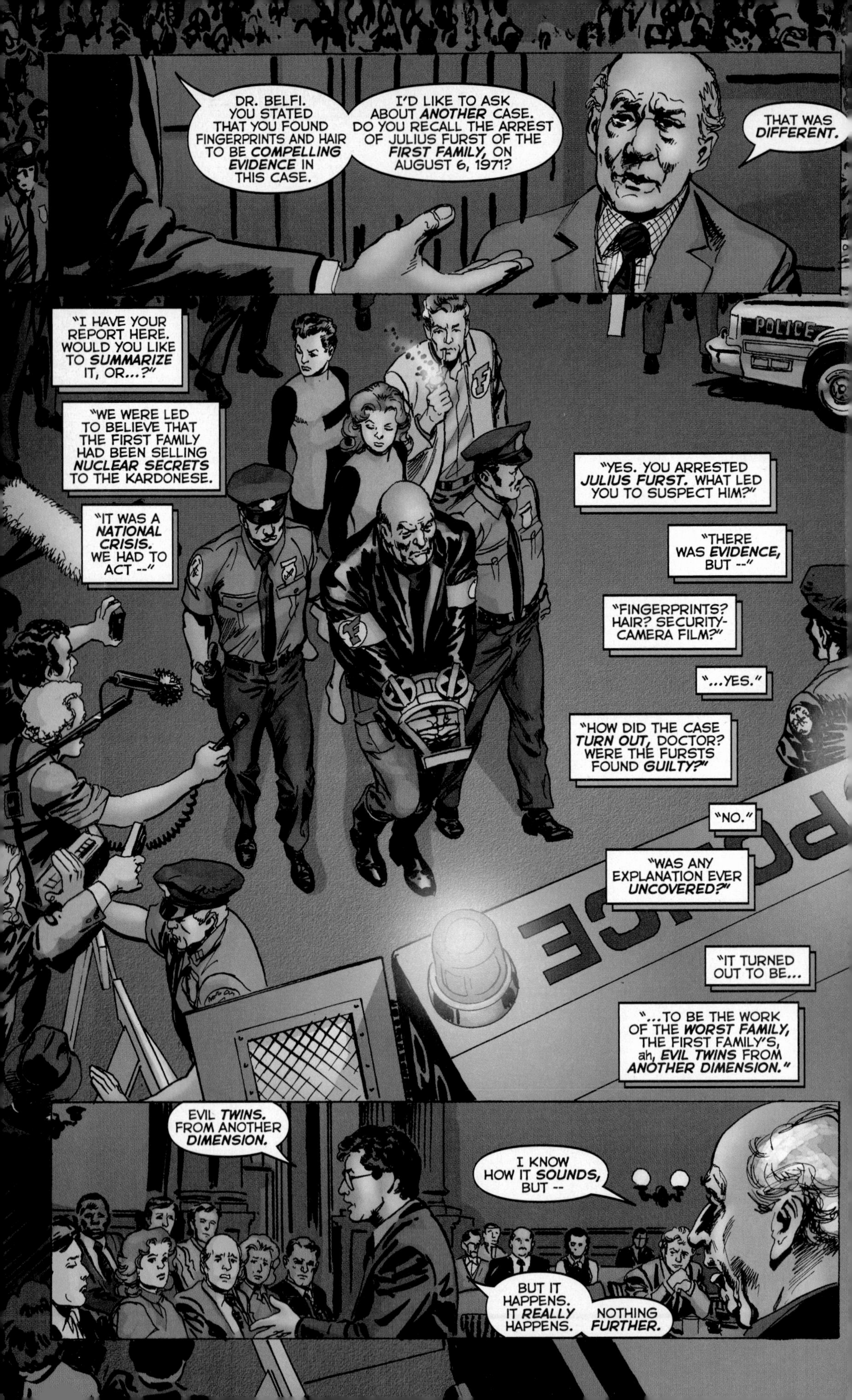

DR. BELFI. YOU STATED THAT YOU FOUND FINGERPRINTS AND HAIR TO BE *COMPELLING EVIDENCE* IN THIS CASE.
I'D LIKE TO ASK ABOUT *ANOTHER* CASE. DO YOU RECALL THE ARREST OF JULIUS FURST OF THE *FIRST FAMILY,* ON AUGUST 6, 1971?
THAT WAS *DIFFERENT.*
POLICE
"I HAVE YOUR REPORT HERE. WOULD YOU LIKE TO *SUMMARIZE* IT, OR...?"
"WE WERE LED TO BELIEVE THAT THE FIRST FAMILY HAD BEEN SELLING *NUCLEAR SECRETS* TO THE KARDONESE.
"IT WAS A *NATIONAL CRISIS.* WE HAD TO ACT --"
"YES. YOU ARRESTED *JULIUS FURST.* WHAT LED YOU TO SUSPECT HIM?"
"THERE WAS *EVIDENCE,* BUT --"
"FINGERPRINTS? HAIR? SECURITY-CAMERA FILM?"
"...YES."
"HOW DID THE CASE *TURN OUT,* DOCTOR? WERE THE FURSTS FOUND *GUILTY?*"
"NO."
"WAS ANY EXPLANATION EVER *UNCOVERED?*"
"IT TURNED OUT TO BE...
"...TO BE THE WORK OF THE *WORST FAMILY,* THE FIRST FAMILY'S, ah, *EVIL TWINS* FROM *ANOTHER DIMENSION.*"
EVIL *TWINS.* FROM ANOTHER *DIMENSION.*
I KNOW HOW IT *SOUNDS,* BUT --
BUT IT HAPPENS. IT *REALLY* HAPPENS.
NOTHING *FURTHER.*

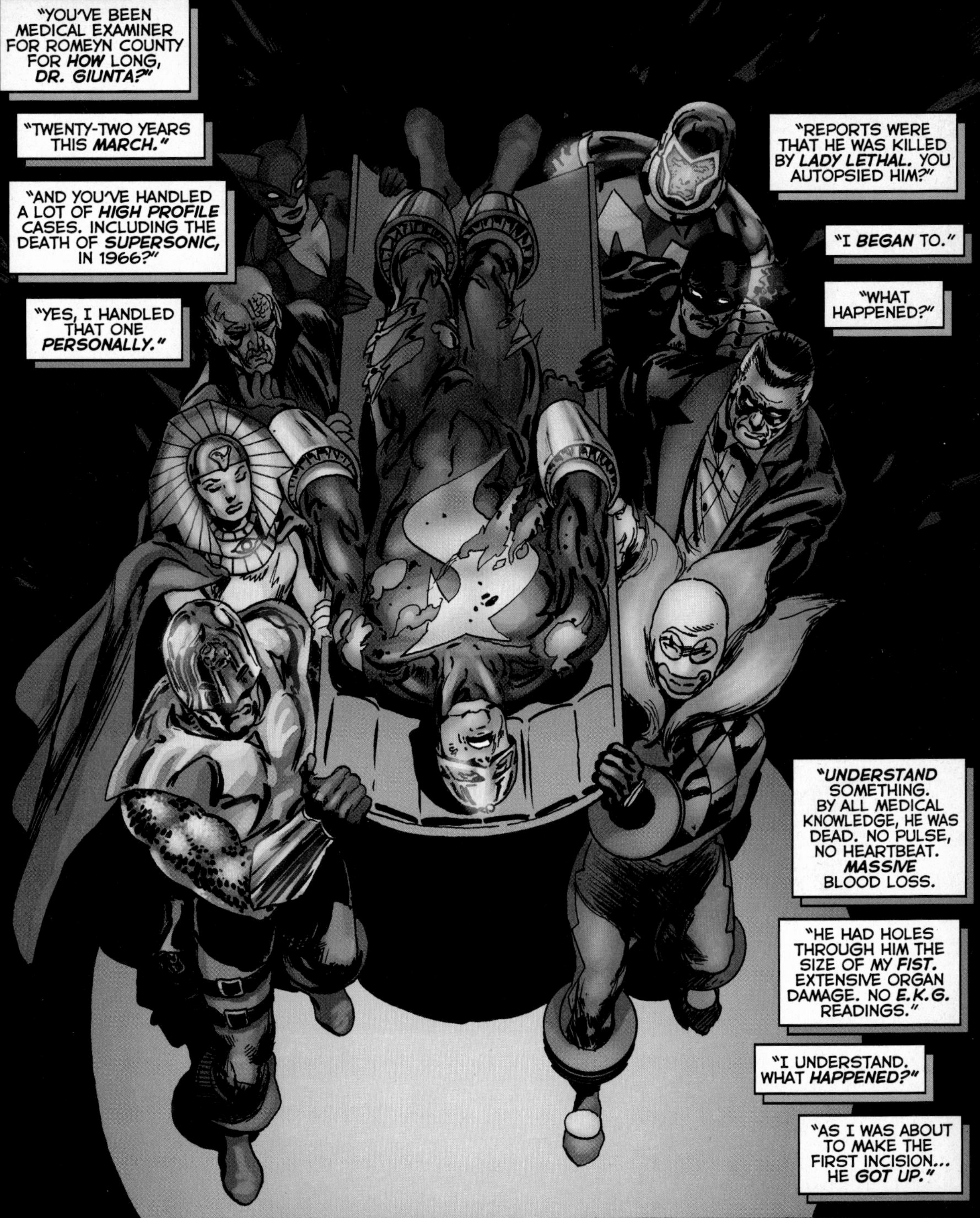
"YOU'VE BEEN MEDICAL EXAMINER FOR ROMEYN COUNTY FOR HOW LONG, DR. GIUNTA?"
"TWENTY-TWO YEARS THIS MARCH."
"AND YOU'VE HANDLED A LOT OF HIGH PROFILE CASES. INCLUDING THE DEATH OF SUPERSONIC, IN 1966?"
"YES, I HANDLED THAT ONE PERSONALLY."
"REPORTS WERE THAT HE WAS KILLED BY LADY LETHAL. YOU AUTOPSIED HIM?"
"I BEGAN TO."
"WHAT HAPPENED?"
"UNDERSTAND SOMETHING. BY ALL MEDICAL KNOWLEDGE, HE WAS DEAD. NO PULSE, NO HEARTBEAT. MASSIVE BLOOD LOSS.
"HE HAD HOLES THROUGH HIM THE SIZE OF MY FIST. EXTENSIVE ORGAN DAMAGE. NO E.K.G. READINGS."
"I UNDERSTAND. WHAT HAPPENED?"
"AS I WAS ABOUT TO MAKE THE FIRST INCISION... HE GOT UP."

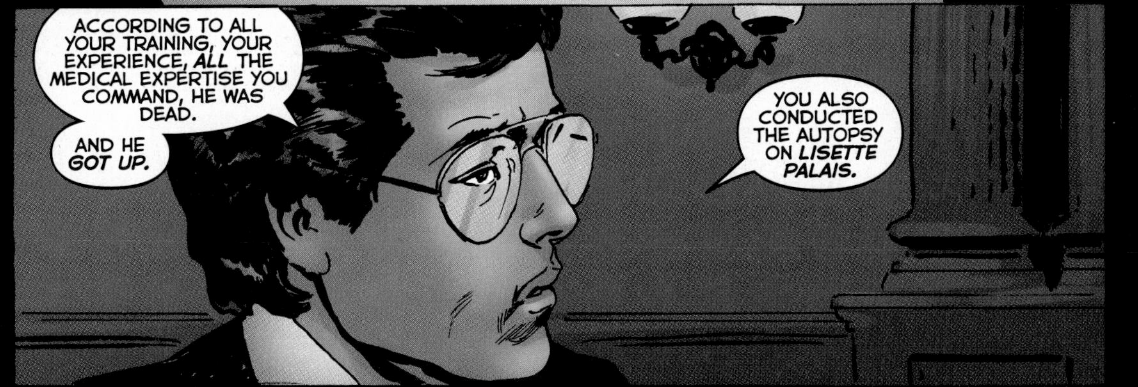
ACCORDING TO ALL YOUR TRAINING, YOUR EXPERIENCE, ALL THE MEDICAL EXPERTISE YOU COMMAND, HE WAS DEAD.
AND HE GOT UP.
YOU ALSO CONDUCTED THE AUTOPSY ON LISETTE PALAIS.

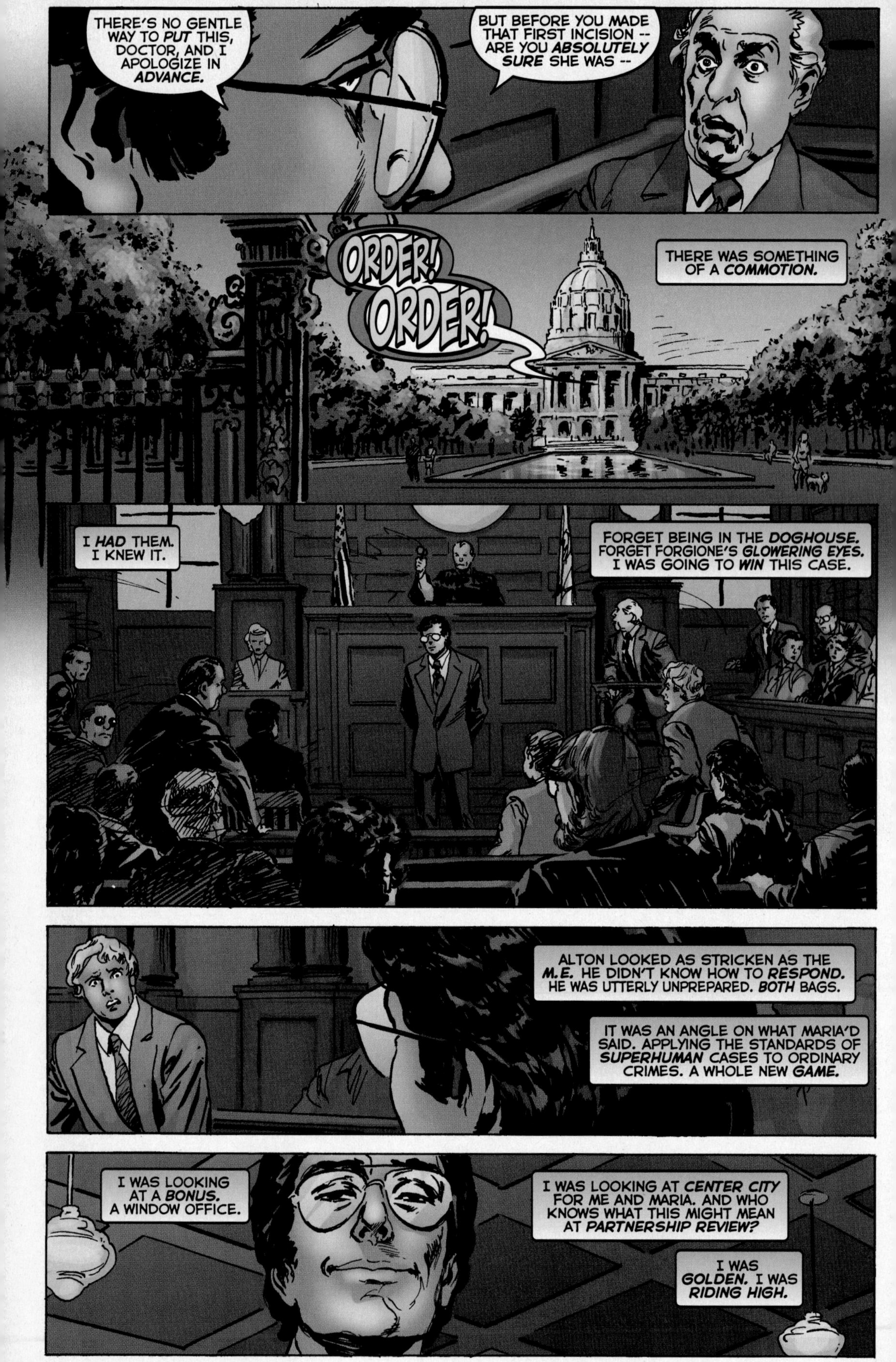

THERE'S NO GENTLE WAY TO *PUT* THIS, DOCTOR, AND I APOLOGIZE IN *ADVANCE.*
BUT BEFORE YOU MADE THAT FIRST INCISION -- ARE YOU *ABSOLUTELY SURE* SHE WAS --
ORDER! ORDER!
THERE WAS SOMETHING OF A *COMMOTION.*
I *HAD* THEM. I KNEW IT.
FORGET BEING IN THE *DOGHOUSE.* FORGET FORGIONE'S *GLOWERING EYES.* I WAS GOING TO *WIN* THIS CASE.
ALTON LOOKED AS STRICKEN AS THE *M.E.* HE DIDN'T KNOW HOW TO *RESPOND.* HE WAS UTTERLY UNPREPARED. *BOTH* BAGS.
IT WAS AN ANGLE ON WHAT MARIA'D SAID. APPLYING THE STANDARDS OF *SUPERHUMAN* CASES TO ORDINARY CRIMES. A WHOLE NEW *GAME.*
I WAS LOOKING AT A *BONUS.* A WINDOW OFFICE.
I WAS LOOKING AT *CENTER CITY* FOR ME AND MARIA. AND WHO KNOWS WHAT THIS MIGHT MEAN AT *PARTNERSHIP REVIEW?*
I WAS *GOLDEN.* I WAS *RIDING HIGH.*

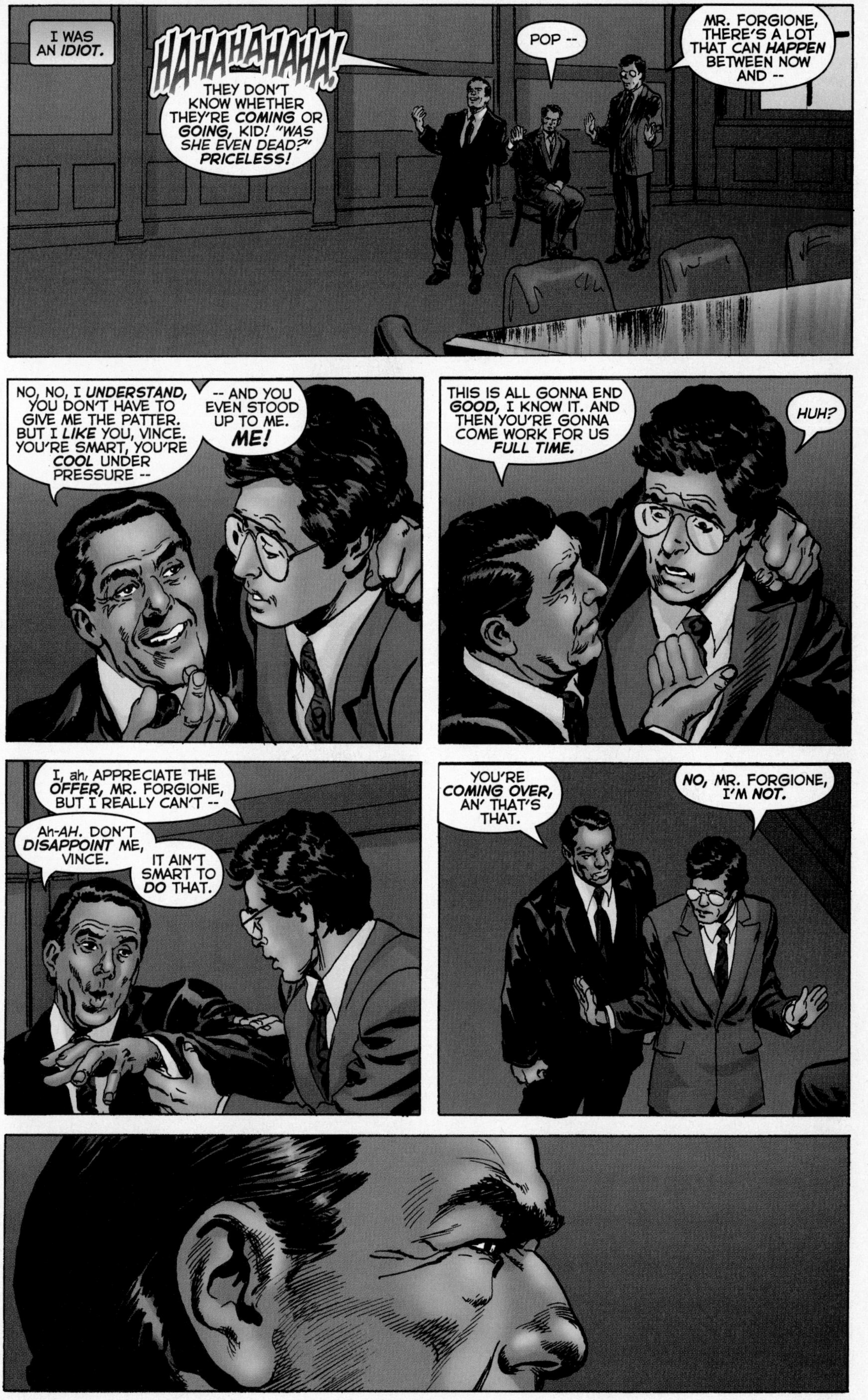

I WAS AN IDIOT.
HAHAHAHAHA!
THEY DON'T KNOW WHETHER THEY'RE COMING OR GOING, KID! "WAS SHE EVEN DEAD?" PRICELESS!
POP --
MR. FORGIONE, THERE'S A LOT THAT CAN HAPPEN BETWEEN NOW AND --
NO, NO, I UNDERSTAND, YOU DON'T HAVE TO GIVE ME THE PATTER. BUT I LIKE YOU, VINCE. YOU'RE SMART, YOU'RE COOL UNDER PRESSURE --
-- AND YOU EVEN STOOD UP TO ME. ME!
THIS IS ALL GONNA END GOOD, I KNOW IT. AND THEN YOU'RE GONNA COME WORK FOR US FULL TIME.
HUH?
I, ah, APPRECIATE THE OFFER, MR. FORGIONE, BUT I REALLY CAN'T --
Ah-AH. DON'T DISAPPOINT ME, VINCE.
IT AIN'T SMART TO DO THAT.
YOU'RE COMING OVER, AN' THAT'S THAT.
NO, MR. FORGIONE, I'M NOT.

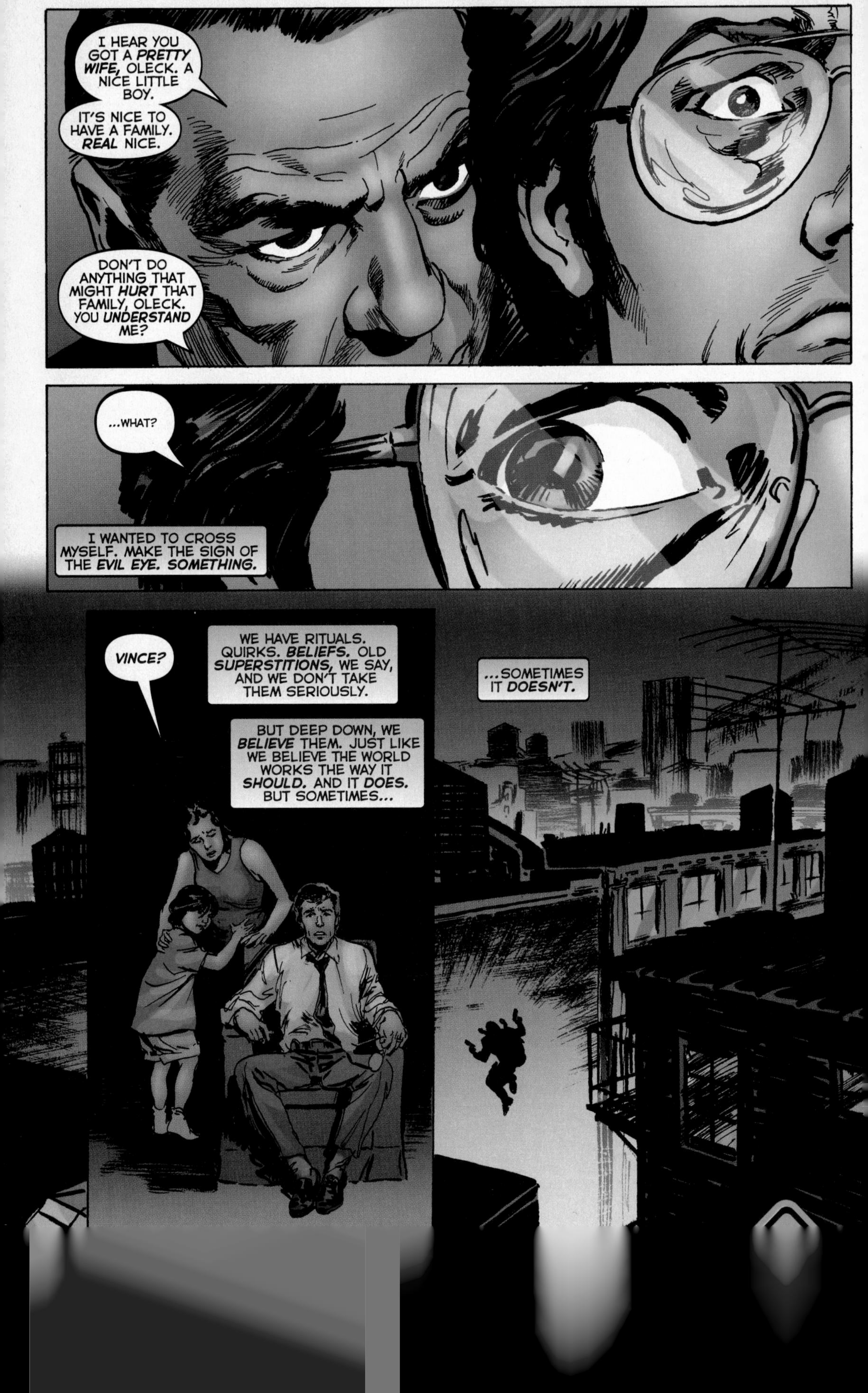
I HEAR YOU GOT A PRETTY WIFE, OLECK. A NICE LITTLE BOY.
IT'S NICE TO HAVE A FAMILY. REAL NICE.
DON'T DO ANYTHING THAT MIGHT HURT THAT FAMILY, OLECK. YOU UNDERSTAND ME?
...WHAT?
I WANTED TO CROSS MYSELF. MAKE THE SIGN OF THE EVIL EYE. SOMETHING.
VINCE?
WE HAVE RITUALS. QUIRKS. BELIEFS. OLD SUPERSTITIONS, WE SAY, AND WE DON'T TAKE THEM SERIOUSLY.
BUT DEEP DOWN, WE BELIEVE THEM. JUST LIKE WE BELIEVE THE WORLD WORKS THE WAY IT SHOULD. AND IT DOES. BUT SOMETIMES...
...SOMETIMES IT DOESN'T.

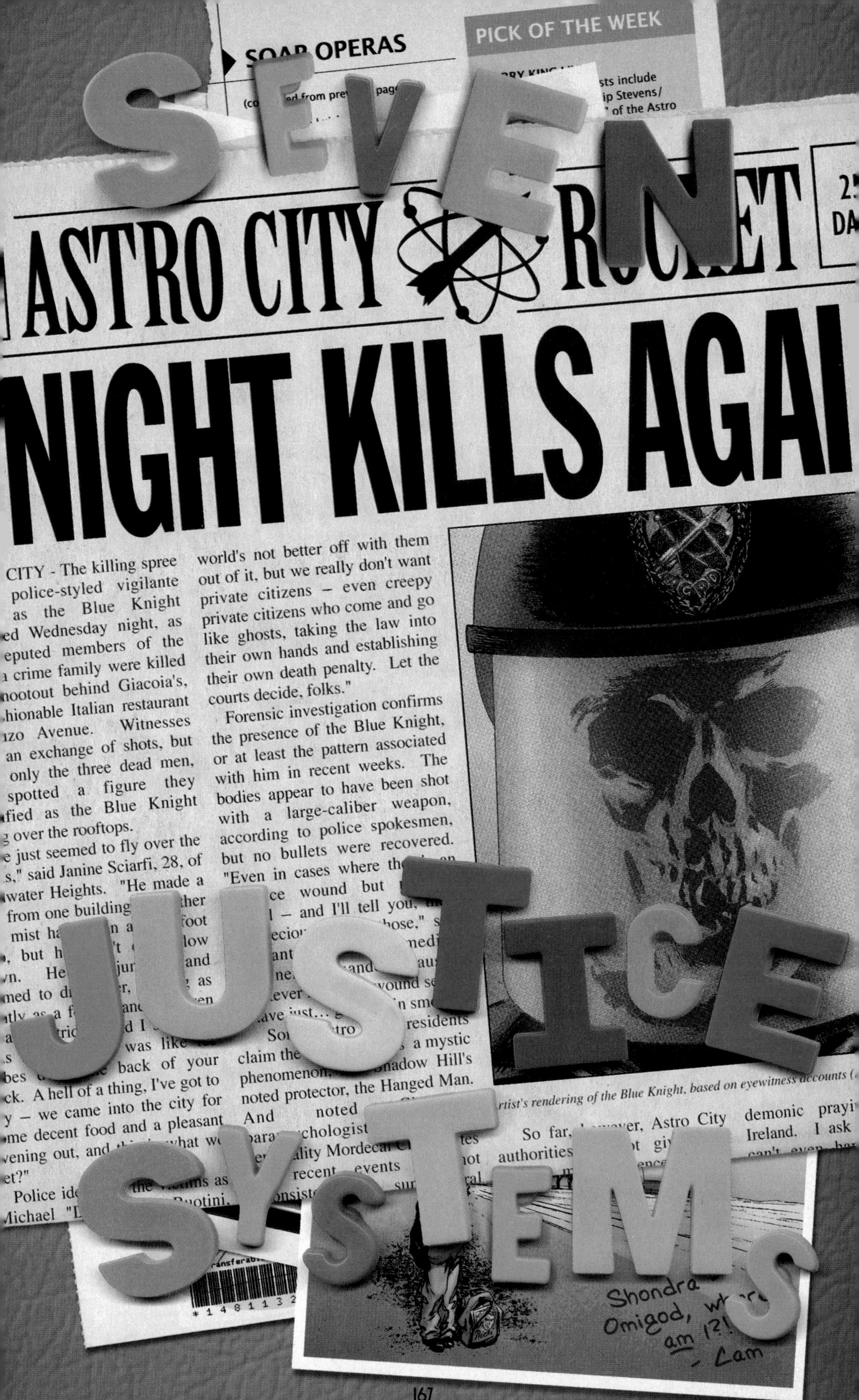
SEVEN
JUSTICE
SYSTEMS
SOAP OPERAS
PICK OF THE WEEK
ASTRO CITY ROCKET
NIGHT KILLS AGAI
CITY - The killing spree
police-styled vigilante
as the Blue Knight
ed Wednesday night, as
eputed members of the
crime family were killed
ootout behind Giacoia's,
hionable Italian restaurant
izo Avenue. Witnesses
an exchange of shots, but
only the three dead men,
spotted a figure they
fied as the Blue Knight
over the rooftops.
e just seemed to fly over the
s," said Janine Sciarfi, 28, of
water Heights. "He made a
world's not better off with them
out of it, but we really don't want
private citizens – even creepy
private citizens who come and go
like ghosts, taking the law into
their own hands and establishing
their own death penalty. Let the
courts decide, folks."
Forensic investigation confirms
the presence of the Blue Knight,
or at least the pattern associated
with him in recent weeks. The
bodies appear to have been shot
with a large-caliber weapon,
according to police spokesmen,
but no bullets were recovered.
back of your
ck. A hell of a thing, I've got to
y – we came into the city for
me decent food and a pleasant
vening out, and
et?"
Police ide
Michael "
phenomenon, Shadow Hill's
noted protector, the Hanged Man.
rtist's rendering of the Blue Knight, based on eyewitness accounts
So far, Astro City
demonic prayi
Ireland. I ask
Shondra
Omigod, where am I?!
- Cam

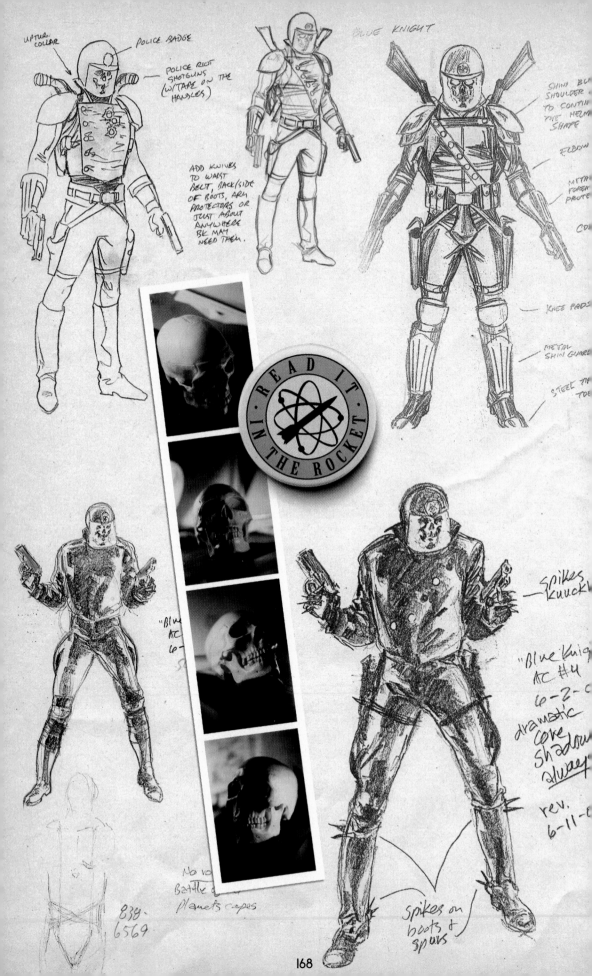

UPTURN
COLLAR

POLICE BADGE

POLICE RIOT
SHOTGUNS
(W/TAPE ON THE
HANDLES)

BLUE KNIGHT

ADD KNIVES
TO WAIST
BELT, BACK/SIDE
OF BOOTS, ARM
PROTECTORS OR
JUST ABOUT
ANYWHERE
BK MAY
NEED THEM.

SHINY BLA
SHOULDER
TO CONTIN
THE HELM
SHAPE

ELBOW

METAL
FOREAR
PROTE

C

KNEE PADS

METAL
SHIN GUARD

STEEL TI
TOE

READ IT IN THE ROCKET

"Blu
AT
6-
S

No vo
Battle o
Planets capes

838.
6569

Spikes
KNUCKL

"Blue Knig
AT #4
6-2-0
dramatic
core
shadow
alway

rev.
6-11-0

spikes on
boots &
spurs

168

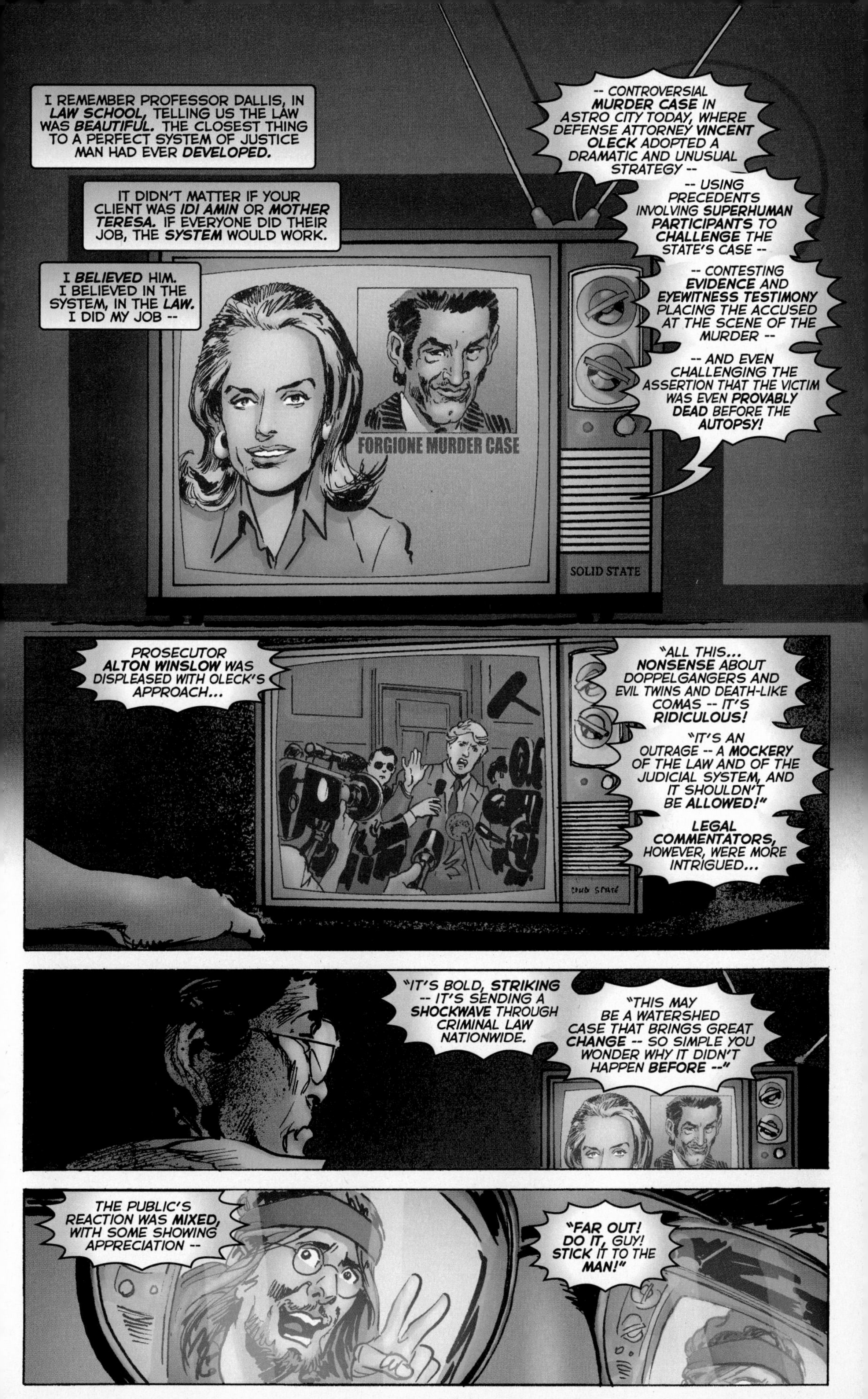
I REMEMBER PROFESSOR DALLIS, IN LAW SCHOOL, TELLING US THE LAW WAS BEAUTIFUL. THE CLOSEST THING TO A PERFECT SYSTEM OF JUSTICE MAN HAD EVER DEVELOPED.
IT DIDN'T MATTER IF YOUR CLIENT WAS IDI AMIN OR MOTHER TERESA. IF EVERYONE DID THEIR JOB, THE SYSTEM WOULD WORK.
I BELIEVED HIM. I BELIEVED IN THE SYSTEM, IN THE LAW. I DID MY JOB --
-- CONTROVERSIAL MURDER CASE IN ASTRO CITY TODAY, WHERE DEFENSE ATTORNEY VINCENT OLECK ADOPTED A DRAMATIC AND UNUSUAL STRATEGY --
-- USING PRECEDENTS INVOLVING SUPERHUMAN PARTICIPANTS TO CHALLENGE THE STATE'S CASE --
-- CONTESTING EVIDENCE AND EYEWITNESS TESTIMONY PLACING THE ACCUSED AT THE SCENE OF THE MURDER --
-- AND EVEN CHALLENGING THE ASSERTION THAT THE VICTIM WAS EVEN PROVABLY DEAD BEFORE THE AUTOPSY!
FORGIONE MURDER CASE
SOLID STATE
PROSECUTOR ALTON WINSLOW WAS DISPLEASED WITH OLECK'S APPROACH...
"ALL THIS... NONSENSE ABOUT DOPPELGANGERS AND EVIL TWINS AND DEATH-LIKE COMAS -- IT'S RIDICULOUS!
"IT'S AN OUTRAGE -- A MOCKERY OF THE LAW AND OF THE JUDICIAL SYSTEM, AND IT SHOULDN'T BE ALLOWED!"
LEGAL COMMENTATORS, HOWEVER, WERE MORE INTRIGUED...
"IT'S BOLD, STRIKING -- IT'S SENDING A SHOCKWAVE THROUGH CRIMINAL LAW NATIONWIDE.
"THIS MAY BE A WATERSHED CASE THAT BRINGS GREAT CHANGE -- SO SIMPLE YOU WONDER WHY IT DIDN'T HAPPEN BEFORE --"
THE PUBLIC'S REACTION WAS MIXED, WITH SOME SHOWING APPRECIATION --
"FAR OUT! DO IT, GUY! STICK IT TO THE MAN!"

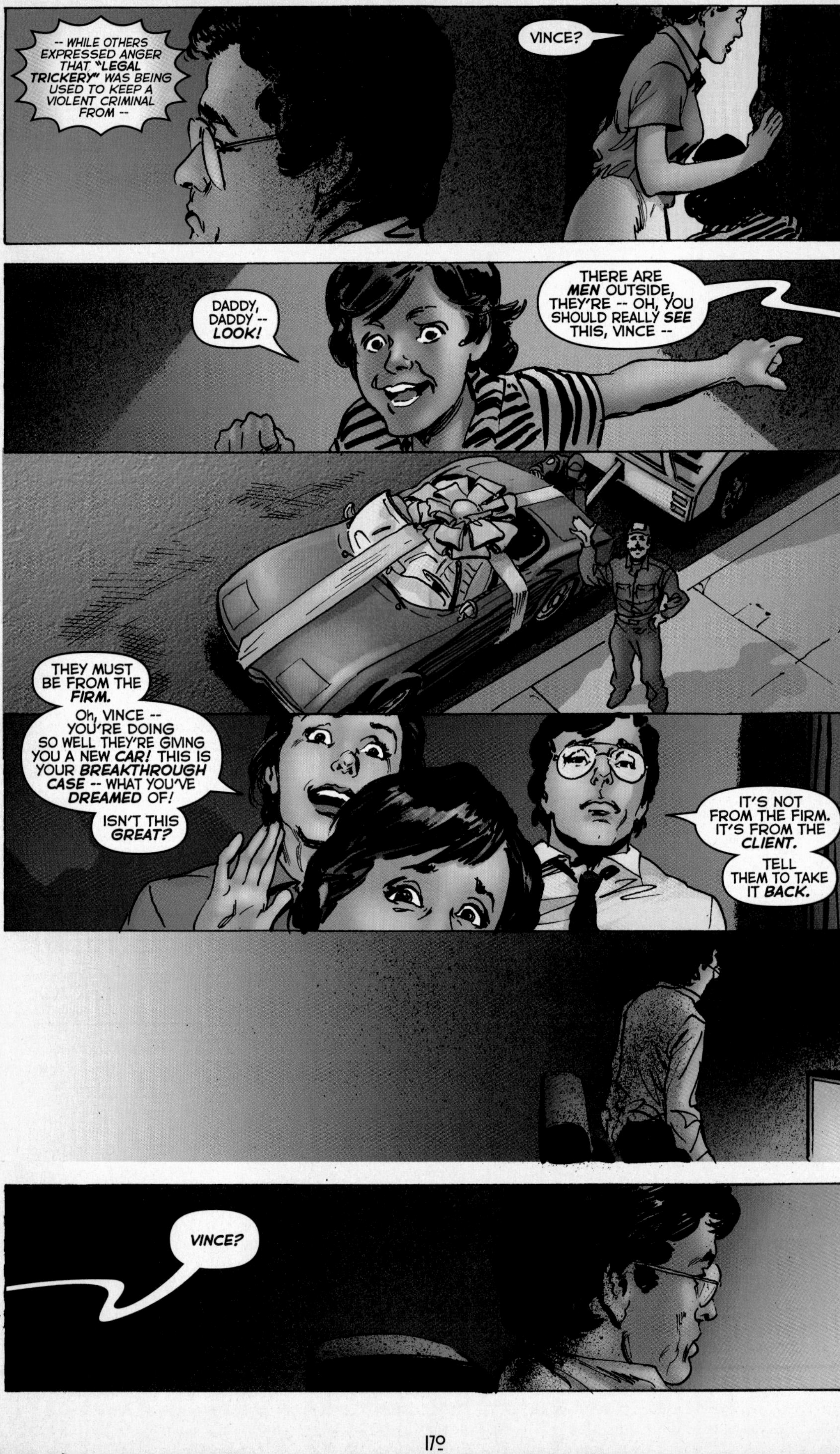
-- WHILE OTHERS EXPRESSED ANGER THAT "LEGAL TRICKERY" WAS BEING USED TO KEEP A VIOLENT CRIMINAL FROM --
VINCE?
DADDY, DADDY -- LOOK!
THERE ARE MEN OUTSIDE, THEY'RE -- OH, YOU SHOULD REALLY SEE THIS, VINCE --
THEY MUST BE FROM THE FIRM.
Oh, VINCE -- YOU'RE DOING SO WELL THEY'RE GIVING YOU A NEW CAR! THIS IS YOUR BREAKTHROUGH CASE -- WHAT YOU'VE DREAMED OF!
ISN'T THIS GREAT?
IT'S NOT FROM THE FIRM. IT'S FROM THE CLIENT.
TELL THEM TO TAKE IT BACK.
VINCE?

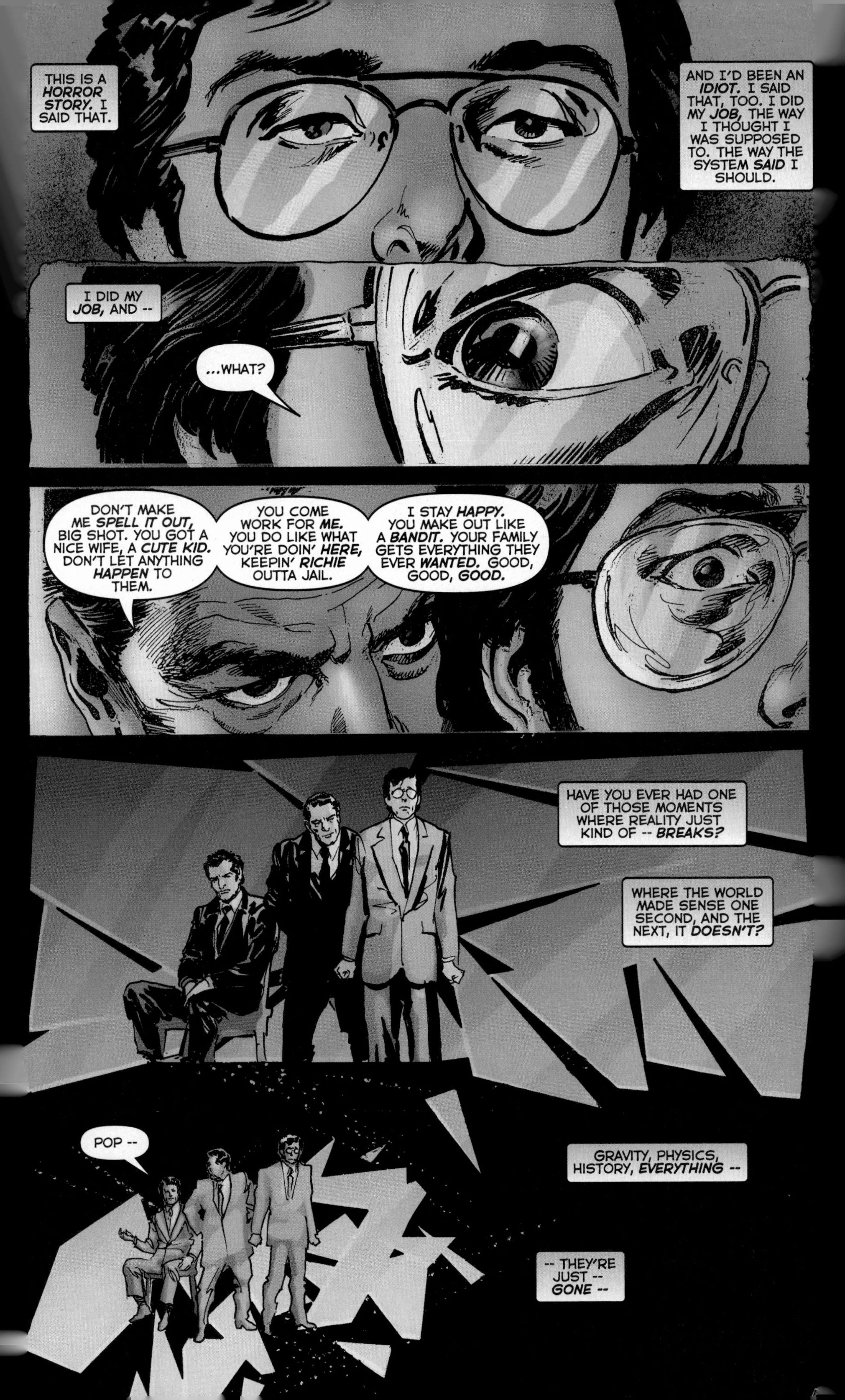

THIS IS A HORROR STORY. I SAID THAT.
AND I'D BEEN AN IDIOT. I SAID THAT, TOO. I DID MY JOB, THE WAY I THOUGHT I WAS SUPPOSED TO. THE WAY THE SYSTEM SAID I SHOULD.
I DID MY JOB, AND --
...WHAT?
DON'T MAKE ME SPELL IT OUT, BIG SHOT. YOU GOT A NICE WIFE, A CUTE KID. DON'T LET ANYTHING HAPPEN TO THEM.
YOU COME WORK FOR ME. YOU DO LIKE WHAT YOU'RE DOIN' HERE, KEEPIN' RICHIE OUTTA JAIL.
I STAY HAPPY. YOU MAKE OUT LIKE A BANDIT. YOUR FAMILY GETS EVERYTHING THEY EVER WANTED. GOOD, GOOD, GOOD.
HAVE YOU EVER HAD ONE OF THOSE MOMENTS WHERE REALITY JUST KIND OF -- BREAKS?
WHERE THE WORLD MADE SENSE ONE SECOND, AND THE NEXT, IT DOESN'T?
POP --
GRAVITY, PHYSICS, HISTORY, EVERYTHING --
-- THEY'RE JUST -- GONE --

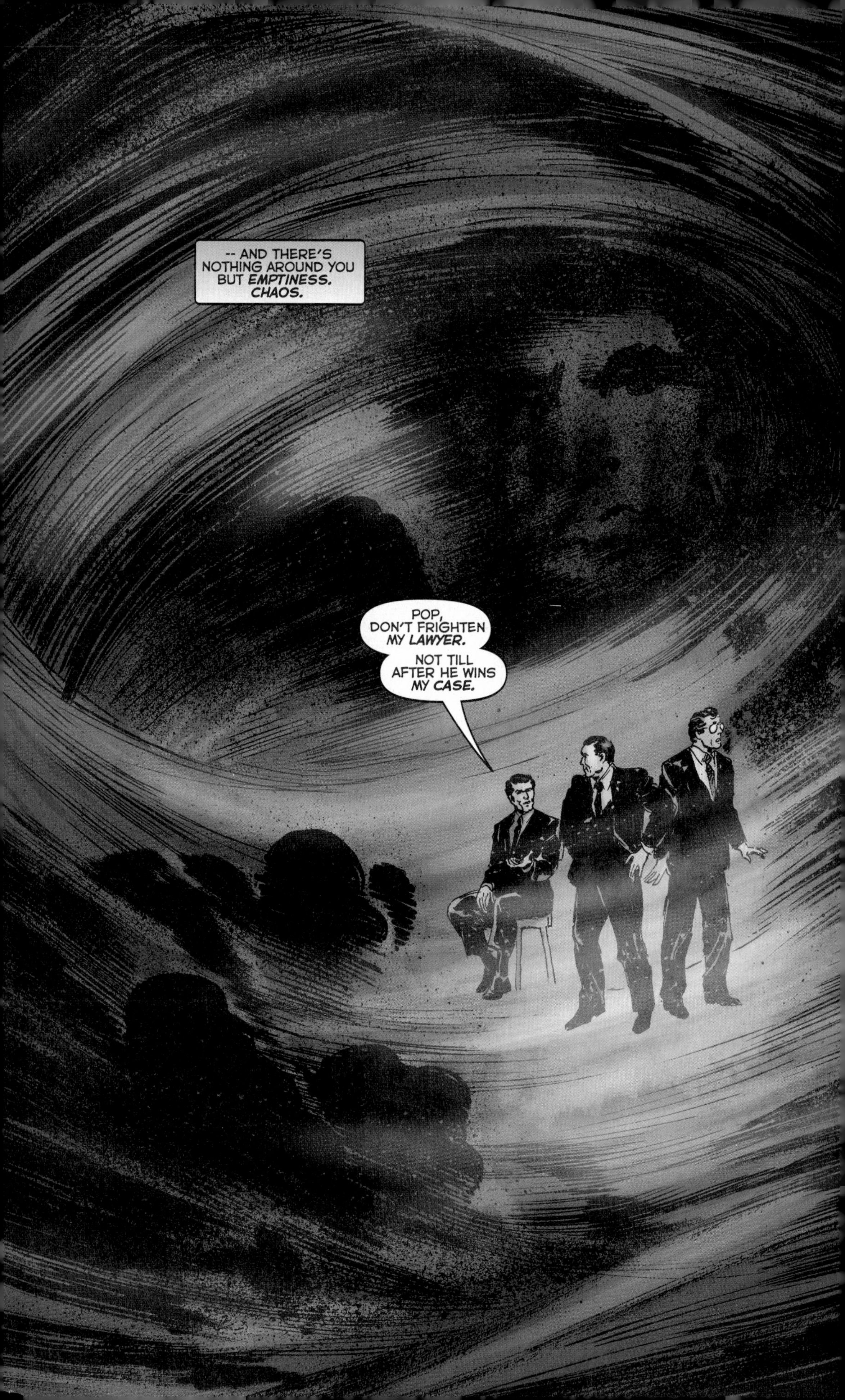
-- AND THERE'S NOTHING AROUND YOU BUT EMPTINESS. CHAOS.
POP, DON'T FRIGHTEN MY LAWYER.
NOT TILL AFTER HE WINS MY CASE.

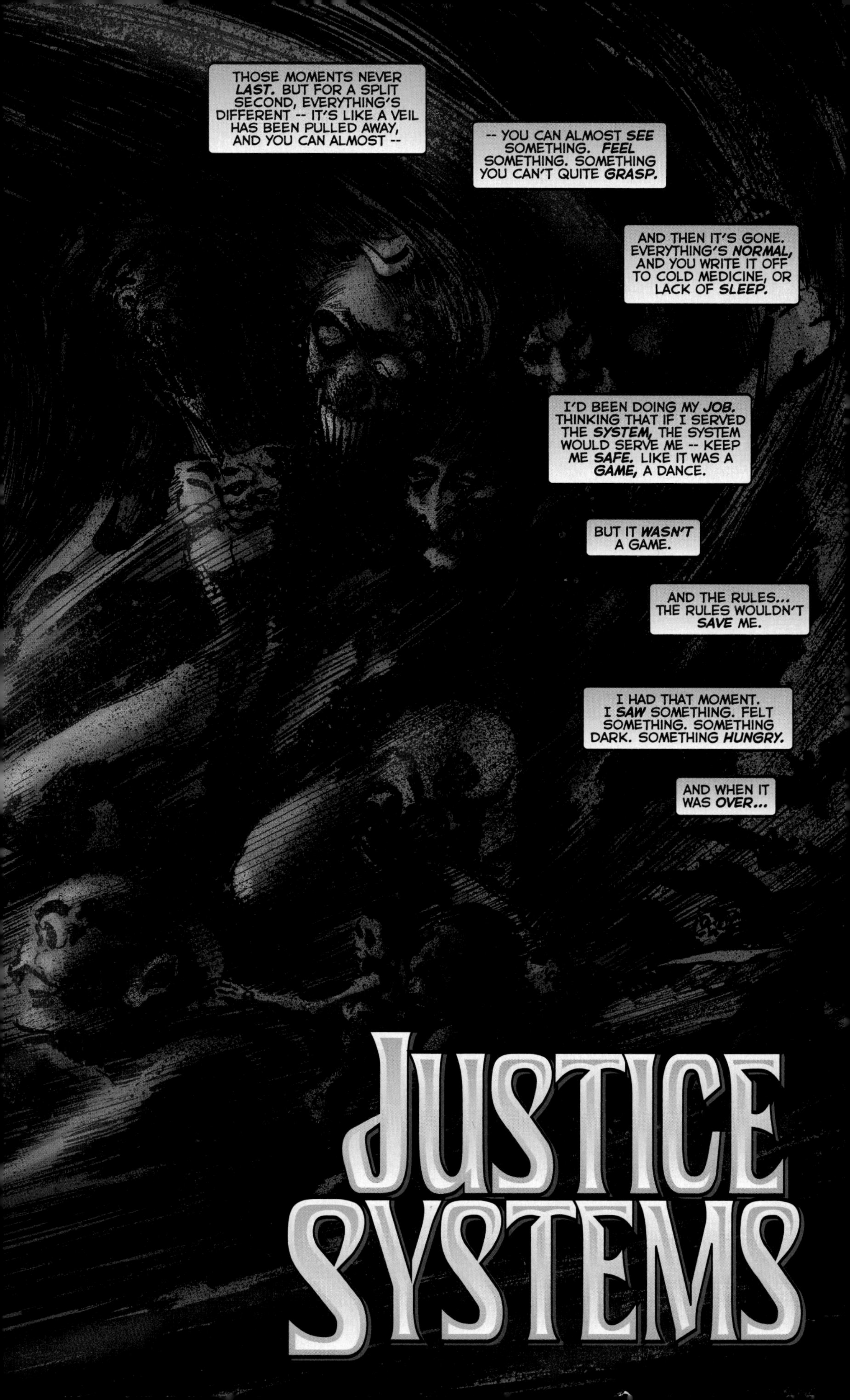
THOSE MOMENTS NEVER LAST. BUT FOR A SPLIT SECOND, EVERYTHING'S DIFFERENT -- IT'S LIKE A VEIL HAS BEEN PULLED AWAY, AND YOU CAN ALMOST --
-- YOU CAN ALMOST SEE SOMETHING. FEEL SOMETHING. SOMETHING YOU CAN'T QUITE GRASP.
AND THEN IT'S GONE. EVERYTHING'S NORMAL, AND YOU WRITE IT OFF TO COLD MEDICINE, OR LACK OF SLEEP.
I'D BEEN DOING MY JOB. THINKING THAT IF I SERVED THE SYSTEM, THE SYSTEM WOULD SERVE ME -- KEEP ME SAFE. LIKE IT WAS A GAME, A DANCE.
BUT IT WASN'T A GAME.
AND THE RULES... THE RULES WOULDN'T SAVE ME.
I HAD THAT MOMENT. I SAW SOMETHING. FELT SOMETHING. SOMETHING DARK. SOMETHING HUNGRY.
AND WHEN IT WAS OVER...
JUSTICE SYSTEMS

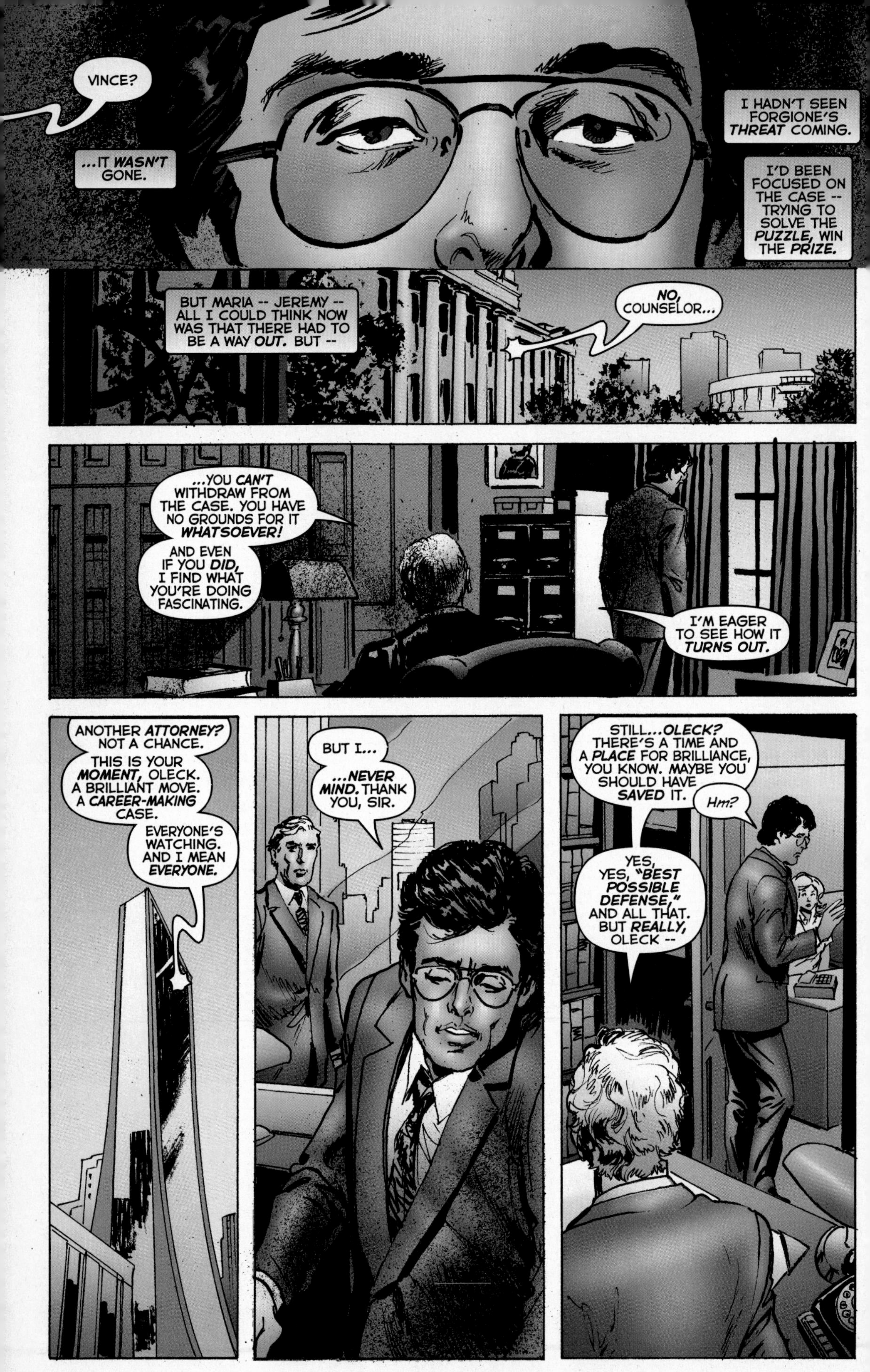
VINCE?
...IT WASN'T GONE.
I HADN'T SEEN FORGIONE'S THREAT COMING.
I'D BEEN FOCUSED ON THE CASE -- TRYING TO SOLVE THE PUZZLE, WIN THE PRIZE.
BUT MARIA -- JEREMY -- ALL I COULD THINK NOW WAS THAT THERE HAD TO BE A WAY OUT. BUT --
NO, COUNSELOR...
...YOU CAN'T WITHDRAW FROM THE CASE. YOU HAVE NO GROUNDS FOR IT WHATSOEVER!
AND EVEN IF YOU DID, I FIND WHAT YOU'RE DOING FASCINATING.
I'M EAGER TO SEE HOW IT TURNS OUT.
ANOTHER ATTORNEY? NOT A CHANCE.
THIS IS YOUR MOMENT, OLECK. A BRILLIANT MOVE. A CAREER-MAKING CASE.
EVERYONE'S WATCHING. AND I MEAN EVERYONE.
BUT I...
...NEVER MIND. THANK YOU, SIR.
STILL...OLECK? THERE'S A TIME AND A PLACE FOR BRILLIANCE, YOU KNOW. MAYBE YOU SHOULD HAVE SAVED IT.
Hm?
YES, YES, "BEST POSSIBLE DEFENSE," AND ALL THAT. BUT REALLY, OLECK --

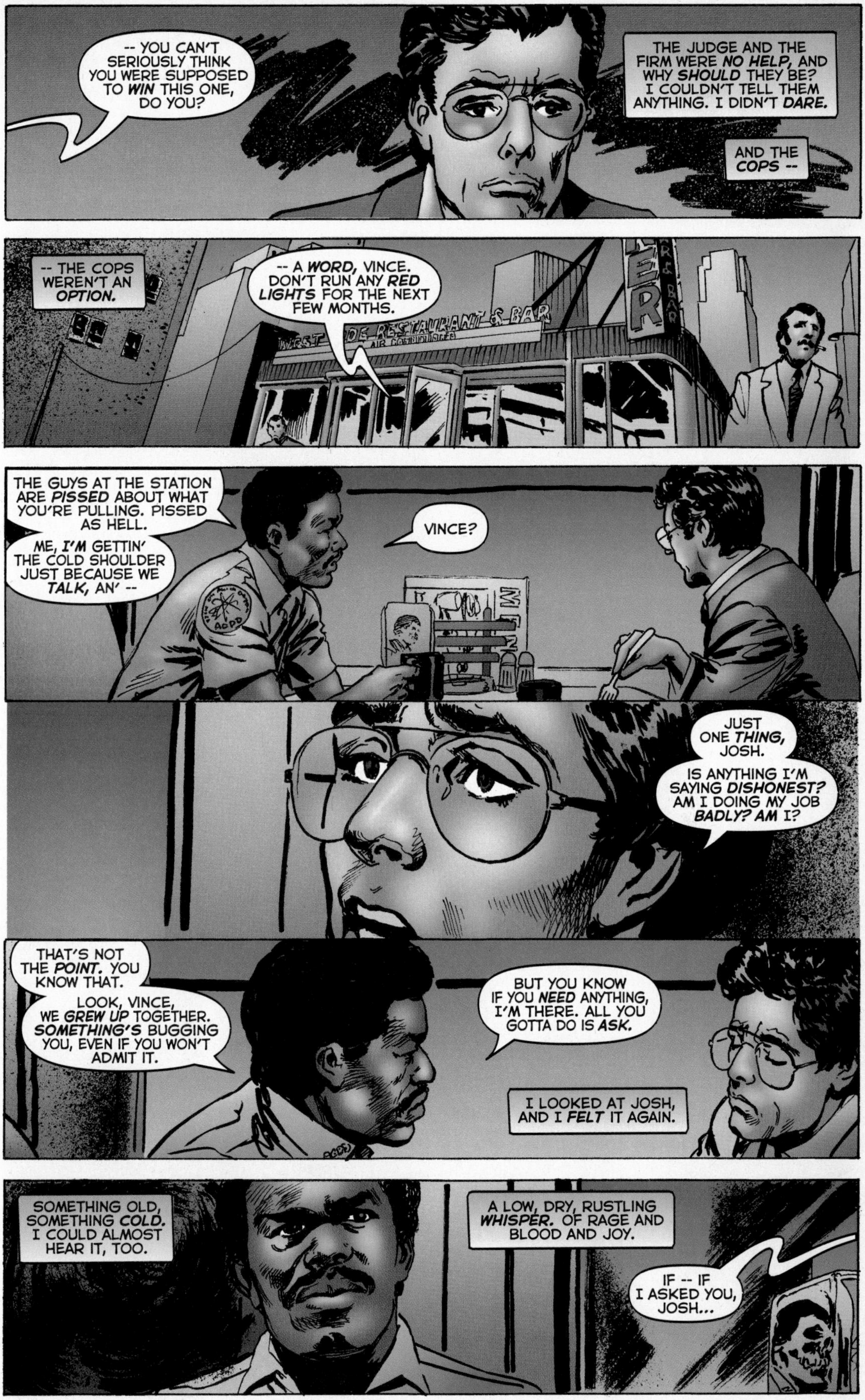
-- YOU CAN'T SERIOUSLY THINK YOU WERE SUPPOSED TO WIN THIS ONE, DO YOU?
THE JUDGE AND THE FIRM WERE NO HELP, AND WHY SHOULD THEY BE? I COULDN'T TELL THEM ANYTHING. I DIDN'T DARE.
AND THE COPS --
-- THE COPS WEREN'T AN OPTION.
-- A WORD, VINCE. DON'T RUN ANY RED LIGHTS FOR THE NEXT FEW MONTHS.
WEST SIDE RESTAURANT & BAR
THE GUYS AT THE STATION ARE PISSED ABOUT WHAT YOU'RE PULLING. PISSED AS HELL.
ME, I'M GETTIN' THE COLD SHOULDER JUST BECAUSE WE TALK, AN' --
VINCE?
JUST ONE THING, JOSH.
IS ANYTHING I'M SAYING DISHONEST? AM I DOING MY JOB BADLY? AM I?
THAT'S NOT THE POINT. YOU KNOW THAT.
LOOK, VINCE, WE GREW UP TOGETHER. SOMETHING'S BUGGING YOU, EVEN IF YOU WON'T ADMIT IT.
BUT YOU KNOW IF YOU NEED ANYTHING, I'M THERE. ALL YOU GOTTA DO IS ASK.
I LOOKED AT JOSH, AND I FELT IT AGAIN.
SOMETHING OLD, SOMETHING COLD. I COULD ALMOST HEAR IT, TOO.
A LOW, DRY, RUSTLING WHISPER. OF RAGE AND BLOOD AND JOY.
IF -- IF I ASKED YOU, JOSH...

...WOULD YOU GET ME A *GUN?*

I WONDERED IF MAYBE I SHOULD JUST *LOSE.* THROW THE CASE, CHEAT -- LET HIM KILL *ME* IF HE WANTED, BUT LEAVE MY FAMILY *OUT* OF IT.

BUT MAYBE THAT WOULDN'T BE *ENOUGH* --

I *STALLED.*

I HAD OTHER *WITNESSES* LINED UP, TO CHALLENGE THE STATE'S METHODS. MOSTLY JUST GOING THROUGH THE *MOTIONS.*

NOW I USED THEM TO BUY TIME TO *THINK* -- HAD THEM SAY THE SAME THINGS IN AS MANY DIFFERENT WAYS AS I COULD --

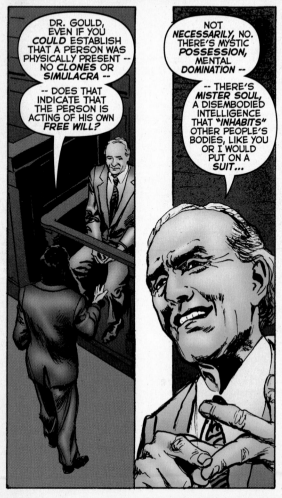

DR. GOULD, EVEN IF YOU *COULD* ESTABLISH THAT A PERSON WAS PHYSICALLY PRESENT -- NO *CLONES* OR *SIMULACRA* --

-- DOES THAT INDICATE THAT THE PERSON IS ACTING OF HIS OWN *FREE WILL?*

NOT *NECESSARILY,* NO. THERE'S MYSTIC *POSSESSION,* MENTAL *DOMINATION* --

-- THERE'S *MISTER SOUL,* A DISEMBODIED INTELLIGENCE THAT "INHABITS" OTHER PEOPLE'S BODIES, LIKE YOU OR I WOULD PUT ON A SUIT...

THE JURY *WANTED* TO CONVICT, BUT THEY WEREN'T *SURE.* I COULD SEE IT IN THEIR FACES, THEIR BODY LANGUAGE.

THE CASE WAS MINE TO *LOSE.* I COULD TIP THEM *ONE* WAY -- TOWARD ACQUITTAL -- OR TIP THEM THE *OTHER.*

IT WAS IN MY *HANDS.*

MR. *OLECK?*

MR. *OLECK?*

Hm?

SORRY, SORRY. NOTHING FURTHER.

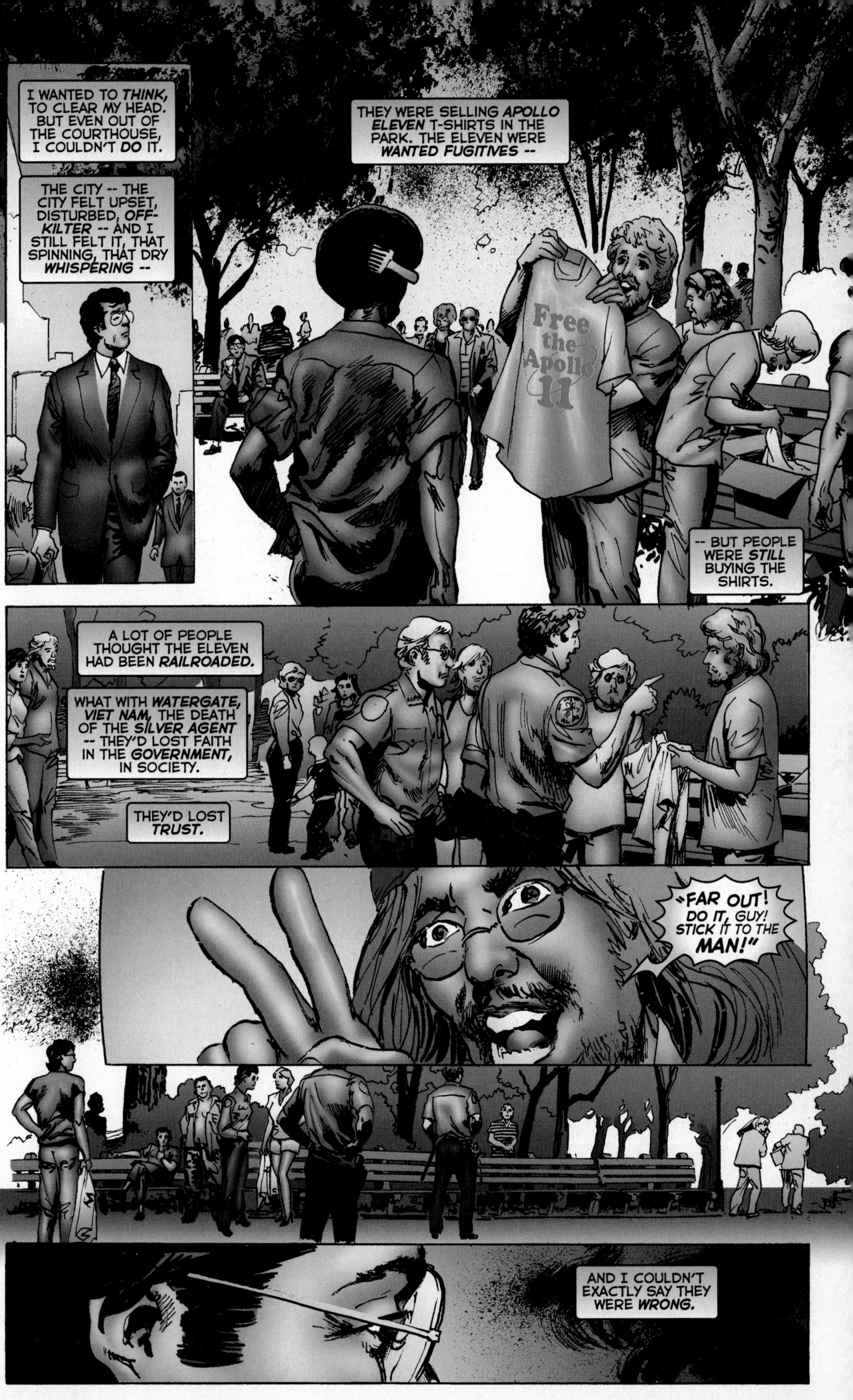
I WANTED TO *THINK*, TO CLEAR MY HEAD. BUT EVEN OUT OF THE COURTHOUSE, I COULDN'T *DO* IT.
THE CITY -- THE CITY FELT UPSET, DISTURBED, *OFF-KILTER* -- AND I STILL FELT IT, THAT SPINNING, THAT DRY *WHISPERING* --
THEY WERE SELLING *APOLLO ELEVEN* T-SHIRTS IN THE PARK. THE ELEVEN WERE *WANTED FUGITIVES* --
Free the Apollo 11
-- BUT PEOPLE WERE *STILL* BUYING THE SHIRTS.
A LOT OF PEOPLE THOUGHT THE ELEVEN HAD BEEN *RAILROADED.*
WHAT WITH *WATERGATE, VIET NAM,* THE DEATH OF THE *SILVER AGENT* -- THEY'D LOST FAITH IN THE *GOVERNMENT,* IN SOCIETY.
THEY'D LOST *TRUST.*
"FAR OUT! DO IT, GUY! STICK IT TO THE *MAN!*"
AND I COULDN'T EXACTLY SAY THEY WERE *WRONG.*

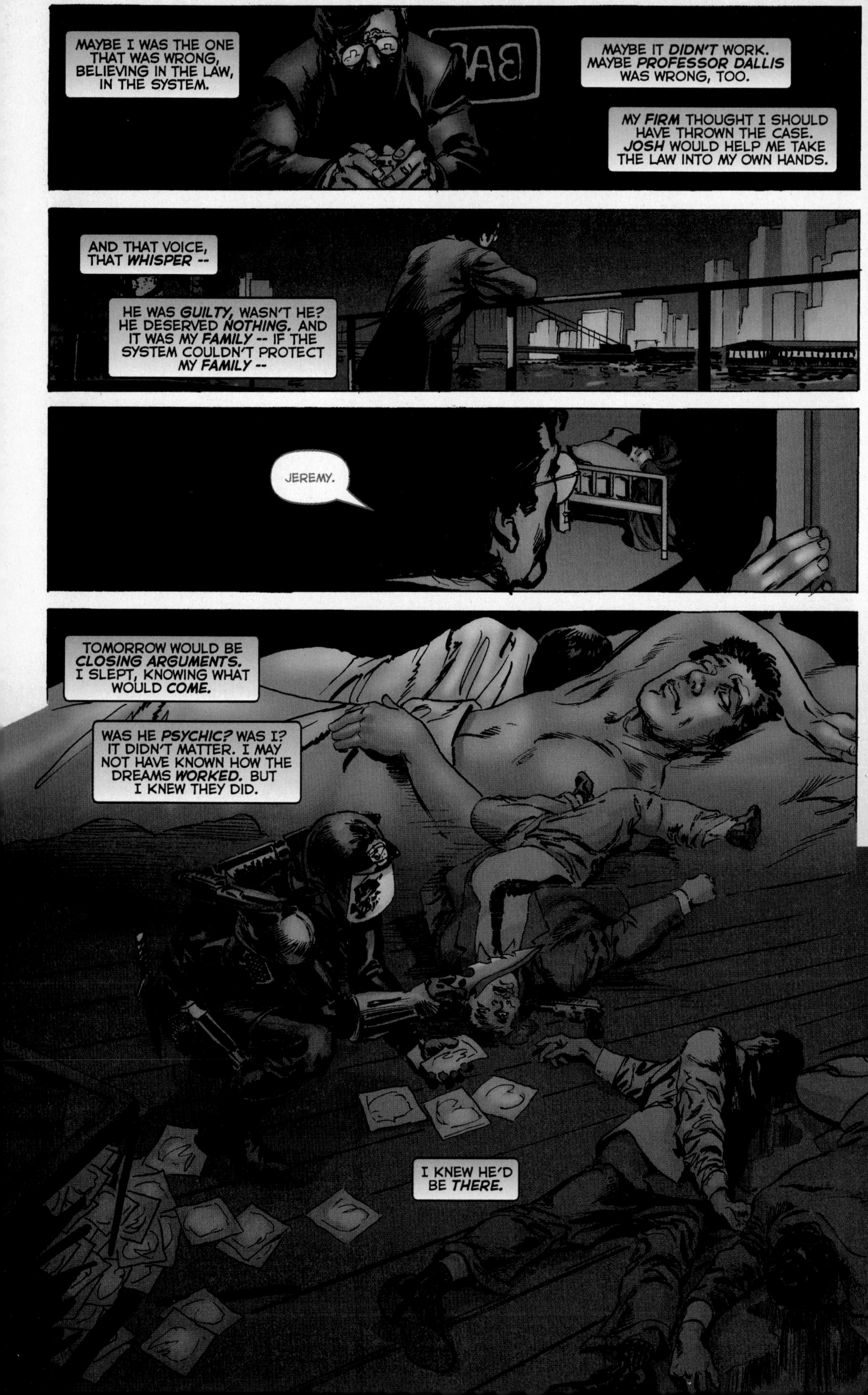
MAYBE I WAS THE ONE THAT WAS WRONG, BELIEVING IN THE LAW, IN THE SYSTEM.
MAYBE IT *DIDN'T* WORK. MAYBE *PROFESSOR DALLIS* WAS WRONG, TOO.
MY *FIRM* THOUGHT I SHOULD HAVE THROWN THE CASE. *JOSH* WOULD HELP ME TAKE THE LAW INTO MY OWN HANDS.
AND THAT VOICE, THAT *WHISPER* --
HE WAS *GUILTY,* WASN'T HE? HE DESERVED *NOTHING.* AND IT WAS MY *FAMILY* -- IF THE SYSTEM COULDN'T PROTECT MY *FAMILY* --
JEREMY.
TOMORROW WOULD BE *CLOSING ARGUMENTS.* I SLEPT, KNOWING WHAT WOULD *COME.*
WAS HE *PSYCHIC?* WAS I? IT DIDN'T MATTER. I MAY NOT HAVE KNOWN HOW THE DREAMS *WORKED.* BUT I KNEW THEY DID.
I KNEW HE'D BE *THERE.*

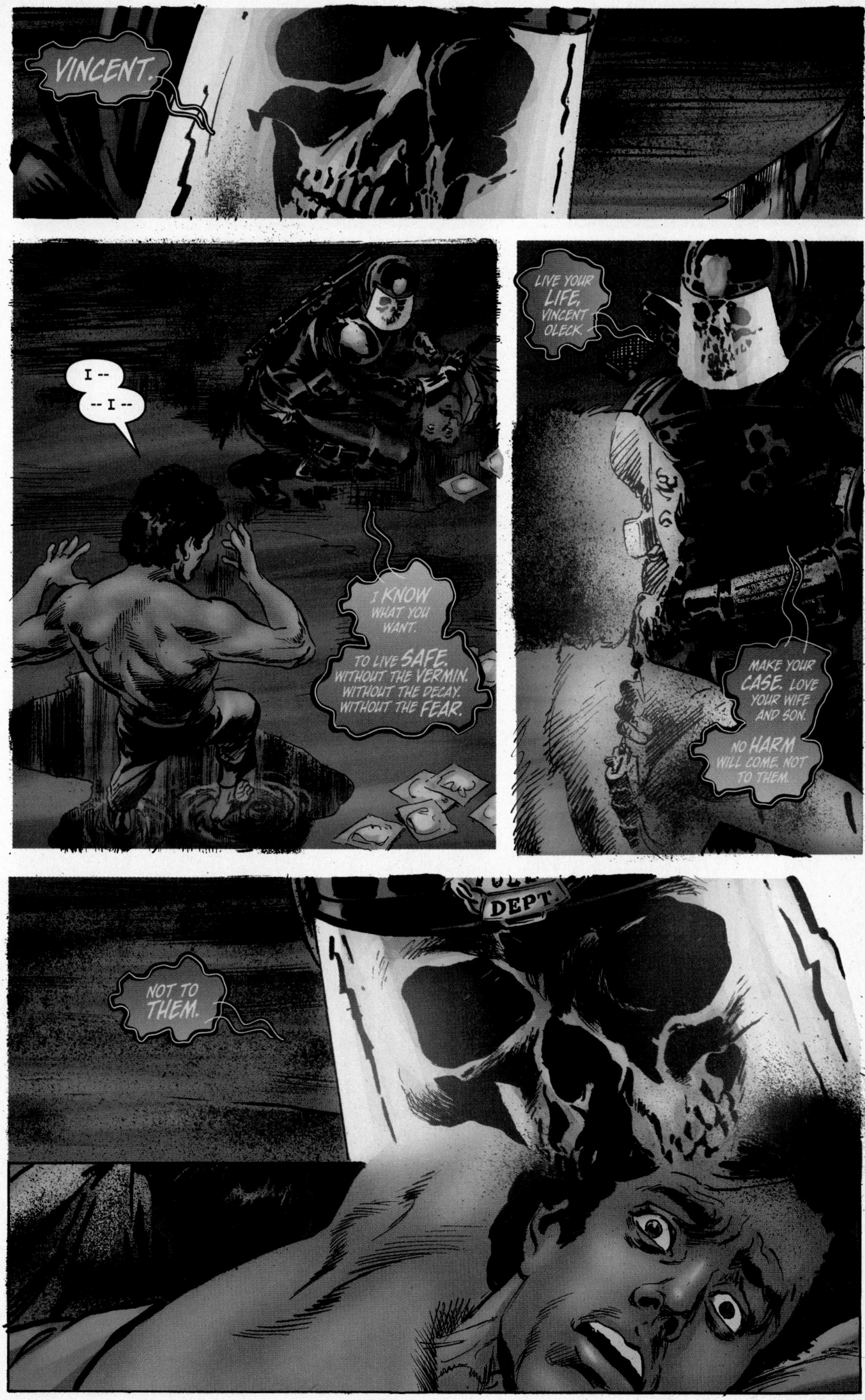
VINCENT.
I --
-- I --
I KNOW WHAT YOU WANT.
TO LIVE SAFE. WITHOUT THE VERMIN. WITHOUT THE DECAY. WITHOUT THE FEAR.
LIVE YOUR LIFE, VINCENT OLECK.
MAKE YOUR CASE. LOVE YOUR WIFE AND SON.
NO HARM WILL COME. NOT TO THEM.
DEPT.
NOT TO THEM.

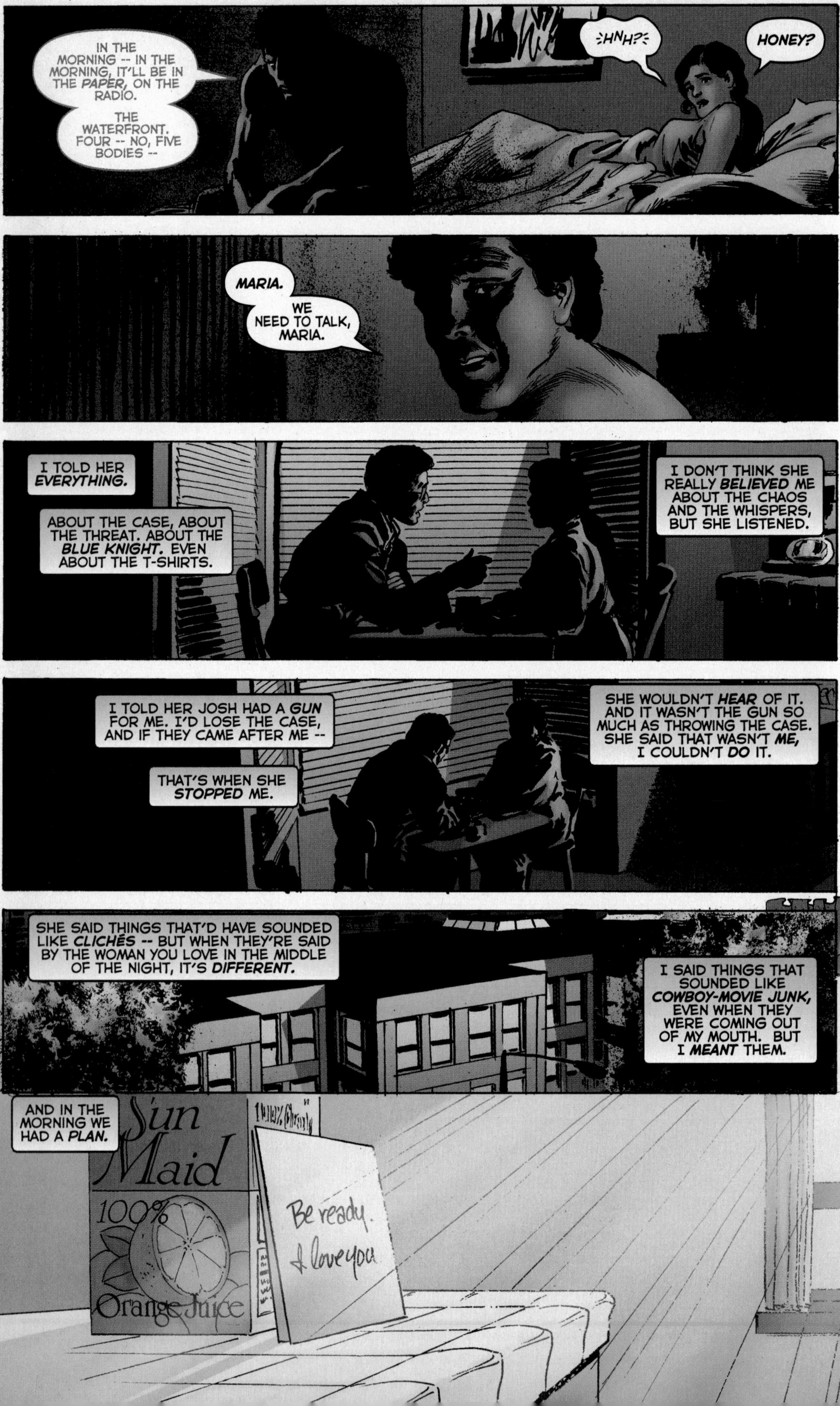
IN THE MORNING -- IN THE MORNING, IT'LL BE IN THE *PAPER,* ON THE RADIO.
THE WATERFRONT. FOUR -- NO, FIVE BODIES --
HNH?
HONEY?
MARIA.
WE NEED TO TALK, MARIA.
I TOLD HER *EVERYTHING.*
ABOUT THE CASE, ABOUT THE THREAT. ABOUT THE *BLUE KNIGHT.* EVEN ABOUT THE T-SHIRTS.
I DON'T THINK SHE REALLY *BELIEVED* ME ABOUT THE CHAOS AND THE WHISPERS, BUT SHE LISTENED.
I TOLD HER JOSH HAD A *GUN* FOR ME. I'D LOSE THE CASE, AND IF THEY CAME AFTER ME --
THAT'S WHEN SHE *STOPPED* ME.
SHE WOULDN'T *HEAR* OF IT. AND IT WASN'T THE GUN SO MUCH AS THROWING THE CASE. SHE SAID THAT WASN'T *ME,* I COULDN'T *DO* IT.
SHE SAID THINGS THAT'D HAVE SOUNDED LIKE *CLICHÉS* -- BUT WHEN THEY'RE SAID BY THE WOMAN YOU LOVE IN THE MIDDLE OF THE NIGHT, IT'S *DIFFERENT.*
I SAID THINGS THAT SOUNDED LIKE *COWBOY-MOVIE JUNK,* EVEN WHEN THEY WERE COMING OUT OF MY MOUTH. BUT I *MEANT* THEM.
AND IN THE MORNING WE HAD A *PLAN.*
Sun Maid
100%
Orange Juice
Be ready.
I love you

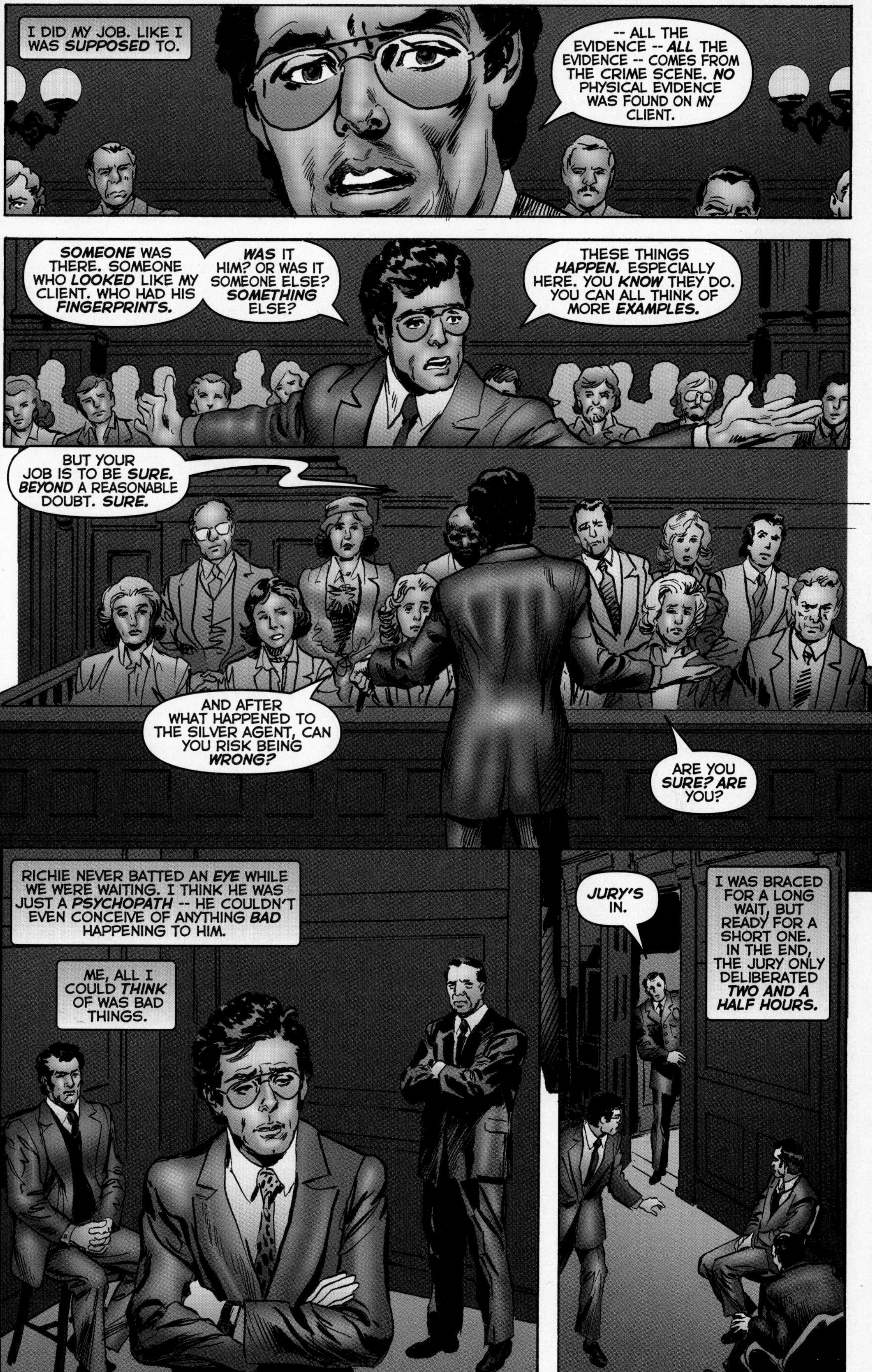
I DID MY JOB. LIKE I WAS SUPPOSED TO.
-- ALL THE EVIDENCE -- ALL THE EVIDENCE -- COMES FROM THE CRIME SCENE. NO PHYSICAL EVIDENCE WAS FOUND ON MY CLIENT.
SOMEONE WAS THERE. SOMEONE WHO LOOKED LIKE MY CLIENT. WHO HAD HIS FINGERPRINTS.
WAS IT HIM? OR WAS IT SOMEONE ELSE? SOMETHING ELSE?
THESE THINGS HAPPEN. ESPECIALLY HERE. YOU KNOW THEY DO. YOU CAN ALL THINK OF MORE EXAMPLES.
BUT YOUR JOB IS TO BE SURE. BEYOND A REASONABLE DOUBT. SURE.
AND AFTER WHAT HAPPENED TO THE SILVER AGENT, CAN YOU RISK BEING WRONG?
ARE YOU SURE? ARE YOU?
RICHIE NEVER BATTED AN EYE WHILE WE WERE WAITING. I THINK HE WAS JUST A PSYCHOPATH -- HE COULDN'T EVEN CONCEIVE OF ANYTHING BAD HAPPENING TO HIM.
ME, ALL I COULD THINK OF WAS BAD THINGS.
JURY'S IN.
I WAS BRACED FOR A LONG WAIT, BUT READY FOR A SHORT ONE. IN THE END, THE JURY ONLY DELIBERATED TWO AND A HALF HOURS.

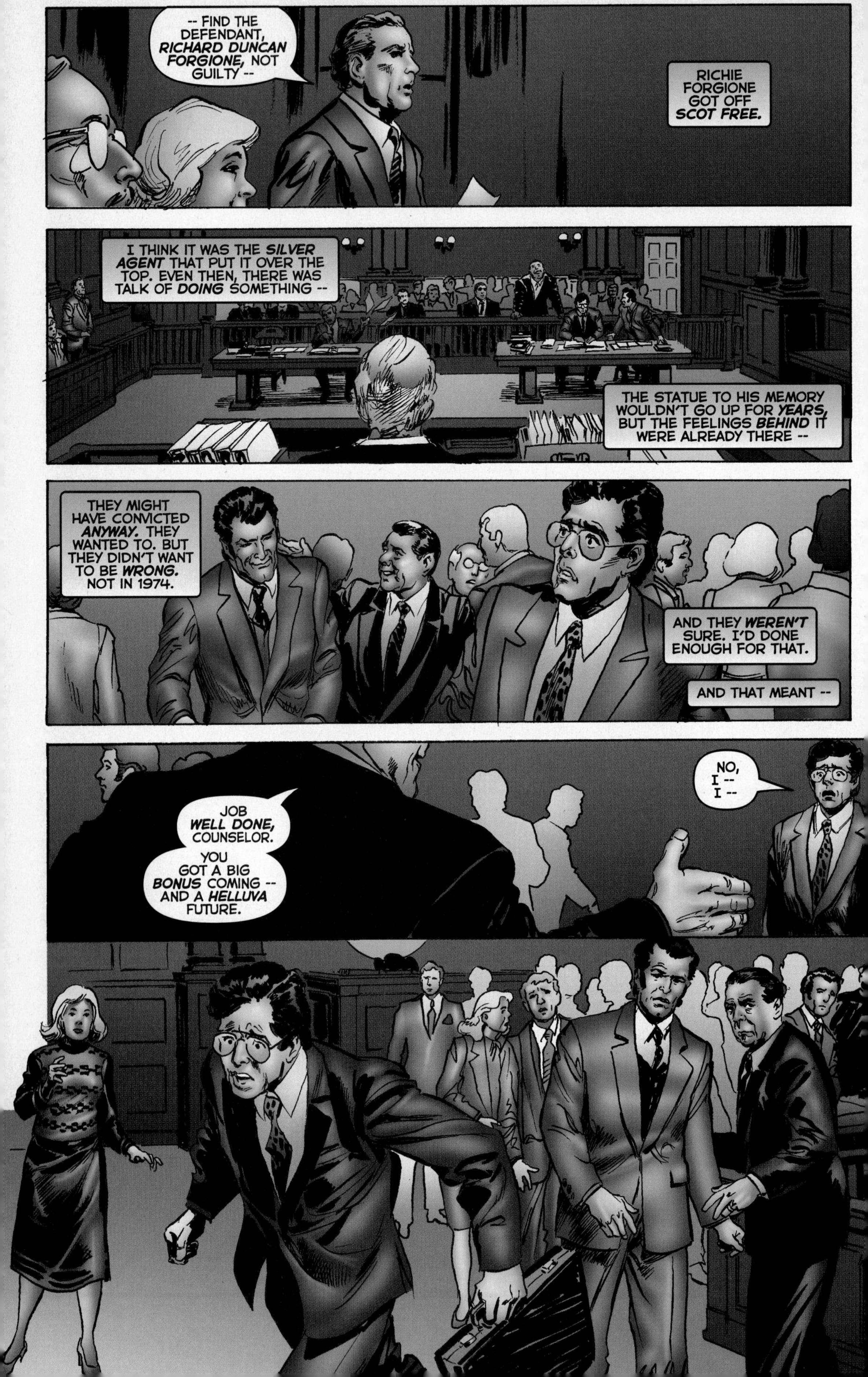
-- FIND THE DEFENDANT, RICHARD DUNCAN FORGIONE, NOT GUILTY --
RICHIE FORGIONE GOT OFF SCOT FREE.
I THINK IT WAS THE SILVER AGENT THAT PUT IT OVER THE TOP. EVEN THEN, THERE WAS TALK OF DOING SOMETHING --
THE STATUE TO HIS MEMORY WOULDN'T GO UP FOR YEARS, BUT THE FEELINGS BEHIND IT WERE ALREADY THERE --
THEY MIGHT HAVE CONVICTED ANYWAY. THEY WANTED TO. BUT THEY DIDN'T WANT TO BE WRONG. NOT IN 1974.
AND THEY WEREN'T SURE. I'D DONE ENOUGH FOR THAT.
AND THAT MEANT --
JOB WELL DONE, COUNSELOR.
YOU GOT A BIG BONUS COMING -- AND A HELLUVA FUTURE.
NO, I -- I --

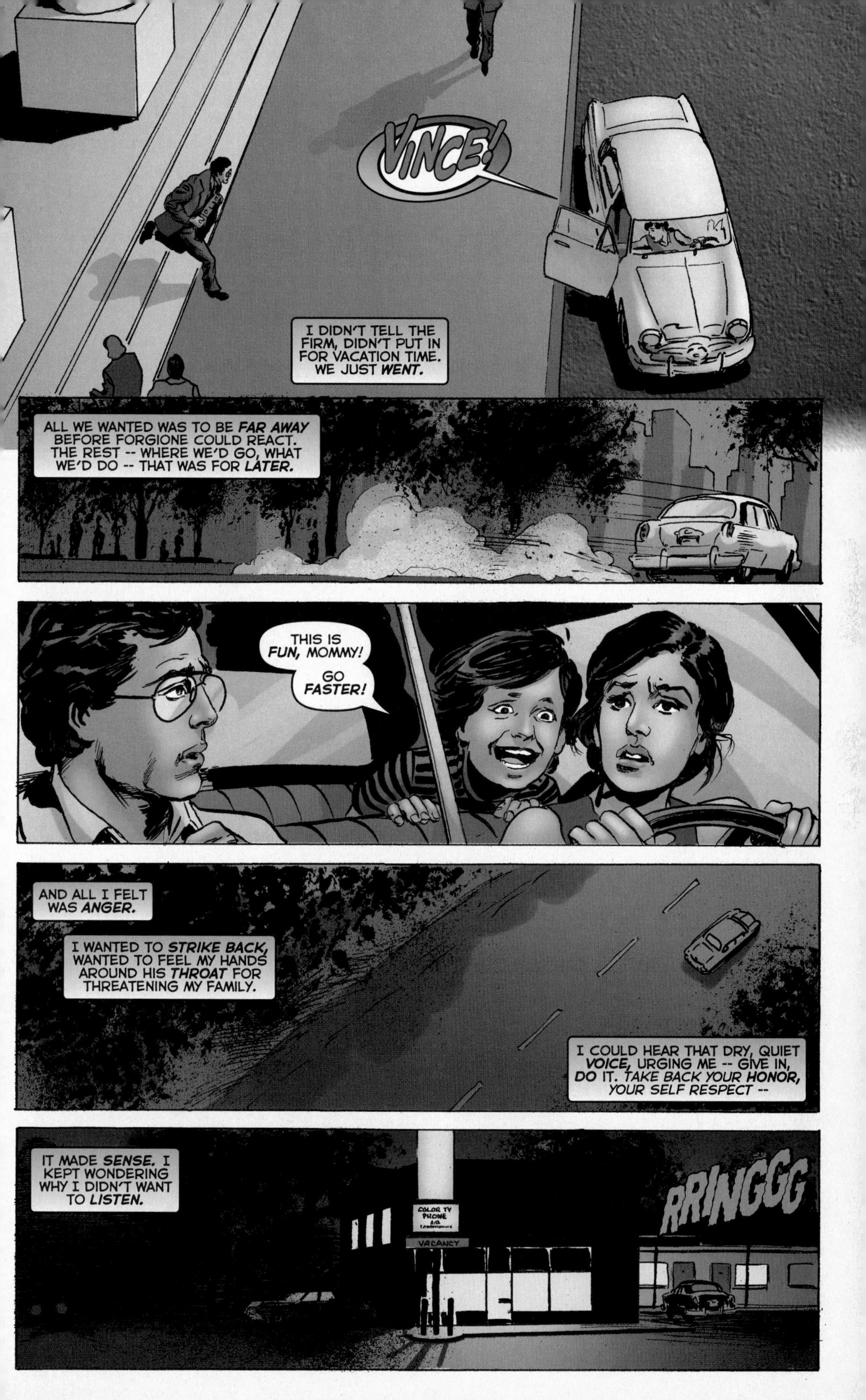
VINCE!
I DIDN'T TELL THE FIRM, DIDN'T PUT IN FOR VACATION TIME. WE JUST WENT.
ALL WE WANTED WAS TO BE FAR AWAY BEFORE FORGIONE COULD REACT. THE REST -- WHERE WE'D GO, WHAT WE'D DO -- THAT WAS FOR LATER.
THIS IS FUN, MOMMY!
GO FASTER!
AND ALL I FELT WAS ANGER.
I WANTED TO STRIKE BACK, WANTED TO FEEL MY HANDS AROUND HIS THROAT FOR THREATENING MY FAMILY.
I COULD HEAR THAT DRY, QUIET VOICE, URGING ME -- GIVE IN, DO IT. TAKE BACK YOUR HONOR, YOUR SELF RESPECT --
IT MADE SENSE. I KEPT WONDERING WHY I DIDN'T WANT TO LISTEN.
COLOR TV
PHONE
VACANCY
RRINGGG

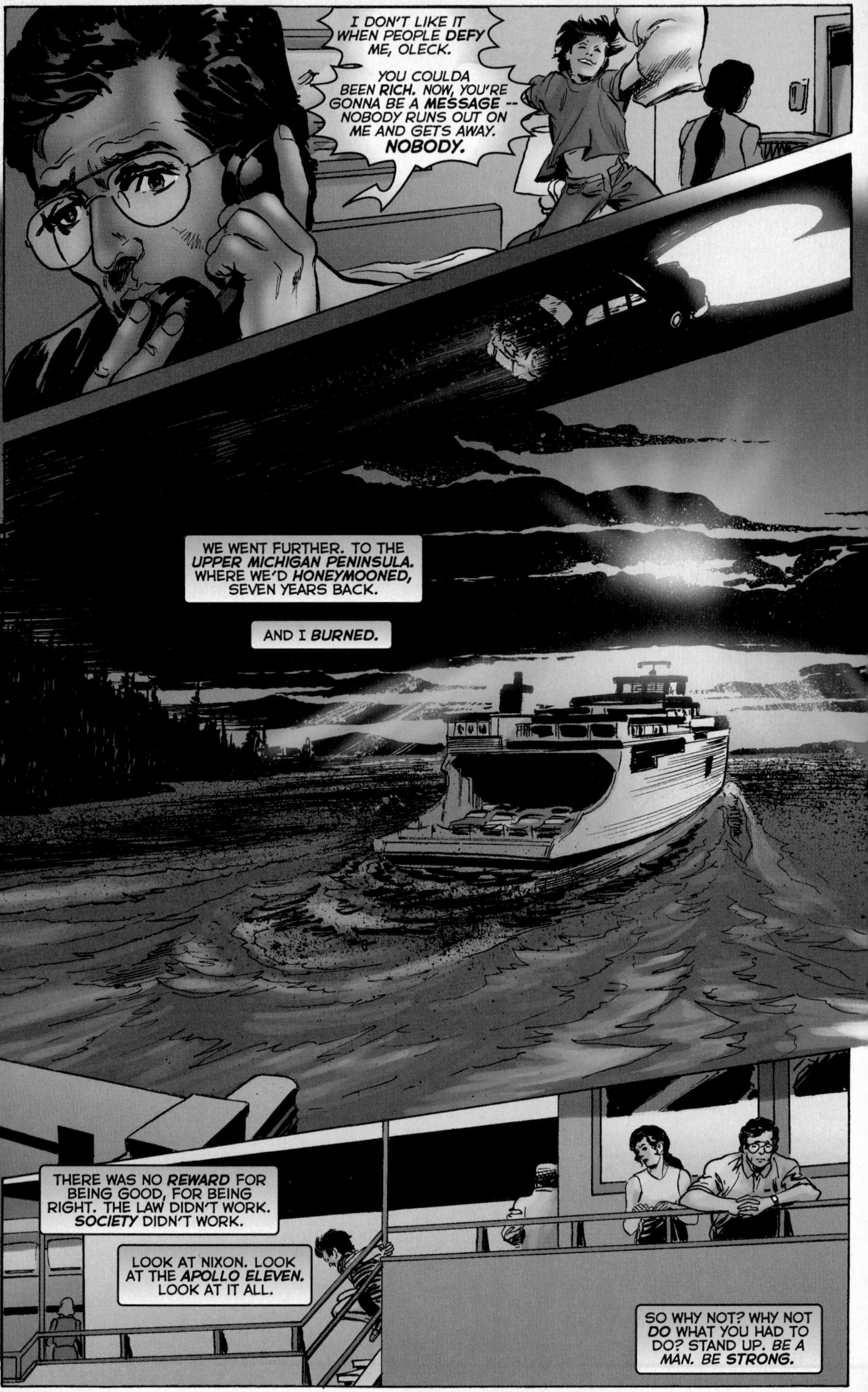
I DON'T LIKE IT WHEN PEOPLE DEFY ME, OLECK.
YOU COULDA BEEN RICH. NOW, YOU'RE GONNA BE A MESSAGE -- NOBODY RUNS OUT ON ME AND GETS AWAY. NOBODY.
WE WENT FURTHER. TO THE UPPER MICHIGAN PENINSULA. WHERE WE'D HONEYMOONED, SEVEN YEARS BACK.
AND I BURNED.
THERE WAS NO REWARD FOR BEING GOOD, FOR BEING RIGHT. THE LAW DIDN'T WORK. SOCIETY DIDN'T WORK.
LOOK AT NIXON. LOOK AT THE APOLLO ELEVEN. LOOK AT IT ALL.
SO WHY NOT? WHY NOT DO WHAT YOU HAD TO DO? STAND UP. BE A MAN. BE STRONG.

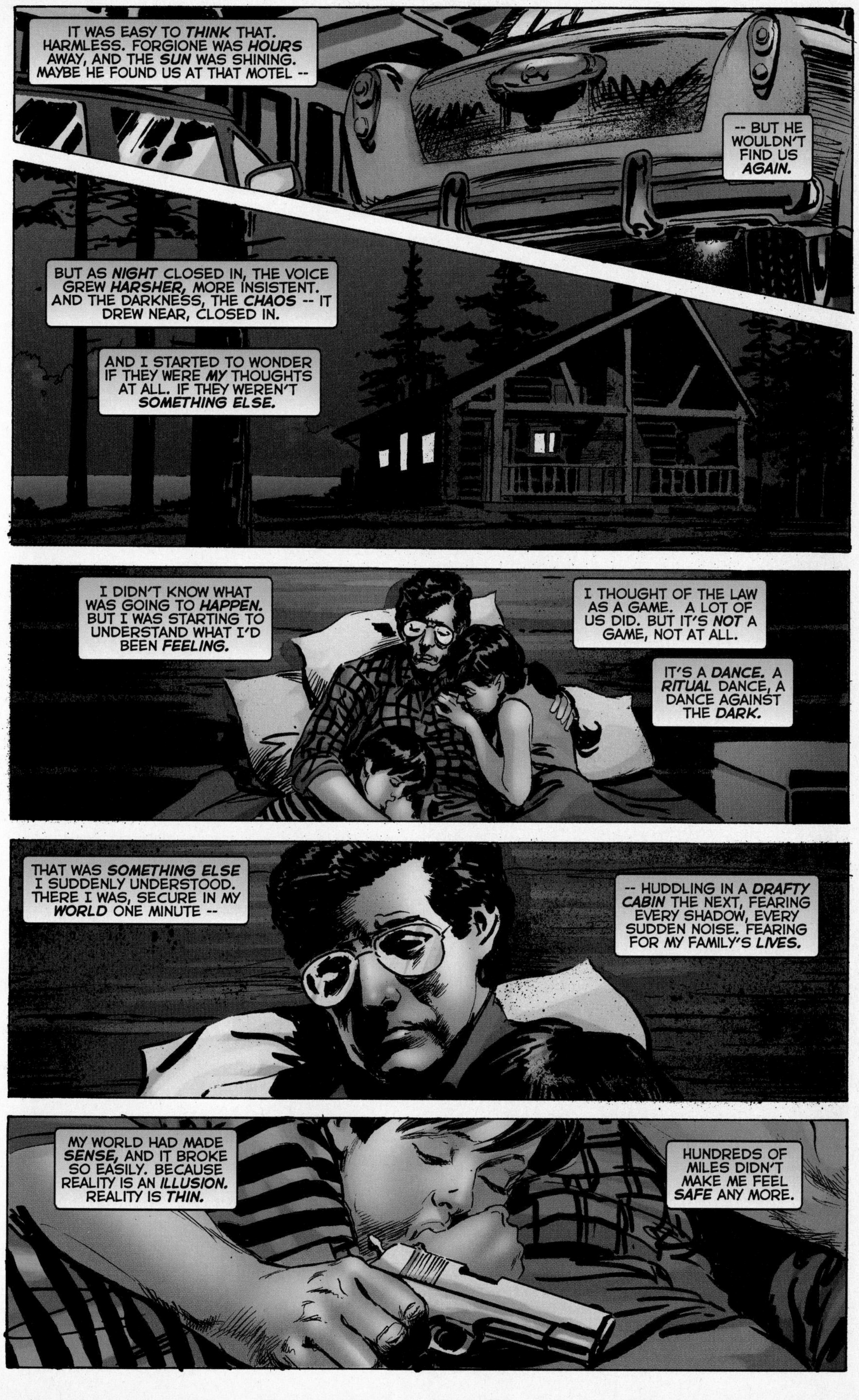
IT WAS EASY TO THINK THAT. HARMLESS. FORGIONE WAS HOURS AWAY, AND THE SUN WAS SHINING. MAYBE HE FOUND US AT THAT MOTEL --
-- BUT HE WOULDN'T FIND US AGAIN.
BUT AS NIGHT CLOSED IN, THE VOICE GREW HARSHER, MORE INSISTENT. AND THE DARKNESS, THE CHAOS -- IT DREW NEAR, CLOSED IN.
AND I STARTED TO WONDER IF THEY WERE MY THOUGHTS AT ALL. IF THEY WEREN'T SOMETHING ELSE.
I DIDN'T KNOW WHAT WAS GOING TO HAPPEN. BUT I WAS STARTING TO UNDERSTAND WHAT I'D BEEN FEELING.
I THOUGHT OF THE LAW AS A GAME. A LOT OF US DID. BUT IT'S NOT A GAME, NOT AT ALL.
IT'S A DANCE. A RITUAL DANCE, A DANCE AGAINST THE DARK.
THAT WAS SOMETHING ELSE I SUDDENLY UNDERSTOOD. THERE I WAS, SECURE IN MY WORLD ONE MINUTE --
-- HUDDLING IN A DRAFTY CABIN THE NEXT, FEARING EVERY SHADOW, EVERY SUDDEN NOISE. FEARING FOR MY FAMILY'S LIVES.
MY WORLD HAD MADE SENSE, AND IT BROKE SO EASILY. BECAUSE REALITY IS AN ILLUSION. REALITY IS THIN.
HUNDREDS OF MILES DIDN'T MAKE ME FEEL SAFE ANY MORE.

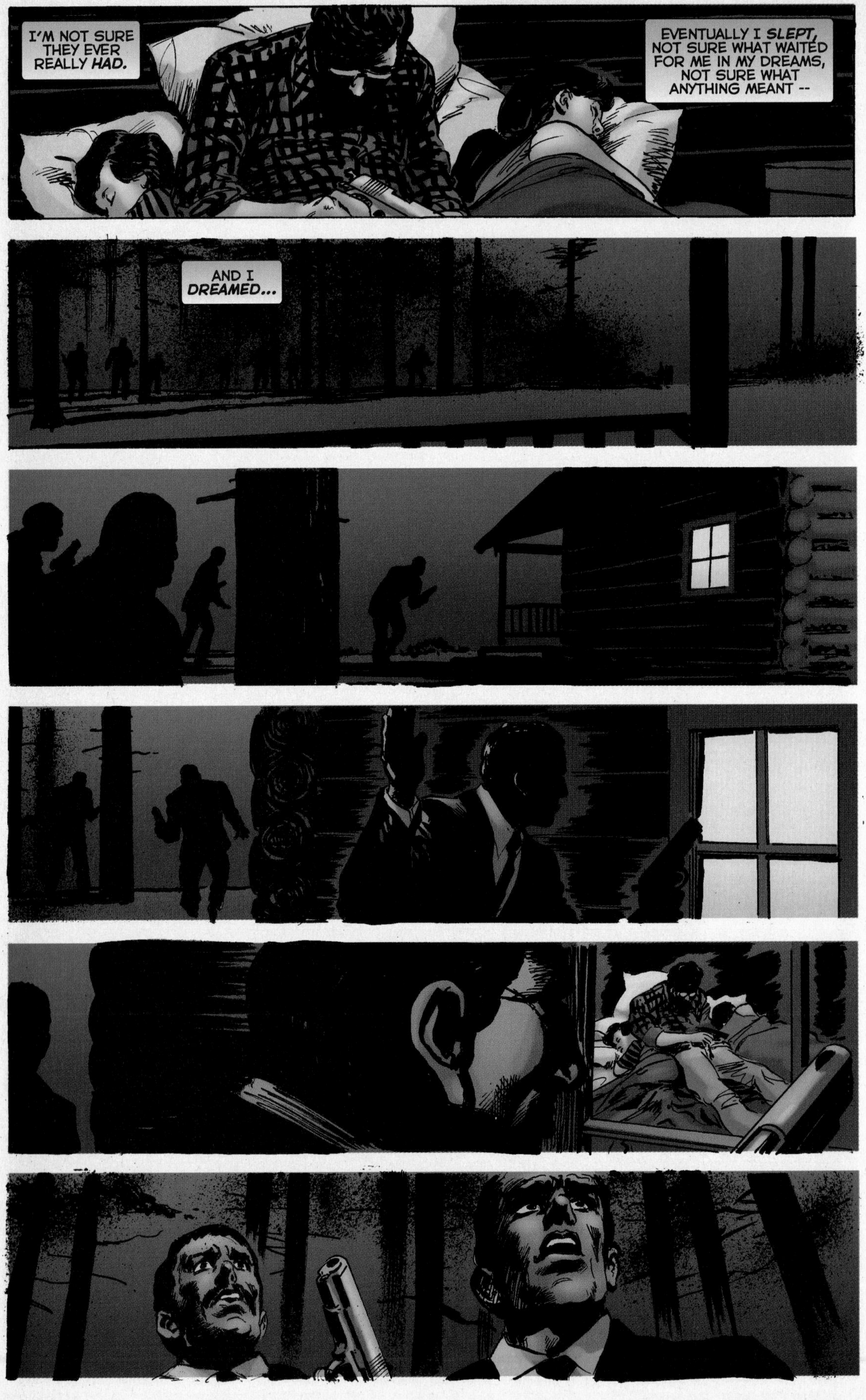
I'M NOT SURE THEY EVER REALLY HAD.
EVENTUALLY I SLEPT, NOT SURE WHAT WAITED FOR ME IN MY DREAMS, NOT SURE WHAT ANYTHING MEANT --
AND I DREAMED...

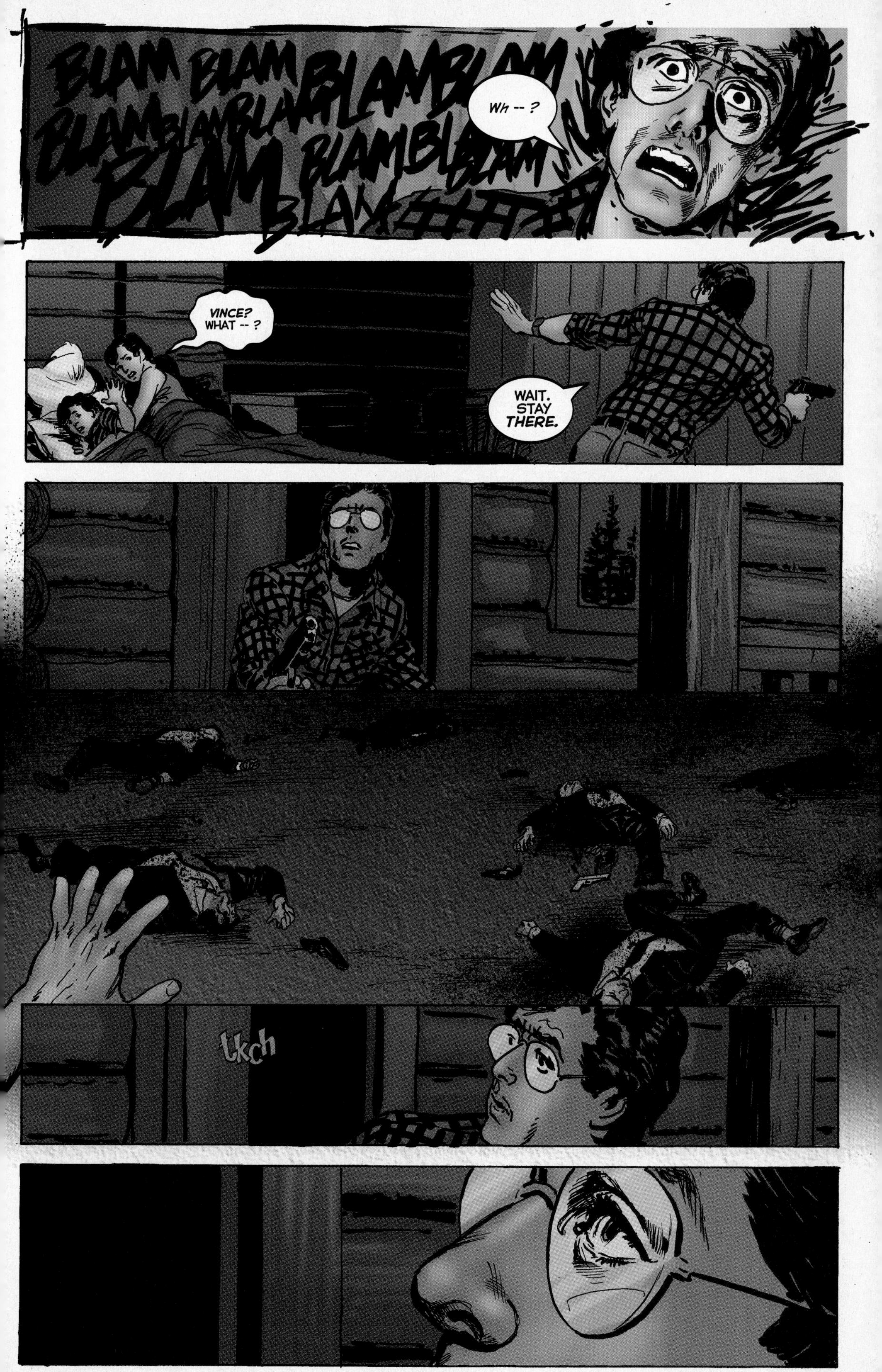
BLAM BLAM BLAMBLAM
BLAMBLAMBLAMBLAMBLAM
BLAM BLAMBLAMBLAM BLAM
Wh -- ?
VINCE? WHAT -- ?
WAIT. STAY THERE.
tkch

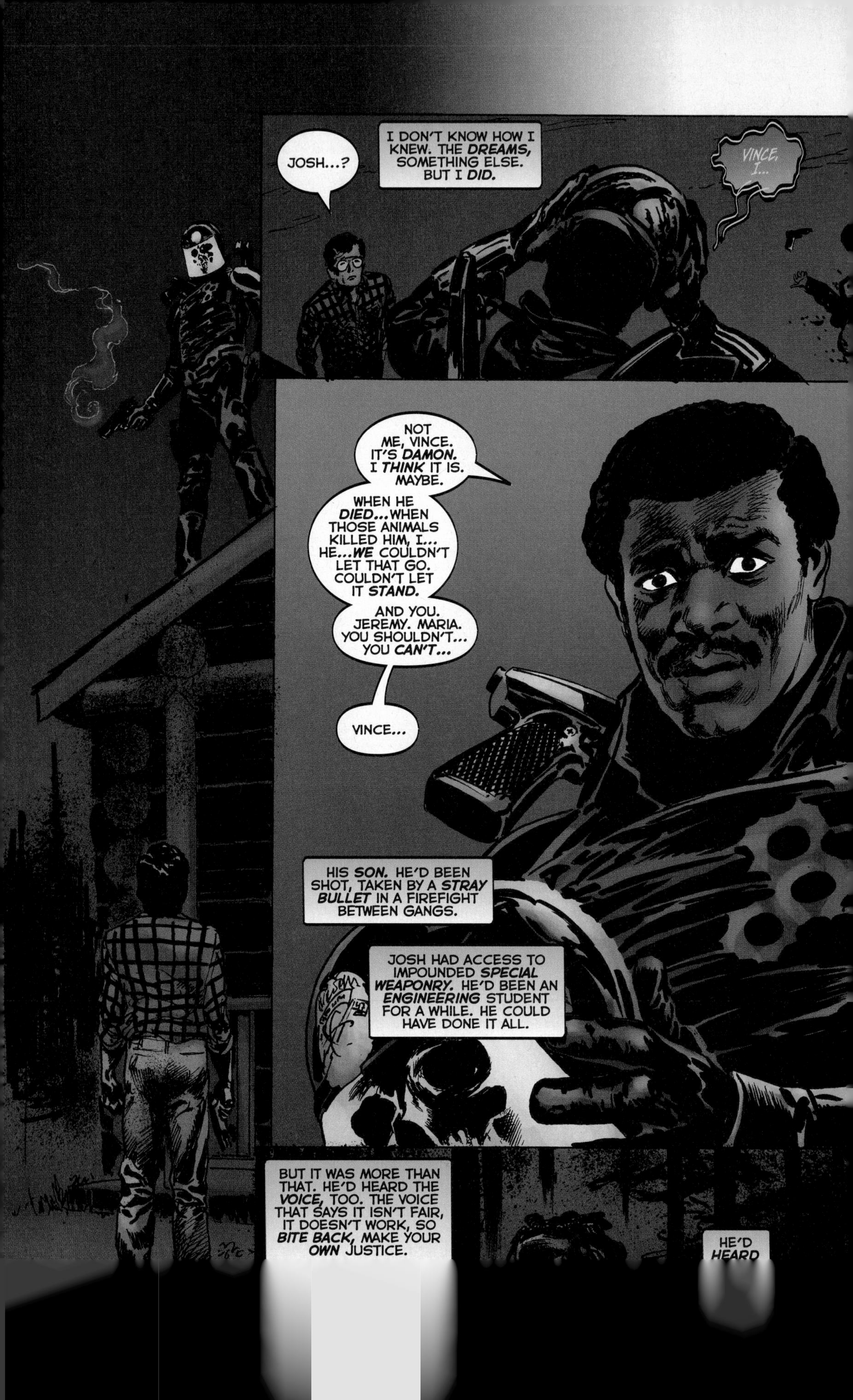
JOSH...?
I DON'T KNOW HOW I KNEW. THE DREAMS, SOMETHING ELSE. BUT I DID.
VINCE, I...
NOT ME, VINCE. IT'S DAMON. I THINK IT IS. MAYBE.
WHEN HE DIED...WHEN THOSE ANIMALS KILLED HIM, I... HE...WE COULDN'T LET THAT GO. COULDN'T LET IT STAND.
AND YOU. JEREMY. MARIA. YOU SHOULDN'T... YOU CAN'T...
VINCE...
HIS SON. HE'D BEEN SHOT, TAKEN BY A STRAY BULLET IN A FIREFIGHT BETWEEN GANGS.
JOSH HAD ACCESS TO IMPOUNDED SPECIAL WEAPONRY. HE'D BEEN AN ENGINEERING STUDENT FOR A WHILE. HE COULD HAVE DONE IT ALL.
BUT IT WAS MORE THAN THAT. HE'D HEARD THE VOICE, TOO. THE VOICE THAT SAYS IT ISN'T FAIR, IT DOESN'T WORK, SO BITE BACK, MAKE YOUR OWN JUSTICE.
HE'D HEARD

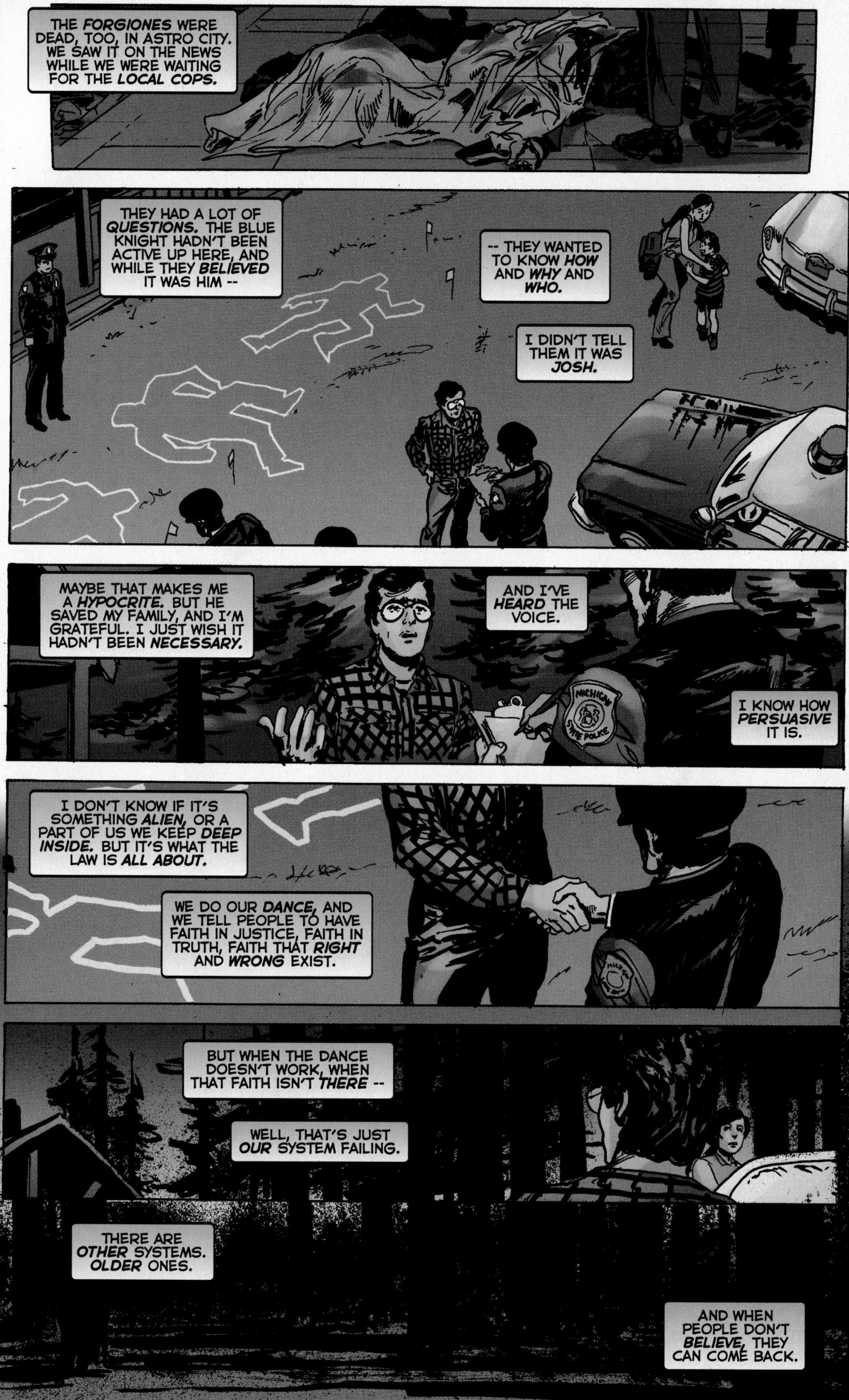
THE FORGIONES WERE DEAD, TOO, IN ASTRO CITY. WE SAW IT ON THE NEWS WHILE WE WERE WAITING FOR THE LOCAL COPS.
THEY HAD A LOT OF QUESTIONS. THE BLUE KNIGHT HADN'T BEEN ACTIVE UP HERE, AND WHILE THEY BELIEVED IT WAS HIM --
-- THEY WANTED TO KNOW HOW AND WHY AND WHO.
I DIDN'T TELL THEM IT WAS JOSH.
MAYBE THAT MAKES ME A HYPOCRITE. BUT HE SAVED MY FAMILY, AND I'M GRATEFUL. I JUST WISH IT HADN'T BEEN NECESSARY.
AND I'VE HEARD THE VOICE.
I KNOW HOW PERSUASIVE IT IS.
I DON'T KNOW IF IT'S SOMETHING ALIEN, OR A PART OF US WE KEEP DEEP INSIDE. BUT IT'S WHAT THE LAW IS ALL ABOUT.
WE DO OUR DANCE, AND WE TELL PEOPLE TO HAVE FAITH IN JUSTICE, FAITH IN TRUTH, FAITH THAT RIGHT AND WRONG EXIST.
BUT WHEN THE DANCE DOESN'T WORK, WHEN THAT FAITH ISN'T THERE --
WELL, THAT'S JUST OUR SYSTEM FAILING.
THERE ARE OTHER SYSTEMS. OLDER ONES.
AND WHEN PEOPLE DON'T BELIEVE, THEY CAN COME BACK.

IT WASN'T *ME*. THE TRIAL, THE CASE. IT WASN'T MY FAULT. I DID WHAT I WAS *SUPPOSED* TO DO. I DID *MY* PART OF THE DANCE.

YOU COULD SAY IT WAS *NIXON'S* FAULT. OR VIET NAM. OR THE *SILVER AGENT'S*, FOR NOT WINNING HIS LAST BATTLE.

OR YOU COULD SAY IT WAS *ALTON WINSLOW'S* FAULT, FOR NOT KEEPING UP WITH ME.

EITHER WAY, I DIDN'T LOSE ANY *SLEEP* OVER THE FORGIONES.

I LOST SLEEP OVER *JOSH.*

I DON'T KNOW IF THE BLUE KNIGHT IS A *SPIRIT*, OR A DEMON. OR A DARK *ANGEL*. OR JUST A TROUBLED *MAN* DRIVEN BY GRIEF.

I JUST KNOW HE WAS BORN BECAUSE THE DANCE *FAILED.*

WE DANCE TO CONVINCE PEOPLE THE SYSTEM *WORKS*. THAT SOCIETY FUNCTIONS AS IT SHOULD. THAT CIVILIZATION *STANDS*, AND WE CAN TAKE CARE OF OURSELVES.

PLEASE... DO NOT HOL[D] CHILDREN A[T] OR OVER RAI[L]

AND IF THEY *BELIEVE* THE DANCE -- AND *ONLY* IF THEY BELIEVE -- IT *DOES.*

WE GOIN' *HOME* NOW, DADDY?

YEAH, SLUGGER...

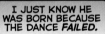

WE'RE GOING *HOME.*

190

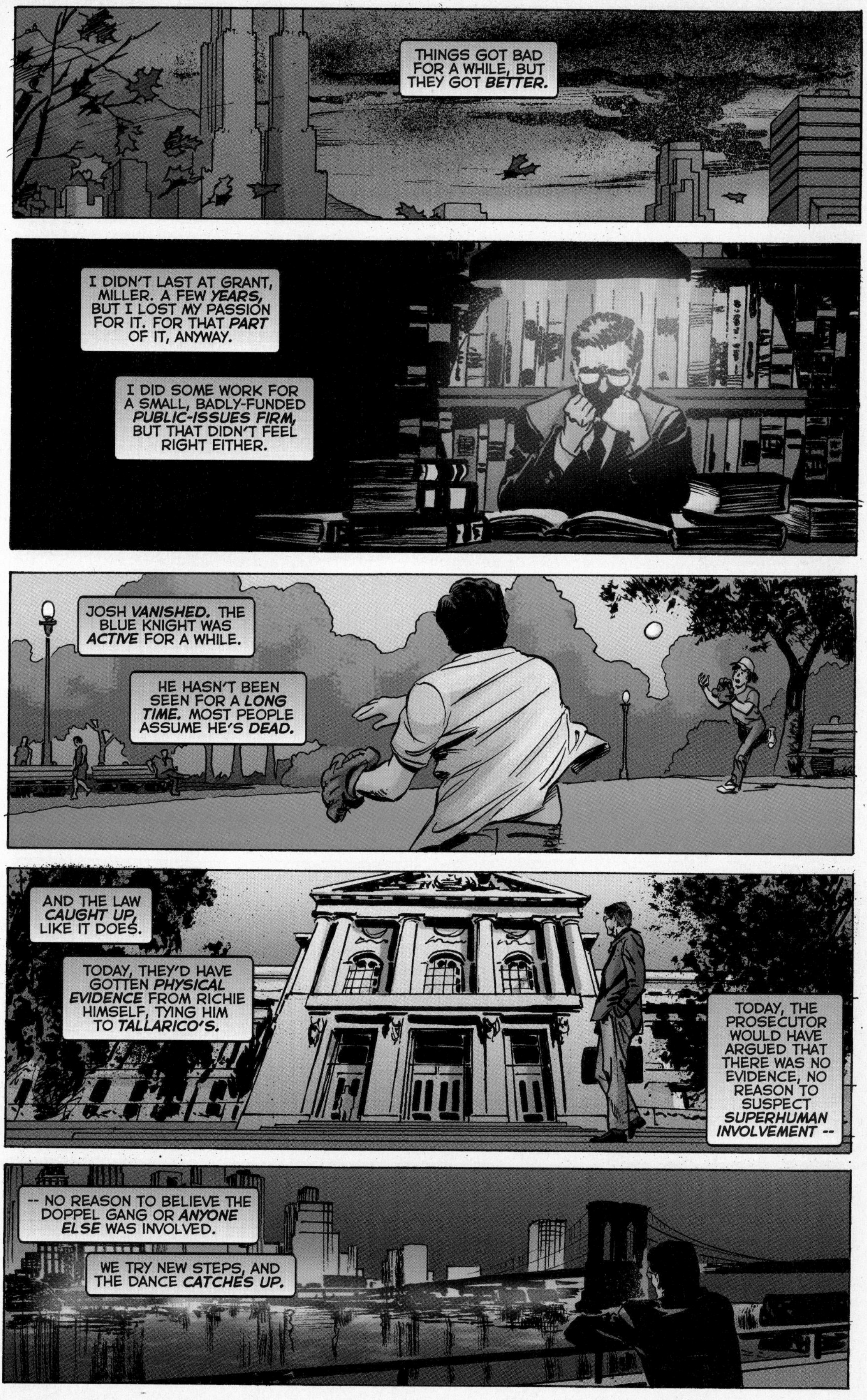
THINGS GOT BAD FOR A WHILE, BUT THEY GOT BETTER.
I DIDN'T LAST AT GRANT, MILLER. A FEW YEARS, BUT I LOST MY PASSION FOR IT. FOR THAT PART OF IT, ANYWAY.
I DID SOME WORK FOR A SMALL, BADLY-FUNDED PUBLIC-ISSUES FIRM, BUT THAT DIDN'T FEEL RIGHT EITHER.
JOSH VANISHED. THE BLUE KNIGHT WAS ACTIVE FOR A WHILE.
HE HASN'T BEEN SEEN FOR A LONG TIME. MOST PEOPLE ASSUME HE'S DEAD.
AND THE LAW CAUGHT UP, LIKE IT DOES.
TODAY, THEY'D HAVE GOTTEN PHYSICAL EVIDENCE FROM RICHIE HIMSELF, TYING HIM TO TALLARICO'S.
TODAY, THE PROSECUTOR WOULD HAVE ARGUED THAT THERE WAS NO EVIDENCE, NO REASON TO SUSPECT SUPERHUMAN INVOLVEMENT --
-- NO REASON TO BELIEVE THE DOPPEL GANG OR ANYONE ELSE WAS INVOLVED.
WE TRY NEW STEPS, AND THE DANCE CATCHES UP.

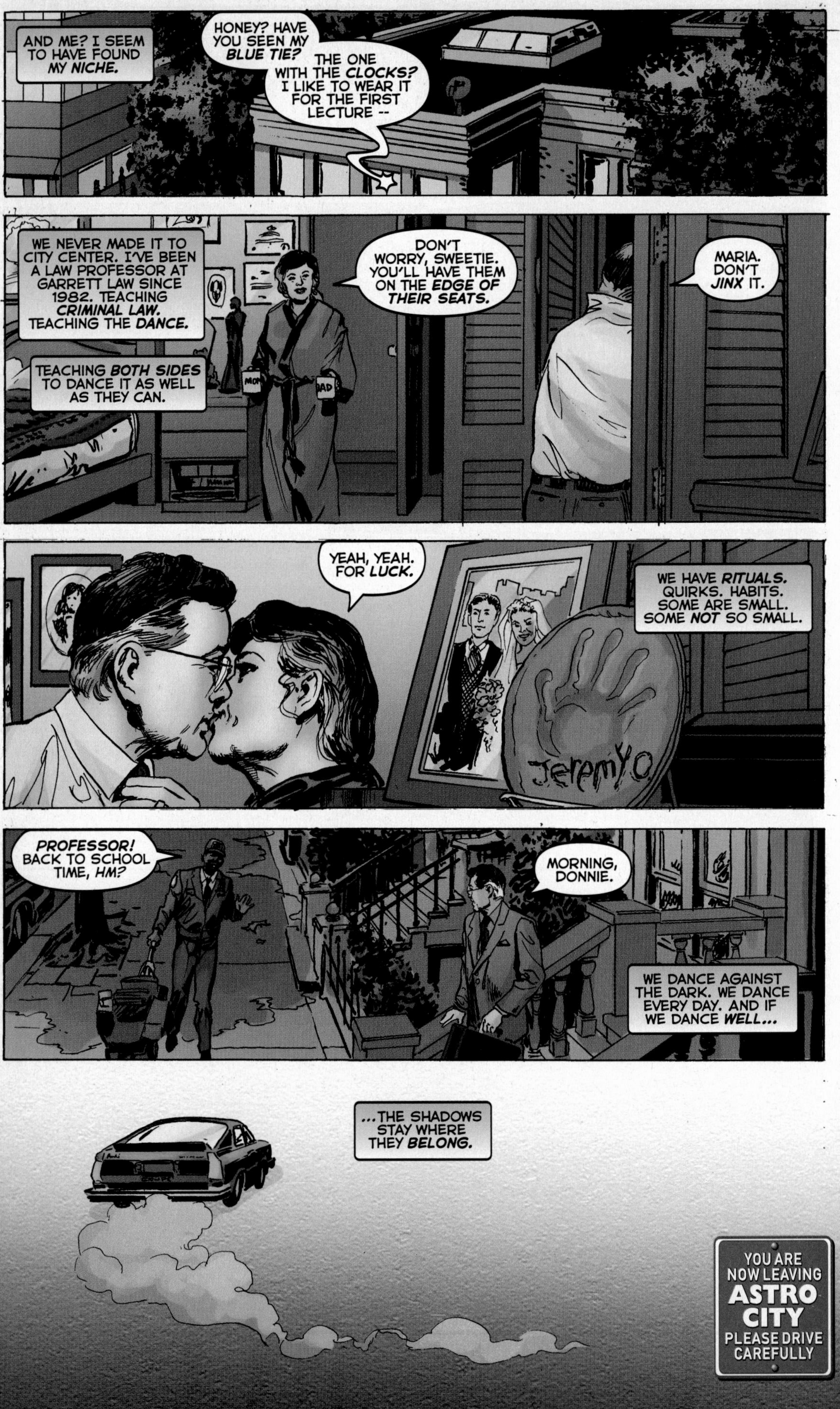
AND ME? I SEEM TO HAVE FOUND MY NICHE.
HONEY? HAVE YOU SEEN MY BLUE TIE?
THE ONE WITH THE CLOCKS? I LIKE TO WEAR IT FOR THE FIRST LECTURE --
WE NEVER MADE IT TO CITY CENTER. I'VE BEEN A LAW PROFESSOR AT GARRETT LAW SINCE 1982. TEACHING CRIMINAL LAW. TEACHING THE DANCE.
TEACHING BOTH SIDES TO DANCE IT AS WELL AS THEY CAN.
DON'T WORRY, SWEETIE. YOU'LL HAVE THEM ON THE EDGE OF THEIR SEATS.
MARIA. DON'T JINX IT.
MOM
DAD
YEAH, YEAH. FOR LUCK.
WE HAVE RITUALS. QUIRKS. HABITS. SOME ARE SMALL. SOME NOT SO SMALL.
JeremY.O.
PROFESSOR! BACK TO SCHOOL TIME, HM?
MORNING, DONNIE.
WE DANCE AGAINST THE DARK. WE DANCE EVERY DAY. AND IF WE DANCE WELL...
...THE SHADOWS STAY WHERE THEY BELONG.
YOU ARE NOW LEAVING ASTRO CITY PLEASE DRIVE CAREFULLY

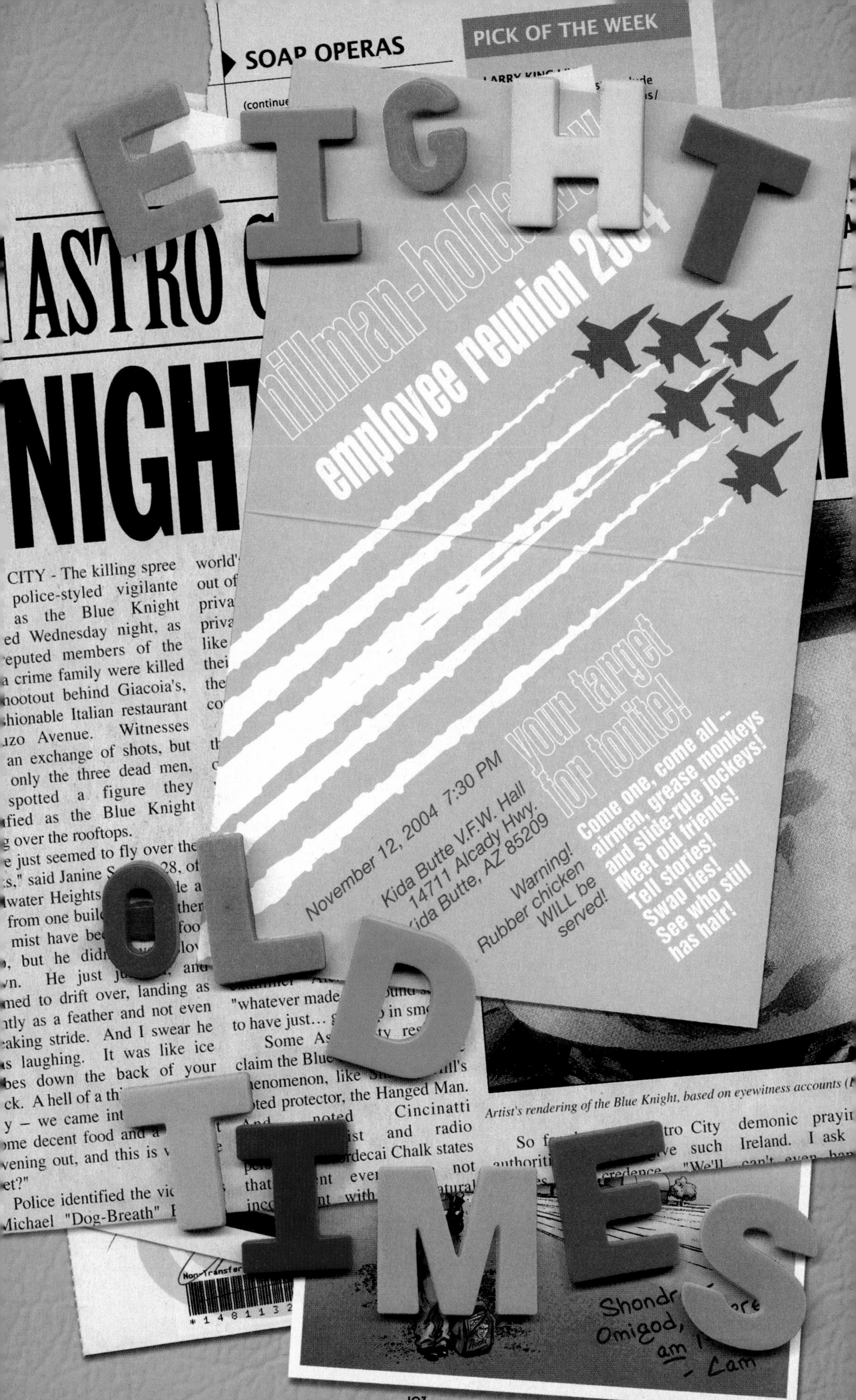
EIGHT
OLD
TIMES
SOAP OPERAS
PICK OF THE WEEK
hillman-holdsworth
employee reunion 2004
your target for tonite!
November 12, 2004 7:30 PM
Kida Butte V.F.W. Hall
14711 Alcady Hwy.
Kida Butte, AZ 85209
Warning!
Rubber chicken
WILL be
served!
Come one, come all --
airmen, grease monkeys
and slide-rule jockeys!
Meet old friends!
Tell stories!
Swap lies!
See who still
has hair!
NIGHT
Artist's rendering of the Blue Knight, based on eyewitness accounts
- Cam

"Supersonic"
rev. 7-7-03

Turbines
up under
jet cuff
arms
legs

SHO
REV.
BLUE & SIL

BLUE HELMET,
EMBLEM AND
BACK OF BODY.
SILVER SUPERSONIC
BODYSUIT
GLOVES &
BOOTS

FRONT OF
BODYSUIT IS
A CHROME BLUE
COMING FROM
THE NECK
DOWN TO THE
ENGINES ON
THE GLOVE &
BOOT CUFFS.

THE BACK
OF THE
BODYSUIT
FROM THE MASK
GOING ALL THE WAY
BEHIND TO THE
BOOTS AND GLOVES
SHOULD BE SILVER.
THE "S" LOGO
WOULD BE
SILVER
OF
COURSE
AND THE
WINDOW
SHAPES
GOING DOWN
THE SIDES OF
THE BODY
WOULD BE
BLUE
CHROME.

FINS
ON THE
BACK OF
BOOTS

GLOVES AND
BOOTS SHOULD
BE SILVER.

IS THE NOSE SHAPE
OKAY?

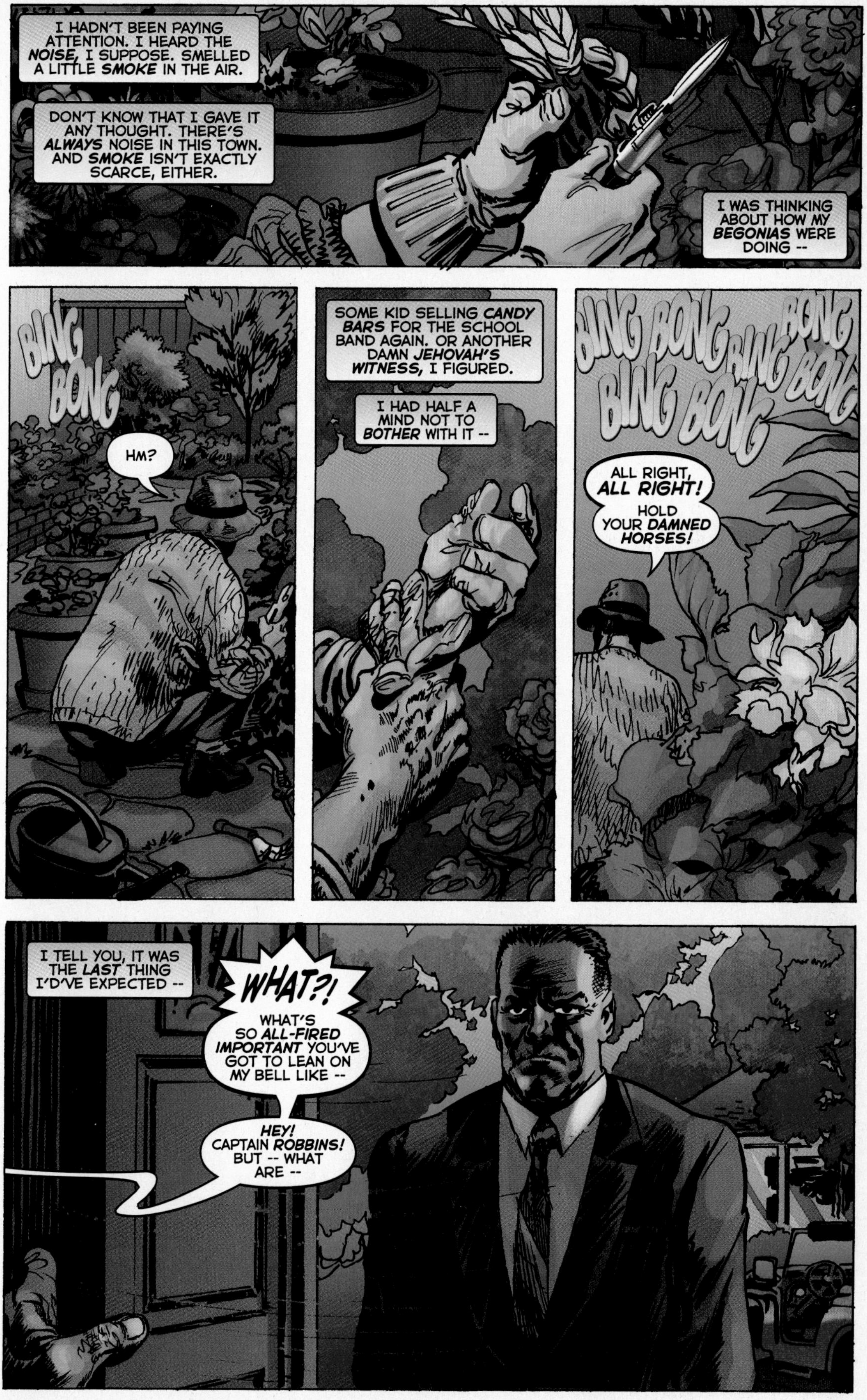
I HADN'T BEEN PAYING ATTENTION. I HEARD THE NOISE, I SUPPOSE. SMELLED A LITTLE SMOKE IN THE AIR.
DON'T KNOW THAT I GAVE IT ANY THOUGHT. THERE'S ALWAYS NOISE IN THIS TOWN. AND SMOKE ISN'T EXACTLY SCARCE, EITHER.
I WAS THINKING ABOUT HOW MY BEGONIAS WERE DOING --
BING BONG
HM?
SOME KID SELLING CANDY BARS FOR THE SCHOOL BAND AGAIN. OR ANOTHER DAMN JEHOVAH'S WITNESS, I FIGURED.
I HAD HALF A MIND NOT TO BOTHER WITH IT --
BING BONG BING BONG BING BONG
ALL RIGHT, ALL RIGHT! HOLD YOUR DAMNED HORSES!
I TELL YOU, IT WAS THE LAST THING I'D'VE EXPECTED --
WHAT?! WHAT'S SO ALL-FIRED IMPORTANT YOU'VE GOT TO LEAN ON MY BELL LIKE --
HEY! CAPTAIN ROBBINS! BUT -- WHAT ARE --

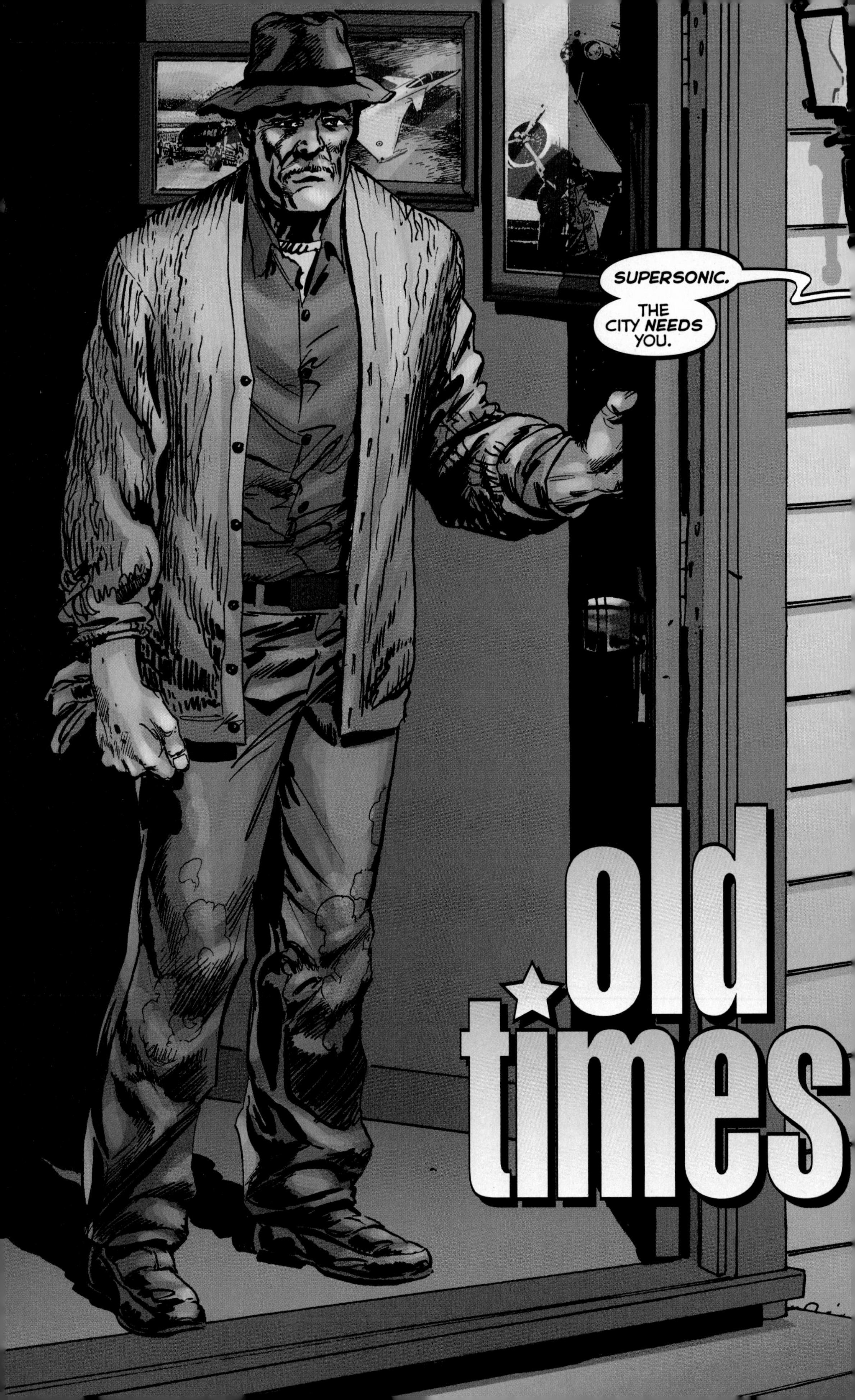
SUPERSONIC.
THE CITY NEEDS YOU.
old times

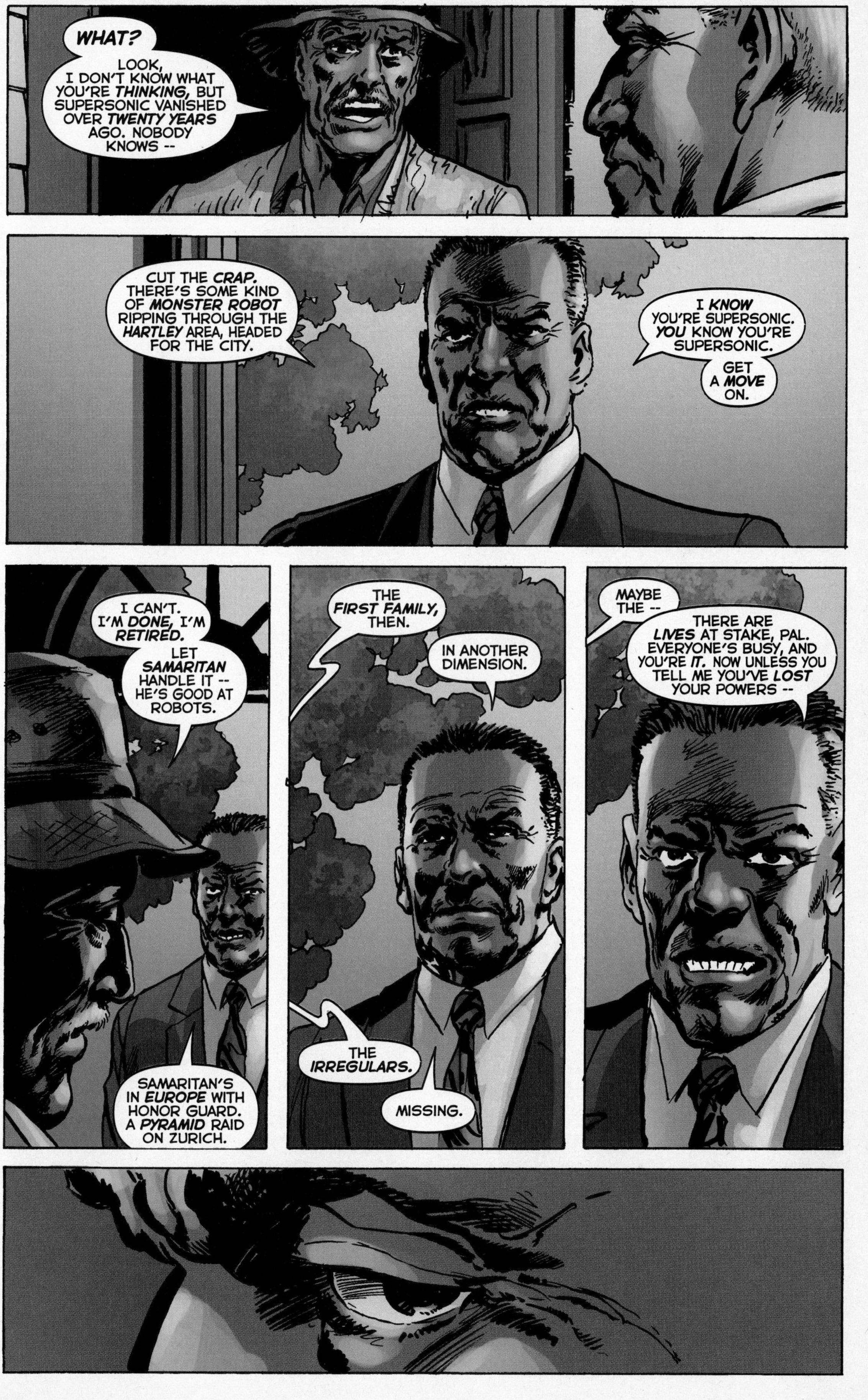
WHAT?
LOOK, I DON'T KNOW WHAT YOU'RE THINKING, BUT SUPERSONIC VANISHED OVER TWENTY YEARS AGO. NOBODY KNOWS --
CUT THE CRAP. THERE'S SOME KIND OF MONSTER ROBOT RIPPING THROUGH THE HARTLEY AREA, HEADED FOR THE CITY.
I KNOW YOU'RE SUPERSONIC. YOU KNOW YOU'RE SUPERSONIC.
GET A MOVE ON.
I CAN'T. I'M DONE, I'M RETIRED.
LET SAMARITAN HANDLE IT -- HE'S GOOD AT ROBOTS.
SAMARITAN'S IN EUROPE WITH HONOR GUARD. A PYRAMID RAID ON ZURICH.
THE FIRST FAMILY, THEN.
IN ANOTHER DIMENSION.
THE IRREGULARS.
MISSING.
MAYBE THE --
THERE ARE LIVES AT STAKE, PAL. EVERYONE'S BUSY, AND YOU'RE IT. NOW UNLESS YOU TELL ME YOU'VE LOST YOUR POWERS --

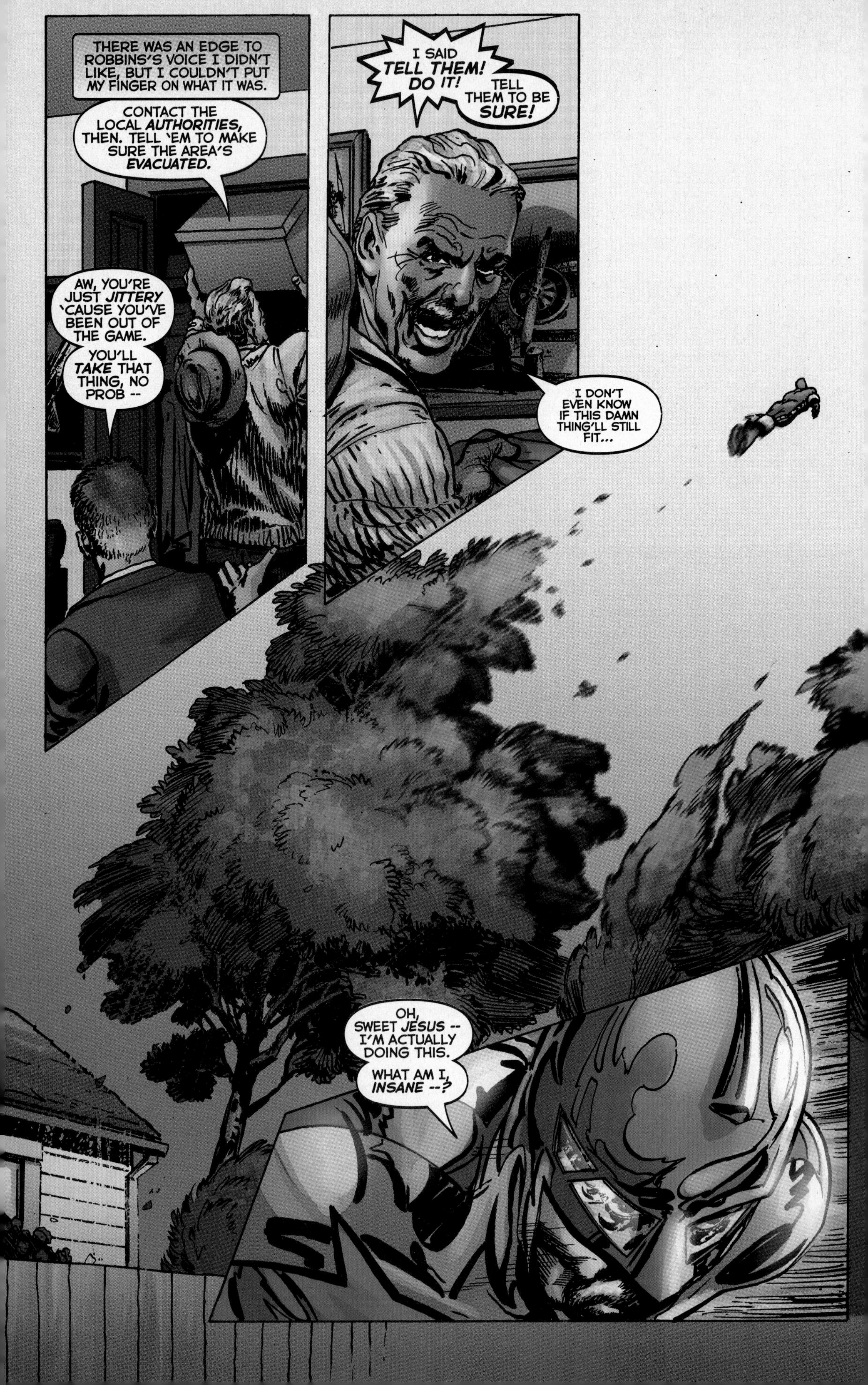
THERE WAS AN EDGE TO ROBBINS'S VOICE I DIDN'T LIKE, BUT I COULDN'T PUT MY FINGER ON WHAT IT WAS.
CONTACT THE LOCAL AUTHORITIES, THEN. TELL 'EM TO MAKE SURE THE AREA'S EVACUATED.
I SAID TELL THEM! DO IT!
TELL THEM TO BE SURE!
AW, YOU'RE JUST JITTERY 'CAUSE YOU'VE BEEN OUT OF THE GAME.
YOU'LL TAKE THAT THING, NO PROB --
I DON'T EVEN KNOW IF THIS DAMN THING'LL STILL FIT...
OH, SWEET JESUS -- I'M ACTUALLY DOING THIS.
WHAT AM I, INSANE --?

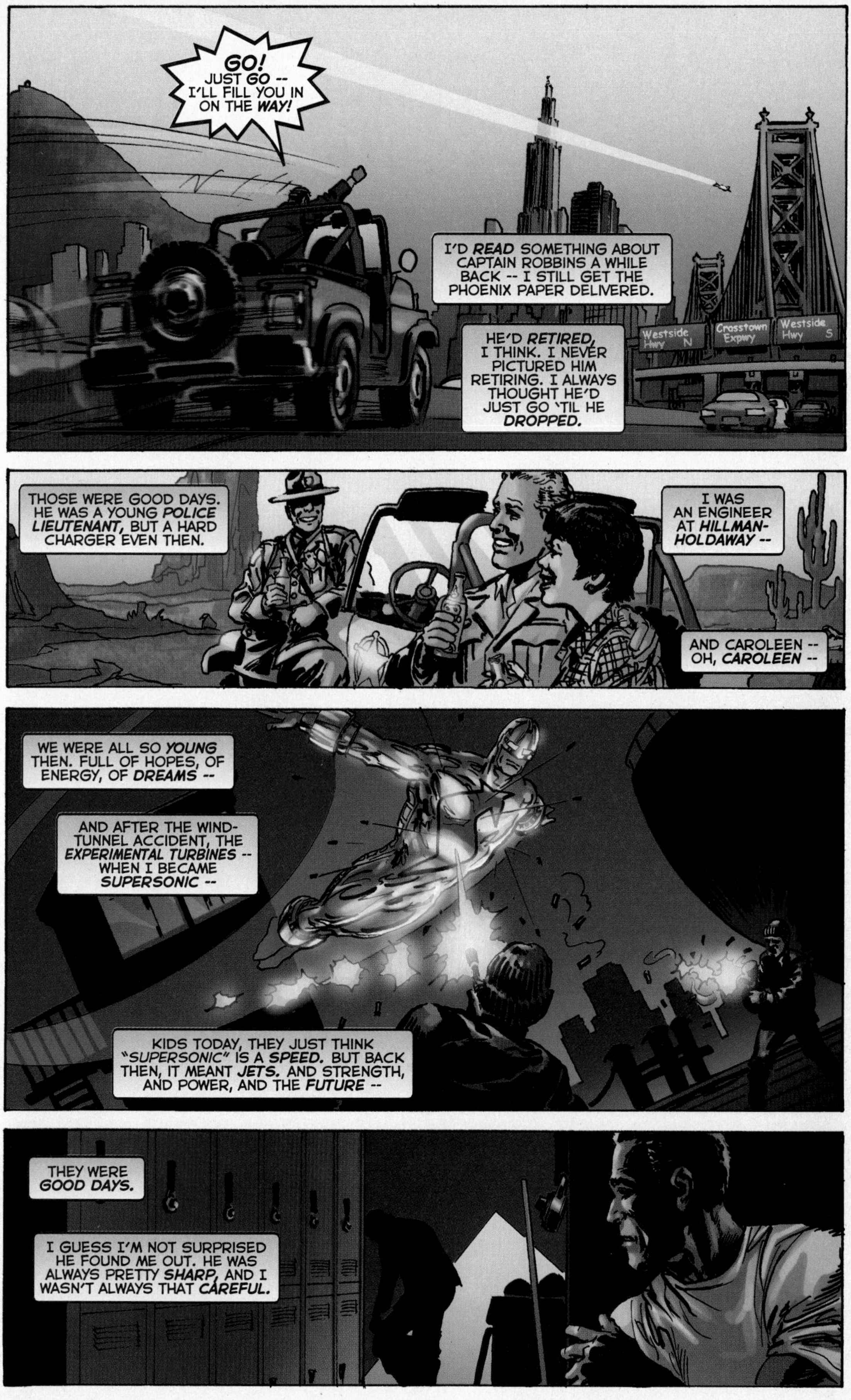
GO! JUST GO -- I'LL FILL YOU IN ON THE WAY!
I'D READ SOMETHING ABOUT CAPTAIN ROBBINS A WHILE BACK -- I STILL GET THE PHOENIX PAPER DELIVERED.
HE'D RETIRED, I THINK. I NEVER PICTURED HIM RETIRING. I ALWAYS THOUGHT HE'D JUST GO 'TIL HE DROPPED.
Westside Hwy N
Crosstown Expwy
Westside Hwy S
THOSE WERE GOOD DAYS. HE WAS A YOUNG POLICE LIEUTENANT, BUT A HARD CHARGER EVEN THEN.
I WAS AN ENGINEER AT HILLMAN-HOLDAWAY --
AND CAROLEEN -- OH, CAROLEEN --
WE WERE ALL SO YOUNG THEN. FULL OF HOPES, OF ENERGY, OF DREAMS --
AND AFTER THE WIND-TUNNEL ACCIDENT, THE EXPERIMENTAL TURBINES -- WHEN I BECAME SUPERSONIC --
KIDS TODAY, THEY JUST THINK "SUPERSONIC" IS A SPEED. BUT BACK THEN, IT MEANT JETS. AND STRENGTH, AND POWER, AND THE FUTURE --
THEY WERE GOOD DAYS.
I GUESS I'M NOT SURPRISED HE FOUND ME OUT. HE WAS ALWAYS PRETTY SHARP, AND I WASN'T ALWAYS THAT CAREFUL.

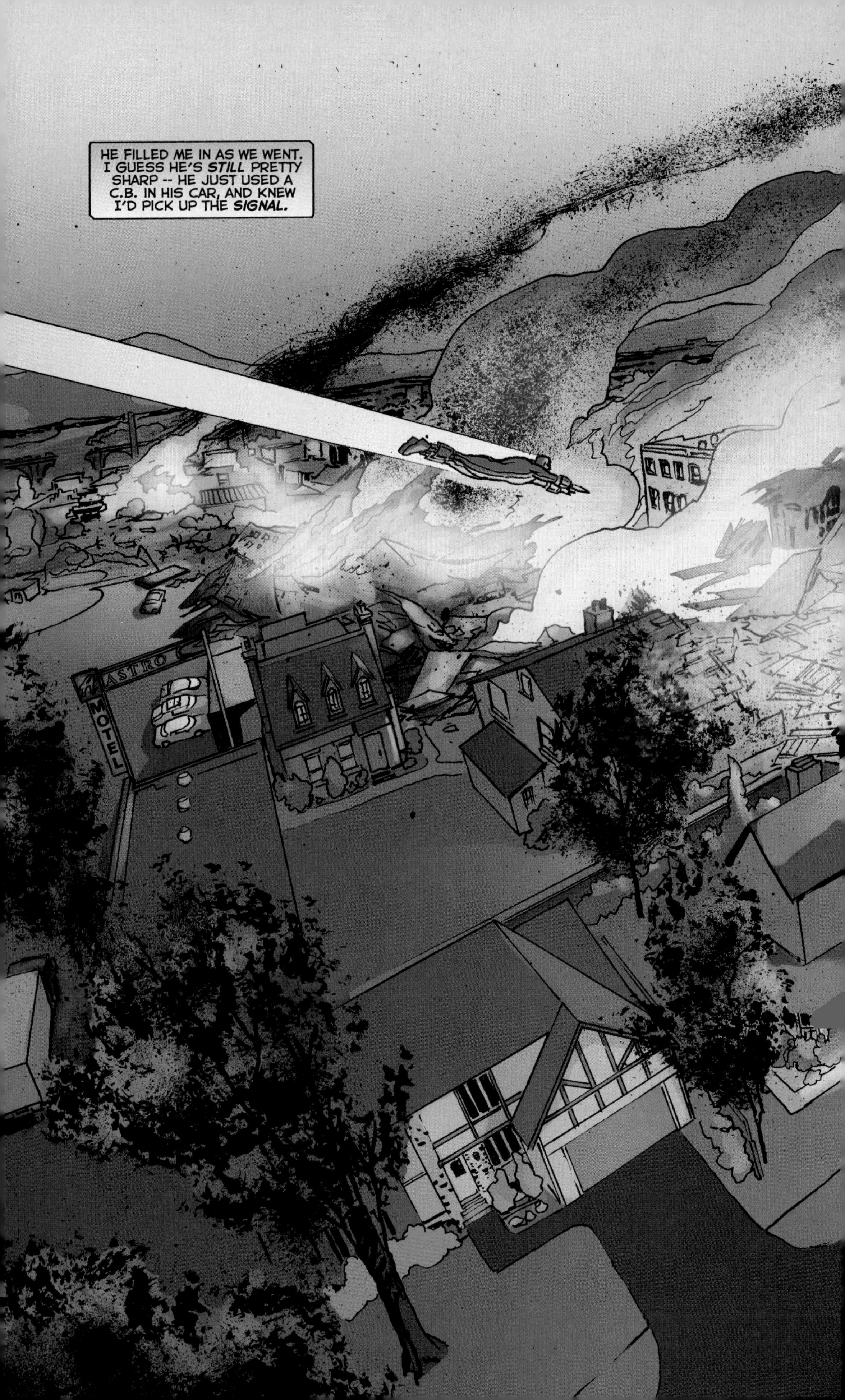
HE FILLED ME IN AS WE WENT. I GUESS HE'S *STILL* PRETTY SHARP -- HE JUST USED A C.B. IN HIS CAR, AND KNEW I'D PICK UP THE *SIGNAL.*
ASTRO
MOTEL

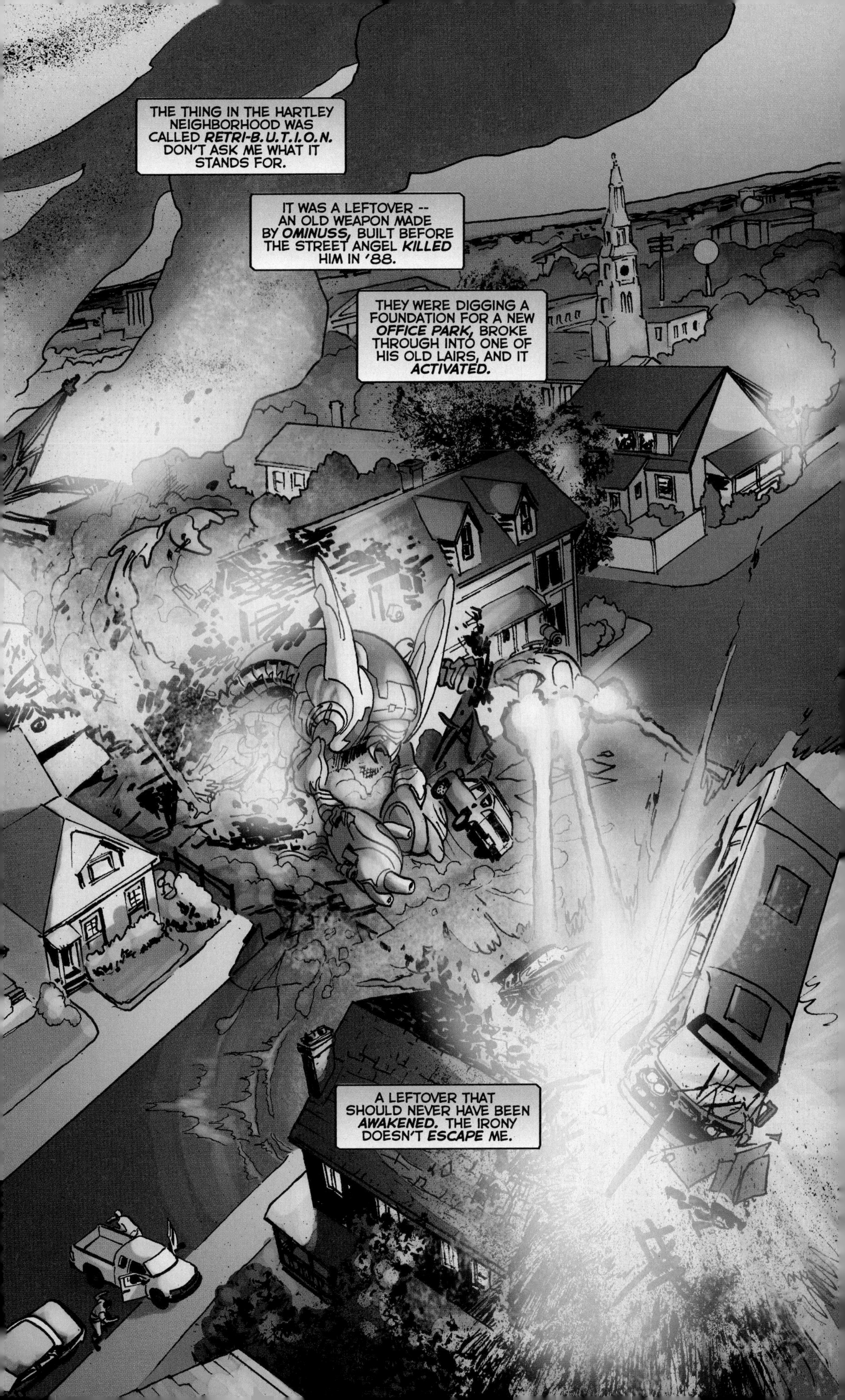
THE THING IN THE HARTLEY NEIGHBORHOOD WAS CALLED *RETRI-B.U.T.I.O.N.* DON'T ASK ME WHAT IT STANDS FOR.
IT WAS A LEFTOVER -- AN OLD WEAPON MADE BY *OMINUSS,* BUILT BEFORE THE STREET ANGEL *KILLED* HIM IN '88.
THEY WERE DIGGING A FOUNDATION FOR A NEW *OFFICE PARK,* BROKE THROUGH INTO ONE OF HIS OLD LAIRS, AND IT *ACTIVATED.*
A LEFTOVER THAT SHOULD NEVER HAVE BEEN *AWAKENED.* THE IRONY DOESN'T *ESCAPE* ME.

RRACHAKKAKA

R3V3NG3!
R3V3NG3!

DO IT, 'SONIC! TAKE 'IM APART!

SHOW ALL THOSE YOUNG PUNKS HOW THE JOB IS DONE!

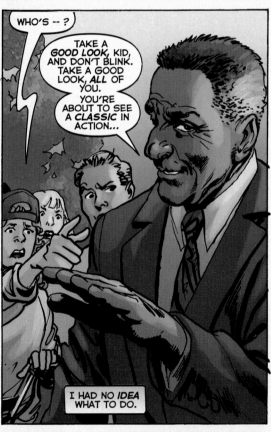

WHO'S -- ?

TAKE A GOOD LOOK, KID, AND DON'T BLINK. TAKE A GOOD LOOK, ALL OF YOU. YOU'RE ABOUT TO SEE A CLASSIC IN ACTION...

I HAD NO IDEA WHAT TO DO.

THERE WAS A DAY I'D HAVE RIGGED A GIANT INDUCTION COIL, DRAINED THE ROBOT'S POWER.

OR WHISKED HIM INTO THE STRATOSPHERE WITH A SUPER-CYCLONE.

TODAY, THOUGH --

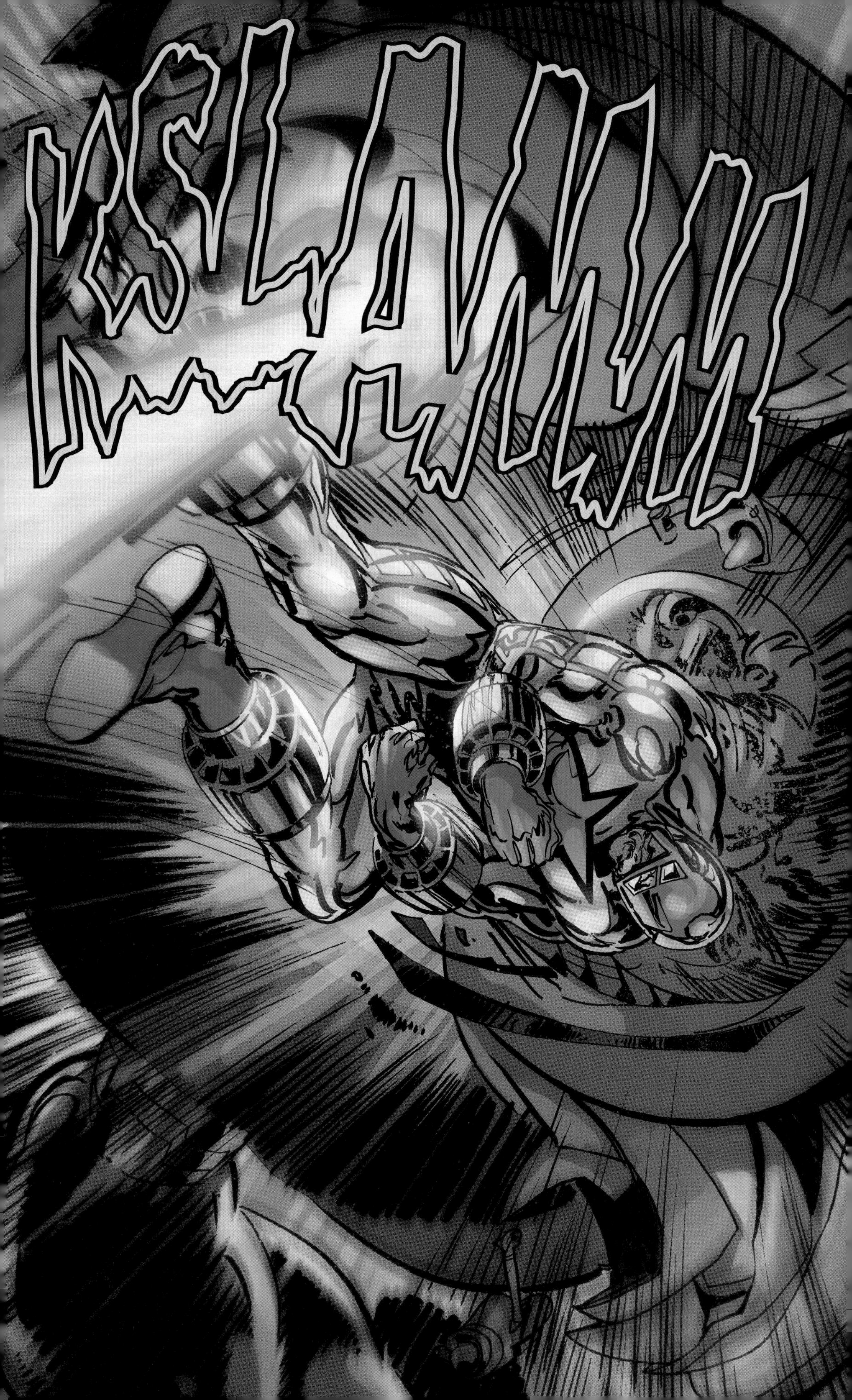
KSLAMMM

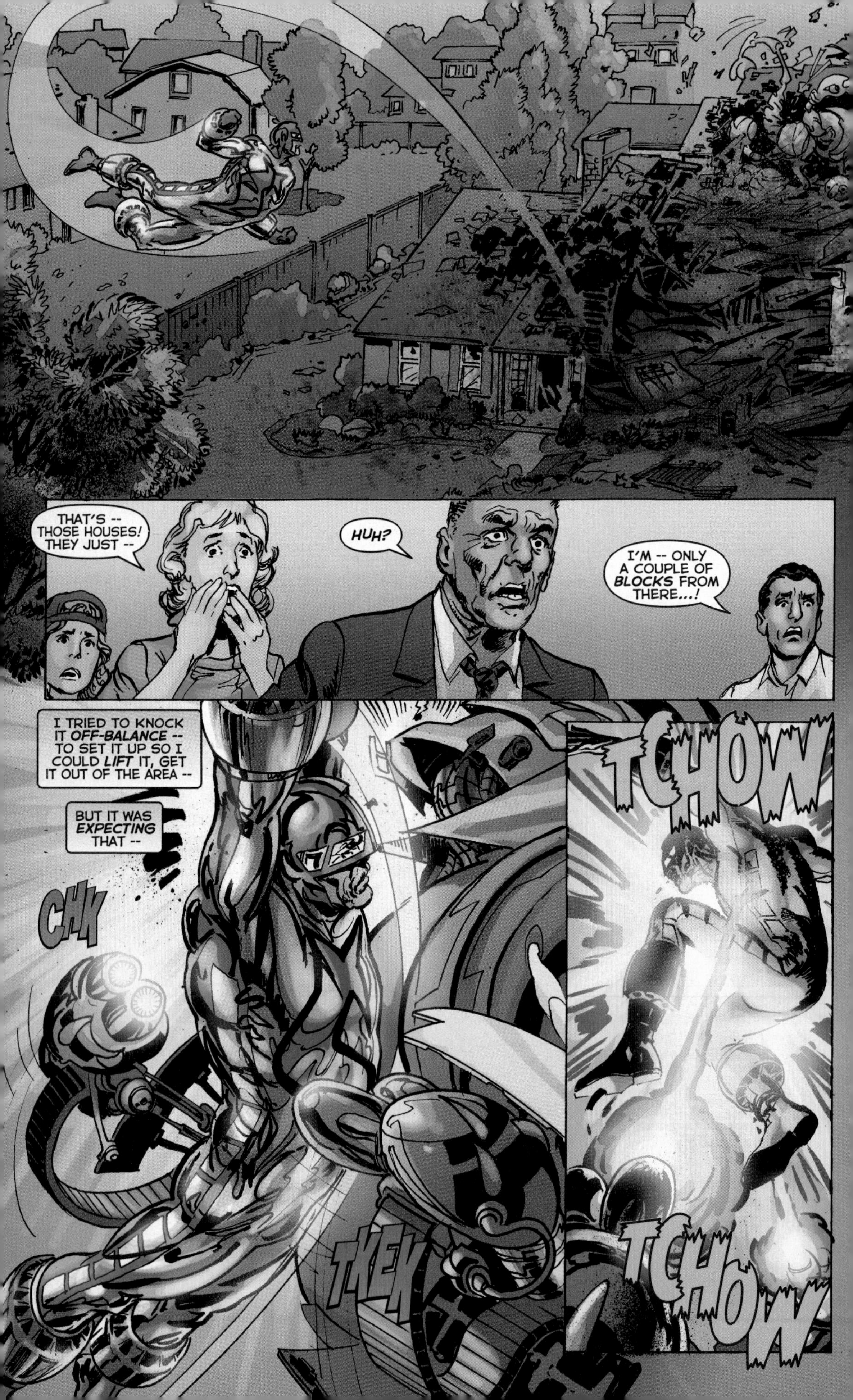
THAT'S -- THOSE HOUSES! THEY JUST --
HUH?
I'M -- ONLY A COUPLE OF BLOCKS FROM THERE...!
I TRIED TO KNOCK IT OFF-BALANCE -- TO SET IT UP SO I COULD LIFT IT, GET IT OUT OF THE AREA --
BUT IT WAS EXPECTING THAT --
CHK
TKEK
TCHOW
TCHOW

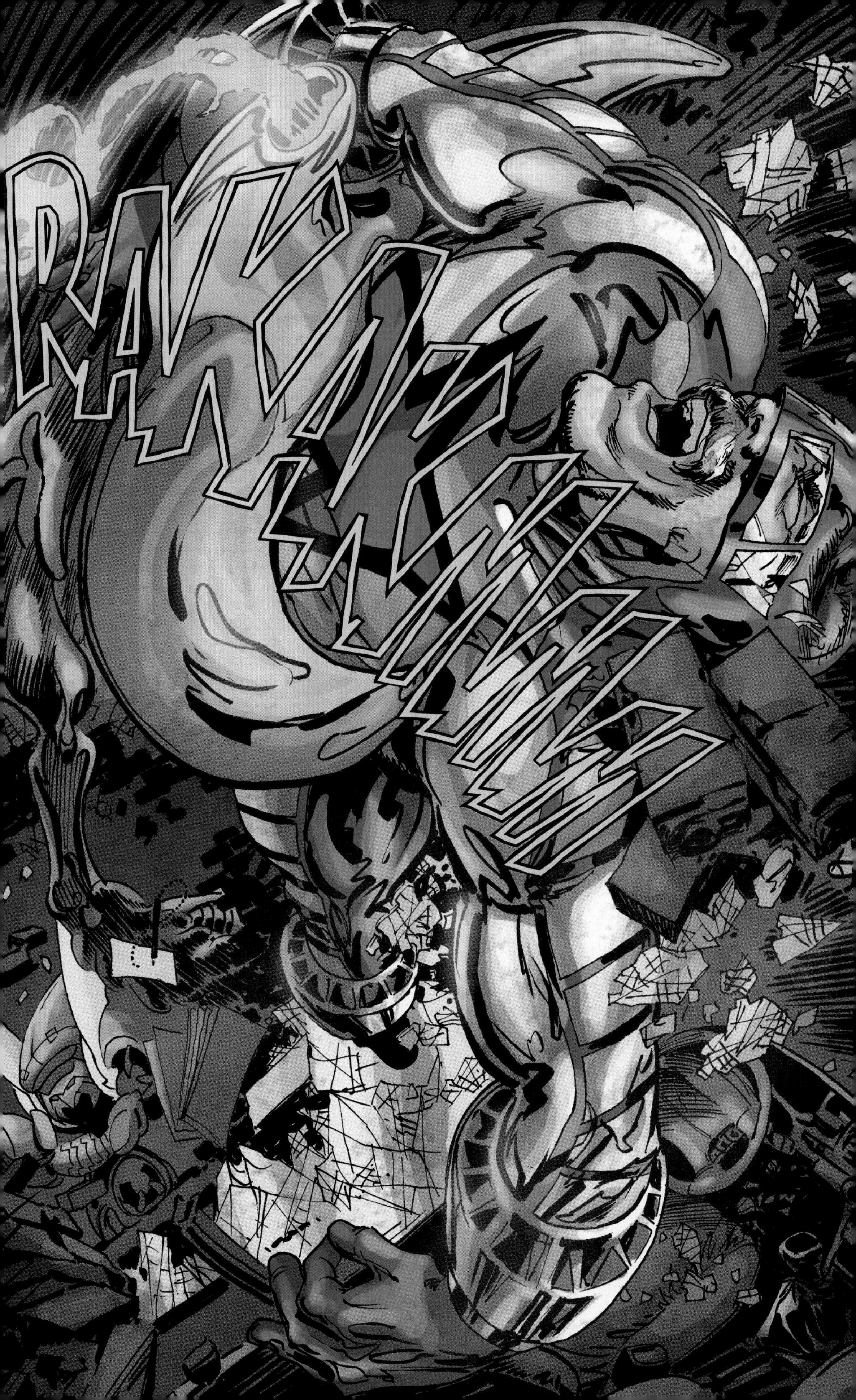

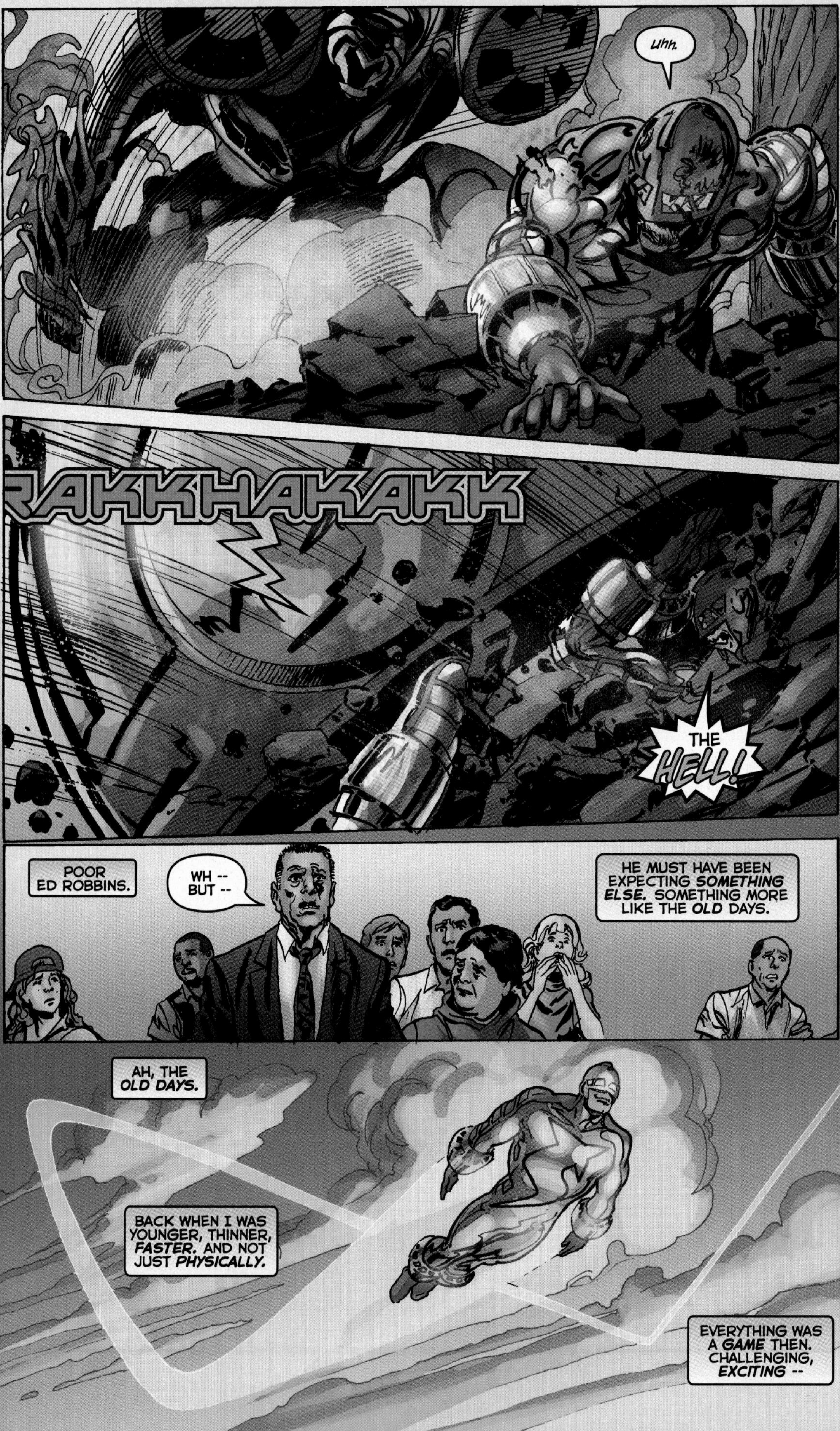
uhh.
RAKKHAKAKK
THE HELL!
POOR ED ROBBINS.
WH -- BUT --
HE MUST HAVE BEEN EXPECTING SOMETHING ELSE. SOMETHING MORE LIKE THE OLD DAYS.
AH, THE OLD DAYS.
BACK WHEN I WAS YOUNGER, THINNER, FASTER. AND NOT JUST PHYSICALLY.
EVERYTHING WAS A GAME THEN. CHALLENGING, EXCITING --

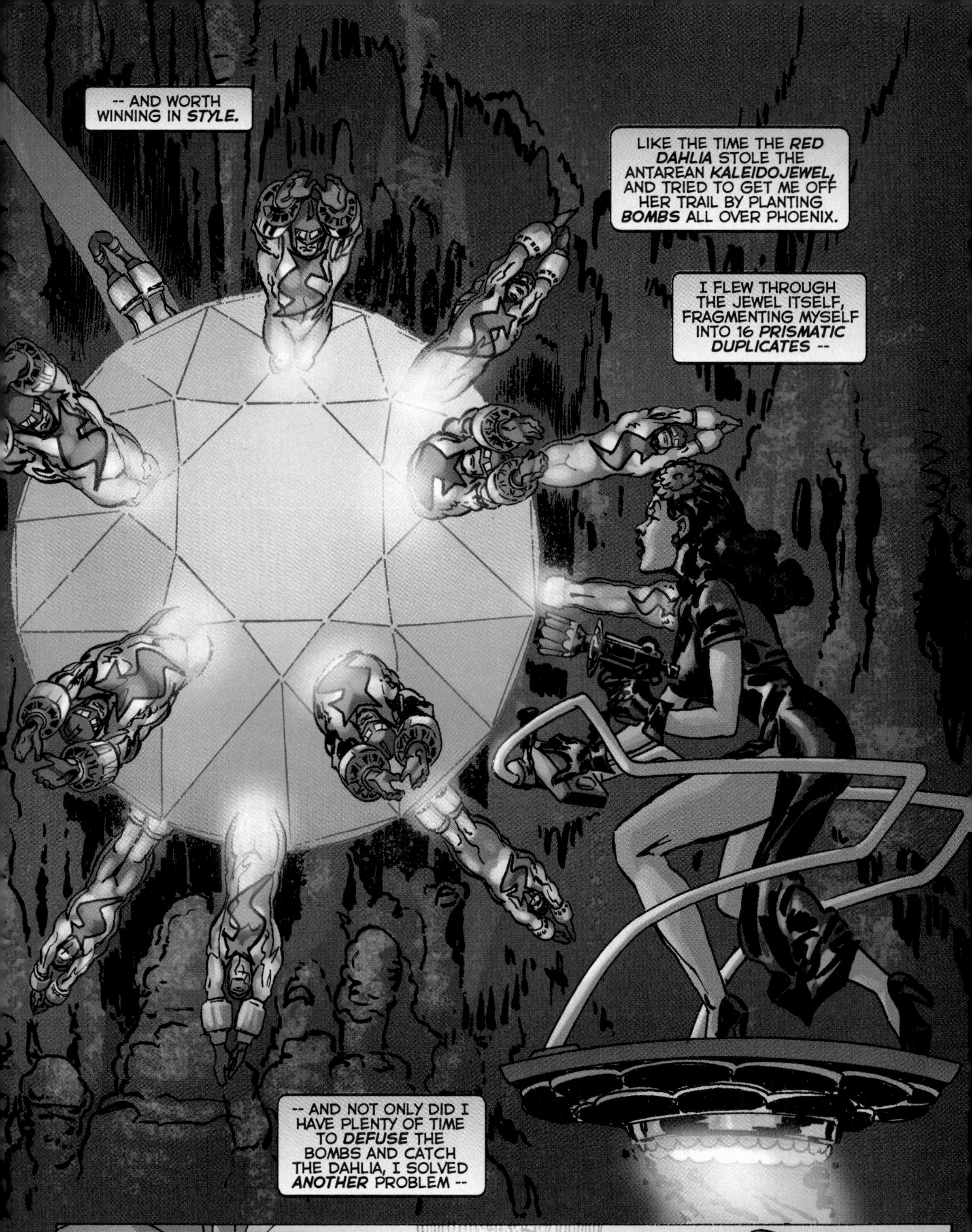
-- AND WORTH WINNING IN STYLE.
LIKE THE TIME THE RED DAHLIA STOLE THE ANTAREAN KALEIDOJEWEL, AND TRIED TO GET ME OFF HER TRAIL BY PLANTING BOMBS ALL OVER PHOENIX.
I FLEW THROUGH THE JEWEL ITSELF, FRAGMENTING MYSELF INTO 16 PRISMATIC DUPLICATES --
-- AND NOT ONLY DID I HAVE PLENTY OF TIME TO DEFUSE THE BOMBS AND CATCH THE DAHLIA, I SOLVED ANOTHER PROBLEM --

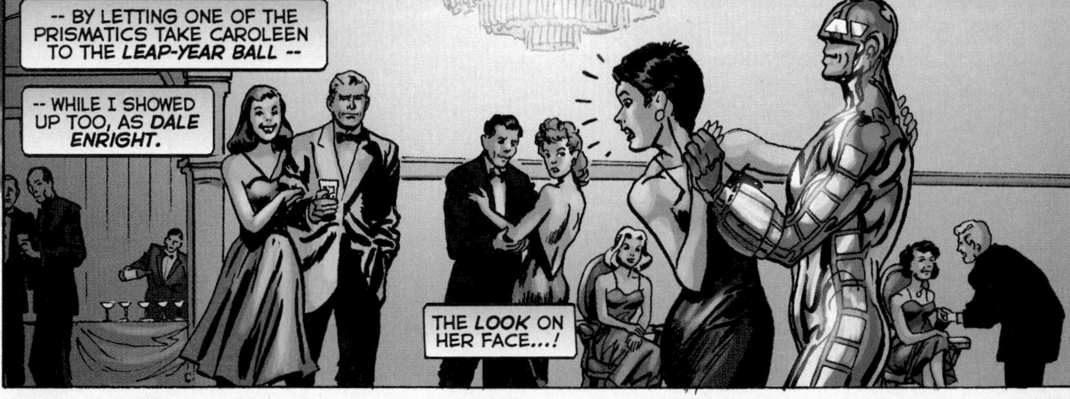
-- BY LETTING ONE OF THE PRISMATICS TAKE CAROLEEN TO THE LEAP-YEAR BALL --
-- WHILE I SHOWED UP TOO, AS DALE ENRIGHT.
THE LOOK ON HER FACE...!

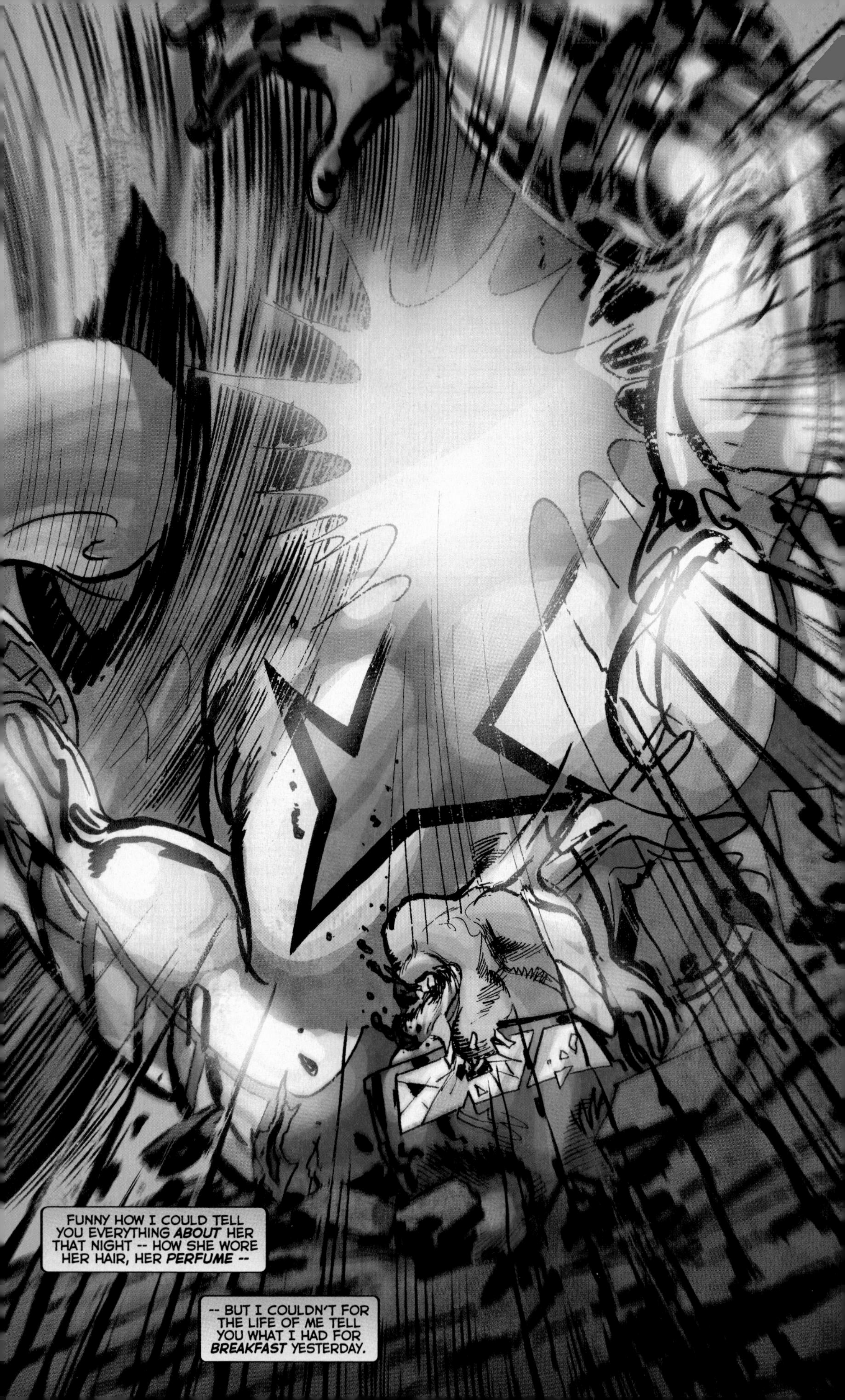
FUNNY HOW I COULD TELL YOU EVERYTHING ABOUT HER THAT NIGHT -- HOW SHE WORE HER HAIR, HER PERFUME --
-- BUT I COULDN'T FOR THE LIFE OF ME TELL YOU WHAT I HAD FOR BREAKFAST YESTERDAY.

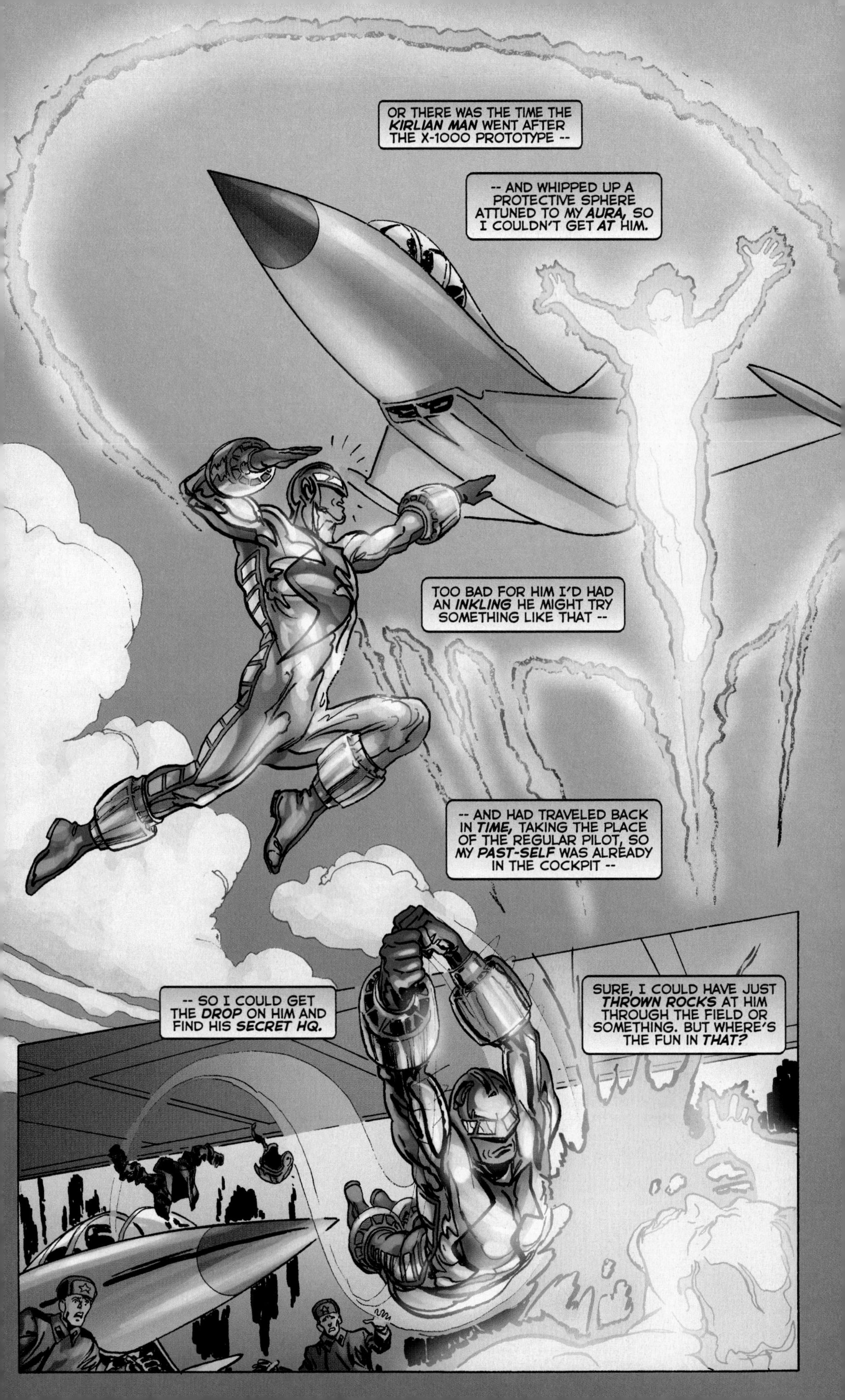
OR THERE WAS THE TIME THE KIRLIAN MAN WENT AFTER THE X-1000 PROTOTYPE --
-- AND WHIPPED UP A PROTECTIVE SPHERE ATTUNED TO MY AURA, SO I COULDN'T GET AT HIM.
TOO BAD FOR HIM I'D HAD AN INKLING HE MIGHT TRY SOMETHING LIKE THAT --
-- AND HAD TRAVELED BACK IN TIME, TAKING THE PLACE OF THE REGULAR PILOT, SO MY PAST-SELF WAS ALREADY IN THE COCKPIT --
-- SO I COULD GET THE DROP ON HIM AND FIND HIS SECRET HQ.
SURE, I COULD HAVE JUST THROWN ROCKS AT HIM THROUGH THE FIELD OR SOMETHING. BUT WHERE'S THE FUN IN THAT?

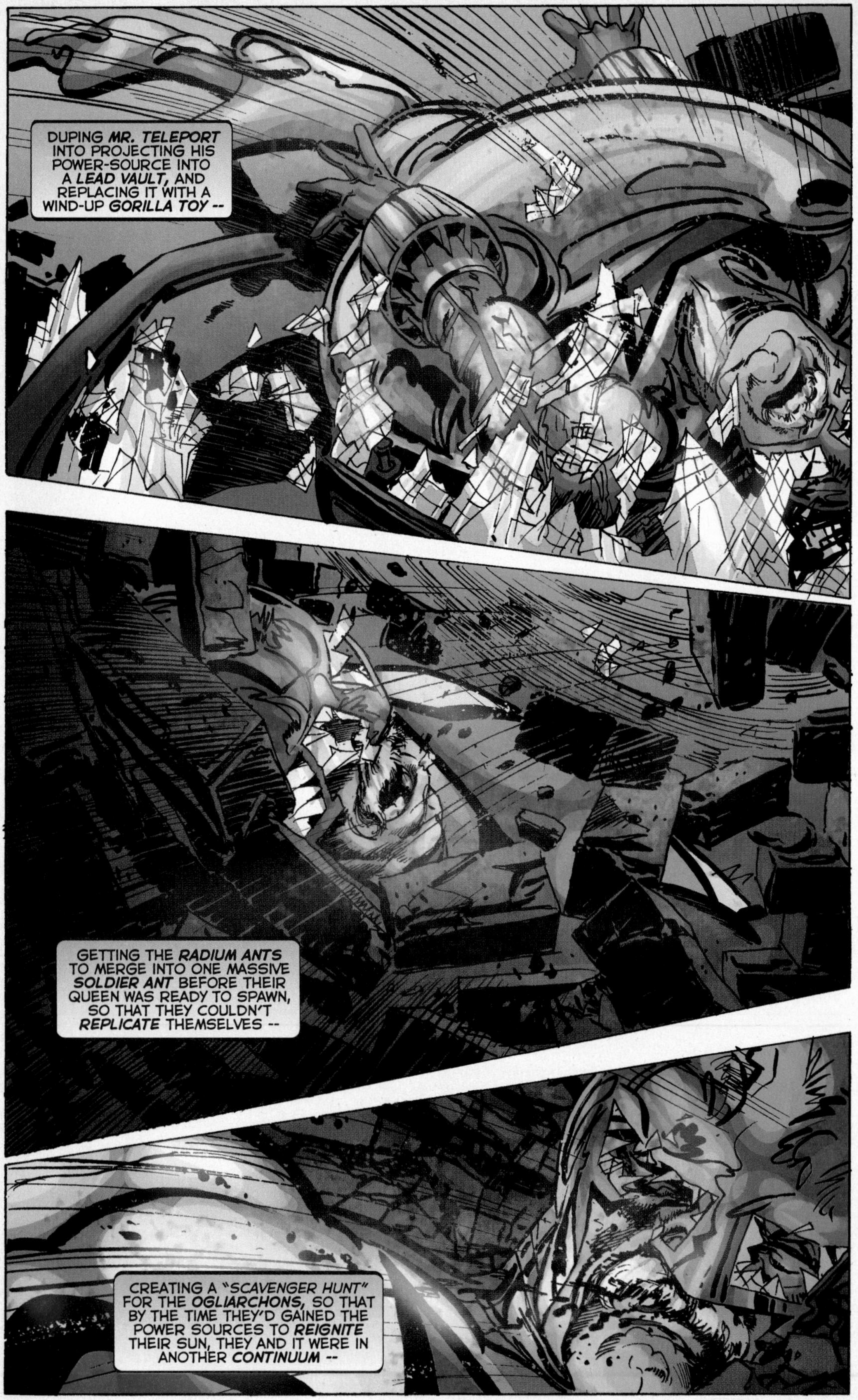
DUPING MR. TELEPORT INTO PROJECTING HIS POWER-SOURCE INTO A LEAD VAULT, AND REPLACING IT WITH A WIND-UP GORILLA TOY --
GETTING THE RADIUM ANTS TO MERGE INTO ONE MASSIVE SOLDIER ANT BEFORE THEIR QUEEN WAS READY TO SPAWN, SO THAT THEY COULDN'T REPLICATE THEMSELVES --
CREATING A "SCAVENGER HUNT" FOR THE OGLIARCHONS, SO THAT BY THE TIME THEY'D GAINED THE POWER SOURCES TO REIGNITE THEIR SUN, THEY AND IT WERE IN ANOTHER CONTINUUM --

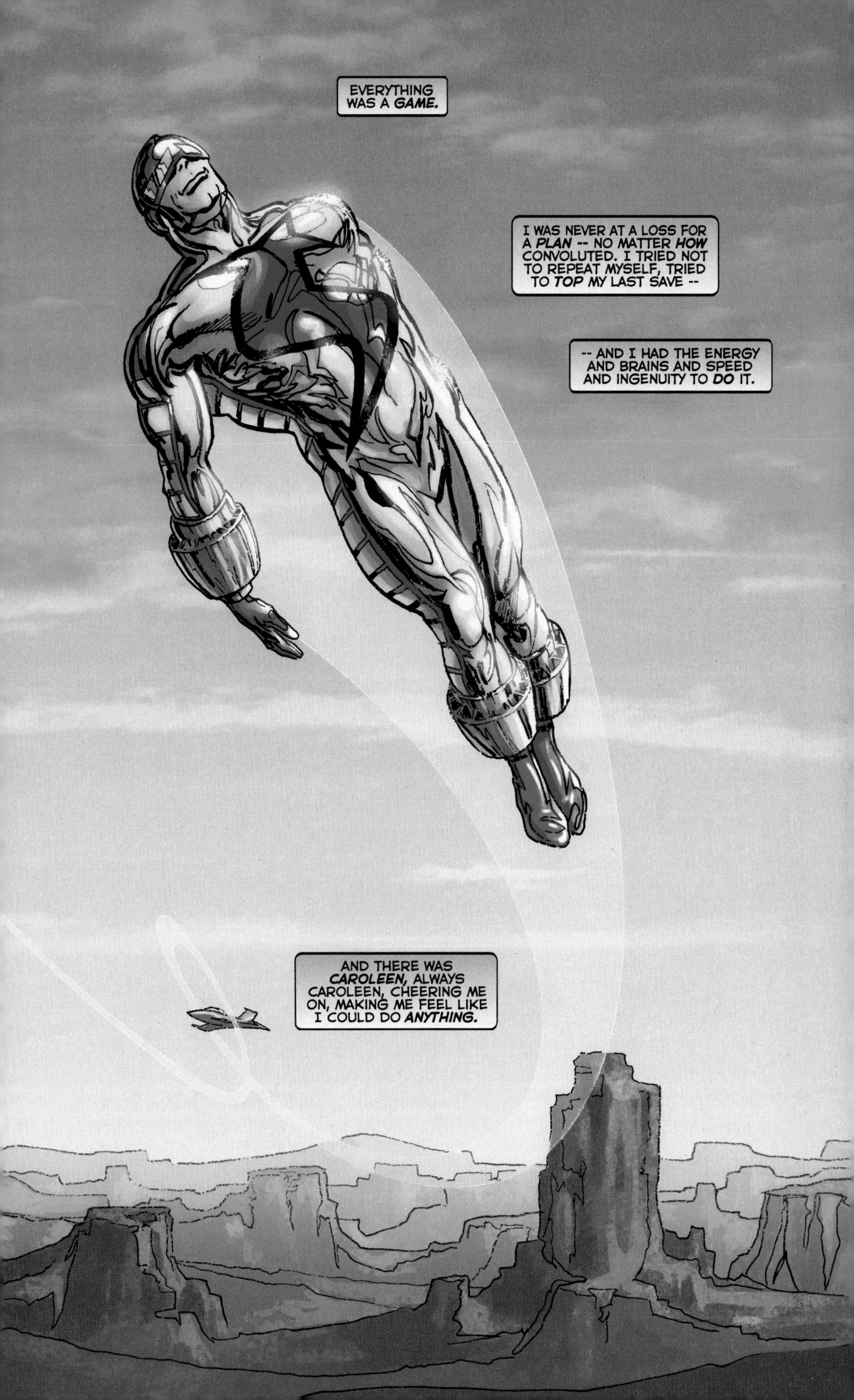
EVERYTHING WAS A GAME.
I WAS NEVER AT A LOSS FOR A PLAN -- NO MATTER HOW CONVOLUTED. I TRIED NOT TO REPEAT MYSELF, TRIED TO TOP MY LAST SAVE --
-- AND I HAD THE ENERGY AND BRAINS AND SPEED AND INGENUITY TO DO IT.
AND THERE WAS CAROLEEN, ALWAYS CAROLEEN, CHEERING ME ON, MAKING ME FEEL LIKE I COULD DO ANYTHING.

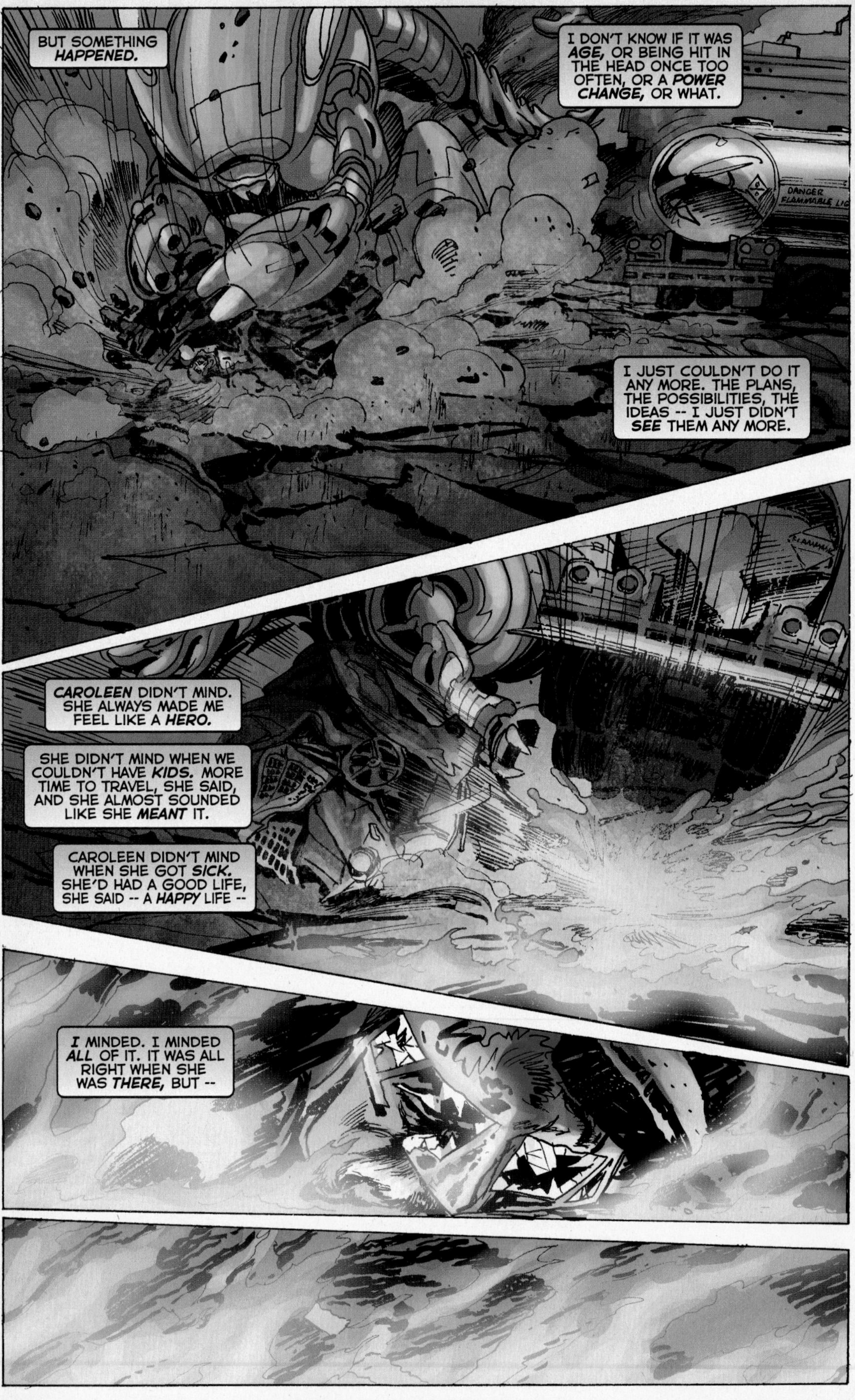
BUT SOMETHING HAPPENED.
I DON'T KNOW IF IT WAS AGE, OR BEING HIT IN THE HEAD ONCE TOO OFTEN, OR A POWER CHANGE, OR WHAT.
DANGER FLAMMABLE LI
I JUST COULDN'T DO IT ANY MORE. THE PLANS, THE POSSIBILITIES, THE IDEAS -- I JUST DIDN'T SEE THEM ANY MORE.
CAROLEEN DIDN'T MIND. SHE ALWAYS MADE ME FEEL LIKE A HERO.
SHE DIDN'T MIND WHEN WE COULDN'T HAVE KIDS. MORE TIME TO TRAVEL, SHE SAID, AND SHE ALMOST SOUNDED LIKE SHE MEANT IT.
CAROLEEN DIDN'T MIND WHEN SHE GOT SICK. SHE'D HAD A GOOD LIFE, SHE SAID -- A HAPPY LIFE --
I MINDED. I MINDED ALL OF IT. IT WAS ALL RIGHT WHEN SHE WAS THERE, BUT --

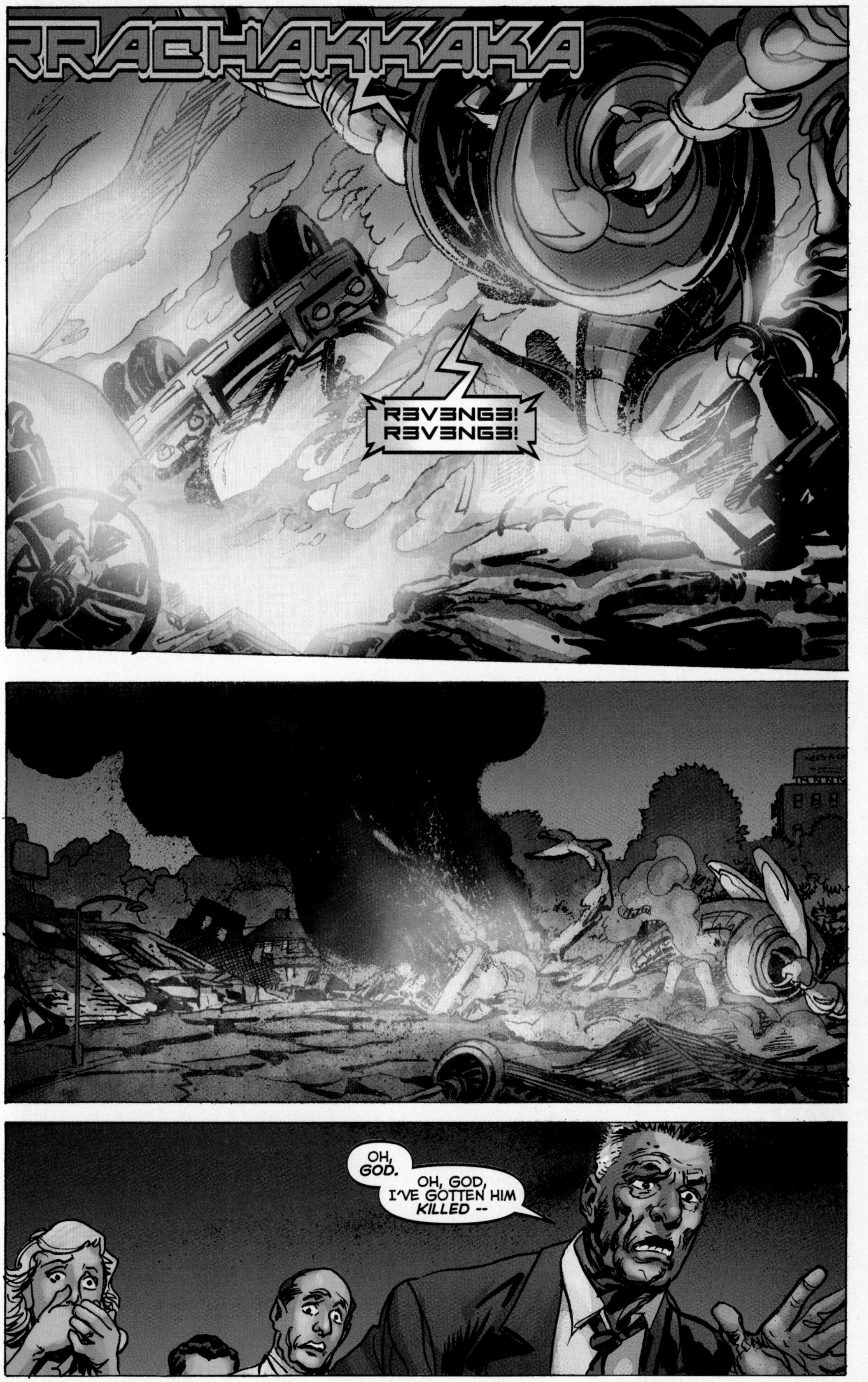
RRACHAKKAKA
R3V3NG3!
R3V3NG3!
OH, GOD.
OH, GOD, I'VE GOTTEN HIM KILLED --

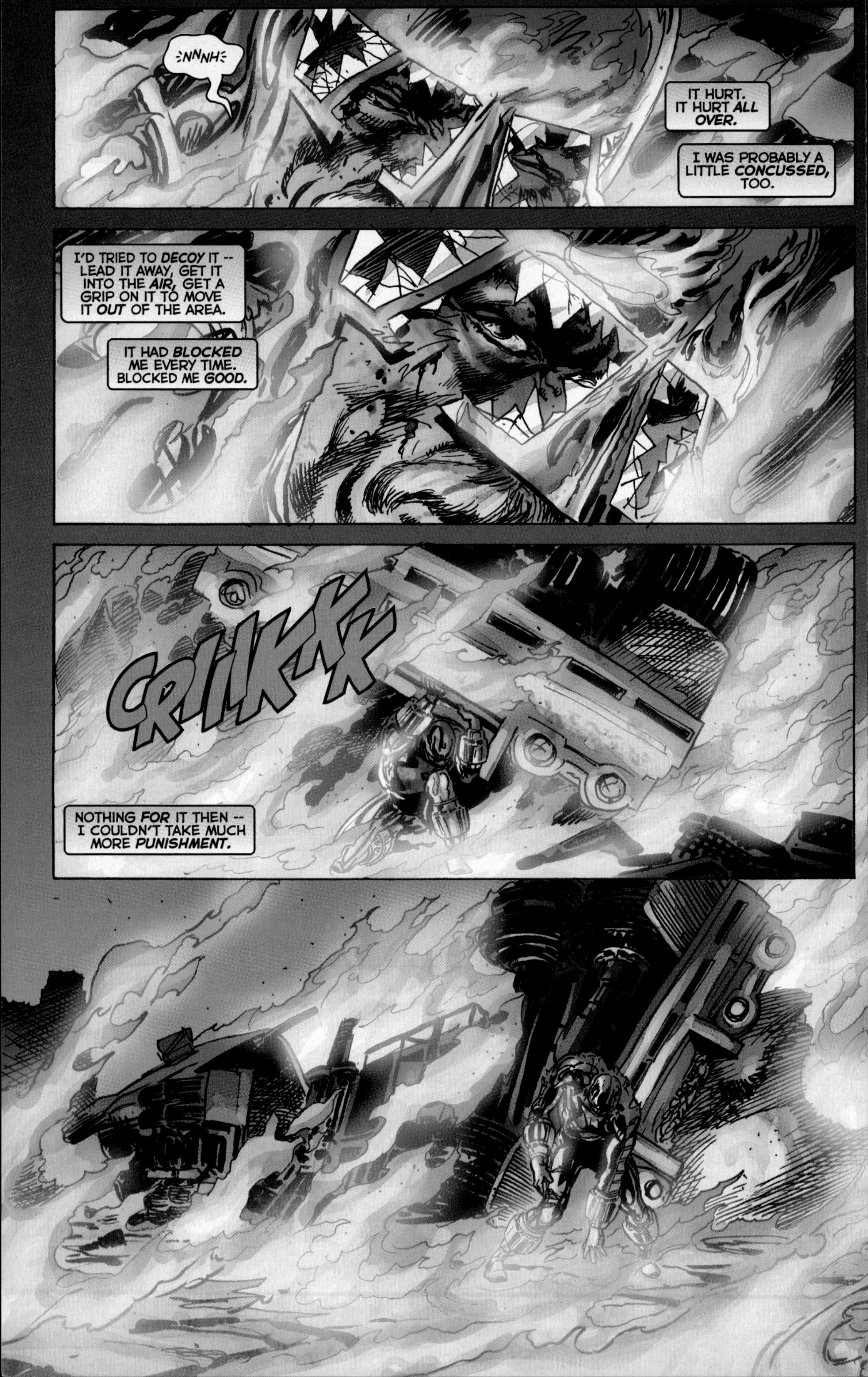
NNNH
IT HURT. IT HURT ALL OVER.
I WAS PROBABLY A LITTLE CONCUSSED, TOO.
I'D TRIED TO DECOY IT -- LEAD IT AWAY, GET IT INTO THE AIR, GET A GRIP ON IT TO MOVE IT OUT OF THE AREA.
IT HAD BLOCKED ME EVERY TIME. BLOCKED ME GOOD.
CRIIKKK
NOTHING FOR IT THEN -- I COULDN'T TAKE MUCH MORE PUNISHMENT.

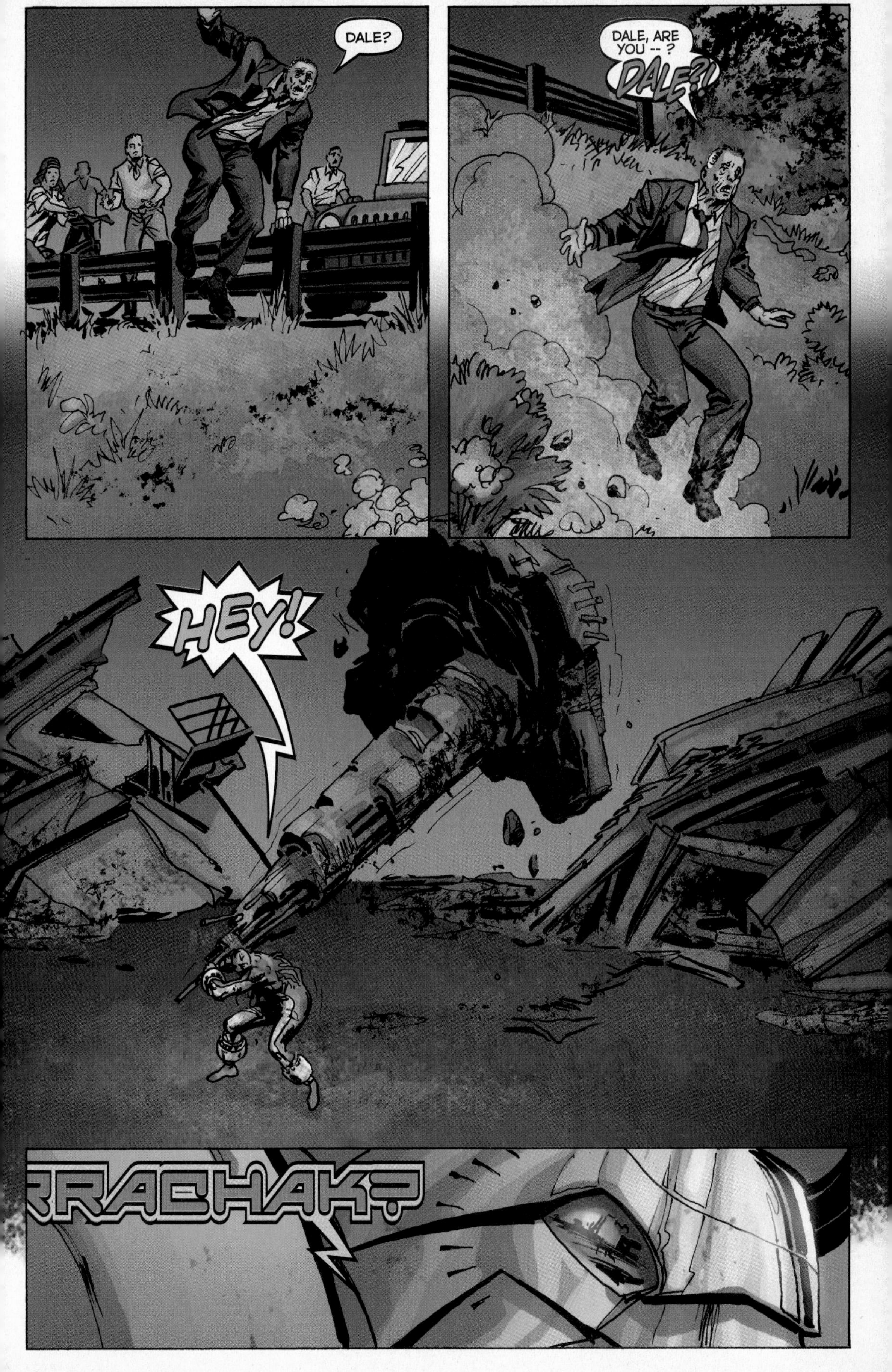
DALE?
DALE, ARE YOU -- ?
DALE?!
HEY!
RRACHAKK

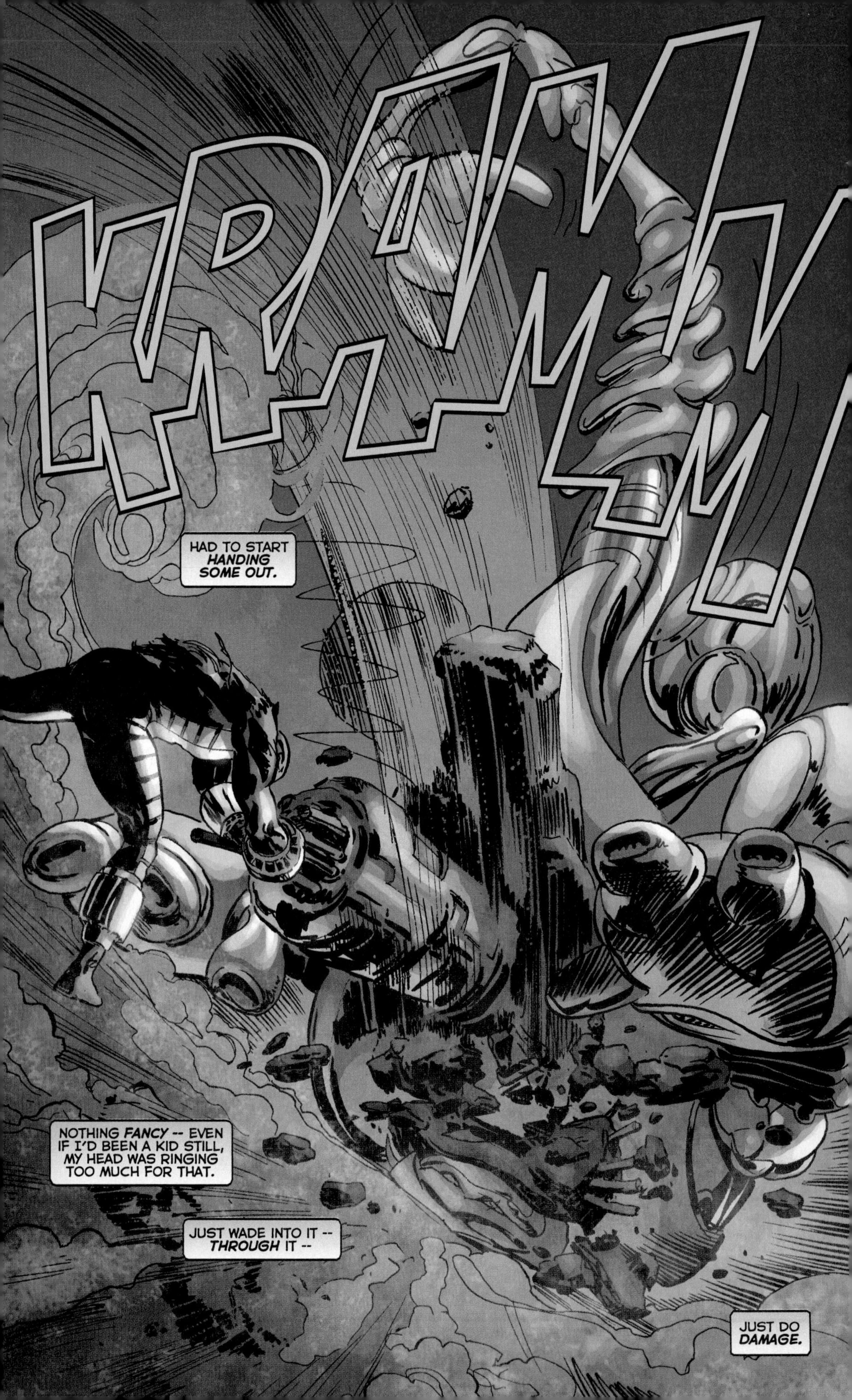

WRAMMM
HAD TO START *HANDING SOME OUT.*
NOTHING *FANCY* -- EVEN IF I'D BEEN A KID STILL, MY HEAD WAS RINGING TOO MUCH FOR THAT.
JUST WADE INTO IT -- *THROUGH* IT --
JUST DO *DAMAGE.*

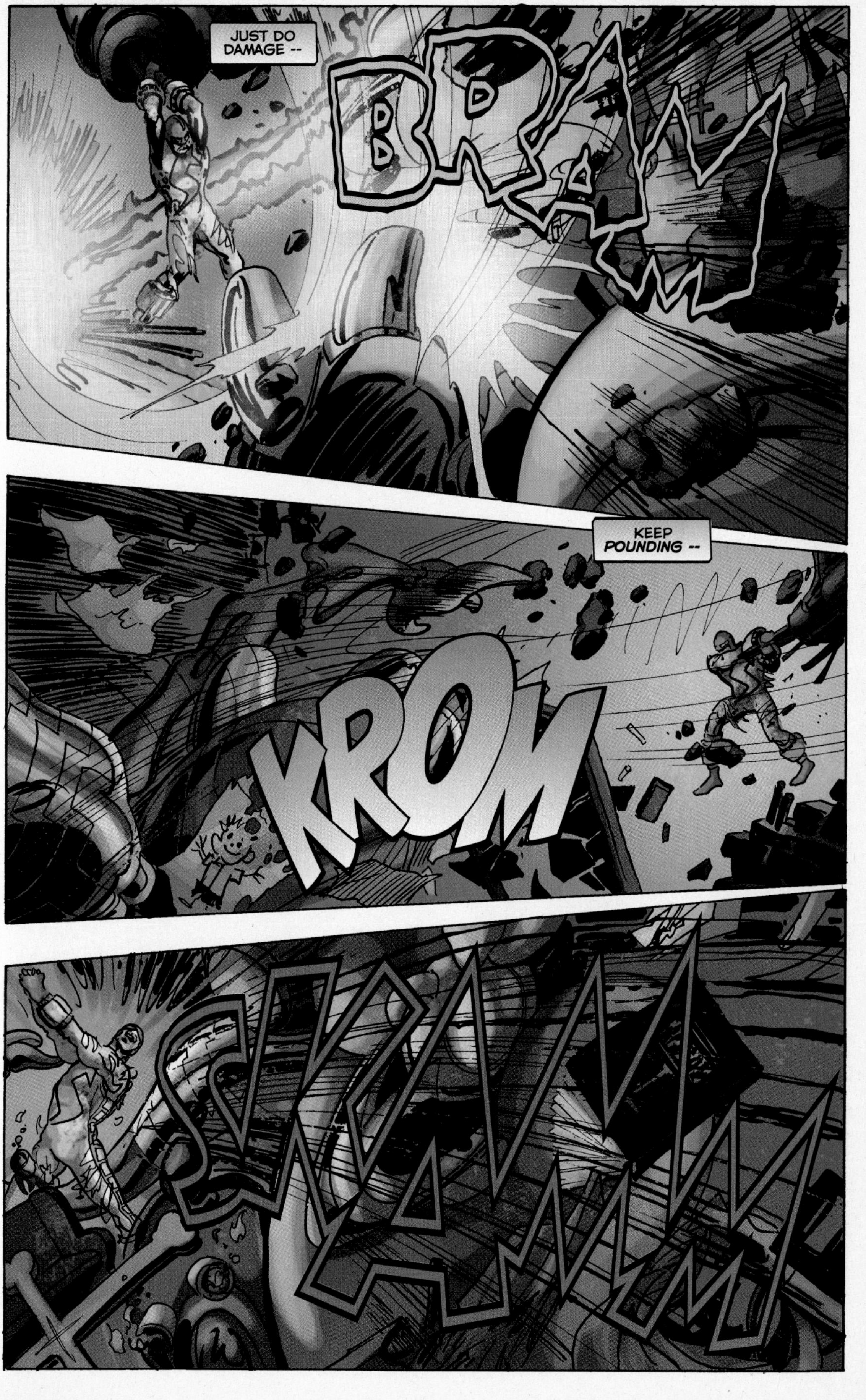
JUST DO DAMAGE --
BDRAAM
KEEP POUNDING --
KROM
SKRAMM

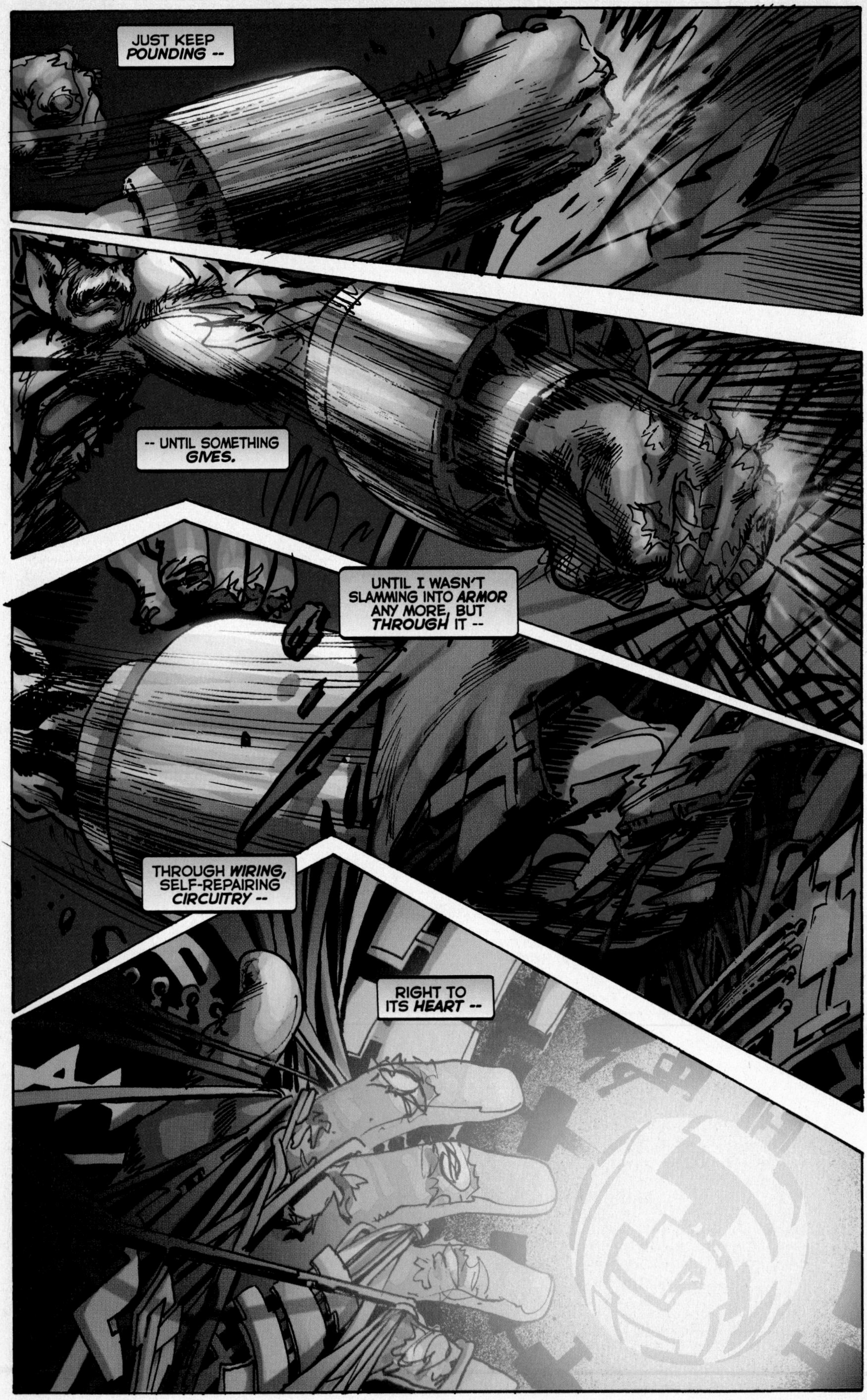
JUST KEEP *POUNDING* --
-- UNTIL SOMETHING *GIVES.*
UNTIL I WASN'T SLAMMING INTO *ARMOR* ANY MORE, BUT *THROUGH* IT --
THROUGH *WIRING,* SELF-REPAIRING *CIRCUITRY* --
RIGHT TO ITS *HEART* --

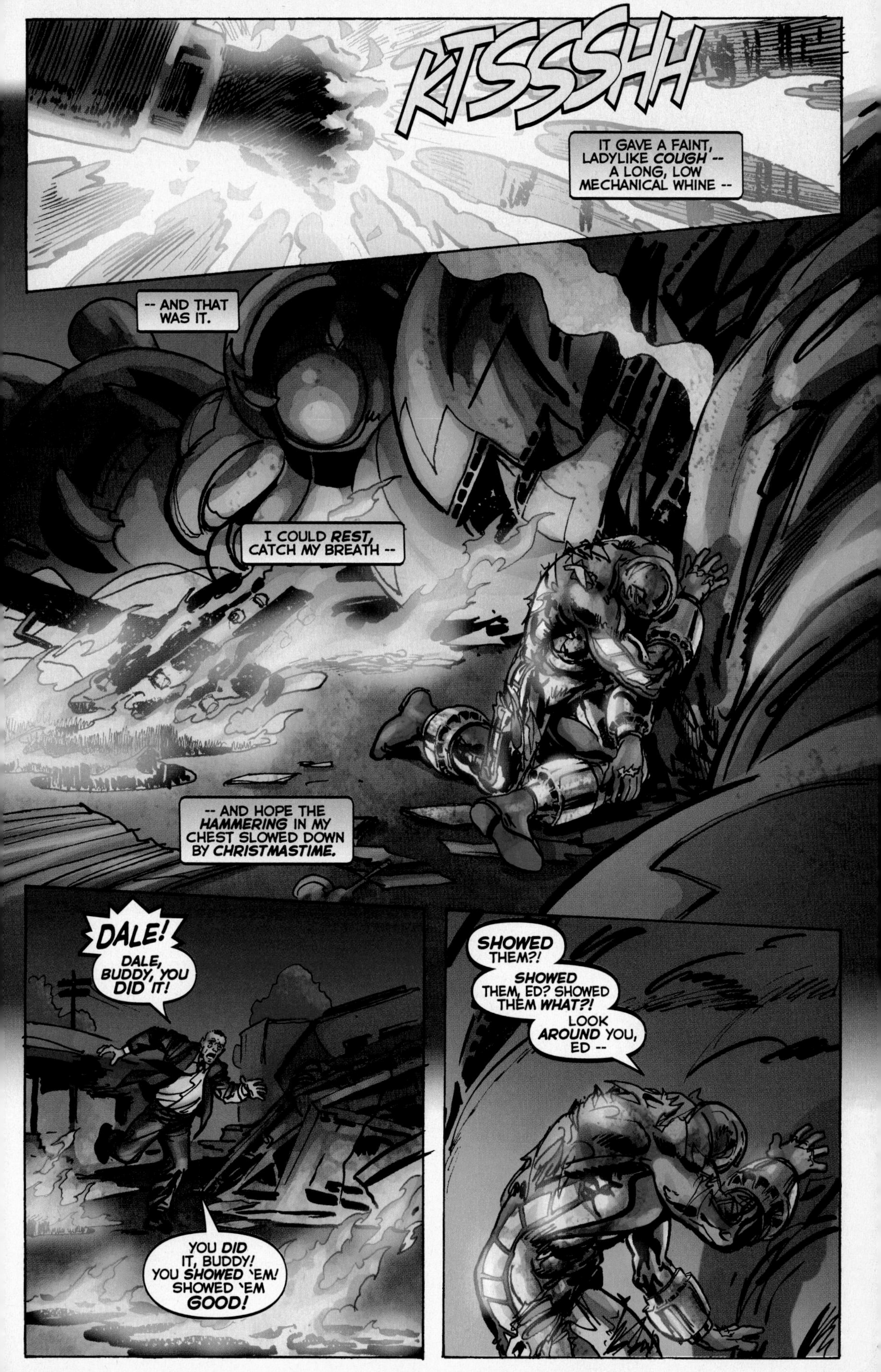
KTSSSHH
IT GAVE A FAINT, LADYLIKE COUGH -- A LONG, LOW MECHANICAL WHINE --
-- AND THAT WAS IT.
I COULD REST, CATCH MY BREATH --
-- AND HOPE THE HAMMERING IN MY CHEST SLOWED DOWN BY CHRISTMASTIME.
DALE!
DALE, BUDDY, YOU DID IT!
YOU DID IT, BUDDY! YOU SHOWED 'EM! SHOWED 'EM GOOD!
SHOWED THEM?!
SHOWED THEM, ED? SHOWED THEM WHAT?!
LOOK AROUND YOU, ED --

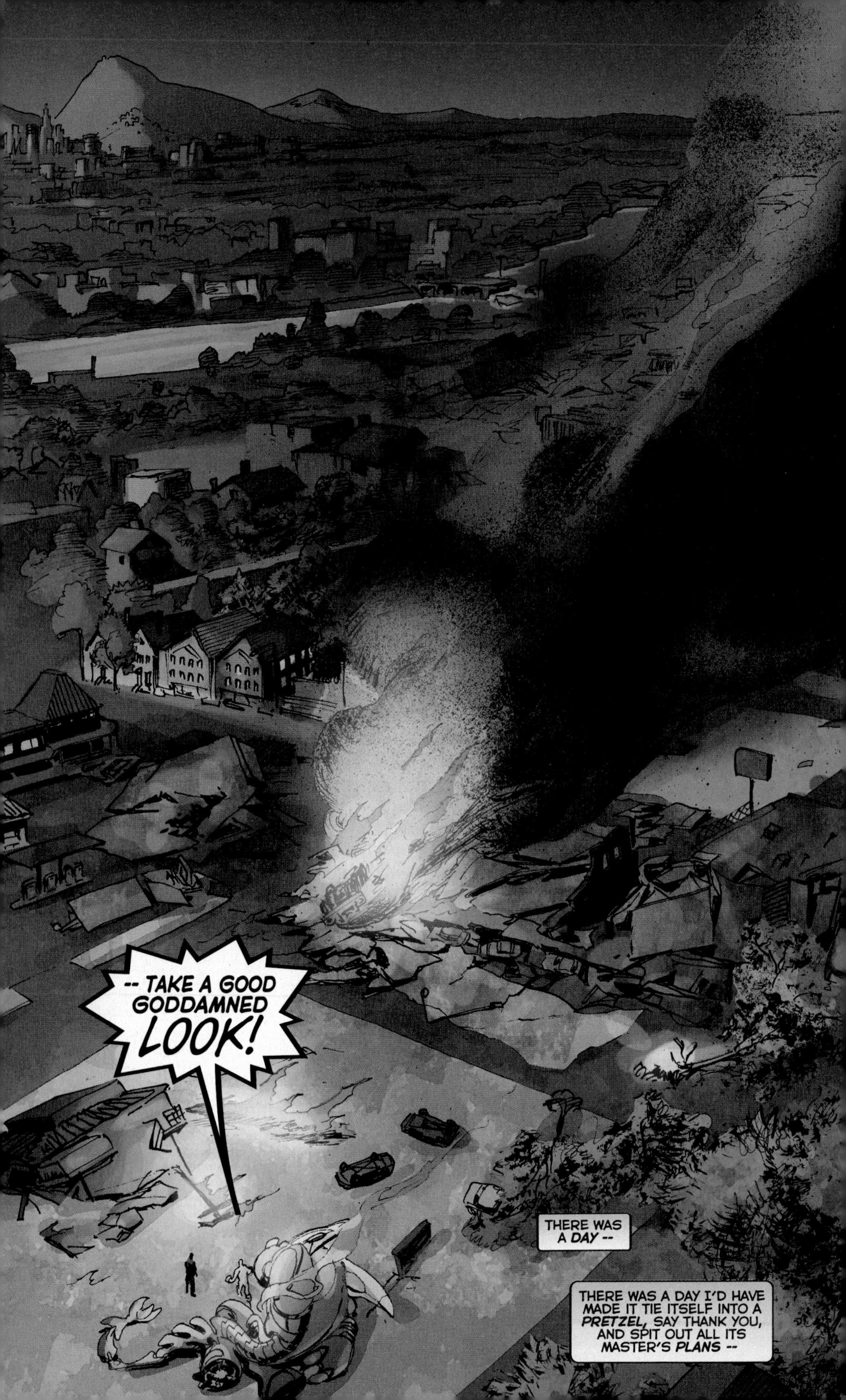
-- TAKE A GOOD GODDAMNED LOOK!
THERE WAS A DAY --
THERE WAS A DAY I'D HAVE MADE IT TIE ITSELF INTO A PRETZEL, SAY THANK YOU, AND SPIT OUT ALL ITS MASTER'S PLANS --

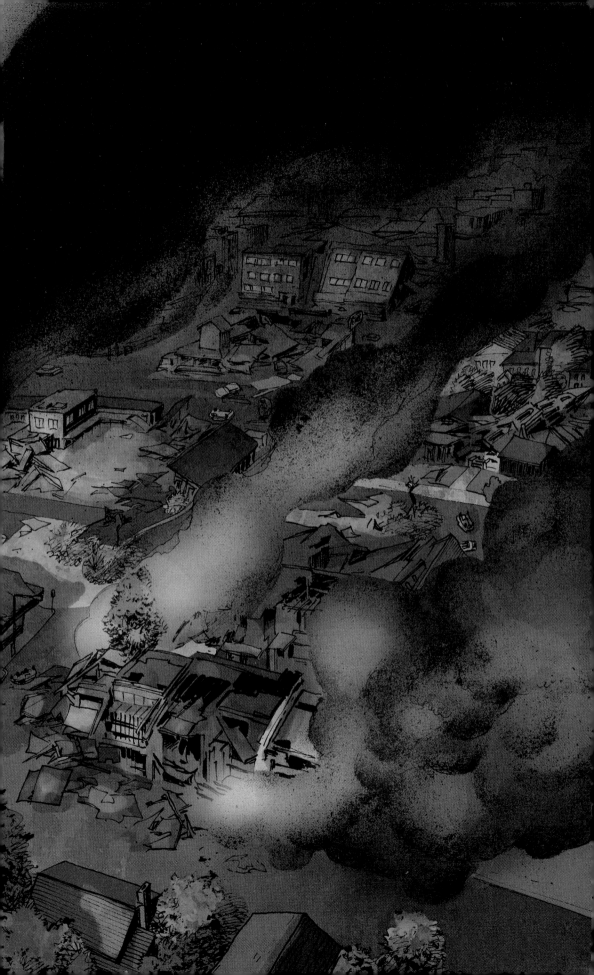

I **TOLD** YOU I WAS DONE. I TOLD YOU I COULDN'T DO IT ANY MORE.

DON'T COME BACK, ED.

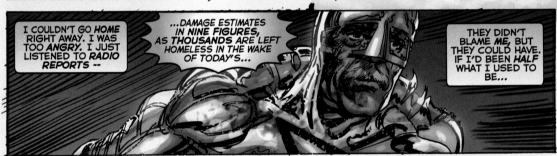

I COULDN'T GO **HOME** RIGHT AWAY. I WAS TOO **ANGRY.** I JUST LISTENED TO **RADIO** REPORTS --

...DAMAGE ESTIMATES IN **NINE FIGURES,** AS **THOUSANDS** ARE LEFT HOMELESS IN THE WAKE OF TODAY'S...

THEY DIDN'T BLAME **ME,** BUT THEY COULD HAVE. IF I'D BEEN **HALF** WHAT I USED TO BE...

HE **MEANT** WELL, BUT HOW COULD HE NOT HAVE KNOWN? IT'D BEEN DECADES. AND I'M YOUNGER THAN **HE** IS, SO HE **HAD** TO KNOW.

ALL HE HAD TO DO WAS **LOOK** IN THE --

Oh.

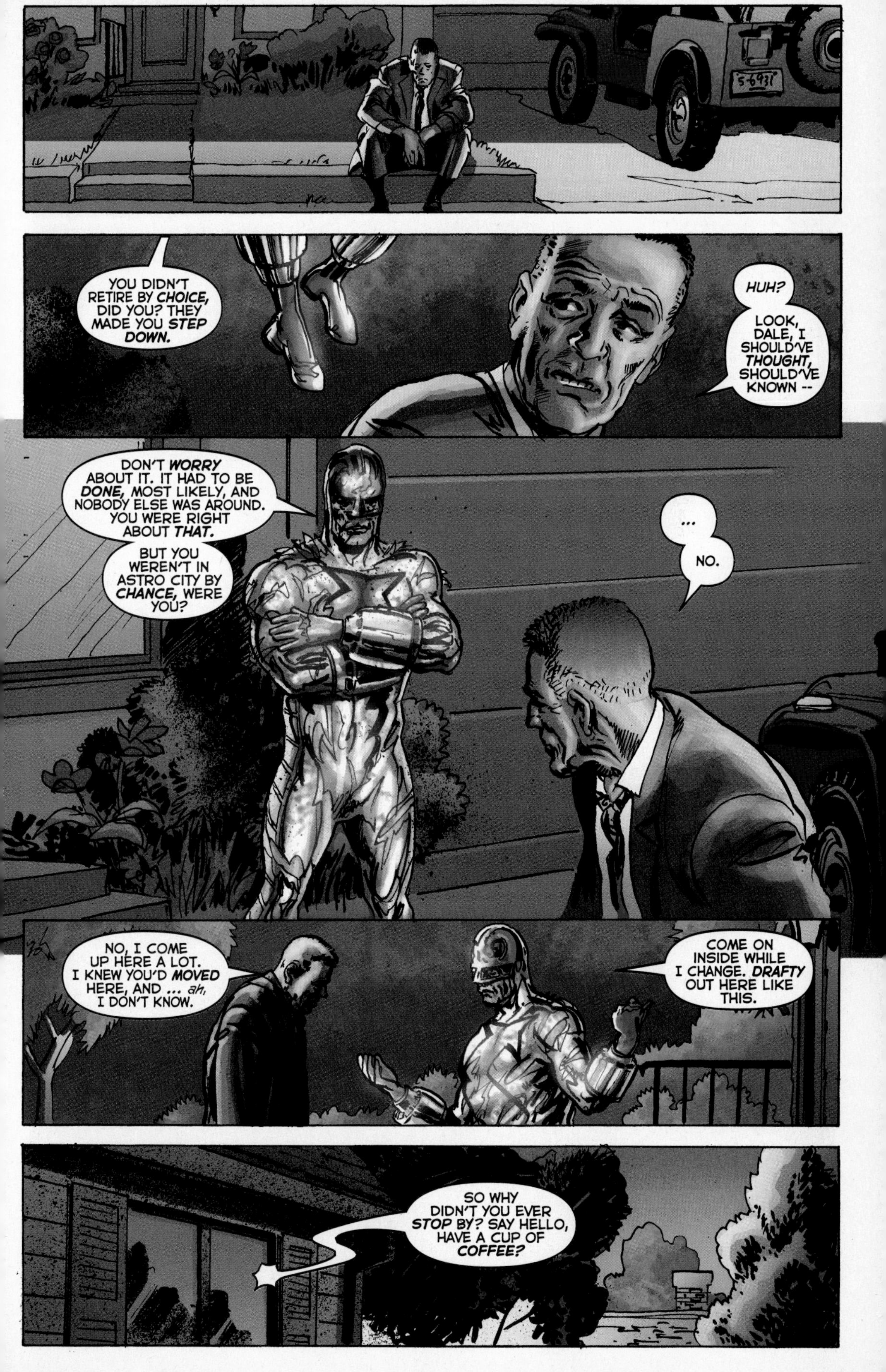
YOU DIDN'T RETIRE BY CHOICE, DID YOU? THEY MADE YOU STEP DOWN.
HUH?
LOOK, DALE, I SHOULD'VE THOUGHT, SHOULD'VE KNOWN --
DON'T WORRY ABOUT IT. IT HAD TO BE DONE, MOST LIKELY, AND NOBODY ELSE WAS AROUND. YOU WERE RIGHT ABOUT THAT.
BUT YOU WEREN'T IN ASTRO CITY BY CHANCE, WERE YOU?
...
NO.
NO, I COME UP HERE A LOT. I KNEW YOU'D MOVED HERE, AND ... ah, I DON'T KNOW.
COME ON INSIDE WHILE I CHANGE. DRAFTY OUT HERE LIKE THIS.
SO WHY DIDN'T YOU EVER STOP BY? SAY HELLO, HAVE A CUP OF COFFEE?

I DIDN'T WANT TO BE JUST *TWO USELESS OLD FARTS* RATTLING AROUND REMEMBERING THEIR *GLORY DAYS.*

I WANTED --

YOU WANTED ME TO STILL *HAVE* IT, BECAUSE IF I DID, MAYBE THEY WERE WRONG ABOUT *YOU.*

BUT THAT'S WHY I MOVED *UP* HERE, AFTER CAROLEEN PASSED.

ALL THOSE *HEROES*, ALL AROUND... THEY'D NEVER NEED *ME*, AND I COULD RETIRE IN PEACE, IGNORE THE RADIO AND THE *TV.*

GROW *ROSES*, LIKE SHE ALWAYS WANTED.

I WAS SORRY TO *HEAR* ABOUT HER. SHE WAS A *GREAT* GIRL.

THEY WANT ME TO *TEACH*, DID YOU KNOW? UP AT THE TROOPER ACADEMY.

CAN YOU *PICTURE* IT? ME LIKE OLD MAN *MULWRAY*, JAWING ON AND ON ABOUT PISSANT CASES NOBODY'D *EVER* CARED ABOUT?

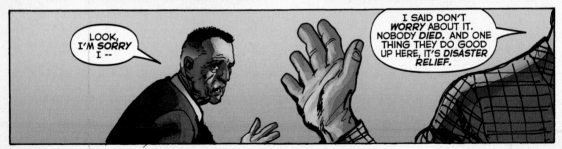

LOOK, I'M *SORRY* I --

I SAID DON'T *WORRY* ABOUT IT. NOBODY *DIED.* AND ONE THING THEY DO GOOD UP HERE, IT'S *DISASTER RELIEF.*

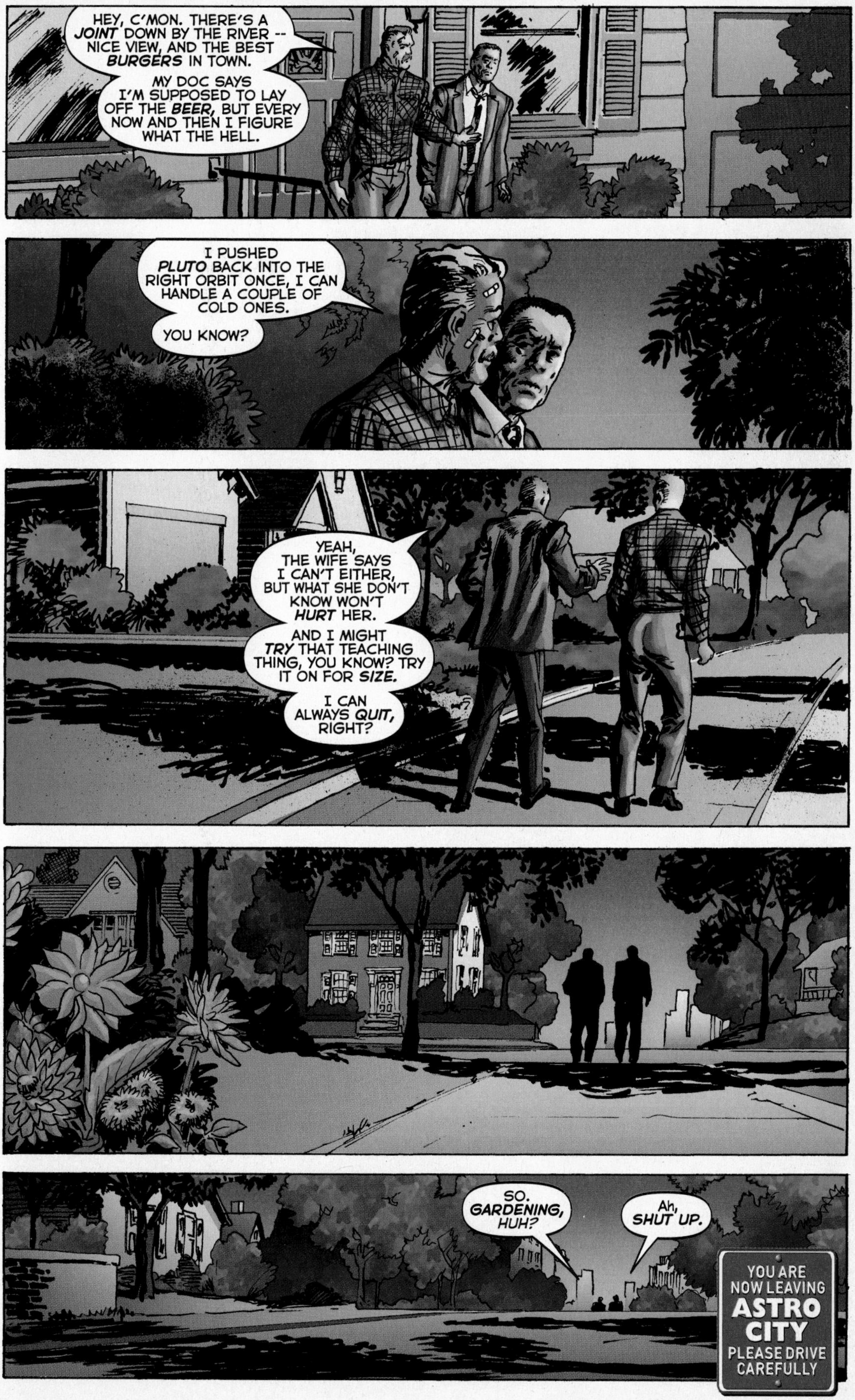
HEY, C'MON. THERE'S A JOINT DOWN BY THE RIVER -- NICE VIEW, AND THE BEST BURGERS IN TOWN.
MY DOC SAYS I'M SUPPOSED TO LAY OFF THE BEER, BUT EVERY NOW AND THEN I FIGURE WHAT THE HELL.
I PUSHED PLUTO BACK INTO THE RIGHT ORBIT ONCE, I CAN HANDLE A COUPLE OF COLD ONES.
YOU KNOW?
YEAH, THE WIFE SAYS I CAN'T EITHER, BUT WHAT SHE DON'T KNOW WON'T HURT HER.
AND I MIGHT TRY THAT TEACHING THING, YOU KNOW? TRY IT ON FOR SIZE.
I CAN ALWAYS QUIT, RIGHT?
SO. GARDENING, HUH?
Ah, SHUT UP.
YOU ARE NOW LEAVING ASTRO CITY PLEASE DRIVE CAREFULLY

NINE

"Since the Fire" was created for and first published in volume 2 of 9-11 - The World's Finest Writers & Artists Tell Stories to Remember, a collection of comics stories and art done in response to the devastating events of September 11th, 2001.

The creative talent, the suppliers, printer and distributor of the book donated their time and effort, and all profits from the book were donated to organizations for the benefit and relief of the victims of that day's brutal attacks on America, and of their families and affected communities, including:

- New York State World Trade Center Relief Fund
- Survivor's Fund of the National Capital Region
- The September 11th Fund of the New York Community Trust and the United Way of New York City
- Twin Towers Fund

The Astro City team of Kurt, Brent, Richard, JG, Alex Sinclair and Alex Ross (who did the cover of that volume) are proud to have been involved with such a worthwhile project.

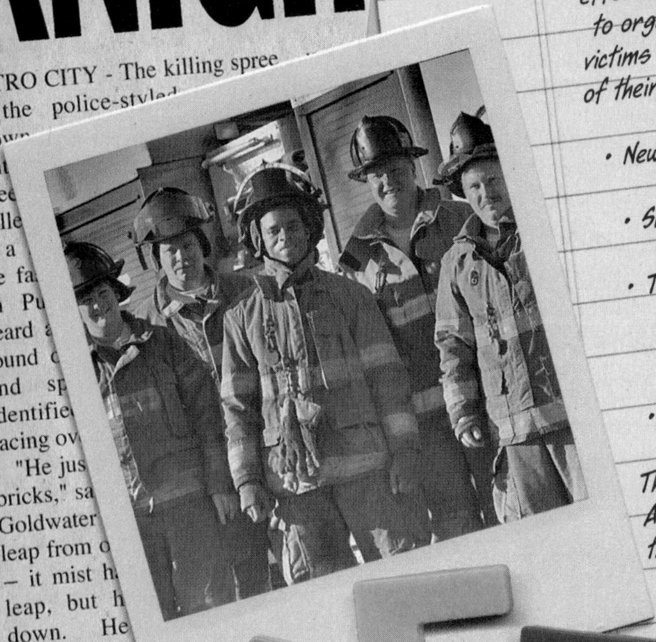

AFTER THE FIRE

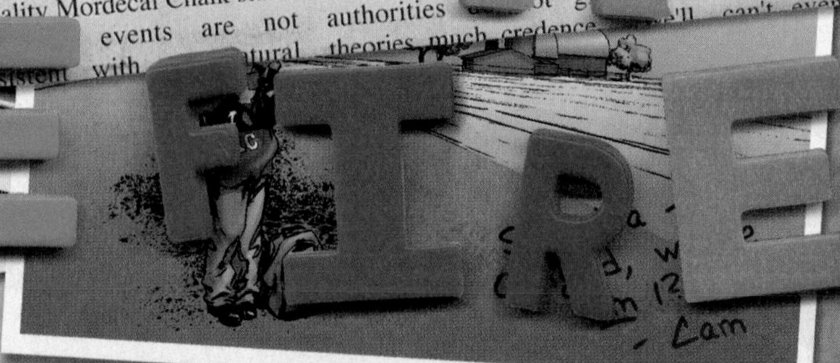

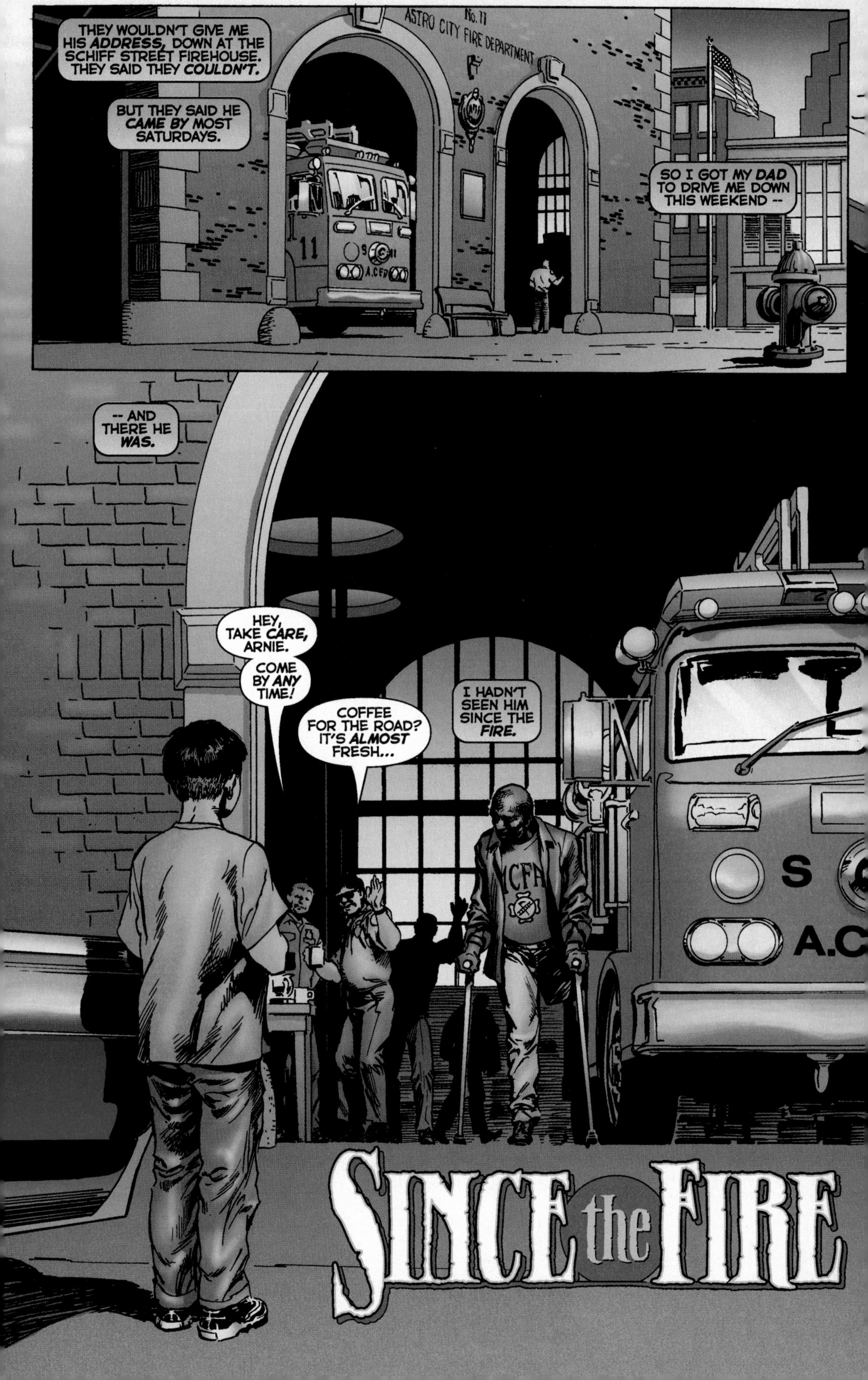
THEY WOULDN'T GIVE ME HIS ADDRESS, DOWN AT THE SCHIFF STREET FIREHOUSE. THEY SAID THEY COULDN'T.
BUT THEY SAID HE CAME BY MOST SATURDAYS.
No. 11 ASTRO CITY FIRE DEPARTMENT
SO I GOT MY DAD TO DRIVE ME DOWN THIS WEEKEND --
-- AND THERE HE WAS.
HEY, TAKE CARE, ARNIE.
COME BY ANY TIME!
COFFEE FOR THE ROAD? IT'S ALMOST FRESH...
I HADN'T SEEN HIM SINCE THE FIRE.
SINCE the FIRE

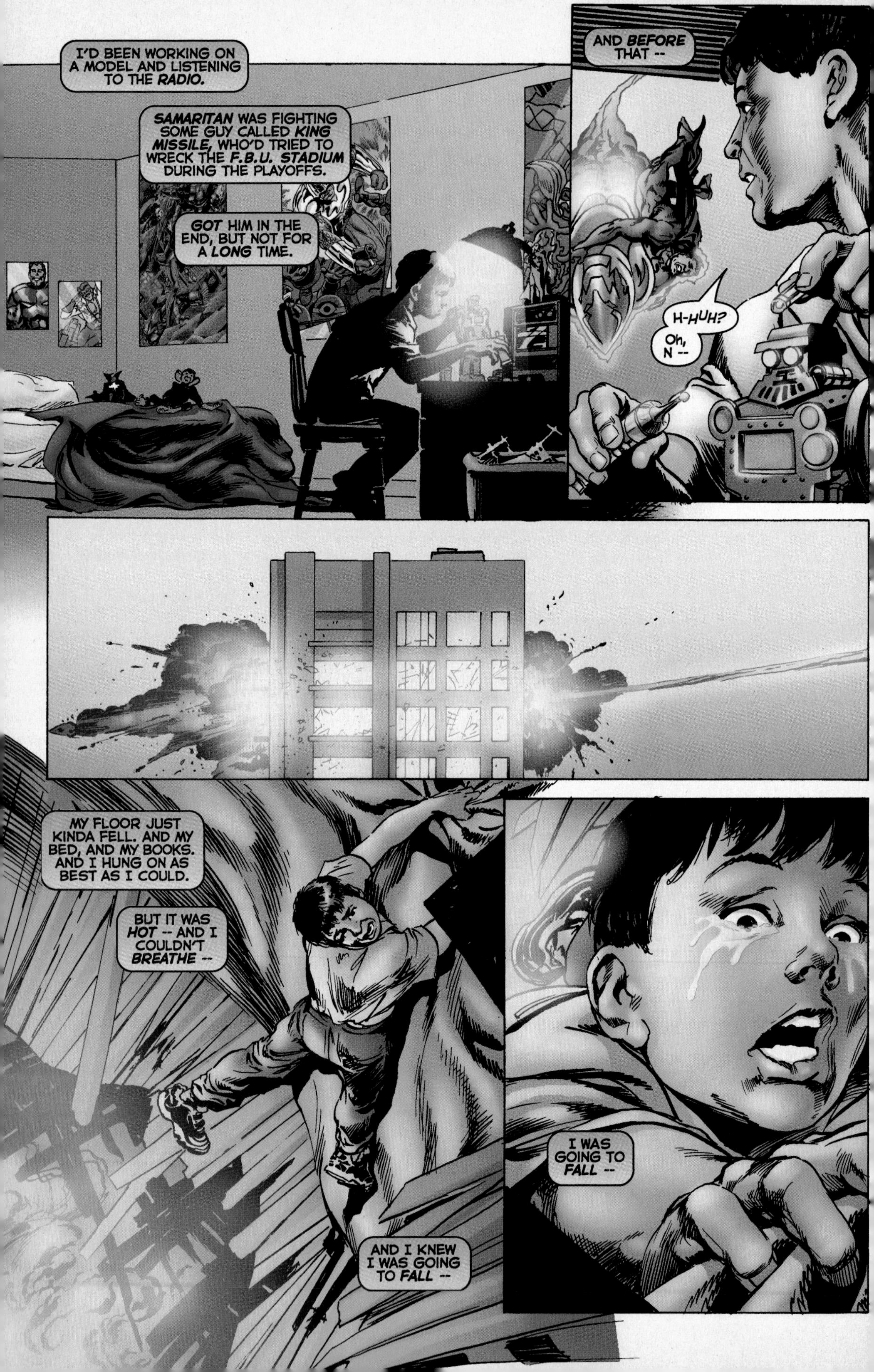
I'D BEEN WORKING ON A MODEL AND LISTENING TO THE RADIO.
SAMARITAN WAS FIGHTING SOME GUY CALLED KING MISSILE, WHO'D TRIED TO WRECK THE F.B.U. STADIUM DURING THE PLAYOFFS.
GOT HIM IN THE END, BUT NOT FOR A LONG TIME.
AND BEFORE THAT --
H-HUH?
Oh, N --
MY FLOOR JUST KINDA FELL. AND MY BED, AND MY BOOKS. AND I HUNG ON AS BEST AS I COULD.
BUT IT WAS HOT -- AND I COULDN'T BREATHE --
AND I KNEW I WAS GOING TO FALL --
I WAS GOING TO FALL --

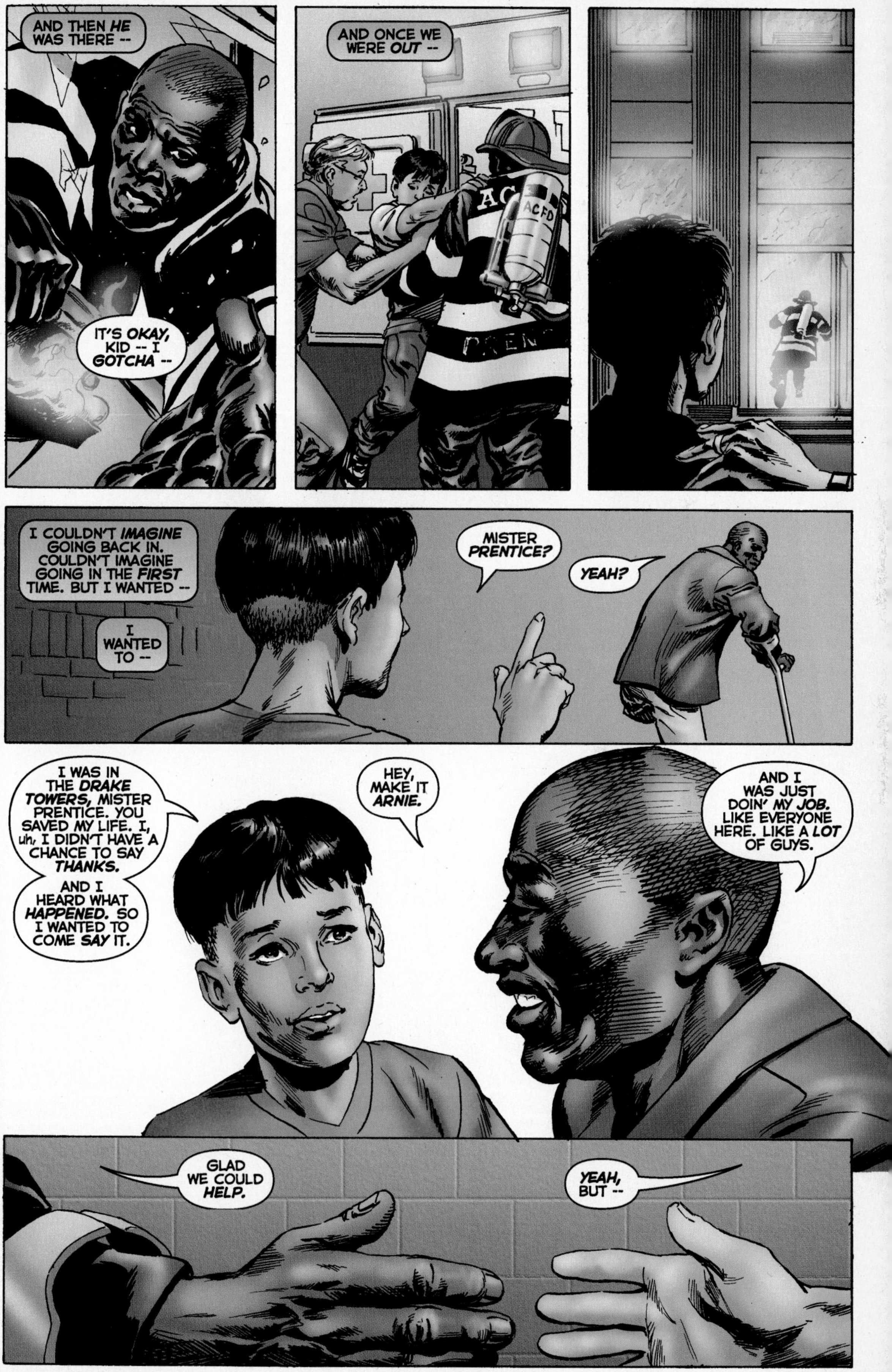
AND THEN HE WAS THERE --
IT'S OKAY, KID -- I GOTCHA --
AND ONCE WE WERE OUT --
I COULDN'T IMAGINE GOING BACK IN. COULDN'T IMAGINE GOING IN THE FIRST TIME. BUT I WANTED --
I WANTED TO --
MISTER PRENTICE?
YEAH?
I WAS IN THE DRAKE TOWERS, MISTER PRENTICE. YOU SAVED MY LIFE. I, uh, I DIDN'T HAVE A CHANCE TO SAY THANKS.
AND I HEARD WHAT HAPPENED. SO I WANTED TO COME SAY IT.
HEY, MAKE IT ARNIE.
AND I WAS JUST DOIN' MY JOB. LIKE EVERYONE HERE. LIKE A LOT OF GUYS.
GLAD WE COULD HELP.
YEAH, BUT --

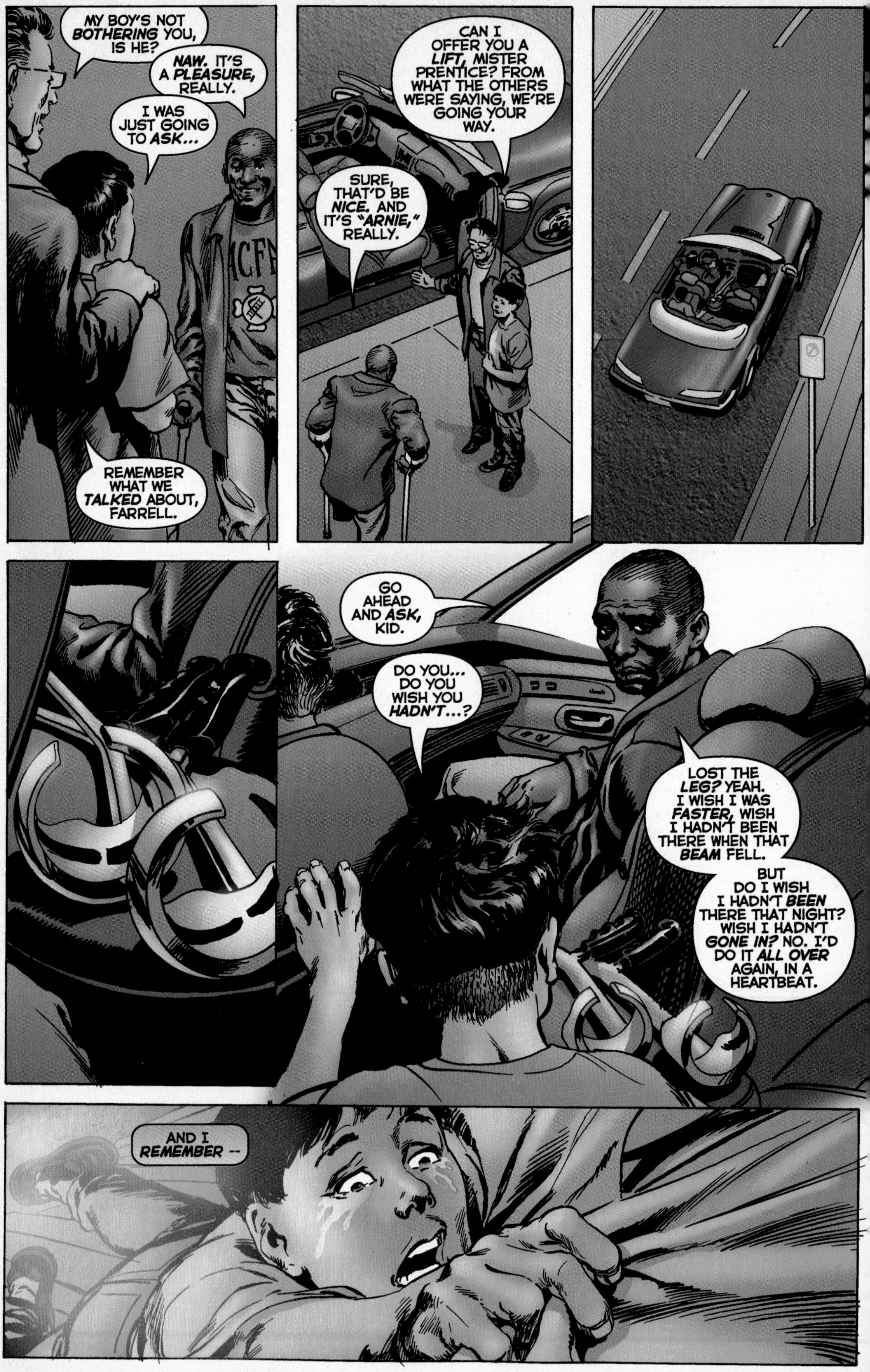
MY BOY'S NOT BOTHERING YOU, IS HE?
NAW. IT'S A PLEASURE, REALLY.
I WAS JUST GOING TO ASK...
REMEMBER WHAT WE TALKED ABOUT, FARRELL.
CAN I OFFER YOU A LIFT, MISTER PRENTICE? FROM WHAT THE OTHERS WERE SAYING, WE'RE GOING YOUR WAY.
SURE, THAT'D BE NICE. AND IT'S "ARNIE," REALLY.
GO AHEAD AND ASK, KID.
DO YOU... DO YOU WISH YOU HADN'T...?
LOST THE LEG? YEAH. I WISH I WAS FASTER, WISH I HADN'T BEEN THERE WHEN THAT BEAM FELL.
BUT DO I WISH I HADN'T BEEN THERE THAT NIGHT? WISH I HADN'T GONE IN? NO. I'D DO IT ALL OVER AGAIN, IN A HEARTBEAT.
AND I REMEMBER --

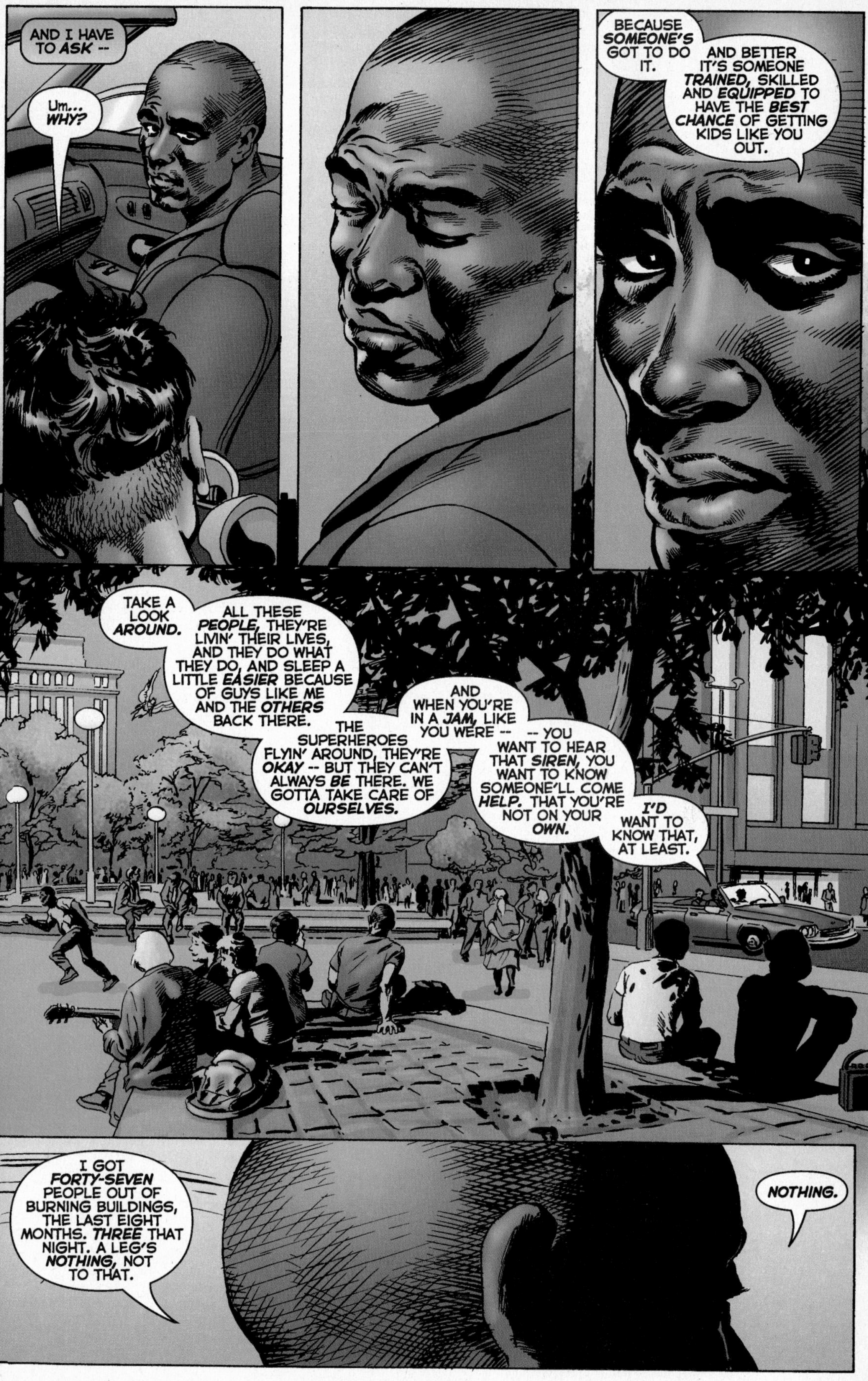
AND I HAVE TO ASK --
Um... WHY?
BECAUSE SOMEONE'S GOT TO DO IT.
AND BETTER IT'S SOMEONE TRAINED, SKILLED AND EQUIPPED TO HAVE THE BEST CHANCE OF GETTING KIDS LIKE YOU OUT.
TAKE A LOOK AROUND.
ALL THESE PEOPLE, THEY'RE LIVIN' THEIR LIVES, AND THEY DO WHAT THEY DO, AND SLEEP A LITTLE EASIER BECAUSE OF GUYS LIKE ME AND THE OTHERS BACK THERE.
THE SUPERHEROES FLYIN' AROUND, THEY'RE OKAY -- BUT THEY CAN'T ALWAYS BE THERE. WE GOTTA TAKE CARE OF OURSELVES.
AND WHEN YOU'RE IN A JAM, LIKE YOU WERE --
-- YOU WANT TO HEAR THAT SIREN, YOU WANT TO KNOW SOMEONE'LL COME HELP. THAT YOU'RE NOT ON YOUR OWN.
I'D WANT TO KNOW THAT, AT LEAST.
I GOT FORTY-SEVEN PEOPLE OUT OF BURNING BUILDINGS, THE LAST EIGHT MONTHS. THREE THAT NIGHT. A LEG'S NOTHING, NOT TO THAT.
NOTHING.

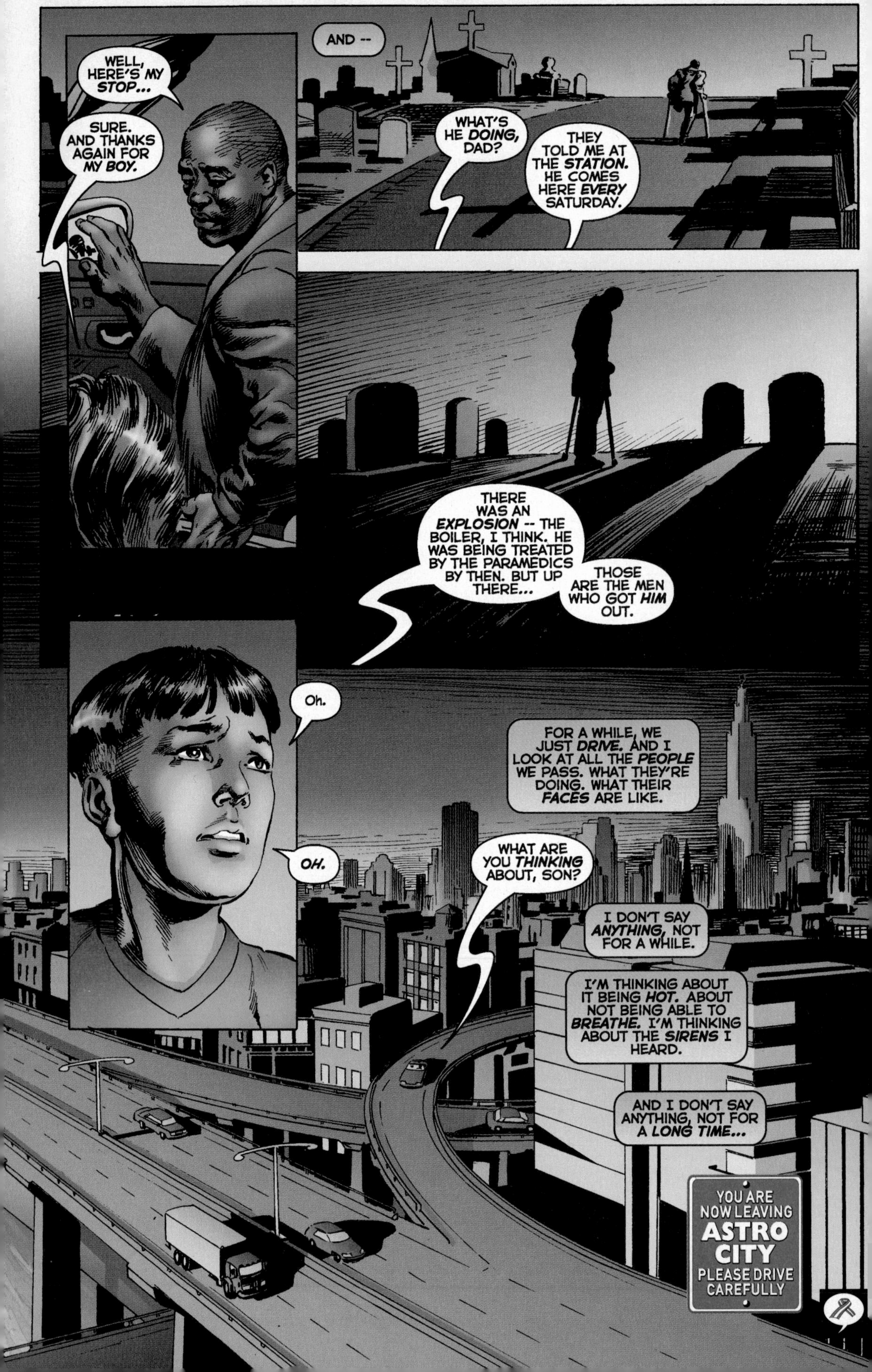
WELL, HERE'S MY STOP...
SURE. AND THANKS AGAIN FOR MY BOY.
AND --
WHAT'S HE DOING, DAD?
THEY TOLD ME AT THE STATION. HE COMES HERE EVERY SATURDAY.
THERE WAS AN EXPLOSION -- THE BOILER, I THINK. HE WAS BEING TREATED BY THE PARAMEDICS BY THEN. BUT UP THERE...
THOSE ARE THE MEN WHO GOT HIM OUT.
Oh.
OH.
FOR A WHILE, WE JUST DRIVE. AND I LOOK AT ALL THE PEOPLE WE PASS. WHAT THEY'RE DOING. WHAT THEIR FACES ARE LIKE.
WHAT ARE YOU THINKING ABOUT, SON?
I DON'T SAY ANYTHING, NOT FOR A WHILE.
I'M THINKING ABOUT IT BEING HOT. ABOUT NOT BEING ABLE TO BREATHE. I'M THINKING ABOUT THE SIRENS I HEARD.
AND I DON'T SAY ANYTHING, NOT FOR A LONG TIME...
YOU ARE NOW LEAVING ASTRO CITY PLEASE DRIVE CAREFULLY

HOME GROWN HEROES

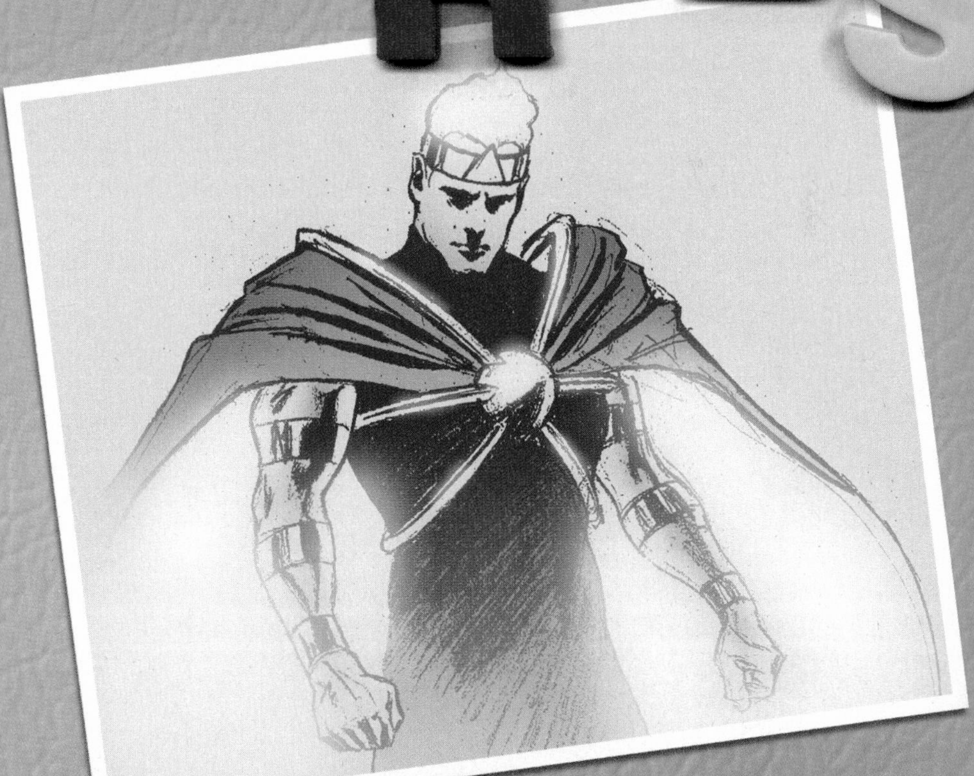

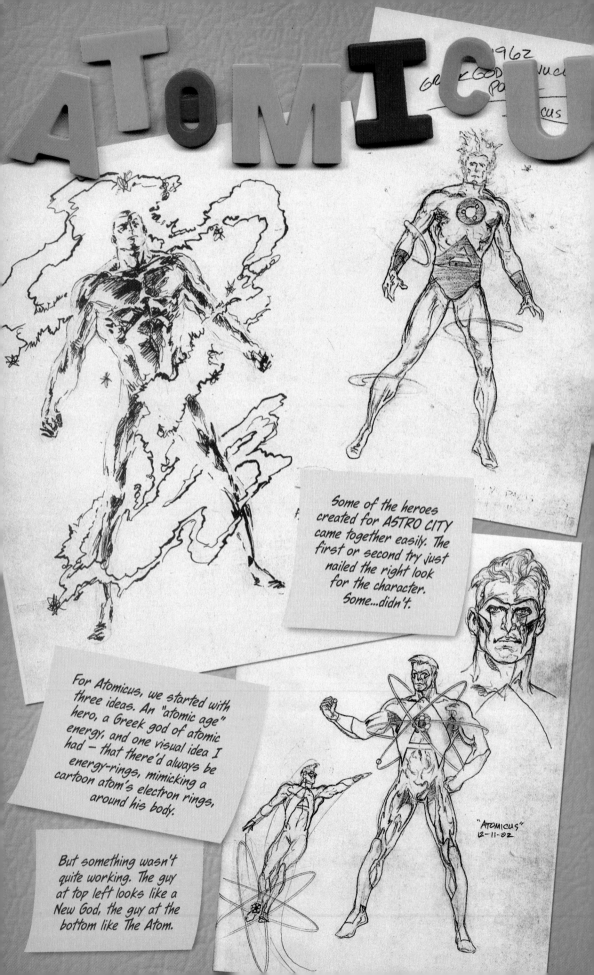

ATOMICU

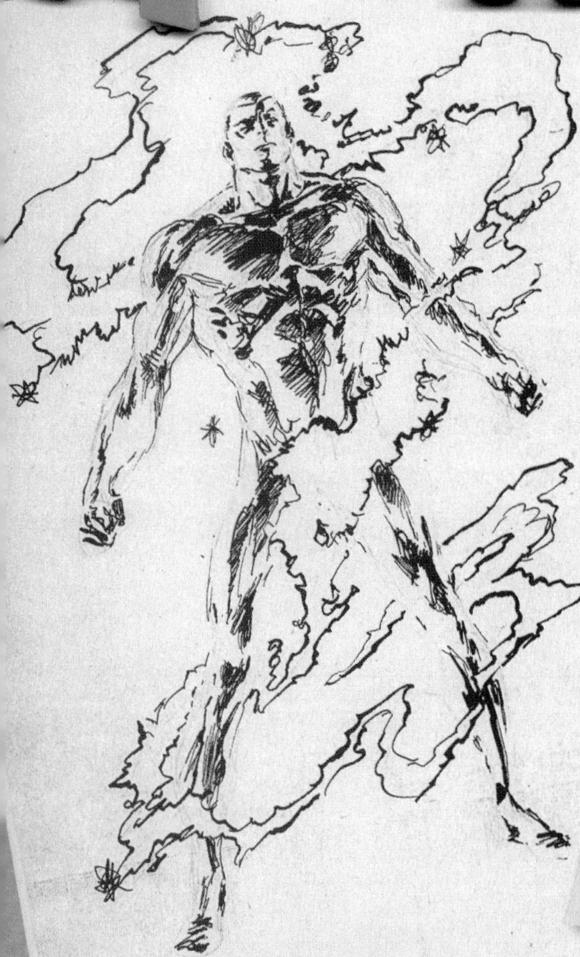

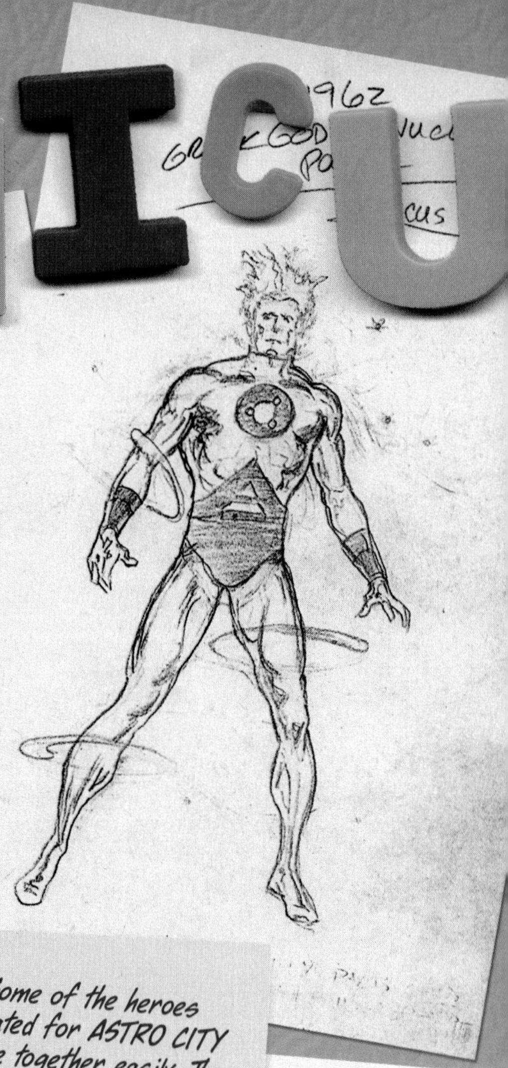

Some of the heroes created for ASTRO CITY came together easily. The first or second try just nailed the right look for the character. Some...didn't.

For Atomicus, we started with three ideas. An "atomic age" hero, a Greek god of atomic energy, and one visual idea I had – that there'd always be energy-rings, mimicking a cartoon atom's electron rings, around his body.

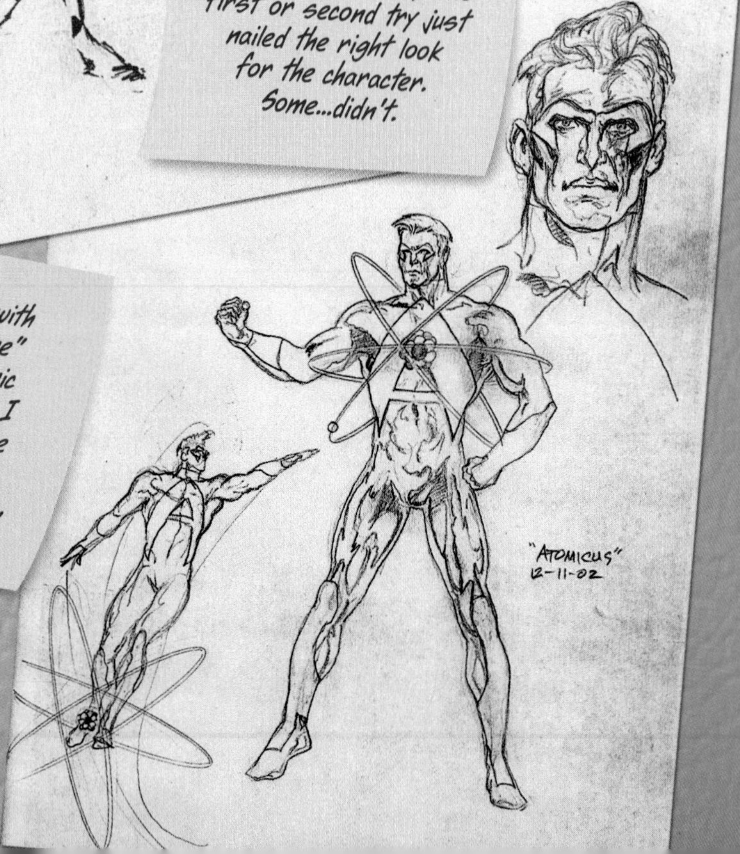
"ATOMICUS"
12-11-02

But something wasn't quite working. The guy at top left looks like a New God, the guy at the bottom like The Atom.

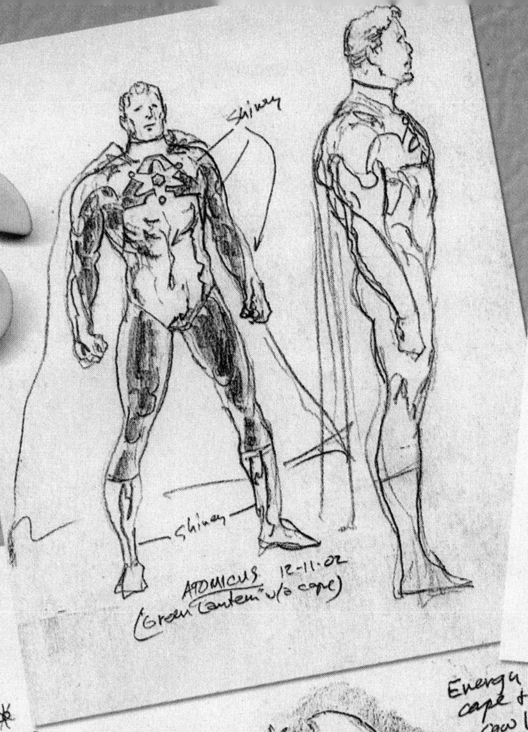
Shiney
Shiney
ATOMICUS 12-11-02
(Green Lantern w/o cape)

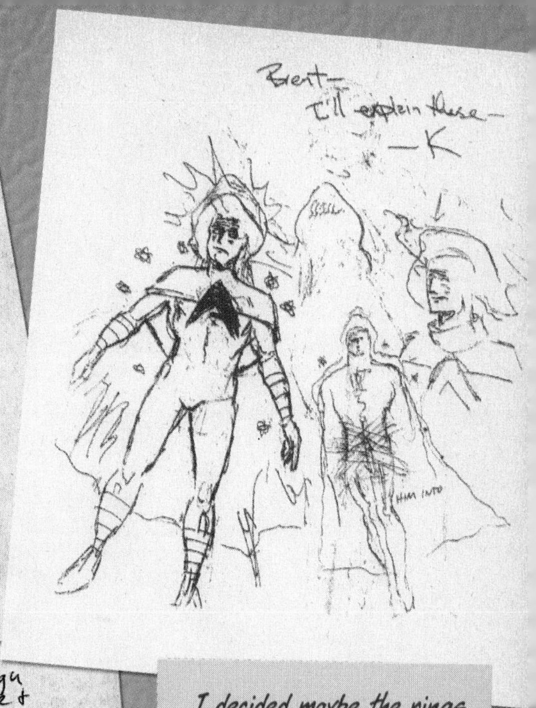
Brent—
I'll explain these—
—K
HIM INTO

I decided maybe the rings weren't working, trying some other ideas, and proving once again why I'm a writer rather than an artist.

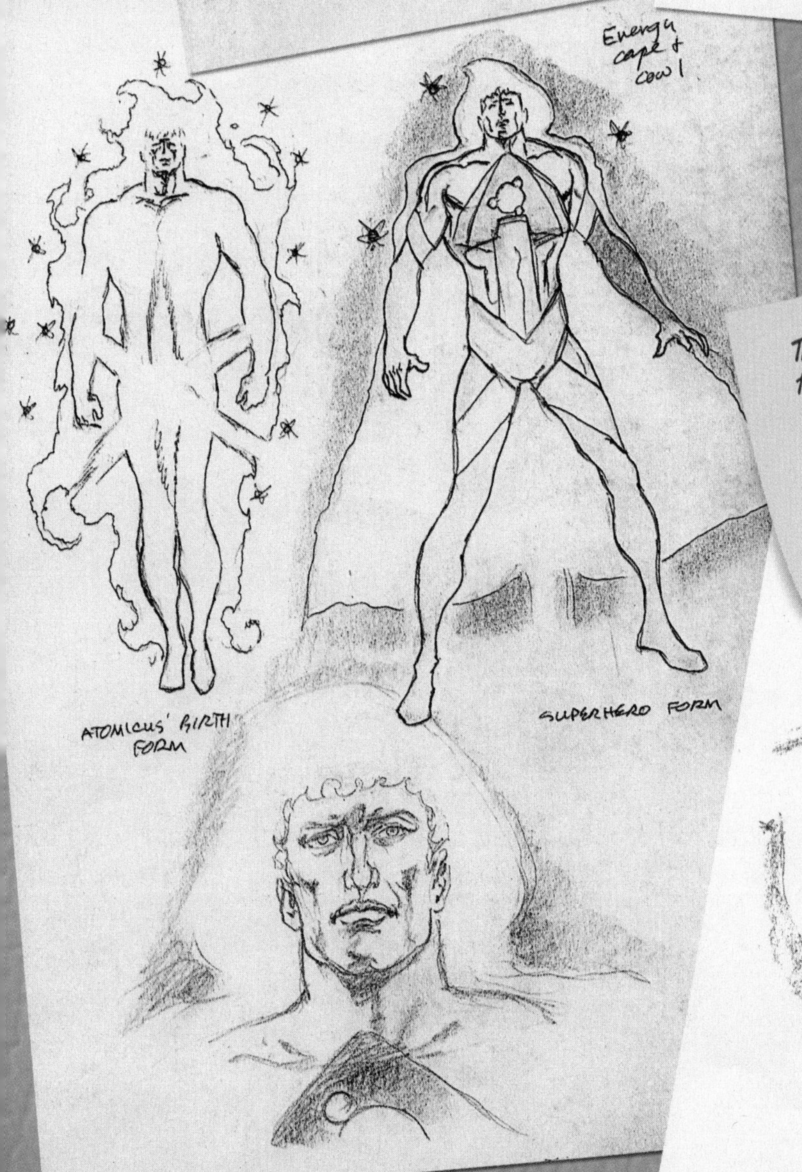
Energy cape + cowl
ATOMICUS' BIRTH FORM
SUPERHERO FORM

The "atomic" was coming through. The "godly" was coming through. But the designs looked too modern, like a character from the Seventies or beyond. Not someone who'd have debuted in 1961.

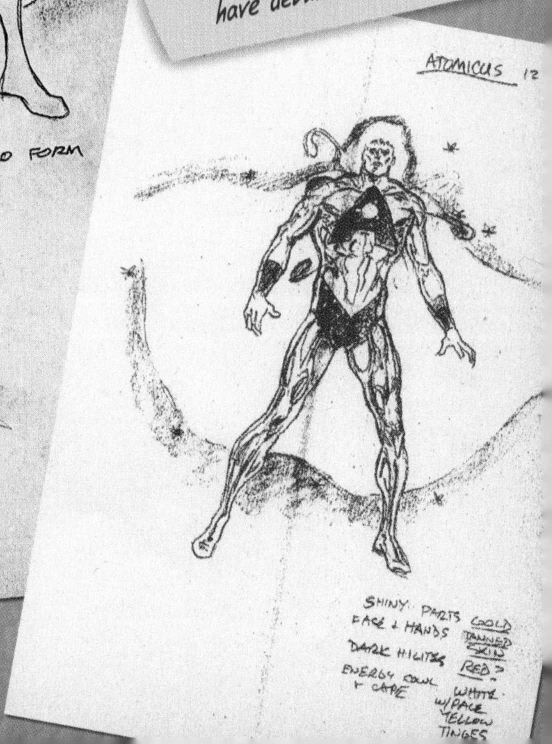
ATOMICUS 12
SHINY PARTS GOLD
FACE + HANDS TANNED SKIN
DARK HILITES RED?
ENERGY COWL + CAPE WHITE W/PALE YELLOW TINGES

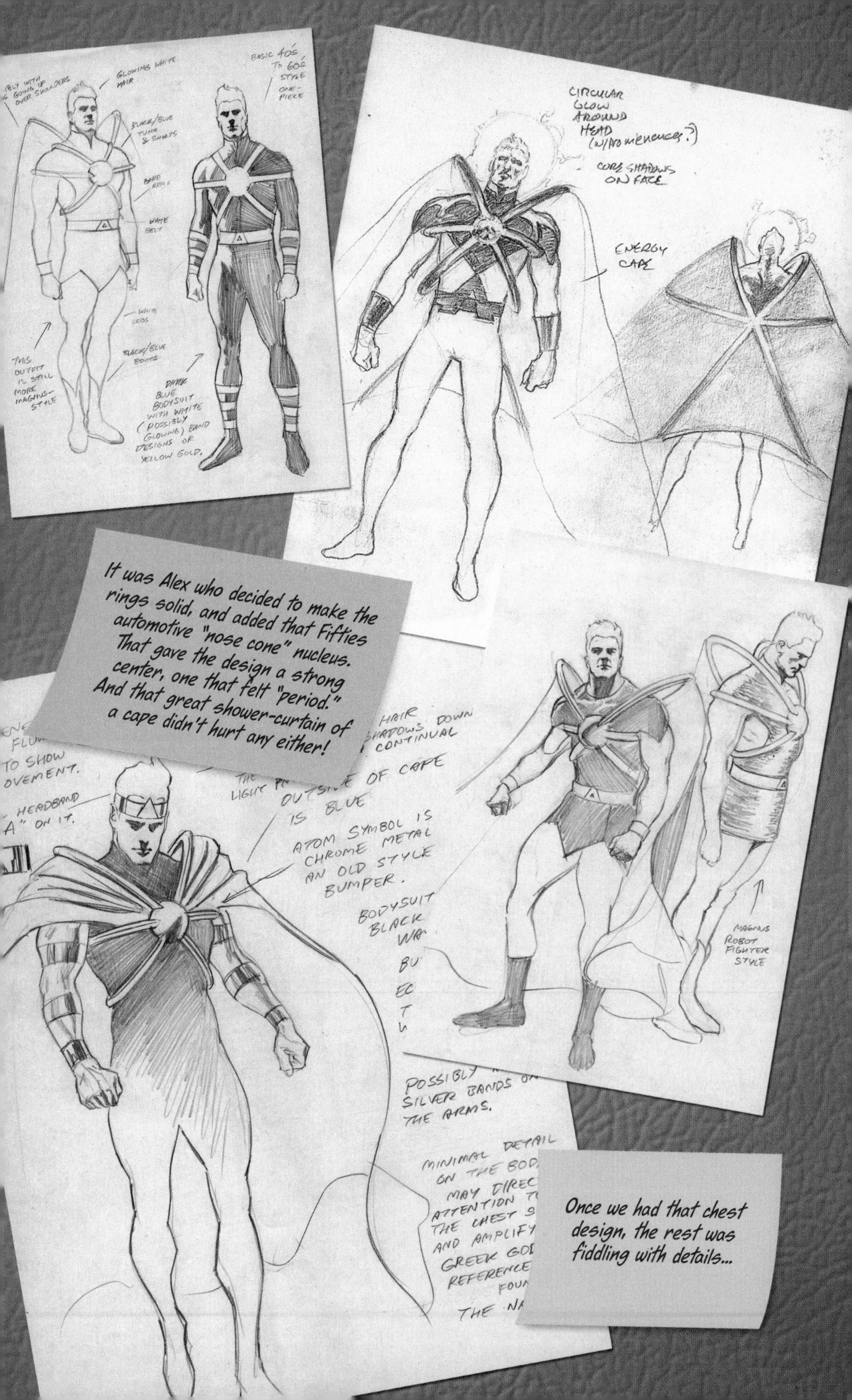
GLOWING WHITE HAIR
BASIC 40'S TO 60'S STYLE ONE-PIECE
BLACK/BLUE TUNIC & SHORTS
BARE ARMS
WHITE BELT
WHITE LEGS
BLACK/BLUE BOOTS
THIS OUTFIT IS STILL MORE MAGNUS-STYLE
DARK BLUE BODYSUIT WITH WHITE (POSSIBLY GLOWING) BAND DESIGNS OR YELLOW GOLD.
CIRCULAR GLOW AROUND HEAD (W/PROMINENCES?)
CORE SHADOWS ON FACE
ENERGY CAPE
MAGNUS ROBOT FIGHTER STYLE
IS BLUE
ATOM SYMBOL IS CHROME METAL AN OLD STYLE BUMPER.
BODYSUIT BLACK
POSSIBLY SILVER BANDS ON THE ARMS.
MINIMAL DETAIL

It was Alex who decided to make the rings solid, and added that Fifties automotive "nose cone" nucleus. That gave the design a strong center, one that felt "period." And that great shower-curtain of a cape didn't hurt any either!

Once we had that chest design, the rest was fiddling with details...

STREET ANGEL

He's only shown up for a couple of panels so far, but that didn't mean we didn't obsess...

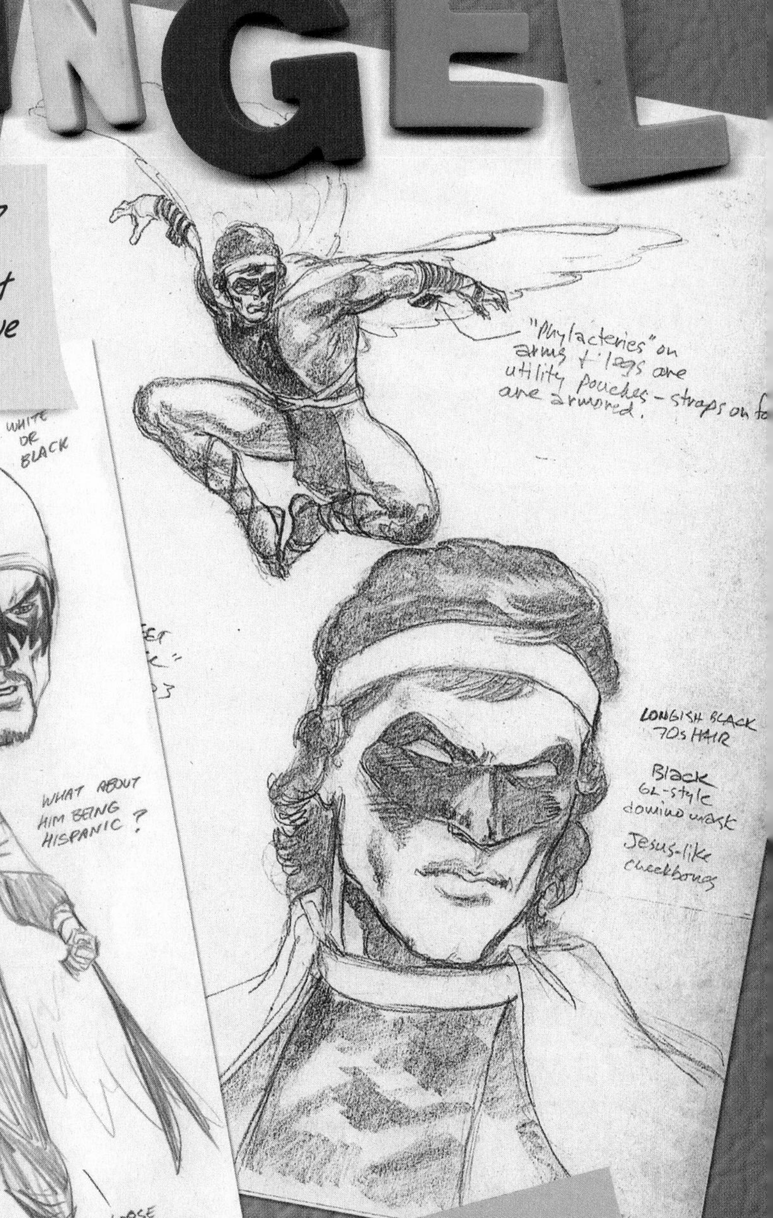

"Phylacteries" on arms + legs are utility pouches - straps on fo
are armored.
LONGISH BLACK 70s HAIR
Black GL-style domino mask
Jesus-like cheekbones

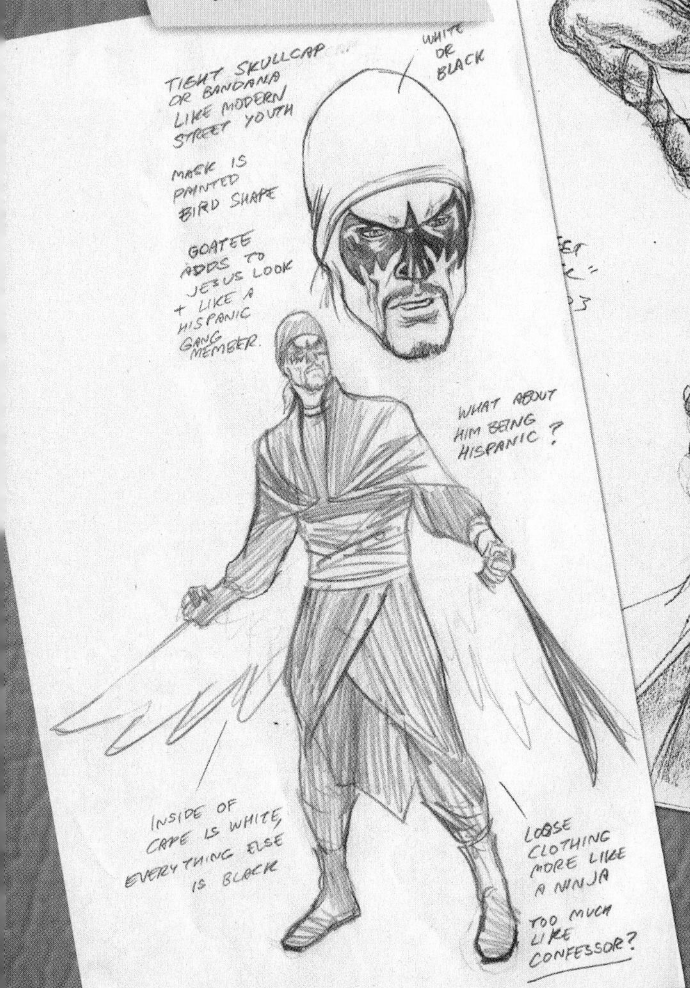

TIGHT SKULLCAP OR BANDANA LIKE MODERN STREET YOUTH
WHITE OR BLACK
MASK IS PAINTED BIRD SHAPE
GOATEE ADDS TO JESUS LOOK + LIKE A HISPANIC GANG MEMBER.
WHAT ABOUT HIM BEING HISPANIC?
INSIDE OF CAPE IS WHITE, EVERYTHING ELSE IS BLACK
LOOSE CLOTHING MORE LIKE A NINJA
TOO MUCH LIKE CONFESSOR?

Nice designs. But too overtly religious, too reminiscent of the Confessor.

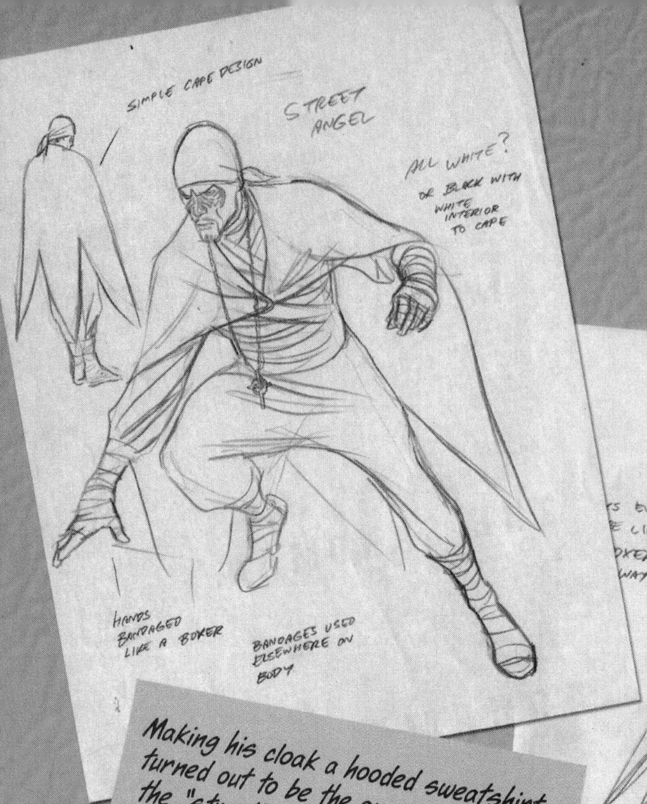
SIMPLE CAPE DESIGN
STREET ANGEL
ALL WHITE? OR BLACK WITH WHITE INTERIOR TO CAPE
HANDS BANDAGED LIKE A BOXER
BANDAGES USED ELSEWHERE ON BODY

Making his cloak a hooded sweatshirt turned out to be the answer. It made the "street" in Street Angel come to the fore, conjuring up thoughts of an inner-city boxer more than a priest. A few touches to say "angel," and we had what I think is one of the most striking-looking characters in the City.

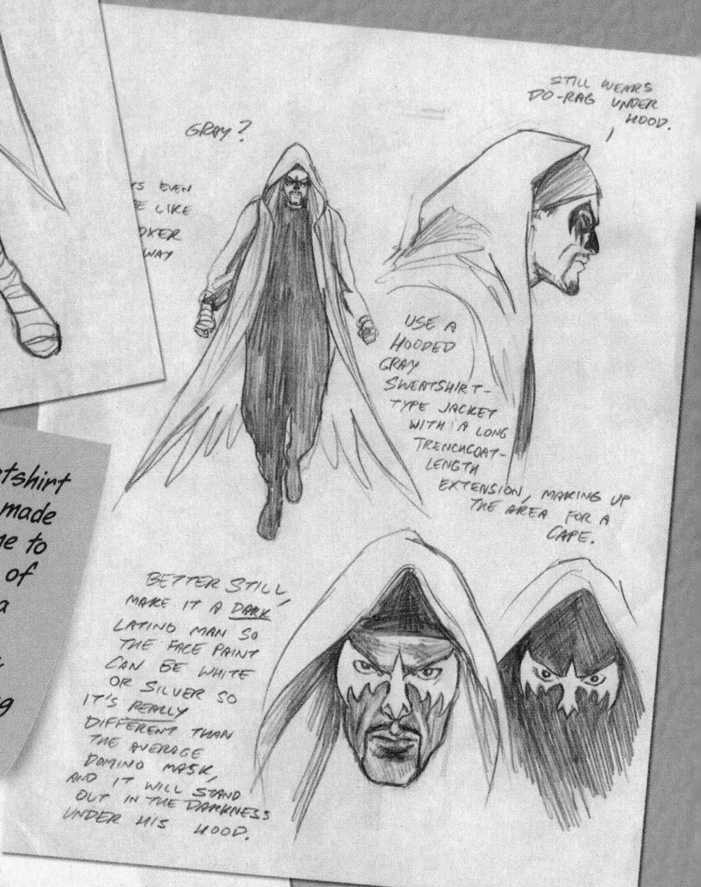
GRAY?
STILL WEARS DO-RAG UNDER HOOD.
USE A HOODED GRAY SWEATSHIRT-TYPE JACKET WITH A LONG TRENCHCOAT-LENGTH EXTENSION, MAKING UP THE AREA FOR A CAPE.
BETTER STILL, MAKE IT A DARK LATINO MAN SO THE FACE PAINT CAN BE WHITE OR SILVER SO IT'S REALLY DIFFERENT THAN THE AVERAGE DOMINO MASK, AND IT WILL STAND OUT IN THE DARKNESS UNDER HIS HOOD.

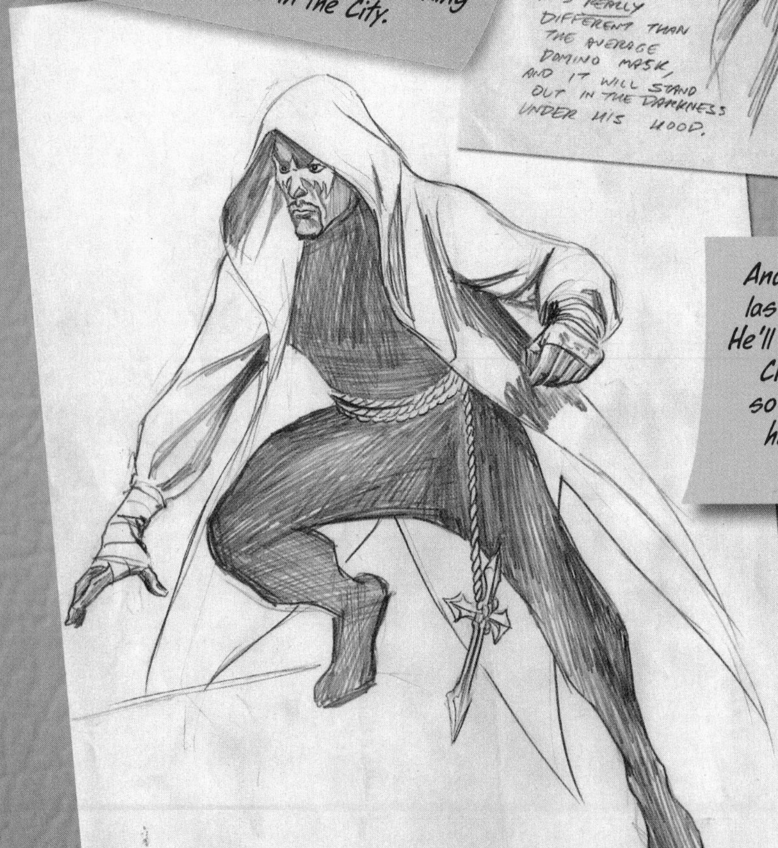

And you haven't seen the last of the Street Angel. He'll be important to ASTRO CITY: THE DARK AGE, so it was worth getting him right, even for a two-panel debut...

COVER GALLERY

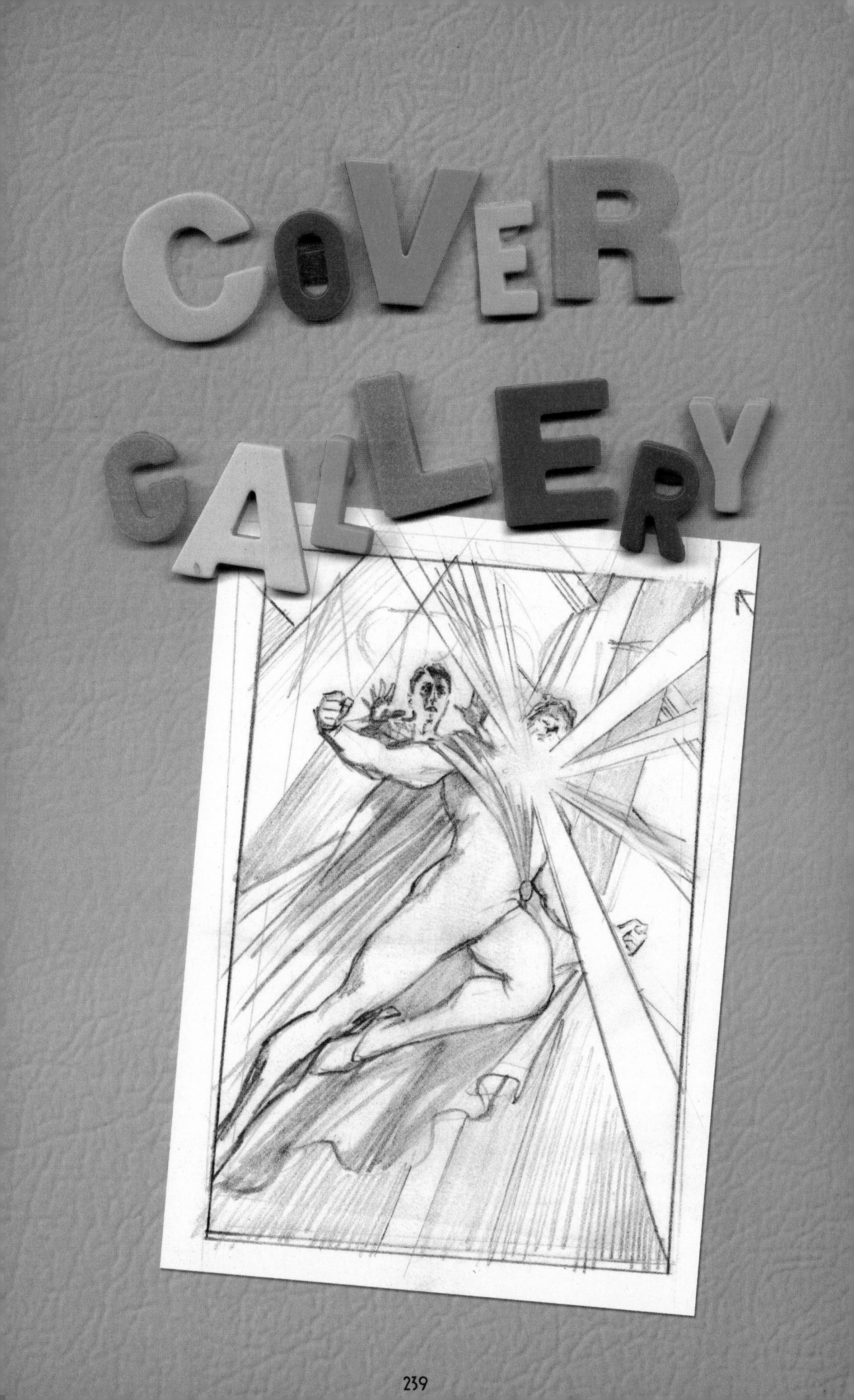

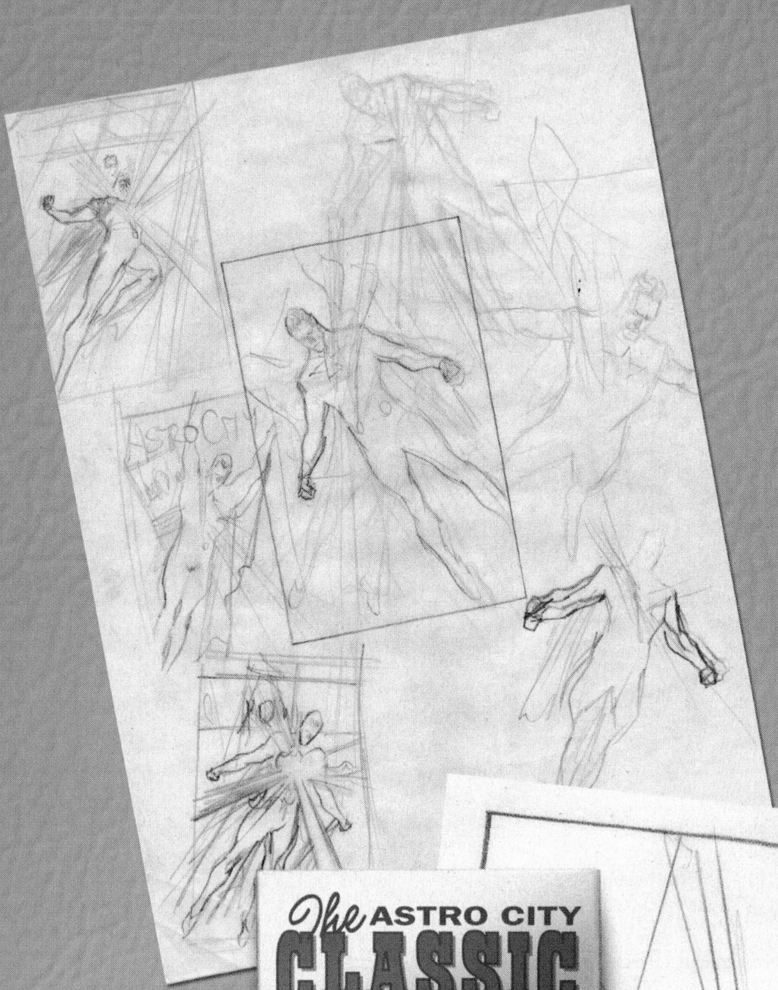

The ASTRO CITY CLASSIC

By any measure... a classic.

BETWEEN CENTER CITY AND OLD TOWN

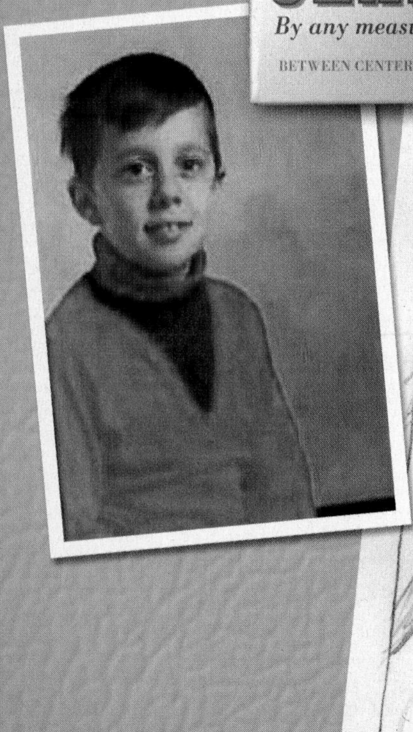

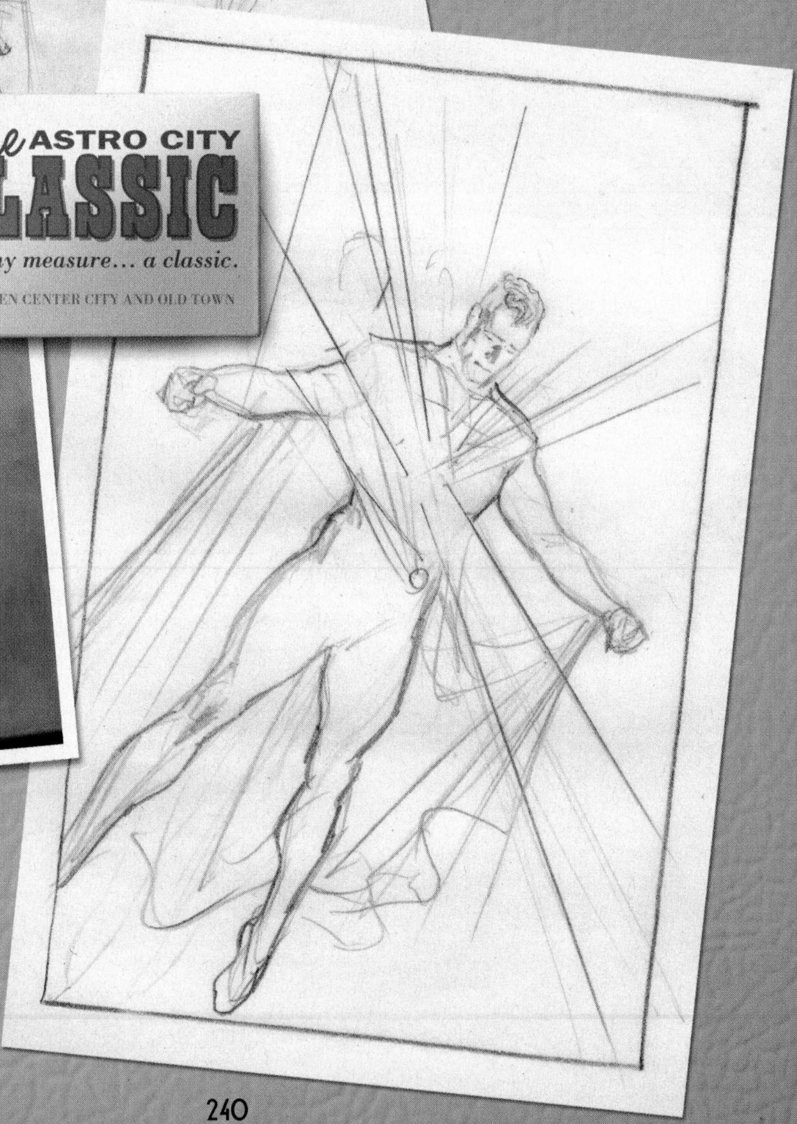

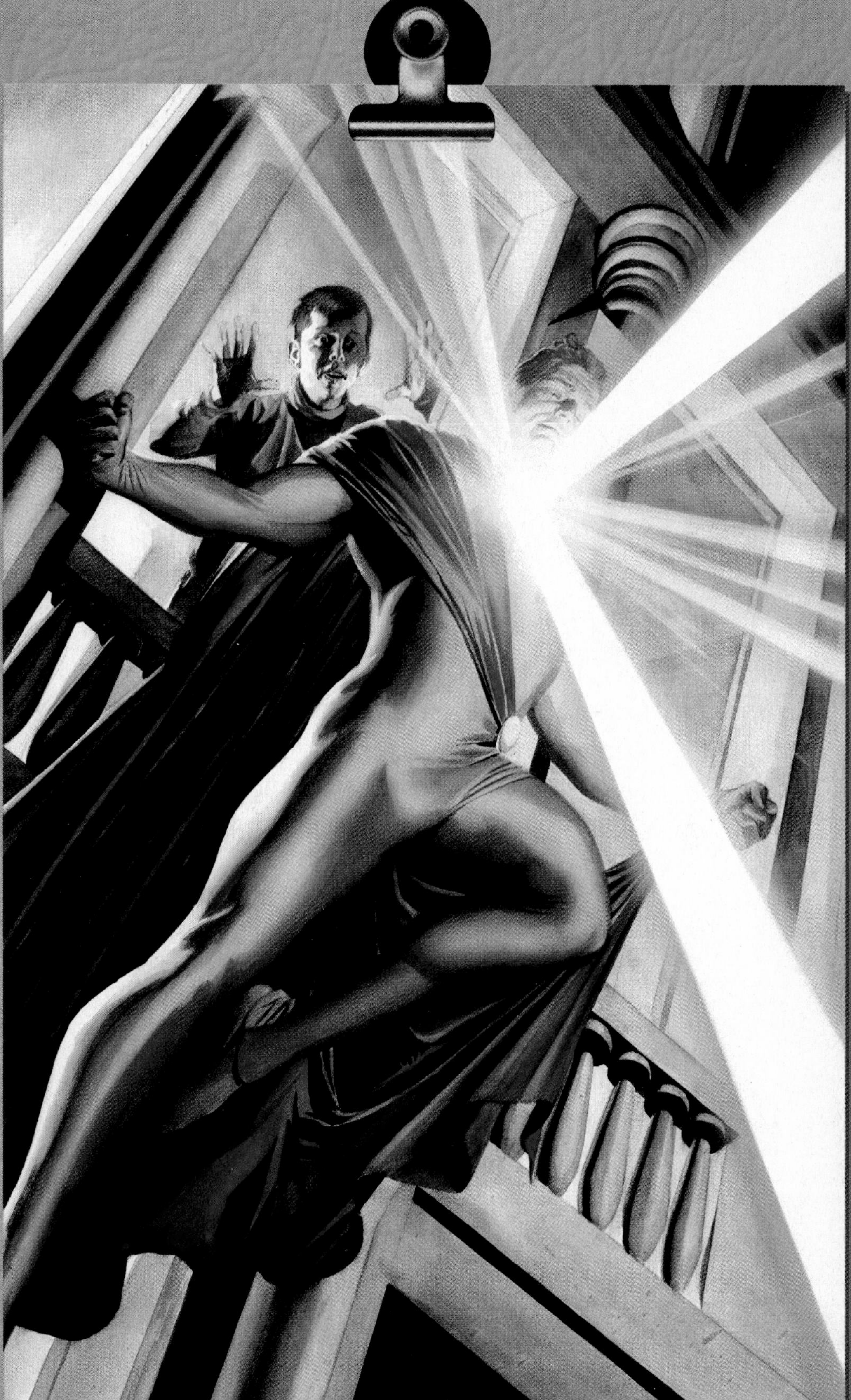

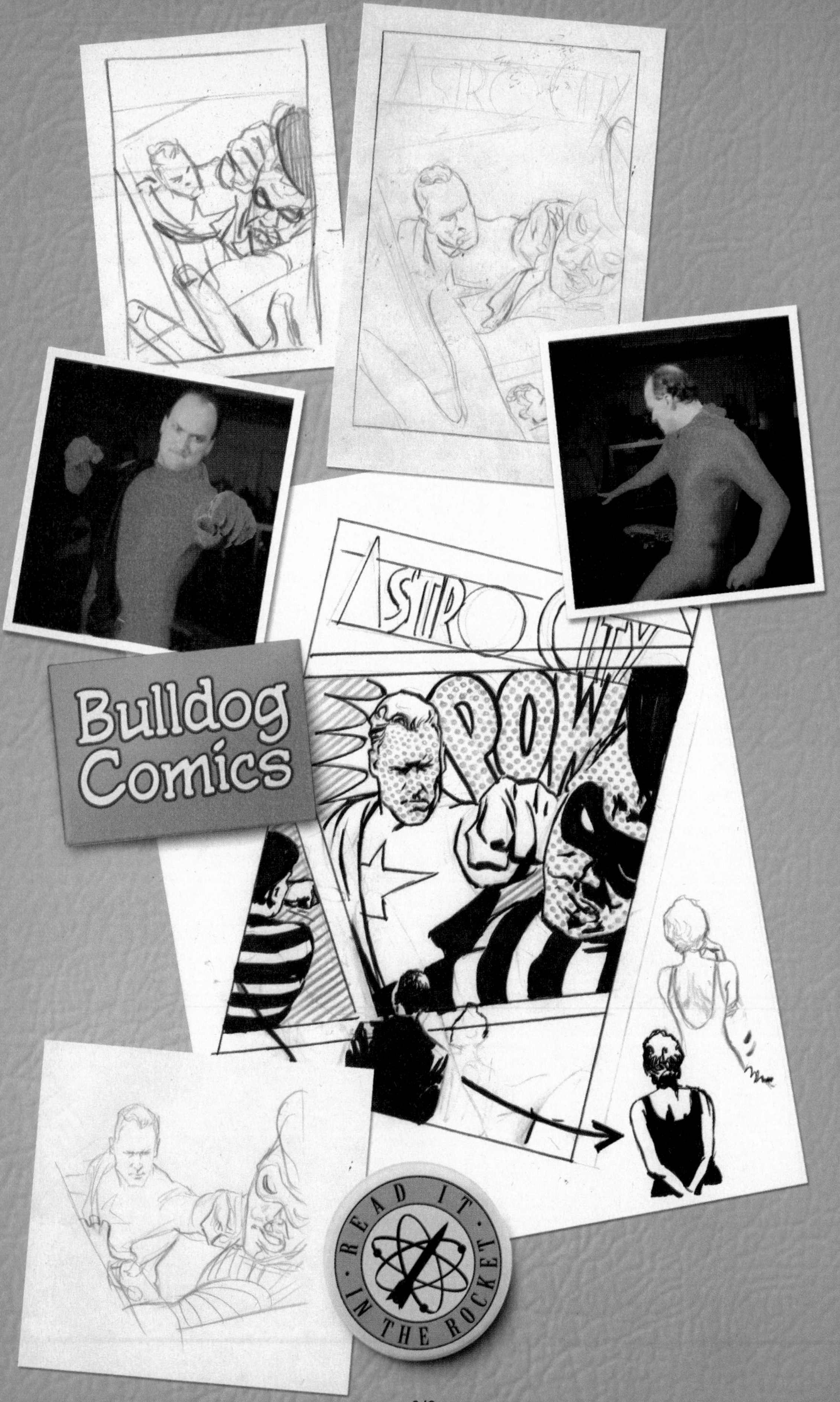
ASTRO CITY
Bulldog Comics
POW
READ IT IN THE ROCKET

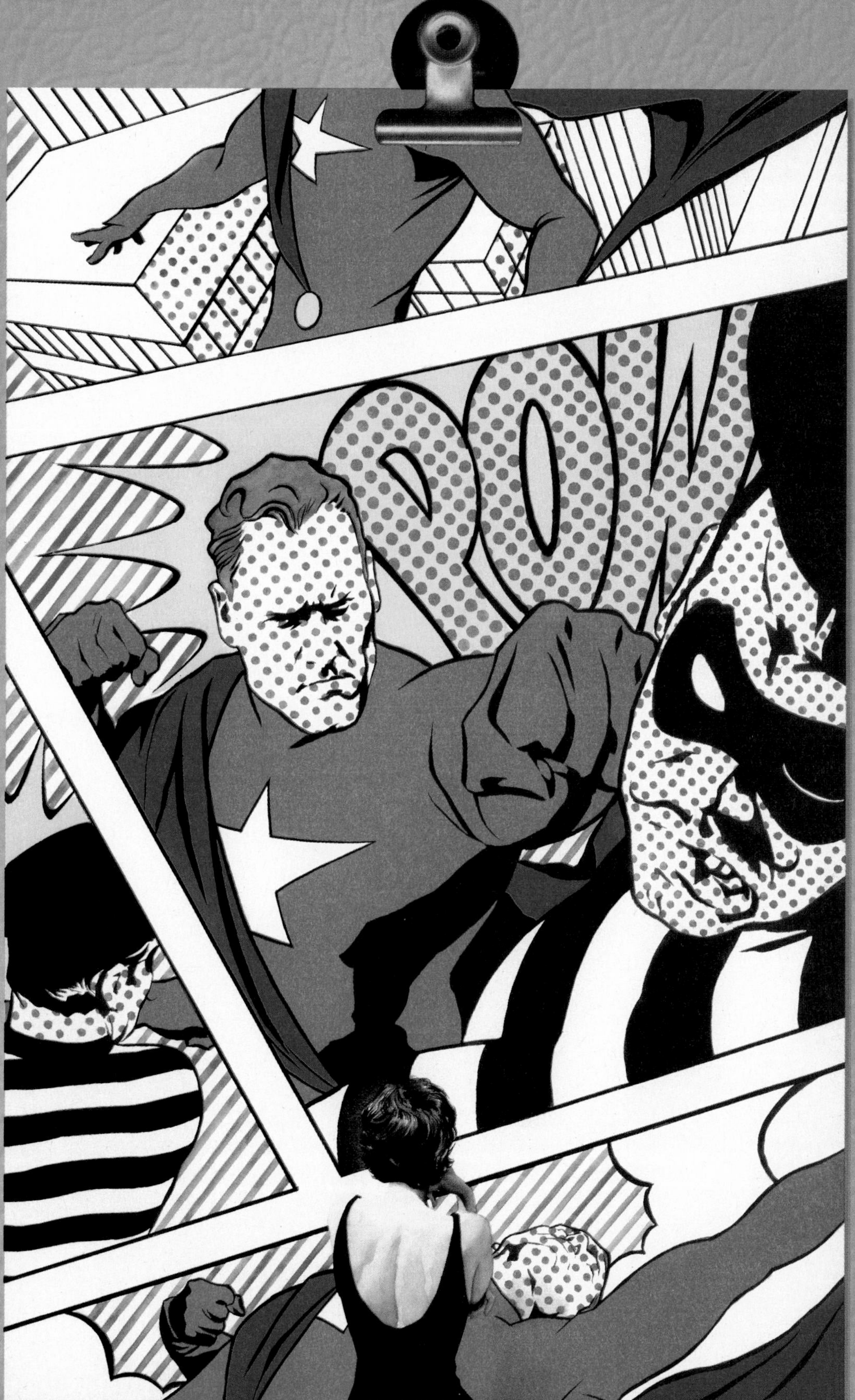
POW

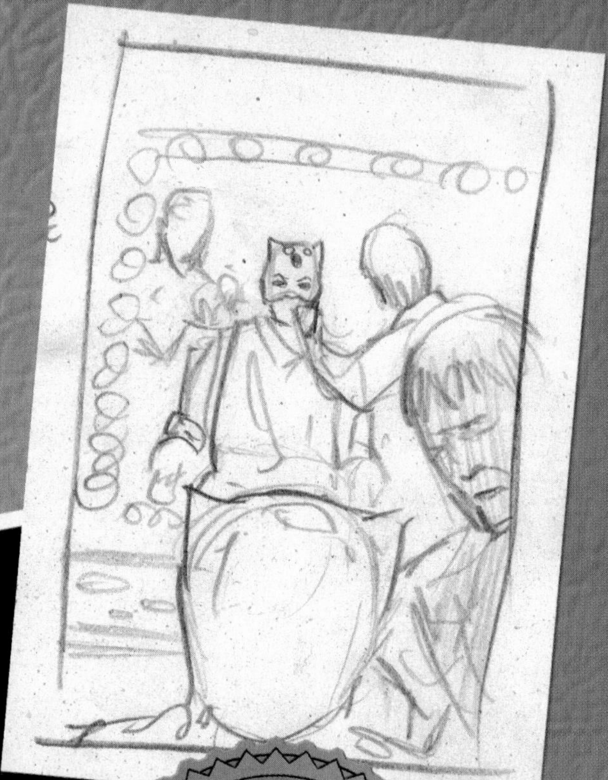

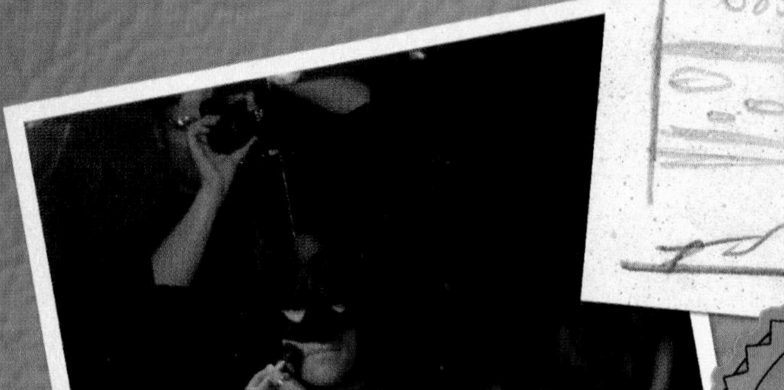

Tomorrow's DAWN™

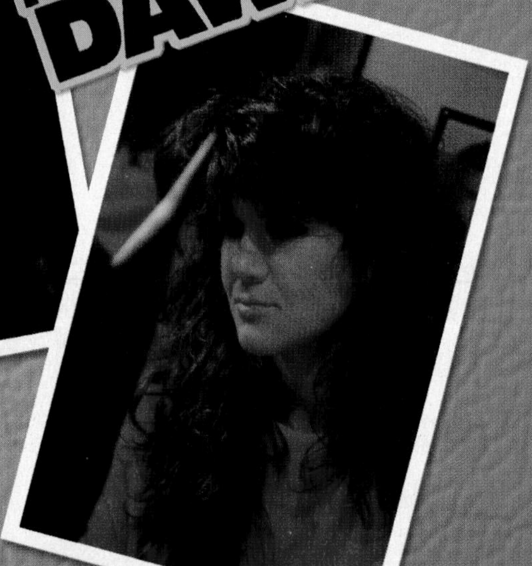

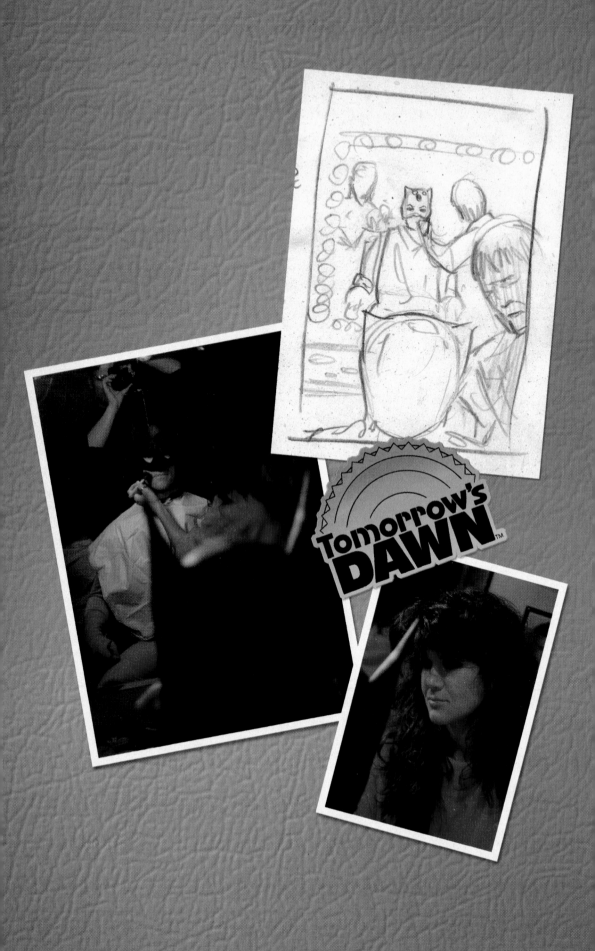

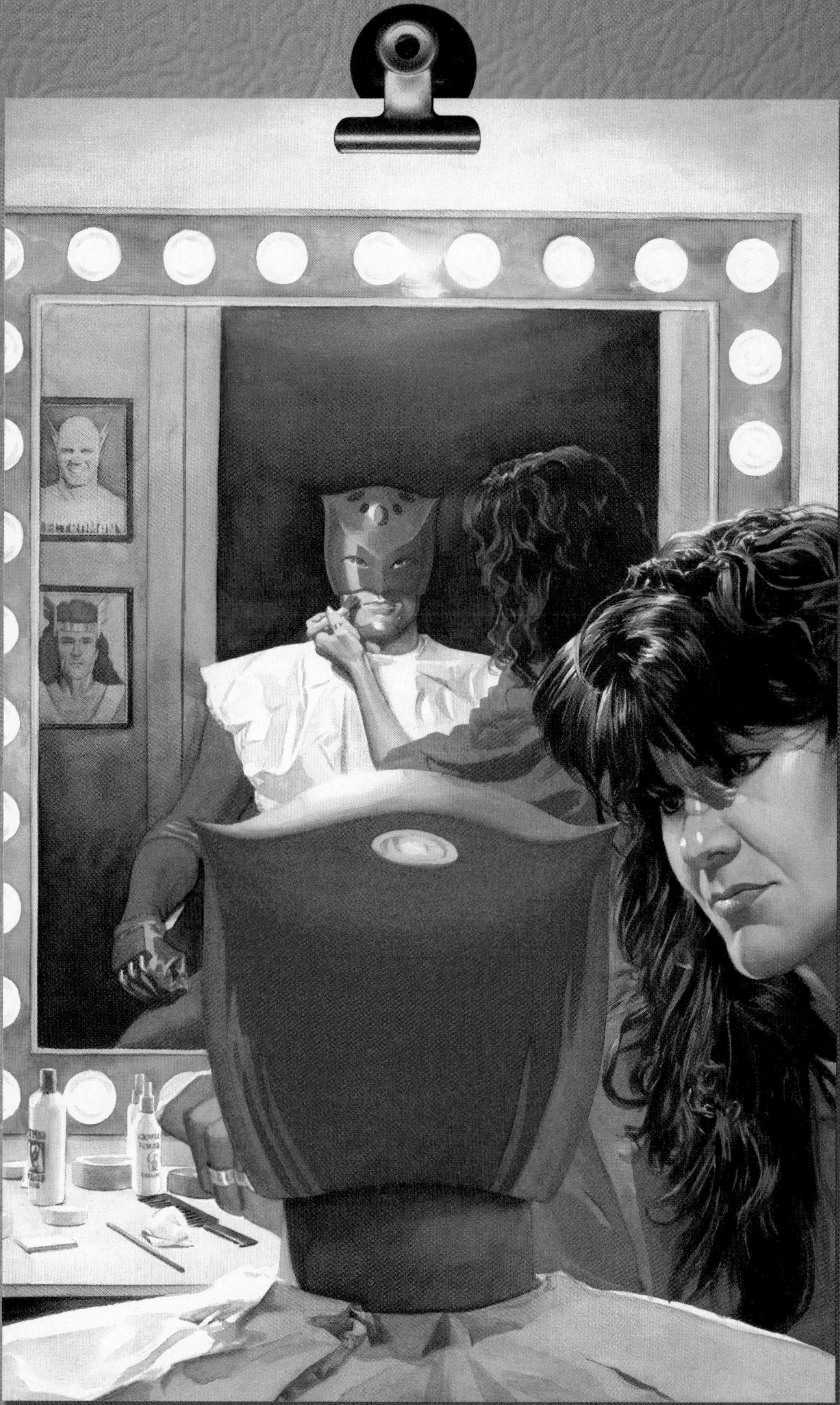

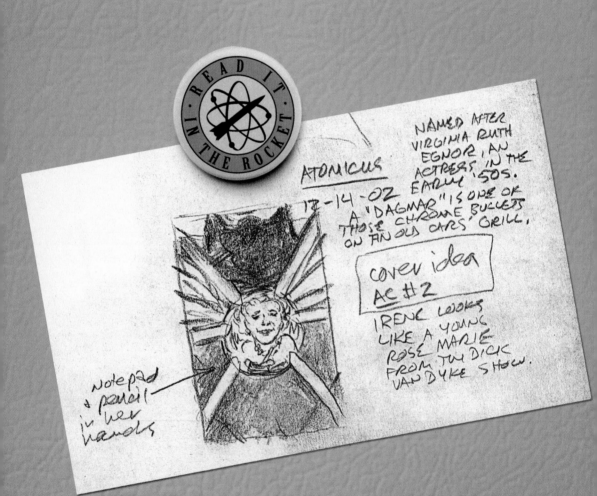

ATOMICUS

12-14-02

NAMED AFTER
VIRGINIA RUTH
EGNOR, AN
ACTRESS, IN THE
EARLY '50s.

A "DAGMAR" IS ONE OF
THOSE CHROME BULLETS
ON AN OLD CARS' GRILL,

cover idea
AC #2

IRENE LOOKS
LIKE A YOUNG
ROSE MARIE
FROM THE DICK
VAN DYKE SHOW.

Notepad
& pencil
in her
hands

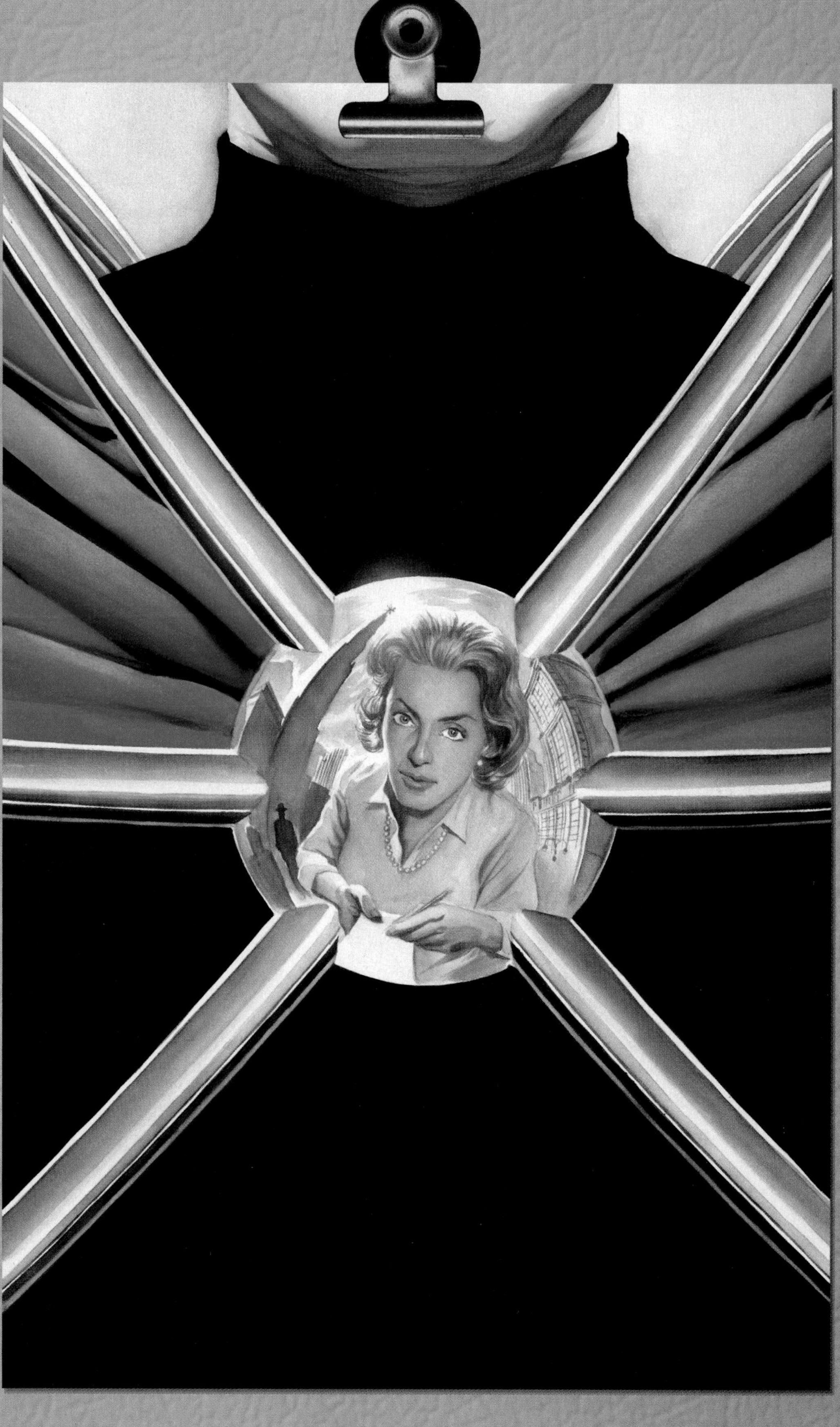

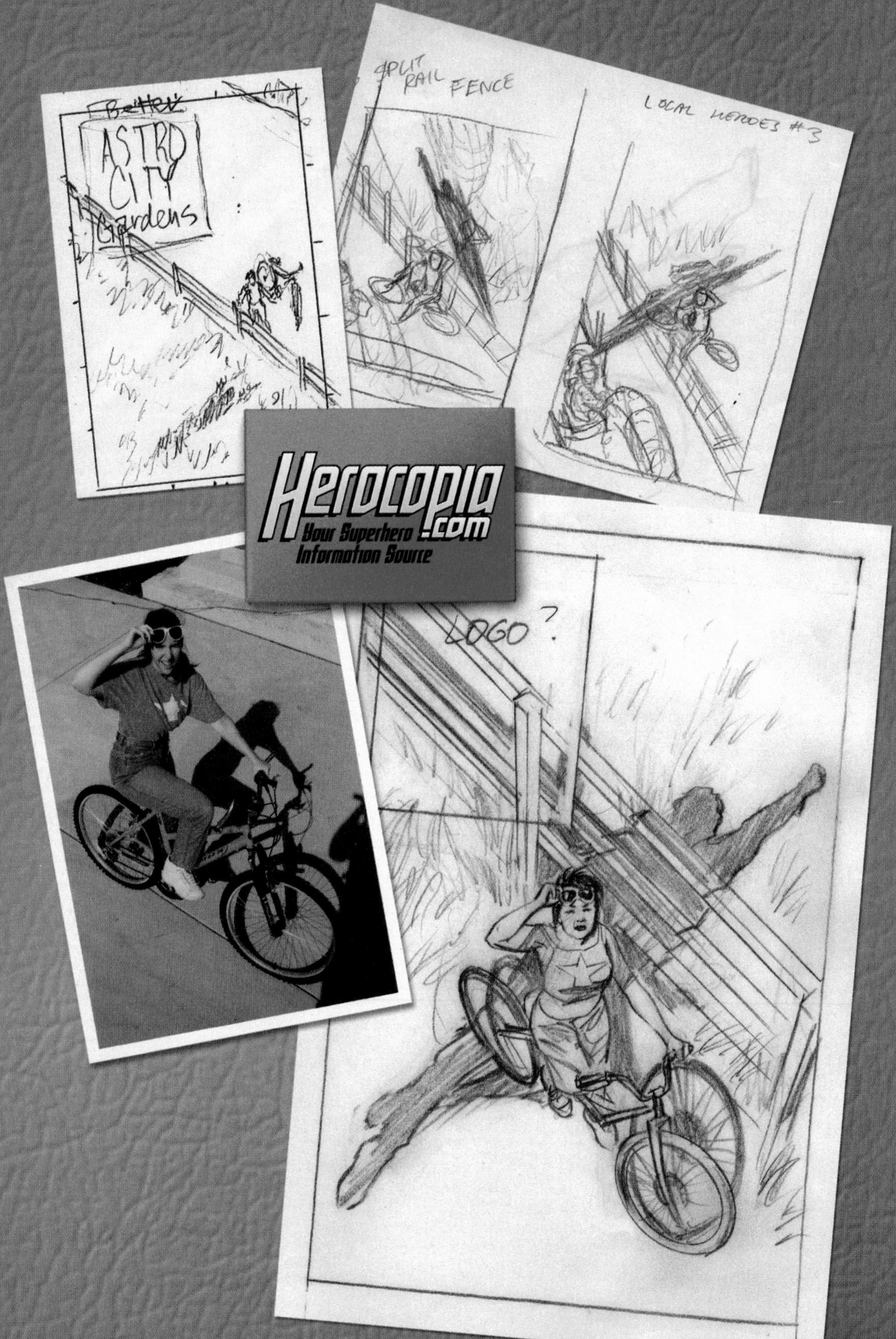
ASTRO CITY Gardens
SPLIT RAIL FENCE
LOCAL HEROES #3
Herocopia .com
Your Superhero Information Source
LOGO?

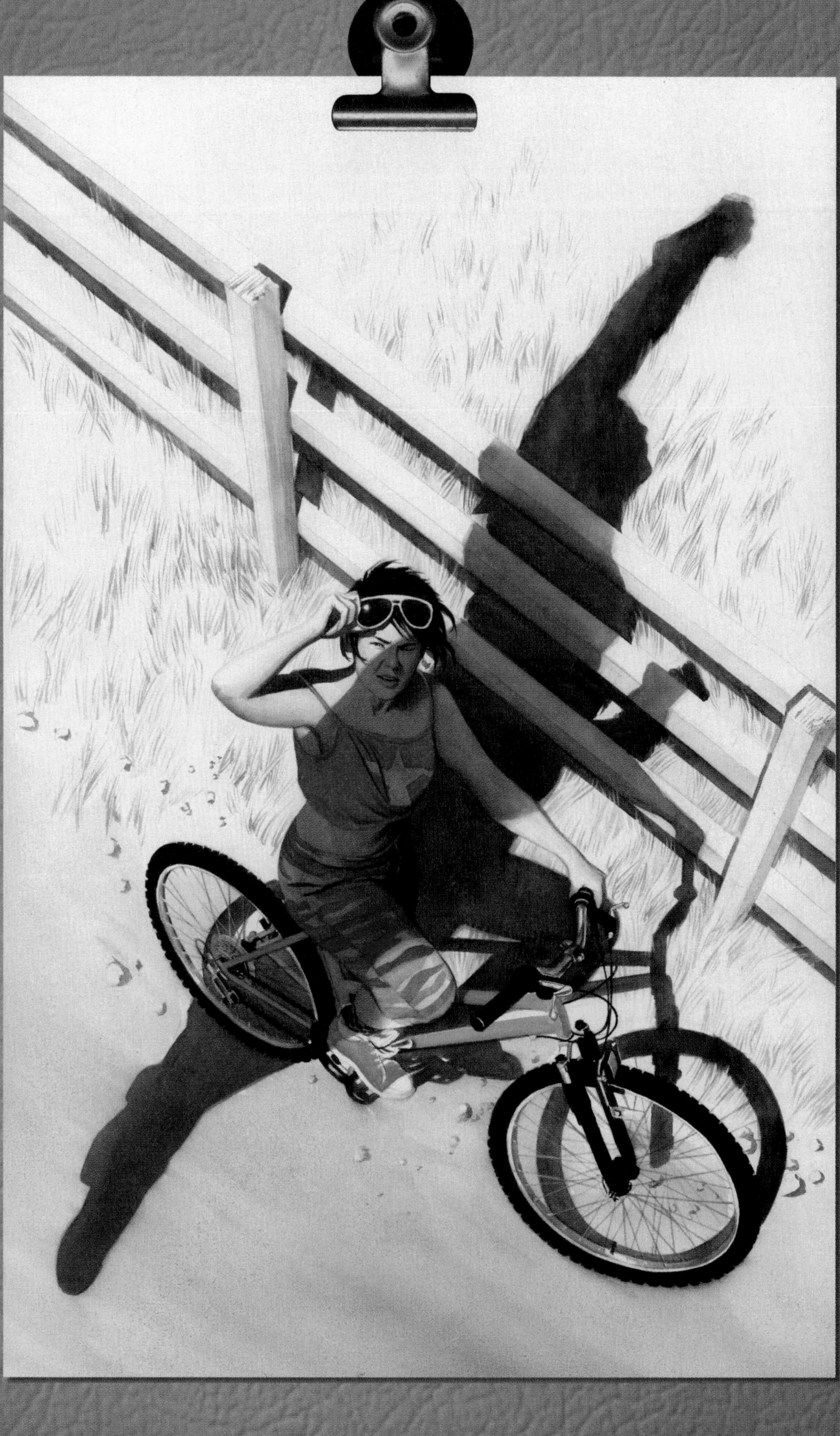

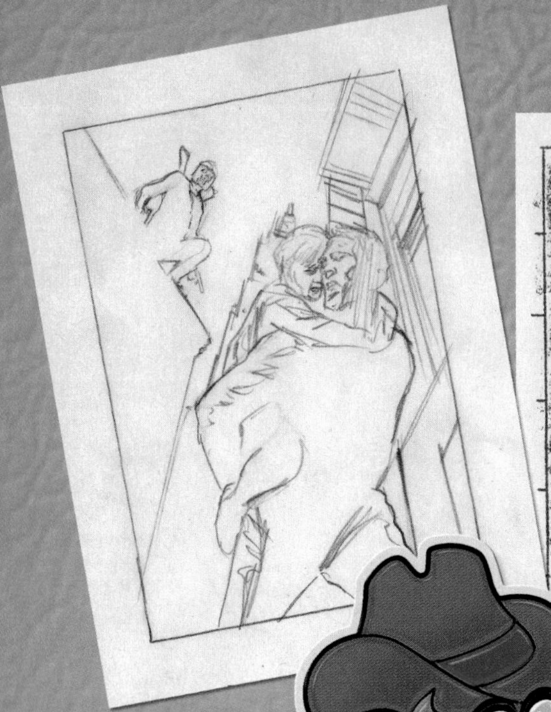

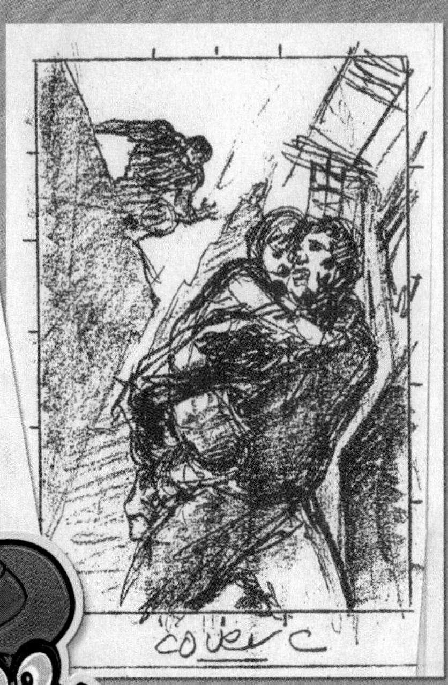
COVER C

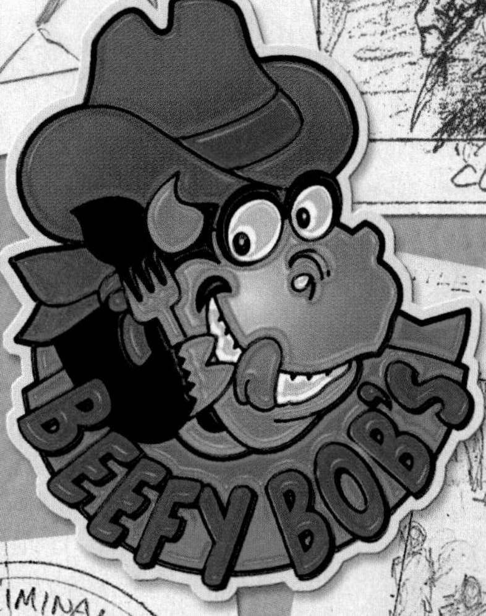
BEEFY BOB'S

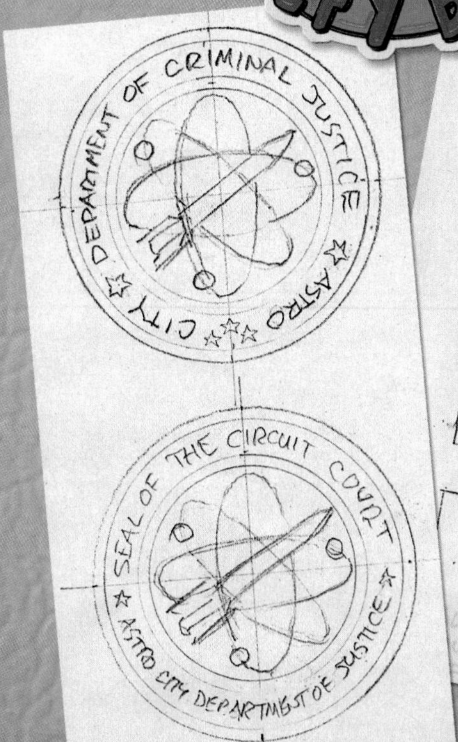
DEPARTMENT OF CRIMINAL JUSTICE
ASTRO CITY
SEAL OF THE CIRCUIT COURT
ASTRO CITY DEPARTMENT OF JUSTICE

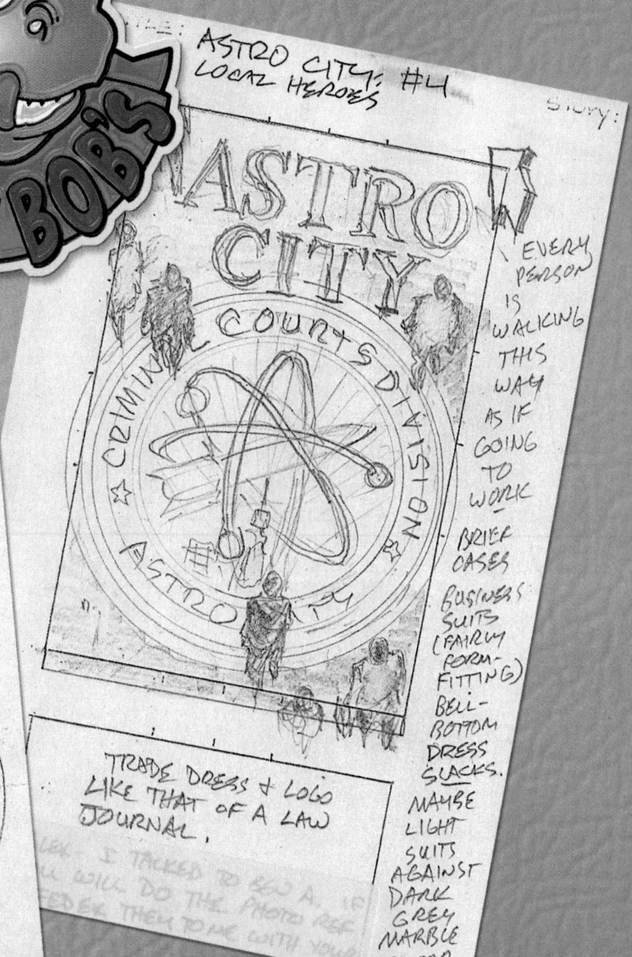
ASTRO CITY: #4
LOCAL HEROES
Story:
ASTRO CITY
CRIMINAL COURTS DIVISION
ASTRO CITY
EVERY PERSON IS WALKING THIS WAY AS IF GOING TO WORK
BRIEF CASES
BUSINESS SUITS (FAIRLY FORM-FITTING)
BELL-BOTTOM DRESS SLACKS.
MAYBE LIGHT SUITS AGAINST DARK GREY MARBLE FLOOR
TRADE DRESS & LOGO LIKE THAT OF A LAW JOURNAL.

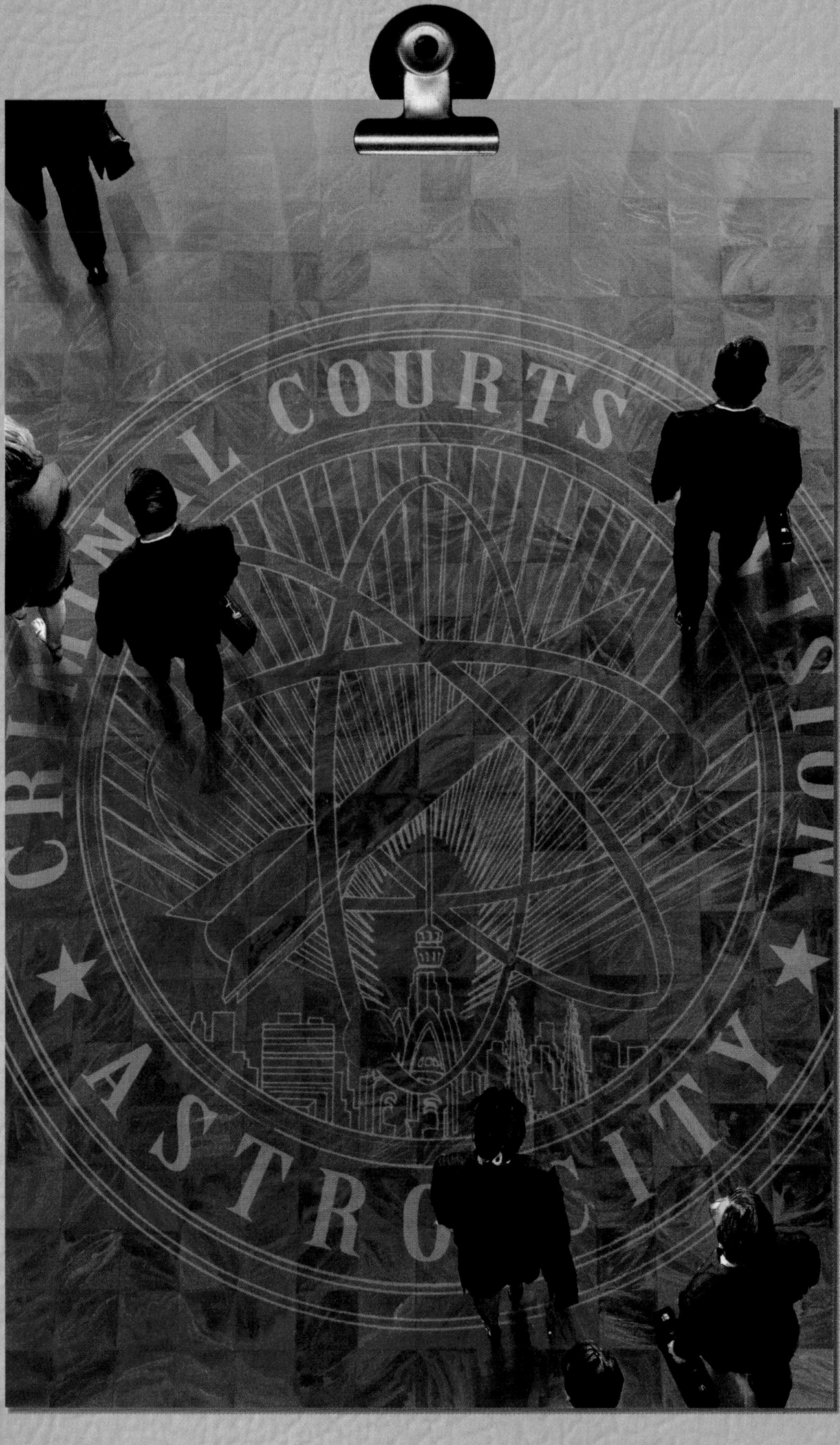
COURTS
ASTRO

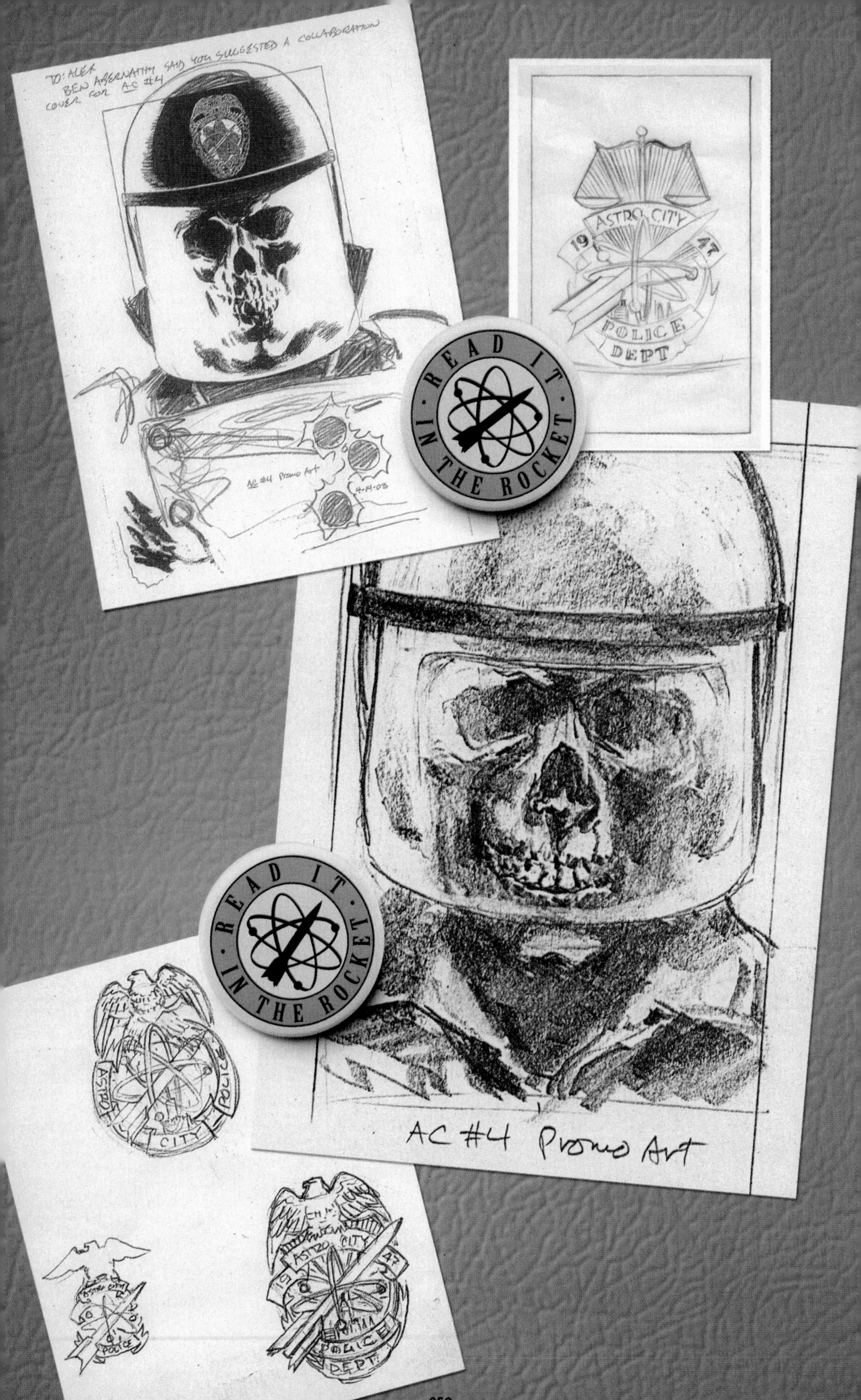
TO: ALEX
BEN ABERNATHY SAID YOU SUGGESTED A COLLABORATION
COVER FOR AC #4
AC #4 Promo Art
4-14-03
READ IT IN THE ROCKET
ASTRO CITY
19 47
POLICE
DEPT
AC #4 Promo Art
READ IT IN THE ROCKET
ASTRO
POLICE
CITY
ASTRO CITY
19 47
POLICE
DEPT

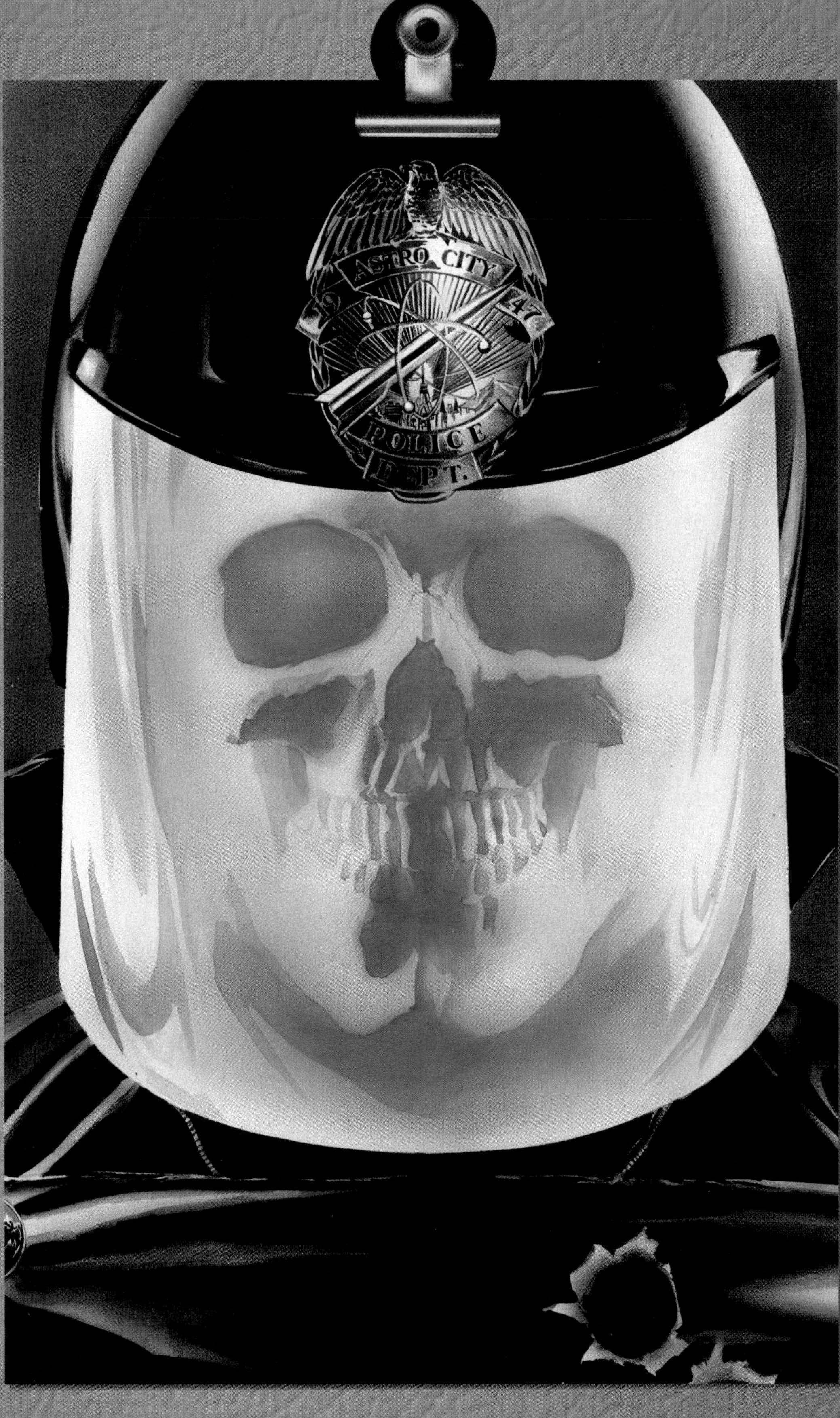
ASTRO CITY
19 47
POLICE
DEPT.

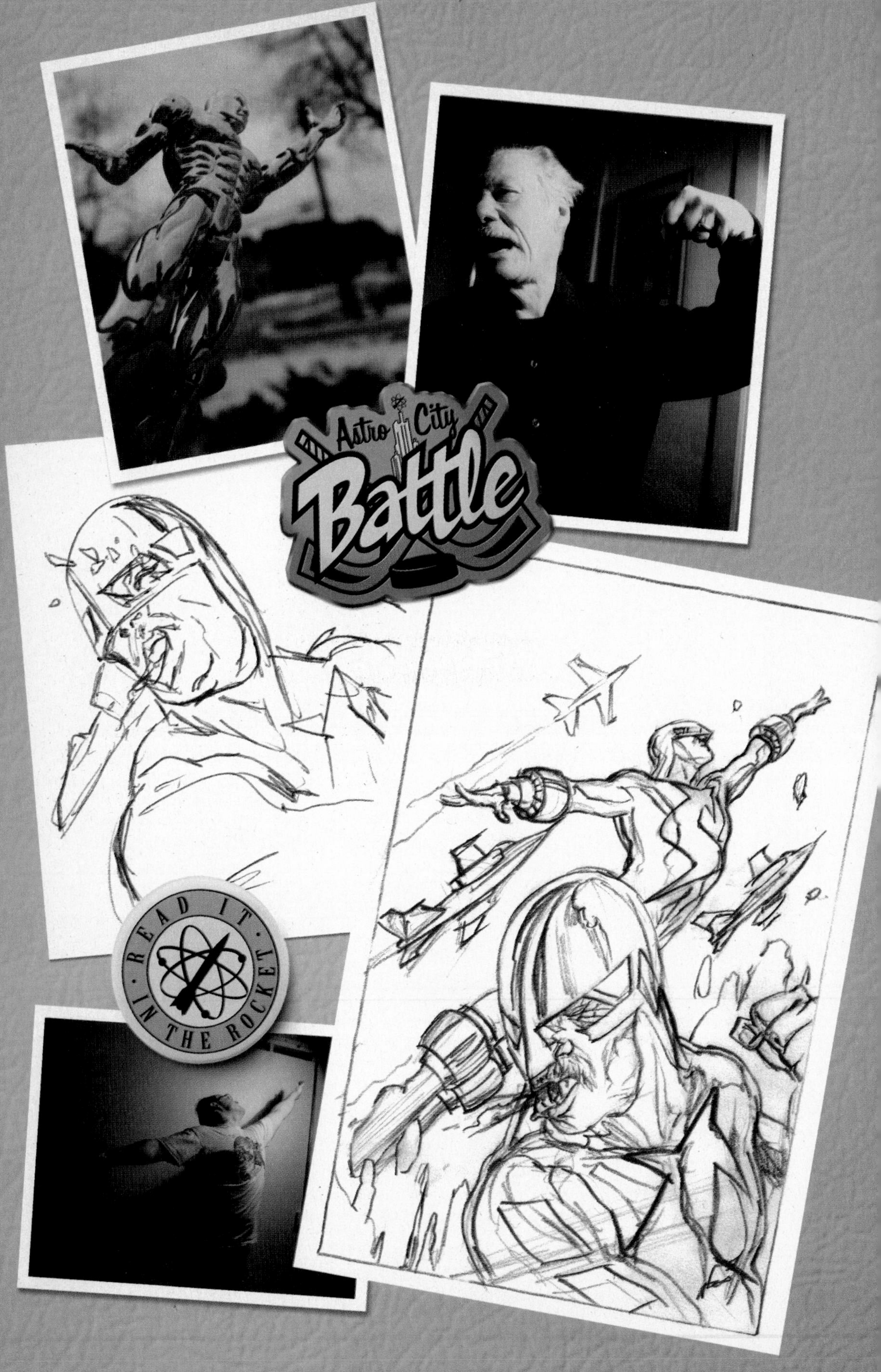
Astro City
Battle
READ IT IN THE ROCKET

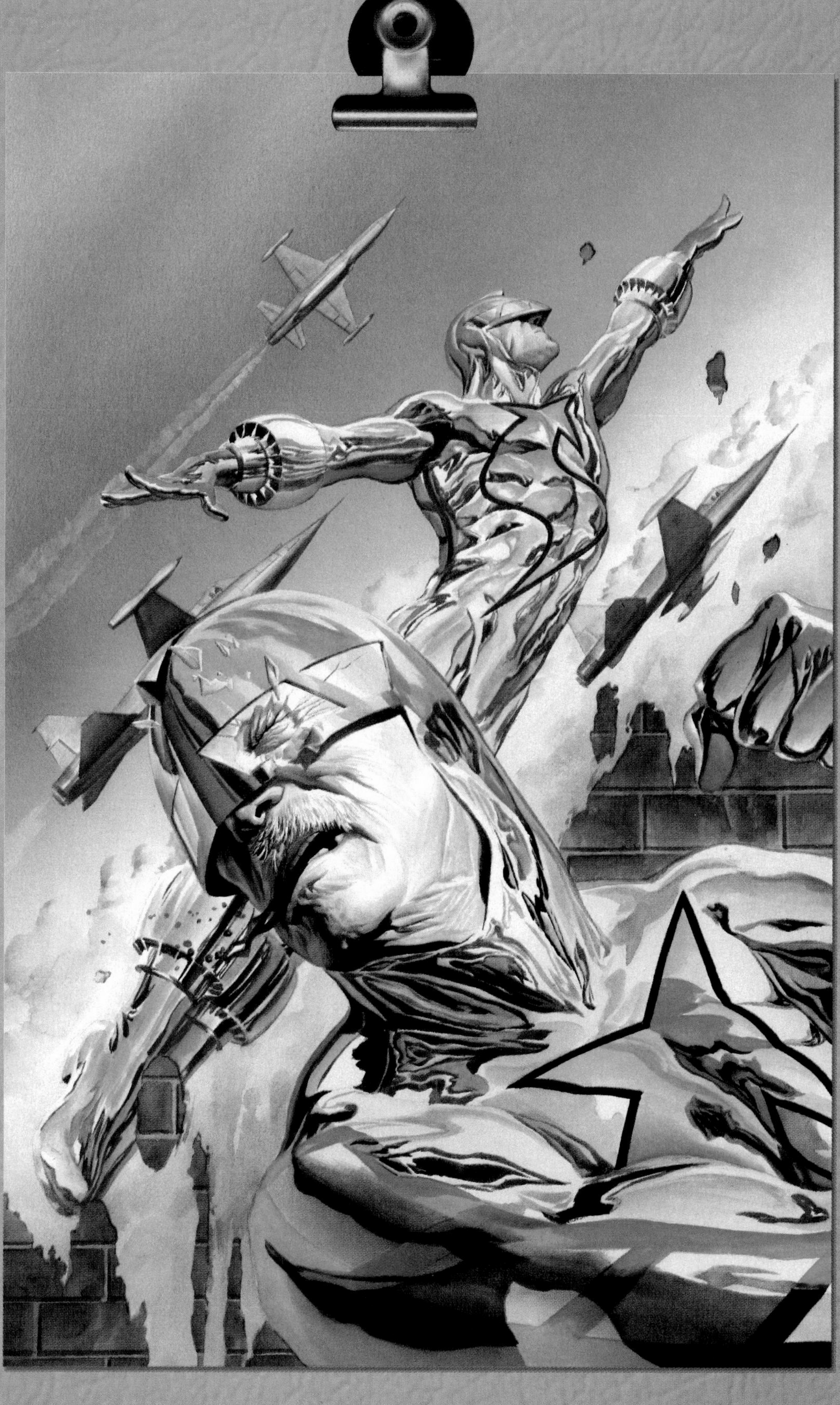

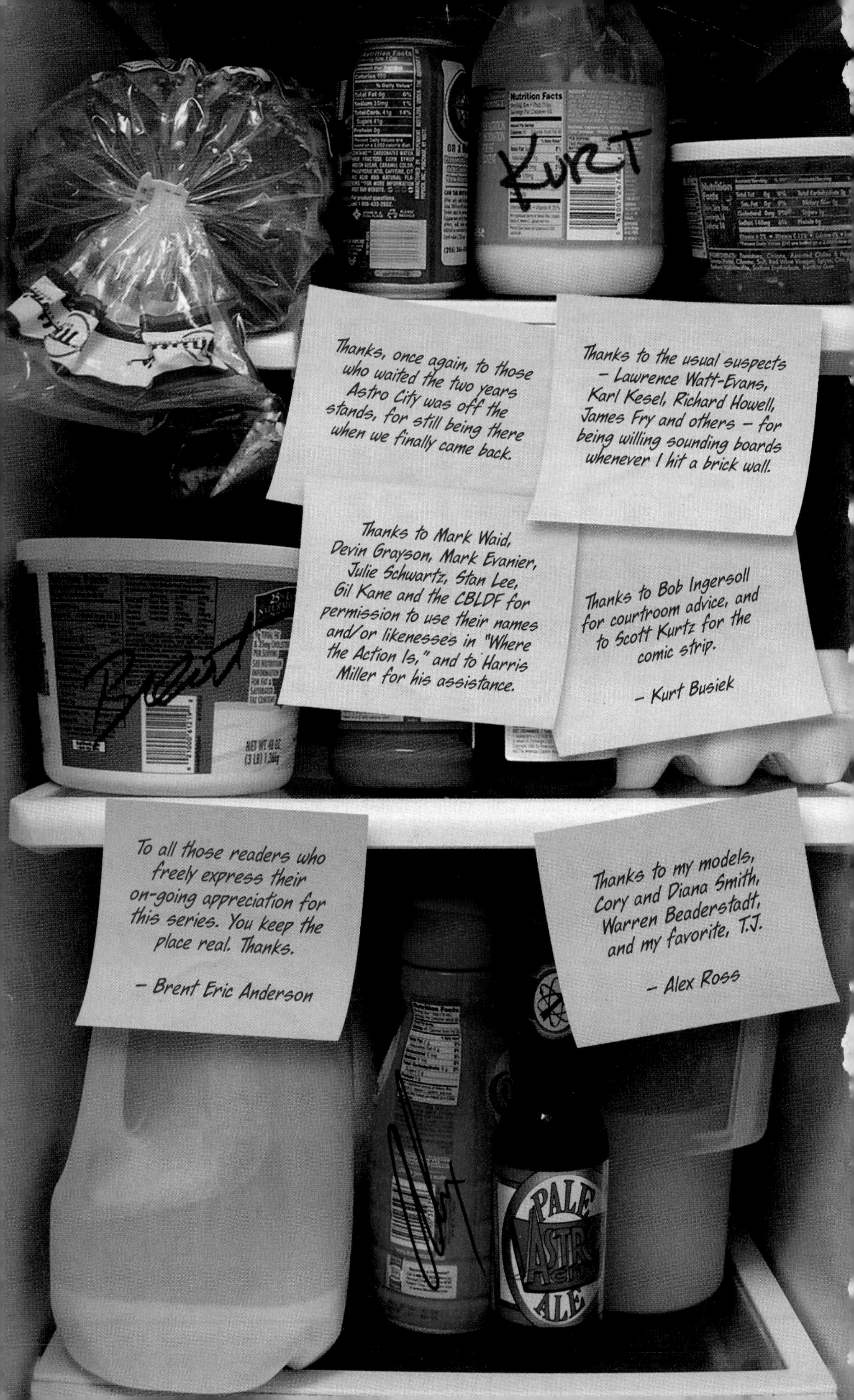

Nutrition Facts
KURT
Thanks, once again, to those who waited the two years Astro City was off the stands, for still being there when we finally came back.
Thanks to the usual suspects – Lawrence Watt-Evans, Karl Kesel, Richard Howell, James Fry and others – for being willing sounding boards whenever I hit a brick wall.
Thanks to Mark Waid, Devin Grayson, Mark Evanier, Julie Schwartz, Stan Lee, Gil Kane and the CBLDF for permission to use their names and/or likenesses in "Where the Action Is," and to Harris Miller for his assistance.
Thanks to Bob Ingersoll for courtroom advice, and to Scott Kurtz for the comic strip.
– Kurt Busiek
To all those readers who freely express their on-going appreciation for this series. You keep the place real. Thanks.
– Brent Eric Anderson
Thanks to my models, Cory and Diana Smith, Warren Beaderstadt, and my favorite, T.J.
– Alex Ross
PALE
ASTRO CITY
ALE